Gender Space Architecture

This significant text brings together for the first time the most important essays concerning the intersecting subjects of gender, space and architecture. Carefully structured and supplied with introductory essays, it guides the reader through theoretical and multi-disciplinary texts to direct considerations of gender in relation to particular architectural sites, projects and ideas.

Gender Space Architecture marks a seminal point in gender and architecture, both summarising core debates and pointing towards new directions and discussions for the future. It will be useful to a wide range of readers wishing to explore this burgeoning new field, including those from architecture, art history, anthropology, cultural studies, gender studies and urban geography.

Jane Rendell is Senior Lecturer in Architecture at the University of Nottingham. **Barbara Penner** is conducting her doctoral research into architecture and romance at Birkbeck College, London. **Iain Borden** is Director of Architectural History and Theory as well as Reader in Architecture and Urban Culture at The Bartlett, University College London.

THE ARCHI*TEXT* SERIES

Edited by Thomas A. Markus and Anthony D. King

Architectural discourse has traditionally represented buildings as art objects or technical objects. Yet buildings are also social objects in that they are invested with social meaning and shape social relations. Recognising these assumptions, the **Architext** series aims to bring together recent debates in social and cultural theory and the study and practice of architecture and urban design. Critical, comparative and interdisciplinary, the books in the series will, by theorising architecture, bring the space of the built environment centrally into the social sciences and humanities, as well as bringing the theoretical insights of the latter into the discourses of architecture and urban design. Particular attention will be paid to issues of gender, race, sexuality and the body, to questions of identity and place, to the cultural politics of representation and language, and to the global and postcolonial contexts in which these are addressed.

Already published:

Framing Places
Mediating power in built form
Kim Dovey

Forthcoming titles:

Moderns Abroad
Italian colonialism and construction
Mia Fuller

The Architecture of Oppression
The SS, forced labor and the Nazi
Monumental Building Economy
Paul Jaskot

Architecture and Language
Thomas A. Markus and Deborah Cameron

Spaces of Global Cultures
Anthony D. King

Beyond the Postcolonial
Architecture, Urban Space and Political Cultures
Abidin Kusno

**Edited by
Jane Rendell, Barbara Penner and
Iain Borden**

Gender Space Architecture

An interdisciplinary introduction

London and New York

First published 2000 by Routledge
2 Park Square, Milton Park, Abingdon, Oxon OX14 4RN

Simultaneously published in the USA and Canada
by Routledge
711 Third Avenue, New York, NY 10017

Routledge is an imprint of the Taylor & Francis Group

Typeset in Frutiger by Solidus (Bristol) Ltd

British Library Cataloguing in Publication Data
A catalogue record for this book is available from the British Library

Library of Congress Cataloging in Publication Data
Gender space architecture : an interdisciplinary introduction / edited
   by Jane Rendell, Barbara Penner, Iain Borden.
       p.   cm. – (Archi*text* series)
   Includes bibliographical references and index.
   ISBN 0-415-17252-7 (hb). — ISBN 0-415-17253-5 (pbk.)
   1. Architecture and women.   2. Space (Architecture)
   3. Gender (Feminism)   I. Rendell, Jane, 1967– . II. Penner, Barbara, 1970– .
   III. Borden, Iain, 1962– IV. Series.
   NA2543.W65G46 1999   99-12322
   720′.82–dc21   CIP

ISBN 0-415-17252-7 (hbk)
ISBN 0-415-17253-5 (pbk)

Contents

Contents ■

Figures

Preface

Architecture is a subject which demands to be understood in context: that is, within the context of its production (society, economics, politics, culture) and the context of its consumption, representation and interpretation (different academic disciplines, interest groups, institutions, users). In the light of enormous and rapid shifts in theoretical, historical and critical debates, particularly with respect to feminism, understanding architecture in relation to gender demands an urgent contextualisation.

A major change in thinking about gender, feminism, space and architecture has occurred in the last five or so years and it has become vital to place current discussions within an intellectual history, enabling some understanding to be gained of the basis and development of these contemporary ideas. *Gender, Space, Architecture* intends to do just that. The purpose of the book is to provide a comprehensive introduction to issues of gender as they pertain to architectural studies. This is the first such book to include a range of key texts from both within and outside architecture published over the last twenty years. It also provides a clear framework by which to investigate the subject. *Gender, Space, Architecture* simultaneously presents closure and aperture – a momentary recapitulation of seminal texts both past and present – as well as providing an opening of the territory to future new ideas and practices.

We imagine readers to come with varying interests from a number of different areas: first from within architecture with an interest in gender; second from within gender studies with an interest in space and architecture; and third from within spatialised disciplines, such as geography and anthropology, with an interest in gender and in architecture.

As with any introductory text, the geographic and historical scope of the subject matter of *Gender, Space, Architecture* is limited to the availability of current research and published material. First, the material is restricted by geography. Most of the writers and the subjects they refer to are western in origin, many in fact from the United States where much of the work has been undertaken. Here, however, we would recall bell hooks' cautionary reminder that rather than undertaking a geographic tour in search of 'difference' and eternal 'otherness', it is better to understand the formation of difference and to find ways of reconciling its divisions and violence. Second, the historical range of the material in *Gender, Space, Architecture* has been similarly constricted to the history of western civilisation, that is, by the conventional boundaries of western architectural history. Where possible, subjects and authors addressing topics outside the realms of Euro-America, as well as questions of cultural hybridity, ethnicity and black politics have therefore been included. We hope that omissions in this context will motivate further research in this field. A similar point needs emphasising in relation to sex and sexuality. While we have included a number of essays by male contributers and material which explores queer theory, homosexuality and masculinity, it is the case that the majority of chapters deal with the feminine and female aspects of gender and consider sexuality from a heterosexual perspective. Such a bias reflects the shape of the subject area historically, although it is important to add that currently there are clear indications of a dramatic increase in research on masculinity, men and architecture, as well as gay politics, queer theory and urban space.

The editors would like to thank Beatriz Colomina, Neil Leach, Katharina Ledersteger-Goodfriend, Sarah Lloyd, Caroline Mallinder, Leslie Kanes Weisman and Sarah Wigglesworth for their support in the project and for valuable suggestions. Many thanks also to Claire Haywood for her invaluable efforts in compiling the index, and to Rebecca Casey, Ruth Jeavons and Bettina Wilkes for their hard work in producing this volume. Over the past five years discussions with students at the Bartlett School of Architecture, Chelsea College of Art and Design, Winchester School of Art, Kingston University and the University of Nottingham have also shaped the final form of this volume. In particular, we have been delighted to work with our series editors, Anthony King and Thomas Markus. From their strategic overviews at the outset of the project to their meticulous comments at the close of the work, Tony and Tom have thoughout shown a keen concern with the development of this book and offered many helpful insights. We would also like to acknowledge the financial support of Chelsea College of Art and Design. Finally, we would like to thank Bridget Smith for her generosity in allowing us to use one of her sumptuous images for the front cover.

Acknowledgements

The editors and publishers gratefully acknowledge the following for permission to reproduce material in this book.

VISUAL MATERIAL

Cover: Bridget Smith, 'Madonna Suite', © 1997
Fig. 16.1:   Michael Saphier, *Office Planning and Design* (New York: McGraw-Hill, 1968)
Fig. 16.2:   John Pile, *Open Office Planning* (London: Architectural Press, 1978)
Fig. 21.1:   National Gallery of Art, Washington
Fig. 27.1:   Iain Borden
Figs 30.1–3:   Dolores Hayden
Figs 31.1–2:   Matrix
Fig. 34.1:   Iain Borden
Fig. 36.1:   National Monuments Records, London
Fig. 36.2:   Alice Friedman
Fig. 37.1–2:   A.J. Downing, *The Architecture of Country Houses* (1850)
Figs 38.1–2:   Special Collections, US Air Force Academy, Colorado Springs
Figs 41.1–6:   Elizabeth Diller

WRITTEN MATERIAL

Leslie Kanes Weisman, 'Women's Environmental Rights: A Manifesto', 'Making Room: Women and Architecture', *Heresies: A Feminist Publication on Art and Politics* (1981), 3(3), issue 11. Reprinted by permission of Leslie Kanes Weisman
Excerpts from Virginia Woolf, *A Room of One's Own* (1929) (London: Flamingo, 1994). By permission of Chatto
Simone de Beauvoir, *The Second Sex* (1949) (London: Vintage, 1997)
Betty Friedan, *The Feminine Mystique* (1963) (London: Penguin Books, 1992)
Audre Lorde, 'The Master's Tools will Never Dismantle the Master's House', *The Audre Lorde Compendium* (1979) (London: Pandora Press, 1996). Published

in *Sister Outsider: Essays and Speeches* by Audre Lorde © 1984, The Crossing Press: Freedom, CA

Excerpts from Michèle Barrett, 'Some Conceptual Problems in Marxist Feminist Analysis', *Women's Oppression Today: Problems in Marxist Feminist Analysis* (1980) (London: Verso, 1988). Reprinted by permission of Verso

Excerpts from Nancy Chodorow, 'Why Women Mother', *The Reproduction of Mothering: Psychoanalysis and the Sociology of Gender* (Berkeley, Los Angeles: University of California Press, 1978). Reprinted by permission of University of California Press

Luce Irigaray, *This Sex which Is Not One* (Ithaca, NY: Cornell University Press, 1985). Reprinted by permission of Editions de Minuit and the University of Massachusetts Press from Elaine Marks and Isabelle Courtivron's *New French Feminisms: An Anthology* (Amherst: University of Massachusetts Press, 1980). © 1980 the University of Massachusetts Press

Excerpts from Joan Wallach Scott, 'Gender: A Useful Category of Historical Analysis', Joan Wallach Scott (ed.), *Feminism and History* (Oxford: Oxford University Press, 1996). Reprinted from Joan Wallach Scott, *Gender and the Politics of History* © 1988 Columbia University Press. Reprinted with the permission of the publisher

Excerpts from Chandra Talpade Mohanty, 'Under Western Eyes: Feminist Scholarship and Colonial Discourses' (1984), Chandra Talpade Mohanty, Ann Russo and Lourdes Torres (eds), *Third World Women and the Politics of Feminism* (Bloomington and Indianapolis: Indiana University Press, 1991), pp. 51–80

Excerpts from Harry Brod, 'The Case for Men's Studies', Harry Brod (ed.), *The Making of Masculinities* (London: Routledge, 1987). Reprinted by permission of Routledge

Judith Butler, 'Subversive Bodily Acts', *Gender Trouble: Feminism and the Subversion of Identity* (London: Routledge, 1990). Reprinted by permission of Routledge and Judith Butler

Excerpts from Shirley Ardener, 'Ground Rules and Social Maps for Women', Shirley Ardener (ed.), *Women and Space: Ground Rules and Social Maps* (Oxford: Berg, 1993). Reprinted by permission of Berg

Excerpts from Daphne Spain, 'The Contemporary Work Place', *Gendered Space* (Chapel Hill, NC Carolina: University of North Carolina Press, 1985). © 1992. Reprinted by permission of University of North Carolina Press

Doreen Massey, 'Space, Place and Gender', *Space, Place and Gender* (Cambridge: Polity Press, 1994), originally published in *LSE Magazine*. Reprinted by permission of *LSE Magazine* and Doreen Massey

Rosalyn Deutsche, 'Men in Space', *Evictions: Art and Spatial Politics* (Cambridge, Mass.: MIT Press, 1996). [An earlier version of this essay appeared in *Strategies* (1990), 3: 130–7, and *Artforum* 28 (February 1990), 6.] Reprinted by permission of the MIT Press © 1996

Susana Torre, 'Claiming the Public Space: The Mothers of Plaza de Mayo', Diana Agrest, Patricia Conway and Leslie Kanes Weisman (eds), *The Sex of*

Architecture (New York: Harry N. Abrams, Inc., Publishers, 1996), pp. 241–50. Reprinted with the permission of Harry N. Abrams, Inc., Publishers, New York

Elizabeth Wilson, 'Into the Labyrinth', *The Sphinx in the City: Urban Life, the Control of Disorder and Women* (London: Virago, 1991). Reprinted by permission of Elizabeth Wilson

Griselda Pollock, 'Modernity and the Spaces of Femininity', *Vision and Difference: Femininity, Feminism and Histories of Art* (London: Routledge, 1992). Reprinted by permission of Routledge

Meaghan Morris, 'Things to Do with Shopping Centres', Susan Sheridan (ed.), *Grafts: Feminist Cultural Criticism* (London: Verso, 1988), pp. 193–208. Reprinted by permission of Verso

Mary McLeod, 'Everyday and "Other" Spaces', Debra L. Coleman, Elizabeth Ann Danze and Carol Jane Henderson (eds), *Feminism and Architecture* (New York: Princeton Architectural Press, 1996), pp. 3–37. Reprinted with permission of the editors and Mary McLeod

bell hooks, 'Choosing the Margin as a Space of Radical Openness', *Yearnings: Race, Gender and Cultural Politics* (London: Turnaround Press, 1989). Reprinted with permission from the publisher, South End Press, 116 Saint Botolph Street, Boston, MA 02115

Elizabeth Grosz, 'Woman, *Chora*, Dwelling', *Space, Time and Perversion, The Politics of the Body* (London: Routledge, 1996). Originally published in *ANY* (April 1991–92), 4. Reprinted by permission of Anyone Corporation and Elizabeth Grosz

Sara Boutelle, 'Julia Morgan', Susana Torre (ed.), *Women in American Architecture: A Historic and Contemporary Perspective* (New York: Whitney Library of Design, 1977), pp. 79–87. © 1977 by Whitney Library of Design. Used by arrangement with Watson-Guptill Publications, a division of BPI Communications, Inc.

Lynne Walker, 'Women and Architecture', Judy Attfield and Pat Kirkham (eds), *A View from the Interior: Feminism, Women and Design* (London: The Women's Press, 1989), pp. 90–105. Reprinted with permission of The Women's Press, 1989, 34 Great Sutton Street, London EC1V 0DX

Denise Scott Brown, 'Room at the Top? Sexism and the Star System in Architecture', Ellen Perry Berkeley (ed.), *Architecture: a Place for Women* (London and Washington: Smithsonian Institution Press, 1989), pp. 237–46. Reprinted by permission of the Smithsonian Institution Press, 1989

Dolores Hayden, 'What Would a Non-sexist City Be Like? Speculations on Housing, Urban Design and Human Work' (1980), Catharine R. Stimpson, Elsa Dixler, Martha J. Nelson and Kathryn B. Yatrakis (eds), *Women and the American City* (Chicago and London: University of Chicago Press, 1981). Reprinted by permission of University of Chicago Press and Dolores Hayden

Frances Bradshaw, 'Working with Women', Matrix, *Making Space: Women and the Man-made Environment* (London: Pluto Press, 1984), pp. 89–105. Reprinted by permission of Pluto Press

Karen A. Franck, 'A Feminist Approach to Architecture: Acknowledging Women's Ways of Knowing', Ellen Perry Berkeley (ed.), *Architecture: A Place for Women* (London and Washington, DC: Smithsonian Institution Press, 1989), pp. 201–16. Reprinted by permission of the Smithsonian Institution Press, 1989

Excerpts from Labelle Prussin, 'The Creative Process', *African Nomadic Architecture: Space, Place and Gender* (Washington, DC: Smithsonian Institution Press, 1995). Reprinted by permission of the Smithsonian Institution Press, 1995

Beatriz Colomina, 'The Split Wall: Domestic Voyeurism', Beatriz Colomina (ed.), *Sexuality and Space* (New York: Princeton Architectural Press, 1992). Reprinted by permission of Beatriz Colomina

Excerpts from Zeynep Çelik, 'Le Corbusier, Orientalism, Colonialism', *Assemblage* (April 1992), 17, pp. 66–77. Reprinted by permission of the Massachusetts Institute of Technology © 1992

Excerpts from Alice T. Friedman, 'Architecture, Authority and the Female Gaze: Planning and Representation in the Early Modern Country House', *Assemblage* (August 1992), 18: 40–61. Reprinted by permission of The Massachusetts Institute of Technology © 1992

Henry Urbach, 'Closets, Clothes, disClosure', Duncan McCorquodale, Katerina Rüedi and Sarah Wigglesworth (eds), *Desiring Practices: Architecture, Gender and the Interdisciplinary* (London: Blackdog, 1996), pp. 246–63. Reprinted by permission of Duncan McCorquodale of Blackdog

Joel Sanders, 'Cadet Quarters, US Air Force Academy, Colorado Springs', Joel Sanders (ed.), *Stud: Architectures of Masculinity* (Princeton: Princeton Architectural Press, 1996), pp. 68–78. Reprinted by permission of Princeton Architectural Press

Diane Agrest, 'Architecture from Without: Body, Logic and Sex', *Architecture from Without: Theoretical Framings for a Critical Practice* (Cambridge, Mass.: MIT Press, 1993). Reprinted by permission of the MIT Press © 1993

Jennifer Bloomer, 'Big Jugs', Arthur Kroker and Marilouise Kroker (eds), *The Hysterical Male: New Feminist Theory* (London: Macmillan, 1991), pp. 13–27. © Arthur Kroker and Marilouise Kroker 1991, from *The Hysterical Male: New Feminist Theory*, by Arthur Kroker and Marilouise Kroker, reprinted (in America) with permission of St. Martin's Press Incorporated; with permission of New World Perspectives (in the UK and Canada)

Elizabeth Diller, 'Bad Press', Francesca Hughes (ed.), *The Architect: Reconstructing her Practice* (Cambridge, Mass.: MIT Press, 1996), pp. 74–94. Reprinted by permission of the MIT Press © 1996

bell hooks, Julie Eizenberg and Hank Koning 'House, 20 June 1994', *Assemblage* (1995), 24. Reprinted with permission of bell hooks

Considerable effort has been made to trace and contact copyright holders and to secure rights prior to publication. However, this has not always been possible. The editors and publisher apologise for any errors and omissions. If notified, the publishers will endeavour to correct these at the earliest opportunity.

Prologue: Leslie Kanes Weisman

'Women's Environmental Rights: A Manifesto'

from *Heresies: A Feminist Publication on Art and Politics* (1981)

> Be it acknowledged:
> The man-made environments which surround us reinforce conventional patriarchal definitions of women's role in society and spatially imprint those sexist messages on our daughters and sons. They have conditioned us to an environmental myopia which limits our self-concepts . . . which limits our visions and choices for ways of living and working . . . which limits us by not providing the environments we need to support our autonomy or by barring our access to them. It is time to open our eyes and see the political nature of this environmental oppression!

Architect Louis Sullivan, often referred to as the 'Father of the Skyscraper', described a building by his colleague Henry Hobson Richardson in this way:

> Here is a man for you to look at, a virile force, an entire male. It stands in physical fact, a monument to trade, to the organized commercial spirit, to the power and progress of the age, to the strength and resource of individuality and force of character. Therefore I have called it, in a world of barren pettiness, a male, for it sings the song of procreant power, as others have squealed of miscegenation.
>
> (Kindergarten Chats 1901)

ARCHITECTURE AS ICON

The built environment is a cultural artifact. It is shaped by human intention and intervention, a living archaeology through which we can extract the priorities and beliefs of the decision-makers in our society. Both the process through which we build and the forms themselves embody cultural values and imply standards of behavior which affect us all.

From the corporate towers of the wizards of industry to the Emerald City of the Wizard of Oz, men have created the built environment in their own self-image. The twentieth-century urban skyscraper, a pinnacle of patriarchal symbology, is rooted in the masculine mystique of the big, the erect, the forceful – the full balloon of the inflated masculine ego. Skyscrapers in our cities compete for individual recognition and domination while impoverishing human identity and the quality of life.

The home, the place to which women have been intimately connected, is as revered an architectural icon as the skyscraper. From early childhood women have been taught to assume the role of 'homemaker', 'housekeeper', and 'housewife'. The home, long considered women's special domain, reinforces sex-role stereotypes and subtly perpetuates traditional views of family. From the master bedroom to the head of the table, the 'man of the house/breadwinner' is afforded places of authority, privacy (his own study), and leisure (a hobby shop, a special lounge chair). A homemaker has no inviolable space of her own. She is attached to spaces of service. She is a hostess in the living room, a cook in the kitchen, a mother in the children's room, a lover in the bedroom, a chauffeur in the garage. The house is a spatial and temporal metaphor for conventional role playing.

The acceptance and expression of these traditional cultural roles and attitudes still persist in the design, if not the use, of almost all domestic architecture. In being exclusively identified with the home, women are associated with traits of nurturance, cooperation, subjectivity, emotionalism, and fantasy, while 'man's world' – the public world of events and 'meaningful' work – is associated with objectivity, impersonalization, competition, and rationality.

This fragmentation, this segregation of the public and private spheres according to sex roles reinforces an emotionally monolithic stereotype of women and men. It excludes each sex from contact and therefore a fuller understanding of each other. It limits each from learning a variety of skills and reflects on our concepts of self and other. I believe one of the most important responsibilities of architectural feminism is to heal this schizophrenic spatial schism – to find a new architectural language in which the 'words', 'grammar', and 'syntax' synthesize work and play, intellect and feeling, action and compassion.

ENVIRONMENT AS BARRIER

Women's lives are profoundly affected by the design and use of public spaces and buildings, transportation systems, neighborhoods, and housing. Discriminatory laws, governmental regulations, cultural attitudes, informal practices, and lack of awareness by professionals have created conditions which reflect and reinforce women's second-class status.

Women are perceived as having very little to do with public space. In public buildings and spaces both physical and cultural barriers exclude women with children. A woman with a child in a stroller, trying to get through a revolving door or a subway turnstile, is a 'handicapped' person. Public places rarely provide space where infants can be breast-fed or have their diapers changed – the implication being that mothers and children should be at home where they belong.

Public transportation is used by those with the least access to automobiles, namely the young, the aged, minorities, and low-income workers. While men also fall into these categories, almost twice as many women as men rely on public transportation to get to their jobs in the 12 largest metropolitan areas of the country. The location of industries and household work in the suburbs, where there is little, if any, public transportation, severely influences job possibilities for both urban low-income female heads of household and suburban women without access to cars.

Women of all socioeconomic classes have been victims of extreme discrimination in the rental and purchase of housing and in obtaining mortgage financing and insurance. Section 8, a federally subsidized housing program, disqualifies single persons who are not elderly or disabled as well as people of the same or opposite sex who live together but are not related by blood or marriage. Standards of this type deny equal access to much-needed low-cost housing for the burgeoning numbers of widows and displaced homemakers, many of whom are likely to have limited or low incomes. It also blatantly discriminates according to sexual preference and marital status. Yet in the past 12 years, households of 'primary individuals' (those who live with persons unrelated to them) have grown four times as fast as households of nuclear families. In 1973, 76 per cent of women over the age of 65 who were heads of households lived alone. The increased longevity of women, combined with undeniable changes in family structure, requires the availability of a wide range of housing types, locations, and prices which respect the diversity of the ageing population and acknowledge varying levels of dependence.

A meaningful environment is necessary and essential to a meaningful existence. Women must demand public buildings and spaces, transportation, and housing, which support our lifestyles and incomes and respond to the realities of our lives, not the cultural fantasies about them.

On New Year's Eve 1971, 75 women took over an abandoned building on Fifth Street owned by the City of New York. They issued the following statement on 29 January:

> Because we want to develop our own culture,
> Because we want to overcome stereotypes,
> Because we refuse to have 'equal rights' in a corrupt society,
> Because we want to survive, grow, be ourselves . . .
>
> We took over a building to put into action
> with women those things essential to women
> – health care, child care, food conspiracy,
> clothing and book exchange, gimme
> women's shelter, a lesbian rights center,
> interarts center, feminist school, drug
> rehabilitation.
>
> We know the city does not provide for us.
> Now we know the city will not allow us to provide for ourselves.
> For this reason we were busted.
> We were busted because we are women acting independently of men, independently
> of the system . . . In other words, we are women being revolutionary.

SPACE AS POWER

The appropriation and use of space are political acts. The kinds of spaces we have, don't have, or are denied access to can empower us or render us powerless. Spaces can enhance or restrict, nurture or impoverish. We must demand the right to architectural settings which will support the essential needs of all women.

The type of spaces demanded by the women involved in the Fifth Street takeover poignantly illustrate those places lacking in our lives. Day-care centers, displaced homemakers' facilities, and women's resource centers are vitally necessary if we are to eliminate existing and potential barriers to employment for all women. Battered women's shelters are essential if we are to provide women and their children with a safe refuge from their abusers and a place to rethink their lives, futures, and the welfare of their children. Emergency housing is needed for women runaways and victims of rape. Halfway houses ought to exist for prostitutes, alcoholics, addicts, and prisoners. Shelters for shopping bag ladies are needed as well. We need decentralized and convenient health care facilities for women. We need to build safe and available abortion clinics. Midwife-run birth centers are crucial if we are to have control over our own bodies and restore our 'birth rights'. These places and spaces represent new architectural settings which reflect both radical changes in our society as well as glaring evidence of women's oppression and disenfranchisement.

WHAT CAN WE DO ABOUT IT?

Women constitute over 50 per cent of the users of our environments, yet we have had a negligible influence on the architectural forms our environments express. Where legislation and funding connected with new spaces for women do exist, it is primarily the result of activism by women, women's movement organizations, and the work of those few but increasing feminists who are in elected or appointed political office. If the future vision for the built and planned environment is to be one in which the totality of women's needs is environmentally supported, then each woman must become her own architect, that is, she must become aware of her ability to exercise environmental judgment and make decisions about the nature of the spaces in which she lives and works. Women must act consciously and politically. We must ask ourselves who will benefit and who will lose in decisions being made about our neighborhoods, homes, and workplaces, and endorse those proposals that make life easier for us and for those groups who have the least.

> Be it affirmed:
> The built environment is largely the creation of white, masculine
> subjectivity. It is neither value-free nor inclusively human. Feminism implies
> that we fully recognize this environmental inadequacy and proceed to think
> and act out of that recognition.

One of the most important tasks of the women's movement is to make visible the full meaning of our experiences and to reinterpret and restructure the built environment in those terms. We will not create fully supportive, life-enhancing environments until our society values those aspects of human experience that have been devalued through the oppression of women, and we must work with each other to achieve this.

These are feminist concerns which have critical dimensions that are both societal and spatial. They will require feminist activism as well as architectural expertise to insure a solution.

1 Jane Rendell, Barbara Penner and Iain Borden

Editors' General Introduction

Research on gender and architecture first started to appear in the late 1970s, largely written by women and from an overtly political feminist angle. Until recently much of this work has remained internal to the discipline, concerned largely with the architectural profession and issues concerning the 'man-made' environment. Published in 1992, Beatriz Colomina's edited volume, *Sexuality and Space*[1] was the first collection of work to bring ideas about gender generated in other fields – such as anthropology, art history, cultural studies, film theory, geography, psychoanalysis and philosophy – to bear on architectural studies. What such work provides is an interdisciplinary context for a gendered critique of architecture, one which expands the terms of the discourse by making links, through gender, with methodological approaches in other academic disciplines. Gender theory, often drawn from other fields of study, provides useful tools and models for critiquing architectural culture – design, theory and history.

Following *Sexuality and Space*, a number of other texts have investigated architecture and gender, taking clearly feminist perspectives, as well as exploring concerns with sex, desire, space and masculinity.[2] What such books have in common is their multifaceted nature. They are all edited collections, compositions of different voices; rather than describe the work of female architects or prescribe the architecture we should be producing, the attitude towards the relationship of architecture and feminism is speculative. *Gender Space Architecture* offers something different: it is an interdisciplinary introduction which consists of a carefully selected, comprehensive collection of seminal texts from the last twenty years, organised both chronologically and thematically. This introduction and the three sectional introductions form an important part of the book, offering a map of the territory and a route-guide through it.

Gender Space Architecture is divided into three parts. Part 1, 'Gender', is a collection of seminal texts from feminism and gender studies, introducing key debates in the development of feminism, women's studies and gender theory. The chapters in Part 2 'Gender, Space' largely derive from more spatial disciplines for whom space is treated as concept as well as context. It – gender, space – covers different ways of thinking about these terms from alternative academic positions, such as anthropology, cultural studies, geography, philosophy and psychoanalysis and the different ways in which gendered representations can be produced and received in different cultural and social practices – including writing, painting and dwelling. Part 3, 'Gender, Space, Architecture', is composed of chapters largely drawn from inside the discipline of architecture which deal with considerations of different architectural practices: design, history and theory. The chapters explore how feminist ideas have influenced the work of women practising within the internal concerns of architectural practice, but also demonstrate the specific effects of applying the gender and spatial theories contained in Parts 1 and 2 of this book to architectural ideas. The result is an elucidation of both the importance of gender to architecture and, conversely, the importance of architecture to gender.

GENDER

Originally used in the 1890s to describe a belief in sexual equality and a commitment to eradicate sexual domination and transform society, feminism depends on an understanding that in all countries where the sexes are divided into separate cultural, political and economic spheres and where women are less valued than men, their sexuality is held as the cause of their oppression. Today, despite the persistence of certain kinds of sexual discrimination in society, few women describe themselves as 'feminists'. Furthermore, in the workplace, and within professional environments such as architecture, the majority of women choose to describe themselves in gender-neutral terms, as architects, rather than as female architects. In academia, although the situation is somewhat different and may appear to embrace issues of sex and gender from a position of radical difference, feminism is still frequently met with a degree of hostility, with resistance to overtly politicised feminist ideas and actions coming both from the establishment and also from women who believe that openly aligning themselves with feminism will result in stereotyping.

On the other hand, in recent years there has been a gradual warming towards gender issues, from both men and women, with an increasing openness to discussing ideas of gender relations – feminine and masculine – as well as sexuality. The terminology has changed: feminist theory has become gender theory, women's studies have become gender studies. It is easy to be cynical, and assume that 'gender' has replaced 'feminism' as a less politicised, more neutral and descriptive rather prescriptive term. But it is also the case – one which this editorial group advocates – that to talk of gender is to take a political position but one which is more sympathetic to difference. As described by Joan Wallach Scott in Chapter 11, gender can be considered as a category of analysis, one which allows us to talk about masculinity and femininity in mutual and dialectic relation. Such an understanding of gender as a form of relationship between men and women is also important in the development of men's studies as outlined by Harry Brod in

Chapter 12. These changes in cultural attitudes towards feminism and gender are part of a more general opening of intellectual discussions – broadly termed 'post-modernism' – towards issues of cultural hybridity and diversity, as well as radical democracy and environmental awareness. Feminism and gender studies have become postmodernised, made interdisciplinary and therefore have to be considered as such.

It is in this context that the first part of *Gender Space Architecture* should be viewed. This first part charts a brief history of western feminist thought over the past century, focusing on the contemporary condition and changing definitions of gender and sex, as well as identifying a number of key positions taken by feminist thinkers – liberal, radical, essentialist, materialist, Marxist, lesbian, psychoanalytic and postcolonial – and introducing the relatively new discipline of men's studies. The early work of feminists fighting for women's equality can be seen to have shifted towards critiques of existing value systems, from understanding why to analysing how oppression occurs. One of the most important aspects of current feminism is the consideration of the interrelationship of a number of different forms of oppression at different times and in different places. Thinking about gender alone is not enough; for current gender theorists, issues of race, class and sexuality are inextricably involved.

In summary, Part 1, 'Gender', introduces some concepts central to an under-standing of feminism and gender studies and the development of this area of study over the last thirty years. The section sets out a simple historical and theoretical framework through which to explore considerations of space and architecture in subsequent chapters.

GENDER, SPACE

A number of academic disciplines – in particular, anthropology, cultural and visual studies, geography, history and philosophy – have now developed extensive and sophisticated methodologies informed by gender concerns and feminist politics. Furthermore, they have embarked on a series of interdisciplinary exchanges, thus not only creating developments in gender within existing disciplines, but also irre-vocably changing the nature of gender discourse.

The second section of this book, 'Gender, Space', identifies those disciplines which might be thought of as spatial and therefore most relevant to discussions of gender, space and architecture. Chapters include contributions from a number of influential thinkers within these key disciplines – such as anthropologist Shirley Ardener (Chapter 15), geographer Doreen Massey (Chapter 17) and cultural theorist Elizabeth Wilson (Chapter 20) – and suggests the relevance of their work to architectural studies. Since discussions about the gendering of space as public and private emerged in relation to the term 'built environment' rather than 'archi-tecture' as it is traditionally defined, as the work of well-known architects, this section focuses on spaces which are not usually considered architectural. For example, in Chapter 22 Meagan Morris looks at shopping malls and suburban developments where, as consumers and mothers, women spend much of their time, while in Chapter 23 Mary McLeod examines so-called 'everyday' places in the city.

Each chapter deals with space, but in a different way. For bell hooks in Chapter 24 and Elizabeth Grosz in Chapter 25, for example, space is at once both real and metaphoric: space exists as a material entity, a form of representation and a conceptual and political construct.

Picking up on such thematic strands in Part 2 allows the reader to consider a number of chapters in Part 1 as explicitly spatial. For example, if we consider space as a metaphor, we can understand how: for Virginia Woolf in Chapter 3, the occupation of a 'room of one's own' is fundamental to female emancipation; for Audre Lorde in Chapter 6, patriarchy is a 'house' which must be deconstructed; and, in a more Utopian moment, for Luce Irigaray, in Chapter 9, it is the specific spatiality of the female sex, the fluidity of 'two lips', which provides inspiration for imagining the shape of a different kind of culture.

It is also possible to take particular ways of thinking about space adopted by authors in Part 2, 'Gender, Space', to set out a framework for considering architecture in Part 3, 'Gender, Space, Architecture'. Discussions of the role of gender in the social production of space, elaborated in Part 2 by authors such as Daphne Spain in Chapter 16 and Rosalyn Deutsche in Chapter 18, provide important ways of understanding various chapters in Part 3, such as the different forms of architectural production considered by Labelle Prussin in Chapter 33 and Elizabeth Diller in Chapter 41, as well as the work of historians such as Zeynep Çelik in Chapter 35 and Alice T. Friedman in Chapter 36. Concerns with issues like public and private or relations of looking and consuming, introduced by various authors in Part 2, such as Susana Torre in Chapter 19 and Elizabeth Wilson in Chapter 20, allow us to think of architecture as a setting for the playing out of gender relations, rather than as a formally styled, immobile object. For some feminist critics in Part 2, such as Griselda Pollock in Chapter 21, the interpretation of various forms of cultural representation as gendered is the focus of their work. Such work has important implications for considering architectural space as a form of gendered representation in Part 3 – for example, by Beatriz Colomina in Chapter 34 and Diane Agrest in Chapter 39.

In this way, links can be made between chapters in the three different sections of this book, *Gender Space Architecture*, as well as between chapters within each section. It is possible therefore to consider how the theoretical positions adopted in Part 1 can be used as critical tools and theoretical frameworks through which to understand architecture in Part 3. For example, Judith Butler's notions of gender as set out in Part 1, Chapter 13, closely inform Henry Urbach's historical and theoretical study of closets and coming out in Part 3, Chapter 37, whereas Harry Brod's summary of the main tenets of men's studies in Part 1, Chapter 12 provides a way of considering SOM's *Cadet Quarters*, US Air Force Academy at Colorado Springs, as a cultural representation of masculinity in Part 3, Chapter 38.

In a similar way, Mohanty's critique of the colonising aspects of western feminism in Part 1, Chapter 10, provides a theoretical backdrop for understanding the ways in which issues of race and gender intersect in the architect Le Corbusier's conflated notions of the ethnic and feminised other in Algiers in Part 3, Chapter 35. Working between Parts 2 and 3, Labelle Prussin's account of African nomad women's involvement in the building process in Part 3, Chapter 33, can be positioned as central to architectural practice by acknowledging bell hooks' call to reclaim and celebrate the margins as centre in Part 2, Chapter 24.

In the United States, the work of Nancy Chodorow on mothering in Part 1, Chapter 8, has provided new ways of thinking about women's creativity for Karen Franck in Part 3, Chapter 32. Equally Betty Friedan's consideration of the problems of women trapped in suburbia in Part 1, Chapter 5 has been highly influential on architectural practitioners in designing places which would allow new relations between men and women in the urban realm, for example, in Part 3, Chapter 30. In the United Kingdom, complex studies of the relation between gender and class oppression in feminist theory, such as those of Michèle Barrett in Part 1, Chapter 6, are manifest in the work of the feminist architectural co-operative Matrix in the 1980s in Part 3, Chapter 31.

GENDER, SPACE, ARCHITECTURE

Traditionally, architecture has been seen as the design and production of buildings by professional architects, which are then discussed by critics, theorists and historians as completed, self-contained objects in terms of style and aesthetics. Marxist critics have extended this field of discussion by examining buildings as the products of the processes of capitalism and architecture as an articulation of the political, social and cultural values of dominant classes and elite social groupings.[3] Although such work has seldom focused on gender difference specifically, many feminists have drawn on the critical methodologies developed through a class-based analysis of architecture in order to consider the ways in which systems of gender and class oppression intersect with one another and with systems of racial, ethnic and sexual domination.

Most recently, architectural criticism has recognised that architecture con-tinues after the moment of its design and construction. The experience, perception, use, appropriation and occupation of architecture need to be considered in two ways: first, as the temporal activity which takes place after the 'completion' of the building, and which fundamentally alters the meaning of architecture, displacing it away from the architect and builder towards the active user; second, as the recon-ceptualisation of architectural production, such that different activities reproduce different architectures over time and space.[4] By recognising that architecture is constituted through its occupation, and that experiential aspects of the occupation of architecture are important in the construction of identity, such work intersects with feminist concerns with aspects of 'the personal', the subject and subjectivity.

Furthermore, in the light of poststructuralist readings of architecture, we must consider that architecture is always in part a representation. As well as existing as a material, three-dimensional object, architecture also exists in the form of architects' drawings (for example, plans, sections, elevations) and publicity/ periodical disseminations (for example, written descriptions and photographs). Architecture also appears indirectly in various forms of cultural documentation, all of which contain representations of gender as well as class, sexuality and race. Considering architecture in this way allows architectural practice to be thought of as buildings, images and written scripts, as well as designs, theories and histories and their various intersections. This position can be and has been subjected to gender and feminist critiques, which show that architecture is gendered in all its representational forms. This can be seen explicitly in the writing of historians such as Beatriz Colomina in Chapter 34, Zeynep Çelik in Chapter 35 and Alice T. Friedman in Chapter 36, as well as in the projects of theorists/designers, such as Diane Agrest in Chapter 39, Jennifer Bloomer in Chapter 40 and Elizabeth Diller in Chapter 41.

The third part of *Gender Space Architecture* takes a broadly chronological look at work which has raised issues of gender in relation to architecture over the past twenty years. The first part of the section, Chapters 27–33, consists of work by female historians, whose research focused on reclaiming the work of women architects, as well as writings by feminist architects on the products and processes involved in designing places by and for women. The later part of the section, Chapters 34–41, consists of recent work which is more theoretically explicit and which openly questions traditional forms of methodology, epistemology and ontology. These authors draw on feminist theory to challenge traditional architectural historical methodology, from the perspective of gender, sexuality and race, to analyse architecture critically as a form of gendered representation and to redefine contemporary notions of design practice. This shift can be identified by comparing the ways in which authors address similar issues; for example, women's relation with the architectural profession. Earlier chapters, for example Sara Boutelle in Chapter 27, Lynne Walker in Chapter 28 and Denise Scott Brown in Chapter 29 – account for women's marginalised experience as practitioners and deal directly with feminist struggles for women's equal access to architectural education and professional status, while later chapters (see, for example, Diane Agrest in Chapter 39, Jennifer Bloomer in Chapter 40 and Elizabeth Diller in Chapter 41) adopt new positions which, as well as implicitly critiquing architectural value systems as inherently patriarchal, advance new forms of feminist architectural practice.

NOTES

1 Beatriz Colomina (ed.), *Sexuality and Space* (New York: Princeton Architectural Press, 1992).

2 See, for example, Diane Agrest, Patricia Conway and Leslie Kanes Weisman (eds), *The Sex of Architecture* (New York: Harry N. Abrams Publisher, 1997); Debra

Coleman, Elizabeth Danze and Carol Henderson (eds), *Architecture and Feminism* (New York: Princeton Architectural Press, 1996); Francesca Hughes (ed.), *The Architect: Reconstructing Her Practice* (Cambridge, Mass.: MIT Press, 1996); Duncan McCorquodale, Katerina Rüedi and Sarah Wigglesworth (eds), *Desiring Practices* (London: Black Dog Publishing Limited, 1996) and Joel Sanders (ed.), *Stud: Architectures of Masculinity* (New York: Princeton Architectural Press, 1996).

3 See, for example, Anthony D. King (ed.), *Buildings and Society* (London: Routledge and Kegan Paul, 1980) and Thomas A. Markus, *Buildings and Power* (London: Routledge, 1993).

4 Iain Borden, Joe Kerr, Alicia Pivaro and Jane Rendell (eds), *Strangely Familiar: Narratives of Architecture in the City* (London: Routledge, 1996); Iain Borden, Joe Kerr, Jane Rendell with Alicia Pivaro (eds), *Unknown City: Contesting Architecture and Social Space* (Cambridge, Mass.: The MIT Press, 1999); Iain Borden and Jane Rendell, *DoubleDecker: Architecture through History, Politics and Poetics* (London: Athlone Press, forthcoming) and Jonathan Hill (ed.), *Occupying Architecture: Between the Architect and the User* (London: Routledge, 1998).

Part 1

Gender

2 Jane Rendell

Introduction: 'Gender'

Composed of a series of diverse practices, feminism can best be described as a form of praxis, a political practice which embraces both action and theory. But possibly the best way of understanding what constitutes the basis of a particular feminist approach is to consider the accounts given of the ways in which differences of sex, gender, race and class and sexuality structure society. The distinction made between the terms 'sex' and 'gender' and the importance ascribed to them, both descriptively and analytically, often defines the basis of a specific theoretical approach or highlights the focus of a practical organisation. In the most simple of summaries, sex – male and female – exemplifies a biological difference between bodies and gender – masculine and feminine – refers to the socially constructed set of differences between men and women. Sex differences are most commonly taken to be differences of a natural and pre-given order, whereas gender differences, although based on sex differences, are taken to be socially, culturally and historically produced differences which change over time and place. Accounts of sex and gender are then important ways of defining different feminist approaches.

Part 1, 'Gender' is composed of a series of chapters, both contemporary and historic, which explore key issues in feminist and gender studies. Each chapter outlines a different approach to ongoing arguments concerning: women's difference from men – equality or difference; differences between women – gender, race, class and sexuality; liberal and radical forms of feminist politics; definitions of being female – materialism, essentialism and constructionism; Anglo-American and French psychoanalytic traditions; modernism and postmodernism; queer theory and men's studies. The chapters are organised chronologically in order to allow readers to trace the historical development of particular debates.

THE PERSONAL IS POLITICAL

The first key issue to emerge in the development of feminism is arguably one of equal rights. First-wave feminism, commencing in the late eighteenth and coming to fruition in the late nineteenth century, sought to oppose the legal inequalities of patriarchy and women's forced dependence on men. As described in the extract by Virginia Woolf in Chapter 3, women's fight for equal rights can be characterised in terms of women's individual and collective exclusion from the public sphere.[1] Second-wave feminism, emerging in the 1960s and 1970s, especially in the United States, placed more importance on understanding why women were different from men, rather than on how women could gain equal status to men. Attempts to evaluate female difference from men, both physically and emotionally, took place through material critiques and the establishment of women-only groups and consciousness-raising workshops. Second-wave feminism recognised that, of equal significance to political and institutional forms of discrimination is discrimination experienced on a personal level – for example, within the home – leading to the phrase 'The personal is political'.

The variation between first-wave and second-wave feminism can be sum-marised as a shift in focus from equality to difference, from addressing the in-equalities of the state, to addressing the differences of women from men and from each other. First-wave feminism can be described as a form of liberal politics, where women's equality is desired but the terms of equality – what it means for a woman to be equal to a man – remain unquestioned. This can be opposed to radical feminist politics, where women's ambition for liberation is defined in terms of differ-ence; what it means to be a woman. The work of Simone de Beauvoir in Chapter 4 is central to this debate; for de Beauvoir, women are 'other' to men – they cannot be defined in male terms since they are different from men.[2]

Definitions and attempts to explain the causes of female difference have come from many different kinds of feminism, but for many, although the precise form of analysis differs, sexual difference has been pin-pointed as the cause, and patriarchy the form, of oppression. One of the most influential and early accounts of the ways in which sex difference marginalised women was by American feminist Betty Friedan, who, as Chapter 5 exemplifies, by attempting to describe 'the problem with no name' produced a critique of the effects of domestic life in the suburbs on women.[3] Almost a decade later, feminists began to develop a more analytic methodology for their critique of sex difference. For example, Shulamith Firestone developed her own version of historical materialism, arguing that women's bodies were the material base of their oppression.[4] With a slightly different twist, Kate Millett posited that the sex difference between men and women created forms of sexual politics and asymmetrical power relations which resulted in the control of women through indoctrination and violence.[5] Possibly the most extreme advocate of female sex difference was American Mary Daly whose work, while following a similar trajectory in its critique of patriarchy, placed great emphasis on the celebration of female difference. Daly's work exemplifies the work of a strand of radical feminism which developed a form of analysis based less on material difference than on essential difference.[6] The feminist most successful in drawing critiques of sex difference from academic and feminist territories into mainstream debate is arguably Australian feminist Germaine Greer, whose powerful account of women's destruction through patriarchy is still a key feminist text.[7] Likewise, Andrea Dworkin's work, most obviously because of its controversial discussion of the objectification of women through male power, sexual aggression and pornography, also occupies a visible and important position in feminist thinking about sex difference.[8]

Due to the explicit political agenda of early feminism and the desire to emphasise women's solidarity and their difference from men, various forms of feminism were critiqued for paying too much attention to the similarities of women, rather than the differences between them. But a variety of feminists working to address forms of oppression other than sex and gender, such as class, race and sexuality, produced work which either implicitly or explicitly criticised this tendency, noting how other factors in women's lives contributed to their experience of sex difference and oppression.

On the agenda of both black and lesbian feminists was a commitment to developing an understanding of the difference among women. The Combahee River Collective (1974) worked to form a more adequate feminist theory of racial difference, which involved developing thematics common to the work of many black women writers, such as a focus on the strength of black women as opposed to their more commonly perceived status as victims, the relation of everyday experience to theoretical concepts and the positive aspects of relationships between women.[9]

For lesbian feminists, the difference between women was to be understood in terms of sexual preference as well as sex. Lesbianism was understood to be a form of female culture and community as well as a sexual practice. For writers such as Adrienne Rich, lesbianism was experienced in the form of both 'continuum' and 'existence',[10] while others emphasised the importance of female friendship.[11] Chapter 7, by the black lesbian poetess Audre Lorde, is exemplary here in that it engages with the emotional as well as the rational in order to draw out the interlocking relations of different forms of oppression due to race and sexuality, as well as class and gender.[12]

In Britain, much feminist study focused on an analysis of capitalism and patriarchy, on understanding the different ways in which class as well as gender operated to oppress women. Questions were raised which specifically addressed the relation of gender and class, such as 'Which came first?', 'Which was more powerful?' and 'Did they always intersect in the same ways?' As argued by Sheila Rowbotham, being working class clearly doubled the oppression of women.[13] Socialist and Marxist feminists put forward different theories which attempted to explain how the two social structures of capitalism and patriarchy, at home and work, in private and in public, operated in relation to one another. In an important essay, Heidi Hartman argued that capitalism and patriarchy were twin social structures which aided each other in oppressing women.[14] But arguably the most influential thinker in this area, was Michèle Barrett, who in Chapter 6, as well as recognising that women's roles at home and work reinforced each other, placed specific emphasis on the ways in which reproduction worked in the service of capitalism.[15]

ONE IS NOT BORN A WOMAN

Understanding the reasons for women's difference from men, in order to re-conceptualise women's knowledge and experience, has been the topic of much feminist discussion and debate. Juliet Mitchell pointed out that women were in need of a psychic revolution and that their oppression needed to be assessed in a different way.[16] The turn to psychoanalysis in order to deal with the differences between women has been criticised for being ahistorical, elitist, universal or for relying too heavily on specific case studies. Psychoanalytic theory operates in an area of overlap between biological and social accounts of sex and gender differ-ence, where differences between men and women cannot be simply explained one way or the other, either as the pre-determined and natural result of biological differ-ence or the socially determined result of various forms of class, gender, racial and sexual relations. Instead, psychoanalytic theory offers an understanding of the unconscious ways in which we acquire sex and gender characteristics, insights into the construction of the gendered subject and subjectivity and various accounts of the connections between the suppressed elements of the unconscious and the feminine.

In America, the psychoanalyst Nancy Chodorow (Chapter 8) based her theories of sexual difference on psychological development. Drawing on, but critiquing, the work of Sigmund Freud, Chodorow argued that women's social role as mothers had a differing effect on the psychological development of boys and girls.[17] Female children learned to connect to objects, since their mother was the same sex as themselves, whereas male children learned to separate themselves from objects, since their primary parent was of a different sex from themselves. This resulted in a difference in psychology, what Carol Gilligan termed an 'ethic of care' in females, a need to empathise, relate and connect.[18]

In France, the situation was somewhat different. Feminist psychoanalysts – namely Hélène Cixious, Luce Irigaray and Julia Kristeva – took a different approach. Again proceeding from, but ultimately rejecting, the work of Freud and Jacques Lacan, these feminists considered the constructions of self and subjectivity in the work of Freud and Lacan to be gendered – based on the male subject and male subjectivity. All three feminists replaced the phallocentricism of Freud and Lacan with new ways of thinking about the construction of the female subject from a position of difference.[19]

The work of Irigaray, included here in Chapter 9, exemplifies a position which argues for a relation between the sexes which is not determined by the equation male/female where female is defined as not-male. This is not to argue for the reversal of the hierarchy of male and female, placing the female in the position of dominance, but to challenge the opposition itself by showing that the feminine and female sexuality exceed the complementary role that they have been assigned in the opposition male/female. Irigaray proposes an alternative female symbolism based metaphorically on the female genitals, a vaginal symbolism, with a different syntax of meaning. The symbolism of two lips – both oral and vaginal – challenges the unity of the phallus because of their self-contained eroticism. From the phallic point of view the vagina is a hole, or a flaw, but when viewed as a founding symbol, a new configuration of meaning occurs. The 'one' of the male subject becomes 'two' constantly in touch with each other, in which they are not separated by negation, but interact and merge – not unitary, but diffuse, diversified, multiple and decentred.[20]

Irigaray's work is located at the centre of a debate over essentialism and constructionism: is being a woman an essential attribute or a constructed one? Feminists who believe that the cause of women's oppression and difference can be found in material circumstances – social and historical – critique the use of psycho-analytic theories for understanding the construction of the female subject as anti-material and ahistorical – as essentialist or pre-given and innate.[21] But to refuse binary oppositions and insist on female difference does not necessarily mean this difference is constructed outside social and historical contexts. The differently sexed female body may still be considered a product of social and physic forces, con-structed or produced, as phallic (in the case of the men) and as castrated (in the case of women).[22]

ANY THEORY OF THE 'SUBJECT' HAS ALWAYS BEEN APPROPRIATED BY THE 'MASCULINE'

Although the term 'postmodernism' is widely used, its meaning is still hotly debated. For some, postmodernism describes a specific historical condition – the economic condition of late capitalism and its associated cultural and intellectual forms; for others, postmodernism is nothing new – the transition from modernism and postmodernism is a repetition of the kind of changes in culture which have occurred in previous epochs. Most agree that postmodernism defines a shift in epistemology, in ways of knowing about truth, reality and history. Postmodernism is characterised by a doubt in one's ability to know the truth – all we can know are different versions of truth; a doubt in one's ability to know reality – all we can know are representations of reality; a doubt in one's ability to know history – all histories are partial and reliant on the relation of historian and reader.[23]

Given the questionable status of truth, reality and history in postmodernism, feminism and postmodernism have had a troubled relation, particularly with respect to a theory of the female subject. Postmodernism has posed a particular challenge for feminism. Since postmodernism provides a critique of the all-knowing modern subject, it cannot allow feminism a female subject cast in the same mould as the modern male subject. On the one hand, for some feminists, this is problematic because it does not allow a stable notion of female subjectivity. In this case postmodernism indicates the abandonment of any kind of political project and instead the acceptance of relativism.[24] On the other hand, some feminists have welcomed the postmodern questioning of traditional categories and embraced the possibility of defining different notions of the subject, truth, reality and history, and argued that this lack of stability is positive.[25] For example, Irigaray has stated that 'any theory of the subject' has always been appropriated by the masculine.[26] Such divergences allow feminism to straddle the divide between the metanarrative of modernism and the relativism of postmodernism, enabling a reconceptualisation of the binary relation between modernism and postmodernism.

Postmodernism's effect on feminism can be described as a transformation from a focus on things to a focus on words, from concern with 'real' things – the everyday realities of women's oppression: rape, unequal wages and the problems of simultaneously working outside the home and trying to raise children – to critiquing representations of these situations. Feminist criticism has drawn on post-structuralist theory, specifically the strategies of Michel Foucault and Jacques Derrida's techniques of deconstruction, in order to discuss the gendering of representations in cultural texts and practices.[27] Foucault, has, among others, shifted the parameters of historical knowledge, from reconstructing a 'real' past and dealing with causation and determination, to focusing instead on the discursive construction of power and knowledge and the political contestation of relations of domination and subordination. Although 'real' problems remain, much recent feminist work has turned from discussing the origins and causes of oppression to examining current repetitions of the origin.

GENDER AS AN ANALYTIC CATEGORY

The fact that women are excluded from the dominant forms of representation and also named as signs within them has required feminist projects to focus on analysing how systems of representation are gendered, as well as why. Feminist historians have been particularly informative in their discussions of the ways in which representations are gendered. While feminist historians writing in the 1970s were concerned with understanding the lives of women, and later the ways in which differences of class and race also impacted on women's lives, more recently feminist historians such as Joan Wallach Scott, in Chapter 11, have recognised that gender is itself an analytic category. Gender not only defines lives as they were lived in the past, but it also constructs the forms of evidence chosen by the historian through which they interpret and explain history. Forms of representation reconstruct particular versions of history; they are gendered according to the viewpoint of their author in the past as well as the historian in the present.[28]

Gendered representations do not only tell of the ways in which sexual difference operates but also how class and race difference are organised.[29] Postmodern theories regarding the construction of the subject and poststructuralist techniques for understanding systems of representation have had an important influence on feminists engaged in studying how class and race interact with gender as multiple forms of oppression. Postcolonial theory, which argues that race as a cultural construction represents notions of the 'other', has been developed by feminists who argue that this 'other' is gendered feminine. Postcolonial feminists – for example, Chandra Talpade Mohanty in Chapter 10 – have also produced important critiques revealing much western feminist study to be 'colonial' and 'essential' in its consideration of race and the construction of the self.[30]

As recent work on masculinity also shows, it is important to consider gender differences as social and cultural representations which vary historically and dialectically.[31] Providing research by men on masculinity, so-called 'men's studies' attempts to redress the balance of feminist work in women's studies. As described by Harry Brod in Chapter 12, such work is often sympathetic to the politics of feminism and also responds methodologically to feminist work by taking gender to be a social construction rather than reinsert the category of man.[32] As contemporary research on men and masculinity increasingly shows, it is important to note both that the categories – men and masculinity, as well as femininity and masculinity – are constructed in mutual relation. It is also necessary to take into account the ways in which differences of class, race and sexuality operate to reinforce or complicate binary notions of sex and gender difference.

Chapter 13, the final chapter in Part 1 by Judith Butler argues that sex and gender are both social and historical constructions. For Butler, gender is not to culture as sex is to nature, sex as natural fact does not precede the cultural inscription of gender. Although gender difference may arise out of the biological or the sex differences between men and women, it is also the case that sex differences are produced through specific material and historical practices. To think of the body only in terms of the biological, anatomical or physiological is limited. Instead, Butler considers gender to be a performance that produces the illusion of an inner sex. Butler suggests that 'gender trouble' is culturally produced through 'subversive body acts' or 'the body in drag' that exhibit the artificiality of gender and so subvert the system from within through parody.[33] This notion of the 'performativity' of gender is paralleled in the work of queer theorists, who argue that if the artificiality of gender is made apparent in exhibitions of display, then the performance of gender may operate subversively to critique radically the naturalness of the biologically sexed body.[34]

NOTES

1 Virginia Woolf, *A Room of One's Own* (1929) (London: Flamingo, 1994). See also Mary Wollstonecraft, *A Vindication of the Rights of Woman* (New York: W. W. Norton, 1792), for an example of a text which marks the emergence of feminism.

2 Simone de Beauvoir, *The Second Sex* (1949) (London: Vintage, 1997).

3 Betty Friedan, 'The problem that has no name', *The Feminine Mystique* (1963) (London: Penguin Books, 1992), pp. 13–16.

4 Shulamith Firestone, *The Dialectic of Sex* (New York: Bantam Books, 1971).

5 Kate Millett, *Sexual Politics* (New York: Doubleday, 1970).

6 Mary Daly, *Gyn/Ecology: the Metaphysics of Radical Feminism* (London: The Women's Press, 1979).

7 Germaine Greer, *The Female Eunuch* (London: Grafton, 1986).

8 Andrea Dworkin, *Intercourse* (London: Arrow Books, 1987).

9 The Combahee River Collective, 'A black feminist statement', G.T. Hull *et al.*, *All the Women are White, all the Blacks are Men, but some of us are Brave: Black Woman's*

Studies (New York: The Feminist Press, 1982). See also later work such as Angela Davis, *Women, Race and Class* (London: The Women's Press, 1982); bell hooks, *Talking Back: Thinking Feminism, Thinking Black* (Boston: South End Press, 1989); and Patricia Hill Collins, *Black Feminist Thought* (London: Unwin Hyman, 1990).

10 See Adrienne Rich, 'Compulsory heterosexuality and lesbian existence', E. Abel and E.K. Abel (eds), *The Signs Reader: Women, Gender and Scholarship* (Chicago: University of Chicago Press, 1983). For an important collection of later work, see Diane Fuss, *Inside/out: Lesbian Theories, Gay Theories* (London: Routledge, 1991).

11 See Charlotte Bunch and S. Pollock (eds), *Learning our Way: Essays in Feminist Education* (New York: The Crossing Press, 1983); Charlotte Bunch, *Passionate Politics: Feminist Theory in Action* (New York: St. Martin's Press, 1987); and Janice Raymond, *A Passion for Friends* (Boston: Beacon Press, 1986).

12 Audre Lorde, 'The master's tools will never dismantle the master's house', *The Audre Lorde Compendium* (1979) (London: Pandora Press, 1996), pp. 158–61.

13 Sheila Rowbotham, *Woman's Consciousness, Man's World* (Harmondsworth: Penguin, 1973).

14 Heidi Hartman, 'The unhappy marrriage of Marxism and feminism', *Women and Revolution* (Boston: South End Press, 1981).

15 Michèle Barrett, 'Some conceptual problems in Marxist feminist analysis', *Women's Oppression Today: Problems in Marxist Feminist Analysis* (1980) (London: Verso, 1988), pp. 8–19.

16 See Juliet Mitchell, *Psychoanalysis and Feminism* (Harmondsworth: Penguin, 1974), and Juliet Mitchell, *Women, the Longest Revolution: Essays on Feminism, Literature and Psychoanalysis* (London: Virago, 1984).

17 Nancy Chodorow, *The Reproduction of Mothering: Psychoanalysis and the Sociology of Gender* (Berkeley, Los Angeles, University of California Press, 1978).

18 Carol Gilligan, *In a Different Voice: Psychological Theory and Women's Development* (Cambridge, Mass.: Harvard University Press, 1982).

19 For the most widely discussed examples of the work of Hélène Cixious and Julia Kristeva, see, for example, Hélène Cixious, 'The laugh of the Medusa', Elaine Marks and Isabelle de Courtivron (eds), *New French Feminisms: An Anthology* (London: Harvester, 1981), pp. 243-64; and Julia Kristeva, *Desire in Language: A Semiotic Approach to Literature and Art* (Oxford: Blackwell, 1980).

20 Luce Irigaray, 'This sex which is not one', *This Sex Which Is Not One* (Ithaca, NY: Cornell University Press, 1985), pp. 23–33.

21 The distinction between materialism and essentialism is a complex one but worth elaborating in a little more detail. For essentialist feminists it is important to argue for innate difference because it strengthens arguments for feminist revolution and the replacing of patriarchy with an improved women-based culture. Materialist feminists find aspects of essentialism disturbing, because it can be seen to encourage certain forms of sexism – if it is the case that women are different from men, then why give women the same rights as men? Instead, materialist feminists argue that if the differences between men and women are considered the result of

material circumstance then 'un-making' such differences will result in a more equal relation between the sexes.

22 The accounts of Irigaray given by Elizabeth Grosz, *Sexual Subversions* (London: Allen and Unwin, 1989), Toril Moi, *Sexual/Textual Politics: Feminist Literary Theory* (London: Methuen, 1985) and Margaret Whitford, *Luce Irigaray: Philosophy in the Feminine* (London: Routledge, 1991) are central to this debate.

23 See, for example, Seyla Benhabib, *Situating the Self: Gender, Community and Post-modernism in Contemporary Ethics* (Cambridge: Polity Press, 1992).

24 See, for example, Susan J. Hekman, *Gender and Knowledge: Elements of a Post-modern Feminism* (Cambridge: Polity Press, 1990).

25 See, for example, the various positions adopted in Linda Nicholson (ed.), *Feminism/ Postmodernism* (London: Routledge, 1990).

26 Luce Irigaray, 'Any theory of the "subject" has always been appropriated by the "masculine"', *The Speculum of the Other Woman* (Ithaca, NY: Cornell University Press, 1985), pp. 133–46.

27 See Michèle Barrett, 'Words and things: materialism and method in contemporary feminist analysis', Michèle Barrett and Anne Phillips (eds), *Destabilising Theory: Contemporary Feminist Debates* (Cambridge: Polity Press, 1992), pp. 201-19. Feminists continue to argue over whether work generated by male theorists can serve as appropriate tools for feminist analysis. See, for example, Jane Flax, *Thinking Fragments: Psychoanalysis, Feminism and Postmodernism in the Contemporary West* (Berkeley, Los Angeles and Oxford: University of California Press, 1991) and Andrea Nye, *Feminist Theory and the Philosophy of Man* (New York: Croom Helm, 1989).

28 See, for example, Catherine Hall, 'Feminism and feminist history', *White, Male and Middle Class: Explorations in Feminism and History* (Cambridge: Polity Press, 1992), pp. 1–42; Joan Wallach Scott, *Gender and the Politics of History* (New York: Columbia University Press, 1988), p. 6; and Joan Wallach Scott, 'Gender: a useful category of historical analysis', Joan Wallach Scott (ed.), *Feminism and History* (Oxford: Oxford University Press, 1996), pp. 152–5.

29 See, for example, Mary Poovey, *Uneven Developments: The Ideological Work of Gender in Mid-Victorian Britain* (Chicago: University of Chicago Press, 1988), and Denise Riley, *Am I that Name? Feminism and the Category of 'Women' in History* (Minneapolis: University of Minnesota Press, 1988).

30 Chandra Talpade Mohanty, 'Under western eyes: feminist scholarship and colonial discourses' (1984), Chandra Talpade Mohanty, Ann Russo and Lourdes Torres (eds), *Third World Women and the Politics of Feminism* (Bloomington and Indianapolis: Indiana University Press, 1991), pp. 51-80. See also Gayatri Chakovorty Spivak, *In Other Worlds: Essays in Cultural Politics* (London: Methuen, 1987); Valentine M. Mooghadam (ed.), *Identity Politics and Women: Cultural Reassertions and Feminisms in International Perspective* (Boulder: Westview Press, 1994); and Chandra Talpade Mohanty and M. Jacqui Alexander (eds), *Feminist Genealogies, Colonial Legacies, Democratic Futures* (London: Routledge, 1997). It is important to note that there is also a good deal of exchange and agreement among worldwide women's

movements. See, for example, Eva Rathgeber, 'WID, WAD, GAD: Trends in Research and Practice', *Journal of Developing Areas* (1990), 24: 489-502.

31 See, for example, Maurice Berger, Brian Wallis and Simon Watson (eds), *Constructing Masculinities* (London: Routledge, 1995); and Andrew Posner and Helaine Perchuk (eds), *The Masculine Masquerade* (Cambridge, Mass.: MIT Press, 1995).

32 See, for example, Harry Brod (ed.), *The Making of Masculinities: The New Men's Studies* (London: Routledge, 1987), and Michael S. Kimmel (ed.), *Changing Men: New Directions in Research on Men and Masculinity* (Newbury Park, Cal.: Sage, 1987).

33 Judith Butler, 'Subversive bodily acts', *Gender Trouble: Feminism and the Subversion of Identity* (London: Routledge, 1990), pp. 139–41.

34 See, for example, Judith Butler, *Gender Trouble: Feminism and the Subversion of Identity* (London: Routledge, 1990). See also Eve Kosofsky Sedgwick, *The Epistemology of the Closet* (New York: Harvester Wheatsheaf, 1991), and Eve Kosofsky Sedgwick, *Tendencies* (London: Routledge, 1994).

3 Virginia Woolf

A Room of One's Own (excerpts from Chapter 1)

from *A Room of One's Own* (1929)

But, you may say, we asked you to speak about women and fiction – what has that got to do with a room of one's own? I will try to explain. When you asked me to speak abut women and fiction I sat down on the banks of a river and began to wonder what the words meant. They might mean simply a few remarks about Fanny Burney; a few more about Jane Austen; a tribute to the Brontës and a sketch of Haworth Parsonage under snow; some witticisms if possible about Miss Mitford; a respectful allusion to George Eliot; a reference to Mrs Gaskell and one would have done. But at second sight the words seemed not so simple. The title women and fiction might mean, and you may have meant it to mean, women and what they are like, or it might mean women and the fiction that they write; or it might mean women and the fiction that is written about them; or it might mean that somehow all three are inextricably mixed together and you want me to consider them in that light. But when I began to consider the subject in this last way, which seemed the most interesting, I soon saw that it had one fatal drawback. I should never be able to come to a conclusion. I should never be able to fulfil what is, I understand, the first duty of a lecturer – to hand you after an hour's discourse a nugget of pure truth to wrap up between the pages of your notebooks and keep on the mantelpiece for ever. All I could do was to offer you an opinion upon one minor point – a woman must have money and a room of her own if she is to write fiction; and that, as you will see, leaves the great problem of the true nature of woman and the true nature of fiction unsolved. I have shirked the duty of coming to a conclusion upon these two questions – women and fiction remain, so far as I am concerned, unsolved problems. But in order to make some amends I am going to do what I can to show you how I arrived at this opinion about the room and the money. I am going to develop in your presence as fully and freely as I can the train of thought which led me to think this. Perhaps if I lay bare the ideas, the prejudices, that lie behind this statement you will find that they have some bearing upon women and some upon fiction. At any rate, when a subject is highly controversial – and any questions about sex is that – one cannot hope to tell the truth. One can only show how one came to hold whatever opinion one does hold. One can only give one's audience the chance of drawing their own conclusions as they observe the limitations, the prejudices, the idiosyncrasies of the speaker. Fiction here is likely to contain more truth than fact. Therefore I propose, making use of all the liberties and licences of a novelist, to tell you the story of the two days that preceded my coming here – how, bowed down by the weight of the subject which you have laid upon my shoulders, I pondered it, and made it work in and out of my daily life. I need not say that what I am about to describe has no existence; Oxbridge is an invention; so is Fernham; 'I' is only a convenient term for somebody who has no real being. Lies will flow from my lips, but there may perhaps be some truth mixed up with them; it is for you to seek out this truth and to decide whether any part of it is worth keeping. If not, you will of course throw the whole of it into the waste-paper basket and forget all about it.

Here then was I (call me Mary Beton, Mary Seton, Mary Carmichael or by any name you please – it is not a matter of importance) sitting on the banks of a river a week or two ago in fine October weather, lost in thought. That collar I have spoken of, women and fiction, the need of coming to some conclusion on a subject that raises all sorts of prejudices and passions, bowed my head to the ground. To the right and left bushes of some sort, golden and crimson, glowed with the colour, even it seemed burnt with the heat, of fire. On the further bank the willows wept in perpetual lamentation, their hair about their shoulders. The river reflected what-ever it chose of sky and bridge and burning tree, and when the undergraduate had oared his boat through the reflections they closed again, completely, as if he had never been. There one might have sat the clock round lost in thought. Thought – to call it by a prouder name than it deserved – had let its line down into the stream. It swayed, minute after minute, hither and thither among the reflections and the weeds, letting the water lift it and sink it until – you know the little tug – the sudden conglomeration of an idea at the end of one's line: and then the cautious hauling of it in, and the careful laying of it out? Alas, laid on the grass how small, how insignificant this thought of mine looked; the sort of fish that a good fisher-man puts back into the water so that it may grow fatter and be one day worth cooking and eating. I will not trouble you with that thought now, though if you look carefully you may find it for yourselves in the course of what I am going to say.

But however small it was, it had, nevertheless, the mysterious property of its kind – put back into the mind, it became at once very exciting, and important; and as it darted and sank, and flashed hither and thither, set up such a wash and tumult of ideas that it was impossible to sit still. It was thus that I found myself walking with extreme rapidity across a grass plot. Instantly a man's figure rose to intercept me. Nor did I at first understand that the gesticulations of a curious-looking object, in a cut-away coat and evening shirt, were aimed at me. His face expressed horror and indignation. Instinct rather than reason came to my help; he was a Beadle; I was a woman. This was the turf; there was the path. Only the Fellows and Scholars are allowed here; the gravel is the place for me. Such thoughts were the work of a moment. As I regained the path the arms of the Beadle sank, his face assumed its usual repose, and though turf is better walking than gravel, no very great harm was done. The only charge I could bring against the Fellows and Scholars of whatever the college might happen to be was that in protection of their turf, which has been rolled for 300 years in succession they had sent my little fish into hiding.

What idea it had been that had sent me so audaciously trespassing I could not now remember. The spirit of peace descended like a cloud from heaven, for if the spirit of peace dwells anywhere, it is in the courts and quadrangles of Oxbridge on a fine October morning. Strolling through those colleges past those ancient halls the roughness of the present seemed smoothed away; the body seemed contained in a miraculous glass cabinet through which no sound could penetrate, and the mind, freed from any contact with facts (unless one trespassed on the turf again), was at liberty to settle down upon whatever meditation was in harmony with the moment. As chance would have it, some stray memory of some old essay about visiting Oxbridge in the long vacation brought Charles Lamb to mind – Saint Charles, said Thackeray, putting a letter of Lamb's to his forehead. Indeed, among all the dead (I give you my thoughts as they came to me), Lamb is one of the most congenial; one to whom one would have liked to say, Tell me then how you wrote your essays? For his essays are superior even to Max Beerbohm's, I thought, with all their perfection, because of that wild flash of imagination, that lightning crack of genius in the middle of them which leaves them flawed and imperfect, but starred with poetry. Lamb then came to Oxbridge perhaps a hundred years ago. Certainly he wrote an essay – the name escapes me – about the manuscript of one of Milton's poems which he saw here. It was *Lycidas* perhaps, and Lamb wrote how it shocked him to think it possible that any word in *Lycidas* could have been different from what it is. To think of Milton changing the words in that poem seemed to him a sort of sacrilege. This led me to remember what I could of *Lycidas* and to amuse myself with guessing which word it could have been that Milton had altered, and why. It then occurred to me that the very manuscript itself which Lamb had looked at was only a few hundred yards away, so that one could follow Lamb's footsteps across the quadrangle to that famous library where the treasure is kept. Moreover, I recollected, as I put this plan into execution, it is in this famous library that the manuscript of Thackeray's *Esmond* is also preserved. The critics often say that *Esmond* is Thackeray's most perfect novel. But the affectation of that style, with its imitation of the eighteenth century, hampers one, so far as I remember; unless indeed the eighteenth-century style was natural to Thackeray – a fact that one might prove by looking at the manuscript and seeing whether the alterations were for the benefit of the style or of the sense. But then one would have to decide what is style and what is meaning, a question which – but here I was actually at the door which leads into the library itself. I must have opened it, for instantly there issued, like a guardian angel barring the way with a flutter of black gown instead of white wings, a deprecating, silvery, kindly gentleman, who regretted in a low voice as he waved me back that ladies are only admitted to the library if accompanied by a Fellow of the College or furnished with a letter of introduction.

That a famous library has been cursed by a woman is a matter of complete indifference to a famous library. Venerable and calm, with all its treasures safe locked within its breasts, it sleeps complacently and will, so far as I am concerned, so sleep for ever. Never will I wake those echoes, never will I ask for that hospitality again, I vowed as I descended the steps in anger. Still an hour remained before luncheon, and what was one to do?

4 Simone de Beauvoir

The Second Sex (excerpts from the Introduction)

from *The Second Sex* (1949)

For a long time I have hesitated to write a book on woman. The subject is irritating, especially to women; and it is not new. Enough ink has been spilled in quarrelling over feminism, and perhaps we should say no more about it. It is still talked about, however, for the voluminous nonsense uttered during the last century seems to have done little to illuminate the problem. After all, is there a problem? And if so, what is it? Are there women, really? Most assuredly the theory of the eternal feminine still has its adherents who will whisper in your ear: 'Even in Russia women still are *women*'; and other erudite persons – sometimes the very same – say with a sigh: 'Woman is losing her way, woman is lost.' One wonders if women still exist, if they will always exist, whether or not it is desirable that they should, what place they occupy in this world, what their place should be. 'What has become of women?' was asked recently in an ephemeral magazine.

But first we must ask: what is a woman? '*Tota mulier in utero*', says one, 'woman is a womb'. But in speaking of certain women, connoisseurs declare that they are not women, although they are equipped with a uterus like the rest. All agree in recognizing the fact that females exist in the human species; today as always they make up about one half of humanity. And yet we are told that femininity is in danger; we are exhorted to be women, remain women, become women. It would appear, then, that every female human being is not necessarily a woman; to be so considered she must share in that mysterious and threatened reality known as femininity. Is this attribute something secreted by the ovaries? Or is it a Platonic essence, a product of the philosophic imagination? Is a rustling petticoat enough to bring it down to earth? Although some women try zealously to incarnate this essence, it is hardly patentable. It is frequently described in vague and dazzling terms that seem to have been borrowed from the vocabulary of the seers, and indeed in the times of St Thomas it was considered an essence as certainly defined as the somniferous virtue of the poppy.

But conceptualism has lost ground. The biological and social sciences no longer admit the existence of unchangeably fixed entities that determine given characteristics, such as those ascribed to woman, the Jew, or the Negro. Science regards any characteristic as a reaction dependent in part upon a *situation*. If today femininity no longer exists, then it never existed. But does the word *woman*, then, have no specific content? This is stoutly affirmed by those who hold to the philosophy of the enlightenment, of rationalism, of nominalism; women, to them, are merely the human beings arbitrarily designated by the word *woman*. Many American women particularly are prepared to think that there is no longer any place for woman as such; if a backward individual still takes herself for a woman, her friends advise her to be psychoanalysed and thus get rid of this obsession. In regard to a work, *Modern Woman: The Lost Sex*, which in other respects has its irritating features, Dorothy Parker has written: 'I cannot be just to books which treat of woman as woman. . . . My idea is that all of us, men as well as women, should be regarded as human beings.' But nominalism is a rather inadequate doctrine, and the anti-feminists have had no trouble in showing that women simply *are not* men. Surely woman is, like man, a human being; but such a declaration is abstract. The fact is that every concrete human being is always a singular, separate individual. To decline to accept such notions as the eternal feminine, the black soul, the Jewish character, is not to deny that Jews, Negroes, women exist today – this denial does not represent a liberation for those concerned, but rather a flight from reality. Some years ago a well-known woman writer refused to permit her portrait to appear in a series of photographs especially devoted to women writers; she wished to be counted among the men. But in order to gain this privilege she made use of her husband's influence! Women who assert that they are men lay claim none the less to masculine consideration and respect. I recall also a young Trotskyite standing on a platform at a boisterous meeting and getting ready to use her fists, in spite of her evident fragility. She was denying her feminine weakness; but it was for love of a militant male whose equal she wished to be. The attitude of defiance of many American women proves that they are haunted by a sense of their femininity. In truth, to go for a walk with one's eyes open is enough to demonstrate that humanity is divided into two classes of individuals whose clothes, faces, bodies, smiles, gaits, interests, and occupations are manifestly different. Perhaps these differences are superficial, perhaps they are destined to disappear. What is certain is that they do most obviously exist.

If her functioning as a female is not enough to define woman, if we decline also to explain her through 'the eternal feminine', and if nevertheless we admit, provisionally, that women do exist, then we must face the question: what is a woman?

To state the question is, to me, to suggest, at once, a preliminary answer. The fact that I ask it is in itself significant. A man would never set out to write a book on the peculiar situation of the human male. But if I wish to define myself, I must first of all say: 'I am a woman'; on this truth must be based all further discussion. A man never begins by presenting himself as an individual of a certain sex; it goes without saying that he is a man. The terms *masculine* and *feminine* are used symmetrically only as a matter of form, as on legal papers. In actuality the relation of the two sexes is not quite like that of two electrical poles, for man represents both the positive and the neutral, as is indicated by the common use of *man* to designate human beings in general; whereas woman represents only the negative, defined by limiting criteria, without reciprocity. In the midst of an abstract discussion it is vexing to hear a man say: 'You think thus and so because you are a woman'; but I know that my only defence is to reply: 'I think thus and so because it is true,' thereby removing my subjective self from the argument. It would be out of the question to reply: 'And you think the contrary because you are a man', for it is understood that the fact of being a man is no peculiarity. A man is in the right in being a man; it is the woman who is in the wrong. It amounts to this: just as for the ancients there was an absolute vertical with reference to which the oblique was defined, so there is an absolute human type, the masculine. Woman has ovaries, a uterus: these peculiarities imprison her in her subjectivity, circumscribe her within the limits of her own nature. It is often said that she thinks with her glands. Man superbly ignores the fact that his anatomy also includes glands, such as the testicles, and that they secrete hormones. He thinks of his body as a direct and normal connection with the world, which he believes he apprehends objectively, whereas he regards the body of woman as a hindrance, a prison, weighed down by everything peculiar to it. 'The female is a female by virtue of a certain *lack* of qualities,' said Aristotle; 'we should regard the female nature as afflicted with a natural defectiveness.' And St Thomas for his part pronounced woman to be an 'imperfect man', an 'incidental' being. This is symbolized in Genesis where Eve is depicted as made from what Bossuet called 'a supernumerary bone' of Adam.

Thus humanity is male and man defines woman not in herself but as relative to him; she is not regarded as an autonomous being. Michelet writes: 'Woman, the relative being . . .' And Benda is most positive in his *Rapport d'Uriel*: 'The body of man makes sense in itself quite apart from that of woman, whereas the latter seems wanting in significance by itself. . . . Man can think of himself without woman. She cannot think of herself without man.' And she is simply what man decrees; thus she is called 'the sex', by which is meant that she appears essentially to the male as a sexual being. For him she is sex – absolute sex, no less. She is defined and differentiated with reference to man and not he with reference to her; she is the incidental, the inessential as opposed to the essential. He is the Subject, he is the Absolute – she is the Other.[1]

NOTE

1   E. Lévinas expresses this idea most explicitly in his essay *Temps et l'Autre*, 'Is there not a case in which otherness, alterity [*altérité*], unquestionably marks the nature of a being, as its essence, an instance of otherness not consisting purely and simply in the opposition of two species of the same genus? I think that the feminine represents the contrary in its absolute sense, this contrariness being in no wise affected by any relation between it and its correlative and thus remaining absolutely other. Sex is not a certain specific difference . . . no more is the sexual difference a mere

contradiction. . . . Nor does this difference lie in the duality of two complementary terms for two complementary terms imply a pre-existing whole. . . . Otherness reaches its full flowering in the feminine, a term of the same rank as consciousness but of opposite meaning.'

I suppose that Lévinas does not forget that woman, too, is aware of her own consciousness, or ego. But it is striking that he deliberately takes a man's point of view, disregarding the reciprocity of subject and object. When he writes that woman is mystery, he implies that she is mystery for man. Thus his description, which is intended to be objective, is in fact an assertion of masculine privilege.

5 Betty Friedan

Excerpts from 'The Problem that Has No Name'

from *The Feminine Mystique* (1963)

The problem lay buried, unspoken, for many years in the minds of American women. It was a strange stirring, a sense of dissatisfaction, a yearning that women suffered in the middle of the twentieth century in the United States. Each suburban wife struggled with it alone. As she made the beds, shopped for groceries, matched slipcover material, ate peanut butter sandwiches with her children, chauffeured Cub Scouts and Brownies, lay beside her husband at night, she was afraid to ask even of herself the silent question: 'Is this all?'

For over fifteen years there was no word of this yearning in the millions of words written about women, for women, in all the columns, books and articles by experts telling women their role was to seek fulfilment as wives and mothers. Over and over women heard in voices of tradition and of Freudian sophistication that they could desire no greater destiny than to glory in their own femininity. Experts told them how to catch a man and keep him, how to breastfeed children and handle their toilet training, how to cope with sibling rivalry and adolescent rebellion; how to buy a dishwasher, bake bread, cook gourmet snails, and build a swimming pool with their own hands; how to dress, look, and act more feminine and make marriage more exciting; how to keep their husbands from dying young and their sons from growing into delinquents. They were taught to pity the neurotic, unfeminine, unhappy women who wanted to be poets or physicists or presidents. They learned that truly feminine women do not want careers, higher education, political rights – the independence and the opportunities that the old-fashioned feminists fought for. Some women, in their forties and fifties, still remembered painfully giving up those dreams, but most of the younger women no longer even thought about them. A thousand expert voices applauded their femininity, their adjustment, their new maturity. All they had to do was devote their lives from earliest girlhood to finding a husband and bearing children.

By the end of the 1950s, the average marriage age of women in America dropped to 20, and was still dropping, into the teens. Fourteen million girls were engaged by 17. The proportion of women attending college in comparison with men dropped from 47 per cent in 1920 to 35 per cent in 1958. A century earlier, women had fought for higher education; now girls went to college to get a husband. By the mid fifties, 60 per cent dropped out of college to marry, or because they were afraid too much education would be a marriage bar. Colleges built dormitories for 'married students', but the students were almost always the husbands. A new degree was instituted for the wives – 'Ph.T.' (Putting Husband Through).

Then American girls began getting married in high school. And the women's magazines, deploring the unhappy statistics about these young marriages, urged that courses on marriage, and marriage counsellors, be installed in the high schools. Girls started going steady at 12 and 13, in junior high. Manufacturers put out brassières with false bosoms of foam rubber for little girls of 10. And an advertisement for a child's dress, size 3–6x, in the *New York Times* in the fall of 1960, said: 'She Too Can Join the Man-Trap Set.'

By the end of the fifties, the United States birthrate was overtaking India's. Statisticians were especially astounded at the fantastic increase in the number of babies among college women. Where once they had two children, now they had four, five, six. Women who had once wanted careers were now making careers out of having babies. So rejoiced *Life* magazine in a 1956 paean to the movement of American women back to the home.

In a New York hospital, a woman had a nervous breakdown when she found she could not breastfeed her baby. In other hospitals, women dying of cancer refused a drug which research had proved might save their lives: its side effects were said to be unfeminine. 'If I have only one life, let me live it as a blonde,' a larger-than-life-sized picture of a pretty, vacuous woman proclaimed from newspaper, magazine, and drugstore ads. And across America, three out of every ten women dyed their hair blonde. They ate a chalk called Metrecal, instead of food, to shrink to the size of the thin young models. Department-store buyers reported that American women, since 1939, had become three and four sizes smaller. 'Women are out to fit the clothes, instead of vice versa,' one buyer said.

Interior decorators were designing kitchens with mosaic murals and original paintings, for kitchens were once again the centre of women's lives. Home sewing became a million-dollar industry. Many women no longer left their homes, except to shop, chauffeur their children, or attend a social engagement with their husbands. Girls were growing up in America without ever having jobs outside the home. In the late fifties, a sociological phenomenon was suddenly remarked: a third of American women now worked, but most were no longer young and very few were pursuing careers. They were married women who held part-time jobs, selling or secretarial, to put their husband through school, their sons through college, or to help pay the mortgage. Or they were widows supporting families. Fewer and fewer women were entering professional work. The shortages in the nursing, social work, and teaching professions caused crises in almost every American city. Concerned over the Soviet Union's lead in the space race, scientists noted that America's greatest source of unused brainpower was women. But girls would not study physics: it was 'unfeminine'. A girl refused a science fellowship at Johns Hopkins to take a job in a real-estate office. All she wanted, she said, was what every other American girl wanted – to get married, have four children, and live in a nice house in a nice suburb.

The suburban housewife – she was the dream image of the young American women and the envy, it was said, of women all over the world. The American housewife – freed by science and labour-saving appliances from the drudgery, the dangers of childbirth, and the illnesses of her grandmother. She was healthy, beautiful, educated, concerned only about her husband, her children, her home. She had found true feminine fulfilment. As a housewife and mother, she was respected as a full and equal partner to man in his world. She was free to choose automobiles, clothes, appliances, supermarkets; she had everything that women ever dreamed of.

In the fifteen years after the Second World War, this mystique of feminine fulfilment became the cherished and self-perpetuating core of contemporary American culture. Millions of women lived their lives in the image of those pretty pictures of the American suburban housewife, kissing their husbands good-bye in front of the picture window, depositing their stationwagonsful of children at school, and smiling as they ran the new electric waxer over the spotless kitchen floor. They baked their own bread, sewed their own and their children's clothes, kept their new washing machines and dryers running all day. They changed the sheets on the beds twice a week instead of once, took the rug-hooking class in adult education, and pitied their poor frustrated mothers, who had dreamed of having a career. They gloried in their role as women, and wrote proudly on the census blank: 'Occupation: housewife'.

For over fifteen years, the words written for women, and the words women used when they talked to each other, while their husbands sat on the other side of the room and talked shop or politics or septic tanks, were about problems with their children, or how to keep their husbands happy, or improve their children's school, or cook chicken, or make slip-covers. Nobody argued whether women were inferior or superior to men; they were simply different. Words like 'emancipation' and 'career' sounded strange and embarrassing; no one had used them for years. When a Frenchwoman named Simone de Beauvoir wrote a book called *The Second Sex*, an American critic commented that she obviously 'didn't know what life was all about', and besides, she was talking about French women. The 'woman problem' in America no longer existed.

If a woman had a problem in the 1950s and 1960s, she knew that something must be wrong with her marriage, or with herself. Other women were satisfied with their lives, she thought. What kind of a woman was she if she did not feel this mysterious fulfilment waxing the kitchen floor? She was so ashamed to admit her dissatisfaction that she never knew how many other women shared it. If she tried to tell her husband, he didn't understand what she was talking about. She did not really understand it herself. For over fifteen years women in America found it harder to talk about this problem than about sex. 'I don't know what's wrong with women today,' a suburban psychiatrist said uneasily. 'I only know something is wrong because most of my patients happen to be women. And their problem isn't sexual.' Most women with this problem did not go to see a psychoanalyst, however. 'There's nothing wrong really,' they kept telling themselves. 'There isn't any problem.'

But on an April morning in 1959, I heard a mother of four, having coffee with four other mothers in a suburban development 15 miles from New York, say in a tone of quiet desperation, 'the problem'. And the others knew, without words, that she was not talking about a problem with her husband, or her children, or her home. Suddenly they realized they all shared the same problem, the problem that has no name. They began, hesitantly, to talk about it. Later, after they had picked up their children at nursery school and taken them home to nap, two of the women cried, in sheer relief, just to know they were not alone.

Gradually I came to realize that the problem that has no name was shared by countless women in America. As a magazine writer I often interviewed women about problems with their children, or their marriages, or their houses, or their communities. But after a while I began to recognize the tell-tale signs of this other problem. I saw the same signs in suburban ranch houses and split-levels on Long Island and in New Jersey and Westchester County; in colonial houses in a small Massachusetts town; on patios in Memphis; in suburban and city apartments; in living-rooms in the Midwest. Sometimes I sensed the problem, not as a reporter, but as a suburban housewife, for during this time I was also bringing up my own three children in Rockland County, New York. The groping words I heard from other women, on quiet afternoons when the children were at school or on quiet evenings when husbands worked late, I think I understood first as a woman long before I understood their larger social and psychological implications.

Just what was this problem that has no name? What were the words women used when they tried to express it? Sometimes a woman would say, 'I feel empty somehow . . . incomplete.' Or she would say, 'I feel as if I don't exist.' Sometimes she blotted out the feeling with a tranquillizer. Sometimes she thought the problem was with her husband, or her children, or that what she really needed was to redecorate her house, or move to a better neighbourhood, or have an affair, or another baby. Sometimes, she went to a doctor with symptoms she could hardly describe: 'A tired feeling . . . I get so angry with the children it scares me . . . I feel like crying without any reason.' (A Cleveland doctor called it 'the housewife's syndrome'.) A number of women told me about great bleeding blisters that break out on their hands and arms. 'I call it the housewife's blight,' said a family doctor in Pennsylvania. 'I see it so often lately in these young women with four, five, and six children, who bury themselves in their dishpans. But it isn't caused by detergent and it isn't cured by cortisone.'

Sometimes a woman would tell me that the feeling gets so strong she runs out of the house and walks through the streets. Or she stays inside her house and cries. Or her children tell her a joke, and she doesn't laugh because she doesn't hear it. I talked to women who had spent years on the analyst's couch, working out their 'adjustment to the feminine role', their blocks to 'fulfilment as a wife and mother'. But the desperate tone in these women's voices, and the look in their eyes, was the same as the tone and look of other women, who were sure they had no problem, even though they did have a strange feeling of desperation.

A mother of four who left college at 19 to get married told me:

> I've tried everything women are supposed to do – hobbies, gardening, pickling, canning, being very social with my neighbours, joining committees, running PTA [Parent–Teacher Association] teas. I can do it all, and I like it, but it doesn't leave you anything to think about – any feeling of who you are. I never had any career ambitions. All I wanted was to get married and have four children. I love the kids and Bob and my home. There's no problem you can even put a name to. But I'm desperate. I begin to feel I have no personality. I'm a server of food and a putter-on of pants and a bedmaker, somebody who can be called on when you want something. But who am I?

A 23-year-old mother in blue jeans said:

> I ask myself why I'm so dissatisfied. I've got my health, fine children, a lovely new home, enough money. My husband has a real future as an electronics engineer. He doesn't have any of these feelings. He says maybe I need a vacation, let's go to New York for a weekend. But that isn't it. I always had this idea we should do everything together. I can't sit down and read a book alone. If the children are napping and I have one hour to myself I just walk through the house waiting for them to wake up. I don't make a move until I know where the rest of the crowd is going. It's as if ever since you were a little girl, there's always been somebody or something that will take care of your life: your parents, or college, or falling in love, or having a child, or moving to a new house. Then you wake up one morning and there's nothing to look forward to.

A young wife in a Long Island development said:

> I seem to sleep so much. I don't know why I should be so tired. This house isn't nearly so hard to clean as the cold-water flat we had when I was working. The children are at school all day. It's not the work. I just don't feel alive.

In 1960, the problem that has no name burst like a boil through the image of the happy American housewife. In the television commercials the pretty house-wives still beamed over their foaming dishpans and *Time*'s cover story on 'The Suburban Wife, an American Phenomenon' protested: 'Having too good a time . . . to believe that they should be unhappy'. But the actual unhappiness of the American housewife was suddenly being reported – from the *New York Times* and *Newsweek* to *Good Housekeeping* and CBS Television ('The Trapped Housewife'), although almost everybody who talked about it found some superficial reason to dismiss it. Some said it was the old problem – education: more and more women had education, which naturally made them unhappy in their role as housewives. 'The road from Freud to Frigidaire, from Sophocles to Spock, has turned out to be a bumpy one,' reported the *New York Times* (28 June 1960).

Many young women – certainly not all – whose education plunged them into a world of ideas feel stifled in their homes. They find their routine lives out of joint with their training. Like shut-ins, they feel left out. In the last year, the problem of the educated housewife has provided the meat of dozens of speeches made by troubled presidents of women's colleges who maintain, in the face of complaints, that sixteen years of academic training is realistic preparation for wifehood and motherhood.

There was much sympathy for the educated housewife. ('Like a two-headed schizophrenic . . . once she wrote a paper on the Graveyard poets; now she writes notes to the milkman. Once she determined the boiling point of sulphuric acid; now she determines her boiling point with the overdue repairman. . . . The housewife often is reduced to screams and tears. . . . No one, it seems, is appreciative, least of all herself, of the kind of person she becomes in the process of turning from poetess into shrew.')

Home economists suggested more realistic preparation for housewives, such as high-school workshops in home appliances. College educators suggested more discussion groups on home management and the family, to prepare women for the adjustment to domestic life. No month went by without a new book by a psychiatrist or sexologist offering technical advice on finding greater fulfilment through sex.

A male humorist joked in *Harper's Bazaar* (July 1960) that the problem could be solved by taking away woman's right to vote. ('In the pre-19th Amendment era, the American woman was placid, sheltered and sure of her role in American society. She left all the political decisions to her husband and he, in turn, left all the family decisions to her. Today a woman has to make both the family *and* the political decisions, and it's too much for her.')

A number of educators suggested seriously that women no longer be admitted to the four-year colleges and universities: in the growing college crisis, the education which girls could not use as housewives was more urgently needed than ever by boys to do the work of the atomic age.

The problem was also dismissed with drastic solutions no one could take seriously. (A woman writer proposed in *Harper's* that women be drafted for compulsory service as nurses' aides and baby-sitters.) And it was smoothed over with the age-old panaceas: 'love is their answer', 'the only answer is inner help', 'the secret of completeness – children', 'a private means of intellectual fulfilment', 'to cure this toothache of the spirit – the simple formula of handing one's self and one's will over to God'.[1]

The problem was dismissed by telling the housewife she doesn't realize how lucky she is – her own boss, no time clock, no junior executive gunning for her job. What if she isn't happy – does she think men are happy in this world? Does she really, secretly, still want to be a man? Doesn't she know yet how lucky she is to be a woman?

The problem was also, and finally, dismissed by shrugging that there are no solutions: this is what being a woman means, and what is wrong with American women that they can't accept their role gracefully? As *Newsweek* put it (7 March 1960):

> She is dissatisfied with a lot that women of other lands can only dream of. Her discontent is deep, pervasive, and impervious to the superficial remedies which are offered at every hand. . . . An army of professional explorers have already charted the major sources of trouble. . . . From the beginning of time, the female cycle has defined and confined woman's role. As Freud was credited with saying: 'Anatomy is destiny.' Though no group of women has ever pushed these natural restrictions as far as the American wife, it seems that she still cannot accept them with good grace. . . . A young mother with a beautiful family, charm, talent and brains is apt to dismiss her role apologetically. 'What do I do?' you hear her say. 'Why nothing. I'm just a housewife.' A good education, it seems, has given this paragon among women an understanding of the value of everything except her own worth.

And so she must accept the fact that 'American women's unhappiness is merely the most recently won of women's rights', and adjust and say with the happy housewife found by *Newsweek*:

> We ought to salute the wonderful freedom we all have and be proud of our lives today. I have had college and I've worked, but being a housewife is the most rewarding and satisfying role. . . . My mother was never included in my father's business affairs . . . she couldn't get out of the house and away from us children. But I am an equal to my husband; I can go along with him on business trips and to social business affairs.

The alternative offered was a choice that few women would contemplate. In the sympathetic words of the *New York Times*:

> All admit to being deeply frustrated at times by the lack of privacy, the physical burden, the routine of family life, the confinement of it. However, none would give up her home and family if she had the choice to make again.

Redbook commented:

> Few women would want to thumb their noses at husbands, children and community and go off on their own. Those who do may be talented individuals, but they rarely are successful women.

The year American women's discontent boiled over, it was also reported (*Look*) that the more than 21 million American women who are single, widowed, or divorced do not cease even after 50 their frenzied, desperate search for a man. And the search begins early – for 70 per cent of all American women now marry before they are 24. A pretty 25-year-old secretary took thirty-five different jobs in six months in the futile hope of finding a husband. Women were moving from one political club to another, taking evening courses in accounting or sailing, learning to play golf or ski, joining a number of churches in succession, going to bars alone, in their ceaseless search for a man.

Of the growing thousands of women currently getting private psychiatric help in the United States, the married ones were reported dissatisfied with their marriages, the unmarried ones suffering from anxiety and, finally, depression. Strangely, a number of psychiatrists stated that, in their experience, unmarried women patients were happier than married ones. So the door of all those pretty suburban houses opened a crack to permit a glimpse of uncounted thousands of American housewives who suffered alone from a problem that suddenly everyone was talking about, and beginning to take for granted, as one of those unreal problems in American life that can never be solved – like the hydrogen bomb. By 1962 the plight of the trapped American housewife had become a national parlour game. Whole issues of magazines, newspaper columns, books learned and frivolous, educational conferences, and television panels were devoted to the problem.

Even so, most men, and some women, still did not know that this problem was real. A bitter laugh was beginning to be heard from American women. They got all kinds of advice from the growing armies of marriage and child-guidance counsellors, psychotherapists, and armchair psychologists, on how to adjust to their role as housewives. No other road to fulfilment was offered to them in the middle of the twentieth century. Most adjusted to their role and suffered or ignored the problem that has no name. It can be less painful, for a woman, not to hear the strange, dissatisfied voice stirring within her.

It is no longer possible to ignore that voice, to dismiss the desperation of so many American women. This is not what being a woman means, no matter what the experts say. For human suffering there is a reason; perhaps the reason has not been found because the right questions have not been asked, or pressed far enough. I do not accept the answer that there is no problem because American women have luxuries that women in other times and lands never dreamed of; part of the strange newness of the problem is that it cannot be understood in terms of the age-old material problems of man: poverty, sickness, hunger, cold. The women who suffer this problem have a hunger that food cannot fill. It persists in women whose husbands are struggling interns and law clerks, or prosperous doctors and lawyers; in wives of workers and executives who make $5,000 a year or $50,000. It is not caused by lack of material advantages; it may not even be felt by women pre-occupied with desperate problems of hunger, poverty, or illness. And women who think it will be solved by more money, a bigger house, a second car, moving to a better suburb, often discover it gets worse.

It is no longer possible today to blame the problem on loss of femininity: to say that education and independence and equality with men have made American women unfeminine. I think, in fact, that this is the first clue to the mystery: the problem cannot be understood in the generally accepted terms by which scientists have studied women, doctors have treated them, counsellors have advised them, and writers have written about them. Women who suffer this problem have lived their whole lives in the pursuit of feminine fulfilment. They are not career women (although career women may have other problems); they are women whose greatest ambition has been marriage and children. For the oldest of these women, these daughters of the American middle class, no other dream was possible. The ones in their forties and fifties who once had other dreams gave them up and threw themselves joyously into life as housewives. For the youngest, the new wives and mothers, this was the only dream. They are the ones who quit high school and college to marry, or marked time in some job in which they had no real interest until they married.

Are the women who finished college, the women who once had dreams beyond housewifery, the ones who suffer the most? According to the experts they are, but listen to these four women:

> My days are all busy, and dull, too. All I ever do is mess around. I get up at eight – I make breakfast, so I do the dishes, have lunch, do some more dishes and some laundry and cleaning in the afternoon. Then it's supper dishes and I get to sit down a few minutes before the children have to be sent to bed. . . . That's all there is to my day. It's just like any other wife's day. Humdrum. The biggest time, I am chasing kids.

> Ye Gods, what do I do with my time? Well, I get up at six. I get my son dressed and then give him breakfast. After that I wash dishes and bathe and feed the baby. Then I get lunch and while the children nap, I sew or mend or iron and do all the other things I can't get done before noon. Then I cook supper for the family and my husband watches TV while I do the dishes. After I get the children to bed, I set my hair and then I go to bed.

> The problem is always being the children's mommy, or the minister's wife and never being myself.

> A film made of any typical morning in my house would look like an old Marx Brothers' comedy. I wash the dishes, rush the older children off to school, dash out in the yard to cultivate the chrysanthemums, run back in to make a phone call about a committee meeting, help the youngest child build a blockhouse, spend fifteen minutes skimming the newspapers so I can be well informed, then scamper down to the washing machines where my thrice-weekly laundry includes enough clothes to keep a primitive village going for an entire year. By noon I'm ready for a padded cell. Very little of what I've done has been really necessary or important. Outside pressures lash me through the day. Yet I look upon myself as one of the more relaxed housewives in the neighbourhood. Many of my friends are even more frantic. In the past sixty years we have come full circle and the American housewife is once again trapped in a squirrel cage. If the cage is now a modern plate-glass-and-broadloom ranch house or a convenient modern apartment, the situation is no less painful than when her grandmother sat over an embroidery hoop in her gilt-and-plush parlour and muttered angrily about women's rights.

The first two women never went to college. They live in developments in Levittown, New Jersey, and Tacoma, Washington, and were interviewed by a team of sociologists studying working-men's wives.[2] The third, a minister's wife, wrote on the fifteenth reunion questionnaire of her college that she never had any career ambitions, but wishes now she had.[3]

The fourth, who has a PhD in anthropology, is today a Nebraska housewife with three children.[4] Their words seems to indicate that housewives of all educational levels suffer the same feeling of desperation.

The fact is that no one today is muttering angrily about 'women's rights', even though more and more women have gone to college. In a recent study of all the classes that have graduated from Barnard College,[5] a significant minority of earlier graduates blamed their education for making them want 'rights', later classes blamed their education for giving them career dreams, but recent graduates blamed the college for making them feel it was not enough simply to be a housewife and mother; they did not want to feel guilty if they did not read books or take part in community activities. But if education is not the cause of the problem, the fact that education somehow festers in these women may be a clue.

If the secret of feminine fulfilment is having children, never have so many women, with the freedom to choose, had so many children, in so few years, so willingly. If the answer is love, never have women searched for love with such determination. And yet there is a growing suspicion that the problem may not be sexual, though it must somehow be related to sex. I have heard from many doctors evidence of new sexual problems between man and wife – sexual hunger in wives so great their husbands cannot satisfy it. 'We have made woman a sex creature,' said a psychiatrist at the Margaret Sanger marriage counselling clinic. 'She has no identity except as a wife and mother. She does not know who she is herself. She waits all day for her husband to come home at night to make her feel alive. And now it is the husband who is not interested. It is terrible for the women, to lie there, night after night, waiting for her husband to make her feel alive.' Why is there such a market for books and articles offering sexual advice? The kind of sexual orgasm which Kinsey found in statistical plenitude in the recent generations of American women does not seem to make this problem go away.

On the contrary, new neuroses are being seen among women – and problems as yet unnamed as neuroses – which Freud and his followers did not predict, with physical symptoms, anxieties, and defence mechanisms equal to those caused by sexual repression. And strange new problems are being reported in the growing generations of children whose mothers were always there, driving them around, helping them with their homework – an inability to endure pain or discipline or pursue any self-sustained goal of any sort, a devastating boredom with life. Educators are increasingly uneasy about the dependence, the lack of self-reliance, of the boys and girls who are entering college today. 'We fight a continual battle to make our students assume manhood,' said a Columbia dean.

A White House conference was held on the physical and muscular deterioration of American children: were they being overnurtured? Sociologists noted the astounding organization of suburban children's lives: the lessons, parties, entertainments, play and study groups organized for them. A suburban housewife in Portland, Oregon, wondered why the children 'need' Brownies and Boy Scouts out here.

> This is not the slums. The kids out here have the great outdoors. I think people are so bored, they organize the children, and then try to hook everyone else on it. And the poor kids have no time left just to lie on their beds and daydream.

When a woman tries to put the problem into words, she often merely describes the daily life she leads. What is there in this recital of comfortable domestic detail that could possibly cause such a feeling of desperation? Is she trapped simply by the enormous demands of her role as modern housewife: wife, mistress, mother, nurse, consumer, cook, chauffeur; expert on interior decoration, child care, appliance repair, furniture refinishing, nutrition, and education? Her day is fragmented; she can never spend more than fifteen minutes on any one thing; she has no time to read books, only magazines; even if she had time, she has lost the power to concentrate. At the end of the day, she is so terribly tired that sometimes her husband has to take over and put the children to bed.

This terrible tiredness took so many women to doctors in the 1950s that one decided to investigate it. He found, surprisingly, that his patients suffering from 'housewife's fatigue' slept more than an adult needed to sleep – as much as ten hours a day – and that the actual energy they expended on housework did not tax their capacity. The real problem must be something else, he decided – perhaps boredom. Some doctors told their women patients they must get out of the house for a day, treat themselves to a movie in town. Others prescribed tranquillizers. Many suburban housewives were taking tranquillizers like cough drops.

> You wake up in the morning, and you feel as if there's no point in going on another day like this. So you take a tranquillizer because it makes you not care so much that it's pointless.

It is easy to see the concrete details that trap the suburban housewife, the continual demands on her time. But the chains that bind her in her trap are chains made up of mistaken ideas and misinterpreted facts, of incomplete truths and unreal choices. They are not easily seen and not easily shaken off.

I found many clues by talking to suburban doctors, gynaecologists, obstetricians, child-guidance clinicians, paediatricians, high-school guidance counsellors, college professors, marriage counsellors, psychiatrists, and ministers – questioning them not on their theories, but on their actual experience in treating American women. I became aware of a growing body of evidence, much of which has not been reported publicly because it does not fit current modes of thought about women – evidence which throws into question the standards of feminine normality, feminine adjustment, feminine fulfilment, and feminine maturity by which most women are still trying to live.

I began to see in a strange new light the American return to early marriage and the large families that are causing the population explosion; the recent movement to natural childbirth and breastfeeding; suburban conformity, and the new neuroses, character pathologies and sexual problems being reported by the doctors. I began to see new dimensions to old problems that have long been taken for granted among women: menstrual difficulties, sexual frigidity, promiscuity, pregnancy fears, childbirth depression, the high incidence of emotional breakdown and suicide among women in their twenties and thirties, the menopause crises, the so-called passivity and immaturity of American men, the discrepancy between women's tested intellectual abilities in childhood and their adult achievement, the changing incidence of adult sexual orgasm in American women, and persistent problems in psychotherapy and in women's education.

If I am right, the problem that has no name stirring in the minds of so many American women today is not a matter of loss of femininity or too much education, or the demands of domesticity. It is far more important than anyone recognizes. It is the key to these other new and old problems which have been torturing women and their husbands and children, and puzzling their doctors and educators for years. It may well be the key to our future as a nation and a culture. We can no longer ignore that voice within women that says: 'I want something more than my husband and my children and my home.'

NOTES

1   See the Seventy-fifth Anniversary Issue of *Good Housekeeping*, May 1960, 'The Gift of Self', a symposium by Margaret Mead, Jessamyn West *et al.*
2   Lee Rainwater, Richard P. Coleman, and Gerald Handel, *Working-man's Wife*, New York, 1959.
3   Betty Friedan, 'If One Generation Can Ever Tell Another', *Smith Alumnae Quarterly*, Northampton, Mass., Winter 1961. I first became aware of 'the problem that has no name' and its possible relationship to what I finally called 'the feminine mystique' in 1957, when I prepared an intensive questionnaire and conducted a survey of my own Smith College classmates fifteen years after graduation. This questionnaire was later used by alumnae classes of Radcliffe and other women's colleges with similar results.
4   Jhan and June Robbins, 'Why Young Mothers Feel Trapped', *Redbook*, September 1960.
5   Marian Freda Poverman, 'Alumnae on Parade', *Barnard Alumnae Magazine*, July 1957.

6 Michèle Barrett

Excerpts from 'Some Conceptual Problems in Marxist Feminist Analysis'

from *Women's Oppression Today: Problems in Marxist Feminist Analysis* (1980)

It is relatively easy to demonstrate that women are oppressed in Britain, as in other contemporary capitalist societies, but more contentious to speak of a 'Marxist feminist' analysis of their oppression. In recent years attempts have been made to develop a theoretical perspective that might confidently be termed 'Marxist feminist', yet the work so generated remains fragmentary and contradictory, lacking a conceptual framework adequate to its project. This, perhaps, is only to be expected, given the magnitude of the task and the obstacles that any synthesis must overcome.

The problem faced by any such analysis can be put simply in terms of the different objects of the two perspectives. Marxism, constituted as it is around relations of appropriation and exploitation, is grounded in concepts that do not and could not address directly the gender of the exploiters and those whose labour is appropriated. A Marxist analysis of capitalism is therefore conceived around a primary contradiction between labour and capital and operates with categories that, as has recently been argued, can be termed 'sex-blind'.[1] Feminism, however, points in a different direction, emphasizing precisely the relations of gender – largely speaking, of the oppression of women by men – that Marxism has tended to pass over in silence. Of course, just as there are many varieties of 'Marxism' so there are many 'feminisms', and indeed one task of any 'Marxist feminism' must be to identify which version of the one is being bracketed with which version of the other. But what is clear is that any feminism must insist on the specific character of gender relations. Some forms of feminism may pose these relations as the primary contradiction of social organization, just as Marxism poses the labour/capital contradiction as primary in the analysis of capitalism, but all must surely pose them as distinct.

What then might be the object of Marxist feminism? In the most general terms it must be to identify the operation of gender relations as and where they may be distinct from, or connected with, the processes of production and reproduction understood by historical materialism. Thus it falls to Marxist feminism to explore the relations between the organization of sexuality, domestic production, the household and so on, and historical changes in the mode of production and systems of appropriation and exploitation. Such questions are now being addressed by Marxist feminists working in anthropology, the sociology of development, and political economy.[2] This book, however, deals with the relations of gender and the oppression of women in a contemporary capitalist society. In this context a Marxist feminist approach will involve an emphasis on the relations between capitalism and the oppression of women. It will require an awareness of the specific oppression of women in capitalist relations of production, but this must be seen in the light of gender divisions which preceded the transition to capitalism and which, as far as we can tell, a socialist revolution would not of itself abolish.

It is immediately clear that these questions must be treated historically. Although the chapters that follow could not attempt to provide a systematic historical account of the topics considered, they do point to the need to look at definitions of sexuality, the structure of the household and so on in concrete historical and empirical terms. Before moving on to more detailed areas we need, however, to discuss the theoretical framework in which the development of a Marxist feminist approach has been located. In order to do this I am going to consider the different uses of three concepts that have proved central to the debate: those of 'patriarchy', 'reproduction' and 'ideology'. These three concepts, as they have been developed in Marxist feminism, bear directly on two issues that have recurred consistently in the discussion. 'Patriarchy', drawn primarily from radical feminist writings, and 'reproduction', drawn from Althusser's emphasis on reproduction of the relations of production, have both been used to address the question of the independence of women's oppression from the general operation of the capitalist mode of production. Developments in the concept of 'ideology', and its use in specific trends of Marxist feminist thought, lead us straight into the question of whether the oppression of women takes place at the level of ideology, and what such a claim would entail.

PATRIARCHY

The concept of patriarchy is perhaps the crucial one with which to begin. The editors of a recent collection entitled *Feminism and Materialism* insist that it 'be seriously addressed in any theoretical practice which claims to be feminist'[3] and indeed the term is used extensively in the women's liberation movement. To get an idea of its theoretical and political force we need to look at the context in which the concept has been used.

The term 'patriarchy' was taken up by the sociologist Max Weber to describe a particular form of household organization in which the father dominated other members of an extended kinship network and controlled the economic production of the household. Its resonance for feminism, however, rests on the theory, put forward by early radical feminism and in particular by American writers such as Kate Millett, of patriarchy as an over-arching category of male dominance.

Millett locates male domination in the following terms: 'groups who rule by birthright are fast disappearing, yet there remains one ancient and universal scheme for the domination of one birth group by another – the scheme that prevails in the area of sex'. She argues that the political power which men wield over women amounts to the fundamental political division in society. Our society, like all other civilizations, is a patriarchy in which the rule of women by men is 'more rigorous than class stratification, more uniform, certainly more enduring'. Millett confronts the thesis that in capitalist society the domination of women by men is mediated by class differences between women, and argues that such differences are transitory and illusory, that 'whatever the class of her birth and education, the female has fewer permanent class associations than does the male. Economic dependency renders her affiliations with any class a tangential, vicarious and temporary matter'. Millett's position here implies that class divisions are relevant only to men; she denies that significant class differences exist between women. Her project is to establish a fundamental system of domination – patriarchy – that is analytically independent of the capitalist or any other mode of production.[4]

Millett's theory of patriarchy resembles that of Shulamith Firestone insofar as it gives not only analytic independence to male domination, but analytic *primacy*. Firestone, however, grounds her account more firmly in biological reproduction, her aim being 'to take the class analysis one step further to its roots in the biological division of the sexes'. Firestone's theoretical goal is to substitute sex for class as the prime motor in a materialist account of history. She paraphrases Engels as follows: 'all past history . . . was the history of class struggle. These warring classes of society are always the product of the modes of organization of the biological family unit for reproduction of the species, as well as of the strictly economic modes of production and exchange of goods and services. The sexual-reproductive organization of society always furnishes the real basis, starting from which we can alone work out the ultimate explanation of the whole superstructure of economic, juridical and political institutions as well as the religious, philosophical and other ideas of a given historical period'.[5]

Although Firestone emphasizes the need to revolutionize reproductive technology in order to free women from the burden of their biologically determined oppression, her account of this determination itself falls into biologistic assumptions.[6] This raises a problem which is often encountered in these early radical feminist uses of the term 'patriarchy': not only do they invoke an apparently universal and transhistorical category of male dominance, leaving us with little hope of change; they also frequently ground this dominance in a supposed logic of biological reproduction. This has paved the way, as we shall see later, for a consideration of patriarchy that tends to stress male supremacy as male control over women's fertility, without a case being made as to why and how men acquired this control. We need to ask whether such an emphasis on the importance of the division of labour between men and women in the reproduction of the species does not amount to a form of biologism, and if so whether 'feminist' biologism escapes the arguments that can be put against other forms of biological explanation of social relations.

Biologistic arguments can be challenged on a number of different grounds. In philosophical terms they tend to be reductionist, in that they subsume complex socially and historically constructed phenomena under the simple category of biological difference, and empiricist, in that they assume that differences in social behaviour are caused by the observed biological differences with which they correlate. The history of social science provides us with examples of various attempts to explain social behaviour with reference to biological determinants – two notorious instances being the alleged connections between criminality and body-type and between intelligence-test scores and racial differences. All such attempts have subsequently been discredited, and psychological findings concerning supposedly innate sex differences have now been subjected to a stringent critique.[7] Furthermore, the political and ideological role of such arguments is inevitably reactionary, since if particular social arrangements are held to be 'naturally' given, there is little we can do to change them.

Although it is important for feminist analysis to locate the question of biological difference in an account of male–female relations, the slide into biological reductionism is an extremely dangerous one. It is regressive in that one of the early triumphs of feminist cross-cultural work – the establishment of a distinction between sex as a biological category and gender as a social one[8] – is itself threatened by an emphasis on the causal role of procreative biology in the construction of male domination. In practice, too, such an analysis may well lead to a feminist glorification of supposedly 'female' capacities and principles and a reassertion of 'separate spheres' for women and men. These dangers are not exclusive to radical feminist analysts of patriarchy – they have surfaced in feminist politics and culture from other sources too – but they are perhaps particularly characteristic of these early radical feminist works.

It has, however, been possible to frame an account of patriarchy from the point of view of social, rather than biological, relations, and a major achievement of the work of Christine Delphy and others has been the development of a more properly materialist analysis of women's oppression. Delphy points to the example of the divorced wife of a bourgeois man as illustrating a system of patriarchal exploitation that cuts across class relations: 'even though marriage with a man from the capitalist class can raise a woman's standard of living, it does not make her a member of that class. She herself does not own the means of production. . . . In the vast majority of cases, wives of bourgeois men whose marriage ends must earn their own living as wage or salaried workers. They therefore become concretely (with the additional handicaps of age and/or lack of professional training) the proletarians that they essentially were.'[9] Delphy argues that women's class position should be understood in terms of the institution of marriage, which she conceptualises as a labour contract in which the husband's appropriation of unpaid labour from his wife constitutes a domestic mode of production and a patriarchal mode of exploitation. Hence she argues that the material basis of women's oppression lies not in capitalist but in patriarchal relations of production. The difficulty here, however, is that the category of patriarchy is assigned analytic independence *vis-à-vis* the capitalist mode of production, but we are not led to a systematic consideration of the relations between them.[10]

A general problem with the concept of patriarchy is that not only is it by and large resistant to exploration within a particular mode of production, but it is redolent of a universal and trans-historical oppression. So, to use the concept is frequently to invoke a generality of male domination without being able to specify historical limits, changes or differences. For a Marxist feminist approach, whose analysis must be grounded in historical analysis, its use will therefore present particular problems.

Before we turn to some general attempts to use the concept of patriarchy in a Marxist feminist theoretical framework, it is worth considering certain specific uses to which the term might be put. Gayle Rubin, for instance, makes the fruitful suggestion that the term 'patriarchy' would be a more valuable one if its use were restricted to societies (and here she cites the nomadic tribes of Abraham's era) where one man wielded absolute power through a socially defined institution of fatherhood.[11] Similarly, it would be possible to argue for a use of the term to describe the ideological aspects of relationships that are predicated on the paradigm, for instance, of a father–daughter relationship. Thus Maria-Antonietta Macciocchi's analysis of female sexuality in the ideology of Italian fascism[12] seems to me to describe an ideological construction of women that might be termed 'patriarchal'. Perhaps Virginia Woolf's account of the pathological attempts of bourgeois fathers to insist on their daughters' dependence, financial and emotional, on themselves, also represents a legitimate use of the term.[13]

These examples, however, are relatively rare in recent theoretical work, which abounds with attempts to represent, more generally, contemporary capitalism as 'patriarchy'. These pose two major problems, as I shall try to illustrate below. First, patriarchy is posed as a system of domination completely independent of the organization of capitalist relations and hence the analyses fall into a universalistic, trans-historical mode which may shade into the biologism discussed earlier. Where attempts are made to constitute patriarchy as a system of male domination in relation to the capitalist mode of production, these frequently founder on the inflexibility and claims to autonomy to which the concept is prone. This problem persists even in the recent, sophisticated formulations of materialist feminism which attempt to incorporate a psychoanalytic perspective. Second, the concept of patriarchy as presently constituted reveals a fundamental confusion, regrettably plain in discussion of it, between patriarchy as the rule of the father and patriarchy as the domination of women by men. Both of these problems can be seen in recent attempts to use the concept of patriarchy in conjunction with a Marxist analysis.

Zillah Eisenstein's collection, *Capitalist Patriarchy and the Case for Socialist Feminism*, includes under this rubric some interesting work on women's oppression and capitalism but ultimately reaches the dilemma of how to reconcile two theoretical approaches with rival claims. Eisenstein herself defines patriarchy as preceding capitalism, as resting today on the 'power of the male through sexual roles', and as institutionalized in the nuclear family. However it is unclear to what extent patriarchy, defined in this way, constitutes an autonomous system, since Eisenstein goes on to refer to it simply in terms of its functions for capital. 'Capitalism uses patriarchy and patriarchy is defined by the needs of capital.'[14] Such a statement can hardly co-exist with the claim that capitalism *is* a patriarchy, and in fact Eisenstein's ensuing analysis of domestic labour is couched extensively in terms of its functions for capital. Her use of the concept of patriarchy, therefore, is one that does not resolve the problem of the analytic independence of 'patriarchy' from capitalism: the analysis vacillates between the assertion of patriarchy as a system of male power external to capitalism and the argument that the organization of patriarchal relations is functional for capital.

Roisin McDonough and Rachel Harrison attempt explicitly to use the concept of patriarchy in a materialist context. Their editors write: 'although it is true that simply to address patriarchy as a concept is in some sense to take its validity for granted, the aim in taking it up here is to displace it, to move the terms of its discussion away from the terrain of universalism and to reappropriate it for material-ism, for an approach to women's situation in its historical specificity'. McDonough and Harrison regard patriarchy as requiring a two-fold definition: first, 'the control of women's fertility and sexuality in monogamous marriage' and second, 'the econ-omic subordination of women through the sexual division of labour (and property)'. They argue that the patriarchal family as such has been eliminated but that patriarchy can be said to exist at present in the operation of these two processes. Their central thesis is that patriarchy as a concept can be historicized through the argument that, in capitalism, patriarchal relations assume a form dictated by capitalist relations of production: 'though women are placed simul-taneously in two separate but linked structures, those of class and patriarchy, it is their class position which limits the conditions of the forms of patriarchy they will be subjected to'.[15] In practice this formulation reduces to an argument that the oppression of women in capitalism presents different contradictions for women, depending upon their social class. Social class, moreover, is ill-defined in this analysis, resting neither on a Marxist nor on a sociological foundation, for the authors argue that 'a woman inhabits her husband's class position, but not the equivalent relation to the means of production'. It is not clear to me what is being claimed here for the concept of patriarchy. For if patriarchal relations assume the form of class relations in capitalism, then however centrally the authors may pose patriarchal relations in the subordination of women, they do not resolve the question of the effectivity of patriarchy as the determinant of women's oppression in capitalism.

Annette Kuhn's paper, 'Structures of Patriarchy and Capital in the Family', from the same volume, constitutes an ambitious attempt to resolve some of these problems. Kuhn argues rightly that many analyses of women's oppression desig-nate the family as the crucial site of oppression and yet reduce it to an entity that is itself the product of the playing out of forces whose real operations lie elsewhere. This tendency she ascribes to functionalism, which characterizes both sociological and Marxist accounts of the family. Such analyses, while claiming a crucial role for the family, in practice 'relegate it, paradoxically, to the status of what may be termed an empty signifier'. Kuhn's project is to demonstrate precisely the reverse, that the psychic and economic mechanisms of the family have an autonomy (or at least a relative autonomy) from capitalist relations. Patriarchy unites psychic and property relations, she argues, and it is by this means that the family gains its autonomous effectivity. Kuhn then presents an analysis of the psychic relations of the family, drawn from psychoanalytic theory, and an account of property relations in the family similar to that of Delphy. She argues that 'the family may be defined exactly as property relations between husbands and wives and those property relations in action', and she concludes that 'the family so defined provides the terms for psychic relations, for the production of sexed and class subjects for representations of relations of patriarchy and capital, that is, for the constitution of subjects in ideology'.

However, there is a fundamental difficulty in Kuhn's attempt to marry a psycho-analytic account of the construction of the gendered subject with an account of the family in terms of a labour contract between husbands and wives. This difficulty lies in a confusion as to whether patriarchy refers to the dominance of men over women or the rule of the father as such. Delphy argues straightforwardly that it is the exploitation of wives' labour by their husbands that constitutes patriarchy, and indeed she explicitly opposes the psychoanalytic position that women's oppression lies in the rule of the father. Kuhn, in common with other writers using the concept of patriarchy, glosses over this central definitional problem, as can be seen in the following passage: 'patriarchy – the rule of the father – is a structure written into particular expressions of the sexual division of labour whereby property, the means of production of exchange values, is appropriated by men, and whereby this property relation informs household and family relations in such a way that men may appropriate the labour and the actual persons of women'.[16] This ambiguity as to the referent of the concept of patriarchy is a serious one. Although the concept may well describe forms of social organization in which economic and social power is vested in the father as such, it is not necessarily a helpful concept with which to explore the oppression of women in capitalist societies, and the difficulties with Marxist feminist work on patriarchy and capitalism illustrate this point. The use of the concept is more consistent in psychoanalytic writing, although the status of this perspective as an account of women's oppression is problematic. It seems admissible in some contexts to refer to patriarchal ideology, describing specific aspects of male–female relations in capitalism, but as a noun the term 'patriarchy' presents insuperable difficulties to an analysis that attempts to relate women's oppression to the relations of production of capitalism. Rather different problems are presented by the concept of 'reproduction', to which I shall now turn.

NOTES

1 See Heidi Hartmann, 'The Unhappy Marriage of Marxism and Feminism: Towards a More Progressive Union', *Capital and Class*, no. 8, 1979 and Mark Cousins, 'Material Arguments and Feminism', *m/f*, no. 2, 1978.

2 See, for instance, the special issue of *Critique of Anthropology*, vol. 3, nos. 9/10, 1977.

3 Annette Kuhn and AnnMarie Wolpe (eds), *Feminism and Materialism*, London, 1978, p. 11.

4 Kate Millett, *Sexual Politics*, London, 1971, pp. 24, 38.

5 Shulamith Firestone, *The Dialectic of Sex*, London, 1972, pp. 20–1.

6 This is particularly clear in her discussion of 'the biological family' as a natural entity.

7 For a feminist critique of this field see Dorothy Griffiths and Esther Saraga, 'Sex Differences and Cognitive Abilities: a Sterile Field of Inquiry?' in O. Hartnett *et al.* (eds), *Sex-Role Stereotyping*, London, 1979; for a more exhaustive and general review see E.E. Maccoby and C.N. Jacklin, *The Psychology of Sex Differences*, London, 1975.

8 See Ann Oakley, *Sex, Gender and Society*, London, 1972.

9 Christine Delphy, *The Main Enemy*, Women's Research and Resources Centre, London, 1977, p. 15.

10 See Michèle Barrett and Mary McIntosh, 'Christine Delphy: Towards a Materialist Feminism?' *Feminist Review*, no. 1, 1979.

11 Gayle Rubin, 'The Traffic in Women: Notes on the "Political Economy" of Sex', in R.R. Reiter (ed.), *Toward an Anthropology of Women*, New York, 1975, p. 168.

12 'Female Sexuality in Fascist Ideology', *Feminist Review*, no. 1, 1979.

13 *Three Guineas*, London, 1938.

14 'Developing a Theory of Capitalist Patriarchy', in Z. Eisenstein (ed.), *Capitalist Patriarchy and the Case for Socialist Feminism*, New York, 1979, p. 28.

15 'Patriarchy and Relations of Production', in *Feminism and Materialism*, pp. 11, 40, 36.

16 'Structures of Patriarchy and Capital in the Family', in *Feminism and Materialism*, pp. 45, 65.

7 Audre Lorde

'The Master's Tools will Never Dismantle the Master's House'

from *The Audre Lorde Compendium* (1979)

I agreed to take part in a New York University Institute for the Humanities conference a year ago, with the understanding that I would be commenting upon papers dealing with the role of difference within the lives of american women: difference of race, sexuality, class, and age. The absence of these considerations weakens any feminist discussion of the personal and the political.

It is a particular academic arrogance to assume any discussion of feminist theory without examining our many differences, and without a significant input from poor women, Black and Third World women, and lesbians. And yet, I stand here as a Black lesbian feminist, having been invited to comment within the only panel at this conference where the input of Black feminists and lesbians is represented. What this says about the vision of this conference is sad, in a country where racism, sexism, and homophobia are inseparable. To read this program is to assume that lesbian and Black women have nothing to say about existentialism, the erotic, women's culture and silence, developing feminist theory, or heterosexuality and power. And what does it mean in personal and political terms when even the two Black women who did present here were literally found at the last hour? What does it mean when the tools of a racist patriarchy are used to examine the fruits of that same patriarchy? It means that only the most narrow perimeters of change are possible and allowable.

The absence of any consideration of lesbian consciousness or the consciousness of Third World women leaves a serious gap within this conference and within the papers presented here. For example, in a paper on material relationships between women, I was conscious of an either/or model of nurturing which totally dismissed my knowledge as a Black lesbian. In this paper there was no examination of mutuality between women, no systems of shared support, no interdependence as exists between lesbians and women-identified women. Yet it is only in the patriarchal model of nurturance that women 'who attempt to emancipate themselves pay perhaps too high a price for the results,' as this paper states.

For women, the need and desire to nurture each other is not pathological but redemptive, and it is within that knowledge that our real power is rediscovered. It is this real connection which is so feared by a patriarchal world. Only within a patriarchal structure is maternity the only social power open to women.

Interdependency between women is the way to a freedom which allows the *I* to *be*, not in order to be used, but in order to be creative. This is a difference between the passive *be* and the active *being*.

Advocating the mere tolerance of difference between women is the grossest reformism. It is a total denial of the creative function of difference in our lives. Difference must be not merely tolerated, but seen as a fund of necessary polarities between which our creativity can spark like a dialectic. Only then does the necessity for interdependency become unthreatening. Only within that interdependency of different strengths, acknowledged and equal, can the power to seek new ways of being in the world generate, as well as the courage and sustenance to act where there are no charters.

Within the interdependence of mutual (nondominant) differences lies that security which enables us to descend into the chaos of knowledge and return with true visions of our future, along with the concomitant power to effect those changes which can bring that future into being. Difference is that raw and powerful connection from which our personal power is forged.

As women, we have been taught either to ignore our differences, or to view them as causes for separation and suspicion rather than as forces for change. Without community there is no liberation, only the most vulnerable and temporary armistice between an individual and her oppression. But community must not mean a shedding of our differences, nor the pathetic pretense that these differences do not exist.

Those of us who stand outside the circle of this society's definition of acceptable women; those of us who have been forged in the crucibles of difference – those of us who are poor, who are lesbians, who are Black, who are older – know that *survival is not an academic skill*. It is learning how to stand alone, unpopular and sometimes reviled, and how to make common cause with those others identified as outside the structures in order to define and seek a world in which we can all flourish. It is learning how to take our differences and make them strengths. *For the master's tools will never dismantle the master's house*. They may allow us temporarily to beat him at his own game, but they will never enable us to bring about genuine change. And this fact is only threatening to those women who still define the master's house as their only source of support.

Poor women and women of Color know there is a difference between the daily manifestations of marital slavery and prostitution because it is our daughters who line 42nd Street. If white american feminist theory need not deal with the differences between us, and the resulting difference in our oppressions, then how do you deal with the fact that the women who clean your houses and tend your children while you attend conferences on feminist theory are, for the most part, poor women and women of Color? What is the theory behind racist feminism?

In a world of possibility for us all, our personal visions help lay the groundwork for political action. The failure of academic feminists to recognize difference as a crucial strength is a failure to reach beyond the first patriarchal lesson. In our world, divide and conquer must become define and empower.

Why weren't other women of Color found to participate in this conference? Why were two phone calls to me considered a consultation? Am I the only possible source of names of Black feminists? And although the Black panelist's paper ends on an important and powerful connection of love between women, what about interracial cooperation between feminists who don't love each other?

In academic feminist circles, the answer to these questions is often, 'We did not know who to ask.' But that is the same evasion of responsibility, the same cop-out, that keeps Black women's art out of women's exhibitions, Black women's work out of most feminist publications except for the occasional 'Special Third World Women's Issue,' and Black women's texts off your reading lists. But as Adrienne Rich pointed out in a recent talk, white feminists have educated themselves about such an enormous amount over the past ten years, how come you haven't also educated yourselves about Black women and the differences between us – white and Black – when it is key to our survival as a movement?

Women of today are still being called upon to stretch across the gap of male ignorance and to educate men as to our existence and our needs. This is an old and primary tool of all oppressors to keep the oppressed occupied with the master's concerns. Now we hear that it is the task of women of Color to educate white women – in the face of tremendous resistance – as to our existence, our differences, our relative roles in our joint survival. This is a diversion of energies and a tragic repetition of racist patriarchal thought.

Simone de Beauvoir once said: 'It is in the knowledge of the genuine conditions of our lives that we must draw our strength to live and our reasons for acting.'

Racism and homophobia are real conditions of all our lives in this place and time. *I urge each one of us here to reach down into that deep place of knowledge inside herself and touch that terror and loathing of any difference that lives there. See whose face it wears.* Then the personal as the political can begin to illuminate all our choices.

NOTES

1   Comments at 'The Personal and the Political Panel,' Second Sex Conference, New York, 29 September 1979.

8 Nancy Chodorow

Excerpts from 'Why Women Mother'

from *The Reproduction of Mothering: Psychoanalysis and the Sociology of Gender* (1978)

> It is woman's biological destiny to bear and deliver, to nurse and to rear children.
>
> *Edith Jacobson*
> 'Development of the Wish for a Child in Boys'

> the problem of maternity cannot be dismissed as a zoological fact . . . the theory of cultural motherhood should have been made the foundation of the general theory of kinship.
>
> *Bronislaw Malinowski*
> 'Parenthood, the Basis of Social Structure'

Mothers are women, of course, because a mother is a female parent, and a female who is a parent must be adult, hence must be a woman. Similarly, fathers are male parents, are men. But we mean something different when we say that someone mothered a child than when we say that someone fathered her or him. We can talk about a man 'mothering' a child, if he is this child's primary nurturing figure, or is acting in a nurturant manner. But we would never talk about a woman 'fathering' a child, even in the rare societies in which a high-ranking woman may take a wife and be the social father of her wife's children. In these cases we call her the child's social father, and do not say that she fathered her child. Being a mother, then, is not only bearing a child – it is being a person who socializes and nurtures. It is being a primary parent or caretaker. So we can ask, why are mothers women? Why is the person who routinely does all those activities that go into parenting not a man?

The question is important. Women's mothering is central to the sexual division of labor. Women's maternal role has profound effects on women's lives, on ideology about women, on the reproduction of masculinity and sexual inequality, and on the reproduction of particular forms of labor power. Women as mothers are pivotal actors in the sphere of social reproduction. As Engels and Marxist feminists, Lévi-Strauss and feminist anthropologists, Parsons and family theorists point out, women find their primary social location within this sphere.

Most sociological theorists have either ignored or taken as unproblematic this sphere of social reproduction, despite its importance and the recognition by some theorists, such as Engels, of its fundamental historical role.[1] As a consequence of ignoring this sphere, most sociological theorists have ignored women, who have been the central figures within it.

Engels helps us to understand this omission through his emphasis on the shift away from kinship-based forms of material production in modern societies. All societies contain both means of producing material subsistence and means of organizing procreation. Earlier societies (and contemporary 'primitive' societies) were centered on kinship relations. Production and reproduction were organized according to the rules of kinship. This does not mean that the relations of production were based entirely on actual biological and affinal ties. In contemporary primitive societies, a kinship idiom can come to describe and incorporate whatever productive relations develop.

In modern societies, ties based on kinship no longer function as important links among people in the productive world, which becomes organized more and more in nonkinship market and class relations. Moreover, the relations of material production, and the extended public and political ties and associations – the state, family – which these relations make possible, dominate and define family relations – the sphere of human reproduction. Many aspects of reproduction are taken over by extrafamilial institutions like schools. Kinship, then, is progressively stripped of its functions and its ability to organize the social world.[2]

Because of their location within and concern with Western capitalist society, most major social theorists have made the recognition of this major historical transformation fundamental to their theories. They have, as a consequence, developed theories which focus on nonfamilial political, economic, and communal ties and have treated familial relations only to point out their declining importance.* This historical transformation also reinforces a tendency in everyday discourse. Social theorists, like societal members, tend to define a society and discuss its social organization in terms of what men do, and where men are located in that society.

It is apparent, however, that familial and kinship ties and family life remain crucial for women. The organization of these ties is certainly shaped in many ways by industrial capitalist development (though the family retains fundamental precapitalist, preindustrial features – that women mother, for instance). However, as production has moved out of the home, reproduction has become even more immediately defining and circumscribing of women's life activities and of women themselves.

Some theorists do investigate the family. Parsons' concern with the 'problem of order' (what accounts for the persistence of social structures over time) and that of the Frankfurt Institute with the reproduction of capitalist relations of production and ideology have led both, in their attempts to understand social reproductive processes, to turn to the family as an area for sociological inquiry.[3] Feminist theorists, including Engels and Charlotte Perkins Gilman,[4] early recognized

---

* Thus, Durkheim describes the shift from mechanical to organic solidarity. Tönnies distinguishes *gemeinschaft* and *gesellschaft* societies. Weber discusses increasing rationalization and the rise of bureaucracy and market relations. Parsons distinguishes particularistic, ascribed, affective role relationships from those based on universalistic, achieved, and nonaffective criteria. Marx gives an account of the way capitalist market relations increasingly dominate all social life.

the family as a central agent of women's oppression as well as the major institution in women's lives. Anthropological theory also, in its concern with societies in which social ties for both men and women are largely defined through kinship, has developed an extensive and sophisticated analysis of kinship and the organization of gender – of rules of descent, marriage rules, residence arrangements, variations in household and family organization, and so forth. Consequently, anthropological theory has informed much family theory, including some feminist theories.[5]

Most of these theories see women's mothering as central. While understanding the importance of this mothering for social reproduction, however, they do not take it as in need of explanation. They simply assume that it is socially, psychologically, and biologically natural and functional. They do not question and certainly do not explain the reproduction of mothering itself either cross-culturally or within modern societies. They understand how women as mothers currently produce men with particular personalities and orientations, and how women's social location and the sexual division of labor generate other features of the social and economic world and of ideology about women. But they do not inquire about how women themselves are produced, how women continue to find themselves in a particular social and economic location

THE ARGUMENT FROM NATURE

Several assumptions underlie this surprising omission. The most prevalent assumptions among nonfeminist theorists is that the structure of parenting is biologically self-explanatory. This assumption holds that what seems universal is instinctual, and that what is instinctual, or has instinctual components, is inevitable and unchanging. Women's mothering as a feature of social structure, then, has no reality separate from the biological fact that women bear children and lactate. These social scientists reify the social organization of gender and see it as a natural product rather than a social construct.

Another explanation from nature is bioevolutionary. This explanation holds that women are primary parents *now* because they always have been. It either assumes that the sexual division of labor – for whatever reason – was the earliest division of labor, and was simply perpetuated; that the sexual division of labor was necessary for species survival in the earliest human communities; or that this species survival division of labor is now built biologically into human sexual dimorphism. In all cases, the implication is that the mode of reproduction of mothering is unchanging, and retains the form of its earliest origins. These accounts argue that women's mothering is, or has been, functional – that children, after all, have been reared – and often imply that what is and has been ought to be – that women ought to mother.

Women's mothering, then, is seen as a natural fact. Natural facts, for social scientists, are theoretically uninteresting and do not need explanation. The assumption is questionable, however, given the extent to which human behavior is not instinctually determined but culturally mediated. It is an assumption in conflict with most social scientists' insistence on the social malleability of biological factors, and it also conflicts with the general reluctance of social scientists to explain existing social forms simply as relics of previous epochs.

In contrast to these assumptions, it seems to me that we must always raise as problematic any feature of social structure, even if – and perhaps especially because – it seems universal. In the case at hand, we are confronted with a sexual division of labor in which women parent, which is reproduced in each generation and in all societies. We must understand this reproduction in order to understand women's lives and the sociology of gender. Why men by and large do not do primary parenting, and women do, is a centrally interesting sociological question.

We must question all assumptions which use biological claims to explain social forms, given the recent rise to prominence of sociobiology and the histor- ically extensive uses of explanations allegedly based on biological sex (or race) differences to legitimate oppression and inequality. That there are undeniable gen- etic, morphological, and hormonal sex differences, which affect our physical and social experiences and are (minimally) the criteria according to which a person's participation in the sexual division of labor and membership in a gender- differentiated world are assigned, only makes this task more necessary.

NOTES

1   See Frederick Engels, 1884, *The Origin of the Family, Private Property, and the State*.
2   For some empirical elucidation of Engels's theory according to this reading, see Heidi Hartmann, 1976, 'Capitalism, Patriarchy, and Job Segregation by Sex,' *Signs*, 1, #3, part 2, pp. 137–169; and Reiter, ed., 1975, *Toward an Anthropology of Women*.
3   Parsons, 1942, 'Age and Sex'; 1943, 'The Kinship System'; 1964, *Social Structure and Personality*; Parsons and Bales, 1955, *Family Socialization and Interaction Process*; Horkheimer, 1936, 'Authority and the Family'; Frankfurt Institute for Social Research, 1972, *Aspects of Sociology*; Mitscherlich, 1963, *Society Without the Father*.
4   Charlotte Perkins Gilman, 1899, *Women and Economics*.
5   On family theory influenced by anthropology, see Coser, ed., 1974b, *The Family*. On feminist theory influenced by anthropology, see Juliet Mitchell, 1974, *Psychoanalysis and Feminism*; and Heidi Hartmann, 1976, 'Capitalism, Patriarchy.' On feminist theory within anthropology, see Rosaldo and Lamphere, eds, 1974, *Women, Culture and Society*, and Reiter, ed., 1975, *Toward an Anthropology*.

9 Luce Irigaray

'This Sex Which Is Not One'[1]

from Elaine Marks and Isabelle Courtivron (eds), *New French Feminisms: An Anthology* (1980)

Female sexuality has always been conceptualized on the basis of masculine parameters. Thus the opposition between 'masculine' clitoral activity and 'feminine' vaginal passivity, an opposition which Freud – and many others – saw as stages, or alternatives, in the development of a sexually 'normal' woman, seems rather too clearly required by the practice of male sexuality. For the clitoris is conceived as a little penis pleasant to masturbate so long as castration anxiety does not exist (for the boy child), and the vagina is valued for the 'lodging' it offers the male organ when the forbidden hand has to find a replacement for pleasure-giving.

In these terms, woman's erogenous zones never amount to anything but a clitoris-sex that is not comparable to the noble phallic organ, or a hole-envelope that serves to sheathe and massage the penis in intercourse: a non-sex, or a masculine organ turned back upon itself, self-embracing.

About woman and her pleasure, this view of the sexual relation has nothing to say. Her lot is that of 'lack,' 'atrophy' (of the sexual organ), and 'penis envy,' the penis being the only sexual organ of recognized value. Thus she attempts by every means available to appropriate that organ for herself: through her somewhat servile love of the father-husband capable of giving her one; through her desire for a child-penis, preferably a boy, through access to the cultural values still reserved by right to males alone and therefore always masculine, and so on. Woman lives her own desire only as the expectation that she may at last come to possess an equivalent of the male organ.

Yet all this appears quite foreign to her own pleasure, unless it remains within the dominant phallic economy. Thus, for example, woman's autoeroticism is very different from man's. In order to touch himself, man needs an instrument: his hand, a woman's body, language . . . And this self-caressing requires at least a minimum of activity. As for woman, she touches herself in and of herself without any need for mediation, and before there is any way to distinguish activity from passivity. Woman 'touches herself' all the time, and moreover no one can forbid her to do so, for her genitals are formed of two lips in continuous contact. Thus, within herself, she is already two – but not divisible into one(s) – that caress each other.

This autoeroticism is disrupted by a violent break-in: the brutal separation of the two lips by a violating penis, an intrusion that distracts and deflects the woman from this 'self-caressing' she needs if she is not to incur the disappearance of her own pleasure in sexual relations. If the vagina is to serve *also*, but *not only*, to take over from the little boy's hand in order to assure an articulation between auto-eroticism and heteroeroticism in intercourse (the encounter with the totally other always signifying death), how, in the classic representation of sexuality, can the perpetuation of autoeroticism for woman be managed? Will woman not be left with the impossible alternative between a defensive virginity, fiercely turned in upon itself, and a body open to penetration that no longer knows, in this 'hole' that constitutes its sex, the pleasure of its own touch? The more or less exclusive – and highly anxious – attention paid to erection in Western sexuality proves to what extent the imaginary that governs it is foreign to the feminine. For the most part, this sexuality offers nothing but imperatives dictated by male rivalry: the 'strong' being the one who has the best 'hard-on,' the longest, the biggest, the stiffest penis, or even the one who 'pees the farthest' (as in little boys' contests). Or else one finds imperatives dictated by the enactment of sadomasochistic fantasies, these in turn governed by man's relation to his mother: the desire to force entry, to penetrate, to appropriate for himself the mystery of this womb where he has been conceived, the secret of his begetting, of his 'origin.' Desire/need, also to make blood flow again in order to revive a very old relationship – intrauterine, to be sure, but also prehistoric – to the maternal.

Woman, in this sexual imaginary, is only a more or less obliging prop for the enact-ment of man's fantasies. That she may find pleasure there in that role, by proxy, is possible, even certain. But such pleasure is above all a masochistic prostitution of her body to a desire that is not her own, and it leaves her in a familiar state of dependency upon man. Not knowing what she wants, ready for anything, even asking for more, so long as he will 'take' her as his 'object' when he seeks his own pleasure. Thus she will not say what she herself wants; moreover, she does not know, or no longer knows, what she wants. As Freud admits, the beginnings of the sexual life of a girl child are so 'obscure,' so 'faded with time,' that one would have to dig down very deep indeed to discover beneath the traces of this civilization, of this history, the vestiges of a more archaic civilization that might give some clue to woman's sexuality. That extremely ancient civilization would undoubtedly have a different alphabet, a different language. . . . Woman's desire would not be ex-pected to speak the same language as man's; woman's desire has doubtless been submerged by the logic that has dominated the West since the time of the Greeks.

Within this logic, the predominance of the visual, and of the discrimination and individualization of form, is particularly foreign to female eroticism. Woman takes pleasure more from touching than from looking, and her entry into a dominant scopic economy signifies, again, her consignment to passivity: she is to be the beautiful object of contemplation. While her body finds itself thus eroticized, and called to a double movement of exhibition and of chaste retreat in order to stimulate the drives of the 'subject,' her sexual organ represents *the horror of nothing to see*. A defect in this systematics of representation and desire. A 'hold' in its scoptophilic lens. It is already evident in Greek statuary that this nothing-to-see has to be excluded, rejected, from such a scene of representation. Woman's genitals are simply absent, masked, sewn back up inside their 'crack.'

This organ which has nothing to show for itself also lacks a form of its own. And if woman takes pleasure precisely from this incompleteness of form which allows her organ to touch itself over and over again, indefinitely, by itself, that pleasure is denied by a civilization that privileges phallomorphism. The value granted to the only definable form excludes the one that is in play in female autoeroticism. The *one* of form, of the individual, of the (male) sexual organ, of the proper name, of the proper meaning ... supplants, while separating and dividing, that contact of *at least two* (lips) which keeps woman in touch with herself, but without any possibility of distinguishing what is touching from what is touched.

Whence the mystery that woman represents in a culture claiming to count everything, to number everything by units, to inventory everything as individualities. *She is neither one nor two*. Rigorously speaking, she cannot be identified either as one person, or as two. She resists all adequate definition. Further, she has no 'proper' name. And her sexual organ, which is not *one* organ, is counted as *none*. The negative, the underside, the reverse of the only visible and morphologically designatable organ (even if the passage from erection to detumescence does pose some problems): the penis.

But the 'thickness' of that 'form,' the layering of its volume, its expansions and contractions and even the spacing of the moments in which it produces itself as form – all this the feminine keeps secret. Without knowing it. And if woman is asked to sustain, to revive, man's desire, the request neglects to spell out what it implies as to the value of her own desire. A desire of which she is not aware, moreover, at least not explicitly. But one whose force and continuity are capable of nurturing repeatedly and at length all the masquerades of 'feminity' that are expected of her.

It is true that she still has the child, in relation to whom her appetite for touch, for contact, has free rein, unless it is already lost, alienated by the taboo against touching of a highly obsessive civilization. Otherwise her pleasure will find, in the child, compensations for and diversions from the frustrations that she too often encounters in sexual relations *per se*. Thus maternity fills the gaps in a repressed female sexuality. Perhaps man and woman no longer caress each other except through that mediation between them that the child – preferably a boy – represents?

Man, identified with his son, rediscovers the pleasure of maternal fondling; woman touches herself again by caressing that part of her body: her baby-penis-clitoris.

What this entails for the amorous trio is well known. But the Oedipal interdiction seems to be a somewhat categorical and factitious law – although it does provide the means for perpetuating the authoritarian discourse of fathers – when it is promulgated in a culture in which sexual relations are impracticable because man's desire and woman's are strangers to each other. And in which the two desires have to try to meet through indirect means, whether the archaic one of a sense-relation to the mother's body, or the present one of active or passive extension of the law of the father. These are regressive emotional behaviors, exchanges of words too detached from the sexual arena not to constitute an exile with respect to it: 'mother' and 'father' dominate the interactions of the couple, but as social roles. The division of labor prevents them from making love. They produce or reproduce. Without quite knowing how to use their leisure. Such little as they have, such little indeed as they wish to have. For what are they to do with leisure? What substitute for amorous resource are they to invent? Still . . .

Perhaps it is time to return to that repressed entity, the female imaginary. So woman does not have a sex organ? She has at least two of them, but they are not identifiable as ones. Indeed, she has many more. Her sexuality, always at least double, goes even further: it is *plural*. Is this the way culture is seeking to characterize itself now? Is this the way texts write themselves/are written now? Without quite knowing what censorship they are evading? Indeed, woman's pleasure does not have to choose between clitoral activity and vaginal passivity, for example. The pleasure of the vaginal caress does not have to be substituted for that of the clitoral caress. They each contribute, irreplaceably, to woman's pleasure. Among other caresses . . . Fondling the breasts, touching the vulva, spreading the lips, stroking the posterior wall of the vagina, brushing against the mouth of the uterus, and so on. To evoke only a few of the most specifically female pleasures. Pleasures which are somewhat misunderstood in sexual difference as it is imagined – or not imagined, the other sex being only the indispensable complement to the only sex.

But *woman has sex organs more or less everywhere*. She finds pleasure almost anywhere. Even if we refrain from invoking the hystericization of her entire body, the geography of her pleasure is far more diversified, more multiple in its differences, more complex, more subtle, than is commonly imagined – in an imaginary rather too narrowly focused on sameness.

'She' is indefinitely other in herself. This is doubtless why she is said to be whimsical, incomprehensible, agitated, capricious . . . not to mention her language, in which 'she' sets off in all directions leaving 'him' unable to discern the coherence of any meaning. Hers are contradictory words, somewhat mad from the standpoint of reason, inaudible for whoever listens to them with ready-made grids, with a fully elaborated code in hand. For in what she says, too, at least when she dares, woman is constantly touching herself. She steps ever so slightly aside from herself with a murmur, an exclamation, a whisper, a sentence left unfinished. . . . When she returns, it is to set off again from elsewhere. From another point of pleasure, or of pain. One would have to listen with another ear, as if hearing an 'other meaning' always in the process of weaving itself, of embracing itself with words, but also of getting rid of words in order not to become fixed, congealed in them. For if 'she' says something, it is not, it is already no longer, identical with what she means. What she says is never identical with anything, moreover; rather, it is contiguous. It touches (upon). And when it strays too far from that proximity, she breaks off and starts over at 'zero': her body-sex.

It is useless, then, to trap women in the exact definition of what they mean, to make them repeat (themselves) so that it will be clear; they are already elsewhere in that discursive machinery where you expected to surprise them. They have returned within themselves. Which must not be understood in the same way as within yourself. They do not have the interiority that you have, the one you perhaps suppose they have. Within themselves means within the intimacy of that silent, multiple, diffuse touch. And if you ask them insistently what they are thinking about, they can only reply: Nothing. Everything.

Thus what they desire is precisely nothing, and at the same time everything. Always something more and something else besides that one – sexual organ, for example – that you give them, attribute to them. Their desire is often interpreted, and feared, as a sort of insatiable hunger, a voracity that will swallow you whole. Whereas it really involves a different economy more than anything else, one that upsets the linearity of a project, undermines the goal-object of a desire, diffuses the polarization toward a single pleasure, disconcerts fidelity to a single discourse . . .

Must this multiplicity of female desire and female language be understood as shards, scattered remnants of a violated sexuality? A sexuality denied? The question has no simple answer. The rejection, the exclusion of a female imaginary certainly puts woman in the position of experiencing herself only fragmentarily, in the little-structured margins of a dominant ideology, as waste, or excess, what is left of a mirror invested by the (masculine) 'subject' to reflect himself, to copy himself. Moreover, the role of 'femininity' is prescribed by this masculine specula(riza)tion and corresponds scarcely at all to woman's desire, which may be recovered only in secret, in hiding, with anxiety and guilt.

But if the female imaginary were to deploy itself, if it could bring itself into play otherwise than as scraps, uncollected debris, would it represent itself, even so, in the form of one universe? Would it even be volume instead of surface? No. Not unless it were understood, yet again, as a privileging of the maternal over the feminine. Of a phallic maternal, at that. Closed in upon the jealous possession of its valued product. Rivaling man in his esteem for productive excess. In such a race for power, woman loses the uniqueness of her pleasure. By closing herself off as volume, she renounces the pleasure that she gets from the nonsuture of her lips: she is undoubtedly a mother, but a virgin mother; the role was assigned to her by mythologies long ago. Granting her a certain social power to the extent that she is reduced, with her own complicity, to sexual impotence.

(Re-)discovering herself, for a woman, thus could only signify the possibility of sacrificing no one of her pleasures to another, of identifying herself with none of them in particular, *of never being simply one*. A sort of expanding universe to which no limits could be fixed and which would not be incoherence nonetheless – nor that polymorphous perversion of the child in which the erogenous zones would lie waiting to be regrouped under the primacy of the phallus.

Woman always remains several, but she is kept from dispersion because the other is already within her and is autoerotically familiar to her. Which is not to say that she appropriates the other for herself, that she reduces it to her own property. Ownership and property are doubtless quite foreign to the feminine. At least sexually. But not *nearness*. Nearness so pronounced that it makes all discrimination of identity, and thus all forms of property, impossible. Woman derives pleasure from what is *so near that she cannot have it, nor have herself*. She herself enters into a ceaseless exchange of herself with the other without any possibility of identifying either. This puts into question all prevailing economies: their calculations are irremediably stymied by woman's pleasure, as it increases indefinitely from its passage in and through the other.

However, in order for woman to reach the place where she takes pleasure as woman, a long detour by way of the analysis of the various systems of oppression brought to bear upon her is assuredly necessary. And claiming to fall back on the single solution of pleasure risks making her miss the process of going back through a social practice that *her* enjoyment requires.

For woman is traditionally a use-value for man, an exchange value among men; in other words, a commodity. As such, she remains the guardian of material substance, whose price will be established, in terms of the standard of their work and of their need/desire, by 'subjects': workers, merchants, consumers. Women are marked phallicly by their fathers, husbands, procurers. And this branding determines their value in sexual commerce. Woman is never anything but the locus of a more or less competitive exchange between two men, including the competition for the possession of mother earth.

How can this object of transaction claim a right to pleasure without removing her/itself from established commerce? With respect to other merchandise in the marketplace, how could this commodity maintain a relationship other than one of aggressive jealousy? How could material substance enjoy her/itself without provoking the consumer's anxiety over the disappearance of his nurturing ground? How could that exchange – which can in no way be defined in terms 'proper' to woman's desire – appear as anything but a pure mirage, mere foolishness, all too readily obscured by a more sensible discourse and by a system of apparently more tangible values?

A woman's development, however radical it may seek to be, would thus not suffice to liberate woman's desire. And to date no political theory or political practice has resolved, or sufficiently taken into consideration, this historical problem, even though Marxism has proclaimed its importance. But women do not constitute, strictly speaking, a class, and their dispersion among several classes makes their political struggle complex, their demands sometimes contradictory.

There remains, however, the condition of underdevelopment arising from women's submission by and to a culture that oppresses them, uses them, makes of them a medium of exchange, with very little profit to them. Except in the quasi monopolies of masochistic pleasure, the domestic labor force, and reproduction. The powers of slaves? Which are not negligible powers, moreover. For where pleasure is concerned, the master is not necessarily well served. Thus to reverse the relation, especially in the economy of sexuality, does not seem a desirable objective.

But if women are to preserve and expand their autoeroticism, their homo-sexuality, might not the renunciation of heterosexual pleasure correspond once again to that disconnection from power that is traditionally theirs? Would it not involve a new prison, a new cloister, built of their own accord? For women to undertake tactical strikes, to keep themselves apart from men long enough to learn to defend their desire, especially through speech, to discover the love of other women while sheltered from men's imperious choices that put them in the position of rival commodities, to forge for themselves a social status that compels recog-nition, to earn their living in order to escape from the condition of prostitute . . . these are certainly indispensable stages in the escape from their proletarization on the exchange market. But if their aim were simply to reverse the order of things, even supposing this to be possible, history would repeat itself in the long run, would revert to sameness: to phallocratism. It would leave room neither for women's sexuality, nor for women's imaginary, nor for women's language to take (their) place.

NOTE

1   This text was originally published as 'Ce sexe qui n'en est pas un,' in *Cahiers du Grif*, no. 5. English translation: 'This Sex Which Is Not One,' trans. Claudia Reeder, in *New French Feminisms*, eds Elaine Marks and Isabelle de Courtivron (New York, 1980), pp. 99–106.

10 Chandra Talpade Mohanty

Excerpts from 'Under Western Eyes: Feminist Scholarship and Colonial Discourses'[1]

from Chandra Talpade Mohanty, Ann Russo and Lourdes Torres (eds), *Third World Women and the Politics of Feminism* (1984)

Any discussion of the intellectual and political construction of 'third world feminisms' must address itself to two simultaneous projects: the internal critique of hegemonic 'Western' feminisms, and the formulation of autonomous, geographically, historically, and culturally grounded feminist concerns and strategies. The first project is one of deconstructing and dismantling; the second, one of building and constructing. While these projects appear to be contradictory, the one working negatively and the other positively, unless these two tasks are addressed simultaneously, 'third world' feminisms run the risk of marginalization or ghettoization from both mainstream (right and left) and Western feminist discourses.

It is to the first project that I address myself. What I wish to analyze is specifically the production of the 'third world woman' as a singular monolithic subject in some recent (Western) feminist texts. The definition of colonization I wish to invoke here is a predominantly *discursive* one, focusing on a certain mode of appropriation and codification of 'scholarship' and 'knowledge' about women in the third world by particular analytic categories employed in specific writings on the subject which take as their referent feminist interests as they have been articulated in the US and Western Europe. If one of the tasks of formulating and understanding the locus of 'third world feminisms' is delineating the way in which it resists and *works against* what I am referring to as 'Western feminist discourse,' an analysis of the discursive construction of 'third world women' in Western feminism is an important first step.

Clearly Western feminist discourse and political practice is neither singular nor homogeneous in its goals, interests, or analyses. However, it is possible to trace a coherence of *effects* resulting from the implicit assumption of 'the West' (in all its complexities and contradictions) as the primary referent in theory and praxis. My reference to 'Western feminism' is by no means intended to imply that it is a monolith. Rather, I am attempting to draw attention to the similar effects of various textual strategies used by writers which codify Others as non-Western and hence themselves as (implicitly) Western. It is in this sense that I use the term *Western feminist*. Similar arguments can be made in terms of middle-class urban African or Asian scholars producing scholarship on or about their rural or working-class sisters which assumes their own middle-class cultures as the norm, and codifies working-class histories and cultures as Other. Thus, while this essay focuses specifically on what I refer to as 'Western feminist' discourse on women in the third world, the critiques I offer also pertain to third world scholars writing about their own cultures, which employ identical analytic strategies.

It ought to be of some political significance, at least, that the term *colonization* has come to denote a variety of phenomena in recent feminist and left-wing writings in general. From its analytic value as a category of exploitative economic exchange in both traditional and contemporary Marxisms – cf. particularly contemporary theorists such as Baran (1962), Amin (1977), and Gunder-Frank (1967) – to its use by feminist women of color in the US to describe the appropriation of their experiences and struggles by hegemonic white women's movements – cf. especially Moraga and Anzaldúa (1983), Smith (1983), Joseph and Lewis (1981), and Moraga (1984) – colonization has been used to characterize everything from the most evident economic and political hierarchies to the production of a particular cultural discourse about what is called the 'third world.'[2] However sophisticated or problematic its use as an explanatory construct, colonization almost invariably implies a relation of structural domination, and a suppression – often violent – of the heterogeneity of the subject(s) in question.

My concern about such writings derives from my own implication and investment in contemporary debates in feminist theory, and the urgent political necessity (especially in the age of Reagan/Bush) of forming strategic coalitions across class, race, and national boundaries. The analytic principles discussed below serve to distort Western feminist political practices, and limit the possibility of coalitions among (usually white) Western feminists and working-class feminists and feminists of color around the world. These limitations are evident in the construction of the (implicitly consensual) priority of issues around which apparently *all* women are expected to organize. The necessary and integral connection between feminist scholarship and feminist political practice and organizing determines the significance and status of Western feminist writings on women in the third world, for feminist scholarship, like most other kinds of scholarship, is not the mere production of knowledge about a certain subject. It is a directly political and discursive *practice* in that it is purposeful and ideological. It is best seen as a mode of intervention into particular hegemonic discourses (for example, traditional anthropology, sociology, literary criticism, etc.); it is a political praxis which counters and resists the totalizing imperative of age-old 'legitimate' and 'scientific' bodies of knowledge. Thus, feminist scholarly practices (whether reading, writing, critical, or textual) are inscribed in relations of power-relations which they counter, resist, or even perhaps implicitly support. There can, of course, be no apolitical scholarship.

The relationship between 'Woman' – a cultural and ideological composite Other constructed through diverse representational discourses (scientific, literary, juridical, linguistic, cinematic, etc.) – and 'women' – real, material subjects of their collective histories – is one of the central questions the practice of feminist scholarship seeks to address. This connection between women as historical subjects and the re-presentation of Woman produced by hegemonic discourses is not a relation of direct identity, or a relation of correspondence or simple implication.[3] It is an arbitrary relation set up by particular cultures. I would like to suggest that the feminist writings I analyze here discursively colonize the material and historical heterogeneities of the lives of women in the third world, thereby producing/re-presenting a composite, singular 'third world woman' – an image which appears arbitrarily constructed, but nevertheless carries with it the authorizing signature of Western humanist discourse.[4]

I argue that assumptions of privilege and ethnocentric universality, on the one hand, and inadequate self-consciousness about the effect of Western scholarship on the 'third world' in the context of a world system dominated by the West, on the other, characterize a sizeable extent of Western feminist work on women in the third world. An analysis of 'sexual difference' in the form of a cross-culturally singular, monolithic notion of patriarchy or male dominance leads to the construction of a similarly reductive and homogeneous notion of what I call the 'third world difference' – that stable, ahistorical something that apparently oppresses most if not all the women in these countries. And it is in the production of this 'third world difference' that Western feminisms appropriate and 'colonize' the constitutive complexities which characterize the lives of women in these countries. It is in this process of discursive homogenization and systematization of the oppression of women in the third world that power is exercised in much of recent Western feminist discourse, and this power needs to be defined and named.

In the context of the West's hegemonic position today, of what Anouar Abdel-Malek (1981) calls a struggle for 'control over the orientation, regulation and decision of the process of world development on the basis of the advanced sector's monopoly of scientific knowledge and ideal creativity,' Western feminist scholarship on the third world must be seen and examined precisely in terms of its inscription in these particular relations of power and struggle. There is, it should be evident, no universal patriarchal framework which this scholarship attempts to counter and resist – unless one posits an international male conspiracy or a monolithic, ahistorical power structure. There is, however, a particular world balance of power within which any analysis of culture, ideology, and socioeconomic conditions necessarily has to be situated. Abdel-Malek is useful here, again, in reminding us about the inherence of politics in the discourses of 'culture':

> Contemporary imperialism is, in a real sense, a hegemonic imperialism, exercising to a maximum degree a rationalized violence taken to a higher level than ever before – through fire and sword, but also through the attempt to control hearts and minds. For its content is defined by the combined action of the military-industrial complex and the hegemonic culture centers of the West, all of them founded on the advanced levels of development attained by monopoly and finance capital, and supported by the benefits of both the scientific and technological revolution and the second industrial revolution itself.
>
> (1981: 145–6)

Western feminist scholarship cannot avoid the challenge of situating itself and examining its role in such a global economic and political framework. To do any less would be to ignore the complex interconnections between first and third world economies and the profound effect of this on the lives of women in all countries. I do not question the descriptive and informative value of most Western feminist writings on women in the third world. I also do not question the existence of excellent work which does not fall into the analytic traps with which I am concerned. In fact I deal with an example of such work later on. In the context of an overwhelming silence about the experiences of women in these countries, as well as the need to forge international links between women's political struggles, such work is both pathbreaking and absolutely essential. However, it is both to the *explanatory potential* of particular analytic strategies employed by such writing, and to their *political effect* in the context of the hegemony of Western scholarships that I want to draw attention here. While feminist writing in the US is still marginalized (except from the point of view of women of color addressing privileged white women), Western feminist writing on women in the third world must be considered in the context of the global hegemony of Western scholarship – i.e., the production, publication, distribution, and consumption of information and ideas. Marginal or not, this writing has political effects and implications beyond the immediate feminist or disciplinary audience. One such significant effect of the dominant 'representations' of Western feminism is its conflation with imperialism in the eyes of particular third world women.[5] Hence the urgent need to examine the *political* implications of our *analytic* strategies and principles.

My critique is directed at three basic analytic principles which are present in (Western) feminist discourse on women in the third world. Since I focus primarily on the Zed Press Women in the Third World series, my comments on Western feminist discourse are circumscribed by my analysis of the texts in this series.[6] This is a way of focusing my critique. However, even though I am dealing with feminists who identify themselves as culturally or geographically from the 'West,' as mentioned earlier, what I say about these presuppositions or implicit principles holds for anyone who uses these methods, whether third world women in the West, or third world women in the third world writing on these issues and publishing in the West. Thus, I am not making a culturalist argument about ethnocentrism; rather, I am trying to uncover how ethnocentric universalism is produced in certain analyses. As a matter of fact, my argument holds for any discourse that sets up its own authorial subjects as the implicit referent, i.e., the yardstick by which to encode and represent cultural Others. It is in this move that power is exercised in discourse.

The first analytic presupposition I focus on is involved in the strategic location of the category 'women' *vis-à-vis* the context of analysis. The assumption of women as an already constituted, coherent group with identical interests and desires, regardless of class, ethnic or racial location, or contradictions, implies a notion of gender or sexual difference or even patriarchy which can be applied universally and cross-culturally. (The context of analysis can be anything from kinship structures and the organization of labor to media representations.) The second analytical presupposition is evident on the methodological level, in the uncritical way 'proof' of universality and cross-cultural validity is provided. The third is a more specifically political presupposition underlying the methodologies and the analytic strategies, i.e., the model of power and struggle they imply and suggest. I argue that as a result of the two modes – or, rather, frames – of analysis described above, a homogeneous notion of the oppression of women as a group is assumed, which, in turn, produces the image of an 'average third world woman.' This average third world woman leads an essentially truncated life based on her feminine gender (read: sexually constrained) and her being 'third world' (read: ignorant, poor, uneducated, tradition-bound, domestic, family-orientated, victimized, etc.). This, I suggest, is in contrast to the (implicit) self-representation of Western women as educated, as modern, as having control over their own bodies and sexualities, and the freedom to make their own decisions.

The distinction between Western feminist re-presentation of women in the third world and Western feminist self-presentation is a distinction of the same order as that made by some Marxists between the 'maintenance' function of the housewife and the real 'productive' role of wage labor, or the characterized by developmentalists of the third world as being engaged in the lesser production of 'raw materials' in contrast to the 'real' productive activity of the first world. These distinctions are made on the basis of the privileging of a particular group as the norm or referent. Men involved in wage labor, first world producers, and, I suggest, Western feminists who sometimes cast third world women in terms of 'ourselves undressed' (Michelle Rosaldo's [1980] term), all construct themselves as the normative referent in such a binary analytic.

NOTES

This essay would not have been possible without S. P. Mohanty's challenging and careful reading. I would also like to thank Biddy Martin for our numerous discussions about feminist theory and politics. They both helped me think through some of the arguments herein.

1   This is an updated and modified version of an essay published in *Boundary 2* 12, no. 3/13, no. 1 (Spring/Fall 1984), and reprinted in *Feminist Review*, no. 30 (Autumn 1988).

2   Terms such as *third* and *first world* are very problematic both in suggesting over-simplified similarities between and among countries labelled thus, and in implicitly reinforcing existing economic, cultural, and ideological hierarchies which are conjured up in using such terminology. I use the term *third world* with full awareness of its problems, only because this is the terminology available to us at the moment. The use of quotation marks is meant to suggest a continuous questioning of the designation. Even when I do not use quotation marks, I mean to use the term critically.

3   I am indebted to Teresa de Lauretis for this particular formulation of the project of feminist theorizing. See especially her introduction in de Lauretis. *Alice Doesn't: Feminism, Semiotics, Cinema* (Bloomington: Indiana University Press, 1984); see also Sylvia Wynter, 'The Politics of Domination,' unpublished manuscript.

4   This argument is similar to Homi Bhabha's definition of colonial discourse as stra-
    tegically creating a space for a subject people through the production of knowl-
    edges and the exercise of power. The full quote reads:

> '[colonial discourse is] an apparatus of power . . . an apparatus that turns on the recognition
> and disavowal of racial/cultural/historical differences. Its predominant strategic function is the
> creation of a space for a subject people through the production of knowledges in terms of which
> surveillance is exercised and a complex form of pleasure/unpleasure is incited. It (i.e. colonial
> discourse) seeks authorization for its strategies by the production of knowledges by coloniser
> and colonised which are stereotypical but antithetically evaluated.   (1983: 23)

5   A number of documents and reports on the UN International Conferences on
    Women, Mexico City, 1975, and Copenhagen, 1980, as well as the 1976 Wellesley
    Conference on Women and Development, attest to this. Nawal el Saadawi, Fatima
    Mernissi, and Mallica Vajarathon (1978) characterize this conference as 'American-
    planned and organized,' situating third world participants as passive audiences.
    They focus especially on the lack of self-consciousness of Western women's implica-
    tion in the effects of imperialism and racism in their assumption of an 'international
    sisterhood.' A recent essay by Valerie Amos and Pratibha Parmar (1984) charac-
    terizes as 'imperial' Euro-American feminism which seeks to establish itself as the
    only legitimate feminism.

6   The Zed Press Women in the Third World series is unique in its conception. I choose
    to focus on it because it is the only contemporary series I have found which assumes
    that 'women in the third world' are a legitimate and separate subject of study and
    research. Since 1985, when this essay was first written, numerous new titles have
    appeared in the Women in the Third World series. Thus, I suspect that Zed has come
    to occupy a rather privileged position in the dissemination and construction of
    discourses by and about third world women. A number of the books in this series
    are excellent, especially those which deal directly with women's resistance struggles.
    In addition, Zed Press consistently publishes progressive feminist, antiracist, and anti-
    imperialist texts. However, a number of the texts written by feminist sociologists,
    anthropologists, and journalists are symptomatic of the kind of Western feminist
    work on women in the third world that concerns me. Thus, an analysis of a few of
    these particular works in this series can serve as a representative point of entry into
    the discourse I am attempting to locate and define. My focus on these texts is
    therefore an attempt at an internal critique: I simply expect and demand more from
    this series. Needless to say, progressive publishing houses also carry their own
    authorizing signatures.

REFERENCES

Anoular Abdel-Malek, *Social Dialectics: Nation and Revolution* (Albany: State University
    of New York Press, 1981).

Samir Amin, *Imperialism and Unequal Development* (New York: Monthly Review Press,
    1977).

Valerie Amos and Patribha Parmar, 'Challenging Imperial Feminism', *Feminist Review* (1984) 17: 3–19.

Paul A. Baran, *The Political Economy of Growth* (New York: Monthly Review Press, 1962).

Nawal el Saadawi, Fatima Mernissi and Mallica Vajarathon, 'A Critical Look at the Wellesley Conference', *Quest* 4, no. 2 (Winter 1978): 101–7.

Audre Gunder-Frank, *Capitalism and Underdevelopment in Latin America* (New York: Monthly Review Press, 1967).

Gloria Joseph and Jill Lewis, *Common Differences; Conflicts in Black and White Feminist Perspectives* (Boston: Beacon Press, 1981).

Cherrie Moraga, *Loving in the War Years* (Boston: South End Press, 1984).

Cherrie Moraga and Gloria Anzalda (eds), *This Bridge called my Back: Writings by Radical Women of Color* (New York: Kitchen Table Press, 1983).

M. A. Rosaldo, 'The Use and Abuse of Anthropology: Reflections of Feminism and Cross-cultural Understanding', *Signs* (1980) 53: 389–417.

Barbara Smith (ed.), *Home Girls: A Black Feminist Anthology* (New York: Kitchen Table Press, 1983).

11 Joan Wallach Scott

Excerpts from 'Gender: A Useful Category of Historical Analysis'[1]

from *Gender and the Politics of History* (1988)

> Gender. *n*. a grammatical term only. To talk of persons or creatures of the
> masculine or feminine gender, meaning of the male or female sex, is either
> a jocularity (permissible or not according to context) or a blunder.
>
> H. W. Fowler, *Dictionary of Modern English Usage*

Those who would codify the meanings of words fight a losing battle, for words, like
the ideas and things they are meant to signify, have a history. Neither Oxford dons
nor the Académie française has been entirely able to stem the tide, to capture and
fix meanings free of the play of human invention and imagination. Mary Wortley
Montagu added bite to her witty denunciation 'of the fair sex' ('my only consola-
tion for being of that gender has been the assurance of never being married to any
one among them') by deliberately misusing the grammatical reference.[2] Through
the ages, people have made figurative allusions by employing grammatical terms to
evoke traits of character or sexuality. For example, the usage offered by the
Dictionnaire de la langue française in 1876 was: 'On ne sait de quel genre il est, s'il
est mâle ou femelle, se dit d'un homme très-caché, dont on ne connait pas les
sentiments.'[3] And Gladstone made this distinction in 1878: 'Athene has nothing of
sex except the gender, nothing of the woman except the form.'[4] Most recently –
too recently to find its way into dictionaries or the *Encyclopedia of the Social
Sciences* – feminists have in a more literal and serious vein begun to use 'gender' as
a way of referring to the social organization of the relationship between the sexes.
The connection to grammar is both explicit and full of unexamined possibilities.
Explicit because the grammatical usage involves formal rules that follow from the
masculine or feminine designation; full of unexamined possibilities because in
many Indo-European languages there is a third category – unsexed or neuter. In
grammar, gender is understood to be a way of classifying phenomena, a socially
agreed-upon system of distinctions rather than an objective description of inherent
traits. In addition, classifications suggest a relationship among categories that
makes distinctions or separate groupings possible.

In its most recent usage, 'gender' seems to have first appeared among
American feminists who wanted to insist on the fundamentally social quality of
distinctions based on sex. The word denoted a rejection of the biological deter-
minism implicit in the use of such terms as 'sex' or 'sexual difference'. 'Gender' also
stressed the relational aspect of normative definitions of femininity. Those who

worried that women's studies scholarship focused too narrowly and separately on women used the term 'gender' to introduce a relational notion into our analytic vocabulary. According to this view, women and men were defined in terms of one another, and no understanding of either could be achieved by entirely separate study. Thus Natalie Davis suggested in 1975:

> It seems to me that we should be interested in the history of both women and men, that we should not be working only on the subjected sex any more than a historian of class can focus entirely on peasants. Our goal is to understand the significance of the *sexes*, of gender groups in the historical past. Our goal is to discover the range in sex roles and in sexual symbolism in different societies and periods, to find out what meaning they had and how they functioned to maintain the social order or to promote its change.[5]

In addition, and perhaps most important, 'gender' was a term offered by those who claimed that women's scholarship would fundamentally transform disciplinary paradigms. Feminist scholars pointed out early on that the study of women would not only add new subject matter but would also force a critical re-examination of the premises and standards of existing scholarly work. 'We are learning', wrote three feminist historians, 'that the writing of women into history necessarily involves redefining and enlarging traditional notions of historical significance, to encompass personal, subjective experience as well as public and political activities. It is not too much to suggest that however hesitant the actual beginnings, such a methodology implies not only a new history of women, but also a new history.'[6] The way in which this new history would both include and account for women's experience rested on the extent to which gender could be developed as a category of analysis. Here the analogies to class and race were explicit; indeed, the most politically inclusive of scholars of women's studies regularly invoked all three categories as crucial to the writing of a new history.[7] An interest in class, race, and gender signalled, first, a scholar's commitment to a history that included stories of the oppressed and an analysis of the meaning and nature of their oppression and, second, scholarly understanding that inequalities of power are organized along at least three axes.

The litany of class, race and gender suggests a parity for each term, but, in fact, that is not at all the case. While 'class' most often rests on Marx's elaborate (and since elaborated) theory of economic determination and historical change, 'race' and 'gender' carry no such associations. No unanimity exists among those who employ concepts of class. Some scholars employ Weberian notions, others use class as a temporary heuristic device. Still, when we invoke class, we are working with or against a set of definitions that, in the case of Marxism, involve an idea of economic causality and a vision of the path along which history has moved dialectically. There is no such clarity or coherence for either race or gender. In the case of gender, the usage has involved a range of theoretical positions as well as simple descriptive references to the relationships between the sexes.

Feminist historians, trained as most historians are to be more comfortable with description than theory, have none the less increasingly looked for usable theoretical formulations. They have done so for at least two reasons. First, the proliferation of case studies in women's history seems to call for some synthesizing perspective that can explain continuities and discontinuities and account for persisting inequalities as well as radically different social experiences. Second, the discrepancy between the high quality of recent work in women's history and its continuing marginal status in the field as a whole (as measured by textbooks, syllabi, and monographic work) points up the limits of descriptive approaches that do not address dominant disciplinary concepts, or at least that do not address these concepts in terms that can shake their power and perhaps transform them. It has not been enough for historians of women to prove either that women had a history or that women participated in the major political upheavals of Western civilization. In the case of women's history, the response of most non-feminist historians has been acknowledgement and then separation or dismissal ('women had a history separate from men's, therefore let feminists do women's history which need not concern us'; or 'women's history is about sex and the family and should be done separately from political and economic history'). In the case of women's participation, the response has been minimal interest at best ('my understanding of the French Revolution is not changed by knowing that women participated in it'). The challenge posed by these responses is, in the end, a theoretical one. It requires analysis not only of the relationship between male and female experience in the past but also of the connection between past history and current historical practice. How does gender work in human social relationships? How does gender give meaning to the organization and perception of historical knowledge? The answers depend on gender as an analytic category.

For the most part, the attempts of historians to theorize about gender have remained within traditional social scientific frameworks, using long-standing formulations that provide universal causal explanations. These theories have been limited at best because they tend to contain reductive or overly simple generalizations that undercut not only history's disciplinary sense of the complexity of social causation but also feminist commitments to analyses that will lead to change. A review of these theories will expose their limits and make it possible to propose an alternative approach.

The approaches used by most historians fall into two distinct categories. The first is essentially descriptive; that is, it refers to the existence of phenomena or realities without interpreting, explaining, or attributing causality. The second usage is causal; it theorizes about the nature of phenomena or realities, seeking an understanding of how and why these take the form they do.

In its simplest recent usage, 'gender' is a synonym for 'women'. Any number of books and articles whose subject is women's history have, in the past few years, substituted 'gender' for 'women' in their titles. In some cases, this usage, though vaguely referring to certain analytic concepts, is actually about the political acceptability of the field. In these instances, the use of 'gender' is meant to denote the scholarly seriousness of a work, for 'gender' has a more neutral and objective sound than does 'women'. 'Gender seems to fit within the scientific terminology of social science and thus dissociates itself from the (supposedly strident) politics of feminism. In this usage, 'gender' does not carry with it a necessary statement about inequality or power nor does it name the aggrieved (and hitherto invisible) party. Whereas the term 'women's history' proclaims its politics by asserting (contrary to customary practice) that women are valid historical subjects, 'gender' includes, but does not name women, and so seems to pose no critical threat. This use of 'gender' is one facet of what might be called the quest of feminist scholarship for academic legitimacy in the 1980s.

But only one facet. 'Gender' as a substitute for 'women' is also used to suggest that information about women is necessarily information about men, that one implies the study of the other. This usage insists that the world of women is part of the world of men, created in and by it. This usage rejects the interpretative utility of the idea of separate spheres, maintaining that to study women in isolation perpetuates the fiction that one sphere, the experience of one sex, has little or nothing to do with the other. In addition, gender is also used to designate social relations between the sexes. Its use explicitly rejects biological explanations, such as those that find a common denominator for diverse forms of female subordination in the facts that women have the capacity to give birth and men have greater muscular strength. Instead, gender becomes a way of denoting 'cultural con-structions' – the entirely social creation of ideas about appropriate roles for women and men. It is a way of referring to the exclusively social origins of the subjective identities of men and women. Gender is, in this definition, a social category imposed on a sexed body.[8] Gender seems to have become a particularly useful word as studies of sex and sexuality have proliferated, for it offers a way of differentiating sexual practice from the social roles assigned to women and men. Although scholars acknowledge the connection between sex and (what the sociol-ogists of the family called) 'sex roles', these scholars do not assume a simple or direct linkage. The use of gender emphasizes an entire system of relationships that may include sex, but is not directly determined by sex nor directly determining of sexuality.

These descriptive usages of gender have been employed by historians most often to map out a new terrain. As social historians turned to new objects of study, gender was relevant for such topics as women, children, families and gender ideologies. This usage of gender, in other words, refers only to those areas – both structural and ideological – involving relations between the sexes. Because, on the face of it, war, diplomacy and high politics have not been explicitly about those relationships, gender seems not to apply and so continues to be irrelevant to the thinking of historians concerned with issues of politics and power. The effect is to endorse a certain functionalist view ultimately rooted in biology and to perpetuate the idea of separate spheres (sex or politics, family or nation, women or men) in the writing of history. Although gender in this usage asserts that relationships between the sexes are social, it says nothing about why these relationships are constructed as they are, how they work or how they change. In its descriptive usage, then, gender is a concept associated with the study of things related to women. Gender is a new topic, a new department of historical investigation, but it does not have the analytic power to address (and change) existing historical paradigms.

Some historians were, of course, aware of this problem, hence the efforts to employ theories that might explain the concept of gender and account for histori- cal change. Indeed, the challenge was to reconcile theory, which was framed in general or universal terms, and history, which was committed to the study of con- textual specificity and fundamental change. The result has been extremely eclectic: partial borrowings that vitiate the analytic power of a particular theory or worse, employ its precepts without awareness of their implications; or accounts of change that, because they embed universal theories, only illustrate unchanging themes; or wonderfully imaginative studies in which theory is none the less so hidden that these studies cannot serve as models for other investigations. Because the theories on which historians have drawn are often not spelled out in all their implications, it seems worthwhile to spend some time doing that. Only through such an exercise can we evaluate the usefulness of these theories and begin to articulate a more powerful theoretical approach.

Feminist historians have employed a variety of approaches to the analysis of gender, but the approaches come down to a choice among three theoretical positions.[9] The first, an entirely feminist effort, attempts to explain the origins of patriarchy. The second locates itself within a Marxian tradition and seeks there an accommodation with feminist critiques. The third, fundamentally divided between French post-structuralist and Anglo-American object-relations theorists, draws on these different schools of psychoanalysis to explain the production and repro- duction of the subject's gendered identity.

Theorists of patriarchy have directed their attention to the subordination of women and found their explanation for it in the male 'need' to dominate the female. In Mary O'Brien's ingenious adaptation of Hegel, she defined male domin- ation as the effect of men's desire to transcend their alienation from the means of the reproduction of the species. The principle of generational continuity restores the primacy of paternity and obscures the real labour and the social reality of women's work in childbirth. The source of women's liberation lies in 'an adequate understanding of the process of reproduction', an appreciation of the contradiction between the nature of women's reproductive labour and (male) ideological mystifications of it.[10] For Shulamith Firestone, reproduction was also the 'bitter trap' for women. In her more materialist analysis, however, liberation would come with transformations in reproductive technology, which might in some not too distant future eliminate the need for women's bodies as the agents of species reproduction.[11]

If reproduction was the key to patriarchy for some, sexuality itself was the answer for others. Catherine MacKinnon's bold formulations were at once her own and characteristic of a certain approach: 'Sexuality is to feminism what work is to Marxism: that which is most one's own, yet most taken away.' 'Sexual objectification is the primary process of the subjection of women. It unites act with word, construction with expression, perception with enforcement, myth with reality. Man fucks woman; subject verb object.'[12] Continuing her analogy to Marx, MacKinnon offered, in the place of dialectical materialism, consciousness-raising as feminism's method of analysis. By expressing the shared experience of objectification, she argued, women come to understand their common identity and so are moved to political action. Although sexual relations are defined in MacKinnon's analysis as social, there is nothing except the inherent inequality of the sexual relation itself to explain why the system of power operates as it does. The source of unequal relations between the sexes is, in the end, unequal relations between the sexes. Although the inequality of which sexuality is the source is said to be embodied in a 'whole system of social relationships', how this system works is not explained.[13]

Theorists of patriarchy have addressed the inequality of males and females in important ways, but, for historians, their theories pose problems. First, while they offer an analysis internal to the gender system itself, they also assert the primacy of that system in all social organization. But theories of patriarchy do not show what gender inequality has to do with other inequalities. Second, whether domination comes in the form of the male appropriation of the female's reproductive labour or in the sexual objectification of women by men, the analysis rests on physical difference. Any physical difference takes on a universal and unchanging aspect, even if theorists of patriarchy take into account the existence of changing forms and systems of gender inequality.[14] A theory that rests on the single variable of physical difference poses problems for historians: it assumes a consistent or inherent meaning for the human body – outside social or cultural construction – and thus the ahistoricity of gender itself. History becomes, in a sense, epiphenomenal, providing endless variations on the unchanging theme of a fixed gender inequality.

Marxist feminists have a more historical approach, guided as they are by a theory of history. But, whatever the variations and adaptations have been, the self-imposed requirement that there be a 'material' explanation for gender has limited or at least slowed the development of new lines of analysis. Whether a so-called dual-systems solution is preferred (one that posits the separate but interacting realms of capitalism and patriarchy) or an analysis based more firmly in orthodox Marxist discussions of modes of production is developed, the explanation for the origins of and changes in gender systems is found outside the sexual division of labour. Families, households and sexuality are all, finally, products of changing modes of production. That is how Engels concluded his explorations of the *Origins of the Family*,[15] that is where economist Heidi Hartmann's analysis ultimately rests. Hartmann insists on the importance of taking into account patriarchy and capitalism as separate but interacting systems. Yet, as her argument unfolds, economic causality takes precedence, and patriarchy always develops and changes as a function of relations of production.[16]

Early discussion among Marxist feminists circled around the same set of problems: a rejection of the essentialism of those who would argue that the 'exigencies of biological reproduction' determine the sexual division of labour under capitalism; the futility of inserting 'modes of reproduction' into discussions of modes of production (it remains an oppositional category and does not assume equal status with modes of production); the recognition that economic systems do not directly determine gender relationships, indeed, that the subordination of women pre-dates capitalism and continues under socialism; the search none the less for a materialist explanation that excludes natural physical differences.[17] An important attempt to break out of this circle of problems came from Joan Kelly in her essay 'The Doubled Vision of Feminist Theory', where she argued that economic and gender systems interact to produce social and historical experiences; that neither system was casual, but both 'operate simultaneously to reproduce the socioeconomic and male-dominant structures of . . . [a] particular social order.' Kelly's suggestion that gender systems have an independent existence provided a crucial conceptual opening, but her commitment to remain within a Marxist framework led her to emphasize the causal role of economic factors even in the determination of the gender system. 'The relation of the sexes operates in accordance with, and through, socioeconomic structures, as well as sex/gender ones.'[18] Kelly introduced the idea of a 'sexually based social reality', but she tended to emphasize the social rather than the sexual nature of that reality, and, most often, 'social', in her usage, was conceived in terms of economic relations of production.

The most far-reaching exploration of sexuality by American Marxist feminists is in *Powers of Desire*, a volume of essays published in 1983.[19] Influenced by increasing attention to sexuality among political activists and scholars, by French philosopher Michel Foucault's insistence that sexuality is produced in historical contexts, and by the conviction that the current 'sexual revolution' requires serious analysis, the authors make 'sexual politics' the focus of their inquiry. In so doing, they open the question of causality and offer a variety of solutions to it; indeed, the real excitement of this volume is its lack of analytic unanimity, its sense of analytic tension. If individual authors tend to stress the causality of social (by which is often meant 'economic') contexts, they none the less include suggestions about the importance of studying 'the psychic structuring of gender identity'. If 'gender ideology' is sometimes said to 'reflect' economic and social structures, there is also a crucial recognition of the need to understand the complex 'link between society and enduring psychic structure'.[20] On the one hand, the editors endorse Jessica Benjamin's point that politics must include attention to 'the erotic, fantastic components of human life', but, on the other hand, no essays besides Benjamin's deal fully or seriously with the theoretical issues she raises.[21] Instead, a tacit assumption runs through the volume that Marxism can be expanded to include discussions of ideology, culture and psychology, and that this expansion will happen through the kind of concrete examination of evidence undertaken in most of the articles. The advantage of such an approach lies in its avoidance of sharp differences of position, the disadvantage in its leaving in place an already fully articulated theory that leads back from relations of the sexes to relations of production.

A comparison of American Marxist-feminist efforts, exploratory and relatively wide-ranging, to those of their British counterparts, tied more closely to the politics of a strong and viable Marxist tradition, reveals that the British have had greater difficulty in challenging the constraints of strictly determinist explanations. This difficulty can be seen most dramatically in the debates in the *New Left Review* between Michèle Barrett and her critics, who charge her with abandoning a materialist analysis of the sexual division of labour under capitalism.[22] It can be seen as well in the replacement of an initial feminist attempt to reconcile psychoanalysis and Marxism with a choice of one or another of these theoretical positions by scholars who earlier insisted that some fusion of the two was possible.[23] The difficulty for both British and American feminists working within Marxism is apparent in the work I have mentioned here. The problem they face is the opposite of the one posed by patriarchal theory. For within Marxism, the concept of gender has long been treated as the by-product of changing economic structures; gender has had no independent analytic status of its own.

A review of psychoanalytic theory requires a specification of schools, since the various approaches have tended to be classified by the national origins of the founders and the majority of the practitioners. There is the Anglo-American school, working within the terms of theories of object-relations. In the United States, Nancy Chodorow is the name most readily associated with this approach. In addition, the work of Carol Gilligan has had a far-reaching impact on American scholarship, including history. Gilligan's work draws on Chodorow's, although it is concerned less with the construction of the subject than with moral development and behaviour. In contrast to the Anglo-American school, the French school is based on structuralist and post-structuralist readings of Freud in terms of theories of language (for feminists, the key figure is Jacques Lacan).

Both schools are concerned with the processes by which the subject's identity is created; both focus on the early stages of child development for clues to the formation of gender identity. Object-relations theorists stress the influence of actual experience (the child sees, hears, relates to those who care for it, particularly, of course, to its parents), while the post-structuralists emphasize the centrality of language in communicating, interpreting and representing gender. (By 'language', post-structuralists do not mean words but systems of meaning – symbolic orders – that precede the actual mastery of speech, reading, and writing.) Another difference between the two schools of thought focuses on the unconscious, which for Chodorow is ultimately subject to conscious understanding and for Lacan is not. For Lacanians, the unconscious is a critical factor in the construction of the subject; it is the location, moreover, of sexual division and, for that reason, of continuing instability for the gendered subject.

In recent years, feminist historians have been drawn to these theories either because they serve to endorse specific findings with general observations or because they seem to offer an important theoretical formulation about gender. Increasingly, those historians working with a concept of 'women's culture' cite Chodorow's or Gilligan's work as both proof of and explanation for their interpretations; those wrestling with feminist theory look to Lacan. In the end, neither of these theories seems to me entirely workable for historians; a closer look at each may help explain why.

My reservation about object-relations theory concerns its literalism, its reliance on relatively small structures of interaction to produce gender identity and to generate change. Both the family division of labour and the actual assignment of tasks to each parent play a crucial role in Chodorow's theory. The outcome of prevailing Western systems is a clear division between male and female: 'The basic feminine sense of self is connected to the world, the basis masculine sense of self is separate.'[24] According to Chodorow, if fathers were more involved in parenting and present more often in domestic situations, the outcome of the Oedipal drama might be different.[25]

This interpretation limits the concept of gender to family and household experience and, for the historian, leaves no way to connect the concept (or the individual) to other social systems of economy, politics or power. Of course, it is implicit that social arrangements requiring fathers to work and mothers to perform most child-rearing tasks structure family organization. Where such arrangements come from and why they are articulated in terms of a sexual division of labour is not clear. Neither is the issue of inequality, as opposed to that of asymmetry, addressed. How can we account within this theory for persistent associations of masculinity with power, for the higher value placed on manhood than on womanhood, for the way children seem to learn these associations and evaluations even when they live outside nuclear households or in households where parenting is equally divided between husband and wife? I do not think we can without some attention to signifying systems, that is, to the ways societies represent gender, use it to articulate the rules of social relationships, or construct the meaning of experience. Without meaning, there is no experience; without processes of signification, there is no meaning.

Language is the centre of Lacanian theory; it is the key to the child's induction into the symbolic order. Through language, gendered identity is constructed. According to Lacan, the phallus is the central signifier of sexual difference. But the meaning of the phallus must be read metaphorically. For the child, the Oedipal drama sets forth the terms of cultural interaction, since the threat of castration embodies the power, the rules of (the Father's) law. The child's relationship to the law depends on sexual difference, on its imaginative (or fantastic) identification with masculinity or femininity. The imposition, in other words, of the rules of social interaction is inherently and specifically gendered, for the female necessarily has a different relationship to the phallus than the male does. But gender identification, although it always appears coherent and fixed, is in fact, highly unstable. As meaning systems, subjective identities are processes of differentiation and distinction, requiring the suppression of ambiguities and opposite elements in order to ensure (create the illusion of) coherence and common understanding. The principle of masculinity rests on the necessary repression of feminine aspects – of the subject's potential for bisexuality – and introduces conflict into the opposition of masculine and feminine. Repressed desires are present in the unconscious and are constantly a threat to the stability of gender identification, denying its unity, subverting its need for security. In addition, conscious ideas of masculine or feminine are not fixed, since they vary according to contextual usage. Conflicts always exists, then, between the subject's need for the appearance of wholeness and the imprecision of terminology, its relative meaning, its dependence on repression.[26] This kind of interpretation makes the categories of 'man' and 'woman' problematic by suggesting that masculine and feminine are not inherent characteristics but subjective (or fictional) constructs. This interpretation also implies that the subject is in a constant process of construction, and it offers a systematic way of interpreting conscious and unconscious desire by pointing to language as the appropriate place for analysis. As such, I find it instructive.

I am troubled, none the less, by the exclusive fixation on questions of the individual subject and by the tendency to reify subjectively originating antagonism between males and females as the central fact of gender. In addition, although there is openness in the concept of how 'the subject' is constructed, the theory tends to universalize the categories and relationship of male and female. The outcome for historians is a reductive reading of evidence from the past. Even though this theory takes social relationships into account by linking castration to prohibition and law, it does not permit the introduction of a notion of historical specificity and variability. The phallus is the only signifier; the process of constructing the gendered subject is, in the end, predictable because always the same. If, as film theorist Teresa de Lauretis suggests, we need to think in terms of the construction of subjectivity in social and historical contexts, there is no way to specify those contexts within the terms offered by Lacan. Indeed, even in de Lauretis's attempts, social reality (that is, 'material, economic and interpersonal [relations] which are in fact social, and in a larger perspective historical') seems to lie outside, apart from the subject.[27] A way to conceive of 'social reality' in terms of gender is lacking.

The problem of sexual antagonism in this theory has two aspects. First, it projects a certain timeless quality, even when it is historicized as well as it has been by Sally Alexander. Alexander's reading of Lacan led her to conclude that 'antagonism between the sexes is an unavoidable aspect of the acquisition of sexual identity. . . . If antagonism is always latent, it is possible that history offers no final resolution, only the constant reshaping, reorganizing of the symbolization of difference, and the sexual division of labour.'[28] It may be my hopeless utopianism that gives me pause before this formulation, or it may be that I have not yet shed the episteme of what Foucault called the Classical Age. Whatever the explanation, Alexander's formulation contributes to the fixing of the binary opposition of male and female as the only possible relationship and as a permanent aspect of the human condition. It perpetuates rather than questions what Denise Riley refers to as 'the dreadful air of constancy of sexual polarity'. She writes: 'The historically constructed nature of the opposition [between male and female] produces as one of its effects just that air of an invariant and monotonous men/women opposition.'[29]

It is precisely that opposition, in all its tedium and monotony, that (to return to the Anglo-American side) Carol Gilligan's work has promoted. Gilligan explains the divergent paths of moral development followed by boys and girls in terms of differences of 'experience' (lived reality). It is not surprising that historians of women have picked up her ideas and used them to explain the 'different voices' their work has enabled them to hear. The problems with these borrowings are manifold, and they are logically connected.[30] The first is a slippage that often happens in the attribution of causality: the argument moves from a statement such as 'women's experience leads them to make moral choices contingent on contexts and relationships' to 'women think and choose this way because they are women'. Implied in this line of reasoning is the ahistorical, if not essentialist, notion of woman. Gilligan and others have extrapolated her description, based on a small sample of late twentieth-century American schoolchildren, into a statement about all women. This extrapolation is evident especially, but not exclusively, in the discussions by some historians of 'women's culture' that take evidence from early saints to modern militant labour activities and reduce it to proof of Gilligan's hypothesis about a universal female preference for relatedness.[31] This use of Gilligan's ideas provides sharp contrast to the most complicated and historicized conceptions of 'women's culture' evident in the *Feminist Studies* 1980 symposium.[32] Indeed, a comparison of that set of articles with Gilligan's formulations reveals the extent to which her notion is ahistorical, defining woman/man as a universal, self-reproducing binary opposition – fixed always in the same way. By insisting on fixed differences (in Gilligan's case, by simplifying data with more mixed results about sex and moral reasoning to underscore sexual difference), feminists contribute to the kind of thinking they want to oppose. Although they insist on the revaluation of the category 'female' (Gilligan suggests that women's moral choices may be more humane than men's), they do not examine the binary opposition itself.

We need a refusal of the fixed and permanent quality of the binary opposition, a genuine historicization and deconstruction of the terms of sexual difference. We must become more self-conscious abut distinguishing between our analytic vocabulary and the material we want to analyze. We must find ways (however imperfect) continually to subject our categories to criticism, our analyses to self-criticism. If we employ Jacques Derrida's definition of deconstruction, this criticism means analyzing in context the way any binary opposition operates, reversing and displacing its hierarchical construction, rather than accepting it as real or self-evident or in the nature of things.[33] In a sense, of course, feminists have been doing this for years. The history of feminist thought is a history of the refusal of the hierarchial construction of the relationship between male and female in its specific contexts and an attempt to reverse or displace its operations. Feminist historians are now in a position to theorize their practice and to develop gender as an analytic category.

NOTES

1 © 1988 Columbia University Press. This essay was first prepared for delivery at the meeting of the American Historical Association in December 1985. It was subsequently published in its current form in the *American Historical Review*, 91/5 (Dec. 1986), and is my *Gender and the Politics of History*, and is reprinted with permission. Discussions with Denise Riley, Janice Doane, Yasmine Ergas, Anne Norton, and

Harriet Whitehead helped formulate my ideas on the various subjects touched in the course of this paper. The final version profited from comments by Ira Katznelson, Charles Tilly, Louise Tilly, Elisabetta Galeotti, Rayna Rapp, Christine Stansell, and Joan Vincent. I am also grateful for the unusually careful editing done at the *AHR* by Allyn Roberts and David Ransell.

2 *The Compact Edition of the Oxford English Dictionary* (Oxford: Oxford University Press, 1971), i. 1126.

3 E. Littré, *Dictionnaire de la langue française* (Paris, 1876).

4 Raymond Williams, *Keywords* (New York: Oxford University Press, 1983), 285.

5 Natalie Zemon Davis, 'Women's History in Transition: The European Case', *Feminist Studies*, 3 (1975–6), 90.

6 Ann D. Gordon, Mari Jo Buhle and Nancy Shrom Dye, 'The Problem of Women's History', in Berenice Carroll (ed.), *Liberating Women's History* (Urbana: University of Illinois Press), 89.

7 The best and most subtle example is from Joan Kelly 'The Doubled Vision of Feminist Theory', in her *Women, History and Theory* (Chicago: University of Chicago Press, 1984), 51–64, esp. p. 61.

8 For an argument against the use of gender to emphasize the social aspect of sexual difference, see Moira Gatens, 'A Critique of the Sex/Gender Distinction', in J. Allen and P. Patton (eds), *Beyond Marxism?* (Leichhardt, NSW: Intervention Publications, 1985), 143–60. I agree with her argument that the sex/gender distinction grants autonomous or transparent determination to the body, ignoring the fact that what we know about the body is culturally produced knowledge.

9 For a different characterization of feminist analysis, see Linda J. Nicholson, *Gender and History: The Limits of Social Theory in the Age of the Family* (New York: Columbia University Press, 1986).

10 Mary O'Brien, *The Politics of Reproduction* (London: Routledge and Kegan Paul, 1981), 8–15, 46.

11 Shulamith Firestone, *The Dialectic of Sex* (New York: Bantam Books, 1970). The phrase 'bitter trap' is O'Brien's (*Politics of Reproduction*, p. 8).

12 Catherine MacKinnon, 'Feminism, Marxism, Method, and the State: An Agenda for Theory', *Signs*, 7 (1982), 515, 541.

13 Ibid., 541, 543.

14 For an interesting discussion of the strengths and limits of the term 'patriarchy', see the exchange among historians Sheila Rowbotham, Sally Alexander and Barbara Taylor in Raphael Samuel (ed.), *People's History and Socialist Theory* (London: Routledge and Kegan Paul, 1981), 363–73.

15 Friedrich Engels, *The Origins of the Family, Private Property, and the State* (1884; repr., New York: International Publishers, 1972).

16 Heidi Hartmann, 'Capitalism, Patriarchy, and Job Segregation by Sex', *Signs*, 1 (1976), 168. See also 'The Unhappy Marriage of Marxism and Feminism: Towards a More Progressive Union', *Capital and Class*, 8 (1979), 1–33; 'The Family as the Locus of Gender, Class, and Political Struggle: The Example of Housework', *Signs*, 6 (1981), 366–94.

17 Discussions of Marxist feminism include Zillah Eisenstein, *Capitalist Patriarchy and the Case for Socialist Feminism* (New York: Longman, 1981); A. Kuhn, 'Structures of Patriarchy and Capital in the Family', in A. Kuhn and A Wolpe (eds), *Feminism and Materialism: Women and Modes of Production* (London: Routledge and Kegan Paul, 1978; Rosalind Coward, *Patriarchal Precedents* (London: Routledge and Kegan Paul, 1983); Hilda Scott, *Does Socialism Liberate Women? Experiences from Eastern Europe* (Boston: Beacon Press, 1974); Jane Humphries, 'Working Class Family, Women's Liberation and Class Struggle: The Case of Nineteenth-century British History', *Review of Radical Political Economics*, 9 (1977), 25–41; Jane Humphries, 'Class Struggle and the Persistence of the Working Class Family', *Cambridge Journal of Economics*, 1 (1971), 241–58; and see the debate on Humphries' work in *Review of Radical Political Economics*, 12 (1980), 76–94.

18 Kelly, 'Doubled Vision of Feminist Theory', 61.

19 Ann Snitow, Christine Stansell and Sharon Thompson (eds), *Powers of Desire: The Politics of Sexuality* (New York: Monthly Review Press, 1983).

20 Ellen Ross and Rayna Rapp, 'Sex and Society: A Research Note from Social History and Anthropology', in *Powers of Desire*, 53.

21 'Introduction', *Powers and Desire*, 12; and Jessica Benjamin, 'Master and Slave: The Fantasy of Erotic Domination', *Powers of Desire*, 297.

22 Johanna Brenner and Maria Ramas, 'Rethinking Women's Oppression', *New Left Review* (1984) 144: 33–71; Michèle Barrett, 'Rethinking Women's Oppression: A Reply to Brenner and Ramas', *New Left Review*, 146 (1984), 123–8; Angela Weir and Elizabeth Wilson, 'The British Women's Movement', *New Left Review*, 148 (1984), 74–103; Michèle Barrett, 'A Response to Weir and Wilson', *New Left Review*, 150 (1985), 143–7; Jane Lewis, 'The Debate on Sex and Class', *New Left Review*, 149 (1985), 108–20. See also Hugh Armstrong and Pat Armstrong, 'Beyond Sexless Class and Classless Sex: Towards Feminist Marxism', *Studies in Political Economy*, 10 (1983), 7–44; Hugh Armstrong and Pat Armstrong, 'Comments: More on Marxist Feminism', *Studies in Political Economy*, 15 (1984), 179–84; and Jane Jenson, 'Gender and Reproduction: Or, Babies and the State', unpub. paper, June 1985, 1–7.

23 For early theoretical formulations, see *Papers on Patriarchy: Conference, London 76* (London: n.p., 1976). I am grateful to Jane Caplan for telling me of the existence of this publication and for her willingness to share with me her copy and her ideas about it. For the psychoanalytic position, see Sally Alexander, 'Women, Class and Sexual Difference', *History Workshop*, 17 (1984), 125–35. In seminars at Princeton University in early 1986, Juliet Mitchell seemed to be returning to an emphasis on the priority of materialist analyses of gender. For an attempt to get beyond the theoretical impasse of Marxist feminism, see Coward, *Patriarchal Precedents*. See also the brilliant American effort in this direction by anthropologist Gayle Rubin, 'The Traffic in Women: Notes on the Political Economy of Sex', ch. 5 this vol., p. 105.

24 Nancy Chodorow, *The Reproduction of Mothering: Psychoanalysis and the Sociology of Gender* (Berkeley: University of California Press, 1978), 169.

25 'My account suggests that these gender-related issues may be influenced during the period of the oedipus complex, but they are not its only focus or outcome. The

negotiation of these issues occurs in the context of broader object-relational and ego processes. These broader processes have equal influence on psychic structure formation, and psychic life and relational modes in men and women. They account for differing modes of identification and orientation to heterosexual objects, for the more asymmetrical oedipal issues psychoanalysts describe. These outcomes, like more traditional oedipal outcomes, arise from the asymmetrical organization of parenting, with the mother's role as primary parent and the father's typically greater remoteness and his investment in socialization especially in areas concerned with gender-typing.' (Nancy Chodorow, *The Reproduction of Mothering*, 166.) It is important to note that there are differences in interpretation and approach between Chodorow and British object-relations theorists who follow the work of D.W. Winnicott and Melanie Klein. Chodorow's approach is best characterized as a more sociological or sociologized theory, but it is the dominant lens through which object-relations theory has been viewed by American feminists. On the history of British object-relations theory in social policy, see Denise Riley, *War in the Nursery* (London: Virago, 1984).

26 Juliet Mitchell and Jacqueline Rose (eds), *Jacques Lacan and the Ecole Freudienne* (New York: Norton, 1983); Alexander, 'Women, Class and Sexual Difference'.

27 Teresa de Lauretis, *Alice Doesn't: Feminism, Semiotics, Cinema* (Bloomington: Indiana University Press, 1984), 159.

28 Alexander, 'Women, Class and Sexual Difference', 135.

29 E.M. Denise Riley, 'Summary of Preamble to Interwar Feminist History Work', unpub. paper, presented to the Pembroke Center Seminar, May 1985, p. 11. The argument is fully elaborated in Riley's brilliant book, *'Am I That Name? Feminism and the Category of 'Women' in History* (London: Macmillan, 1988).

30 Carol Gilligan, *In a Different Voice: Psychological Theory and Women's Development* (Cambridge, Mass.: Harvard University Press, 1982).

31 Useful critiques of Gilligan's book are: J. Auerbach *et al.*, 'Commentary on Gilligan's In a Different Voice', *Feminist Studies*, 11 (1985), 149–62, and 'Women and Morality', a special issue of *Social Research*, 50 (1983). My comments on the tendency of historians to cite Gilligan come from reading unpublished manuscripts and grant proposals, and it seems unfair to cite those here. I have kept track of the references for over five years, and they are many and increasing.

32 *Feminist Studies*, 6 (1980), 26–64.

33 For a succinct and accessible discussion of Derrida, see Jonathan Culler, *On Deconstruction: Theory and Criticism after Structuralism* (Ithaca, NY: Cornell University Press, 1982), esp. 156–79. See also Jacques Derrida, *Of Grammatology*, trans. Gayatri Chakravotry Spivak (Baltimore: Johns Hopkins University Press, 1974); Jacques Derrida, *Spurs* (Chicago: University of Chicago Press, 1979); and a transcription of Pembroke Center Seminar, 1983, in *Subjects/Objects* (Fall 1984).

12 Harry Brod

Excerpts from 'The Case for Men's Studies'

from Harry Brod (ed.) *The Making of Masculinities* (1987)

> After all, men have been the subject of nearly all research to date, which
> has constituted 'men's studies,' so why should feminists add to this?
>
> *Sue Wise and Liz Stanley*, 'Sexual Politics'

In this chapter I attempt to establish the validity of the emerging field of men's
studies, primarily by articulating its distinctive contributions to the ongoing feminist
reconstruction of knowledge. I contend that men's studies perspectives are essential to, not merely compatible with, the academic and political projects initiated by
women's studies two decades ago. In the course of this discussion, I propose a
general theory of men's studies as an academic field, analyze some illustrative
examples of men's studies research, and contrast various political perspectives on
men's studies.

MEN'S STUDIES DEFINED

To assess men's studies claims to inclusion in the academy, its specific contributions
must first be articulated. Given the women's studies critique of traditional
scholarship, it may seem, at least initially, that men's studies represents an attempt
to undermine rather than contribute to feminist scholarship, since it appears to
threaten the fundamental premise of women's studies. Briefly, women's studies
emerges from the proposition that traditional scholarship embodies a bias that is
male oriented or androcentric. Women's experiences and perspectives have been
systematically not incorporated into, or written out of, what has been accepted as
knowledge. Thus traditional scholarship, while claiming to be objective and
neutral, has been a *de facto* program of 'men's studies.'[1] The goal of women's
studies, then, is to reconstitute knowledge to rectify that deficiency, by supplementing the traditional canon with additional information about women and, in
many cases, by bringing about a fundamental revision of the form and content of
traditional academic disciplines to produce a gynocentric rather than androcentric
vision. 'Men's studies' appears as the problem, not the solution.

The new men's studies, however, does not recapitulate traditionally male-
biased scholarship. Like women's studies, men's studies aims at the emasculation of
patriarchal ideology's masquerade as knowledge. Men's studies argues that while

women's studies corrects the exclusion of women from the traditional canon caused by androcentric scholarship's elevation of *man* as male to *man* as generic human, the implications of this fallacy for our understanding of men have gone largely unrecognized. While *seemingly* about men, traditional scholarship's treatment of generic man as the human norm in fact systematically excludes from consideration what is unique to men *qua* men. The overgeneralization from male to generic human experience not only distorts our understanding of what, if anything, is truly generic to humanity but also precludes the study of masculinity as a *specific male* experience, rather than a universal paradigm for *human* experience. The most general definition of men's studies is that it is the study of masculinities and male experiences as specific and varying social–historical–cultural formations. Such studies situate masculinities as objects of study on a par with femininities, instead of elevating them to universal norms.

For the feminist project that undergirds both to be completed, men's studies then emerges as a necessary complement to women's studies. For not only do old soldiers not die, they do not even fade away. No feminist theory can move women from the margin to the center, if one accepts this central metaphor of bell hooks's recent book on feminist theory, by ignoring men.[2] If men are to be removed from center stage and a feminist vision fulfilled, that feminist vision must be explicitly focused on men to move them off center. Men's studies views men precisely in this manner. While women have been obscured from our vision by being too much in the background, men have been obscured by being too much in the foreground.[3] Without a particular focus on men, the danger remains that even new knowledge about women will remain knowledge of the 'other,' not quite on a par with knowledge of men. The 'women question' must be supplemented by the 'man question' for either to be addressed fully.

Men's studies raises new questions and demonstrates the inadequacy of established frameworks in answering old ones. I here allude only to several illustrative questions guiding research in various key areas.

Work and Family

Why are women parents in the paid labor force seen as working mothers, while statistics on levels of fatherhood in the workforce are unavailable, not even collected by the Census Bureau?[4] Is there an unacknowledged darker side to fathers' feelings toward their sons – what could be called a *Laius complex* – in which men fear their sons' impending ascension to power?[5] Has new research on fathering simply changed pronouns from earlier research on mothering, uncritically using concepts that speak more to female than male life cycles, thereby failing fully to capture male dimensions of parenting?[6] To focus this problem more sharply, take cognizance of how dual labor market analysis has shown that the working mother concept means not only that some women have children but that the work women as a group do, even in the paid labor force, is a 'mothering' (i.e., service) kind of work.[7] The noun *mother* remains as women's putative essence, in some cases modified by the adjective *working* and in other cases not. To coin a phrase, the analogous concept for men would be *fathering workers*, not *working fathers*. With parenting conceived on the female model, where the private is seen as antecedent to and constitutive of the public, we have not sufficiently investigated how men's supposedly essential public roles have an impact on their private fathering functions. For example, do men see parenting as more of a 'job,' with discrete tasks, than women do? Further, on the normative female model, male differences in parenting styles inevitably appear as deficiencies. They may well be, but this would need to be established, not assumed. Nor have we investigated how fathering relates to men's life cycles and career development patterns, as we have investigated mothering in women's lives.[8]

Violence

What is the connection between masculinity and militarism? Consider, for example, the change in rhetoric of the peace movement in the relatively short time from the early days of Vietnam draft resistance when the profile of the hero changed from the soldier to the resister, but women's function as support and trophy remained unquestioned ('Girls say yes to guys who say no,' as the slogan then had it), to the current climate in which the women's peace movement has made a critical analysis of masculinity part of mainstream rhetoric, to the extent that Helen Caldicott published an antinuclear book entitled *Missile Envy*, with all its Freudian connotations.[9] Further, what concepts of men as citizen-warriors have shaped our traditions of political theory and practice in which questions of war and peace, as well as questions of the general welfare, are framed?[10]

Health

How much more would we know about health science if gender bias had not prevented us from looking for DES sons, for example, and the miscarriages and birth defects among offspring of males working with hazardous genotoxic substances as quickly as we moved to protect the supposedly frailer vessels of female bodies?[11] How are codes of masculinity and Type A cardiovascular disease personalities related?[12]

Sexuality

What are the determinants of heterosexuality and homosexuality, as activities and identities?[13] Is pornography constitutive, expressive, or distortive of male sexuality?[14] Is 'womb envy' an adequate explanatory concept for much of male behavior?[15]

Culture

What do changing styles in genres such as adventure and detective stories tell us about masculinities?[16] How have concepts of the hero been shaped by the rhythms of male life cycles, with their particular patterns of separation and return and distinctive individuating trajectories, and by male predilections for clearly demarcated, agonistic situations?[17] The literature solely on gender and Shakespearean protagonists has practically become a subgenre. Several books focus on masculinity.[18]

As Kahn writes of Shakespeare's plays, 'Much of their enduring value also lies in how they present specifically masculine experience.'[19]

These and many other questions form some of the core concerns of men's studies. In the following section, I discuss two such problematics at greater length. First, however, it may be helpful to discuss the propitiousness of such inquiries.

Current interest in the new men's studies has identifiable academic, social, and political roots. Academically, women's studies has for some time been broadening its goal from supplementing or compensating for the traditional curriculum to fundamentally revising that curriculum. This shift has engendered deeply probing questions, not simply about the status of women in sexist society, but about the nature of the gender division itself. Such questions inevitably focus attention on masculinity as well as femininity. Men's studies extends and highlights such trends in feminist scholarship.

Socially, numerous factors contribute to interest in male role changes. Forces are at work specific to male spheres of activity, in addition to the more obvious demands for change occasioned by the women's movement. The breadwinner role, arguably the traditional core of male identity, is threatened not only by the increased entry of women into the paid workforce but also by changes in the nature of work, such as increasing emphasis on mental rather than manual labor. Such changes are especially notable in advanced industrial nations undergoing a shift from manufacturing to service economies, paradigmatically the United States. This shift is accompanied by a change from a work ethic, emphasizing renunciation or delayed gratification of one's desires in the interests of efficient production, to a consumer ethic, emphasizing the cultivation and satisfaction of desires through consumption. Greater consciousness of and interest in more personal and psychological aspects of male roles arises in response to the new status of men as consumers.[20] Moreover, the traditional heroism of the male warrior is rendered obsolete by the advent of the electronic battlefield and nuclear weaponry. Proving one's identity by sexual conquest has also been rendered problematic by the women's and gay liberation movements, and by other changes in sexual ethics. The benchmarks of masculinity are noticeably in flux, giving rise to interest in examining male identities.

Politically, men's studies is rooted in the pro-feminist men's movement, analogously to women's studies rootedness in feminism. (It should nonetheless be noted that not all men's studies practitioners are male, just as not all women's studies practitioners are female.) There is, in the United States as elsewhere, a small but growing men's movement. The Men's Studies Association is the largest organizational component of the movement's major national organization, the National Organization for Changing Men. The association has been instrumental in organizing men's studies activities since its inception in 1983.[21] This connection should not be disavowed in the new field's quest for academic respectability. Women's studies gains much of its vitality from its connection to the feminist movement, whereby its feminist commitments have not been minimized or negated in pursuit of an ephemeral goal of apolitical objectivity. Similarly, men's studies should be unabashedly explicit about its roots in the search for progressive, pro-feminist change in male roles. If certain traditionalists wish to castigate men's studies as 'merely' a form of political activism and not a scholarly pursuit, the response of men's studies should be to wear its activism as a badge of honor rather than shame. Such a charge can be made only by practitioners ignorant of the history of their own disciplines, for all knowledge, even that stemming from disciplines now firmly ensconced in the academic establishment, originates in the search for human betterment. To provide an example: When it was founded more than a hundred years ago, the Modern Language Association, now perhaps the quintessential professional organization, was self-consciously the product of a social movement aimed at democratizing higher education and making it relevant to then-current needs. Then, too, there were those who argued that teaching modern languages instead of the classics would destroy the integrity of the university, since such teaching was clearly a passing fad.

I have more to say of the politics of men's studies later in the chapter. Because I believe knowledge cannot ultimately be served from its social roots and reper-cussions, in the discussion of men's studies research perspectives that follows I intertwine analysis of scholarly paradigm shifts with analysis of their political ramifications.

MASCULINITY DEMYSTIFIED

New women's history, written since the 1960s, has decisively changed the under-standing and writing of history, not by elevating a few select women to the ranks of the 'great men' of male historiography, but by joining ranks with the social history emergent since the early twentieth century to change the construction of historical narratives. The new women's social history focuses on the lives led by the majority of women in all strata at society, based on a wide range of sources from diaries to demographies. Similarly, the new men's history, as practised by men's studies, is not a succession of biographies of great men; neither is it a tale of campaigns, military and political, won and lost. Instead, new men's history deals with the daily lives of the majority of men in the past. Just as one of the leading questions raised by women's history has been the extent to which women acted *as women*, on the basis of some more or less articulated normative femininity, so too men's history questions how specific concepts and social forms of masculinity interacted in men's lives and either formed the basis of or emerged as reflections on their actions. While the dominant trend in the new men's history is in the tradition of social history, some psychohistorical studies, augmented by a more critical analysis of masculinity than that found in mainstream psychoanalytic literature, also have been incorporated into men's studies.

Men's history lays decisive emphasis on dispelling the commonly held belief that the contemporary period is uniquely tumultuous and troubling for be-leaguered male egos. It reveals that constructs of masculinity have always resulted from conflicting pressures. To cite the contemporary example: The nostalgic male eye that looks longingly back to the 1950s, ostensibly the last time when men were men and everyone knew what that meant, forgets that this was also a period of pervasive fear among the white middle class that men were being emasculated by being turned into robotized organization men in indistinguishable gray flannel suits. One of the apotheotic films of the decade, *Rebel without a Cause*, contains scenes in which the James Dean character's juvenile delinquency is clearly attributed to his father's wearing an apron. The 1950s were also the era of the beatniks, and the decade was ushered in by the 1949 premiere of Arthur Miller's *Death of a Salesman*, to my mind still the most eloquently profound single statement of mainstream contemporary American male dilemmas. These are but a few among many signs that all was not well in the kingdom.

NOTES

1 See Dale Spender, ed., *Men's Studies Modified: The Impact of Feminism on the Academic Discipline* (Elmsford, NY: Pergamon, 1981); Janice G. Raymond, 'Women's Studies: A Knowledge of One's Own,' in *Gendered Subjects: The Dynamics of Feminist Teaching*, ed. Margo Culley and Catherine Portuges (London: Routledge & Kegan Paul, 1985), pp. 49–50; Judith Shapiro, 'Anthropology and the Study of Gender,' in *A Feminist Perspective in the Academy: The Difference It Makes*, ed. Elizabeth Langland and Walter Gove (Chicago: University of Chicago Press, 1981), p. 111.

2 bell hooks, *Feminist Theory: From Margin to Center* (Boston: South End Press, 1984).

3 The metaphor is from David Morgan, 'Men, Masculinity and the Process of Sociological Enquiry,' in *Doing Feminist Research*, ed. Helen Roberts (London: Routledge & Kegan Paul, 1981), p. 94.

4 See Lorna McKee and Margaret O'Brien, eds., *The Father Figure* (London: Tavistock, 1982).

5 See Samuel Osherson, *Finding Our Fathers: The Unfinished Business of Manhood* (New York: Free Press, 1986), chap. 1.

6 This argument is made in Martin P. M Richards, 'How Should We Approach the Study of Fathers?' in McKee and O'Brien, eds., *Father Figures*.

7 See Ruth Milkman, 'Organizing the Sexual Division of Labor: Historical Perspectives on "Women's Work" and the American Labor Movement,' *Socialist Review* 49, no. 1 (January–February 1980): 95–150.

8 Good steps in this direction are Byran E. Robinson and Robert L. Barrett, *The Developing Father* (New York: Guilford, 1986); Joseph H. Pleck, 'The Work–Family Role System,' in *Work and Family: Changing Roles of Men and Women*, ed. Patricia Voydanoff (Palo Alto, Calif.: Mayfield, 1984); Robert A. Lewis and Robert E. Salt, eds., *Men in Families* (Beverly Hills, Calif.: Sage, 1986); Robert A. Lewis and Marvin B. Sussman, eds., *Men's Changing Roles in the Family* (New York: Haworth, 1986).

9 Helen Caldicott, *Missile Envy* (New York: Bantam, 1985). In Caldicott's own words: 'That's why I call my book *Missile Envy*, after Freud. That's the dynamic: mine's bigger than yours, or I want one that's as big as yours. ' 'Nuclear Madness: Excerpts

from Helen Caldicott's Farewell Speech,' *National Women's Studies Association Perspectives* 4, no. 4 (Fall 1986): 3. See also Brian Easlea, *Fathering the Unthinkable: Masculinity, Scientists, and the Nuclear Arms Race* (London: Pluto, 1983).

10 See Judith Stiehm, ed. *Women and Men's Wars* (Elmsford, NY: Pergamon, 1983) and *Women's Views of the Political World of Men* (Transnational, 1984). For studies which revise standard interpretations of major political theorists by establishing the centrality of their views on masculinity, see *Fortune Is a Woman: Gender and Politics in the Thought of Niccolo Machiavelli*, Hanna Fenichel Pitkin (University of California Press, 1984) and *The Orwell Mystique: A Study in Male Ideology*, Daphne Patai (University of Massachusetts, 1984).

11 Janice M. Swanson and Katharine A. Forrest, eds., *Men's Reproductive Health* (New York: Springer, 1984); Michael Castlemen, 'Why Johnny Can't Have Children,' in Francis Baumli, ed., *Men Freeing Men* (Jersey City, NJ: New Atlantis Press, 1985); and Phil Korman, 'Hazards in the Workplace,' *Changing Men: Issues in Gender, Sex and Politics* 16 (Summer 1986).

12 See Meyer Friedman and Ray H. Rosenman, *Type A Behavior and Your Heart* (New York: Knopf, 1974). For a critical analysis of how this question was raised, see 'Dreams of the Heart: Cardiology Rewrites the Masculine Script,' chap. 6 in Barbara Ehrenreich, *The Hearts of Men: American Dreams and the Flight from Commitment* (New York: Anchor-Doubleday, 1983).

13 See, for example, Andy Metcalf and Martin Humphries, eds., *The Sexuality of Men* (London: Pluto, 1985); Alan P. Bell and Martin S. Weinberg, *Homosexualities: A Study of Diversity among Men and Women* (New York: Simon & Schuster, 1978); or John D'Emilio, *Sexual Politics: The Making of a Homosexual Minority in the United States, 1940–1970* (Chicago: University of Chicago Press, 1983).

14 See the chapter on 'Male and Female Sexuality in Capitalism' in Alan Soble's *Pornography: Marxism, Feminism and the Future of Sexuality* (New Haven: Yale University Press, 1986); and Harry Brod, 'Eros Thanatized: Pornography and Male Sexuality,' *Humanities in Society* 7, nos. 1–2 (Winter–Spring 1984).

15 Eva Feder Kittay, 'Womb Envy: An Explanatory Concept,' in *Mothering: Essays in Feminist Theory*, ed. Joyce Trebilcot (Totowa, NJ: Rowman & Allanheld, 1984).

16 See the chapter on 'Gender and Genre: Mens Stories' in *Rewriting English: Cultural Politics of Gender and Class*, ed. Janet Batsleer, Tony Davies, Rebecca O'Rourke, and Chris Weedon (London: Methuen, 1985). See also Ernest Mandel, *Delightful Murder: A Social History of the Crime Story* (Minneapolis: University of Minnesota Press, 1984).

17 Men's studies has yet fully to integrate such earlier works as Joseph Campbell's *The Hero with a Thousand Faces* (New York: Meridian–World, 1956) or the title essay in Otto Rank's *The Myth of the Birth of the Hero and Other Writings*, ed. Philip Freund (New York: Vintage–Random, 1964). Published before *The Second Sex*, Simone de Beauvior's *The Ethics of Ambiguity*, trans. Bernard Frechtman (Secaucus, NJ: Citadel, 1970), prefigures contemporary discussion such as Carol Gilligan's of women's greater tolerance for ambiguity, for *both – and* rather than *either – or* categories. See also Eugene R. August, ' "Modern Men," or Men's Studies in the 80s,' *College*

English 44, no. 6 (October 1982); and William J. Goode, *The Celebration of Heroes: Prestige as a Control System* (Berkeley: University of California Press, 1978).

18 Coppélia Kahn, *Man's Estate: Masculine Identity in Shakespeare* (Berkeley: University of California Press, 1981); Marilyn French, *Shakespeare's Division of Experience* (New York: Summit, 1981); Marianne L. Novy, *Love's Argument: Gender Relations in Shakespeare* (Chapel Hill: University of North Carolina Press, 1984); Diane E. Dreher, *Domination and Defiance: Fathers and Daughters in Shakespeare* (Lexington: University Press of Kentucky, 1986); Peter Erickson, *Patriarchal Structures in Shakespeare's Drama* (Berkeley: University of California Press, 1985).

19 Kahn, *Man's Estate*, p. 20. On masculinity in modern literature, see Peter Schwenger, *Phallic Critiques: Masculinity and Twentieth-Century Literature* (London: Routledge & Kegan Paul, 1984) and Bruce Woodcock, *Male Mythologies: John Fowles and Masculinity* (Susses: Harvester, 1984).

20 An example of the advertising industry's response to changes in men is *Men's Changing Role in the Family of the 80s: An American Consensus Report* (New York: Benton & Bowles Research Services, 1980).

21 The full address is: National Organization for Changing Men, PO Box 451, Watseka, IL 60970.

13 Judith Butler

Excerpts from 'Subversive Bodily Acts'

from *Gender Trouble: Feminism and the Subversion of Identity* (1990)

If the body is not a 'being,' but a variable boundary, a surface whose permeability is politically regulated, a signifying practice within a cultural field of gender hierarchy and compulsory heterosexuality, then what language is left for understanding this corporeal enactment, gender, that constitutes its 'interior' signification on its surface? Sartre would perhaps have called this act 'a style of being,' Foucault, 'a stylistics of existence.' And in my earlier reading of Beauvior, I suggest that gendered bodies are so many 'styles of the flesh.' These styles all never fully self-styled, for styles have a history, and those histories condition and limit the possibilities. Consider gender, for instance, as *a corporeal style*, an 'act,' as it were, which is both intentional and performative, where '*performative*' suggests a dramatic and contingent construction of meaning.

Wittig understands gender as the workings of 'sex,' where 'sex' is an obligatory injunction for the body to become a cultural sign, to materialize itself in obedience to a historically delimited possibility, and to do this, not once or twice, but as a sustained and repeated corporeal project. The notion of a 'project,' however, suggests the originating force of a radical will, and because gender is a project which has cultural survival as its end, the term *strategy* better suggests the situation of duress under which gender performance always and variously occurs. Hence, as a strategy of survival within compulsory systems, gender is a performance with clearly punitive consequences. Discrete genders are part of what 'humanizes' individuals within contemporary culture; indeed, we regularly punish those who fail to do their gender right. Because there is neither an 'essence' that gender expresses or externalizes nor an objective ideal to which gender aspires, and because gender is not a fact, the various acts of gender create the idea of gender, and without those acts, there would be no gender at all. Gender is, thus, a construction that regularly conceals its genesis; the tacit collective agreement to perform, produce, and sustain discrete and polar genders as cultural fictions is obscured by the credibility of those productions – and the punishments that attend not agreeing to believe in them; the construction 'compels' our belief in its necessity and naturalness. The historical possibilities materialized through various corporeal styles are nothing other than those punitively regulated cultural fictions alternately embodied and deflected under duress.

Consider that a sedimentation of gender norms produces the peculiar phenomenon of a 'natural sex' or a 'real woman' or any number of prevalent and compelling social fictions, and that this is a sedimentation that over time has produced a set of corporeal styles which, in reified form, appear as the natural configuration of bodies into sexes existing in a binary relation to one another. If these styles are enacted, and if they produce the coherent gendered subjects who pose as their originators, what kind of performance might reveal this ostensible 'cause' to be an 'effect'?

In what senses, then, is gender an act? As in other ritual social dramas, the action of gender requires a performance that is *repeated*. This repetition is at once a re-enactment and re-experiencing of a set of meanings already socially estab-lished; and it is the mundane and ritualized form of their legitimation. Although there are individual bodies that enact these significations by becoming stylized into gendered modes, this 'action' is a public action. There are temporal and collective dimensions to these actions, and their public character is not inconsequential; indeed, the performance is effected with the strategic aim of maintaining gender within its binary frame – an aim that cannot be attributed to a subject, but, rather, must be understood to found and consolidate the subject.

Gender ought not to be construed as a stable identity or locus of agency from which various acts follow; rather, gender is an identity tenuously constituted in time, instituted in an exterior space through a *stylized repetition of acts*. The effect of gender is produced through the stylization of the body and, hence, must be understood as the mundane way in which bodily gestures, movements, and styles of various kinds constitute the illusion of an abiding gendered self. This formulation moves the conception of gender off the ground of a substantial model of identity to one that requires a conception of gender as a constituted *social temporality*. Significantly, if gender is instituted through acts which are internally discontinuous, then the *appearance of substance* is precisely that, a constructed identity, a performative accomplishment which the mundane social audience, including the actors themselves, come to believe and to perform in the mode of belief. Gender is also a norm that can never be fully internalized; 'the internal' is a surface signification, and gender norms are finally phantasmatic, impossible to embody. If the ground of gender identity is the stylized repetition of acts through time and not a seemingly seamless identity, then the spatial metaphor of a 'ground' will be displaced and revealed as a stylized configuration, indeed, a gendered cor-porealization of time. The abiding gendered self will then be shown to be structured by repeated acts that seek to approximate the ideal of a substantial ground of identity, but which, in their occasional *dis*continuity, reveal the temporal and contingent groundlessness of this 'ground.' The possibilities of gender trans-formation are to be found precisely in the arbitrary relation between such acts, in the possibility of a failure to repeat, a de-formity, or a parodic repetition that exposes the phantasmatic effect of abiding identity as a politically tenuous construction.

If gender attributes, however, are not expressive but performative, then these attributes effectively constitute the identity they are said to express or reveal. The distinction between expression and performativeness is crucial. If gender attributes and acts, the various ways in which a body shows or produces its cultural signification, are performative, then there is no pre-existing identity by which an act or attribute might be measured; there would be no true or false, real or distorted acts of gender, and the postulation of a true gender identity would be revealed as a regulatory fiction. That gender reality is created through sustained social performances means that the very notions of an essential sex and a true or abiding masculinity or femininity are also constituted as part of the strategy that conceals gender's performative character and the performative possibilities for proliferating gender configurations outside the restricting frames of masculinist domination and compulsory heterosexuality.

Genders can be neither true nor false, neither real nor apparent, neither original nor derived. As credible bearers of those attributes, however, genders can also be rendered thoroughly and radically *incredible*.

Part 2

Gender, Space

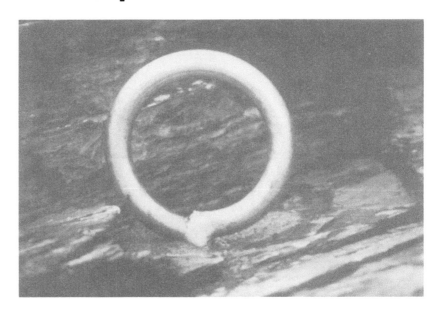

14 Jane Rendell

Introduction: 'Gender, Space'

The issue of whether space is gendered and, if so, how it is gendered, is a problematic one. A whole series of questions can be asked about whether gendered space is produced through intentional acts of architectural design according to the sex of the architect, or whether it is produced through the interpretative lens of architectural criticism, history and theory. Such issues are dealt with explicitly in Part 3: 'Gender, Space, Architecture'. The collection of essays in Part 2: 'Gender, Space' addresses the gendering of space from another perspective – through use. Specific places may be 'sexed' according to the biological sex of the people who occupy them, or gendered according to the 'gender' associated with the different kinds of activities which occur in them. For example, toilets (rest rooms in the US) are 'sexed' male or female because they are occupied by men or women, while the domestic kitchen is gendered feminine because the activity of cooking is something that is socially connected with women. However, how do we consider the kitchen of the public restaurant where the cooking is done by the chef who is usually male?

The study of gender and space is an interdisciplinary one. Currently, those looking at gender in architecture have started to take their inspiration from the work of feminists in other fields: namely, geography, anthropology, cultural studies, film theory and art history, psychoanalysis, identity politics and philosophy. Such fields are those concerned with space, the representation of space and spatial metaphors. This is not space as it has traditionally been defined by architecture – the space of architect-designed buildings – but rather space as it is found, as it is used, occupied and transformed through everyday activities.

GENDER AND SPACE

In defining the dialectical relationship between society and space, the work of Marxist geographers – namely, David Harvey and Edward Soja – is of critical importance in positing that space is socially produced, but that space is also a condition of social production.[1] Anthropologists have also argued that space is materially and culturally produced, and architecture is here taken to be one of many culturally produced artefacts. As material culture, space is not innate and inert, measured geometrically, but an integral and changing part of daily life, intimately bound up in social and personal rituals and activities. This kind of work in anthropology and geography implicitly critiques the status of architecture and the role of the architect, investigating all aspects of the built environment, rather than one-off pieces, as architecture, and defining the users of buildings, as well as their designers and builders, as producers of space. Such work has been influential for architectural historians and theorists in critiquing the privileged status of architecture and the role of the architect, and in suggesting that architecture is continually re-produced through use and everyday life.[2]

Anthropology was one of the first disciplines to suggest that there was a relation between gender and space, and that it was defined through power relations. It was the work done by feminist anthropologists on 'public' and 'private' realms, kinship networks and social relations of exchange which has been critical to feminism, particularly to those interested in spatial boundaries, such as urbanists and historians.[3] The work of Shirley Ardener, for example, in Chapter 15, has been particularly important in developing studies which examine the differing spaces men and women are allocated culturally, and the particular role space has in symbolising, maintaining and reinforcing gender relations.[4] More recently, particular attention has been paid to the ways in which the relationship between gender and space is defined through power – how power relations are inscribed in built space. See, for example, Daphne Spain's discussion in Chapter 16 of how women's social status defines, and is defined by, the work spaces that they occupy.[5]

Making connections between the spaces occupied by women and their social status relates to the work of feminist geographers, such as Liz Bondi, Doreen Massey, Linda McDowell and Gillian Rose, who maintain that space is produced by and productive of gender relations. These feminists argue that if gender makes a difference to the society we live in, to how we are treated and how we consider ourselves, this social condition must make some impact on the spaces we make and use. Drawing on her own experience and describing aspects of everyday life, Massey, for example, in Chapter 17 describes the spatial dimension of gendered and social relations in an account of the ways in which space is patterned by gender.[6] Geographers such as Massey and Rose have produced important critiques of the work of male geographers Harvey and Soja on postmodern space, arguing that their accounts overlook the ways gender operates to structure space and society. Perhaps the most influential of these critiques has been provided by cultural theorist Rosalyn Deutsche, whose attack, in Chapter 18, on postmodern geographers, as well as Fredric Jameson and his seminal text on postmodernism,[7] is a sustained analysis of the various ways in which gender issues are either excluded from their work or appropriated within it.[8]

To summarise, if from an anthropological and geographical perspective space is socially and culturally produced and gender relations are socially, culturally and spatially constructed, then this raises two key questions: 'how are gender relations manifest in space?' and equally, 'how are spatial relations manifest in constructions of gender?'

PUBLIC AND PRIVATE

Although important for thinking about the dialectical relation of gender and space, studies in geography and anthropology are largely silent on ways in which gender and space are represented. With few exceptions, such work is lacking in any explicit discussion of the role of representation in negotiating the complex relation between gendered identities and urban spaces.[9] It is important to note that as well as being gendered through physical occupation – the different inhabitation of space by men or women – space is also produced as gendered through representation. Descriptions of gendered space make use of words and images which have cultural associations with particular genders to invoke comparisons to the biological body – for example, soft, curvaceous interiors are connected with women and phallic towers with men.

The work of the Marxist philosopher Henri Lefebvre provides a useful theoretical framework to consider how representation helps produce, and is produced by, social space. Rather than considering the production of the urban realm simply through the activity of the building industry and urban design professions, Lefebvre is interested in how space is produced conceptually as well as materially. Lefebvre suggests that the social production of space works through three different, yet interactive processes: 'spatial practice' (material or functional space), 'representations of space' (space as codified language), and 'representational space' (the lived everyday experience of space).[10] How might we relate this to issues of gender and space?

The most pervasive representation of gendered space is the paradigm of the 'separate spheres', an oppositional and an hierarchical system consisting of a dominant public male realm of production (the city) and a subordinate private female one of reproduction (the home). The origins of this ideology which divides city from home, public from private, production from reproduction, and men from women is both patriarchal and capitalist. But, as an ideology, it does not describe the full range of lived experience of all urban dwellers. This is problematic for feminists because assumptions regarding sex, gender and space contained within this binary hierarchy are continually reproduced.

Feminist work in gender and space has taken this prevailing intellectual framework as a starting point for critiquing the limited definitions of gendered space offered by the separate spheres ideology and providing alternative ways for thinking about how space is gendered. It is possible to read the work of Susana Torre in Chapter 19, Elizabeth Wilson in Chapter 20 and Griselda Pollock in Chapter 21 as 'deconstructions' of the male/female polarity of the separate spheres. Implicit within the work of such feminists are strategies which have been developed as part of the intellectual project of the French philosopher Jacques Derrida, whose work has aimed to expose the ways in which binary systems allow things to be only 'like' or 'not like' the dominant category and instead replace such prevailing intellectual norms with new formulations.[11]

Following Derrida, the first step in the process of deconstruction would be the strategic reversal of binary terms, so that the term occupying the negative position in a binary pair is placed in the positive position and the positive term is placed in the negative position. The reversal of the binary pairing has been key to the work of feminists who have been involved in reassessing the importance of the female side of the binary . Examples can be found in projects which reassert the importance of the private domestic sphere and family life,[12] as well as those which study the patriarchal mechanisms which exclude women from public life.[13]

Second, there must also be a movement of displacement in which the negative term is displaced from its dependent position and located as the very condition of the positive term. The work of some feminists has implicitly involved such a movement of displacement, displacing the negative term from its dependent position, and showing it to be the condition of the positive term. For example, feminist urban historians exploring women's occupation of cities have shown the importance of understanding how ideological mechanisms such as patriarchy and capitalism marginalise women's relation to public space. Susana Torre's examination of the mothers of Plaza de Mayo in Chapter 19 is an exemplary demonstration of how the appropriation of public space by women is an empowering and political act.[14]

Alternatively, it is possible to re-evaluate the negative status of the female private sphere of the suburb by reconsidering the activities of production rather than reproduction which have taken place in domestic sites.[15] More recently, constructions of public masculinity have been re-defined in ways which connect male identity with models of domesticity.[16] In all these cases, one of patriarchy's positive terms (production, public, male, city) is re-interpreted by showing its previously obscured connections with a term originally represented negatively in patriarchal ideology (reproduction, private, female, home).

It is clear that the separation of the public and private spheres problematises the relationship of women to the city on both a material and ideological level. In Chapter 20, Wilson's concern is with re-establishing a positive connection between women and the public realm by reclaiming the city as a space of female enjoyment through literary evidence.[17] Reacting to sociologists like Janet Wolff, who have claimed that literary and visual forms represent the separate spheres ideology in such a powerful way that the liberating potential of lived experience as a counter-practice is denied or at least obscured, Wilson warns of the dangers of subscribing to an anti-urban bias in much feminist literature and advocates the role of the city in providing a space of liberation for women.[18]

While feminist analysis recognises both that representations may be gendered and that gender is itself a form of representation, the emphasis accorded to representations of gender and space is a matter of feminist debate. It is possible to use literature produced by women, as Wilson does, to provide positive representations of their life in cities, and to assert therefore, as Wolff does, that women occupied and enjoyed urban public space. Equally, it is possible to argue that the almost exclusively male literature of modernity, promoted the ideology of the separate spheres and so worked to deny the connection of women to the city. Clearly, women's relationship to the city and urban experience can only be understood through cultural representations, and it is important to consider how gender ideology does not precede, but is produced through, historical documentation and cultural forms of representation.[19]

Feminists working in art, film and literary criticism have developed sophisticated techniques of textual analysis in order to understand how gender difference operates as a mechanism in the construction of various cultural representations. In visual systems of signification, such as fine art, photography and film, feminist research has considered the representational roles of the female and the 'feminine'.[20] Feminists have drawn on semiotics and psychoanalysis in order to discuss how gender difference is structured by the relations of desiring and being-desired, looking and being-looked-at – the female spectacle and the male gaze.[21] The dominance of the male subject in visual regimes has ramifications for the gendering of urban space, producing representations of urban space where only men do the looking, and women are looked at as objects of visual consumption.

In Chapter 21, art historian Griselda Pollock draws heavily on feminist psychoanalytic and semiotic theory to consider how women's relation to public space, specifically Paris as the city of modernity, is mediated through visual representations – in her study, the paintings of male Impressionists. Pollock discusses three ways of thinking about gender and space in relation to visual representations: the gendering of the location depicted, the gendering of the representational codes, and the gendering of the ideological context.[22] Pollock constructs a model of gendered space which shows how the paintings of a number of Impressionist artists correlate certain kinds of women with particular spaces in the city: 'ladies' are found in parks and theatres; 'fallen women' are discovered in the backstage of theatres, cafés, follies and brothels.[23]

Pollock's analysis suggests that the gendering of space is configured in a far more complicated manner than the separate spheres ideology suggests, one which pays greater attention to relations of looking and moving.[24] Pollock's work is arguably an example of the third, and most important, strategy of deconstruction, that of an intervention – the creation or discovery of a new term which is undecidable within a binary logic. Such a term operates simultaneously as both and neither of the binary terms; it may include both and yet exceed their scope, so indicating the inadequacy of the separate spheres as a description of gendered space. The spaces and activities of consumption and the everyday described in Chapters 22 and 23 may also be considered as terms which move beyond the binary logic of the separate spheres.

CONSUMPTION AND THE EVERYDAY

For Marxist work in many disciplines, an interrogation of the sites and modes of production has shifted to those of consumption.[25] Consumption is also raising interesting questions for feminism. An increasing number of studies of women and shopping reflect the important role that spaces of consumption play in the public lives of women and the construction of femininity. Women, in their capacity as workers, provide cheap labour in shops. In their role as consumers, women buy items for themselves and commodities for the home. In these ways women have close daily contact with urban spaces outside the home. Spatially, the activity of consumption shows that a 'woman's place' is simultaneously both in the home and in the city, going beyond the bounds of the separate spheres.

The role of consumer may be seen as an empowering one for women, a source of self-identity and pleasure in the public realm.[26] But such a view is complicated by patriarchal ideologies and practices, which do not allow for such straightforward self-interest on the part of the female subjects. Instead of consuming for themselves, it can be argued that female consumers consume in order to reproduce capitalism and also in order to represent male status.[27] In patriarchy, where women's role can be compared to that of a commodity, places of consumption reinforce such an ideology by representing women as objects of visual consumption in order to sell goods.

One of the most important bodies of emerging research on gender and spaces of consumption is currently situated in Australian schools of cultural studies and geography.[28] As one of the key contemporary thinkers in cultural theory, Meaghan Morris discusses in Chapter 22 the relevance of semiotic theory to a study of women's occupation of the everyday spaces of consumption.[29] A complex piece of writing, Morris's attempt to draw out the explicit relevance of areas of theory, in this case semiotic theory, for understanding the built environment provides an excellent example of the problems inherent in applying theoretical models developed in academic settings to the analysis of everyday places. Morris's work is attentive to the problems faced by feminists in understanding the ways in which representational systems hold gendered meanings, since gender is itself a form of representation.

Shopping malls and other places of consumption constitute the kind of spaces which can be characterised as everyday. Everyday space, formulated as 'other' to architecture, in the same way as women to men, has surfaced as a recent critical trend in cultural and spatial disciplines.[30] In Chapter 23, Mary McLeod provides both an overview and a critique of how the everyday has been used and interpreted in architectural theory and practice.[31] McLeod investigates the influence of Michel Foucault and Derrida on architectural thinking in relation to notions of the other, difference and subjectivity. Ultimately, McLeod argues that the work of Foucault and Derrida falls short for feminists since these theorists ignore the role of consumption and gender. Instead McLeod proposes that we examine the work of the situationists and Henri Lefebvre in relation to their understandings of 'everyday space'. This approach, which appears in non-gender-specific writing about architecture, closely intersects with feminist interests in personal experience and in the study of places which are not designed by (male) architects, so allowing a rethinking about women's relation to space.

REAL AND METAPHORIC

Space is also important in the construction of the female subject and gendered subjectivity and identity. The role of place in gender politics is important in determining relations between knowledge, position and vision. In theorising subjectivity, identity and experience, feminists suggest that positioning is integral to knowing.[32] The opposition of essentialism and constructivism discussed in Part 1: 'Gender' can be reformulated by considering the subject as positioned or placed, using spatial references in order to deal with knowledge through positionality. Our position, where we live and where we work, where we come from and where we are going, is important in understanding ourselves as human subjects. How people define their own spaces and experience them is important in constructing identities. Discussions of gender difference are described in spatial language, such as 'standpoint', 'locality' and 'margins'.[33]

bell hooks looks at the role of space, both real and metaphorical, in shaping us as human beings in terms of lived experience and aspiration. In Chapter 24, hooks considers the importance of a different binary in describing the politics and spaces of location – that of margin and centre.[34] For hooks, centre and margin are occupied simultaneously. For hooks, theory is emancipatory, it allows the margin to be looked at in a different way, as a positive space, a site of resistance not domination, of both radical possibility and oppression. 'Choosing' the margin, rather than being assigned it, makes a difference.

Spatial metaphors are epistemological statements which can highlight the importance of space in the construction of identity, both conceptually and materially, in the abstract and in the concrete. Space itself has always been seen as feminine and devalued in relation to the masculine active element of time; even the reassertion of the importance of space in postmodern studies has not resulted in a revaluing of the feminine. Instead, the femininity is connected with chaotic and disorderly space, while logocentric space remains masculine.[35]

In the three-dimensional space of the city, representations of gender work in different ways. The female body may be used as a sign, an empty signifier, to represent abstract concepts such as liberty or patriotism in the form of public statues. Cities and buildings may also embody qualities associated with the female body or feminine attributes in terms of their form, shape, colour, texture.[36] For example, in the association of the city with the feminine and the labyrinthine, a connection is made between the chaos of the city, the uterine form of the female body and the patriarchal notion of the unknown as feminine, as other, as unknowable entity. Here work of feminist philosophers has been important in providing critiques of the gendering of space and time in the work of male philosophers,[37] and in exploring new conceptions of time, space and subjects.[38]

As in cultural geography, it is the work of Australian feminist philosophers which is emerging as the leading area in this kind of research. Possibly the most influential thinker, especially within architectural circles, has been Elizabeth Grosz.[39] In Chapter 25, the last essay in Part 2: 'Gender, Space', Grosz, following the work of Irigaray, considers the erasure of women in western philosophy.[40] Grosz argues that women are not mentioned in philosophy but are the foundations of philosophic value. Drawing on the philosophical concept of *chora*, a term which has no qualities of its own, Grosz shows how in the work of both Plato, where *chora* is the receptacle which allows the passage between form and matter, and Derrida, where *chora* is an undefinable and transgressive element, the concept is gendered in the feminine, either as maternal or subversive and 'other'. For Grosz, the work of feminist philosophers is to return women to the places from which they have been dispelled, those spaces named as feminine by men. Women need to re-conceptualise time and space from their own perspective, and for this task it is the role of the conceptual and the imaginary in the work of feminist philosophers that is perhaps the most relevant for architectural practice.

NOTES

1 See for example, David Harvey, *The Condition of Postmodernity* (Oxford: Blackwell, 1989), and Edward Soja, *Postmodern Geographies: the Reassertion of Space in Social Theory* (London: Verso, 1989).

2 See, for example, Anthony D. King (ed.), *Buildings and Society: Essays on the Social Development of the Built Environment* (London: Routledge & Kegan Paul, 1980); Anthony King, *The Bungalow* (Oxford: Oxford University Press, 1995); Amos Rapoport, *House Form and Culture* (Englewood Cliffs, NJ: Prentice Hall, 1969) and Amos Rapoport, *Human Aspects of Urban Form* (Oxford: Pergamon Press, 1977).

3 See, for example, Shirley Ardener, *Defining Females* (London: Croom Helm, 1978); Eva Gamamikow *et al.* (eds), *The Public and the Private* (London: Heinemann, 1983); Rayna R. Reiter (ed.), *Toward an Anthropology of Women* (New York: Monthly Review Press, 1975) and Michelle Rosaldo and Louise Lamphere, *Women, Culture and Society* (Stanford, CA: Stanford University Press, 1974).

4 Shirley Ardener, 'Ground Rules and Social Maps for Women', Shirley Ardener (ed.), *Women and Space: Ground Rules and Social Maps* (Oxford: Berg, 1993), pp. 1–30.

5 Daphne Spain, *Gendered Spaces* (Chapel Hill, NC: University of North Carolina Press, 1992).

6 See, for example, Liz Bondi, 'Feminism, Postmodernism, and Geography: a Space for Women?' *Antipode* (August 1990), 22(2): 156–67; Liz Bondi, 'Gender Symbols and Urban Landscapes' *Progress in Human Geography* (1992), 16(2): 157–70; Liz Bondi, 'Gender and Geography: Crossing Boundaries', *Progress in Human Geography* (1993), 17(2): 241–6; Doreen Massey, *Space, Place and Gender* (Cambridge: Polity Press, 1994); Linda McDowell, 'Space, Place and Gender Relations, Parts 1 and 2', *Progress in Human Geography* (1993), 17(2): 157–79 and 17(3): 305–18, and Gillian Rose, *Feminism and Geography: the Limits of Geographical Knowledge* (Cambridge: Polity Press, 1993).

7 See Fredric Jameson, *Postmodernism, or, the Cultural Logic of Late Capitalism* (London: Verso, 1991).

8 See Rosalyn Deutsche, 'Men in Space', *Strategies* (1990), 3: 130–7; Rosalyn Deutsche,

'Boys Town', *Environment and Planning D: Space and Society* (1991), 9: 5–30; Doreen Massey, 'Flexible Sexism', *Environment and Planning D: Society and Space* (1991), 9: 31–57, and Gillian Rose, 'Review of Edward Soja, *Postmodern Geographies* and David Harvey, 'The Condition of Postmodernity', *Journal of Historical Geography* (January 1991), 17(1): 118–21.

9 See, for example, Liz Bondi, 'Gender Symbols and Urban Landscapes', *Progress in Human Geography* (1992), 16(2): 157–70 and Gillian Rose, 'Making Space for the Female Subject of Feminism', Steve Pile and Nigel Thrift (eds), *Mapping the Subject* (London: Routledge, 1995), pp. 332–54.

10 Henri Lefebvre, *The Production of Space* (Oxford: Blackwell, 1991), p. 33.

11 Derrida's aim is not to destroy the categories themselves but to 'de-stabilise, challenge, subvert, reverse or over-turn some of the hierarchical binary oppositions (including those implicating sex and gender) of Western culture'. Derrida uses the term 'deconstruction' to describe a three-fold intervention which destabilises the metaphysical structures of binary oppositions. See Elizabeth Grosz, *Sexual Subversions* (London: Allen & Unwin, 1989), p. xv.

12 See, for example, Michelle Perrot (ed.), *A History of Private Life: From the Fires of the Revolution to the Great War* (Cambridge, Mass.: The Belknap Press of Harvard University Press, 1990).

13 Nancy Fraser, *Unruly Practices: Power, Discourse and Gender in Contemporary Social Theory* (Cambridge: Polity Press, 1989); Carole Pateman, *The Sexual Contract* (Cambridge: Polity Press, 1988); Carole Pateman, *The Disorder of Women* (Cambridge: Polity Press, 1989); and Mary P. Ryan, *Women in Public: Between Banners and Ballots, 1825–80* (London: Johns Hopkins University Press, 1990).

14 Susana Torre, 'Claiming the Public Space: The Mothers of Plaza de Mayo', Diana Agrest, Patricia Conway and Leslie Kanes Weisman (eds), *The Sex of Architecture* (New York: Harry N. Abrams, Inc., Publishers, 1996), pp. 241–50.

15 See, for example, Kathleen Adler, 'The Suburban, the Modern and une Dame de Paissy', *Oxford Art Journal* (1989), 12(1): 3–13.

16 See, for example, John Tosh, 'Domesticity and Manliness in the Victorian Middle-class', Michael Roper and John Tosh (eds), *Manful Assertions: Masculinities in Britain since 1800* (London: Routledge, 1991), pp. 43–73.

17 Elizabeth Wilson, *The Sphinx in the City: Urban Life, the Control of Disorder, and Women* (London: Virago Press, 1991). See also the seminal text, Elizabeth Wilson, 'The Invisible Flaneur', *New Left Review* (1992), 191: 90–110, and Elizabeth Wilson, 'The Rhetoric of Urban Space', *New Left Review* (1995), 209: 146-60.

18 Janet Wolff, 'The Invisible *Flâneuse*: Women and the Literature of Modernity', *Theory, Culture and Society* (1985), 2(3): 36–46.

19 See, for example, Leonore Davidoff and Catherine Hall, 'The Architecture of Public and Private Life', Derek Fraser and Anthony Sutcliffe (eds.), *The Pursuit of Urban History* (London: Edward Arnold Publishers Ltd, 1983), pp. 327–45; and Leonore Davidoff and Catherine Hall, *Family Fortunes* (Chicago: University of Chicago Press, 1987).

20 In art history, key texts include Lynda Nead, *Myths of Sexuality: Representations of*

Women in Victorian Britain (Oxford: Blackwell, 1988); Linda Nochlin (ed.), *The Politics of Vision: Essays on Nineteenth-century Art and Society* (London: Thames & Hudson, 1991); and Griselda Pollock, *Vision and Difference: Femininity, Feminism and the Histories of Art* (London: Routledge, 1988), pp. 5–26. In film studies, see, for example, Ann E. Kaplan, *Women and Film: Both Sides of the Camera* (New York: Methuen, 1983); Annette Kuhn, *Women's Pictures; Feminism and Cinema* (London: Verso, 1994); and Laura Mulvey (ed.), *Visual and Other Pleasures* (London: Macmillan, 1989). There is less work in photography, but for an example, see Abigail Solomon-Godeau, 'The Legs of the Countess', *October* (Winter 1986), pp. 65–108.

21 See Laura Mulvey, 'Visual Pleasure and Narrative Cinema', Laura Mulvey (ed.), *Visual and Other Pleasures* (London: Macmillan, 1989), pp. 14–26 and Jacqueline Rose, *Sexuality in the Field of Vision* (London: Verso, 1986).

22 Pollock, *Vision*, pp. 5–26.

23 Ibid., p. 73.

24 Pollock's work has been influential on the development of feminist architectural history. See, for example, Jane Rendell, 'Subjective Space: A Feminist Architectural History of the Burlington Arcade', Duncan MacCorquodale, Katerina Rüedi and Sarah Wigglesworth (eds), *Desiring Practices: Architecture, Gender and the Inter-disciplinary* (London: Black Dog Publishing Ltd, 1996), pp. 216–33, and Jane Rendell, 'Displaying Sexuality: Gendered Identities in the Early Nineteenth Century Street', Nick Fyfe (ed.), *Images of the Street: Representation, Experience, and Control in Public Space* (London: Routledge, 1998), pp. 74–91.

25 See, for example, Daniel Miller (ed.), *Acknowledging Consumption* (London: Routledge, 1995); Rob Shields (ed.), *Lifestyle Shopping* (London: Routledge, 1992), and John Urry, *Consuming Places* (London: Routledge, 1995).

26 See, for example, Rachel Bowlby, *Shopping with Freud* (London: Routledge, 1993); Robyn Dowling, 'Femininity, Place and Commodities: A Retail Case Study', *Antipode* (October 1993), 25(4): 295–319; Anne Friedberg, *Window Shopping* (Oxford: University of California Press, 1993); Hilary Radner, *Shopping Around: Feminine Culture and the Pursuit of Pleasure* (New York: Routledge, 1995); Jenny Ryan, 'Women, Modernity and the City', *Theory, Culture and Society* (November 1994), 11(4): 35–64; and Judith Williamson, *Consuming Passions: The Dynamics of Popular Culture* (London: Marian Boyers, 1986).

27 Thorstein Veblen, *The Theory of the Leisure Class* (London: Penguin, 1979).

28 Hilary Winchester, 'The Construction and Deconstruction of Women's Roles in the Urban Landscape', Kay Anderson and Fay Gale (eds.), *Inventing Places* (Australia: Longman Cheshire, 1992), pp. 139–55; and Gillian Swanson, 'Drunk with the Glitter: Consuming Spaces and Sexual Geographies', Sophie Watson and Katherine Gibson (eds), *Postmodern Cities and Spaces* (Oxford: Blackwell, 1995), pp. 80–99.

29 Meaghan Morris, 'Things to Do with Shopping Centres', Susan Sheridan (ed.), *Grafts: Feminist Cultural Criticism* (London: Verso, 1988), pp. 193-208.

30 See, for example, Michael Sorkin (ed.), *Variations on a Theme Park* (New York: Hill & Wang, 1992), and Steven Harris and Deborah Berke (eds), *Architecture of the Everyday* (New York: Princeton Architecture Press, 1998). In architectural circles, the

most influential text has been Michael de Certeau, *The Practice of Everyday Life* (Berkeley: University of California Press, 1988).

31 Mary McLeod, 'Everyday and "Other" Spaces', Debra L. Coleman, Elizabeth Ann Danze and Carol Jane Henderson (eds), *Feminism and Architecture* (New York: Princeton Architectural Press, 1996), pp. 3–37.

32 See, for example, Liz Bondi and Mona Domosh, 'Other Figures in the Other Places: on Feminism, Postmodernism and Geography', *Environment and Planning D: Society and Space* (1992), 10: 199–213.

33 See, for example, Jane Flax, 'Postmodernism and Gender Relations in Feminist Theory', Linda Nicholson (ed.), *Feminism/Postmodernism* (London: Routledge, 1990), pp. 39–62, p. 56; Jane Flax, *Thinking Fragments: Psychoanalysis, Feminism and Postmodernism in the Contemporary West* (Berkeley, Los Angeles and Oxford: University of California Press, 1991), p. 232; Donna Haraway, 'Situated Knowledges: The Science Question in Feminism and the Privilege of Partial Knowledge', *Feminist Studies* (Fall 1988), 14(3): 575–603, especially, pp. 583–8; Linda Nicholson, 'Introduction', Nicholson (ed.), *Feminism/Postmodernism*, pp. 1–16; and Elspeth Probyn, 'Travels in the Postmodern: Making Sense of the Local', Nicholson (ed.), *Feminism/Postmodernism*, pp. 176–89, p. 178.

34 bell hooks, *Yearnings: Race, Gender, and Cultural Politics* (London: Turnaround Press, 1989), pp. 145-53.

35 Doreen Massey, *Space, Place and Gender* (Cambridge: Polity Press, 1994), p. 258.

36 See, for example, Marina Warner, *Monuments and Maidens* (London: Picador, 1988).

37 See, for example, Moira Gatens, *Feminism and Philosophy: Perspectives on Difference and Equality* (Cambridge: Polity Press, 1992); Genevieve Lloyd, *The Man of Reason: 'Male' and 'Female' in Western Philosophy* (London: Methuen, 1984); and Andrea Nye, *Feminist Theory and the Philosophy of Man* (New York: Croom Helm, 1989).

38 See, for example, Gillian Rose, 'Progress in Geography and Gender: or Something Else', *Progress in Human Geography* (1993), 17(4): 531–7.

39 See Elizabeth Grosz, *Sexual Subversions* (London: Allen and Unwin, 1989) and Elizabeth Grosz, *Space, Time and Perversion* (London: Routledge, 1996).

40 Elizabeth Grosz, 'Women, Chora, Dwelling', 'Architecture and the Feminine: Mop-up Work', *ANY* (January–February 1994), 4: 22–7.

15 Shirley Ardener

'The Partition of Space'

from *Women and Space: Ground Rules and Social Maps* (1993)

THE PARTITION OF SPACE

A restricted area like a club, a theatre or a nation-state has a set of rules to determine how its boundary shall be crossed and who shall occupy that space. Those who enter it will share certain defining features: they will perhaps have met specific criteria of club membership, bought a ticket or passed a citizenship test. In some way they must be recognised, say by a gate-keeper, such as a hall porter, an usherette or an Immigration Officer, or by the other members of the category. So, too, other systems of classification will be decided by taxonomic rules of some kind, which will define 'X' in contrast to 'non-X'. Thus, in studying the way people pattern their perceptions, attention has been especially drawn to the significance of the perimeters of the categories that we make in order to codify and confront the worlds we create, in which we then live, and how we cope with some of the problems that arise from the existence of these boundaries (see, for example, Douglas 1966; S. Ardener 1978).

These few words have already found us deeply involved with the point on which the chapters in this volume depend: space. For in discussing ways in which humans perceive and pattern their social worlds a notion (the boundary) has been seized and applied to the meaning of concepts, and to classification into groups, whose label is taken from the register of terms which is used primarily for the three-dimensional 'real' world. The extended use of such spatial terms is firmly embedded in the language in which this is written. Obvious cases would be 'high society', 'wide application', 'spheres of interest', 'narrow-mindedness', 'political circles', 'deep divides of opinion', and so forth. Such practices merely remind us that much of social life is given shape, and that when dimension or location are introduced we assert a correspondence between the so-called 'real' physical world and its 'social reality' (cf. Durkheim and Mauss 1903). There is, of course, an inter-action such that appreciation of the *physical* world is in turn dependent on *social* perceptions of it. Measurements, and what is measured, for instance, are neither totally imperative nor just random; choice enters 'reality'. Societies have generated their own rules, culturally determined, for making boundaries on the ground, and have divided the social into spheres, levels and territories with invisible fences and platforms to be scaled by abstract ladders and crossed by intangible bridges with as much trepidation or exultation as on a plank over a raging torrent.

This brief preamble is by way of indicating why this book on 'women and space' links 'ground rules' with 'social maps' and why such ambiguous pairs of terms were selected for the sub-title. As a preliminary to introducing the chapters and to giving special consideration to women, a few more general points may quickly be raised, in condensed form. It will become apparent that, while divisions of space and social formations are intimately associated, no simple one-way 'cause and effect' pertains, and their cumulative interdependence suggests that we should think rather in terms of 'simultaneities' (see E. Ardener 1971, 1977, 1978, 1989), and this should be remembered when considering the following section.

Communication systems are primarily associated in our minds with words. Nevertheless, it is by now well recognised, of course, that society has also devised many other symbolic codes. Of one, Edwin Ardener has written:

> We might visualise a semiotic system that depended, in the absence of the power of speech, upon the apperception by the human participants of contextually defined logical relations among themselves in space. Let us say: the relevant position of each participant to another in a gathering, and to items in a fixed environment.
>
> (1971: xliii–xliv)

Thus people may 'jockey for position' knowing that their fellows may 'read' from this their social importance. Thus, as Hall puts it, *space speaks*.

Goffman suggests that 'the division and hierarchies of social structure are depicted microecologically, that is, through the use of small-scale spatial meta-phors' (1979: 1). This suggests that *space reflects social organisation*, but of course, once space has been bounded and shaped it is no longer merely a neutral background: it exerts its own influence. A dozen people in a small room 'is not the same thing' as a dozen people in a great hall; seating-space shaped by a round, rather than square, table, may influence the nature of social interaction among those seated. The 'theatre of action' to some extent determines the action. The environment imposes certain restraints on our mobility, and, in turn, our percep-tions of space are shaped by our own capacity to move about, whether by foot or by mechanical or other transport. So: *behaviour and space are mutually dependent*.

As Judy Matthews in her study of community action has noted, social identity is partly determined by 'the physical and spatial constituents of the groups' en-vironment' (1980: 4); that is to say: *space defines the people in it*. At the same time, however (again reflexively), the presence of individuals in space in turn deter-mines its nature. For example, the entry of a stranger may change a private area into a public one (see S. Ardener 1978: 32; 1993 edn.: 18, and Rodgers, below); similarly, 'the Court is where the king is'. Thus: *people define space*.

Not only people, but, as Goffman has said,

> Objects are thought to structure the environment immediately around themselves; they cast a shadow, heat up the surround, strew indications, leave an imprint, they impress a part of themselves, a portrait that is unintended and not dependent on being attended, yet, of course, informing nonetheless to whomsoever is properly placed, trained and inclined.
>
> (1979: 1)

Further, as anyone who has played chess will know, *objects are affected by the place in space of other objects*; not only their presence, and their position, but even their absence, or 'negative presence', may be important.

Structural relationships, such as in hierarchies or other ranking patterns, and systems of relationships like those of kinship, are treated in this volume as 'social maps', which are frequently, but not necessarily, realised on 'the ground' by the placing of individuals in space. In many situations we find (real or metaphysical) 'spaces within spaces', or 'overlapping universes'. To understand them we may be required to 'pull them apart' in order first to identify each simple map (of, say 'X' and 'non-X'), before reconsidering the way these correspond or are interrelated. It is as if we provide one map showing only where the roads are (or are not), and another setting out the water courses, and so on, before we compile a complex map of all the features of the terrain. Correspondingly, ideally we may 'map', say, the relationships between a wife and her husband (where they draw the various limits) before 'mapping' the same woman's relationships to her children, in order to compile a complete picture of her family life.

Individuals (and things) belong, then, to many pairs, groups or sets, each of which may be thought of as occupying its own 'space', or as sharing a particular 'universe'. Members of one group may be 'dominant' relative to members of another group in one 'universe', while in turn being 'muted' in relation to members of a third group sharing with them a universe differently defined. A woman may be 'muted' relative to her husband and 'dominant' in relation to her children; gypsy men are 'dominant' in their own culture and structurally 'muted' *vis-à-vis* the English (Okely 1978). In a society where, say, (a) men take precedence over women and (b) the religious is dominant in relation to the secular, the following ordering is possible: *monks ← lay-men ← nuns ← lay-women* (where *gender* is the predominant critical distinction). Alternatively (as in some Buddhist processions), where the space is primarily *religious* (but gender counts), we may find a redistribution of space between the poles: *monks ← nuns ← lay-men ← lay-women*. The second ordering is interesting because the (religious) precedence of *nuns* over *lay-women* may tend to obscure the priority of males between the sexes. This might be particularly so if, at any time or place, no *monks* or *lay-women* are present (that is, the sequence is incomplete). This may account for the inability of some to distinguish asymmetries, that even bear upon them disadvantageously. In other 'real' or 'social' spaces femaleness may be the dominant determinant, but in others yet again, gender may be irrelevant, or insignificant. Age, class and many other features may add further complexities in situations of multiple dimensions (see S. Ardener 1992). If relationships (say between *monks*, *nuns* and *lay-persons*) are expressed by the distribution of people on the ground, then the application of the term 'map' is probably unambiguous to most readers of this book. If, however, the relationships cannot be actually 'seen' in physical arrangements, but only detected in other ways (such as by who speaks first, or in what manner, or by who bows to whom), then possibly the use of the term 'map' may be challenged. Even when an ordering is 'jumbled up' to the eye, or intangible, it may, however, still be *convenient* to our understanding to think of that ordering as a 'map' on which the 'jumble' has been simplified by a logical rearrangement of the information. No map corresponds to what can be seen: the London underground system is not accurately and completely portrayed on the map provided to the public.

Thus, in this volume the term 'social map' has been used broadly, and sometimes in different ways. The concept is applied to 'historical time' (in which 'yesterday' may seem 'closer' than the 'distant' past; just as some kin, living or dead, may seem 'close' relative to other kin). The notion of 'private' as opposed to 'public' is seen as a criterion for 'mapping' metaphysical space, as 'inner' does in opposition to 'outer', *regardless* of the fact that some 'private places' can really be walked into. No emphasis has been given to the distinction between 'place' and 'space', as used by geographers. The term 'social map', as used in this book, may be taken, perhaps, as a temporary and handy 'folk' term, rather than as having the status of a definitive scientific label.

Space, then, is not a simple concept. In certain societies it is coloured. Thus, among the Zuni of America, north is thought of as blue, south as red, and east as white (Durkheim and Mauss [1903] 1963: 44; Needham 1973: 33). Among the Atoni of Indonesia, south is again red (it is also associated with rulers), east is again white (and is connected with warriors), west is black (and is associated with village headman) and the north is – not blue (Zuni) – but yellow. The Irish have coloured space (E. Ardener 1975). Here, however, south is black (and the sphere of music, slaves, witches and the dead).

If space is an ordering principle, so, of course, is gender. These principles are often also linked, though not always in the same way. For the Irish, south is associated with women. In contrast, the Chinese see the south as male and the north as female.

In 1909 Robert Hertz wrote a classic text, 'The Pre-eminence of the Right Hand'. It is available in Needham's 1973 translation from French into English. Thus over 80 years ago Hertz wrote:

> Society and the whole universe have a side which is sacred, noble and precious, and another which is profane and common; a male side, strong and active, and another, female, weak and passive; or, in two words, a right side and a left side.
>
> (Needham 1973: 10)

He also equated the right with 'rectitude', 'dexterity', 'the juridical norm' (p. 11), 'life' (p. 12), 'the 'inside' (p. 13), 'the 'sacred' (p. 12), 'good', and 'beauty' (p. 12).

He associated the left with the 'profane' (p. 12), the 'ugly' (p. 12); with 'bad' (p. 12), 'death' (p. 12), the 'outside, the infinite, hostile and the perpetual menace of evil' (p. 13).

Hertz (drawing on Wilson's report of 1891) noted that among North American Indians 'The right hand stands for me, the left for not-me, others'. Drawing on Mallery (1881), Hertz noted that 'The raised right hand signifies bravery, power, and virility, while on the contrary the same hand, carried to the left and placed below the left hand, signifies, according to context, the ideas of death, destruction, and burial'.

After discussing Australian beliefs (of the Wulwanga), Hertz concludes it is not chance that God took one of Adam's left ribs to create Eve, 'for one and the same essence characterises woman and the left side of the body – two parts of a weak and defenceless being, somewhat ambiguous and disquieting, destined by nature to a passive and receptive role and to a subordinate condition'.

Since Hertz, social anthropologists have travelled the world collecting world-views from different cultures. Many have described systems of dual classification, and a selection of studies can be found in Needham (1973). These schemes of perception which elsewhere Bourdieu (1977: 15) speaks of finding, include those 'which divide the world up in accordance with the oppositions between male and female, east and west, future and past, top and bottom, right and left.' To which we may add public/private and inside/outside (a particular concern of modern Greeks, as shown by Hirschon below). Thus Faron (Needham 1973: 196) provides two lists from Chile demonstrating the 'Mapuche inferior–superior, left–right hand associations' adding that 'There are many indications of male superiority and association with the right as well as with good and the sacred'. There is also 'an unmistakable and literal connection between left and evil, right and good'. Again, van der Kroef (ibid.: 180) correlates pairs of oppositions among the people of Amboyna in Indonesia. Other sets of dual classification for the Gogo of Tanzania, for the Kaguru of Tanzania, for the Meru of Kenya, and for the Fulani of West Africa, document this approach.

Now it would be a diversion to go into further details on dual classification here; it is a field requiring delicate handling – especially of the relationship between concepts placed in vertical lists. There is, indeed, no attempt here at a compre-hensive analysis of all the characteristics of space; the literature is in any case already extensive. McDowell, for example, has provided a useful review of material on the gender division of urban space. For some Marxist analyses of place and space see the work of David Harvey. The few simple, but fundamental points raised above are merely reminders of the general context in which the following discus-sions are to be viewed. The chapters below provide illustrations of them, and give some examples of their special relevance to women. Although there is no pretence at comprehensiveness, one more aspect must, nevertheless, be mentioned: the re-lationship of time and space. When we speak of 'the world getting smaller' through the advent of air travel, or of a distance being 'five minutes' walk away', we clearly acknowledge that time and space are 'mutually affecting spheres of reality', where 'reality' is understood to depend upon human apperceptions. Paine quotes a resident of Israel who felt that by settling in Israel he had taken a leap back in time which made him closer to David and Uzziah than to the contemporary *shtetl* in Poland. One could say that by a change of place time had been collapsed, or elided. This reminds us of Harvey's comment that 'nearness does not consist of shortness of distance' (1990) and Edwin Ardener's study of 'remoteness' (1987). 'Time-systems occupy spaces which are generated by and with the physical and social space' (E. Ardener 1975: 11).

REFERENCES

E. Ardener, 'Introductory Essay', E. W Ardener (ed.), *Social Anthropology and Language* (London: Tavistock Press, 1971).
———— 'The Voice of Prophecy', The Munro Lecture, delivered in Edinburgh, 1975.
———— ' " Remote Areas", Some Theoretical Considerations', A. Jackson (ed.), *Anthropology at Home* (London: Tavistock, 1987).
———— *The Voice of Prophesy* (ed.) Malcolm Chapman (Oxford: Basil Blackwell, 1989).
S. Ardener (ed.), *Persons and Powers of Women in Diverse Cultures* (Oxford and Providence, RI: Berg, 1992).
———— (ed.), *Defining Females* (London: Croom Helm, 1979; reprinted, Berg, 1993).
P. Bourdieu, *Outline of a Theory of Practice* (Cambridge University Press, 1977).
Mary Douglas, *Purity and Danger: An Analysis of Concepts of Pollution and Taboo* (London: Routledge & Kegan Paul, 1966).
E. Durkheim and M. Mauss (1903) *Primitive Classification*, trans. R. Needham (London: Cohen & West, 1963).
E. Goffman, *Gender Advertisements* (London: Macmillan, 1979).
D. Harvey, 'Between Space and Time: Reflections on the Geographical Imagination', *Annals of the Association of American Geographers* (September 1990), 3.
———— 'From Space to Place and Back Again: Reflections on the Condition of Postmodernity', 'Futures' Symposium, Tate Gallery (November 1990).
R. Hertz, 'The Pre-eminence of the Right Hand', originally in French, 1909, translated in R. Needham (ed.), *Death and the Right Hand* (London: Cohen & West, 1973).
J.A. Matthews, 'Environment Change and Community Identity', paper delivered at Conference on Threatened Identities, under the auspices of the British Psychological Society, Oxford (April 1980).
R. Needham (ed.), *Introduction to Right and Left: Essays on Dual Symbolic Classification* (Chicago: University of Chicago Press, 1973).
J. Okely, 'Privileged, Schooled and Finished: Boarding School for Girls', S. Ardener (ed.), *Defining Females* (London: Croom Helm, 1978; reprinted Berg, 1993), pp. 109–39; (1993 edn, pp. 93–122).

16 Daphne Spain

Excerpts from 'The Contemporary Workplace'

from *Gendered Space* (1985)

SPATIAL SEGREGATION IN THE WORKPLACE

To what extent do women and men who work in different occupations also work in different spaces? Baran and Teegarden (1987: 206) propose that occupational segregation in the insurance industry is 'tantamount to spatial segregation by gender' since managers are overwhelmingly male and clerical staff are predominantly female. This section examines the spatial conditions of women's work and men's work and proposes that working women and men come into daily contact with one another very infrequently. Further, women's jobs can be classified as 'open floor,' but men's jobs are more likely to be 'closed door.' That is, women work in a more public environment with less control of their space than men. This lack of spatial control both reflects and contributes to women's lower occupational status by limiting opportunities for the transfer of knowledge from men to women.

It bears repeating that my argument concerning space and status deals with structural workplace arrangements of women as a group and men as a group, *not* with occupational mobility for individual men and women. Extraordinary people always escape the statistical norm and experience upward mobility under a variety of circumstances. The emphasis here is on the ways in which workplaces are structured to provide different spatial arrangements for the typical working woman and the typical working man and how those arrangements contribute to gender stratification. . . .

Typical Women's Work: 'Open-Floor Jobs'

A significant proportion of women are employed in just three occupations: teaching, nursing, and secretarial work. In 1990 these three categories alone accounted for 16.5 million women, or 31 per cent of all women in the labor force (US Department of Labor 1991: 163, 183). Aside from being concentrated in occupations that bring them primarily into contact with other women, women are also concentrated spatially in jobs that limit their access to knowledge. The work of elementary schoolteachers, for example, brings them into daily contact with children, but with few other adults. When not dealing with patients, nurses spend their time in a lounge separate from the doctors' lounge. Nursing and teaching share common spatial characteristics with the third major 'women's job' – that of secretary.

Secretarial/clerical work is the single largest job category for American women. In 1990, 14.9 million women, or more than one of every four employed women, were classified as 'administrative support, including clerical'; 98 per cent of all secretaries are female (US Department of Labor 1991: 163, 183). Secretarial and clerical occupations account for over three-quarters of this category and epitomize the typical 'woman's job.' It is similar to teaching and nursing in terms of the spatial context in which it occurs.

Two spatial aspects of secretarial work operate to reduce women's status. One is the concentration of many women together in one place (the secretarial 'pool') that removes them from observation of and/or input into the decision-making processes of the organization. Those decisions occur behind the 'closed doors' of the managers' offices. Second, paradoxically, is the very public nature of the space in which secretaries work. The lack of privacy, repeated interruptions, and potential for surveillance contribute to an inability to turn valuable knowledge into human capital that might advance careers or improve women's salaries relative to men's.

Like teachers and nurses, secretaries process knowledge, but seldom in a way beneficial to their own status. In fact, secretaries may wield considerable informal power in an organization, because they control the information flow. Management, however, has very clear expectations about how secretaries are to handle office information. Drawing from their successful experience with grid theory, business consultants Robert Blake, Jane Mouton, and Artie Stockton have outlined the ideal boss–secretary relationship for effective office teamwork. In the first chapter of *The Secretary Grid*, an American Management Association publication, the following advice is offered:

> The secretary's position at the center of the information network raises the issue of privileged communications and how best to handle it. Privileged communication is information the secretary is not free to divulge, no matter how helpful it might be to others. And the key to handling it is the answer to the question 'Who owns the information?' The answer is, 'The boss does.' . . . The secretary's position with regard to this information is that of the hotel desk clerk to the contents of the safety deposit box that stores the guest's valuables. She doesn't own it, but she knows what it is and what is in it. The root of the word *secretary* is, after all, *secret*: something kept from the knowledge of others.
>
> (Blake *et al*. 1983: 4–5; emphasis in original)

In other words, secretaries are paid *not* to use their knowledge for personal gain, but only for their employers' gain. The workplace arrangements that separate secretaries from managers within the same office reinforce status differences by exposing the secretary mainly to other secretaries bound by the same rules of confidentiality. Lack of access to and interaction with managers inherently limits the status women can achieve within the organization.

The executive secretary is an exception to the rule of gendered spatial segregation in the workplace. The executive secretary may have her own office, and she has access to more aspects of the managerial process than other secretaries. According to another American Management Association publication titled *The Successful Secretary*:

> Probably no person gets to observe and see management principles in operation on a more practical basis than an executive secretary. She is privy to nearly every decision the executive makes. She has the opportunity to witness the gathering of information and the elements that are considered before major decisions are made and implemented.
>
> (Belker 1981: 191)

Yet instructions to the successful executive secretary suggest that those with the closest access to power are subject to the strictest guidelines regarding confidentiality. When physical barriers are breached and secretaries spend a great deal of time with the managers, rules governing the secretary's use of information become more important. The executive secretary is cautioned to hide shorthand notes, remove partially typed letters from the typewriter, lock files, and personally deliver interoffice memos to prevent unauthorized persons from gaining confidential information from the boss's office (Belker 1981: 66).

The executive secretary has access to substantial information about the company, but the highest compliment that can be paid her is that she does not divulge it to anyone or use it for personal gain. Comparing the importance of confidentiality to the seal of the confessional, Belker counsels secretaries that

> the importance of confidentiality can't be over-emphasized. Your company can be involved in some delicate business matters or negotiations, and the wrong thing leaked to the wrong person could have an adverse effect on the result. . . . Years ago, executive secretaries were sometimes referred to as confidential secretaries. It's a shame that title fell out of popular usage, because it's an accurate description of the job.
>
> (Belker 1981: 73–4)

Typical Men's Work: 'Closed-Door Jobs'

The largest occupational category for men is that of manager. In 1990, 8.9 million men were classified as 'executive, administrative, and managerial.' This group constituted 14 percent of all employed men (US Department of Labor 1991: 163, 183). Thus, more than one in ten men works in a supervisory position.

Spatial arrangements in the workplace reinforce these status distinctions, partially by providing more 'closed-door' potential to managers than to those they supervise. Although sales and production supervisors may circulate among their employees, their higher status within the organization is reflected by the private offices to which they can withdraw. The expectation is that privacy is required for making decisions that affect the organization. Rather than sharing this privacy, the secretary is often in charge of 'gate-keeping' – protecting the boss from interruptions.

Just as there are professional manuals for the successful secretary, there are also numerous guidelines for the aspiring manager. Harry Levinson's widely read *Executive* (1981) (a revision of his 1968 *The Exceptional Executive*) stresses the importance of managerial knowledge of the entire organization. A survey of large American companies asking presidents about suitable qualities in their successors revealed the following profile:

> A desirable successor is a person with a general knowledge and an understanding of the whole organization, capable of fitting specialized contributions into profitable patterns. . . . The person needs a wide range of liberal arts knowledge together with a fundamental knowledge of business. . . . A leader will be able to view the business in global historical and technical perspective. Such a perspective is itself the basis for the most important requisite, what one might call 'feel' – a certain intuitive sensitivity for the right action and for handling relationships with people.
>
> (Levinson 1981: 136)

The importance of knowledge is stressed repeatedly in this description. The successful manager needs knowledge of the organization, of liberal arts, and of business in general. But equally important is the intuitive ability to carry out actions. This 'feel' is not truly intuitive, of course, but is developed through observation and emulation of successful executives. Levinson identifies managerial leadership and 'an art to be cultivated and developed,' which is why it cannot be learned by the book; rather, 'it must be learned in a relationship, through identification with a teacher' (Levinson 1981: 145).

Because the transfer of knowledge and the ability to use it are so crucial to leadership, Levinson devotes a chapter to 'The Executive as Teacher.' He advises that there is no prescription an executive can follow in acting as a teacher. The best strategy is the 'shine and show them' approach – the manager carries out the duties of office as effectively as possible and thereby demonstrates to subordinates how decisions are made. There are no formal conditions under which teaching takes place; it is incorporated as part of the routine of the business day. In Levinson's words,

> The process of example-setting goes on all the time. Executives behave in certain ways, sizing up problems, considering the resources . . . that can be utilized to meet them, and making decisions about procedure. Subordinates, likewise, watch what they are doing and how they do it.
>
> (Levinson 1981: 154)

Just as in the ceremonial men's huts of nonindustrial societies, constant contact between elders and initiates is necessary for the transmission of knowledge. Levinson implies that it should be frequent contact to transfer most effectively formal and informal knowledge. Such frequent and significant contact is missing from the interaction between managers and secretaries. Given the spatial distance between the closed doors of managers and the open floors of secretaries, it is highly unlikely that sufficient contact between the two groups could occur for secretaries to alter their positions within the organization.

In addition to giving subordinates an opportunity to learn from the boss, spatial proximity provides opportunities for subordinates to be seen by the boss. This opportunity has been labelled 'visiposure' by the author of *Routes to the Executive Suite* (Jennings 1971: 113). A combination of 'visibility' and 'exposure,' visiposure refers to the opportunity to 'see and be seen by the right people' (Jennings 1971: 113). Jennings counsels the rising executive that 'the abilities to see and copy those who can influence his career and to keep himself in view of those who might promote him are all-important to success.' The ultimate form of visiposure is for the subordinate's manager to be seen by the right managers as well. Such 'serial visiposure' is the 'sine qua non of fast upward mobility' and is facilitated by face-to-face interaction among several levels of managers and subordinates (Jennings 1971: 113–14).

Both Levinson and Jennings acknowledge the importance of physical proximity to achieving power within an organization, yet neither pursues the assumptions underlying the transactions they discuss – that is, the spatial context within which such interactions occur. To the extent that women are segregated from men, the transfer of knowledge – with the potential for improving women's status – is limited.

OFFICE DESIGN AND GENDER STRATIFICATION

Contemporary office design clearly reflects the spatial segregation separating women and men. Secretaries (almost all of whom are women) and managers (nearly two-thirds of whom are men) have designated areas assigned within the organization. The following diagram prepared by an architectural firm for a business client demonstrates the open floorplan for secretaries and the closed doors behind which managers work. This diagram is typical of those in other books on office design (Black *et al.* 1986; Duffy *et al.* 1976; Mogulescu 1970).

Although salesmen have been given an open floorplan similar to that for secretaries (room 2b), their space is beside the managers' offices. Thus, salesmen are subject to less scrutiny than secretaries, whose desks are placed directly in front of the managers' doors. Indeed, the secretaries in this 'pool' are potentially observable by four managers (from rooms 3, 4, 5, and 6). In an ironic twist of the panoptic principle, members of the subordinate group (secretaries) have now been placed at the center to enhance supervision by managers at the periphery.

Privacy can be a scarce resource in the modern office. Empirical studies have shown that privacy in the office involves 'the ability to control access to one's self or group, particularly the ability to *limit others' access to one's workspace*' (Sundstrom 1986: 178; emphasis added). Business executives commonly define privacy as the ability to control information and space. In other words, privacy is connected in people's minds with the spatial reinforcement of secrecy. Studies of executives, managers, technicians, and clerical employees have found a high correlation between enclosure of the work space (walls and doors) and perceptions of privacy; the greater the privacy, the greater the satisfaction with work. Employees perceive spatial control as a resource in the workplace that affects their job satisfaction and performance (Sundstrom et al. 1980; Sundstrom 1986).

Not surprisingly, higher status within an organization is accompanied by greater control of space. In the Sundstrom study, most secretaries (75 percent) reported sharing an office; about one-half (55 percent) of bookkeepers and accountants shared an office; and only 18 percent of managers and administrators shared space. Secretaries had the least physical separation from other workers, while executives had the most (Sundstrom 1986: 184).

Two aspects of the work environment are striking when the spatial features of the workplaces for secretaries and executives are compared: the low number of walls or partitions surrounding secretaries (an average of 2.1), compared with executives (an average of 3.5), and the greater surveillance that accompanies the public space of secretaries. Three-quarters of all secretaries were visible to their supervisors, compared with only one-tenth of executives. As one would expect given the physical description of their respective offices, executives report the greater sense of privacy and secretaries the least (Sundstrom 1986: 185). Doors do not necessarily have to be closed or locked in order to convey the message of differential power; they merely have to be available for closing and be seen as controlled at the executive's discretion (Steele 1986: 46).

The spatial distribution of employees in an office highlights the complex ways in which spatial segregation contributes to gender stratification. Workers obviously are not assigned space on the basis of sex, but on the basis of their positions within the organization. Theoretically, managers have the most complex jobs and secretaries have the least complex, yet research on secretaries and managers with equal

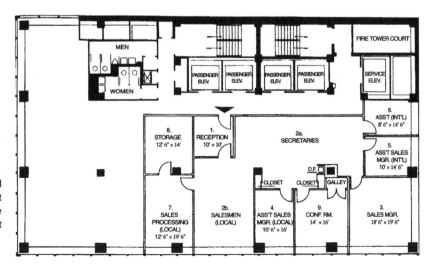

Figure 16.1
The office architect is cautioned that the initial space study must illustrate the 'relationships of the organization' clearly to the client

degrees of office enclosure suggests that women's space is still considered more public than men's space. Sundstrom found that

> in the workspaces with equivalent enclosure – private offices – [respondents] showed different ratings of privacy, with lowest ratings by secretaries. This could reflect social norms. Secretaries have low ranks, and co-workers or visitors may feel free to walk unannounced into their work-spaces. However, they may knock respectfully at the entrance of the work-spaces of managers. . . . *Perhaps a private office is more private when occupied by a manager than when occupied by a secretary.*
>
> (Sundstrom 1986: 191; emphasis added).

This passage suggests that even walls and a door do not insure privacy for the typical working woman in the same way they do for the typical working man. Features that should allow control of work space do not operate for secretaries as they do for managers.

What of the new 'open planning' intended to eliminate all spatial status distinctions in the office? Known by its German name of *Bürolandschaft*, or 'office landscape,' this design was introduced in the 1960s and featured offices without partitions or walls (Becker 1981; Pile 1978). It was characterized by the extensive use of plants to represent the openness of outdoors and furniture grouped together to 'suggest working relationships.' Diagrams of such offices at first strike the American eye as chaotic, but these plans were adopted by such corporations as DuPont, Eastman Kodak, Corning Glass, and the Ford Motor Company (Pile 1978).

For all its emphasis on increased communication, easier traffic flow, and an egalitarian environment, there were subtle spatial status distinctions built into the most open of offices. The German Quickborner Team that promoted the plan so vigorously illustrated a design describing an area for the manager 'screened by plants, files, and screens' and 'assigned extra space to symbolize status and increase[d] sense of privacy' (Pile 1978: 26).

Office landscaping, while apparently creating an environment totally opposite that of the Panopticon, served a similar function. The Quickborner Team explained to executives skeptical of the reduced privacy inherent in open planning that efficiency would be improved by their design, since 'most demands for privacy really cover a desire to hide from contacts and from work. An effective manager finds that his performance is enhanced, not hampered, when he moves into well-planned open space' (Pile 1978: 27).

By the end of the 1970s office landscaping had lost its novelty. Many companies had adopted its principles because it was relatively inexpensive and created an image of modernity in a competitive market. But the 'new democracy' supposedly characteristic of landscaped office design with more open space did not materialize. Those who had power in conventional offices still had it (Becker 1981: 59). The open office facilitates the ability of managers to supervise secretaries by creating greater enclosure for managers than for clerical staff. To the extent that there are fewer plants to provide privacy for secretaries, spatial segregation reinforces women's lower status.

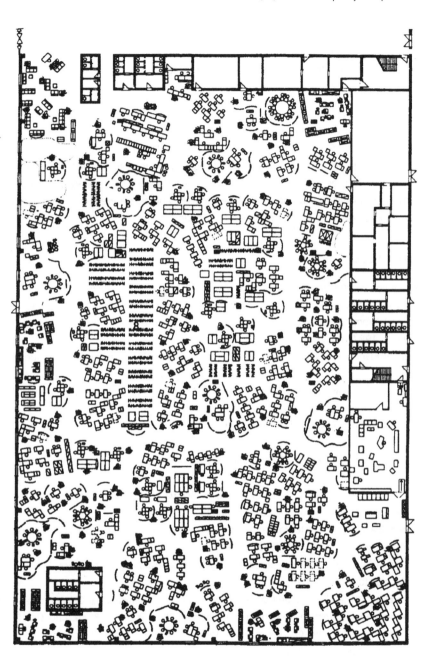

Figure 16.2
This design represents the German
Quickborner Team's approach to
Bürolandschaft

What of the office of the future, characterized by advanced information technology and a reduced need for spatial proximity? These work arrangements appeal to a minority of employees as a way of controlling their own environments by working at home (less than 2 percent of the labor force worked at home in 1980 [Kraut and Grambsch 1987]). Regardless of the costs or benefits to employees, a spatially dispersed labor force presents problems of control for management. In an analysis of the impact of computer technology on the workplace, Ellis observes that much of the authority and control exercised by managers and supervisors stem from the physical integrity of the organization. . . . If the organization becomes too abstract, so too do many of the traditional tools of management. . . . How does one motivate, control, and evaluate the distant employee?

(Ellis 1986: 46)

Tracing workplace design from the Panopticon up through the home office reveals the common thread of reinforcement of stratification systems through spatial arrangements. Whether the spatial segregation is overt, as with the Panopticon, or covert, as with landscaped offices, the effect is similar. Managers retain control of knowledge by use of enclosed spaces, and secretaries remain on open floors that allow little control of space or knowledge.

REFERENCES

Barbara Baran and Suzanne Teegarden, 'Women's Labour in the Office of the Future: A Case Study of the Insurance Industry', Lourdes Beneria and Catharine R. Stimpson (eds), *Women, Households and the Economy* (New Brunswick, NJ: Rutgers University Press, 1987), pp. 201–24.

Suzanne Bianchi and Nancy Rytina, 'The Decline in Occupational Sex Segregation during the 1970s: Census and CPS Comparisons', *Demography* (February 1986), 23: 79–83.

Suzanne Bianchi and Daphne Spain, *American Women in Transition* (New York: Russell Sage Foundation, 1986).

D. Franklin Becker, *Workspace: Creating Environments in Organisations* (New York: Praeger, 1981).

Loren Belker, *The Successful Secretary* (New York: American Management Association, 1981).

J. Thomas Black, Kelly S. Roark and Lisa S. Schwartz (eds), *The Changing Office Workplace* (Washington, DC: Urban Land Institute, 1986).

Robert Blake, Jane S. Mouton and Artie Stockton, *The Secretary Grid* (New York: American Management Association, 1983).

Francis Duffy, Colin Cave and John Worthington (eds), *Planning Office Space* (London: Architectural Press, 1976).

Peter Ellis, 'Office Planning and Design: The Impact of Organizational Change due to Advanced Information Technology', J. Thomas Black, Kelly S. Roark and Lisa S. Schwartz (eds), *The Changing Office Workplace* (Washington, DC: Urban Land Institute, 1986), pp. 37–52.

Eugene Emerson Jennings, *Routes to the Executive Suite* (New York: McGraw-Hill, 1971).

Robert Kraut and Patricia Grambsch, 'Home-based White Collar Employment: Lessons from the 1980 Census', *Social Forces* 66 (December 1987): 410–26.

Harry Levinson, *Executive* (Cambridge, Mass.: Harvard University Press, 1981).

Maurice Mogulescu, *Profit through Design: Rx for Effective Office Space Planning* (New York: American Management Association, 1970).

John Pile, *Open Office Planning: A Handbook for Interior Designers and Architects* (London: Architectural Press, 1978).

Fritz Steele, 'The Dynamics of Power and Influence in Workplace Design and Management', Jean D. Wineman (ed.), *New Behavioral Issues in Office Design* (New York: Van Nostrand Reinhold, 1986).

Eric Sundstrom, 'Privacy in the Office', Jean D. Wineman (ed.), *New Behavioral Issues in Office Design* (New York: Van Nostrand Reinhold, 1986), pp. 177–202.

Eric Sundstrom, Robert Burt and Douglas Kemp, 'Privacy at Work: Architectural Correlations of Job Satisfaction and Job Performance', *Academy of Management Journal* 23 (March 1980): 101–17.

US Department of Education, *Digest of Education Statistics 1990* 26th edition, (Washington D.C.: Natinal Center for Education Statistics) January.

US Department of Labor, *Employment and Earnings* 38 (Washington, DC: Bureau of Labor Statistics, January 1991).

17 Doreen Massey

'Space, Place and Gender'

from *Space, Place and Gender* (1994)

I can remember very clearly a sight which often used to strike me when I was nine or ten years old. I lived then on the outskirts of Manchester, and 'Going into Town' was a relatively big occasion; it took over half an hour and we went on the top deck of a bus. On the way into town we would cross the wide, shallow valley of the River Mersey, and my memory is of dank, muddy fields spreading away into a cold, misty distance. And all of it – all of these acres of Manchester – was divided up into football pitches and rugby pitches. And on Saturdays, which was when we went into Town, the whole vast area would be covered with hundreds of little people, all running around after balls, as far as the eye could see. (It seemed from the top of the bus like a vast, animated Lowry painting, with all the little people in rather brighter colours than Lowry used to paint them, and with cold red legs.)

I remember all this very sharply. And I remember, too, it striking me very clearly – even then as a puzzled, slightly thoughtful little girl – that all this huge stretch of the Mersey flood plain had been entirely given over to boys.

I did not go to those playing fields – they seemed barred, another world (though today, with more nerve and some consciousness of being a space-invader, I do stand on football terraces – and love it). But there were other places to which I did go, and yet where I still felt that they were not mine, or at least that they were designed to, or had the effect of, firmly letting me know my conventional subordination. I remember, for instance, in my late teens being in an Art Gallery (capital A capital G) in some town across the Channel. I was with two young men, and we were hitching around 'the Continent'. And this Temple of High Culture, which was one of The Places To Be Visited, was full of paintings, a high proportion of which were of naked women. They were pictures of naked women painted by men, and thus of women seen through the eyes of men. So I stood there with these two young friends, and they looked at these pictures which were of women seen through the eyes of men, and I looked at them, my two young friends, looking at pictures of naked women as seen through the eyes of men. And I felt objectified.

This was a 'space' that clearly let me know something, and something ignominious, about what High Culture thought was my place in Society. The effect on me of being in that space/place was quite different from the effect it had on my male friends. (I remember that we went off to a café afterwards and had an argument about it. And I lost that argument, largely on the grounds that I was 'being silly'. I had not then had the benefit of reading Griselda Pollock, or Janet Wolff, or Whitney Chadwick . . . maybe I really *was* the only person who felt like that . . .)

I could multiply such examples, and so I am sure could anyone here today, whether woman or man. The only point I want to make is that space and place, spaces and places, and our senses of them (and such related things as our degrees of mobility) are gendered through and through. Moreover they are gendered in a myriad different ways, which vary between cultures and over time. And this gendering of space and place both reflects *and has effects back on* the ways in which gender is constructed and understood in the societies in which we live.

When I first started 'doing geography' these things were just not talked about. What I want to do here is simply to give one example of how issues of gender began to creep into our subject matter. The example is perhaps quite mundane; it concerns empirical issues of regional development which are now well established in debate; but in spite of that some interesting lessons can be drawn.

The example, then, is from studies of regional employment in the United Kingdom. It concerns the story of the regional decentralization of jobs which took place in this country between the mid-1960s and the early 1970s. There are some facts which ought to be known before the story begins. This was a period largely of Labour government, with Harold Wilson as Prime Minister. There were major losses of jobs in coal mining, in the north-east of England, in south Wales and in central Scotland. It was the great era of regional policy, when there were numerous incentives and inducements to firms to invest in the regions where job loss was taking place. And it was also an era of the decentralization of jobs from the high employment areas of the south-east and the west midlands to these 'northern' regions of high *un*employment. And the question which preoccupied many of us at that time was: how were we to put these facts together? Or, specifically, how were we to explain the decentralization of jobs to the regions of the north and the west?

The argument went through a series of stages. Or, at least, I shall present it as a series of stages – there are many occupants in what I label as the early stages who will doubtless disagree with what I say. Intellectual change is just not as linear as that.

The analysis, then, in 'stage one' was led primarily by people with computers and statistical packages, who correlated the timing and size of the decentralization of employment with the timing and distribution of regional policy. They found a high correlation between the two, and deduced that they were causally related: namely (although this was of course not directly shown by the statistics themselves) that regional policy was the cause of the decentralization of jobs. Thus regional policy, on this reading, was seen as having been quite successful.

But then came stage two. It was provoked by political rumblings of discontent, from male-dominated trade unions and local councils, and from evidence given to a parliamentary sub-committee. For jobs were not just jobs, it seemed: they were gendered. While the jobs which had been lost had been men's, the new jobs, arriving on the wave of decentralization, were largely being taken by women. And within academe, a whole new line of inquiry started as to *why* these jobs were for women. The answers which were found are now well known. Women workers were cheap; they were prepared to accept low wages, the result of years of negotiating in terms of 'the family wage'. Women were also more available than men for part-time work, an effect of the long-established domestic division of labour within the household. Both of these reasons were characteristic of male/female relations, within the home and within the employment market, across the country. But some reasons were more specific, or at least more important, to these particular regions to which the jobs had been decentralized. Thus, the women in these regions had very low rates of organization into trade unions, a result of the very low levels of their previous incorporation into paid employment. The female economic activity rates there were indeed amongst the lowest in the country. These women, in other words, were classic 'green labour'.

With this development of the argument a slightly more complex story evolved which recognized some differences within the labour market, which recognized certain constraints and specificities of women as potential employees, which, in brief, recognized that women and women's jobs were different. Such a revised understanding led also to a revised evaluation of the effectivity of regional policy. It was now clearly necessary to be more muted in any claims for its success. There were two versions of this re-evaluation. One, clearly sexist, persisted in its claim that the new jobs being made available in the regions should be criticized for being 'not real jobs', or for being 'only for women'. There was, however, also another form of re-evaluation, more academically respectable although still worrying in its implications: that the fact that the new jobs were for women was unfortunate in the sense that, because women's jobs were less well paid than were men's, aggregate regional income was still lower.

And yet there was a further stage in the development of this argument: stage three. For the more that one thought about it, the more the story seemed more complicated than that. Why, for example, had the economic activity rate for women in these regions been historically so low? This raised the whole question of local gender cultures. Many people, writing in both geography and sociology, commented upon the domestic labour burden of being a wife or mother to miners. They commented also on how the length and irregularity of shift-work made it problematical for the other partner in a couple also to seek paid employment outside the home. There was much detailed investigation of the construction of particular forms of masculinity around jobs such as mining. And all these investigations, and others besides, pointed to a deeper explanation of why, more than in most other regions of the country, there was in these areas a culture of the man being the breadwinner and of the women being the homemaker.

We had, in other words, moved through a series of approaches; from not taking gender into account at all, we had moved first to looking at women, and from there to looking at gender roles, men, and locally constructed gender relations. Moreover this gave us, once again, both a different story of what had happened and a different evaluation of regional policy. The new story was again more complicated and more nuanced. Harold Wilson had come to power in 1964 on a programme of modernizing social democracy, part of which centred on the rationalization of old industries such as coal mining. Contradictorily for him, however, the loss of jobs which would be consequent upon that rationalization would occur precisely in the regions which were his main geographical power base – regions such as the north-east of England, south Wales, and the central area of Scotland. In order, therefore to proceed with this reconstruction of the old basic sectors of these regions, it was necessary to have as the other side of the deal a strong regional policy. Given this, acquiescence might be won from the trade unions and their members. However, it was the very fact that the men in the region were being made redundant which was important in creating the availability of female labour. For women were now for the first time in decades 'freed' on to the labour market. They needed paid employment, most particularly now in the absence of work for men, and there was less of a domestic labour burden upon them restraining them from taking it. Moreover these women had been constructed over the years, precisely by the specificity of the local gender culture, into just the kind of workforce the decentralizing industries were looking for.

Moreover, there was yet again a different evaluation of regional policy. For regional policy could no longer be accepted as the single dominant factor in the explanation of decentralization of employment because the labour-force which had been part of the attraction to the incoming industries had been created not by regional policy but by the simultaneous decline of men's jobs and as a result of the previous gender culture. It certainly remained true that regional policy had brought with it only low-paid jobs, but on the other hand there were some positive aspects to the jobs it did bring, which previously had been unrecognized. Most importantly, it did bring some independent income for women, and for the first time in decades. Moreover, as the very fact of the initial complaints indicated, precisely by bringing in those jobs it began to disrupt some of the old gender relations. In other words, on this score (though not on many others) regional policy can be seen to have had some quite positive effects – though in a wholly different way from that initially claimed in stage one of the development of the argument.

There are a number of reflections which can be drawn from this story of a developing analysis. First, and most obviously, taking gender seriously produced a more nuanced evaluation of regional policy, a far better understanding of the organization and reorganization of our national economic space, and indeed – since these decentralizing industries were moving north to cut costs in the face of increasing international competition – it has shown us how British industry was actively *using* regional differences in systems of gender relations in an early attempt to get out of what has become the crisis of the British economy. Second, this understanding was arrived at not just by looking at women – although that was a start – but by investigating geographical variations in the construction of masculinity and femininity and the relations between the two. Feminist geography is (or should be) as much about men as it is about women. Third, moreover, the very focus on geographical variation means that we are not here dealing with some essentialism of men and women, but with how they are constructed as such.

The fourth reflection is a rather different one. It is easy now to look back and criticize this old-time patriarchy in the coalfields. Indeed it has become a stick with which to beat 'the old labour movement'. But that should not let us slide into an assumption that because the old was bad the new is somehow unproblematical. So, partly in response to the last three reflections (the need to look at men and masculinity, the importance of recognizing geographical variations and of constructing a non-essentialist analysis, and the feeling that it is important to look at new jobs as well as at old) I am now involved in research on a 'new' region of economic growth – Cambridge. Cambridge: the very name of the place gives rise to thoughts of 'the Cambridge phenomenon' of high-technology growth, of science and innovation, and of white-collar work. It is all a million miles from coal mines, geographically, technologically, and – you would think – socially. In fact the picture is not as clear as that.

It is the highly qualified workers in high-technology sectors on which this new research is concentrating. Well over 90 per cent of these scientists and technologists are men. They frequently love their work. This is no bad thing, until one comes across statements like 'the boundary between work and play disappears', which immediately gives pause for thought. Is the only thing outside paid employment 'play'? Who does the domestic labour? These employees work long hours on knotty problems, and construct their image of themselves as people around the paid work that they do. But those long hours, and the flexibility of their organization, is someone else's constraint. Who goes to the launderette? Who picks up the children from school? In a previous project, from which this one derived, and from which we have some initial information, only one of these employees, and that one of the few women whom we found, mentioned using the flexibility of work hours in any relation to domestic labour – in this case she said that on occasions she left work at six o'clock to nip home to feed the cat![1] The point is that the whole design of these jobs requires that such employees do not do the work of reproduction and of caring for other people; indeed it implies that, best of all, they have someone to look after *them*. It is not therefore just the old labour movement, it is also the regions of the 'new man' which have their problems in terms of the construction of gender relations. What is being constructed in this region of new economic growth is a new version of masculinity, and a new – and still highly problematical – set of gender roles and gender relations.[2]

NOTES

1   See Doreen Massey, Paul Quintas and David Wield, *High-Tech Fantasies: Science Parks in Society, Science and Space*, London: Routledge, 1992.
2   This research is being undertaken with Nick Henry at the Open University and with funding from the Economic and Social Research Council (Grant no. R000233004, High-status growth? Aspects of home and work around high technology sectors).

18 Rosalyn Deutsche

'Men in Space'[1]

from *Evictions, Art and Spatial Politics* (1996)

With the publication of two new books – both by geographers – urban studies has decisively entered 'the postmodern debate,' determined, apparently, to win. Indeed, Edward Soja's *Postmodern Geographies: The Reassertion of Space in Critical Social Theory* and David Harvey's *The Condition of Post-modernity: An Enquiry into the Origins of Cultural Change*[2] possess a winning combination: they bring together critical discourses about space, culture and aesthetics within the framework of a social theory that purports to explain postmodern life. This formula has been used before, though never so thoroughly, by a disparate group of scholars who, over the last decade, have written not only about postmodern culture but about modernism as well.

For anyone in the art world eager to escape the control that traditional aesthetic categories exercise over how art is defined, such interdisciplinary approaches have a strong, even a fatal, attraction. Strong for many reasons, but especially because they permit us to view art from previously excluded perspectives within which, linked to new elements, it modifies its very identity. That shift is illuminating for what it reveals about art but also for what it suggests about knowledge: for an instant *all* explanation appears to be uncertain since objects of knowledge are themselves indeterminable, fixed only by discursive relationships and exclusions. Knowledge is 'complete' when it conceals this process. The interdisciplinary approach is appealing, then, because momentarily, it undermines the authority of all knowledge that claims to know definitively the things it studies. But interdisciplinary holds dangers, too, because it does not *automatically* become anti-disciplinary. More often, disciplines unite in alliances that fortify an authoritarian epistemology – by adding to its appearance of completeness – instead of relinquishing it for a more democratic one. Is the current synthesis of urban studies, cultural theory and sociology such a defensive formation? If so, what are its casualties?

In 1985, sociologist Janet Wolff raised a similar question. Investigating the biases that had shaped her profession's definitions of both the modern urban experience and the culture of modernism, she drew a succinct conclusion: 'The literature of modernity describes the experience of men'.[3] Seconding Wolff's opinion and reiterating her assertion that modernity is a product of the city, Griselda Pollock later extended Wolff's thesis to evaluate another field – art history – and, in particular, T. J. Clark's 'exemplary' text of social art history, *The Painting of Modern Life: Paris in the Art of Manet and his Followers* (1984). Here, Clark compared the spatial compositions and iconography of late nineteenth-century modernist painting to modern city spaces. He described, with sophistication, Haussmann's spatial renovation of Paris and fit his analysis into a sociological pattern popularized in Marshall Berman's influential book, *All that Is Solid Melts into Air* (1982): modernization is a process of capitalist socioeconomic restructuring; modernity, the experience produced by that process; and modernism, a cultural form developing from the historical modern experience. Adhering to this model of society in which so-called levels – sets of relations and political practices – are, in the end, hierarchically compartmentalized, Clark explains that, for him, economic life is not a given reality but, like the cultural realm, consists of representations. He neglected, nonetheless, to consider the political meaning produced by his own representation of society, one which, in fact, he didn't really examine as a representation at all. Instead, he felt free to 'insist,' unproblematically, 'on the determinate weight in society of those arrangements we call economic' and to state that 'the class of an individual . . . is the determinant fact of social life.'[4] Consequently, Clark interpreted nineteenth-century modernist painting as an artistic response to the experience produced by Haussmann's spatial reorganization of Paris which was determined, in turn, by the restructuring of capitalism during the Second Empire. Modernism 'failed,' in Clark's view, because it did not map the class divisions of modern Paris but only obscured them by recreating in painting what Haussmann produced in the actual built environment – a mythologization of the city as 'spectacle.'

Not surprisingly, this account produces, as Pollock notes, 'peculiar closures on the issue of sexuality.'[5] However, Clark's descriptions of cities and paintings don't entirely discount women's 'experience' or even gender relations. What his book dismisses is feminism as a requisite, rather than expendable, mode of social analysis. *This* repression is necessitated less by Clark's interest in class than by his image of the social as an 'a priori' totality in which a single set of social relations are privileged as determinate – the foundation of social totality. Feminism, of course, challenged this kind of totalizing depiction long ago; it has also contributed indispensably to aesthetics precisely in Clark's principal area of concern – the visual image. Clark, after all, addresses both the city as an image and images of the city. For years, feminist theories have differentiated vision – pleasure in looking – from the notion of seeing as a process of perceiving the real world. The image and the act of looking are understood to be relations highly mediated by fantasies that structure and are structured by sexual difference. Visual space is, *in the first instance,* a set of social relations; it can never be innocent or assumed to reflect, either directly or through contrived mediations, 'real' social relations, that reside elsewhere: in Clark's account, they reside in the economic relations producing the built environment. In fact, that environment, created in part by capitalism, becomes an image – becomes what Raymond Ledrut calls 'the locus of a certain "investment" by the ego'[6] – its meaning is no longer reducible to nor fixed by the economic circumstances of its production. At this point, feminist theories of visual space intersect with and complicate the political economy of urban space, which does not *inherently* exclude feminism. That relation of exclusion takes place in an epistemological field where grandiose claims are made on theoretical space, where only *one* theory is allowed to explain social relations of subordination. Refusing difference in social theory, the literature about modernity issuing from a synthesis of urban and cultural disciplines has, in this manner, constructed a coherent field by eliminating feminist criticism.

Will the same be true for urban postmodernity? This question has hovered at the margins of cultural discourse since 1984, when Fredric Jameson, drawing eclectically from spatial and aesthetic discourses, published his famous article, 'Post-modernism or the Cultural Logic of Late Capitalism.' Jameson negatively assessed postmodernism as a cultural 'pathology,'[7] a symptom produced by postmodern fragmentations – of space, society, the body, the subject – caused, in his view, solely by the economic and spatial restructuring that constitute capitalism's third stage. The proper activity for radical artists, he prescribed, is an 'aesthetic of cognitive mapping' – the production of spatial *imageability* – by means of which inhabitants of 'hyperspace' might overcome fragmentation, recover the ability to perceive the underlying totality and, concomitantly, find their place in the world. Jameson contends that he is suggesting how radical forces can engage in political battles over representation. Yet his proposal for analyzing space as a visual image begs, just as Clark's does, all political questions raised by feminist critiques of representation – most notably, the issue of positionality. A commanding position on the battleground of representation – one that denies the partial and fragmented conditions of vision by claiming to 'perceive' a *total* truth – is an illusory place whose construction, motivated by wishes, entails hallucinations and hysterical blindness. It is a position constructed in a form of knowledge that produces total – unfragmented – subjects. This realization cannot be wished away by stating, as Jameson has, that his concepts are, of course, representations; the forms of representations matter since they are always constituted by acts of differentiation. If representations are relationships, rather than embodiments of essential meanings, then the high ground of total knowledge can only be gained by a particular encounter with differences – the violent relegation of other subjectivities to positions of invisibility or, what amounts to the same thing, subordination. Jameson's image of society and his desire for accurate maps illustrate the mechanism. Fragmentation, in his account, is only a pathology and the ability to find 'our' place has been destroyed by late capitalism alone. Because he disavows the importance and complexity of other social relations, Jameson confuses capital's fragmentations with the 'fragmentations' caused by challenges – from feminists, gays, lesbians, postcolonials, antiracists – to the types of discursive power Jameson himself exercises; universalizing thought, essentialist discourses, constructions of unitary subjectivity. Such challenges expose Jameson's fragmented unity and coherent subject as fictions from the start and he responds by silencing them. Accordingly, he has recently dispelled any doubts about the nature of what he calls 'cognitive mapping', by revealing that what he actually means by this procedure for uncovering total reality is 'class consciousness,'[8] thereby definitively wiping feminism off the map of radical social theory. How does it resurface? As just another force fragmenting our ability to apprehend the 'real' unified political field.

The Jameson School of Interdisciplinarity has yet to receive sustained attention from art critics. Its relation to feminism is placed on the agenda again by Harvey's and Soja's books about postmodernism. Leading figures in Marxist geography, the authors of these texts have each contributed invaluably to analyses of the social production of space as the very condition of capitalist restructuring. They have turned to cultural theory in response to several provocations: arguments taking place within their own fields; postmodernism's divergences from traditional Marxism; and, perhaps, sociology's inability to address the built environment as a signifying system. The seriousness of Harvey's and Soja's desire to embrace the cultural field is, however, compromised by their bibliographies of postmodernism which are *very* exclusive, virtually restricted to texts by white, western males and, of those, none that deal with feminism and postmodernism. To note these similarities is not to equate the two books. Indeed, Soja is uncomfortable with Harvey's rigid economistic formulas for explaining the production of space and, to define space as social from the beginning, he advances, first, a concept he calls the 'socio-spatial dialectic' and then, a 'spatialized ontology.' He seems willing to disintegrate boundaries between disciplines and, at the same time, to avoid reducing their specificity, but his readings of 'postmodern landscapes' actually leave the cultural and economic realms curiously unmodified by their encounter; the 'essential' identities of each remain intact. Further, by organizing the city into a landscape brought into existence by an outside viewer and by refusing to consider the politics of such spatializations as objectifying representations, Soja clings tenaciously to a belief in the total vantage point, despite, as Liz Bondi writes, the interest he expresses in postmodern decentering.[9]

Harvey sets out even more resolutely on the path followed by Clark and Jameson, defending political economy against postmodern fragmentation. With him, Jameson is no longer alone in the strength of the negative evaluation he brings to postmodernity. Postmodernism, for Harvey, is endowed with a monolithic identity; it mirrors fragmented, dislocated, compressed and abstracted experiences of space and time, experiences wrought by post-Fordist capitalism's regime of flexible accumulations – the condition of postmodernity. The concern of some strands of postmodernism with difference and specificty, their rejection of universalizing thought, complies with the concealment of capitalism's global penetration, which Harvey equates with total reality. So does the interest of artists in what Harvey terms 'image creation.' Attention to images, he believes, represents a turn away from the 'real' social, because it fetishistically rejects 'essential' social meanings; it doesn't provide us with Jamesonian 'mental maps' to match current realities or a 'trajectory out of the condition of postmodernity.'[10]

Here, Harvey is seriously confused. It is certainly true that contemporary art has explored the image. But critical practices have done so neither to assert the status of the image as a container of universal aesthetic meanings nor to celebrate the dominant images that circulate in our society. Rather, they reveal the identity of images as part of a realm of representation where meanings and subjects are socially and hierarchically produced as, among other things, gendered. To the extent that this is its goal, postmodernism's concentration on images is emphatically *not* a turn away from, but rather toward, the social. If, that is, gender relations count as more than epiphenomena of society. But Harvey, ignorant of contemporary materialist discourses about images and blind to the fact that some of the art he criticizes *contests* the fetishistic representation of woman, argues – in the name of anti-fetishism – *for* seemingly transparent images that reveal 'essential' meanings. This – truly fetishistic – conception in which representations are produced by subjects who discover, rather than project, that meaning corresponds to Harvey's own image of society: a metatheory that purports to perceive the single, absolute foundation of social coherence. Postmodernism interferes with that depiction. 'Postmodernism,' he complains, 'takes matters too far. It takes them beyond the point where any coherent politics are left. . . . Postmodernism has us . . . denying that king of meta-theory which can grasp the political-economic processes.'

Everyone knows by now that postmodernism means different things to different people. Distaste for this 'complication' is no excuse for reducing, as Harvey does, all critiques of totalization to an undifferentiated mass or for ignoring, in the process, the persistence of feminism within postmodern culture. Given that presence, what can it possibly mean to characterize postmodernity, *negatively,* as fragmented? Such assertions veer dangerously close to right-wing tenets that feminists disrupt 'our' unified heritage.

It would be a shame if urban studies intervened in cultural theory only to reinstate such ideas. Non-subordinated feminisms would, then, only be equated with political escapism. Feminist contributions to analyses of the visual environment would evade 'real' urban politics. If, unreceptive to the politics of representation analyzed in contemporary art, urban discourse continues to construct space as a feminized object surveyed by mastering subjects and if spatialization goes unexamined as a mode of analysis, the discipline will reproduce oppressive forms of knowledge. Artists don't need more directives for the 'cognitive mapping' of global space or exhortations to take the position of the totality. Postmodernists who problematize the image – artists like Cindy Sherman, Barbara Kruger, Silvia Kilbowski, Mary Kelly, Connie Hatch – reject such vanguard roles. They have been saying for years that, thanks to the recognition that representations are *situated*, not universal, subjects, the world is not so easily mapped any more. They don't seek to conquer this complexity but to multiply the fragmentations, mapping the configurations of fantasy that produce coherent images, including coherent images of politics. Geographers will have to consider that space.

NOTES

1 A modified version of an article which first appeared as a column in *Artforum* (February 1990).

2 Edward W. Soja, *Postmodern Geographies: The Reassertion of Space in Critical Social Theory,* London and New York, Verso, 1989; David Harvey, *The Condition of Postmodernity: An Enquiry into the Origins of Cultural Change,* Oxford and Cambridge, Mass., 1989.

3 Janet Wolff, 'The Invisible *Flaneuse:* Women and the Literature of Modernity', *Theory, Culture and Society* 2, 3 (1985): 37.

4 T.J. Clark, *The Painting of Modern Life: Paris in the Art of Manet and his Followers,* New York, Alfred A. Knopf, 1985, pp. 6–7.

5 Griselda Pollock, *Vision and Difference: Femininity, Feminism and the Histories of Art,* London and New York, Routledge, 1988, p. 53.

6 Raymond Ledrut, *Les images de la ville,* Paris, Anthropos, 1973, p. 21; translated in Gottdiener and Lagopoulous, eds, *The City and the Sign: An Introduction to Urban Semiotics,* New York, Columbia University Press, 1986, p. 223.

7 Frederic Jameson, 'Postmodernism, or the Cultural Logic of Late Capitalism', *New Left Review* 146 (July/August 1984): 63.

8 Jameson, 'Marxism and Postmodernism', *New Left Review* 146 (July/August 1984): 44; also in Douglas Kellner, ed. *Postmodernism, Jameson, Critique,* Washington, D.C., Maisonneuve Press, 1989, pp. 367–87.

9 Liz Bondi, 'On Gender Tourism in the Space Age: A Feminist Response to *Postmodern Geographies*', paper presented at Association of American Geographers Conference, Toronto, 1990.

10 Harvey, *Condition of Postmodernity,* pp. 116–17.

19 Susana Torre

'Claiming the Public Space: The Mothers of Plaza de Mayo'

from Diana Agrest, Patricia Conway and Leslie Kanes Weisman (eds), *The Sex of Architecture* (1996)

To my 'disappeared' Argentinian classmates, and to their mothers

The role of women in the transformation of cities remains theoretically problematic. While women's leadership in organizations rebuilding communities and neighborhoods and their creation of new paradigms for monumentality are sometimes noted in the press, these interventions have yet to inform cultural discourse in the design disciplines or in the history and theory of art and architecture.

The largest body of current feminist scholarship on women in urban settings is concerned with the construction of bourgeois femininity in nineteenth-century European capitals.[1] Within this framework, women are seen as extensions of the male gaze and as instruments of the emerging consumer society and its transformative powers at the dawn of modernity. In other words, they are described as passive agents rather than engaged subjects.[2] When women have assumed transformative roles, feminist critics and biographers have seen them as exceptional individuals or female bohemians, publicly flaunting class and gender distinctions; in contrast, women in general, and working-class women in particular, are presented as unintentional agents of a collective social project, acting out assigned scripts. As a class, women share the problematic status of politically or culturally colonized populations. Both are seen as passively transformed by forced modernization rather than as appropriating modernity on their own and, through this appropriation, being able to change the world that is transforming them.

From this perspective it is difficult to see the current individual and collective struggle of women to transform urban environments as anything of cultural significance, or to re-evaluate the enduring influence of traditional female enclaves originated in the premodern city. Many of these enclaves continue to serve their traditional functional and social roles, like the public washing basins in major Indian cities or the markets in African villages, while others have persisted as symbolic urban markings, like the forest of decorated steel poles that once held clotheslines in Glasgow's most central park. Some of these enclaves have even become a city's most important open space, like River Walk in San Antonio, Texas, where women once congregated to wash laundry and socialize.

A literature is now emerging, focused on the participation by marginalized populations in the transformation of postmodern cities and establishing the critical connection between power and spatiality, particularly within the disciplines of art and architectural history and architectural and urban design.[3] To these contributions, which have revealed previously unmarked urban sites as well as the social consequences of repressive urban planning ideologies, should be added feminist analyses of women's traditional urban enclaves and of women's appropriations of public sites that symbolized their exclusion or restricted status. These appropriations, whether in the form of one of the largest mass demonstrations ever held on the Washington Mall (in favor of abortion rights) or in the display of intimacy in very public settings (such as the private offerings and mementos that complete Maya Lin's Vietnam Memorial and compose the monumental Names Quilt commemorating Aids victims), continue to establish women's rights not merely to inhabit but also to transform the public realm of the city. It is in such situations that women have been most effective in constructing themselves as transformative subjects, altering society's perception of public space and inscribing their own stories into the urban palimpsest.[4]

As in all instances where the topic of discussion is as complex as the transformative presence of women in the city – and particularly when this topic does not yet operate within an established theoretical framework – the main difficulty is to establish a point of entry. In the present essay I propose entering this territory through the examination of one dramatic case of a successful, enduring appropriation: the Mothers of the Plaza de Mayo in Argentina.[5] This small but persistent band of women protestors first captured international attention in the mid-1970s with their sustained presence in the nation's principal 'space of public appearance,' as Hanna Arendt has called the symbolic realm of social representation, which is controlled by the dominant political or economic structures of society. This case illustrates the process that leads from the embodiment of traditional roles and assigned scripts as wives and mothers to the emergence of the active, transformative subject, in spite of – or perhaps because of – the threat or actuality of physical violence that acts of protest attract in autocratic societies. As we will see, this case is also emblematic of architecture's complicity with power in creating a symbolic system of representation, usually of power hierarchies. The hegemony of this system has been threatened ever since the invention of the printing press and is now claimed by electronic media and its virtual space of communication. Finally, the Mothers of Plaza de Mayo's appropriation of the public square as a stage for the enactment of their plea is a manifestation of *public space* as social production. Their redefinition of that space suggests that the public realm neither resides in nor can be represented by buildings and spaces bur rather is summoned into existence by social actions.

THE MOTHERS OF THE PLAZA DE MAYO

In March 1976, after a chaotic period following Juan Perón's death, a military junta wrested power from Perón's widow, Isabel, in order (as the junta claimed) to restore order and peace to the country. The first measures toward achieving this goal were similar to those of General Pinochet in Chile three years earlier, and included the suspension of all civil rights, the dissolution of all political parties, and the placement of labor unions and universities under government control. It would take seven long, dark years for a democratically elected government to be restored to Argentina, which at last permitted an evaluation of the extent of open kidnappings, torture, and executions of civilians tolerated by the military. Because of the clandestine, unrecorded activities of the para-military groups charged with these deeds, and because many burial sites still remain undisclosed, agreement as to the exact number of 'disappeared' may never be achieved, but estimates range from 9,000 to 30,000. Inquiries to the police about the fate of detainees went unanswered. Luis Puenzo's 1985 film, *The Official Story*, offers glimpses into the torture and degradation endured by thousands of men, women, and even babies, born in detention, some of whom were adopted by the torturers' families.

'Disappearances' were very effective in creating complicitous fear: many kidnappings were conducted in broad daylight, and the victims had not necessarily demonstrated open defiance of the military. In fact, later statistics show that almost half of the kidnappings involved witnesses, including children, relatives, and friends of those suspected of subversion. Given the effectiveness of arbitrary terror in imposing silence, it is astonishing that the public demands of less than a score of bereaved women who wanted to know what had happened to their children contributed so much to the military's fall from power. Their silent protest, opposed to the silence of the authorities, eventually had international resonance, prompting a harsh denunciation of the Argentinean military, which led, finally, to the demise of state terrorism and the election of a democratic government.

The actions of the 'Mothers,' as they came to be known, exemplified a kind of spatial and urban appropriation that originates in private acts that acquire public significance, thus questioning the boundaries of these two commonly opposed concepts. Gender issues, too, were not unimportant. The Mothers' appropriation of the plaza was nothing like a heroic final assault on a citadel. Instead, it succeeded because of its endurance over a protracted period, which could only happen because the Mothers were conspicuously ignored by the police, the public, and the national press. As older women they were no longer sexually desirable, and as working-class women they were of an inferior ilk. Nevertheless, their motherhood status demanded conventional respect. Communicating neither attraction nor threat, they were characterized by the government as 'madwomen.' The result of their public tenacity, which started with the body exposed to violence, eventually evolved into a powerful architecture of political resistance.

Plaza de Mayo is Argentina's symbolic equivalent of the Washington Mall. It is, however, a much smaller and very different kind of space: an urban square that evolved from the Spanish Plaza de Armas, a space that has stood for national unity since Creoles gathered there to demand independence from Spain in May of 1810. The national and international visibility of Plaza de Mayo as *the* space of public appearance for Argentineans is unchallenged. Originally, as mandated by the planning ordinances of the Law of the Indies, its sides were occupied by the colonial Cabildo, or city council, and the Catholic Cathedral. Today the most distinctive structure is the pink, neoclassical Casa Rosada, the seat of government.

Military exercises, executions, and public market commingled in the plaza until 1884, when Torcuato de Alvear, the aristocratic mayor, embarked on a Haussmanian remodeling of the center of Buenos Aires shortly after important civic structures – such as Congress and the Ministries of Finance and Social Welfare – had been completed. A major element of Alvear's plan was Avenida de Mayo, an east–west axis that put Congress and the Casa Rosada in full view of each other. Such a potent urban representation of the checks and balances of the modern, democratic state was achieved through selective demolition, including the removal of the plaza's market stalls and the shortening of the historic Cabildo's wings by half their original length. Currently, the plaza's immediate area includes several government offices, the financial district, and the city's most famous commercial street, Florida. This densely populated pedestrian thoroughfare links Avenida de Mayo to Plaza San Martín, another major urban square. A plastered masonry obelisk, the May Pyramid, erected on the square in 1811 to mark the first anniversary of the popular uprising for independence, was rebuilt as a taller, more ornate structure and placed on the axis between Congress and the Casa Rosada. In this new position, it became a metaphorical fulcrum in the balance of powers.

The now well-known image of a ring of women with heads clad in white kerchiefs circling the May Pyramid evolved from earlier spontaneous attempts at communication with government officials. At first, thirteen wives and mothers of the 'disappeared' met one another at the Ministry of the Interior, having exhausted all sources of information about their missing children and husbands. There a small office had been opened to 'process' cases brought by those who had filed writs of *habeas corpus*. One woman well in her sixties, Azucena Villaflor de Vicente, rallied the others: 'It is not here that we ought to be,' she said. 'It's the Plaza de Mayo. And when there are enough of us, we'll go to the Casa Rosada and see the president about our children who are missing.'[6] At the time, popular demonstrations at the plaza, frequently convened by the unions as a show of support during Juan Perón's tenure, were strictly forbidden, and gatherings of more than two people were promptly dispersed by the ever-present security forces. The original group of thirteen women came to the plaza wearing white kerchiefs initially to identify themselves to one another. They agreed to return every Thursday at the end of the business day in order to call their presence to the attention of similarly aggrieved women. The Mothers moved about in pairs, switching companions so that they could exchange information while still observing the rule against demonstrations. Eventually they attracted the interest of the international press and human rights organizations, one of which provided an office where the women could congregate privately. Despite this incentive to abandon the plaza for a safer location, the Mothers sustained a symbolic presence in the form of a silent march encircling the May Pyramid. That form, so loaded with cultural and sexual associations, became the symbolic focus of what started as a literal response to the police's demand that the women 'circulate.'

The white kerchiefs were the first elements of a common architecture evolved from the body. They were adopted from the cloth diapers a few of the Mothers had worn on their heads in a pilgrimage to the Virgin of Luján's sanctuary. The diapers were those of their own missing children, whose names were embroidered on them, and formed a headgear that differentiated the Mothers from the multitude of other women in kerchiefs on that religious march. In later demonstrations the Mothers constructed full-size cardboard silhouettes representing their missing children and husbands, and shielded their bodies with the ghostly blanks of the 'disappeared.'

By 1982, the military had proven itself unable to govern the country or control runaway inflation of more than 1000 percent per year. The provision of basic services was frequently disrupted by the still powerful Peronista labor unions, and many local industries had gone bankrupt due to the comparative cheapness of imported goods under an economic policy that eliminated most import taxes. Then, in the same year, the military government embarked on an ultimately ruinous war with Great Britain over the sovereignty of the Falkland/Malvinas Islands. With the help of the United States satellite intelligence and far superior naval might, Great Britain won with few casualties, while Argentina lost thousands of ill-equipped and ill-trained soldiers. The military government, which had broadcast a fake victory on television using old movie reels rather than current film footage, was forced to step down in shame by the popular outcry that followed. Following the collapse of the military government, the Mothers were a prominent presence at the festivities in Plaza de Mayo, their kerchiefs joyously joined as bunting to create a city-sized tent over the celebrants. They have continued their circular march to this day, as a kind of living memorial and to promote their demands for full accountability and punishment for those responsible for the disappearance of their husbands and children.

After the election of a democratic government, the military leadership was prosecuted in a civil rather than military court, resulting in jail sentences for a few generals and amnesty for other military personnel. Although the amnesty was forcefully contested by the Mothers and other organizations, the protest was seen by many as divisive. Nevertheless, the Mothers and a related organization of grandmothers pressed on with attempts to find records about disappearances and fought in the courts to recover their children and grandchildren. Then, early in 1995, more than a decade after the restoration of democratic government, a retired lieutenant publicly confessed to having dumped scores of drugged but still living people from a helicopter into the open ocean, and he invited other military men on similar assignments to come forth. The Mothers were present to demonstrate this time as well, but now the bunting had become a gigantic sheet that was waved overhead as an angry, agitated sea.

The Mothers were able to sustain control of an important urban space much as actors, dancers, or magicians control the stage by their ability to establish a presence that both opposes and activates the void represented by the audience. To paraphrase Henri Lefebvre, bodies produce space by introducing direction, rotation, orientation, occupation, and by organizing a *topos* through gestures, traces, and marks.[7] The formal structure of these actions, their ability to refunctionalize existing urban spaces, and the visual power of the supporting props contribute to the creation of public space.

What is missing from the current debate about the demise of public space is an awareness of the loss of architecture's power to represent the *public*, as a living, acting, and self-determining community. Instead, the debate focuses almost exclusively on the *physical space* of public appearance, without regard for the social action that can make the environment come alive or change its meaning. The debate appears to be mired in regrets over the replacement of squares (for which Americans never had much use) with shopping malls, theme parks, and virtual space. But this focus on physical space – and its ideological potential to encompass the public appearance of all people, regardless of color, class, age, or sex – loses credibility when specific classes of people are denouncing their exclusion and asserting their presence and influence in public life. The claims of these excluded people underscore the roles of *access* and *appearance* in the production and representation of public space, regardless of how it is physically or virtually constituted. They also suggest that public space is produced through public discourse, and its representation is not the exclusive territory of architecture, but is the product of the inextricable relationship between social action and physical space.

NOTES

1 An excellent example is Elizabeth Wilson's *The Sphinx and the City* (London: Virago, 1991).

2 See Alain Touraine, *Critique of Modernity* (Oxford: Blackwell, 1995), especially the chapter entitled 'The Subject.'

3 See Sophia Watson and Katherine Gibson (eds), *Postmodern Cities and Spaces* (Oxford: Blackwell, 1995).

4 A different approach has been taken by Jennifer Bloomer in her Urban Still Life project, which proposes to replace heroic (male) statues with domestic (female) tableaux, apparently without challenging the symbolic order of the nineteenth-century city.

5 The Mothers of Plaza de Mayo's activities have been extensively documented from a human rights point of view. See Josephine Fisher, *Mothers of the Disappeared* (Boston: South End Press, 1989), for interviews with the leaders and bibliographical references.

6 Quoted in John Simpson and Jana Bennett, *The Disappeared and the Mothers of the Plaza: The Story of the 11,000 Argentinians who Vanished* (New York: St. Martin's Press, 1985).

7 Henri Lefebvre, *The Production of Space* (Oxford and Cambridge, Mass.: Blackwell, 1991).

20 Elizabeth Wilson

'Into the Labyrinth'

from *The Sphinx in the City: Urban Life, the Control of Disorder and Women*
(1991)

> Autobiography has to do with time, with sequence and with what makes
> up the continuous flow of life. Here, I am talking of a space, of moments
> and discontinuities.
>
> Walter Benjamin, *One Way Street* (1932)

'Now let me call back those who introduced me to the city', wrote Walter Benjamin
in the 1930s, remembering his childhood in old Berlin. In his case, it was nurse-
maids; in mine, my mother. She planted within me, never to be eradicated, a
conviction of the fateful pleasures to be enjoyed and the enormous anxieties to be
overcome in discovering the city.

Every excursion we made together was an immense labour, a strenuous and
fraught journey to the treacherous destination: we waited for buses that never
came, were marshalled into queues that never grew shorter, walked down endless
streets in the hot sun. Our destinations also were terrible. The Tower of London,
Hampton Court and Madame Tussaud's were theatres of cruelty: *here* was the
exact spot upon which Anne Boleyn was beheaded; *this* was the gallery along
which Catherine Howard ran desperately to beg Henry the Eighth for mercy; here
was the Chamber of Horrors with its electric chair.

There were also the crowds of that first, weary, hot, London summer. I had
never seen crowds like those. The insolence, the promiscuity of the crowd, jostling
my mother and myself, seemed like a vast yawn of indifference. The stale suits and
rayon dresses brushed against us, bodies against bodies. The air seemed yellow
with a kind of blasé fatigue. My mother tried to keep her hat tipped forward, her
little veil in place, her corsage of soft suede anemones – blue, rose-red and purple
– crisply pinned against the navy crêpe of her dress, but I felt the vulnerability of her
pretensions exposed, and together we seemed so insignificant and lost.

I saw and snatched a pound note from beneath the feet that tramped across
a mosaic floor in the food hall of our local department store. I was offered the
forbidden chewing gum by departing American soldiers. We took boat trips down
the Thames. And on one occasion there were fireworks: the crowd swarmed darkly,
softly, beneath the trees; there was a hiss, and gold, white and magenta stars burst
silently towards us, to melt away just out of reach.

Our visits to the Zoo and Kensington Gardens expressed some longing for
what was so absent from the stony streets in which we lived and wandered: a

memory of the rural life we had left behind. Walter Benjamin recalled the park as a scene of bourgeois domestic harmony:

> There were serpentine paths near the lake and . . . benches . . . at the edge of the sand
> pit with its ditches, where toddlers dig or stand sunk in thought until bumped by a
> playmate or roused by the voice of a nursemaid from the bench of command; there she
> sits stern and studious, reading her novel and keeping the child in check while hardly
> raising an eyelid until, her labour done, she changes places with the nurse at the other
> end of the bench, who is holding the baby between her knees and knitting. Old, solitary
> men found their way here, paying due honour, amid these scatterbrained womenfolk,
> among the shrieking children, to the serious side of life: the newspaper.[1]

And perhaps my mother hoped to find a lost tranquillity in the green vista with its lines of trees in faultless perspective. The flowers and especially the spring blossoms, like all flowers in cities, appeared as a luxury item set against the urban fabric, rather than as an invasion of nature or a rural enclave; they symbolised some other, idealised world.

The Zoo was a very different experience, for there again were the crowds, jostling to stare at the infant gorilla and the apes. This was an old-time crowd, more of an eighteenth-century 'mob' come to stare at whatever exotic spectacle was on offer – a hanging, lunatics at Bedlam. Screams of laughter greeted the antics of the chimpanzees, those caricatures of humanity. Family groups approached the tiger's cage with a frisson of fear. Always for me the great question was whether to brave the reptile house, where huge snakes lay so creepily still. Their malevolent, horrible inertia gave me nightmares, yet I could never resist. 'I won't look' – but I always did.

The reptile house was for me that Minotaur's chamber cited by so many writers who liken the city to a labyrinth. Benjamin's Minotaur was 'three-headed', being the three prostitutes in a small Parisian brothel. In either case, fear mixed with an obscure or suspect pleasure lay at the heart of the city's secret courtyards and alleyways.

In Benjamin's adolescence the Berlin cafés played their part in introducing him to the world of pleasure that is one layer in the geology of the social city, and years later he remembered the names of those cafés like an incantation: the Romanisches Café, the Viktoria, the West End Café. Those salons were neither exactly public nor private space, and yet partook of both, and in them bohemia and the bourgeoisie mingled as part of the quintessential urban spectacle:

> For one of the most elementary and indispensable diversions of the citizen of a great
> metropolis, wedged, day in, day out, in the structure of his office and family amid an
> infinitely variegated social environment, is to plunge into another world, the more exotic
> the better. Hence the bars haunted by artists and criminals. The distinction between the
> two, from this point of view, is slight. The history of the Berlin coffeehouses is largely
> that of different strata of the public, those who first conquered the floor being obliged
> to make way for others gradually pressing forward, and thus to ascend the stage.[2]

There were, of course, no comparable cafés in London in the mid-1950s, when I was myself of an age to explore the city alone, coffee bars and jazz clubs offering a poor substitute. Soho drinking clubs were barred to me, in any case unknown. I nevertheless roamed London, solitary, engaged in that urban search for mysteries, extremes and revelations, a quest quite other than that of the wanderer through the natural landscape: a search less hallowed, yet no less spiritual.

Christine Mallet Joris's *Into the Labyrinth* was the title of the second lesbian novel I ever read (the first being, of course, Radclyffe Hall's *The Well of Loneliness*). *Into the Labyrinth* was French, and, unlike Radclyffe Hall's Edwardian romance, fitted precisely into my aimless, desperate walks and rides round London's streets, squares and inner suburbs. The heroine, a schoolgirl, discovered love in a house on a street called, romantically – and inappropriately – the *Rempart des Béguines* (the Rampart of Nuns). The adventures and sufferings attendant upon her sexual initiation took place in the bedrooms, hotels, the theatres and cafés of a great city – a city like a magic set of boxes, with, inside each box, a yet smaller and more secret one.

This recurring image, of the city as a maze, as having a secret centre, contradicts that other and equally common metaphor for the city as labyrinthine and centreless. Even if the labyrinth does have a centre, one image of the discovery of the city, or of exploring the city, is not so much finally reaching this centre, as of an endlessly circular journey, and of the retracing of the same pathways over time.

Yet one never retraces the same pathway twice, for the city is in a constant process of change, and thus becomes dreamlike and magical, yet also terrifying in the way a dream can be. Life and its certainties slither away from underfoot. This continual flux and change is one of the most disquieting aspects of the modern city. We expect permanence and stability from the city. Its monuments are solid stone and embody a history that goes back many generations. Rome was known as the 'Eternal City'. Yet, far from being eternal, in the sense of being outside time, Rome, like all cities, is deeply time-bound.[3] Although its history gives it its character, and a patina of durability, in modernity especially the city becomes ever more changing. That which we thought was most permanent dissolves as rapidly as the kaleidoscopic spectacle of the crowds and vehicles that pass through its streets. As Siegfried Kracauer wrote of Berlin in the 1920s:

> If some street blocks seem to be created for eternity, then the present-day
> Kurfurstendam is the embodiment of empty, flowing time in which nothing is allowed to
> last. . . . Many buildings have been shorn of the ornaments which formed a kind of
> bridge to yesterday. . . . Only the marble staircases that glimmer through the doorways
> preserve memories: those of the pre-war world.[4]

Walter Benjamin noted this constant destruction and replacement in his inventory of the cafés he had once frequented. The Viktoria Café 'no longer exists. Its place – on the corner of Friedrichstrasse and Unter den Linden – has been taken by one of the noisiest luxury cafés of new Berlin, against which the earlier one, however luxurious it may have been in its day, stands out with all the magic of the age of chandeliers, mirrored walls and plush comfort.'[5]

Even if the building itself – a café, hotel or department store – survives, its life may have long departed. It is still possible to visit some of the original Vienna cafés, famous at the turn of the century for their astonishing intellectual and bohemian life. Today they are almost empty, and dust floats down the bars of sunshine that reveal worn velvet and threadbare carpet, while a bad-tempered waitress surveys her deserted realm.

The London of the 1990s, for all the destruction that has occurred, is a livelier place than gloomy 1950s London. Today I am nevertheless sometimes conscious of a nostalgia for that vanished city: for the hushed interior spaces of long-defunct department stores with their carpeted trying-on rooms; for the French provision stores of Soho, replaced first by stripshows, later by fashion boutiques; but most of all for the very gloom and shabbiness now banished by gentrification, redevelopment and the commercialisation of leisure. It felt safe, and as you wandered through the streets you sensed always that pervasive English privacy, of lives veiled by lace curtains, of a prim respectability hiding strange secrets behind those inexpressive Earls Court porticoes.

In my mid-teens I was unfamiliar with the writings of Benjamin, but I intuitively identified with an urban consciousness of which his reminiscences are one of the most beautiful examples. This consciousness had been developed by the dandies and *'flâneurs'* (strollers, loiterers) of mid-nineteenth-century Paris. They had relished the kaleidoscope of urban public life and had created from it a new aesthetic, perceiving a novel kind of beauty in streets, factories and urban blight. In the 1930s the anthropologist Claude Lévi-Strauss discovered this beauty in an even more intense form in the Latin American cities he visited. He wrote that although 'São Paulo was said at the time to be an ugly town . . . I never thought São Paulo was ugly; it was a "wild" town, as are all American towns.' This quality of 'wildness' was, Lévi-Strauss felt, due to exaggerated and surreal contrasts. Extremes of wealth and poverty, of enjoyment and misery, made an essential contribution to this perception of the city. It was just those things that were shoddy and awful about city life that constituted its seduction, its peculiar beauty. What Lévi-Strauss found strange and evocative about the cities of the New World was their premature decrepitude, the incongruity of concrete skyscrapers alongside shanty towns, of Victorian Gothic churches jumbled up with bleak warehouses, creating a stone landscape as melancholy as it was striking.[6]

His perception, like that of the dandies, 'makes strange' the familiar and disregarded aspects of city life. It inverts our values: what was once seen as marginal becomes the essence of city life and that which makes it truly beautiful, even if its beauty is a beauty of ugliness. This new definition of beauty and meaning places the underside or 'Other' of city existence at the centre of consciousness. The nineteenth-century Parisian *flâneur* did not care about the pomp of the 'official', public city being created by Napoleon III and Baron Haussmann; it was the trivial, fragmented aspects of street life that appealed to him.

Lévi-Strauss was a latterday *flâneur* who discovered in the streets of São Paulo and Chicago a heartrending nostalgia not for the past but for the future. Their street canyons and windswept vistas suggested a lost future that was never to be, and ached with the yearning of human aspirations destined ever to fall short of the grandiose hopes that inspired them.

This sophisticated urban consciousness, which, as we shall see, reached a high point in central Europe in the early twentieth century, was an essentially male consciousness. Sexual unease and the pursuit of sexuality outside the constraints of the family were one of its major preoccupations.

This in itself made women's very presence in the cities a problem. The city offers untrammelled sexual experience; in the city the forbidden – what is most feared and desired – becomes possible. Woman is present in cities as temptress, as whore, as fallen woman, as lesbian, but also as virtuous womanhood in danger, as heroic womanhood who triumphs over temptation and tribulation. Writers such as Benjamin concentrated upon their own experience of strangeness in the city, on their own longings and desires, but many writers more definitely and clearly posed the presence of women as a problem of order, partly *because* their presence symbolised the promise of sexual adventure. This promise was converted into a general moral and political threat.

Nineteenth-century planning reports, government papers and journalism created an interpretation of urban experience as a new version of Hell, and it would even be possible to describe the emergent town-planning movement – a movement that has changed our cities almost beyond recognition – as an organised campaign to exclude women and children, along with other disruptive elements – the working class, the poor, and minorities – from this infernal urban space altogether.

Sexuality was only one source of threatening ambiguity and disorder in the city. The industrial city became a crucible of intense and unnerving contrasts. The hero, or less often the heroine, of urban literature was lured by the astonishing wealth and opportunity, threatened by the crushing poverty and despair of city life. Escape and entrapment, success and disaster offered heightened, exaggerated scenarios of personal triumph or loss of identity.

There was another contradictory aspect of city life. The sociologist Max Weber argued that the western city developed a typical form of political organisation: democracy. Feudal lords found that they were unable to retain their hold over their vassals, bondsmen and serfs once these had settled in cities. It was in the western late medieval city that men and women for the first time came together as individuals rather than as members of a kin group, clan or feudal entourage. The western city evolved political organisations which displaced existing paternalistic and patriarchal forms, and so the way was opened both to individualism and to democracy during the transition from feudalism to capitalism.

By the nineteenth century this had become contradictory because commentators and reformers of that period claimed to value individualism and democracy, but as cities grew, the mob became a revolutionary threat. The dangers seemed especially clear in American cities, already becoming for Europeans a paradigm of all that was new, and Alexis de Tocqueville was one of the first to voice this heightened, paranoid fear of the crowd in the nineteenth-century city, reporting that:

> the lowest classes in these vast cities are a rabble more dangerous even than that of European towns. The very lowest are the freed Negroes, condemned by law and opinion to a hereditary state of degradation and wretchedness. Then, there is a crowd of Europeans driven by misfortune or misbehaviour to the shores of the New World; such men carry our worst vices to the United States.

As he saw it, it was 'the size of some American cities and especially the nature of their inhabitants' that constituted a danger, even 'threatening the future of the democratic republics of the New World'. He predicted that the new urban crowd would destroy those infant republics 'unless their government succeeds in creating an armed force . . . capable of suppressing their excesses'.[7]

There were women as well as men in the urban crowd. Indeed the crowd was increasingly invested with female characteristics, while retaining its association with criminals and minorities. The threatening masses were described in feminine terms: as hysterical, or, in images of feminine instability and sexuality, as a flood or swamp. Like women, crowds were liable to rush to extremes of emotion. As the rightwing theorist of the crowd, Le Bon, put it, 'Crowds are like the sphinx of ancient fable; it is necessary to arrive at a solution of the problems offered by their psychology or to resign ourselves to being devoured by them.' At the heart of the urban labyrinth lurked not the Minotaur, a bull-like male monster, but the female Sphinx, the 'strangling one', who was so called because she strangled all those who could not answer her riddle: female sexuality, womanhood out of control, lost nature, loss of identity.[8]

Yet the city, a place of growing threat and paranoia to men, might be a place of liberation for women. The city offers women freedom. After all, the city normalises the carnivalesque aspects of life. True, on the one hand it makes necessary routinised rituals of transportation and clock watching, factory discipline and timetables, but despite its crowds and the mass nature of its life, and despite its bureaucratic conformity, at every turn the city dweller is also offered the opposite – pleasure, deviation, disruption. In this sense it would be possible to say that the male and female 'principles' war with each other at the very heart of city life. The city is 'masculine' in its triumphal scale, its towers and vistas and arid industrial regions; it is 'feminine' in its enclosing embrace, in its indeterminacy and labyrinthine uncentredness. We might even go so far as to claim that urban life is actually based on this perpetual struggle between rigid, routinised order and pleasurable anarchy, the male–female dichotomy.

Perhaps the 'disorder' of urban life does not so much disturb women. If this is so, it may be because they have not internalised as rigidly as men a need for overrationalistic control and authoritarian order. The socialisation of women renders them less dependent on duality and opposition; instead of setting nature against the city, they find nature *in* the city. For them, that invisible city, the 'second city', the underworld or secret labyrinth, instead of being sinister or diseased as in the works of Charles Dickens and many of the writers we will encounter later on, is an Aladdin's cave of riches. Yet at the same time, it is a place of danger for women. Prostitutes and prostitution recur continually in the discussion of urban life, until it almost seems as though to be a woman – an individual, not part of a family or kin group – in the city, is to become a prostitute – a public woman.

The city – as experience, environment, concept – is constructed by means of multiple contrasts: natural, unnatural; monolithic, fragmented; secret, public; pitiless, enveloping; rich, poor; sublime, beautiful. Behind all these lies the ultimate and major contrast: male, female; culture, nature; city, country. In saying this I am not arguing (as do some feminists) that male–female difference creates the deepest and most fundamental of all political divisions. Nor am I arguing that the male/female stereotypes to which I refer accurately reflect the nature of actual, individual men and women. In the industrial period, nonetheless, that particular division became inscribed on urban life and determined the development and planning of cities to a surprising degree and in an extraordinarily unremarked way. It will be one purpose of this book to explore how underlying assumptions, based both on this unconscious division and on consciously spelt-out ideas about women's rightful place, have determined the shape of contemporary cities.

We shall also explore how women have lived out their lives on sufferance in the metropolis. For although women, along with minorities, children, the poor, are still not full citizens in the sense that they have never been granted full and free access to the streets, industrial life still drew them into public life, and they have survived and flourished in the interstices of the city, negotiating the contradictions of the city in their own particular way.

The contradictions and intensity of urban life have produced strong responses, one of which has been a corrosive anti-urbanism. For many years I took for granted the assumption that a great city was the best place to live, and Paris and New York seemed the only possible – and even more magical – alternatives to the shabbier but comfortable and accommodating ambience of sub-bohemian London. It was only my involvement in 'alternative' radical politics in the 1970s which alerted me to the hatred many 'progressive' people feel for cities, and to an alien point of view, which self-righteously attacked the ugliness and vulgarity of urban life while setting out some rural or small-town idyll as the desired alternative. I had known that many rightwing writers feared the modern city as destructive of the traditional patriarchal order; but to me the anti-urbanism of the left seemed like a betrayal, and made me permanently disillusioned with utopianism. William Morris in particular – a writer who seems exempt from any criticism by socialists to this day – demonstrated in his utopian *News from Nowhere* a retreat from modernity and a nostalgia for patriarchalism that I found suffocating.

Anti-urbanism has a long history, partly related to industrialisation; developments in the 1980s and early 1990s have served to make such ideas even more threatening and more plausible. One development is our growing ecological consciousness; another the redevelopment of inner cities as uninhabited office or business districts; a third the parallel growth of inner-city ghettoes inhabited by a so-called 'underclass'; fourthly, the simultaneous suburbanisation of more and more of the countryside. The result is that today in many cities we have the worst of all worlds: danger without pleasure, safety without stimulation, consumerism without choice, monumentality without diversity. At the same time, larger and larger numbers of people inhabit zones that are no longer really either town or countryside.

We need a radically new approach to the city. We will never solve the problems of living in cities until we welcome and maximise the freedom and autonomy they offer and make these available to all classes and groups. We must cease to perceive the city as a dangerous and disorderly zone from which women – and others – must be largely excluded for their own protection. There are other issues, of course, equally important. Leisure and consumption must cease to be treated purely as commodities controlled by market forces, nor can adequate housing ever be provided so long as it is regarded as a mere byproduct of urban development and property speculation.

Yet at the 'commonsense' level of our deepest philosophical and emotional assumptions, the unconscious bedrock of western culture, it is the male–female dichotomy that has so damagingly translated itself into a conception of city culture as pertaining to men. Consequently, women have become an irruption in the city, a symptom of disorder, and a problem: the Sphinx in the city.

Women are placed at the centre of my argument for this reason.

NOTES AND REFERENCES

1 Walter Benjamin, *One Way Street* (London: New Left Books, 1979), p. 296.
2 Ibid., p. 312.
3 See Burton Pike, *The Image of the City in Modern Literature* (Princeton, NJ: Princeton University Press, 1981), passim, to which I am indebted for the ideas developed in this section. See also Christine Sizemore, 'Reading the City as Palimpsest: The Experiential Perception of the City in Doris Lessing's *The Four Gated City*', Susan Merrill Squier (ed.), *Women Writers and the City: Essays in Feminist Literary Criticism* (Knoxville: University of Tennessee Press, 1984).
4 David Frisby, *Fragments of Modernity: theories of Modernity in the work of Simmel, Kracauer and Benjamin* (Oxford: Polity Press, 1985), p. 139, quoting Siegfried Kracauer (1932), 'Strasse ohne Erinnerung', *Frankfurter Zeitung*, 16 December.
5 Benjamin, op. cit., p. 309.
6 Claude Lévi-Strauss, *Tristes Tropiques* (Harmondsworth: Penguin, 1976), pp. 120–1.
7 Charles Alexis de Tocqueville, *Democracy in America* [1835] (New York: Harper and Row, 1966), p. 256, footnote.
8 Andreas Huyssen, *After the Great Divide: Modernism, Mass Culture, Postmodernism* (London: Macmillan, 1986), pp. 52–3, quoting Gustave Le Bon (1981), *The Crowd* (Harmondsworth: Penguin), pp. 39, 52.

21 Griselda Pollock

Excerpts from 'Modernity and the Spaces of Femininity'

from *Vision and Difference: Femininity, Feminism and Histories of Art* (1992)

> Investment in the look is not as privileged in women as in men. More than
> other senses, the eye objectifies and masters. It sets at a distance, and
> maintains a distance. In our culture the predominance of the look over
> smell, taste, touch and hearing has brought about an impoverishment of
> bodily relations. The moment the look dominates, the body loses its
> materiality.
>
> > (Luce Irigaray (1978), interview in M.F. Hans and G. Lapouge (eds)
> > *Les Femmes, la pornographie et l'érotisme*, Paris, p. 50)

INTRODUCTION

The schema which decorated the cover of Alfred H. Barr's catalogue for the exhibition *Cubism and Abstract Art* at the Museum of Modern Art, New York, in 1936 is
paradigmatic of the way modern art has been mapped by modernist art history.
Artistic practices from the late nineteenth century are placed on a chronological
flow chart where movement follows movement connected by one-way arrows
which indicate influence and reaction. Over each movement a named artist pre-
sides. All those canonized as the initiators of modern art are men. Is this because
there were no women involved in early modern movements? No.[1] Is it because
those who were, were without significance in determining the shape and character
of modern art? No. Or is it rather because what modernist art history celebrates is
a selective tradition which normalizes, as the *only* modernism, a particular and
gendered set of practices? I would argue for this explanation. As a result any
attempt to deal with artists in the early history of modernism who are women
necessitates a deconstruction of the masculinist myths of modernism.[2]

These are, however, widespread and structure the discourse of many
counter-modernists, for instance in the social history of art. The recent publication
The Painting of Modern Life: Paris in the Art of Manet and his Followers, by T.J.
Clark,[3] offers a searching account of the social relations between the emergence of
new protocols and criteria for painting – modernism – and the myths of modernity
shaped in and by the new city of Paris remade by capitalism during the Second
Empire. Going beyond the commonplaces about a desire to be contemporary in
art, 'il faut être de son temps',[4] Clark puzzles at what structured the notions of
modernity which became the territory for Manet and his followers. He thus indexes
the impressionist painting practices to a complex set of negotiations of the ambiguous and baffling class formations and class identities which emerged in Parisian

society. Modernity is presented as far more than a sense of being 'up to date' – modernity is a matter of representations and major myths – of a new Paris for recreation, leisure and pleasure, of nature to be enjoyed at weekends in suburbia, of the prostitute taking over and of fluidity of class in the popular spaces of entertainment. The key markers in this mythic territory are leisure, consumption, the spectacle and money. And we can reconstruct from Clark a map of impressionist territory which stretches from the new boulevards via Gare St Lazare out on the suburban train to La Grenouillère, Bougival or Argenteuil. In these sites, the artists lived, worked and pictured themselves.[5] But in two of the four chapters of Clark's book, he deals with the problematic of sexuality in bourgeois Paris and the canonical paintings are *Olympia* (1863, Paris, Musée du Louvre) and *A bar at the Folies-Bergère* (1881–82, London, Courtauld Institute of Art).

It is a mighty but flawed argument on many levels but here I wish to attend to its peculiar closures on the issue of sexuality. For Clark the founding fact is class. Olympia's nakedness inscribes her class and thus debunks the mythic classlessness of sex epitomized in the image of the courtesan.[6] The fashionably blasé barmaid at the Folies evades a fixed identity as either bourgeois or proletarian but none the less participates in the play around class that constituted the myth and appeal of the popular.[7]

Although Clark nods in the direction of feminism by acknowledging that these paintings imply a masculine viewer/consumer, the manner in which this is done ensures the normalcy of that position, leaving it below the threshold of historical investigation and theoretical analysis.[8] To recognize the gender-specific conditions of these paintings' existence one need only imagine a female spectator and a female producer of the works. How can a woman relate to the viewing positions proposed by either of these paintings? Can a woman be offered, in order to be denied, imaginary possession of Olympia or the barmaid? Would a woman of Manet's class have a familiarity with either of these spaces and its exchanges which could be evoked so that the painting's modernist job of negation and disruption could be effective? Could Berthe Morisot have gone to such a location to canvass the subject? Would it enter her head as a site of modernity as she experienced it? Could she as a woman experience modernity as Clark defines it at all?*

---

* While accepting that paintings such as *Olympia* and *A bar at the Folies-Bergère* come from a tradition which invokes the spectator as masculine, it is necessary to acknowledge the way in which a feminine spectator is actually implied by these paintings. Surely one part of the shock, of the transgression effected by the painting *Olympia* for its first viewers at the Paris Salon was the presence of that 'brazen' but cool look from the white woman on a bed attended by a black maid in a space in which women, or to be historically precise bourgeois ladies, would be presumed to be present. That look, so overtly passing between a seller of woman's body and a client/viewer signified the commercial and sexual exchanges specific to a part of the public realm which should be invisible to ladies. Furthermore, its absence from their consciousness structured their identities as ladies. In some of his writings T.J. Clark correctly discusses

For it is a striking fact that many of the canonical works held up as the founding monuments of modern art treat precisely with this area, sexuality, and this form of it, commercial exchange. I am thinking of innumerable brothel scenes through to Picasso's *Demoiselles d'Avignon* or that other form, the artist's couch. The encounters pictured and imagined are those between men who have the freedom to take their pleasures in many urban spaces and women from a class subject to them who have to work in those spaces often selling their bodies to clients, or to artists. Undoubtedly these exchanges are structured by relations of class but these are thoroughly captured within gender and its power relations. Neither can be separated or ordered in a hierarchy. They are historical simultaneities and mutually inflecting.

So we must enquire why the territory of modernism so often is a way of dealing with masculine sexuality and its sign, the bodies of women – why the nude, the brothel, the bar? What relation is there between sexuality, modernity and modernism? If it is normal to see paintings of women's bodies as the territory across which men artists claim their modernity and compete for leadership of the avant-garde, can we expect to rediscover paintings of women in which they battled with their sexuality in the representation of the male nude? Of course not; the very suggestion seems ludicrous. But why? Because there is a historical asymmetry – a difference socially, economically, subjectively between being a woman and being a man in Paris in the late nineteenth century. This difference – the product of the social structuration of sexual difference and not any imaginary biological distinction – determined both what and how men and women painted.

I have long been interested in the work of Berthe Morisot (1841–96) and Mary Cassatt (1844–1926), two of the four women who were actively involved with the impressionist exhibiting society in Paris in the 1870s and 1880s who were regarded by their contemporaries as important members of the artistic group we now label the Impressionists.[9] But how are we to study the work of artists who are women so that we can discover and account for the specificity of what they

---

the meanings of the sign woman in the nineteenth century as oscillating between two poles of the *fille publique* (woman of the streets) and the *femme honnête* (the respectable married woman). But it would seem that the exhibition of *Olympia* precisely confounds that social and ideological distance between two imaginary poles and forces the one to confront the other in that part of the public realm where ladies do go – still within the frontiers of femininity. The presence of this painting in the Salon – not because it is a nude but because it displaces the mythological costume or anecdote through which prostitution was represented mythically through the courtesan – transgresses the line on my grid derived from Baudelaire's text, introducing not just modernity as a manner of painting a pressing contemporary theme, but the spaces of modernity into a social territory of the bourgeoisie, the Salon, where viewing such an image is quite shocking because of the presence of wives, sisters and daughters. The understanding of the shock depends upon our restoration of the female spectator to her historical and social place.

produced as individuals while also recognizing that, as women, they worked from different positions and experiences from those of their colleagues who were men?

Analysing the activities of women who were artists cannot merely involve mapping women on to existing schemata, even those which claim to consider the production of art socially and address the centrality of sexuality. We cannot ignore the fact that the terrains of artistic practice and of art history are structured in and structuring of gender power relations.

As Roszika Parker and I argued in *Old Mistresses: Women, Art and Ideology* (1981), feminist art history has a double project. The historical recovery of data about women producers of art coexists with and is only critically possible through a concomitant deconstruction of the discourses and practices of art history itself.

Historical recovery of women who were artists is a prime necessity because of the consistent obliteration of their activity in what passes for art history. We have to refute the lies that there were no women artists, or that the women artists who are admitted are second-rate and that the reason for their indifference lies in the all-pervasive submission to an indelible femininity – always proposed as unquestionably a disability in making art. But alone historical recovery is insufficient. What sense are we to make of information without a theorized framework through which to discern the particularity of women's work? This is itself a complicated issue. To avoid the embrace of the feminine stereotype which homogenizes women's work as determined by natural gender, we must stress the heterogeneity of women's art work, the specificity of individual producers and products. Yet we have to recognize what women share – as a result of nurture not nature, i.e. the historically variable social systems which produce sexual differentiation.

This leads to a major aspect of the feminist project, the theorization and historical analysis of sexual difference. Difference is not essential but understood as a social structure which positions male and female people asymmetrically in relation to language, to social and economic power and to meaning. Feminist analysis undermines one bias of patriarchal power by refuting the myths of universal or general meaning. Sexuality, modernism or modernity cannot function as given categories to which we add women. That only identifies a partial and masculine viewpoint with the norm and confirms women as other and subsidiary. Sexuality, modernism or modernity are organized by and organiz-ations of sexual difference. To perceive women's specificity is to analyse historically a particular configuration of difference.

This is my project here. How do the socially contrived orders of sexual difference structure the lives of Mary Cassatt and Berthe Morisot? How did that structure what they produced? The matrix I shall consider here is that of space.

Space can be grasped in several dimensions. The first refers us to spaces as locations. What spaces are represented in the paintings made by Berthe Morisot and Mary Cassatt? And what are not? A quick list includes:

dining-rooms
drawing-rooms
bedrooms
balconies/verandas
private gardens

The majority of these have to be recognized as examples of private areas or domestic space. But there are paintings located in the public domain, scenes for instance of promenading, driving in the park, being at the theatre, boating. They are the spaces of bourgeois recreation, display and those social rituals which constituted polite society, or Society, *Le Monde*. In the case of Mary Cassatt's work, spaces of labour are included, especially those involving child care. In several examples, they make visible aspects of working-class women's labour within the bourgeois home.

I have previously argued that engagement with the impressionist group was attractive to some women precisely because subjects dealing with domestic social life hitherto relegated as mere genre painting were legitimized as central topics of the painting practices.[10] On closer examination it is much more significant how little of typical impressionist iconography actually reappears in the works made by artists who are women. They do not represent the territory which their colleagues who were men so freely occupied and made use of in their works, for instance bars, cafés, backstage and even those places which Clark has seen as participating in the myth of the popular – such as the bar at the Folies-Bergère or even the Moulin de la Galette. A range of places and subjects was closed to them while open to their male colleagues who could move freely with men and women in the socially fluid public world of the streets, popular entertainment and commercial or casual sexual exchange.

The second dimension in which the issue of space can be addressed is that of the spatial order within paintings. Playing with spatial structures was one of the defining features of early modernist painting in Paris, be it Manet's witty and calculated play upon flatness or Degas's use of acute angles of vision, varying viewpoints and cryptic framing devices. With their close personal contacts with both artists, Morisot and Cassatt were no doubt party to the conversations out of which these strategies emerged and equally subject to the less conscious social forces which may well have conditioned the predisposition to explore spatial ambiguities and metaphors.[11] Yet although there are examples of their using similar tactics, I would like to suggest that spatial devices in the work of Morisot and Cassatt work to a wholly different effect.

A remarkable feature in the spatial arrangements in paintings by Morisot is the juxtaposition on a single canvas of two spatial systems – or at least of two compartments of space often obviously boundaried by some device such as a balustrade, balcony, veranda or embankment whose presence is underscored by facture. In *The harbour at Lorient*, 1869, Morisot offers us at the left a landscape view down the estuary represented in traditional perspective while in one corner, shaped by the boundary of the embankment, the main figure is seated at an oblique angle to the view and to the viewer. A comparable composition occurs in *On the terrace*, 1874, where again the foreground figure is literally squeezed off-centre and compressed within a box of space marked by a heavily brushed-in band of dark paint forming the wall of the balcony on the other side of which lies the outside world of the beach. In *On the balcony*, 1872, the viewer's gaze over Paris is obstructed by the figures who are none the less separated from that Paris as they look over the balustrade from the Trocadéro, very near to her home.[12] The point can be underlined by contrasting the painting by Monet, *The garden of the princess*, 1867, where the viewer cannot readily imagine the point from which the painting has been made, namely a window high in one of the new apartment buildings, and instead enjoys a fantasy of floating over the scene. What Morisot's balustrades demarcate is not the boundary between public and private but between the spaces of masculinity and of femininity inscribed at the level of both what spaces are open to men and women and what relation a man or woman has to that space and its occupants.

In Morisot's paintings, moreover, it is as if the place from which the painter worked is made part of the scene creating a compression or immediacy in the foreground spaces. This locates the viewer in that same place, establishing a notional relation between the viewer and the woman defining the foreground, therefore forcing the viewer to experience a dislocation between her space and that of a world beyond its frontiers.

Proximity and compression are also characteristic of the works of Cassatt. Less often is there a split space, but it occurs, as in *Susan on a balcony*, 1883. More common is a shallow pictorial space which the painted figure dominates as in *Young woman in black: portrait of Mrs Gardner Cassatt*, 1883. The viewer is forced into a confrontation or conversation with the painted figure while dominance and familiarity are denied by the device of the averted head of concentration on an activity by the depicted personage. What are the conditions for this awkward but pointed relation of the figure to the world? Why this lack of conventional distance and the radical disruption of what we take as the normal spectator–text relations? What has disturbed the 'logic of the gaze?'

In a previous monograph on Mary Cassatt I tried to establish a correspondence between the social space of the represented and the pictorial space of the representation.[13] Considering the painting *Lydia, at a tapestry frame*, 1881, I noted the shallow space of the painting which seemed inadequate to contain the embroidery frame at which the artist's sister works. I tried to explain its threatened protrusion beyond the picture's space into that of the viewer as a comment on the containment of women and read the painting as a statement of resistance to it. In *Lydia crocheting in the garden*, 1880, the woman is not placed in an interior but in a garden. Yet this outdoor space seems to collapse towards the picture plane, again creating a sense of compression. The comfortable vista beyond the figure, opening out to include a view and the sky beyond as in Caillebotte's *Garden at Petit Gennevilliers with dahlias*, 1893, is decisively refused.

I argued that despite the exterior setting the painting creates the intimacy of an interior and registers the garden, a favoured topic with impressionist artists, not as a piece of private property but as the place of seclusion and enclosure. I was searching for some kind of homology between the compression of pictorial space and the social confinement of women within the prescribed limits of bourgeois codes of femininity. Claustrophobia and restraint were read into the pressurized placement of figures in shallow depth. But such an argument is only a modified form of reflection theory which does not explain anything (though it does have the saving grace of acknowledging the role of signifiers in the active production of meaning).

In the case of Mary Cassatt I would now want to draw attention to the disarticulation of the conventions of geometric perspective which had normally governed the representation of space in European painting since the fifteenth century. Since its development in the fifteenth century, this mathematically calcu-lated system of projection had aided painters in the representation of a three-dimensional world on a two-dimensional surface by organizing objects in relation to each other to produce a notional and singular position from which the scene is intelligible. It establishes the viewer as both absent from and indeed independent of the scene while being its mastering eye/I.

It is possible to represent space by other conventions. Phenomenology has been usefully applied to the apparent spatial deviations of the work of Van Gogh and Cézanne.[14] Instead of pictorial space functioning as a notional box into which objects are placed in a rational and abstract relationship, space is represented according to the way it is experienced by a combination of touch, texture, as well as sight. Thus objects are patterned according to subjective hierarchies of value for the producer. Phenomenological space is not orchestrated for sight alone but by means of visual cues refers to other sensations and relations of bodies and objects in a lived world. As experiential space this kind of representation becomes susceptible to different ideological, historical as well as purely contingent, subjective inflections.

These are not necessarily unconscious. For instance, in *Little girl in a blue armchair*, 1878, by Cassatt, the viewpoint from which the room has been painted is

Figure 21.1
Mary Cassatt, 'Little Girl in a Blue Armchair', (1878). National Gallery of Art, Washington. Collection of Mr & Mrs Paul Mellon

low so that the chairs loom large as if imagined from the perspective of a small person placed amongst massive upholstered obstacles. The background zooms sharply away indicating a different sense of distance from that which a taller adult would enjoy over the objects to an easily accessible back wall. The painting therefore not only pictures a small child in a room but evokes that child's sense of the space of the room. It is from this conception of the possibilities of spatial structure that I can now discern a way through my earlier problem in attempting to relate space and social processes. For a third approach lies in considering not only the spaces represented, or the spaces *of* the representation, but the social spaces from which the representation is made and its reciprocal positionalities. The producer is herself shaped within a spatially orchestrated social structure which is lived at both psychic and social levels. The space of the look at the point of production will to some extent determine the viewing position of the spectator at the point of consumption. This point of view is neither abstract nor exclusively personal, but ideologically and historically construed. It is the art historian's job to re-create it – since it cannot ensure its recognition outside its historical moment.

The spaces of femininity operated not only at the level of what is represented, the drawing-room or sewing-room. The spaces of femininity are those from which femininity is lived as a positionality in discourse and social practice. They are the product of a lived sense of social locatedness, mobility and visibility, in the social relations of seeing and being seen. Shaped within the sexual politics of looking they demarcate a particular social organization of the gaze which itself works back to secure a particular social ordering of sexual difference. Femininity is both the condition and the effect.

How does this relate to modernity and modernism? As Janet Wolff has convincingly pointed out, the literature of modernity describes the experience of men.[15] It is essentially a literature about transformations in the public world and its associated consciousness. It is generally agreed that modernity as a nineteenth-century phenomenon is a product of the city. It is a response in a mythic or ideological form to the new complexities of a social existence passed amongst strangers in an atmosphere of intensified nervous and psychic stimulation, in a world ruled by money and commodity exchange, stressed by competition and formative of an intensified individuality, publicly defended by a blasé mask of indifference but intensely 'expressed' in a private, familial context.[16] Modernity stands for a myriad of responses to the vast increase in population leading to the literature of the crowds and masses, a speeding up of the pace of life with its attendant changes in the sense and regulation of time and fostering that very modern phenomenon, fashion, the shift in the character of towns and cities from being centres of quite visible activities – manufacture, trade, exchange – to being zoned and stratified, with production becoming less visible while the centres of cities such as Paris and London become key sites of consumption and display, producing what Sennett has labelled the spectacular city.[17]

All these phenomena affected women as well as men, but in different ways. What I have described above takes place within and comes to define the modern forms of the public space changing, as Sennett argues in his book significantly titled *The Fall of Public Man*, from the eighteenth century formation to become more mystified and threatening but also more exciting and sexualized. One of the key figures to embody the novel forms of public experience of modernity is the flâneur or impassive stroller, the man in the crowd who goes, in Walter Benjamin's phrase, 'botanizing on the asphalt'.[18] The flâneur symbolizes the privilege or freedom to move about the public arenas of the city observing but never interacting, consuming the sights through a controlling but rarely acknowledged gaze, directed as much at other people as at the goods for sale. The flâneur embodies the gaze of modernity which is both covetous and erotic.

But the flâneur is an exclusively masculine type which functions within the matrix of bourgeois ideology through which the social spaces of the city were reconstructed by the overlaying of the doctrine of separate spheres on to the division of public and private, which became as a result a gendered division. In contesting the dominance of the aristocratic social formation they were struggling to displace, the emergent bourgeoisies of the late eighteenth century refuted a social system based on fixed orders of rank, estate and birth and defined themselves in universalistic and democratic terms. The pre-eminent ideological figure is MAN, which immediately reveals the partiality of their democracy and universalism. The rallying cry, liberty, equality and fraternity (again note its gender partiality), imagines a society composed of free, self-possessing male individuals exchanging with equal and like. Yet the economic and social conditions of the existence of the bourgeoisie as a class are structurally founded upon inequality and difference in terms both of socio-economic categories and of gender. The ideological formations of the bourgeoisie negotiate these contradictions by diverse tactics. One is the appeal to an imaginary order of nature which designates as unquestionable the hierarchies in which women, children, hands and servants (as well as other races) are posited as naturally different from and subordinate to white European man. Another formation endorsed the theological separation of spheres by fragmentation of the problematic social world into separated areas of gendered activity. This division took over and reworked the eighteenth-century compartmentalization of the public and private. The public sphere, defined as the world of productive labour, political decision, government, education, the law and public service, increasingly became exclusive to men. The private sphere was the world, home, wives, children and servants.[19] As Jules Simon, moderate republican politician, explained in 1892:

> What is a man's vocation? It is to be a good citizen. And woman's? To be a good wife and a good mother. One is in some way called to the outside world, the other is *retained* for the interior.[20]

(My italics)

Woman was defined by this other, non-social space of sentiment and duty from which money and power were banished.[21] Men, however, moved freely between the spheres while women were supposed to occupy the domestic space alone. Men came home to be themselves but in equally constraining roles as husbands and fathers, to engage in affective relationships after a hard day in the brutal, divisive and competitive world of daily capitalist hostilities. We are here defining a mental map rather than a description of actual social spaces. In her introduction to the essays on *Women in Space*, Shirley Ardener has, however, emphasized that

> societies have generated their own culturally determined ground rules for making boundaries on the ground and have divided the social into spheres, levels and territories with invisible fences and platforms to be scaled by abstract ladders and crossed by intangible bridges with as much trepidation and exultation as on a plank over a raging torrent.[22]

There was none the less an overlap between the purely ideological maps and the concrete organization of the social sphere. As social historians, Catherine Hall and Lee Davidoff have shown in their work on the formation of the British middle class in Birmingham, the city was literally reshaped according to this ideal divided. The new institutions of public governance and business were established as being exclusively masculine preserves, and the growing separation of work and home was made real by the building of suburbs such as Edgbaston to which wives and daughters were banished.[23]

As both ideal and social structure, the mapping of the separation of the spheres for women and men on to the division of public and private was powerfully operative in the construction of a specifically bourgeois way of life. It aided the production of the gendered social identities by which the miscellaneous components of the bourgeoisie were helped to cohere as a class, in difference from both aristocracy and proletariat. Bourgeois women, however, obviously went out in public, to promenade, go shopping or visiting or simply to be on display. And working-class women went out to work, but that fact presented a problem in terms of definition as woman. For instance Jules Simon categorically stated that a woman who worked ceased to be a woman.[24] Therefore, across the public realm lay another, less often studied map which secured the definitions of bourgeois womanhood – femininity – in difference from proletarian women.

For bourgeois women, going into town mingling with crowds of mixed social composition was not only frightening because it became increasingly unfamiliar, but because it was morally dangerous. It has been argued that to maintain one's respectability, closely identified with femininity, meant *not* exposing oneself in public. The public space was officially the realm of and for men; for women to enter it entailed unforeseen risks. For instance in *La Femme* (1858–60) Jules Michelet exclaimed:

> How many irritations for the single woman! She can hardly ever go out in the evening; she would be taken for a prostitute. There are a thousand places where only men are to be seen, and if she needs to go there on business, the men are amazed, and laugh like fools. For example, should she find herself delayed at the other end of Paris and hungry, she will not dare to enter into a restaurant. She would constitute an event; she would be

a spectacle: All eyes would be constantly fixed on her, and she would overhear uncomplimentary and bold conjectures.[25]

The private realm was fashioned for men as a place of refuge from the hurly-burly of business, but it was also a place of constraint. The pressures of intensified individuality protected in public by the blasé mask of indifference, registered in the equally socially induced roles of loving husband and responsible father, led to a desire to escape the overbearing demands of masculine domestic personae. The public domain became also a realm of freedom and irresponsibilty if not immorality. This, of course, meant different things for men and for women. For women, the public spaces thus construed were where one risked losing one's virtue, dirtying oneself; going out in public and the idea of disgrace were closely allied. For the man going out in public meant losing oneself in the crowd away from both demands of respect-ability. Men colluded to protect this freedom. Thus a woman going out to dine at a restaurant even with her husband present was scandalous, whereas a man dining out with a mistress, even in the view of his friends, was granted a fictive invisibility.[26]

The public and private division functioned on many levels. As a metaphorical map in ideology, it structured the very meaning of the terms 'masculine' and 'feminine' within its mythic boundaries. In practice, as the ideology of domesticity became hegemonic, it regulated women's and men's behaviour in the respective public and private spaces. Presence in either of the domains determined one's social identity and therefore, in objective terms, the separation of the spheres problem-atized women's relation to the very activities and experiences we typically accept as defining modernity.

In the diaries of the artist Marie Bashkirtseff, who lived and worked in Paris during the same period as Morisot and Cassatt, the following passage reveals some of the restraints:

> What I long for is the freedom of going about alone, of coming and going, of sitting in the seats of the Tuileries, and especially in the Luxembourg, of stopping and looking at the artistic shops, of entering churches and museums, of walking about old streets at night; that's what I long for; and that's the freedom without which one cannot become a real artist. Do you imagine that I get much good from what I see, chaperoned as I am, and when, in order to go to the Louvre, I must wait for my carriage, my lady companion, my family?[27]

These territories of the bourgeois city were however not only gendered on a male/female polarity. They became the sites for the negotiation of gendered class identities and class gender positions. The spaces of modernity are where class and gender interface in critical ways, in that they are the spaces of sexual exchange. The significant spaces of modernity are neither simply those of masculinity, nor are they those of femininity which are as much the spaces of modernity for being the negative of the streets and bars. They are, as the canonical works indicate, the marginal or interstitial spaces where the fields of the masculine and feminine intersect and structure sexuality within a classed order.

NOTES

1 For substantive evidence, see Lea Vergine, *L'Autre moitié de l'avant-garde, 1910– 1940*, translated by Mireille Zanuttin (Italian edn 1980), Paris, Des Femmes, 1982.

2 See Nicole Dubreuil-Blondin, 'Modernism and feminism: some paradoxes', in Benjamin H. D. Bluchloh (ed.), *Modernism and Modernity*, Halifax, Nova Scotia, Press of Nova Scotia College of Art and Design, 1983. Also Lillian Robinson and Lisa Vogel, 'Modernism and history', *New Literary History*, 1971–2, iii (1): 177–99.

3 T.J. Clark, *The Painting of Modern Life: Paris in the Art of Manet and his Followers*, New York, Knopf, and London, Thames & Hudson, 1984.

4 George Boas, 'Il faut être de son temps', *Journal of Aesthetics and Art Criticism*, 1940, 1, 52–65; reprinted in *Wingless Pegasus: A Handbook for Critics*, Baltimore, Johns Hopkins University Press, 1950.

5 The itinerary can be fictively reconstructed as follows: a stroll on the *Boulevard des Capucines* (C. Monet, 1873, Kansas City, Nelson Atkins Museum of Art), across the *Pont de l'Europe* (G. Caillebotte, 1876, Geneva, Petit Palais), up to the *Gare St Lazare* (Monet, 1877, Paris, Musée d'Orsay), to catch a suburban train for the twelve-minute ride out to walk along the *Seine at Argenteuil* (Monet, 1875, San Francisco, Museum of Modern Art) or to stroll and swim at the bathing-place on the Seine, *La Grenouillère* (A. Renoir, 1869, Moscow, Pushkin Museum), or to *Dance at Bougival* (A. Renoir, 1883, Boston, Museum of Fine Arts). I was privileged to read early drafts of Tim Clark's book now titled *The Painting of Modern Life* and it was here that this impressionist territory was first lucidly mapped as a field of leisure and pleasure on the metropolitan/suburban axis. Another study to undertake this work is Theodore Reff, *Manet and Modern Paris*, Chicago, University of Chicago Press, 1982.

6 Clark, op. cit., 146.

7 Ibid., 253.

8 The tendency is the more marked in earlier drafts of material which appears in *The Painting of Modern Life*, e.g. 'Preliminaries to a possible teatment of *Olympia* in 1865', *Screen*, 1980, 21 (1), especially 33–7, and 'Manet's *Bar at the Folies-Bergère*' in Jean Beauroy *et al.* (eds), *The Wolf and the Lamb: Popular Culture in France*, Saratoga, Anma Libri, 1977. See also Clark, op. cit., 250–2, and contrast the radical reading of Manet's paintings which results from acknowledging the specificity of the presumed masculine spectator in Eunice Lipton's 'Manet and radicalised female imagery', *Art Forum*, March, 1975, 13 (7), and also Beatrice Farwell, 'Manet and the nude: a study of the iconography of the Second Empire', University of California, Los Angeles, PhD, 1973, published New York, Garland Press, 1981.

9 Tamar Garb, *Women Impressionists*, Oxford, Phaidon Press, 1987. The other two artists involved were Marie Bracquemond and Eva Gonzales.

10 Roszika Parker and Griselda Pollock, *Old Mistresses: Women, Art and Ideology*, London, Routledge & Kegan Paul, 1981, 38.

11 I refer for example to Edouard Manet, *Argenteuil Les Canotiers*, 1874 (Tournai, Musée des Beaux Arts) and to Edgar Degas, *Mary Cassatt at the Louvre*, 1879–80,

etching, third of twenty states (Chicago, Art Institute of Chicago). I am grateful to Nancy Underhill of the University of Queensland for raising this issue with me. See also Clark, op. cit., 165, 239 ff., for further discussion of this issue of flatness and its social meanings.

12 See also Berthe Morisot, *View of Paris from the Trocadéro*, 1872 (Santa Barbara, Museum of Art), where two women and a child are placed in a panoramic view of Paris but fenced off in a separate spatial compartment precisely from the urban landscape. Reff, op. cit., 38, reads this division quite (in)differently and finds the figures merely incidental, unwittingly complying with the social segregation upon which the painting's structure comments. It is furthermore interesting to note that both these scenes are painted quite close to the Morisot home in the Rue Franklin.

13 Griselda Pollock, *Mary Cassatt*, London, Jupiter Books, 1980. Contrast G. Cailebotte, *Portraits*, 1877 (New York, private collection).

14 See, for instance, M. Merleau-Ponty, 'Cézanne's doubt', in *Sense and Non-Sense*, translated by Hubert L. Dreyfus and Patricia Allen Dreyfus, Evanston, Illinois, Northwestern University Press, 1961.

15 Janet Wolff, 'The invisible *flâneuse*; women and the literature of modernity', *Theory, Culture and Society*, 1985, 2 (3): 37–48.

16 See George Simmel, 'The metropolis and mental life', in Richard Sennett (ed.), *Classic Essays in the Culture of the City*, New York, Appleton-Century-Crofts, 1969.

17 Richard Sennett, *The Fall of Public Man*, Cambridge, Cambridge University Press, 1977, 126.

18 Walter Benjamin, *Charles Baudelaire: Lyric Poet in the Era of High Capitalism*, London, New Left Books, 1973, chap. II, 'The flâneur', 36.

19 'What was new in the nineteenth century was not the ideal of the woman by the hearth, *la femme au foyer*, in itself, but the unprecedented scale on which it was propogated and diffused.' John MacMillan, *From Housewife to Harlot, French Nineteenth-Century Women*, Brighton, Harvester Press, 1981, 9. For an excellent study of the English case see Catherine Hall, 'The early formation of Victorian domestic ideology', in Sarah Burman (ed.), *Fit Work for Women*, London, St Martin's Press, 1979.

20 Jules Simon, *La Femme au vingtième siècle*, Paris, 1892, 67.

21 A fascinating interpretation of his process is offered in Bonnie G. Smith, *Ladies of the Leisure Class: The Bourgeoises of Northern France in the Nineteenth Century*, Princeton, Princeton University Press, 1981. She documents the shift from married women's active involvement in family business and management of financial affairs common in the early nineteenth century to the completed practice of domesticity, which involved total dissociation from family businesses and money, accomplished by the 1870s. See especially chapters 2–3.

22 Shirley Ardener, *Women and Space*, London, Croom Helm, 1981, 11–12

23 Catherine Hall and Leonore Davidoff, 'The architecture of public and private life: English middle-class society in a provincial town 1780–1850', in Derek Fraser and Anthony Sutcliffe (eds), *In Pursuit of Urban History*, London, Edward Arnold, 1983, 326–46.

24 Jules Simon, op. cit., quoted in MacMillan, op. cit., 37. MacMillan also quotes the novelist Daniel Lesuer, 'Le travail de la femme la déclasse', *L'Evolution Feminine: ses résultats economiques,* 1900, 5. My understanding of the complex ideological relations between public labour and the insinuation of immorality was much enhanced by Kate Stockwell's contributions to seminars on the topic at the University of Leeds, 1984–85.

25 Jules Michelet, *La Femme,* in *Oeuvres complètes* (Vol. XVIII, 1858–60), Paris, Flammarion, 1985, 413. In passing we can note that in a drawing for a print on the theme of omnibus travel, Mary Cassatt initially placed a man on the bench beside the woman, child and female companion (c. 1891, Washington, National Gallery of Art). In the print itself this masculine figure is erased.

26 Sennett, op. cit., 23.

27 *The Journals of Marie Bashkirtseff* (1890), introduced by Rozsika Parker and Griselda Pollock, London, Virago Press, 1985, entry for 2 January 1879, 347.

22 Meaghan Morris

'Things to Do with Shopping Centres'

from Susan Sheridan (ed.) *Grafts: Feminist Cultural Criticism* (1988)

The first thing I want to do is to cite a definition of modernity. It comes not from recent debates in feminist theory or aesthetics or cultural studies, but from a paper called 'Development in the Retail Scene' given in Perth in 1981 by John Lennen of Myer Shopping Centres. To begin his talk (to a seminar organized by the Australian Institute of Urban Studies), Lennen told this fable: 'As Adam and Eve were leaving the Garden of Eden, Adam turned to Eve and said, "Do not be distressed, my dear, we live in times of change."'[1] After quoting Adam, Lennen went on to say, 'Cities live in times of change. We must not be discouraged by change, but rather we must learn to manage change.' He meant that the role of shopping centres was changing from what it had been in the 1970s, and that retailers left struggling with the consequences (planning restrictions, post-boom economic conditions, new forms of competition) should not be discouraged, but should change their practices accordingly.

I want to discuss some issues for feminist criticism that emerge from a study I'm doing of the management of change in certain sites of 'cultural production' involving practices regularly, if by no means exclusively, carried out by women – shopping, driving, the organization of leisure, holiday and/or unemployment activities. By 'sites', I mean shopping centres, cars, highways, 'homes' and motels. It's a large project, and this essay is a kind of preface to one or two of its problems. The essay has a framing theme, however – the 'Edenic' allegories of consumerism in general, and of shopping centres in particular, that one can find elaborated in a number of different discourses (and cultural 'sites'). It also has an argument, which will take the form of a rambling response to three questions that I've often been asked by women with whom I've discussed the project.

One of these is very general: 'what's feminist about it?' I can't answer that in any direct or immediate way, since obviously 'feminism' is not a set of approved concerns and methods, a kind of planning code, against which one can measure one's own interests and aspirations. To be frank, it's a question that I find almost unintelligible. While I do understand the polemical, and sometimes theoretical, value of arguing that something is *not* feminist, to demand a definition of positive feminist identity seems to me to require so many final decisions to be taken, and to assume so much about shared and settled values, that it makes the very concept of a 'project' – undecided and unsettled – impossible. So I shall take this question here as an invitation to make up answers as I go, and the essay will be the response. (That's a way of saying that for me, the answer to 'what's feminist about it?' should be 'I don't know yet'.)

The other two questions are more specific, and relate particularly to shopping centres.[2]

The first question is asked almost invariably by women with whom I've discussed the topic of shopping. They say: 'Yes, you do semiotics . . . are you looking at how shopping centres are all the same everywhere? – laid out systematically, everyone can read them?' They don't ask about shopping centres and change, or about a semiotics of the management of change.

In fact, my emphasis is rather the opposite. It's true that at one level of analysis (and of our 'practice' of shopping centres), layout and design principles ensure that all centres are minimally readable to anyone literate in their use – that is, to almost if not quite everybody in the Western suburban culture I'm concerned with here. This 'readability' may be minimal indeed: many centres operate a strategy of alternating surprise and confusion with familiarity and harmony; and in different parts of any one centre, clarity and opacity will occur in different degrees of intensity for different 'users'. To a newcomer, for example, the major supermarket in an unfamiliar centre is usually more difficult to read than the spatial relations between the speciality food shops and the boutiques. Nevertheless, there are always some basic rules of contiguity and association at work to assist you to make a selection (of shops, as well as products).

However, I am more interested in a study that differentiates particular shopping centres. Differentiating shopping centres means, among other things, looking at how particular centres produce and maintain what the architectural writer Neville Quarry calls (in an appreciation of one particular effort) 'a unique sense of place'[3] – in other terms, a myth of identity. I see this as a 'feminist' project because it requires the predication of a more complex and localized affective relation to shopping spaces (and to the links between those spaces and other sites of domestic and familial labour) than does the scenario of the cruising grammarian reading similarity from place to place. In one way, all shoppers may be cruising grammarians. I do not need to deny this, however, in order to choose to concentrate instead on the ways that particular centres strive to become 'special', for better or for worse, in the everyday lives of women in local communities. Men, of course, may have this relation to *a* shopping centre, too. So my 'feminism' at this stage is defined in non-polemical and non-exclusive (that is, non-self-identical) terms.

Obviously, shopping centres produce a sense of place for economic, 'come-*hither*' reasons, and sometimes because the architects and planners involved may be committed, these days, to an aesthetics or even a politics of the local. But we cannot derive commentary on their function, people's responses to them, or their own cultural production of 'place' in and around them, from this economic rationale. Besides, shopping-centre identities aren't fixed, consistent or permanent. Shopping centres do get facelifts, and change their image – increasingly so as the great classic structures in any region begin to age, fade and date.

But the cost of renovating them (especially the larger ones) means that the identity effect produced by any one centre's spatial play in time is not only complex, highly nuanced and variable in detail, but also simple, massive and relatively enduring overall, and over time, in space. At every possible 'level' of analysis – and there are very many indeed with such a complex, continuous social event – shopping centres are overwhelmingly and constitutively paradoxical. This is one of the things that makes it very hard to differentiate them. On the one hand, they seem so monolithically present – solid, monumental, rigidly and indisputably on the landscape, and in our lives. On the other hand, when you try to dispute with them, they dissolve at any one point into a fluidity and indeterminacy that might suit any philosopher's delirium of an abstract femininity – partly because the shopping centre 'experience' at any one point includes the experience of crowds of people (or of their relative absence), and so of all the varied responses and uses that the centre provokes and contains.

To complicate matters, this *dual* quality is very much a part of shopping-centre strategies of appeal, their 'seductiveness', and also of their management of change. The stirring tension between the massive stability of the structure, and the continually shifting, ceaseless spectacle within and around the 'centre', is one of the things that people who like shopping centres really love about shopping centres. At the same time, shopping-centre management methods (and contracts) are very much directed towards organizing and unifying – at the level of admini-strative control, if not of achieved aesthetic effect – as much of this spectacle as possible by regulating tenant mix, signing and advertising styles, common space decor, festivities, and so on. This does not mean, however, that they succeed in 'managing' either the total spectacle (which includes what people do with what they provide) or the responses it provokes (and may include).

So the task of analysing shopping centres partly involves on the one hand exploring common sensations, perceptions and emotional states aroused by them (which can be negative, of course, as well as delirious), and on the other hand, battling against those perceptions and states in order to make a place from which to speak other than that of the fascinated describer – either standing 'outside' the spectacle *qua* ethnographer, or (in a pose which seems to me to amount to much the same thing) ostentatiously absorbed in her own absorption in it, *qua* celebrant of 'popular culture'.

If the former mode of description may be found in much sociology of con-sumerism, or 'leisure', the latter mode is the more common today in cultural studies – and it has its persuasive defenders. Iain Chambers, for example, has argued strongly that to appreciate the democratic 'potential' of the way that people live through (not 'alongside') culture – appropriating and transforming everyday life – we must first pursue the 'wide-eyed presentation of actualities' that Adorno disapproved of in some of Benjamin's work on Baudelaire.[4] It's difficult to disagree with this as a general orientation, and I don't. But if we look more closely at the terms of Adorno's objection (and leave aside here the vexed question of its pertinence to Benjamin's work), it's possible to read in them now a description of shopping-centre mystique: 'your study is located at the crossroads of magic and positivism. That spot is bewitched'.[5] With a confidence that feminist philosophers have taught us to question, Adorno continues that 'Only theory could break the spell . . .' (although in context, he means Benjamin's own theoretical practice, not a force of theory-in-general).

In my view, neither a strategy of 'wide-eyed presentation' nor a faith in theory as the exorcist is adequate to dealing with the critical problems posed by feminism in the analysis of 'everyday life'. If we locate our own study at that 'crossroads of magic and positivism' to be found in the grand central court of any large regional mall, then social experiences more complex than wide-eyed bewitchment are certain to occur – and to elicit, for a feminist, a more critical response than 'presentation' requires. If it is today fairly easy to reject the rationalist and gynophobic prejudice implied by Adorno's scenario (theory breaking the witch's spell), and if it is also easy to refuse the old critiques of 'consumption' as false consciousness (bewitchment by the mall), then it is perhaps not so easy at the moment *also* to question the 'wide-eyed' pose of critical amazement at the performance of the everyday.

There's a great deal to be said about that, but my one point here must be that at the very least, a feminist analysis of shopping centres will insist initially upon ambivalence about its objects rather than a simple astonishment 'before' them. Ambivalence allows a thinking of relations between contradictory states: it is also a 'pose', no doubt, but one that is probably more appropriate to an everyday practice of using the same shopping centres often, for different reasons (rather than visiting several occasionally, just in order to see the sights). Above all, it does not eliminate the moment of everyday discontent – of anger, frustration, sorrow, irritation, hatred, boredom, fatigue. Feminism is minimally a movement of discontent with 'the everyday' and with wide-eyed definitions of the everyday as 'the way things are'. While feminism too may proceed by 'staring hard at the realities of the contemporary world we all inhabit', as Chambers puts it, feminism also allows the possibility of rejecting what we see and refusing to take it as 'given'. Like effective shopping, feminist criticism includes moments of sharpened focus, narrowed gaze – of sceptical, if not paranoid, assessment. (This is a more polemical sense in which I shall consider this project to be 'feminist' in the context of cultural studies.)

Recent feminist theory in a number of academic domains has provided a great many tools for any critical study of myths of identity and difference, and the rhetoric of 'place' in everyday life. But in using them in shopping centres, I strike another difficulty: a rhetorical one this time, with resonances of interdisciplinary conflict. It's the difficulty of what can seem to be a lack, or lapse, of appropriateness between my discourse as feminist intellectual and my objects of study.

To put it bluntly: isn't there something really 'off' about mobilizing the weapons (and I use that violent metaphor deliberately) of an elite, possibly still fashionable but definitely *un*popular theoretical discourse against a major element in the lived culture of 'ordinary women' to whom that discourse might be as irrelevant as a stray copy of a book by Roland Barthes chosen to decorate a simulated yuppy apartment on display at Canberra's FREEDOM furniture showroom? And wouldn't using that discourse, and its weapons, be 'off' in a way that it isn't off to use them to reread Gertrude Stein, or other women modernists, or indeed to rewrite devalued and non-modernist writings by women so that they may be used to revise existing concepts of the literary canon?

Of course, these are not questions that any academic, even feminist, is obliged to ask or to answer. One can simply define one's 'object' strategically, in the limited way most appropriate to a determined disciplinary, and institutional, context. They are also questions that it's impossible to answer without challenging their terms – by pointing out, for example, that a politics of 'relevance', and 'appropriateness' (in so far as it can be calculated at all) depends as much on the 'from where' and the 'to whom' of any discourse as it does on its relations to an 'about'. For example, the reason that I referred to 'interdisciplinary conflict' above is that during my research, I have found the pertinence or even the 'good taste' of using a theoretical vocabulary derived from semiotics to discuss 'ordinary women's lives' questioned more severely by sociologists or historians (for whom the question becomes more urgent, perhaps, as so-called 'theory' becomes more respectable) than by non-academic (I do not say 'ordinary') women – who have been variously curious, indifferent or amused.

Nevertheless, these are questions that feminist intellectuals do ask each other; and we will no doubt continue to do so as long as we retain some sense of a wider social (as well as 'interdisciplinary') context and political import for our work. So I want to suggest the beginnings of an answer, one 'appropriate' to a cross-disciplinary gathering of feminist intellectuals, by questioning the function of the 'ordinary woman' as a figure in our polemics. As a feminist, I cannot and do not wish the image, or the reality, of other women away. As a semiotician, however, I must notice that 'images' of other women, even those which I've just constructed in mentioning 'them' as problem ('sociologists and historians' for me, rather than 'ordinary women'), are, in fact, images.

Take a visual image of the unnamed 'ordinary woman' walking through a shopping centre. Some image like this is perhaps what we have in mind if we talk about the gap between a feminist intellectual's discourse on shopping centres and her 'object of study'. But this particular image was originally published in an Australian government report on *The Shopping Centre as a Community Leisure Resource*.[6] It was in fact taken, without its subject's knowledge or consent, by a sociological surveillance camera at Sydney's Blacktown Westpoint shopping centre in 1977 or 1978. Framed as a still image, it proclaims its realist status: the candid-camera effect of capturing an iconic moment of spontaneity and joy is reinforced by bits of accessory reality protruding casually into the frame (stroller, vertical section of a 'companion'). These details help us to imagine that we *know what is happening here*: a young mother is strolling in the mall, enjoying herself enormously in its ambience, and sharing her pleasure with a friend. She becomes 'representative' of the leisure-resource potential of 'the shopping centre' for working-class women. ('The shopping centre', too, is abstracted as representative, since all we see of it is the speckled floor found in any downmarket centre any- where.) But of course, we only know what is happening in the image. We don't know what she is laughing at, how she felt about her companion – or her child – at that instant, what her expression was like two seconds before and after the moment she passed the camera, or what her ideas about shopping centres, or Blacktown Westpoint in particular, might have been.

This image of an ordinary woman, then, is not a glimpse of her reality, but a polemical declaration *about* reality mobilized between the authors (or better, the authority) of a governmental report and its readership. I can deduce very little about that woman at Blacktown, let alone about 'women' in 'shopping centres', from it. Nor can I adopt the pretence (as some sociologists still might) that my discourse, my camera or even my 'questionnaire', if I really had the real woman here to talk to now, would give me unmediated access to or true knowledge of her thoughts and feelings. Even her thoughts and feelings about shopping at Blacktown Westpoint now, or ten years ago. Above all, I cannot try to look through this image of a woman to my imaginary Real Woman and ask of her, '*What does shopping-woman want?*'.

So one possible step away from being 'off' is to construct my initial object of study as neither 'that woman', nor even her image, but the image of shopping-woman framed as illustration to the sociological *text*.

The study of shopping centres today is necessarily involved in a history of the positioning of women as objects of knowledges, indeed as targets for the man- oeuvres of retailers, planners, developers, sociologists, market researchers and so on. There's a lot of feminist research available now on precisely that, especially in relation to fashion and the history of department stores – research which also takes the further necessary step of writing histories of how the target *moves*, how the object *evades*: this is the study of women's resistance, action, creativity, or if you like, of cultural production, understood as the transformation of initially imposed constraints.[7]

But I would need then to take a second step away from being off, and also away from trying to be on target with/about women (as the Blacktown Westpoint image attempts to be), by challenging my initial question about the gap between my theoretical speech and its object. For having said that the text–image relation could be my object, the gap narrows too easily to a purely professional dispute (a critique of sociological constructions, for example). My difficulty in the shopping-centre project will thus be not simply my relation as intellectual to the culture I'm speaking 'about', but to whom I will imagine that I will be speaking. So if, in a first instance, the task of differentiating shopping centres involves a struggle with fascinated description – consuming and consumerist list-making, attempts to freeze and fix a spectacular reality – my second problem will be to produce a mode of address that will 'evade' the fascinated or mirroring relationship to both the institutional discourses 'about' women that I'm contesting, and the imaginary figure of Everywoman that those discourses – along with many feminist arguments – keep on throwing up.

However, in making that argument, I also evaded the problem of 'other' (rather than 'ordinary') women. I slid from restating the now conventional case that an image of a woman shopping is not a 'real' (or really representative) woman shopping to talking as though that difference absolved me from thinking about other women's ideas about their experience in shopping centres, as 'users' and as workers there. This is a problem of method, to which I'd like to return. First, I want to make a detour to consider the second enquiry I've had from 'other' women: 'What's the point of differentiating shopping centres? So what if they're *not* all the same?'

Here I want to make two points about method. The first is that if this project on 'Things To Do with Shopping Centres' could have a subtitle, it would be *'Pedestrian Notes on Modernity'*. I agree with Alice Jardine's argument in her book *Gynesis* that feminist criticism has much to gain from studying recent debates about 'modernity' in thought (that is, 'modernity' in the general European sense of life after industrialization – a sense which includes but is broader than the American aesthetic term 'postmodernity'). Those debates are important, not only because of the history of 'women' as an object of power-knowledge in the terms I described above, but because of the function of images of 'Woman' to signify the *problem* of (power) knowledge. I also agree with Jardine that as well as looking at how 'woman' or 'femininity' came to function as a fulcrum metaphor in those debates, especially in the 1970s, we need now to make a history of women modernists – instead of only and continually talking about mainly male philosophers (give or take a few female feminists) and the masculine avant gardes of nearly a century ago. However I don't think I do quite agree with Jardine that there's a risk of women becoming, as she puts it, 'that profoundly archaic silhouette – poet and madwoman – who finally took a peek at modernity and then quickly closed the door'.[8]

I think that if the broad impact of modernization in culture is seen as what's beyond the door, not just aesthetic and philosophical modern*ism* (a distinction which Jardine herself is careful to make), then women have had to go through that door *en masse* a long time ago; or, if we consider that the home has been one of the major experimental sites of modernization,[9] then 'modernity' has rather come through our doors whether we wished it so or not: and that if any archaic silhouette is peeking and hovering at a door, it's perhaps that of the theorist (feminist or otherwise) looking back, longingly, at aesthetic and philosophical dilemmas you can find made redundant on television, or on remainder at shoppingtown, any old day of the week. That's one sense in which I'd claim the word 'pedestrian'. Studying shopping centres should be (like studying women modernists) one way to contest the idea that you can find, for example, at moments in the work of Julia Kristeva, that the cultural production of 'actual women' has historically fallen short of a modernity understood as, or in terms derived from, the critical construction of modern*ism*.[10] In this project, I prefer to study instead the everyday, the so-called banal, the supposedly un- or non-experimental, asking not, 'why does it fall short of modernism?' but 'how do classical theories of modernism fall short of women's modernity?'

Secondly, the figure of the pedestrian gives me a way of imaging a critical method for analysing shopping centres that doesn't succumb unequivocally to the lure of using the classical images of the Imaginary, in the psychoanalytic sense, as a mirror to the shoppingtown spectacle. Such images are very common now in the literature about shopping centres: especially about big, enclosed, enveloping, 'spectacular' centres like one of those I'm studying, Indooroopilly Shoppingtown. Like department stores before them (and which they now usually contain), they are described as palaces of dreams, halls of mirrors, galleries of illusion ... and the fascinated analyst becomes identified as a theatre critic, reviewing the spectacle, herself in the spectacle, and the spectacle in herself. This rhetoric is closely related, of course, to the vision of shoppingtown as Eden, or paradise: the shopping centre is figured as, if not exactly utopian, then a mirror to utopian desire, the desire of fallen creatures nostalgic for the primal garden, yet aware that their paradise is now an illusion.

The pedestrian, or the woman walker, doesn't escape this dreamy ambivalence. Indeed, sociological studies suggest that women who don't come in cars to shopping centres spend much more time in them than those that do. The slow, evaluative, appreciatively critical relation is not enjoyed to the same extent by women who hit the carpark, grab the goods, and head on out as fast as possible. Obviously, different women do both at different times. But if walking around for a long time in one centre creates engagement with and absorption in the spectacle, then one sure way at least to begin from a sharply defined sense of critical estrangement is to arrive at a drive-in centre on foot – and have to find a way to walk in. (Most women non-drivers, of course, don't arrive on foot, especially with children – but by public transport: which can, in Australia, produce an acutely estranging effect.)

I have to insert a qualification here about the danger of constructing exemplary allegorical figures (even that of the 'woman walker') if they're taken to refer to some model of the 'empirical social user' of shopping centres. It's a fairly futile exercise to try to make generalizations, beyond statistical averaging, about the users of shopping centres at any particular time – even in terms of class, race, age or gender. It's true that where you find a centre in a socially homogenized area (very common in some suburban regions of most Australian cities), you do find a high incidence of regular use by specific social groups (which may contribute strongly to the centre's identity effect). At a lot of centres, nevertheless, that's not the case. And even where it is, such generalizations remain abstractions, for concrete reasons:

cars, public transport, visiting and tourist practices (since shopping centres can be used for sightseeing), and day-out patterns of movement, all mean that centres do not automatically 'reflect' the composition of their immediate social environment. Also, there are different practices of use in one centre on any one day: some people may be there for the one and only time in their lives; there are occasional users choosing that centre rather than this on that day for particular, or quite arbitrary reasons; people may shop at one centre and go to another to socialize or hang around. The use of centres as meeting places (and sometimes for free warmth and shelter) by young people, pensioners, the unemployed and the homeless is a familiar part of their social function – often planned for, now, by centre management (distribution of benches, video games, security guards). And many of a centre's habitual users may not always live in its vicinity.

Shopping centres illustrate very well, I think, the argument that you can't treat a public at a cultural event as directly expressive of social groups and classes, or their supposed sensibility.[11] Publics aren't stable, homogeneous entities – and polemical claims assuming that they are tell us little beyond the display of political position and identification being made by the speaker. These displays may be interesting in themselves, but they don't necessarily say much about the wider social realities such polemics often invoke.

Shopping-centre designers know this very well, in fact – and some recent retailing theory talks quite explicitly about the marketing need to break down the old standardized predication of a 'vast monolithic middle-class market' for shopping-centre product, that characterized the strategy of the 1970s.[12] The prevailing marketing philosophy for the 1980s (especially in the United States, but visible also in parts of Australia) has been rather to develop spectacles of 'diversity and market segmentation'. That is, to produce images of class, ethnic, age and gender *differentiation* in particular centres – not because a Vietnamized centre, for example, would better 'express' the target culture and better serve Vietnamese (though it may well do so, particularly since retail theorists seem to have pinched the idea partly from the forms of community politics), but because the display of difference will today increase a centre's 'tourist' appeal to everyone else from elsewhere.[13]

This is a response, of course, to the disintegration of the postwar 'middle class', and the ever-growing disparity in the developed nations between rich and poor. This change is quite menacing to the suburban shopping centres, however structurally complicit the companies that profit from them may have been in bringing the change about; and what's interesting is the attempt to 'manage' the change in terms of a differential thematization of 'shoppers' – and thus of the centres to serve them. Three years ago, one theorist imagined the future thus: 'Centres will be designed specifically to meet demands of the *economic* shopper, the *recreational* shopper, or the *pragmatic* shopper, and so on.'[14] His scenario is already being realized, although once again this does not mean that as 'shoppers' we do in fact conform to, let alone become, the proffered image of our 'demands'.

That said, I want to make one more point about pedestrian leisureliness and critical time. One thing that it's important to do with particular centres is to write them a (differential) history. This can be surprisingly difficult and time-consuming. The shopping centre 'form' itself – a form often described as 'one of the few new building types created in our time'[15] – certainly has had its histories written, mostly in heroic and expansive terms. But I've found empirically that while some local residents are able to tell stories of a particular development and its effects on their lives, the people who manage centres in Australia are often disconcerted at the suggestion that *their* centre could have a history. There are several obvious reasons for that – short-term employment patterns, employee and even managerial in-difference to the workplace, ideologies about what counts as proper history, the consecration of shopping centres to the perpetual present of consumption ('now-ness'), suspicion of 'media enquiries' (that is, of me) in centres hostile to publicity they don't control, and also the feeling that in many cases, the history is best forgotten. For example, the building of Indooroopilly Shoppingtown required the blitzing of a huge chunk of old residential Indooroopilly.

But there's a parallel avoidance of local shopping-centre histories in much of the critical writing on centres – except for those which (like Southdale Mall or Faneuil Hall Marketplace in the United States, and Roselands in Australia) figure as pioneers in the history of development. Leaving aside for the moment the material produced by commercial interests (which tends to be dominated, as one might expect, by complex economic and futuristic speculation developed, in relation to particular centres, along interventionist lines), I'd argue that an odd gap usually appears between, on the one hand, critical writing where the shopping place becomes the metaphorical site for a practice of personal reminiscence (auto-biography, the production of a written self), and on the other, the purely formal description of existing structures found in architectural criticism.[16] Walter Benjamin's *A Berlin Chronicle* (for older market forms) and Donald Horne's memoir of the site of Miranda Fair in *Money Made Us* are examples of the first practice, and the article by Neville Quarry that I've mentioned an example of the second.

The gap between these two genres (reminiscence and formal description) may in turn correspond to one produced by so-called 'Man-Environment' studies. For example, Amos Rapoport's influential book *The Meaning of the Built Environment* depends entirely on the humanist distinction between 'users' meanings' (the personal) and 'designers' meanings' (the professional).[17] I think that a feminist study of shopping centres should *occupy* this user/designer, memory/aesthetics gap, not, of course, to 'close' or to 'bridge' it, but to dislocate the relationship between the poles that create it, and so dissolve their imaginary autonomy. Of course, any vaguely anti-humanist critique would want to say as much. What is of particular interest to me as a feminist is to make relations between on the one hand those competing practices of 'place' (which Michel de Certeau calls 'spatial stories')[18] that by investing sites with meaning make them sites of social conflict, and on the other, women's discourses of memory and local history.

A shopping centre is a 'place' combining an extreme project of general 'planning' competence (efforts at total unification, total management) with an intense degree of aberrance and diversity in local performance. It is also a 'place' consecrated to timelessness and stasis (no clocks, perfect weather ...) yet lived and celebrated, lived and loathed, in intimately historic terms: for some, as ruptural event (catastrophic or Edenic) in the social experience of a community, for others, as the enduring scene (as the cinema once was, and the home still may be) of all the changes, fluctuations and repetitions of the passing of everyday life. For both of these reasons, a shopping centre seems to me to be a good place to begin to consider women's 'cultural production' of modernity.

This is also why I suggested that it can be important to write a history of particular shopping centres. It is one way in which the clash of conflicting pro-grammes for the management of change, and for resisting, refusing or evading 'management', can better be understood.

Such a history can be useful in other ways. It helps to denaturalize the myths of spectacular identity-in-place that centres produce in order to compete with each other, by analysing how these myths, those spectacles, are constructed for particular spaces over time. The qualification 'particular' is crucial, I think, because like many critics now I have my doubts that polemical demonstrations of the fact that such 'myth-making' takes place have much to offer a contemporary cultural politics. Like revelations of essentialism or, indeed, 'naturalism' in other people's arguments, simple demythologization all too often retrieves, at the end of the process, its own untransformed basic premises now masked as surprising conclu-sions. I also think that the project itself is anachronistic: commercial culture today proclaims and advertises, rather than 'naturalizes', its powers of artifice, myth invention, simulation.[19] In researching the history of myth-making in a particular place, however, one is obliged to consider how it works in concrete social circum-stances that inflect, in turn, its workings – and one is obliged to learn from that place, make discoveries, change the drift of one's analysis, rather than use it as a site of theoretical self-justification.

Secondly, such a history must assume that centres and their myths are actively transformed by their 'users' (although in very ambiguous ways) and that the history itself would count as one such transformation by a user. In my study this will mean, in practice, that I'm only going to analyse shopping centres that I know personally.

I'm not going to use them to tell my life story, but I am going to refuse the discursive position of externalized visitor/observer, or ethnographer/celebrant, by setting up as my objects only those centres where I have, or have had, some practice other than that of analyst – places I've lived near or used as consumer, window-shopper, tourist, or as escapee from a passing mood (since refuge, or R&R, is one of the social functions of shopping centres, though women who just hate them may find that hard to accept). As the sociologist John Carroll reports with the cheerfulness of the true conservative, 'The Promotions Manager of one of the Shopping World chains in Australia has speculated that these centres may replace Valium.'[20] Carroll doesn't add anything about their role in creating needs for Valium, or in selling it, but only if you combine all three functions do you get a sense, I think, of Shopping World's lived ambiguity.

And here I return to the question of 'other women' and my relation to their relation to these shopping centres. I've argued quite clearly, I hope, my objections in the present context to procedures of sampling 'representative' shoppers, framing exemplary figures, targeting empirical 'user groups', and so on. That doesn't mean that I think there's anything 'wrong' with those methods, that I wouldn't use them in another context or borrow, in this context, from studies which have used them. Nor does it mean that I think there's no way to produce knowledge of shopping centres except from 'personal experience' (which would preclude me, for example, from considering what it's like to work in one for years).

However I'm interested in something a little more fugitive – or pedestrian – than either a professionally based informatics, or a narcissistically enclosed reverie, can give me. I'm interested in impromptu shopping-centre encounters: chit-chat, with women I meet in and around and because of these centres that I know personally (ranging from close family friends at some to total strangers at others). Collecting chit-chat *in situ* is, of course, a pedestrian professional practice ('journalism'). But I also want to analyse it in terms of the theoretical concerns I've outlined (rather than as 'evidence' of how others really feel) as a means of doubting and revising, rather than confirming, my own 'planning' programme.

NOTES

1 Australian Institute of Urban Studies, *Shopping for a Retail Policy*, Canberra: AIUS Publication 99, 1982.

2 In this paper I normally use the term 'shopping centre' as the most common Australian synonym for what is elsewhere called a 'shopping mall'. 'Mall' is in one way less ambiguous, because less easily confused with the central 'shopping district' or 'downtown' (usually called in Australia, 'town' or 'the city'). However while 'mall' in Australia may be used in this sense, it more usually refers to a shopping street – mostly in 'town' – which is now closed to traffic.

3 Review of The Jam Factory in 'A Shopping Guide', unpublished paper. A different section of this paper is published as 'Knox City Shopping Centre: a review', *Architecture Australia*, November 1978, vol. 67, no. 5, p. 68.

4 Iain Chambers, *Popular Culture: The Metropolitan Experience*, New York and London 1986, p. 13.

5 Theodor Adorno, 'Letters to Walter Benjamin', in *Aesthetics and Politics* (translation editor Ronald Taylor, afterword by Fredric Jameson), London 1977, p. 129.

6 Department of Environment, Housing and Community Development, *The Shopping Centre as a Community Leisure Resource*, Australian Government Publishing Service, Canberra 1978.

7 A few examples are Rosalind Coward, *Female Desire*, London 1984; Angela McRobbie and Mica Nava (eds), *Gender and Generation*, London 1984 (especially the essay by Erica Carter, 'Alice in the Consumer Wonderland: West German case studies in gender and consumer culture', pp. 185–214): Judith Williamson,

Consuming Passions: The Dynamics of Popular Culture, London and New York 1986; Elizabeth Wilson, *Adorned in Dreams: Fashion and Modernity*, London 1985. For an essay with less emphasis on consumer evasiveness, see David Chaney, 'The Department Store as a Cultural Form', *Theory, Culture and Society*, vol. 1, no. 3, 1983, pp. 22–31. A more recent account of the debate about consumer 'productivity' is Mica Nava. 'Consumerism and its Contradictions', *Cultural Studies*, vol. 1, no. 2, 1987, pp. 204–10.

8 Alice Jardine, *Gynesis: Configurations of Woman and Modernity*, Ithaca, NY, and London 1985, p. 49.

9 See Stuart Ewen, *Captains of Consciousness: Advertising and the Social Roots of the Consumer Culture*, New York 1976; Stuart and Elizabeth Ewen, *Channels of Desire: Mass Images and the Shaping of American Consciousness*, New York 1982; Kerreen M. Reiger. *The Disenchantment of the Home: Modernizing the Australian Family 1880–1940*, Oxford 1985.

10 See for example the interview with Françoise van Rossum-Guyon, 'Questions à Julia Kristeva – A partir de Polylogue', *Revue des sciences humaines*, 168 (*Ecriture, fémininité, feminisme*) 1977, pp. 495–501.

11 See John Frow, 'Accounting for Tastes: Some Problems in Bourdieu's Sociology of Culture', *Cultural Studies*, vol. 1. no. 1, 1987, pp. 59–73.

12 George Sternlieb and James W. Hughes, 'Introduction: The Uncertain Future of Shopping Centres', in Sternlich and Hughes (eds), *Shopping Centers, USA*, New Jersey 1981, p. 3.

13 For an excellent early study of the relationship between tourism and 'social structural differentiation', see Dean MacCannell, *The Tourist: A New Theory of the Leisure Class*, New York 1975.

14 John A. Dawson, *Shopping Centre Development*, London and New York 1983, chap. 7.

15 Victor Gruen and Larry Smith, *Shopping Town USA*, New York 1960, p. 11. Victor Gruen is widely regarded as the inventor of the modern enclosed mall, and his book was influential on subsequent accounts. See for example, Nadine Beddington, *Design for Shopping Centres*, London 1982, p. 22.

16 This essay was written before I had an opportunity to read William Severini Kowinski's wonderful 'odyssey' of shopping-centre life in the USA, *The Malling of America: An Inside Look at the Great Consumer Paradise*, New York 1985.

17 For Rapoport, 'meanings are in people, not in objects or things. However *things do elicit meanings*. . . . Put differently, the question is how (and, of course, whether) meanings can be encoded in things in such a way that they can be decoded by intended users'. (*The Meaning of the Built Environment: A Nonverbal Communication Approach*, Beverly Hills 1982, p. 19.)

   In this approach, 'meaning' is treated as a sort of independent existing substance exchanged, or channelled, between complete, autonomous subjects. In spite of Rapoport's stress on 'nonverbal communication', his concept of 'meaning' corresponds to the perfectly conventional humanist model of verbal communication – precisely because it is a *communication* model rather than a theory of discourses.

18 Michel de Certeau, *The Practice of Everyday Life*, Berkeley and London 1984, pp. 115–31. I have tried to develop this notion further in my essay 'At Henry Parkes Motel', *Cultural Studies*, vol. 2, no. 1 1988 pp. 1–16, 29–47.

19. I have argued this in more detail via a critique of Roland Barthes's *Mythologies* in 'Sydney Tower', *Island Magazine*, 9/10, March 1982, pp. 53–66. Barthes's own well-known critique of his early work is 'Change the Object Itself', in Roland Barthes, *Image-Music-Text* (essays selected and translated by Stephen Heath), Glasgow, 1977, pp. 165–9; also available as 'Mythology Today', Roland Barthes, *The Rustle of Language*, trans. Richard Howard, Oxford 1986, pp. 65–8.

20 John Carroll, 'Shopping World: An Afternoon in the Palace of Modern Consumption', *Quadran*, August 1979, p. 15.

23 Mary McLeod

'Everyday and "Other" Spaces'

from Debra L. Coleman, Elizabeth Ann Danze and Carol Jane Henderson (eds),
Feminism and Architecture (1996)

One of the primary preoccupations of contemporary architecture theory is the concept of 'other' or 'otherness.' Members of the so-called neo-avant-garde – architects and critics frequently affiliated with publications such as *Assemblage* and *ANY* and with architecture schools such as Princeton, Columbia, SCI-Arc, and the Architectural Association – advocate the creation of a *new* architecture that is somehow totally 'other.' While these individuals repeatedly decry utopianism and the morality of form, they promote novelty and marginality as instruments of political subversion and cultural transgression. The spoken and unspoken assumption is that 'different' is good, that 'otherness' is automatically an improvement over the *status quo*.

While the formal and ideological allegiances of these advocates vary considerably, most fall into two broad categories. The first consists of self-identified proponents of deconstruction in architecture, who seek to find an architectural equivalent or parallel to the writings of Jacques Derrida. This group includes the so-called deconstructivists Peter Eisenman, Bernard Tschumi, Andrew Benjamin, Geoff Bennington, Mark Wigley, and Jeffrey Kipnis.[1] The second category is a diverse group of critics and theorists without any collective identity but who are all adherents of Michel Foucault's notion of 'heterotopia.' These include Anthony Vidler, Demetri Porphyrios, Aaron Betsky, Catherine Ingraham, and Edward Soja.[2]

The desire for 'otherness,' shared by these two groups, raises a series of questions concerning theory's political and cultural role that have been largely unexplored in recent architectural debate. To what extent is this preoccupation with 'otherness' a product of critics' and practitioners' own identity and status? Does it elucidate or support groups considered socially marginal or 'other'? Are there positions in architecture outside these two tendencies that address concerns of 'otherness' relevant to 'ordinary' people – those for whom the avant-garde has little significance?

The deconstructivists have argued that Derrida's notion of *différance* (a word play on 'differ' and 'defer') challenges the canons of architecture, such as function, structure, enclosure – in other words, that his claim that meaning is infinitely deferred and has no extra-linguistic beginning or end undermines any notion of architectural truth or foundation. Proponents, such as Eisenman and Wigley, value the disclosure of this instability as an end in itself. They claim that by revealing how binary oppositions such as form and content or structure and decoration are inscribed within a seemingly fixed, hierarchical structure and then eroded by the second or subordinate term in the opposition, the value system of architecture itself is eroded and put into flux. The second term is then seen as a condition of possibility for the whole system. For the most part, these theorists view the 'secondary,' the 'other,' as something largely internal to architecture. They assert that binary oppositions in architecture can be undone, or dismantled from within, through an investigation of the object. In his essay 'En Terror Firma: In Trails of Grotextes,' published in 1988 (the year of the Museum of Modern Art's *Deconstructivist Architecture* exhibition), Eisenman makes this explicit:

> Textual or textuality is that aspect of text which is a condition of otherness or secondarity. An example of this condition of otherness in architecture is a trace. If architecture is primarily presence – materiality, bricks and mortar – then otherness or secondarity would be trace, as the presence of absence. . . . This other architecture . . . this second text will always be within the first text and thus between traditional presence and absence, between being and non-being.[3]

Eisenman's discourse is itself slippery, and the buzz words change every six months: 'presence of absence,' 'grotesque,' 'monstrous,' 'the fold,' 'weak form,' 'slim mold,' 'anti-memory,' and, most recently, 'ungrounding the desire for grounding.' With the possible exception of the writings of his palimpsest phase, coincident with the design of the Wexner Center, his rhetoric, whether structuralist or post-structuralist, has consistently proclaimed architecture as 'independent discourse.' In his essay 'The End of the Classical, the End of the Beginning, the End of the End' (1984), he asserts that architecture is 'free of external values – classical or any other; that is, the intersection of the *meaning-free*, the *arbitrary*, and the *timeless* in the artificial.'[4] Bernard Tschumi has made similar claims in his oft-published account of La Villette. Although Tschumi alludes to intertextuality and applauds programmatic juxtaposition and experimentation, he asserts that 'La Villette . . . aims at an architecture that *means nothing*, an architecture of the significant other than the signified, one that is pure trace or play of language.'[5] Otherness is confined here to form (language) and textuality, refusing any reality outside the object (text).

As I have argued elsewhere, several of these deconstructivist practitioners have based their political claims on this strategy and its discourse.[6] Using words such as 'unease,' 'disintegration,' 'decentering,' 'dislocation,' and 'violation,' they have stated that their work subverts the *status quo* through formal disruptions and inversions within the object. Describing his Carnegie-Mellon Research Institute, Eisenman writes, for instance,

The presence of a 40' frame over a 45' solid leaves the outline of the 40' N-cube as a trace on the surface of the 45' cube. In this way the fallibility of man is seen as undercutting the hyperrationality of the forms of knowledge systems, leading to a new and complex condition of the beautiful.[7]

In other words, while such architecture forsakes the modern movement's political agenda, including the transformation of productive processes and institutional boundaries, it now gains political power simply through the cultural sign, or, more precisely, through revealing the disintegration of that sign. Newness and 'otherness' – traditional claims of the avant-garde – are largely an issue of formal strategy.

Although this tendency in architecture has found its most important theoretical source in Jacques Derrida's philosophy of deconstruction, other contemporary architecture critics have linked this new fragmented architecture (and what are sometimes considered its historical precedents, such as Piranesi's *Carceri* or *Campo Marzio*) with Foucault's more politicized concept of 'heterotopia' – literally 'other places.'[8] Here the notion of 'other' refers to that which is both formally and socially 'other.' Difference is a function of different locations and distributions of power, as well as formal or textual inversion. 'Other' is therefore not always an issue of 'within' but of arenas outside of or marginal to our daily life.

Foucault gives his most complete discussion of heterotopia in his essay 'Des Espaces autres,' a lecture that he delivered at a French architecture research institute in 1967 and which was not published in English until 1985.[9] Since it was written as a lecture, it lacks Foucault's usual rigor; his argument seems loose, almost conflicted at times, as if he were groping for examples. But it is also his most comprehensive discussion of physical space,[10] and its very looseness may account for its influence in recent architecture discourse.

In 'Des Espaces autres' Foucault distinguishes heterotopias from imaginary spaces – utopias – and from everyday landscapes. He proposes that certain unusual or out-of-the-ordinary places – the museum, the prison, the hospital, the cemetery, the theater, the church, the carnival, the vacation village, the barracks, the brothel, the place of sexual initiation, the colony – provide our most acute perceptions of the social order. These perceptions might derive either from a quality of disorder and multiplicity, as in the brothel, or from a kind of compensation, a laboratory-like perfection, as in the colony, which exposes the messy, ill-constructed nature of everyday reality. Many of the spaces cited, such as the prison or asylum, are exactly the arenas that Foucault condemns in his institutional studies for their insidious control and policing of the body. In this essay, however, his tone is neutral or even laudatory of those 'other' spaces. Foucault suggests that these heterotopic environments, by breaking with the banality of everyday existence and by granting us insight into our condition, are both privileged and politically charged. He asserts that they 'suspend, neutralize, or invert the set of relationships' that they designate.[11]

What are explicitly omitted in his list of 'other' spaces, however, are the residence, the workplace, the street, the shopping center, and the more mundane areas of everyday leisure, such as playgrounds, parks, sporting fields, restaurants, and cafés. (Cinemas, paradoxically, are both excluded and included as hetero-topias.) Indeed, in his emphasis on isolated institutions – monuments, asylums, or pleasure houses – he forsakes all the messy, in-between urban spaces that might be considered literally heterotopic. For most contemporary architecture critics, the political ambiguity and two-sided nature of Foucault's notion of heterotopia (its diversity or its extreme control) have been ignored. Following Foucault's alluring account of Borges' Chinese encyclopedia in *The Order of Things*, they interpret the concept simply as incongruous juxtaposition, all too frequently equating Foucault's notion of 'otherness' with Derrida's concept of *différance*.[12] With a kind of postmodern ease, critics have created a heterotopic tableau of these theories seeking to undermine order.

However, my objective here is not to expound upon the distinctions between Foucault's and Derrida's versions of poststructuralism in terms of architecture, although at times distinctions will be made. Nor is there the opportunity to expand on the philosophical differences in the meaning of the word 'other,' namely the differences between Sartre's reworking of a Hegelian other in existentialism and Lacan's notions of split subjectivity and linguistic drift.[13] Though certainly significant in philosophical and literary discourse, these distinctions, for better or worse, are typically blurred in architecture theory. The subject of this essay is a more basic issue: What are some of the limitations of a political and social vision of architecture that so exclusively focuses on 'otherness,' 'disruption,' and 'break,' and thus posits its political role as negation?

'GETTING A BIT OF THE OTHER' (WITH A DEBT TO SUZANNE MOORE)[14]

A paramount problem in poststructuralist theory generally and contemporary architecture theory specifically is the omission of any connections between an abstract notion of 'other' and women's actual social situation – connections that would seem to follow from their proponents' initial preoccupations. As critics have frequently noted, the positions taken by both Derrida and Foucault (and, one might add, the sometime poststructuralists Roland Barthes and Jacques Lacan) have much in common with feminist theories, especially in their rejection of a universal subject, originary essence, and the notion of objective truth – too often the viewpoint of the white Western male. In fact, one of the most continually repeated refrains in poststructuralist theory is the reassertion, indeed celebration, of the secondary or marginal that had been previously repressed. Focusing more specifically on a Derridean/Lacanian strain of poststructuralism (and momentarily leaving aside Foucault's more social model), femininity becomes 'lack,' 'absence,' the 'uncon-scious,' 'that which cannot be represented' – in short, the 'other.' It would appear, following this line of thought, that an architecture that seeks to represent 'the presence of absence,' an 'other' architecture, might be about women.

But how can an absence be about anyone? And is 'other' genuinely an 'other', or is it simply the all-too-common perspective of a repressed masculine discourse? These two questions – the first raising issues of subjecthood, the second alluding to the homogenizing quality of 'otherness' – point to the difficulties some feminist theorists have had with aspects of Derrida's and Lacan's legacy. As Nancy Hartstock has asserted:

> Why is it, exactly at the moment when so many of us who have been silenced begin to demand the right to name ourselves, to act as subjects rather than objects of history, that just then the concept of subjecthood becomes 'problematic.'[15]

The frequent equation of woman with 'lack' recalls Luce Irigaray's caustic critique of psychoanalysis as part of phallocentric culture. Is 'woman' the unconscious, as Lacan claims, or does a woman have one?[16] Do women have any positive identities apart from masculine models? What are women's own desires and social realities? For many women architects, the critical point is not just the undermining of binary oppositions, but the denial of women *per se*. Can you play Eisenman's game if you're not permitted to play, or not even recognized as a potential player? Or more importantly, can you create *different* games – new forms and spaces – if your very existence is denied? Must the rejection of essentialism imply absence?

Paradoxically, the poststructuralist rejection of masculine hierarchies has tended to essentialize all that is 'feminine.' All women become subsumed into the category of Woman, which then embodies all that is mystical, dark, and otherworldly. For deconstructivist architects, if they recognize the issue of Woman at all, to enter this 'dark continent' is in itself transgressive. Whereas modernism's universal subject excluded women, poststructuralism's celebration of 'otherness' presents another problem: Too often it consigns women to being the means of constructing the identity of men.[17] It is no accident that Peter Eisenman pays homage to *Blue Velvet*, in which women exist primarily as choices for men, as their 'other.'[18] However aesthetically alluring and richly ambiguous the film, part of its appeal for men (especially 'with-it' men) is that they can have 'their sex, their myths, their violence, and their politics, all at the same time.'[19] Instead of celebrating the avant-garde's desire for 'otherness,' architects and critics might investigate the desires of those multiple others, those actual, flesh-and-blood women. The feminine is experienced differently, at different times, in different cultures, by different people. The point is not just recognizing 'difference,' but all kinds of difference.

Foucault's conception of 'other' (*autre*) stands apart from Lacanian and Derridean models in that it suggests actual places and actual moments in time. It acknowledges that power is not simply an issue of language. And this insistence on seeing institutions and practices in political and social terms has been welcomed by many feminist theorists.[20] Yet, one of the most striking aspects of Foucault's notion of heterotopia is how his concept of 'other' spaces, in its emphasis on rupture, seems to exclude the traditional arenas of women and children, two of the groups that most rightly deserve the label 'other' (if by now one can abide the term's universalizing effect). Women have a place in his discussion primarily as sex objects – in the brothel, in the motel rented by the hour. (And what might be even harder for most working mothers to accept with a straight face is his exclusion of the house as a heterotopia because it is a 'place of rest.') Foucault seems to have an unconscious disdain for aspects of everyday life such as the home, the public park, and the department store that have been provinces where women have found not only oppression but also some degree of comfort, security, autonomy, and even freedom. In fact, the writings of Foucault and some of his architecture-critic followers (most notably, Mike Davis)[21] display an almost callous disregard for the needs of the less powerful – older people, the handicapped, the sick – who are more likely to seek security, comfort, and the pleasures of everyday life than to pursue the thrills of transgression and 'difference.' In applauding the rest home, for instance, as a microcosm elucidating social structures, Foucault never considers it from the eyes of the resident. Insight seems to be the privilege of the powerful.

Another major, and all-too-obvious, problem is the exclusion of minorities, the third world – indeed, most non-Western culture in architects' discussions of 'other.' Some of the same issues surrounding the end of subjectivity and the tourism of 'otherness' raised with regard to women are relevant here.[22] One of the most paradoxical aspects of Foucault's notion of heterotopia is his example of the colony. Although the concept of the 'other' has had a powerful influence since World War II on third-world political and cultural theorists (from Frantz Fanon to Edward Said),[23] Foucault himself never attempts to see the colony through the eyes of the colonized, just as in his earlier institutional studies he avoids the prisoner's viewpoint in his rejection of experiential analysis.[24] In philosophical and literary deconstruction, a major claim for political validity is the notion of dismantling European logocentricism. Yet despite this embrace of 'otherness' in some of its theoretical sources, poststructuralist tendencies in architecture posit a notion of 'other' that is solely a question of Western dismantling of Western conventions for a Western audience. Again, 'other' seems confined exclusively to a Western avant-garde. And once more, deconstructivist currents and the unconscious biases of Foucault appear to converge in architecture discourse.

Thus far, this argument about the exclusion of 'others' in the concept of 'other' has been restricted to theoretical propositions that have at best – perhaps fortunately – only marginal relation to the architecture produced by these practitioners, or by those that have been loosely grouped with them (such as Zaha Hadid, Daniel Libeskind, and Coop Himmelblau).[25] And by no means is the negative tone of these remarks meant to disparage the incredible aesthetic energy and invention of many of these designs. What is disturbing is the link between theory and the architecture culture surrounding this theory. In the United States the focus on transgression in contemporary architecture circles seems to have contributed to a whole atmosphere of machismo and neo-avant-garde aggression. The theoretical language of deconstructivist theory is violent and sharp; the architecture milieu is exclusive – like a boys' club. One is reminded how often avant-gardism is a more polite label for angry young men, sometimes graying young men. All too frequently, lecture series and symposia have at best a token representation of women – and no African Americans or non-Western architects from anywhere but Japan. One of the most telling examples was the first 'Anyone' conference, staged at the

Getty Center at immense expense. Among the twenty-five speakers, at a conference supposedly about the multiplicity, diversity, and fluidity of identity, there were only two women; and the men were all white American, white European, and Japanese.[26] In fairness, it should be noted that this exclusionary attitude is not the sole province of the deconstructivists. American and European postmodernists and proponents of regionalism are equally blind to the issues of the non-Western world beyond Japan. Most recently, the same charge might be brought against the Deleuzean 'de-form' nexus, despite its rhetoric of continuity and inclusion.[27]

These blatant social exclusions, under the mantle of a discourse that celebrates 'otherness' and 'difference,' raise the issue of whether contemporary theorists and deconstructivist architects have focused too exclusively on formal transgression and negation as a mode of practice. Undoubtedly, the difficult political climate of the past two decades and the economic recession of the late 1980s and early 1990s in the United States have contributed to the profession's hermeticism (namely, its rejection of constructive political strategies and institutional engagement), but the consequences of this retreat are now all too clear. Are there other formal and social options – options beyond transgression and nostalgia, deconstructivism and historicist postmodernism – that embrace the desires and needs of those outside the avant-garde?

EVERYDAY LIFE

The seduction and power of the writings of Derrida and Foucault, and their very dominance in American academic intellectual life, may have encouraged architects and theorists to leave unexplored another position linking space and power: the notion of 'everyday life' developed by French philosopher Henri Lefebvre from the 1930s through the 1970s and by cultural theorist Michel de Certeau shortly thereafter.[28] A peculiar synthesis of Surrealist and Marxist notions, Lefebvre's concept of everyday life might be best understood as a series of paradoxes. While the 'object of philosophy,' it is inherently nonphilosophical; while conveying an image of stability and immutability, it is transitory and uncertain; while unbearable in its monotony and routine, it is festive and playful. It is at once 'sustenance, clothing, furniture, homes, neighborhoods, environment' – material life – but with a 'dramatic attitude' and 'lyrical tone.' In short, everyday life is 'real life,' the 'here and now,' not abstract truth.[29] De Certeau, in his book *The Practice of Everyday Life* (*L'Invention du quotidien*, 1980) gives the notion of everyday life a somewhat more particularist, less Marxist cast, stressing the localized and transitory qualities of daily existence.

In contrast to Foucault, both these theorists not only analyze the tyranny and controls that have imposed themselves on 'everyday life,' but also explore the freedoms, joys, and diversity – what de Certeau describes as 'the network of anti-discipline' within everyday life.[30] Their concern is not only to depict the power of disciplinary technology, but also to reveal how society resists being reduced by it, not just in the unusual or removed places but in the most ordinary. And here, they place an emphasis on consumption without seeing it as solely a negative force, as some leftists have, but also as an arena of freedom, choice, creativity, and invention. De Certeau, who dedicated his seminal work *The Practice of Everyday Life* to the 'ordinary man,' is strangely silent on the issue of women (except for one female *flâneur* in his chapter 'Walking the City').[31] Lefebvre, however, despite moments of infuriating sexism and disturbingly essentialist rhetoric, seems to have an acute understanding of the role of the everyday in woman's experience and how consumption has been her demon but also her liberator, offering an arena of action that grants her entry and power in the public sphere. This argument has been further developed by several contemporary feminist theorists, including Janet Wolff, Elizabeth Wilson, Anne Friedberg, and Kristin Ross.[32] What these critics share, despite their many differences, is an emphasis on pleasure, the intensification of sensory impressions, the freedom and positive excesses of consumption as experiences that counter the webs of control and monotony in daily life. Here, 'other' is not so much a question of what is outside everyday life – events characterized by rupture, transgression, difference – but what is contained, and *potentially* contained, within it. In short, their emphasis is populist, not avant-garde.[33] They articulate a desire to bring happiness and pleasure to many, rather than merely to jolt those who have the textual or architectural sophistication to comprehend that a new formal break has been initiated. Of course, these two goals need not be exclusive.

EVERYDAY AND OTHER ARCHITECTURE

This notion of an 'intensification of the everyday' – and even an appreciation of the pleasures of consumption – is not something totally new to architecture or architecture criticism. Groups and individuals as diverse as the Situationists, the Independent Group, Denise Scott Brown and Robert Venturi, and Jane Jacobs have all addressed these issues. Tracing this lineage, however, requires a critical distance. While some of the attempts to embrace the 'everyday' have succeeded, or have at least suggested promising strategies, others now appear ineffectual or regressive, frequently carrying overtones of adolescent rebellion and machismo. Especially in the case of the Situationists, the differences between certain positions – notably, the celebration of shock, transgression, and violence – and deconstructivist theory are not so clear.

The Situationists, indebted to Lefebvre and to whom Lefebvre himself was indebted, proposed a complicated mixture of long-standing avant-garde practices involving negation and innovative strategies emphasizing everyday pleasure and its intensification.[34] Formally launched in July 1957, the Situationist project might be summarized as 'the liberation of everyday life.' This involved studying the whole range of diverse sensations that 'one encounters *by chance* in everyday life' and then proposing acts, situations, and environments that transformed the world in those same terms.[35] One of the major Situationist techniques was *dérive* – literally, 'drift' – a kind of mindless wandering in the city which would open up the existing environment to new considerations. Guy Debord's *Mémoires*, published in 1959, evoke, through a montage of assorted quotations, the nature of these new perceptions. The investigations of chance urban encounters, everyday locales (streets, cafés, bars), and the latent desires and techniques of mass culture (comics, film, advertising) – all for radical, new ends – convey a milieu more accessible and literally heterotopic than Foucault's 'other' spaces. The Situationists attacked both bourgeois art (high modernism) and earlier avant-gardist movements, explicitly denouncing the Futurists' 'technological optimism,' the Surrealists' 'ostentatious "weirdness,"' and Duchamp's 'gamelike rebellions.'[36] But as much as those of their predecessors, their visions of pleasure are permeated with sexism, a sexism inextricably entwined with their revulsion against bourgeois family life. They categorically ignore issues such as domesticity, childcare, reproduction – indeed, all aspects of women's situation in society; and their insistent allusions to sex, debauchery, violence, cruelty, and madness suggest a kind of puerile avant-gardism, one that may have unfortunately left its heritage in the deconstructivist movement.[37] The *Mémoires* feel, as critic Greil Marcus notes, 'like a drunken sprawl through the encyclopedia of common knowledge.'[38] (A quotation that appears on the first collage is 'our talk is full of booze.'[39]) Debord calls women 'girls'; and among his 'girls' are a model named Sylvie, a 'beautiful wife,' and 'poor' Ann – the young prostitute in Thomas De Quincey's *Confessions of an English Opium Eater*. Here, 'other' seems again to be for the benefit of male identity.

The few architecture projects by Dutch painter and architect Constant are among the most evocative and exhilarating aesthetic visions of the 1950s, anticipating the formal vocabulary of much deconstructivist work.[40] The Situationists' designs, in contrast to those of their formal heirs, are assertively constructive. Debord once claimed that his objective was to negate negation.[41] Yet, their program presents other difficulties. Although Constant's utopian scheme, New Babylon, dedicated to a postrevolutionary society of play, proposes a communal and festive use of space, it also carries peculiarly behavioralist connotations in its attempt to manufacture emotions.[42] What he calls the yellow sector shelters a complete zone of play, including labyrinthine houses for endless adventure; and there is also a deaf room, a screaming room, an echo room, a room of reflection, a room of rest, and a room of erotic play. The project's flexible walls and fluid modes of circulation are supposed to allow inhabitants to change their milieux, but pyschogeography's correlation between physical environment and emotion, and the suffocating sense of there being 'no exit' from this brave new world, seem to kill the very freedom of discovery and chance so celebrated by the group. Indeed, New Babylon's programmed indeterminacy eliminates privacy, domesticity, social obligations, and loyalties to locales – most of everyday life as we know it. Notions of drift, so difficult to make architectural, are reduced to a project for an admittedly seductive 'gypsy camp.'

Less overtly revolutionary and less rooted in philosophy, but with a stronger grasp of daily life as experienced by most, is the work of the Independent Group (IG) in London. In contrast to the Situationists' fascination with vagrants and bars, the participants of the IG examined more 'normative' conditions of working-class and lower middle-class domestic and commercial life. They embraced American mass culture as a foil to both the deprivations of postwar Britain and the sterility of modernist abstraction, and were especially attracted to an aspect of mass culture that had been largely neglected in the first phase of the modern movement: advertising. This break with the imagery of Machine Age production was a stand self-consciously proclaimed by Alison and Peter Smithson in their 1956 manifesto: 'Gropius wrote a book on grain silos, Le Corbusier one on aeroplanes.... But today we collect ads.'[43] Nor did the Smithsons overlook the feminine overtones of this new vision of mass culture when they alluded to the 'patron's wife who leafs through the magazines.'[44] The writings and designs of the Independent Group being to suggest the double nature of consumption as oppression and liberation, and its particular meaning to women.

The Smithsons' architecture clearly embodies an early critique of avant-garde elitism and its neglect of 'everyday' concerns. However inclusive the modern move- ment's initial objectives, by the 1950s it stood for stylistic formalism and abstract functionalism removed from actual human needs. Reyner Banham dubbed the Smithsons' work an *architecture autre* – not because of its iconoclastic margin- ality, but for its very insistence on banality and realism.[45] Housing, the street (not just the traffic corridor), and the playground were arenas to explore; and if their sensibility of pop humor meant including images of Joe Dimaggio and Marilyn Monroe in a photomontage of Golden Lane's street deck, the exterior views of this unbuilt housing complex showed existing urban blight with a poignant realism. Photographs of their few built projects included actual inhabitants (children, old people), not avant-garde drifters. The Smithsons' designs struck a delicate balance between invention and appreciation of the ordinary – a balance that was undoubt- edly appreciated by architects more than the population at large. While their refusal to compromise may have itself carried elitist overtones, their inclusive vision began to address (in the sphere of their profession at least) what Andreas Huyssen has called 'the Great Divide' between modernism and mass culture.[46] However, the IG's embrace of consumerist culture was not without its own political ambiguity. As Banham noted, 'We dig Pop which is acceptance – culture, capitalist, and yet in our formal politics, if I may use the phrase, most of us belong firmly on the other side.'[47]

Denise Scott Brown (one of the Smithson's ambivalent heirs) and Robert Venturi break even more definitively with modernist dogma in their advocacy of consumerist culture. In their publications, exhibitions, and teachings of the 1970s (most notably, *Learning from Las Vegas* and the Smithsonian Institution exhibition *Signs of Life*),[48] they allude to a world neglected in both modern architecture and Foucault's heterotopic landscape: the A & P supermarket, Levittown, mobile homes, fast-food stores – the milieu of ordinary middle- and lower-class people. *Learning from Las Vegas* does contain an overdose of honeymoon motels and gambling casinos, but in contrast to Foucault's heterotopic spaces or Anthony Vidler's ex- amples of the uncanny, this landscape is not privileged for its difference or strange- ness but taken as part of a continuum of daily existence. Like the Independent Group, Scott Brown and Venturi grant the world of women, children, and elderly people – domestic culture – a place in aesthetic culture. Even Dr Seuss receives homage in Scott Brown's 1971 *Casabella* essay, with its slogan 'Hop on pop.'[49]

What has been noted less frequently is that Scott Brown also gives one of the sharpest, and wittiest, critiques of the machismo underlying modern architecture and the profession at large. In *Learning from Las Vegas*, the authors characterize the modern movement as 'heroic and original,' 'violent, high adventure,' 'a bunch of angry young men under 30,' 'imposing on the whole landscape heroic representations of the masters' unique creations.' No less acerbic are their remarks about contemporary architecture in 1970. While the stalwart modern architects of that era are 'aging architectural revolutionaries who man the review boards and who have achieved aesthetic certainty,' avant-garde designers such as Archigram are the 'last, megalomaniac gasps' of a puerile rebellion: 'look Ma, no buildings.'[50] Scott Brown and Venturi's critique of the heroic gestural designs of the 1960s might apply equally well to more recent deconstructivist works:

> Our heroic and original symbols, from *carceri* to Cape Kennedy, feed our late Romantic egos and satisfy our lust for expressionistic, acrobatic space for a new age in architecture.[51]

Throughout *Learning from Las Vegas* Scott Brown and Venturi convey an intuitive understanding of the problems of universal subjectivity, an insight that some current architecture theorists would like to claim as their own. They use the term 'Man' sarcastically, for example, alluding to the aesthetic experts who 'build for Man rather than for people.'[52]

However, Scott Brown and Venturi's populism, which seems so removed from the iconoclastic *épater la bourgeoisie* of so much avant-gardism, raises other political issues. While they challenge the stance of heroic originality embedded in so much of modernism, their very preoccupation with the everyday becomes at times precariously close to an endorsement of the *status quo*. Must the affirmation of those groups traditionally neglected by the avant-garde necessarily preclude substantial invention and change? And does 'ordinary' necessarily have to be ugly or mundane? In short, one yearns for a bit more 'other' – another other, a new vision emerging from their very sensitivity to the everyday.

Arguably, the most influential critic to stress issues of the 'everyday' in architecture was a non-architect, Jane Jacobs, whose 1961 book *The Death and Life of Great American Cities* (published nearly a decade before *Learning from Las Vegas*) had a powerful impact on a whole generation of social and architecture critics that emerged in the 1960s and 1970s.[53] While the book preceded the advent of modern feminism in the United States and does not make gender a specific issue, Jacobs' urban landscape comes, as Elissa Rosenberg has argued, explicitly from a woman's experience.[54] A domestic perspective is critical to Jacobs' development of the idea of mixed use. This proposal is not only an attack on modern architecture's functional segregation but also an implicit challenge to the traditional split between domestic and public life.[55] Jacobs deliberately rejects theoretical models and relies on empirical observation to examine how space is actually used. Of the individuals discussed in this essay, she comes closest to realizing de Certeau's plea for an account of cities, not from the bird's-eye view, but from the experience of the pedestrian, the everyday user. And the terrain she describes is very different from that traversed by Baudelaire's *flâneurs*, from Foucault's prisons and brothels, or from the Situationist bars and gypsy encampments. What is evoked in her descriptions of New York City's West Village and Boston's North End is an informal public life: the world of the stoop, the neighborhood bakery, the dry-cleaning establishment, and, most importantly, the street; and with these come new subjects – mothers in the park, children, grocers, and newsstand attendants. In contrast to Foucault and Mike Davis, who are preoccupied with policing and control (a reflection, I would argue, of their own unspoken subjecthood as men, relatively strong men), Jacobs is concerned with freedom and safety for children, elderly people, and those most vulnerable to attack. She grants a public meaning to domestic life – one that refuses a segregation of the sexes as well as of functions.

This is a vision that shares much with postmodern thought: an interest in blurring categories, in diversity, in understanding and enjoying a genuinely heterotopic milieu. Jacobs' detailed and vibrant picture of daily urban life opens the door for a critical re-evaluation of social and functional divisions that are embodied in the physical form of modern economic development. But there is also a nostalgia and a conservative dimension to her interpretation of Hudson Street as a natural order. Her depiction of the city as a 'self-regulating system' overlooks the positive potential of human agency and cultural transformation, and despite her acute analysis of many aspects of daily life, the book offers few insights into confronting the connections between space and power.[56]

'OTHER' ARCHITECTURES

What I have tried to do in this brief survey is to point to another series of concerns that have somehow been forgotten in the plethora of recent theoretical writings surrounding deconstructivism. These examples are cited not as endorsement but as territory for rethinking. On the positive side, they offer models of architectural production that counter notions of both cultural elitism and isolated artistic rebellion, finding a stratum of creativity and invention in more familiar terrains. They explore – with different degrees of success – the gap between architecture and what people make of it, seeing its occupants no longer simply as passive consumers or victims but also as vital actors contributing a multiplicity of new images and modes of occupation. Although these groups and individuals cannot provide a framework for political action (nor would any except the Situationists claim to), they articulate a range of concerns neglected in traditional political analyses and theoretical critiques. Most optimistically, these architecture positions embody new social and cultural formations. Yet it must also be stated that any facile rehabilitation of the 'ordinary' readily becomes problematic. There is, of course, no 'common man,' just as there is no universal 'other.' Despite Lefebvre's and de Certeau's recognition of the polymorphous fluidity of the 'everyday,' populist tenets frequently homogenize and subsume stratifications of power, such as class, gender, and race, in the fray of contemporary architectural practice and polemics.

The 'ordinary' becomes a rationalization for market forces and passive consumption; 'common sense' becomes a means to avoid the rigors of ideological critique. However progressive and radically generative the proposals of Scott Brown and Jacobs were at their inception, the subsequent history of postmodern architecture, and its easy compliance with the boom forces of the 1980s, invites caution. Indeed, the blatant commodification of postmodernism fueled the attraction to deconstructivism's subversive claims.

But that time has passed, and now deconstructivism itself faces co-option. Transgression and shock have themselves become part of commodity culture (grunge, deconstructionist clothing, the 'junky' look, MoMA exhibitions, Decon coffee-table books); deconstructivist practitioners are firmly entrenched members of the cultural establishment. In this light, it appears that a reconsideration of everyday life might serve as an antidote not only to the solipsism and implicit biases in much contemporary architecture theory but also to the commodification of 'avant-garde' rebellion.

Recently, there have been a few signs of a shifting mentality in American architecture. 'Politics' – feminism, issues of gay and lesbian identity, race, ethnicity – have themselves begun to gain a certain fashionability in academic circles, though often in the framework of previous Derridean currents. It would seem these developments too might gain in vitality and breadth by a reconsideration of themes such as consumption, mass culture, and popular taste. Are there politically and aesthetically constructive positions beyond pure negation? Can buildings and urban space also be seen in terms of pleasure, comfort, humor, and emotion? Are there 'other' architectures to explore – ones that are less hermetic and more engaged in individuals' emotional and physical lives?

AFTERWORD

It is always safer for an architecture critic to avoid showing exemplary or instrumental images; not only does it save the critic from embarrassment (the examples rarely seem to live up to the grandiose claims), but it also invites closure. Nevertheless, I would like to propose – modestly – two urban places that I believe escape the mechanisms of discipline, and not primarily through negation or transgression. They are cited here neither as social prescriptions nor as formal models, but simply as places that might suggest other urban tactics. Both sites, perhaps not coincidentally, were designed in part by women, women not exactly at the forefront of the avant-garde culture (one early in her career, the other later). Both sites are populist, and highly popular with ordinary people. One is humorous, witty; the other is deeply contemplative involving participation. The first is Niki de Saint-Phalle and Jean Tinguely's Stravinsky Fountain adjacent to Centre Pompidou in Paris. The second is Maya Lin's Vietnam Veterans Memorial in Washington, DC. They present possibilities of architectural space beyond conformity or disruption, both everyday and other.

NOTES

1 By now, the publications of this group are numerous. Among the most notable are: Philip Johnson and Mark Wigley, *Deconstructivist Architecture* (New York: Museum of Modern Art and Boston: Little, Brown, 1988); Andreas Papadakis, Catherine Cooke, and Andrew Benjamin (eds), *Deconstruction: Omnibus Volume* (New York: Rizzoli, 1989); and Mark Wigley, *The Architecture of Deconstruction: Derrida's Haunt* (Cambridge, Mass.: MIT Press, 1993). Needless to say, any label such as 'deconstructivist' is reductive; not only do the positions of individual proponents vary, but they have also changed over time. Nonetheless, all the individuals cited have frequently published their writings and designs under the rubric of 'deconstruction' or 'deconstructivism.'

2 See Anthony Vidler, *The Architectural Uncanny: Essays in the Modern Unhomely* (Cambridge, Mass.: MIT Press, 1992); Demetri Porphyrios, *Sources of Modern Eclecticism: Studies of Alvar Aalto* (London: Academy Editions, 1982); Aaron Betsky, *Violated Perfection: Architecture and the Fragmentation of the Modern* (New York: Rizzoli, 1990); Catherine Ingraham, 'Utopia/Heterotopia' (course description of class given at Columbia University), in *Deconstruction III*, ed. Andreas Papadakis, Architectural Design Profile No. 87 (London: Academy Editions, 1994); and Edward Soja, *Postmodern Geographies: The Reassertion of Space in Critical Social Theory* (London: Verso, 1989). To the best of my knowledge, Porphyrios's book, based on his Princeton doctoral dissertation, was the first architecture publication in the English-speaking world to cite Foucault's notion of heterotopia. Anthony Vidler was his doctoral advisor. Although Vidler does not specifically mention heterotopia in *The Architectural Uncanny*, he cites Foucault on numerous occasions and adopts David Carroll's notion of 'paraesthetics,' which is indebted to Foucault. See David Carroll, *Paraesthetics: Foucault, Lyotard, Derrida* (New York: Methuen, 1987). In several publications, Manfredo Tafuri also alludes sympathetically to Foucault's notion of heterotopia, and Tafuri's interpretation of Piranesi's work as encapsulating the crisis of Enlightenment reason reveals certain parallels with Foucault's claims for heterotopic environments. See especially Manfredo Tafuri, "'The Wicked Architect": G.B. Piranesi, Heterotopia, and the Voyage,' in *The Sphere and the Labyrinth: Avant-Gardes and Architecture from Piranesi to the 1970s*, trans. Pellegrino d'Acierno and Robert Connolly (Cambridge, Mass.: MIT Press, 1987). The complexity of Tafuri's project of ideological demystification and its multiplicity of intellectual sources, however, separates his interest in Foucault from the instrumental applications of many architecture critics.

3 Peter Eisenman, 'En Terror Firma: In Trails of Grotextes,' *Pratt Journal of Architecture*, no. 2 (Spring 1988), reprinted in *Deconstruction: Omnibus Volume*, 153.

4 Peter Eisenman, 'The End of the Classical, the End of the Beginning, the End of the End,' *Perspecta*, no. 21 (1984): 166.

5 Bernard Tschumi, *Cinégramme Folie: Le Parc de la Villette* (Princeton: Princeton Architectural Press, 1987), vii. This essay has been frequently republished, most recently in Bernard Tschumi, *Architecture and Disjunction* (Cambridge, Mass.: MIT

Press, 1994). Although the essay was significantly rewritten in this last publication, it retains the quoted passage.

6 Mary McLeod, 'Architecture and Politics in the Reagan Era: From Postmodernism to Deconstructivism,' *Assemblage*, no. 8 (February 1989): 50–1.

7 Peter Eisenman, 'Carnegie-Mellon Research Institute,' in *Deconstruction: Omnibus Volume*, 172–3. In a 1992 interview Eisenman makes the nature of his 'critical' position explicit: 'My desire is to displace from within, from the center.' See Alan Balfour *et al.*, 'Conversation with Peter Eisenman,' in *Cities of Artificial Excavation: The Work of Peter Eisenman*, 1978, 1988, ed. Jean-François Bédard (Montreal: Centre Canadien d'Architecture and Rizzoli, 1994), 128.

8 Italian philosopher Gianni Vattimo also uses the notion 'heterotopia,' though in a different manner from Foucault. For Vattimo, 'heterotopia' alludes to the plurality of norms that distinguishes late-modern art (since the 1960s) from modern art. Gianni Vattimo, 'From Utopia to Heterotopia,' in *Transparent Society*, trans. David Webb (Baltimore: Johns Hopkins University Press, 1992), 62–75. Vattimo's writings have influenced European architecture debate, but have had little impact on American architecture theory.

9 Michel Foucault, 'Of Other Spaces: Utopias and Heterotopias,' in *Architecture, Culture, 1943–1968: A Documentary Anthology*, ed. Joan Ockman with Edward Eigen (New York: Columbia Books of Architecture and Rizzoli, 1993), 420–26. The paper was first delivered at the Centre d'études architecturales, Paris, March 1967. A brief account of the essay's publishing history is given in Ockman, 419.

10 Despite Foucault's interest in institutions and his insistent use of spatial metaphors, discussions of physical urban space such as cities, streets, and parks are rare in his work. Philosopher Henri Lefebvre charged, probably legitimately, that Foucault was more concerned with a metaphorical notion of space – 'mental space' – than with lived space, 'the space of people who deal with material things'. See Henri Lefebvre, *The Production of Space*, trans. Donald Nicholson-Smith (Oxford: Blackwell, 1991; original French ed., 1974), 3–4. Besides his paper 'Les Espaces autres,' Foucault's most concrete discussions of physical space can be found in interviews from the last decade of his life. See, for instance, 'Questions on Geography' (1976) and 'The Eye of Power' (1977), in *Power/Knowledge: Selected Interviews and Other Writings 1972–77*, ed. Colin Gordon (New York: Pantheon Books, 1980); 'Space, Knowledge, and Power' (1982) in *The Foucault Reader*, ed. Paul Rabinow (New York: Pantheon Books, 1984); and, especially, 'An Ethics of Pleasure', in *Foucault Live (Interviews, 1966–84)*, ed. Sylvère Lotringer (New York: Semiotext(e), 1989), 257–77. In this last interview, Foucault distinguishes architects from doctors, priests, psychiatrists, and prison wardens, claiming that the architect does not exercise (or serve as a vehicle of) as much power as the other professionals. Foucault's own class status and power are revealed when he states, 'After all, the architecture has no power over me. If I want to tear down or change a house he built for me, put up new partitions, add a chimney, the architect has no control' (267). Surely, few occupants of public housing projects or nursing homes could or would make the same statement.

11 Foucault, 'Of Other Spaces,' 421–22.

12 Michel Foucault, preface to *The Order of Things: An Archaeology of Human Sciences* (New York: Vintage Books, 1970), xv–xx. Foucault's notion of heterotopia outlined in his oft-quoted preface from 1966 is more abstract than that given in his 1967 essay. In the earlier account, Foucault describes heterotopias as 'impossible to think' – spaces without 'site' which challenge the order and the language that allow 'words and things . . . to "hold together" . . . [They] desiccate speech, stop words in their tracks, contest the very possibility of language at its sources.' Architects have largely ignored the fluidity and radicality of Foucault's concept in *The Order of Things* (as well as its theoretical shortcomings), adopting it as a catch-all term for postmodern plurality and as a means to validate discordant geometries and frag-mented forms. See Porphyrios, *Sources of Modern Eclecticism*; Georges Teyssot, 'Heterotopias and the History of Spaces,' *A+U* (October 1980): 80–100; and Stanley Allen, 'Piranesi's *Campo Marzio*: An Experimental Design', *Assemblage*, no. 10 (December 1989): 77. A more nuanced historical application is provided by Georges Teyssot in 'Heterotopias and the History of Spaces,' *A+U* (October 1980): 80–100. Teyssot distinguishes between Foucault's epistemological and spatial notions of heterotopia but does not elaborate on the tensions between them.

13 For concise accounts of the 'problem of other,' see Vincent Descombes, *Modern French Philosophy*, trans. L. Scott-Fox and J.M. Harding (Cambridge: Cambridge University Press, 1980), and Elizabeth Grosz, *Sexual Subversions* (Sydney: Allen and Unwin, 1989), 1–38. For a discussion of the 'problem of other' and its relation to gender and colonial/postcolonial theory in the context of architecture, see Zeynep Çelik and Leila Kinney, 'Ethnography and Exhibitionism at the Expositions Universelles,' *Assemblage*, no. 13 (December 1990), esp. 54–6.

14 Suzanne Moore, 'Getting a Bit of the Other: The Pimps of Postmodernism,' in *Male Order*, eds Rowena Chapman and Jonathan Rutherford (Oxford: Wichart, 1988), 165–92. I am indebted to this strong and witty argument for articulating some of my own long-standing frustrations with the masculine biases of some post-structuralist theory.

15 Nancy Hartsock, 'Rethinking Modernism,' *Cultural Critique*, no. 7 (Fall 1987), 187–206. Similarly, Andreas Huyssen asks, 'Isn't the "death of the subject/author" position tied by mere reversal to the very ideology that invariably glorifies the artist as genius? . . . Doesn't poststructuralism, where it simply denies the subject alto-gether, jettison the chance of challenging the *ideology of the subject* (as male, white, and middle-class) by developing alternative and different notions of subj-ectivity?' Andreas Huyssen, 'Mapping the Postmodern,' in *After the Great Divide: Modernism, Mass Culture, Postmodernism* (Bloomington: Indiana University Press, 1986), 213. See also Frances E. Mascia-Lees, Patricia Sharpe, and Colleen Ballerino Cohen, 'The Postmodern Turn in Anthropology: Cautions from a Feminist Perspec-tive,' *Signs* 15, no. 1 (1989): 15.

16 Irigaray argues that Lacan's revision of Freud is even more constraining for women than his predecessor's biological model, where anatomy served as proof/alibi for the differences between the sexes. She reminds us that language presents its own

prison, given that its laws 'have been prescribed by male subjects for centuries.' Irigaray further charges that Lacan seeks woman out only 'as lack, as fault or flaw,' and that 'it is inasmuch as she [woman] does not exist that she sustains the desire of these "speaking beings" that are called men.' Luce Irigaray, 'Cosi Fan Tutti' (1975), in *This Sex which Is Not One*, trans. Catherine Porter (Ithaca: Cornell University Press, 1985), 87, 89. See also Moore, 190.

17 Already in 1949, Simone de Beauvoir in *The Second Sex* argued that men gained their own identity as subjects by constructing woman as the 'other'. Simone de Beauvoir, *The Second Sex*, trans. H.M. Parshley (New York: Knopf, 1952).

18 This was a major theme in the three lectures that Eisenman delivered at Columbia University in the spring of 1991 (March 25, March 28, April 1, April 4), entitled 'Weak Form: Architecture in a Mediated Environment.'

19 Norman K. Denzin, '*Blue Velvet*: Postmodern Contradictions,' *Theory, Culture and Society* 5, no. 4 (1988): 472. In Denzin's essay this passage alludes to 'postmodern individuals,' but his assertion seems most relevant to male viewers.

20 Although many feminists have appreciated Foucault's analyses of power and his emphasis on the body as a target of disciplinary practices, some feminists have criticized him for failing to provide a normative basis for action and for bypassing the problem of political agency. See especially Nancy Fraser, *Unruly Practice: Power, Discourse and Gender in Contemporary Social Theory* (Minneapolis: University of Minnesota Press, 1989). For other feminist interpretations of Foucault, see Irene Diamond and Lee Quinby, eds, *Feminism and Foucault: Reflections on Resistance* (Boston: Northeastern University Press, 1988), and Jana Sawicki, *Disciplining Foucault: Feminism, Power, and the Body* (New York: Routledge, 1991).

21 Mike Davis, *City of Quartz: Excavating the Future in Los Angeles* (London and New York: Verso, 1990). This aspect of Davis's eloquent and moving text has been largely ignored by critics.

22 Kristin Ross's observation about the struggles of colonized peoples parallels the quotation of Hartsock cited earlier: 'Precisely at the moment that colonized peoples demand and appropriate to themselves the status of men … French intellectuals announce "the death of man."' Kristin Ross, *Fast Cars, Clean Bodies: Decolonization and the Reordering of French Culture* (Cambridge, Mass.: MIT Press, 1995), 163.

23 Recently, postcolonial critics such as Homi Bhabha and Gayatri Spivak have challenged the manichaeism or binary logic implicit in Fanon's and Said's understanding of colonial identity. See especially Homi K. Bhabha's essay 'The Other Question: Stereotype, Discrimination and the Discourse of Colonialism,' in *The Location of Culture* (London and New York: Routledge, 1994) for a critique of phenomenology's opposition between subject and object and its extension into the discourse of colonialism as a rigid division between colonizer and colonized.

24 Although one can be sympathetic to Foucault's wish to avoid speaking for others, his magisterial tone and his refusal to acknowledge voice and perspective in his early institutional studies give the impression that he is stating universal truths, despite his own demystification of conventional Enlightenment truths. Too often his ex-

clusion of certain 'others' (for instance, his medical study gives only the briefest reference to issues of reproduction and women's health) results in myopia.

25 Certainly, La Villette and the Wexner Center, the two iconic built projects most cited by deconstructivist theorists, are enjoyed by women and children as much as men, with the possible exception of the predominantly female staff at the Wexner, who are squeezed into extremely tight quarters.

26 One of the women speakers, Maria Nordman, limited her remarks to a request that the windows be opened to let in light and that the method of seating be decentralized; she chose to sit in the audience during her presentation. *Anyone* (New York: Rizzoli, 1991), 198–9. A third woman – Cynthia Davidson, the editor of *Anyone* – might arguably be included in the list of participants, although this publication does not provide a short biographical statement for her, as it does for the speakers. Subsequent *ANY* events have included more women, perhaps in response to public outrage, but minority architects have yet to be substantially involved. In the 1994 catalogue of Eisenman's architecture, *Cities of Artificial Excavation*, none of the eight authors is a woman, nor are any of the seven interviewers. Just as scandalous is the track record of the evening lecture series at Columbia University's architecture school (an institution that prides itself on being avant-garde). Not once in the past six years has the semester series included more than two women as speakers; and there have been no African Americans.

27 On another occasion, I hope to address the masculine assumptions underlying this new current in architecture theory, which seems to have its greatest energy in New York, and almost exclusively among young men. While Deleuze and Guattari reject the bipolarity latent in much Derridean thought and are more materially grounded, their 'becoming – animal, becoming – woman' again suggests their (*male*) desire. As in Foucault's work, what is neglected in their exhilarating vision of fluidity and flow (for instance, domesticity, children, the elderly) is telling, and strikingly reminiscent of the machismo of some male leaders of the New Left in the 1960s.

28 The notion of 'everyday life' can be a frustratingly amorphous concept, and Lefebvre's intensely dialectical approach, combined with his rejection of traditional philosophical rationalism ('truth without reality'), makes it all the more difficult to decipher. His encompassing vision of daily life contrasts sharply with Foucault's concept of heterotopias as isolated and removed spaces. Although Lefebvre's and de Certeau's notions of everyday life both counter Foucault's bleaker, more paranoid vision of disciplinary controls, it must also be acknowledged that there are important differences between the two theorists which become more pronounced after 1968. More than de Certeau, Lefebvre acknowledges the tyrannies, monotonies, and inertia of daily existence as well as its spontaneous moments of invention and festival. Although in the wake of 1968 de Certeau frequently alluded to '*quadrillage*' and the disciplinary surveillance of mass society, by 1980 his vision was more optimistic – indeed idealistic – seeing daily life primarily as endlessly creative, useful, and efficacious. See Henri Lefebvre, *Everyday Life in the Modern World*, trans. Sacha Rabinovitch (New Brunswick, NJ, and London: Transaction Publishers, 1984); Henri Lefebvre, *The Production of Space*; Michel de Certeau, *The Practice of*

Everyday Life, trans. Steven Rendall (Berkeley: University of California Press, 1984); and Michel de Certeau, *Heterologies: Discourse on the Other*, trans. Brian Massumi (Minneapolis: University of Minnesota Press, 1986).

29 Lefebvre, *Everyday Life in the Modern World*, 17–22.

30 De Certeau, *The Practice of Everyday Life*, xv. When he uses this phrase, de Certeau cites in a footnote Lefebvre's work on everyday life as a 'fundamental source.'

31 In his introduction there is also one parenthetical reference to a housewife shopping in a supermarket (ibid., xix). Although de Certeau discusses many activities in which women are central – leisure, consumption, cooking – he rarely considers these subjects in terms of their particular implications for women. Nonetheless, his interest in resistance and in minority positions and his insistence on the specificity of place and the particularity of subject positions makes his writing especially relevant to those groups whose creative activities and tactics of resistance have been traditionally obscured.

32 See Janet Wolff, *Feminine Sentences: Essays on Women and Culture* (Berkeley: University of California Press, 1990), esp. 34–50; Elizabeth Wilson, *The Sphinx in the City: Urban Life, the Control of Disorder, and Women* (Berkeley: University of California Press, 1991); Anne Friedberg, *Window Shopping: Cinema and the Postmodern* (Berkeley: University of California Press, 1993); Kristin Ross, introduction to *The Ladies' Paradise*, by Emile Zola (Berkeley: University of California Press, 1992); and Ross, *Fast Cars, Clean Bodies*. Of the critics cited here, Ross is the most indebted to Lefebvre, and, like Lefebvre, she stresses consumption's double-sided nature. For an insightful discussion of consumption and women's role with regard to architecture, see Leila Whitemore, 'Women and the Architecture of Fashion in nineteenth-century Paris,' *a/r/t*, 'Public Space,' no. 5 (1994–95): 14–25.

33 In contrast to a lineage of French theorists prior to 1968, I am not opposing popular culture to mass culture; rather, like de Certeau, I see them as increasingly synonymous.

34 Despite the Situationists' obvious debt to Lefebvre, by the mid-1960s they were frequently critical of Lefebvre, accusing him of presenting an 'appearance' of freedom in place of an 'authentic' experience. Lefebvre continued to praise Constant's projects in his writings, but by 1960 Constant himself had left the Situationists due to his differences with Debord about the role of artistic production. The best overview of the Situationists can be found in the catalogue of an exhibition sponsored by the Institute of Contemporary Art in Boston, *On the Passage of a Few People Through a Rather Brief Moment in Time: The Situationist International 1957–1972*, ed. Elisabeth Sussman (Cambridge, Mass.: MIT Press, 1989). Peter Wollen's essay 'Bitter Victory: The Art and Politics of the Situationists', is especially useful. See also Sadie Plant, *The Most Radical Gesture: The Situationist International in a Postmodern Age* (London and New York: Routledge, 1992), and Ken Knabb, ed. and trans., *Situationist International Anthology* (Berkeley: Bureau of Public Secrets, 1981 [orig. publication date, no copyright]; 2nd print, 1989).

35 Ivan Chtcheglov, 'Formulary for a New Urbanism,' 1953, in *Situationist International Anthology*, 4.

36 Guy Debord, 'Report on the Construction of Situations and on the International Situationist Tendency's Conditions of Organization and Action', 1957, in *Situationist International Anthology*, 18,19.

37 Some of the themes of Bernard Tschumi's early writings and projects (transgression, lust, violence, murder) recall those of Situationist works. See, for example, *Space: A Thousand Words* (London: Royal College of Art Gallery, 1975); *The Manhattan Transcripts* (New York and London: St Martin's Press/Academy Editions, 1981); and *Questions of Space*, Text 5 (London: Architectural Association, 1990). It should also be noted that Tschumi acknowledges Lefebvre as a source in his writings of the early and mid-1970s.

38 Greil, Marcus, in *On the Passage*, 127.

39 Ibid., 128.

40 Constant's full name was Constant Nieuwenhuys. In 1953 he collaborated with Dutch architect Aldo Van Eyck on a color–space installation. The most complete account of Constant, including a selection of his writings, is Jean-Clarence Lambert, *Constant: Les Trois Espaces* (Paris: Editions Cercle d'Art, 1992). Despite the obvious influence of Constant's work on Tschumi and other so-called deconstructivists, the Situationists are not mentioned in the Museum of Modern Art's catalogue *Deconstructivist Architecture*.

41 In an article written with Gil J. Wolman, Debord states: 'It is necessary to go beyond any idea of scandal. Since the negation of the bourgeois conception of art and artistic genius has become pretty much old hat, [Duchamp's] drawing of a mustache on the *Mona Lisa* is no more interesting than the original version of that painting. We must now push this process to the point of negating the negation.' Guy Debord and Gil J. Wolman, 'Methods of Detournement,' *Les Lèvres nues*, no. 8 (May 1956), reprinted in Knabb, ed., *Situationist Anthology*, 9.

42 Constant, 'New Babylon,' in *Programs and Manifestos on Twentieth Century Architecture*, ed. Ulrich Conrads, trans. Michael Bullock (Cambridge, Mass.: MIT Press, 1970), 177–8; Constant, 'Description de la zone jaune,' *Internationale situationniste*, no. 4 (June 1960): 23–6. See also the suggestive commentary by Anthony Vidler, 'Vagabond Architecture,' in *The Architectural Uncanny: Essays in the Modern Unhomely*, 212–13, and Hilde Heynen, 'New Babylon: The Antinomies of Utopia', *Assemblage*, no. 29 (April 1996), 24–39.

43 Alison and Peter Smithson, 'But Today We Collect Ads,' *Ark* 18 (November 1956), reprinted in David Robbins, ed. *The Independent Group: Postwar Britain and the Aesthetics of Plenty* (Cambridge, Mass.: MIT Press, 1990), 185.

44 Ibid., 186. It is perhaps not coincidental that women played an active, if less overtly public, role in the Independent Group. Mary Banham wrote: 'The women, all young and some with children, believed most strongly of all. We threw our best efforts into the ongoing discussion; opened our homes to provide the places; worked on publicity; designed and installed exhibitions; and talked, listened, and wrote.' Mary Banham, 1990, in *Retrospective Statements, The Independent Group*, 187.

45 Reyner Banham first used the term *une architecture autre* in his essay 'The New Brutalism,' *Architectural Review* 118, no. 708 (December 1955): 361.

46 Andreas Huyssen, *After the Great Divide*.

47 Reyner Banham, 'The Atavism of the Short Distance MiniCyclist,' *Living Arts* (1963); reprinted in *The Independent Group*, 176. In the preceding paragraph, Banham makes it clear that 'the other side "is" in some way Left-oriented, even protest-oriented.'

48 Robert Venturi, Denise Scott Brown, and Steven Izenour, *Learning from Las Vegas* (Cambridge, Mass.:MIT Press, 1981 [orig. 1972, 2nd ed. 1977]) and *Signs of Life, Symbols in the American City*, Smithsonian Institution, Renwick Gallery, February 26–September 30, 1976. While Scott Brown and Venturi stress the intensely collaborative nature of their writing (Denise Scott Brown and Robert Venturi, interview by Mary McLeod and Stanislaus von Moos, March 18, 1996, Philadelphia), the populist strains and sharpest polemical passages attacking architects' machismo and heroic posturing are more reminiscent of Scott Brown's independent writings than of Venturi's. One would never characterize these passages as part of a 'gentle manifesto' (Venturi's own description of *Complexity and Contradiction*).

49 Denise Scott Brown, 'Learning from Pop,' *Casabella*, nos 359–360 (December 1971); reprinted in Robert Venturi and Denise Scott Brown, *A View from the Campidoglio* (Cambridge: Icon Editions, Harper and Rowe, 1984), 32. Many have argued that Scott Brown and Venturi's populism is compromised by their irony and 'pop' sensibility, especially in a project such as the Guild House, where symbolism sometimes seems more a product of aesthetic provocation than of a sensitivity to the occupants' own sensibilities or needs. Nonetheless, Scott Brown and Venturi's appreciation of mass culture and attention to lower- and middle-class taste has served as an important antidote to the modern movement's aesthetic strictures.

50 Venturi, Scott Brown, and Izenour, *Learning from Las Vegas*, 165, 149.

51 Ibid., 148.

52 Ibid., 154.

53 Jane Jacobs, *The Death and Life of Great American Cities* (New York: Vintage Books, 1961). Jacobs is quoted in *Learning from Las Vegas*, 81.

54 Elissa Rosenberg, 'Public and Private: Rereading Jane Jacobs,' *Landscape Journal* 13, no. 2 (Fall 1994): 139–44. I am indebted to Rosenberg's insightful reading of Jacobs for several significant points in my analysis of *The Death and Life of Great American Cities*.

55 Ibid., 139.

56 Ibid., 143–4. See also Thomas Bender, 'Jane in the Cities', *The Nation* 238, no. 21 (2 June 1984): 678.

24 bell hooks

'Choosing the Margin as a Space of Radical Openness'

from *Yearnings: Race, Gender and Cultural Politics* (1989)

As a radical standpoint, perspective, position, 'the politics of location' necessarily calls those of us who would participate in the formation of counter-hegemonic cultural practice to identify the spaces where we begin the process of re-vision. When asked, 'What does it mean to enjoy reading *Beloved*, admire *Schooldaze*, and have a theoretical interest in post-structuralist theory?' (one of the 'wild' questions posed by the Third World Cinema Focus Forum), I located my answer concretely in the realm of oppositional political struggle. Such diverse pleasures can be experienced, enjoyed even, because one transgresses, moves 'out of one's place.' For many of us, that movement requires pushing against oppressive boundaries set by race, sex, and class domination. Initially, then, it is a defiant political gesture. Moving, we confront the realities of choice and location. Within complex and ever shifting realms of power relations, do we position ourselves on the side of colonizing mentality? Or do we continue to stand in political resistance with the oppressed, ready to offer our ways of seeing and theorizing, of making culture, towards that revolutionary effort which seeks to create space where there is unlimited access to the pleasure and power of knowing, where transformation is possible? This choice is crucial. It shapes and determines our response to existing cultural practice and our capacity to envision new, alternative, oppositional aesthetic acts. It informs the way we speak about these issues, the language we choose. Language is also a place of struggle.

To me, the effort to speak about issues of 'space and location' evoked pain. The questions raised compelled difficult explorations of 'Silences' – unaddressed places within my personal political and artistic evolution. Before I could consider answers, I had to face ways these issues were intimately connected to intense personal emotional upheaval regarding place, identity, desire. In an intense all-night-long conversation with Eddie George (member of Black Audio Film Collective) talking about the struggle of oppressed people to come to voice, he made the very 'down' comment that 'ours is a broken voice.' My response was simply that when you hear the broken voice you also hear the pain contained within that brokenness – a speech of suffering; often it's that sound nobody wants to hear. Stuart Hall talks about the need for a 'politics of articulation.' He and Eddie have engaged in dialogue with me in a deeply soulful way, hearing my struggle for words. It is this dialogue between comrades that is a gesture of love; I am grateful.

I have been working to change the way I speak and write, to incorporate in the manner of telling a sense of place, of not just who I am in the present but where I am coming from, the multiple voices within me. I have confronted silence, inarticulateness. When I say, then, that these words emerge from suffering, I refer to that personal struggle to name that location from which I come to voice – that space of my theorizing.

Often when the radical voice speaks about domination we are speaking to those who dominate. Their presence changes the nature and direction of our words. Language is also a place of struggle. I was just a girl coming slowly into womanhood when I read Adrienne Rich's words, 'This is the oppressor's language, yet I need it to talk to you.' This language that enabled me to attend graduate school, to write a dissertation, to speak at job interviews, carries the scent of oppression. Language is also a place of struggle. The Australian aborigines say 'that smell of the white man is killing us.' I remember the smells of my childhood, hot water corn bread, turnip greens, fried pies. I remember the way we talked to one another, our words thickly accented black Southern speech. Language is also a place of struggle. We are wedded in language, have our being in words. Language is also a place of struggle. Dare I speak to oppressed and oppressor in the same voice? Dare I speak to you in a language that will move beyond the boundaries of domination – a language that will not bind you, fence you in, or hold you? Language is also a place of struggle. The oppressed struggle in language to recover ourselves, to reconcile, to reunite, to renew. Our words are not without meaning, they are an action, a resistance. Language is also a place of struggle.

It is no easy task to find ways to include our multiple voices within the various texts we create – in film, poetry, feminist theory. Those are sounds and images that mainstream consumers find difficult to understand. Sounds and scenes which cannot be appropriated are often that sign everyone questions, wants to erase, to 'wipe out.' I feel it even now, writing this piece when I gave it talking and reading, talking spontaneously, using familiar academic speech now and then, 'talking the talk' – using black vernacular speech, the intimate sounds and gestures I normally save for family and loved ones. Private speech in public discourse, intimate intervention, making another text, a space that enables me to recover all that I am in language, I find so many gaps, absences in this written text. To cite them at least is to let the reader know something has been missed, or remains there hinted at by words – there in the deep structure.

Throughout *Freedom Charter*, a work which traces aspects of the movement against racial apartheid in South Africa, this statement is constantly repeated: *our struggle is also a struggle of memory against forgetting*. In much new, exciting cultural practice, cultural texts – in film, black literature, critical theory – there is an effort to remember that is expressive of the need to create spaces where one is able to redeem and reclaim the past, legacies of pain, suffering, and triumph in ways that transform present reality. Fragments of memory are not simply represented as flat documentary but constructed to give a 'new take' on the old, constructed to move us into a different mode of articulation. We see this in films like *Dreaming Rivers* and *Illusions*, and in books like *Mama Day* by Gloria Naylor. Thinking again about space and location, I heard the statement 'our struggle is also a struggle of memory against forgetting'; a politicization of memory that distinguishes nostalgia, that longing for something to be as once it was, a kind of useless act, from that remembering that serves to illuminate and transform the present.

I have needed to remember, as part of a self-critical process where one pauses to reconsider choices and location, tracing my journey from small-town Southern black life, from folk traditions, and church experience to cities, to the university, to neighborhoods that are not racially segregated, to places where I see for the first time independent cinema, where I read critical theory, where I write theory. Along that trajectory, I vividly recall efforts to silence my coming to voice. In my public presentation I was able to tell stories, to share memories. Here again I only hint at them. The opening essay in my book, *Talking Back*, describes my effort to emerge as critical thinker, artist, and writer in a context of repression. I talk about punishment, about mama and daddy aggressively silencing me, about the censorship of black communities. I had no choice. I had to struggle and resist to emerge from that context and then from other locations with mind intact, with an open heart. I had to leave that space I called home to move beyond boundaries, yet I needed also to return there. We sing a song in the black church tradition that says, 'I'm going up the rough side of the mountain on my way home.' Indeed the very meaning of 'home' changes with experience of decolonization, of radicalization. At times, home is nowhere. At times, one knows only extreme estrangement and alienation. Then home is no longer just one place. It is locations. Home is that place which enables and promotes varied and everchanging perspectives, a place where one discovers new ways of seeing reality, frontiers of difference. One confronts and accepts dispersal and fragmentation as part of the construction of a new world order that reveals more fully where we are, who we can become, an order that does not demand forgetting. 'Our struggle is also a struggle of memory against forgetting.'

This experience of space and location is not the same for black folks who have always been privileged, or for black folks who desire only to move from underclass status to points of privilege; not the same for those of us from poor backgrounds who have had to continually engage in actual political struggle both within and outside black communities to assert an aesthetic and critical presence. Black folks coming from poor, underclass communities, who enter universities or privileged cultural settings unwilling to surrender every vestige of who we were before we were there, all 'sign' of our class and cultural 'difference,' who are unwilling to play the role of 'exotic Other,' must create spaces within that culture of domination if we are to survive whole, our souls intact. Our very presence is a disruption. We are often as much an 'Other,' a threat to black people from privileged class backgrounds who do not understand or share our perspectives, as we are to uninformed white folks. Everywhere we go there is pressure to silence our voices, to co-opt and undermine them. Mostly, of course, we are not there. We never 'arrive' or 'can't stay.' Back in those spaces where we come from, we kill ourselves in despair, drowning in nihilism, caught in poverty, in addiction, in every postmodern mode of dying that can be named. Yet when we few remain in that 'other' space, we are often too isolated, too alone. We die there, too. Those of us who live, who 'make it,' passionately holding on to aspects of that 'downhome' life we do not intend to lose while simultaneously seeking new knowledge and experience, invent spaces of radical openness. Without such spaces we would not survive. Our living depends on our ability to conceptualize alternatives, often improvised. Theorizing about this experience aesthetically, critically is an agenda for radical cultural practice.

For me this space of radical openness is a margin – a profound edge. Locating oneself there is difficult yet necessary. It is not a 'safe' place. One is always at risk. One needs a community of resistance.

In the preface to *Feminist Theory: From Margin to Center*, I expressed these thoughts on marginality:

> To be in the margin is to be part of the whole but outside the main body. As black Americans living in a small Kentucky town, the railroad tracks were a daily reminder of our marginality. Across those tracks were paved streets, stores we could not enter, restaurants we could not eat in, and people we could not look directly in the face. Across those tracks was a world we could work in as maids, as janitors, as prostitutes, as long as it was in a service capacity. We could enter that world but we could not live there. We had always to return to the margin, to cross the tracks to shacks and abandoned houses on the edge of town.
>
> There were laws to ensure our return. Not to return was to risk being punished. Living as we did – on the edge – we developed a particular way of seeing reality. We looked both from the outside in and from the inside out. We focused our attention on the center as well as on the margin. We understood both. This mode of seeing reminded us of the existence of a whole universe, a main body made up of both margin and center. Our survival depended on an ongoing public awareness of the separation between margin and center and an ongoing private acknowledgement that we were a necessary, vital part of that whole.
>
> This sense of wholeness, impressed upon our consciousness by the structure of our daily lives, provided us with an oppositional world-view – a mode of seeing unknown to most of our oppressors, that sustained us, aided us in our struggle to transcend poverty and despair, strengthened our sense of self and our solidarity.

Though incomplete, these statements identify marginality as much more than a site of deprivation; in fact I was saying just the opposite, that it is also the site of radical possibility, a space of resistance. It was this marginality that I was naming as a central location for the production of a counter-hegemonic discourse that is not just found in words but in habits of being and the way one lives. As such,

I was not speaking of a marginality one wishes to lose – to give up or surrender as part of moving into the center – but rather of a site one stays in, clings to even, because it nourishes one's capacity to resist. It offers to one the possibility of radical perspective from which to see and create, to imagine alternatives, new worlds.

This is not a mythic notion of marginality. It comes from lived experience. Yet I want to talk about what it means to struggle to maintain that marginality even as one works, produces, lives, if you will, at the center. I no longer live in that segregated world across the tracks. Central to life in that world was the ongoing awareness of the necessity of opposition. When Bob Marley sings, 'We refuse to be what you want us to be, we are what we are, and that's the way it's going to be,' that space of refusal, where one can say no to the colonizer, no to the downpressor, is located in the margins. And one can only say no, speak the voice of resistance, because there exists a counter-language. While it may resemble the colonizer's tongue, it has undergone a transformation, it has been irrevocably changed. When I left that concrete space in the margins, I kept alive in my heart ways of knowing reality, which affirm continually not only the primacy of resistance but the necessity of a resistance that is sustained by remembrance of the past, which includes recollections of broken tongues giving us ways to speak that decolonize our minds, our very beings. Once mama said to me as I was about to go again to the predominantly white university, 'You can take what the white people have to offer, but you do not have to love them.' Now understanding her cultural codes, I know that she was not saying to me not to love people of other races. She was speaking about colonization and the reality of what it means to be taught in a culture of domination by those who dominate. She was insisting on my power to be able to separate useful knowledge that I might get from the dominating group from participation in ways of knowing that would lead to estrangement, alienation, and worse – assimilation and co-optation. She was saying that it is not necessary to give yourself over to them to learn. Not having been in those institutions, she knew that I might be faced again and again with situations where I would be 'tried,' made to feel as though a central requirement of my being accepted would mean participation in this system of exchange to ensure my success, my 'making it.' She was reminding me of the necessity of opposition and simultaneously encouraging me not to lose that radical perspective shaped and formed by marginality.

Understanding marginality as position and place of resistance is crucial for oppressed, exploited, colonized people. If we only view the margin as sign marking the despair, a deep nihilism penetrates in a destructive way the very ground of our being. It is there in that space of collective despair that one's creativity, one's imagination is at risk, there that one's mind is fully colonized, there that the freedom one longs for as lost. Truly the mind that resists colonization struggles for freedom one longs for is lost. Truly the mind that resists colonization struggles for freedom of expression. The struggle may not even begin with the colonizer; it may begin within one's segregated, colonized community and family. So I want to note that I am not trying to romantically re-inscribe the notion of that space of marginality where the oppressed live apart from their oppressors as 'pure.' I want to say that these margins have been both sites of repression and sites of resistance. And since we are well able to name the nature of that repression we know better the margin as site of deprivation. We are more silent when it comes to speaking of the margin as site of resistance. We are more often silenced when it comes to speaking of the margin as site of resistance.

Silenced. During my graduate years I heard myself speaking often in the voice of resistance. I cannot say that my speech was welcomed. I cannot say that my speech was heard in such a way that it altered relations between colonizer and colonized. Yet what I have noticed is that those scholars, most especially those who name themselves radical critical thinkers, feminist thinkers, now fully participate in the construction of a discourse about the 'Other.' I was made 'Other' there in that space with them. In that space in the margins, that lived-in segregated world of my past and present. They did not meet me there in that space. They met me at the center. They greeted me as colonizers. I am waiting to learn from them the path of their resistance, of how it came to be that they were able to surrender the power to act as colonizers. I am waiting for them to bear witness, to give testimony. They say that the discourse on marginality, on difference has moved beyond a discussion of 'us and them.' They do not speak of how this movement has taken place. This is a response from the radical space of my marginality. It is a space of resistance. It is a space I choose.

I am waiting for them to stop talking about the 'Other,' to stop even describing how important it is to be able to speak about difference. It is not just important what we speak about, but how and why we speak. Often this speech about the 'Other' is also a mask, an oppressive talk hiding gaps, absences, that space where our words would be if we were speaking, if there were silence, if we were there. This 'we' is that 'us' in the margins, that 'we' who inhabit marginal space that is not a site of domination but a place of resistance. Enter that space. Often this speech about the 'Other' annihilates, erases: 'No need to hear your voice when I can talk about you better than you can speak about yourself. No need to hear your voice. Only tell me about your pain. I want to know your story. And then I will tell it back to you in a new way. Tell it back to you in such a way that it has become mine, my own. Re-writing you, I write myself anew. I am still author, authority. I am still the colonizer, the speaking subject, and you are now at the center of my talk.' Stop. We greet you as liberators. This 'we' is that 'us' in the margins, that 'we' who inhabit marginal space that is not a site of domination but a place of resistance. Enter that space. This is an intervention. I am writing to you. I am speaking from a place in the margins where I am different, where I see things differently. I am talking about what I see.

Speaking from margins. Speaking in resistance. I open a book. There are words on the back cover, *Never in the Shadows Again*. A book which suggests the possibility of speaking as liberators. Only who is speaking and who is silent. Only who stands in the shadows – the shadow in a doorway, the space where images of black women are represented voiceless, the space where our words are invoked to serve and support, the space of our absence. Only small echoes of protest. We are re-written. We are 'Other.' We are the margin. Who is speaking and to whom. Where do we locate ourselves and comrades.?

Silenced. We fear those who speak about us, who do not speak to us and with us. We know what it is like to be silenced. We know that the forces that silence us, because they never want us to speak, differ from the forces that say speak, tell me your story. Only do not speak in a voice of resistance. Only speak from that space in the margin that is a sign of deprivation, a wound, an unfulfilled longing. Only speak your pain.

This is an intervention. A message from that space in the margin that is a site of creativity and power, that inclusive space where we recover ourselves, where we move in solidarity to erase the category colonized/colonizer. Marginality as site of resistance. Enter that space. Let us meet there. Enter that space. We greet you as liberators.

Spaces can be real and imagined. Spaces can tell stories and unfold histories. Spaces can be interrupted, appropriated, and transformed through artistic and literary practice.

As Pratibha Parma notes, 'The appropriation and use of space are political acts.'

To speak about that location from which work emerges, I choose familiar politicized language, old codes, words like 'struggle, marginality, resistance.' I choose these words knowing that they are no longer popular or 'cool' – hold onto them and the political legacies they evoke and affirm, even as I work to change what they say, to give them renewed and different meaning.

I am located in the margin. I make a definite distinction between that marginality which is imposed by oppressive structures and that marginality one chooses as site of resistance – as location of radical openness and possibility. This site of resistance is continually formed in that segregated culture of opposition that is our critical response to domination. We come to this space through suffering and pain, through struggle. We know struggle to be that which pleasures, delights, and fulfills desire. We are transformed, individually, collectively, as we make radical creative space which affirms and sustains our subjectivity, which gives us a new location from which to articulate our sense of the world.

25 Elizabeth Grosz

'Woman, *Chora*, Dwelling'

from *Space, Time and Perversion, The Politics of the Body* (1991)

> Everywhere you shut me in. Always you assign a place to me. Even outside
> the frame that I form with you. . . . You set limits even to events that could
> happen with others. . . . You mark out boundaries, draw lines, surround,
> enclose. Excising, cutting out. What is your fear? That you might lose your
> property. What remains is an empty frame. You cling to it, dead.
>
> Luce Irigaray (1992:24–5)

A feminist might take many different approaches in exploring the theme of women
and architecture. For the purposes of this brief analysis, I will remain silent regarding most of them, leaving undiscussed the sometimes crucial issues of sexism
and the often manifest discrimination against women in architectural training,
apprenticeship, and practice. Such issues are best discussed and understood by
those actively involved in the profession, who have not only first hand experience
of the operations of discriminatory practices, but also have insights into the internal
exigencies of the system in which they work, and an understanding of the various
strategies pragmatically at hand in architectural institutions to transform them into
sites of contestation. My concern here is with a series of narrower and more
theoretical issues that link the very *concept* of architecture with the phallocentric
effacement of women and femininity, the cultural refusal of women's specificity or
corporeal and conceptual autonomy and social value.

I wish to make some indirect and tenuous connections between architecture,
deconstruction, and feminist theory, forge some rudimentary links, and point out
some of the rather awkward points of dis-ease between these various concerns.
My goal here will be to present an initial exploration of the cultural origins of
notions of spatiality in the writings of the Classical period, most notably in Plato's
Timaeus, which invokes a mythological bridge between the intelligible and the
sensible, mind and body, which he calls *chora*. *Chora* has been the object of considerable philosophical reflection, especially in contemporary French philosophy,
having taken on the status of a master term in the writings of Julia Kristeva, in her
understanding of the stabilization and destabilization of the speaking subject and,
more recently in the writings of Jacques Derrida, particularly in his various theoretical exchanges with architecture,in his commentaries on and contributions to
the work of the architects and architectural theorists Bernard Tschumi and Peter
Eisenman. *Chora*, which Derrida insists must be understood without any definite
article, has an acknowledged role at the very foundations of the concept of
spatiality, place and placing: it signifies, at its most literal level, notions of 'place,'

'location,' 'site,' 'region,' 'locale,' 'country'; but it also contains an irreducible, yet often overlooked connection with the function of femininity, being associated with a series of sexually-coded terms – 'mother,' 'nurse,' 'receptacle,' and 'imprint-bearer.' Derrida is interested in *chora* in keeping with the larger and more general features of 'deconstructive reading,' that always seek out terms that disturb the logic, the *logos*, of the text under examination, in order to show that it exceeds and cannot be contained by the logic, explicit framework, and overt intentions of the text. Derrida continually seeks out these terms – impossible to assimilate into the text's logic – which are nonetheless necessary for it to function. They are thus ineliminable from the text's operations and exert a disruptive force, an aporetic effect, on the apparent claims and concerns of the text in question. *Chora* thus follows a long line of deconstructively privileged terms in Derrida's texts, from 'writing,' 'trace,' 'pharmakon,' 'dissemination,' 'supplement,' 'parergon,' in his earlier writings, to 'cinders,' 'ghost,' 'remainder,' 'residue' (among others) in his more recent texts. Each term designates and locates a point of indeterminacy or undecidability, a point at which the text's own writing exceeds its explicit goals and logic, where the text turns in on itself and ties itself into a strategically positioned knot.

It will be my argument here, reading Plato and Derrida on *chora*, that the notion of *chora* serves to produce a founding concept of femininity whose connections with women and female corporeality have been severed, producing a disembodied femininity as the ground for the production of a (conceptual and social) universe. In outlining the unacknowledged and unremitting debt that the very notion of space, and the built environment that relies on its formulation, owes to what Plato characterizes as the 'femininity' of the *chora* (a characterization he both utilizes and refuses to commit himself to), I will develop some of the insights of Luce Irigaray in her critical analysis of the phallocentric foundations of Western philosophy. Irigaray's reading of the history of philosophy as the erasure or covering over of women's specificity has served to demonstrate that even where women and femininity are not explicitly mentioned or evoked in philosophical and architectural texts, nonetheless they, and concepts associated with them, serve as the unconscious, repressed or unspoken foundations of and guarantee for philosophical value. This essay may be understood as the confrontation of one strand of contemporary architectural theory, represented by Derrida's relatively small and admittedly oblique contributions to architecture, and Irigaray's sweeping analysis of the investment that all modes of knowledge have in perpetuating the secondary and subordinate social positions accorded to women and femininity. Irigaray *contra* Derrida in the domain of the dwelling: where and how to live, as whom, and with whom?

DWELLING: BETWEEN THE INTELLIGIBLE AND THE SENSIBLE

Timaeus represents Plato's attempt to produce a basic explanation of the universe as we know it – a *modest* attempt on the part of a philosopher who believed that only philosophers were fit to rule the well-ordered *polis* – an explanation of the divine creation of the cosmos and the earth. In an age when myth is not yet definitively separated from science or philosophy, Plato presents an account of the genesis of the universe from divine and rational metaphysical principles. He sets up a series of binary oppositions that will mark the character of Western thought: the distinctions between being and becoming, the intelligible and the sensible, the ideal and the material, the divine and the mortal, which may all be regarded as versions of the distinction between the (perfect) world of reason and the (imperfect) material world.

This opposition between what is intelligible and unchanging, being (the world of Forms or Ideas), and what is sensible (which Plato describes as visible) and subject to change, becoming, seems relatively straightforward; but, it is difficult to use as an explanatory model, a ground of ontology, unless there is the possibility of some mediation, some mode of transition or passage from one to the other. Plato complicates and indeed problematizes and undoes this opposition by devising a third or intermediate category, whose function is to explain the passage from the perfect to the imperfect, from the Form to the reality: *chora*. This category, it is claimed, shares little in common with either term in the opposition. Plato does suggest at some points that it shares in the properties of both the Forms and material reality; yet at other points, he claims that it has nothing in common with either. Rather enigmatically and impossibly, he suggests that it has both no attributes of its own, and that it shares some of the attributes of the Forms: '. . . we shall not be wrong if we describe it as invisible and formless, all-embracing, possessed in a most puzzling way of intelligibility, yet very hard to grasp (Plato, 1977: 70).

Somehow, in a 'puzzling way,' it participates in intelligibility yet is distinct from the intelligible; it is also distinct from the material world insofar as it is 'invisible and formless,' beyond the realm of the senses. It dazzles the logic of non-contradiction, it insinuates itself between the oppositional terms, in the impossible no-man's land of the excluded middle. This is already enough to indicate to Derrida, no less than to Irigaray, that there is something odd at stake here, something that exceeds what Plato is able to legitimately argue using his own criteria.

Plato cannot specify any particular properties or qualities for *chora*: if one could attribute it any specificity it would immediately cease to have its status as intermediary or receptacle and would instead become an object (or quality or property). It is thus by definition impossible to characterize. It is the mother of all qualities without itself having any – except its capacity to take on, to nurture, to bring into existence any other kind of being. Being a kind of pure permeability, infinitely transformable, inherently open to the specificities of whatever concrete it brings into existence, *chora* can have no attributes, no features of its own. Steeped in paradox, its quality is to be quality-less, its defining characteristic that it lacks any defining feature. It functions primarily as the receptacle, the storage point, the locus of nurturance in the transition necessary for the emergence of matter, a kind of womb of material existence, the nurse of becoming, an incubator to ensure the transmission or rather the copying of Forms to produce matter that resembles them. Matter bears a likeness to the Forms. This relation (like the paternal bond between father and son) depends on the minimalized contributions of the receptacle/space/mother in the genesis of becoming. Moreover, it becomes less clear as the text proceeds whether something like *chora* is necessary for the very genesis of the Forms themselves, i.e. whether *chora* can be conceived as a product or copy of the Forms, or contrarily, whether the Forms are themselves conditioned on *chora*:

> It can always be called the same because it never alters its characteristics. For it continues to receive all things, and never itself takes a permanent impress from any of the things that enter it, making it appear different at different times. And the things which pass in and out of it are copies of the eternal realities, whose form they take in a wonderful way that is hard to describe.
>
> (Plato, 1977: 69)

Chora can only be designated by its, by her, function: to hold, nurture, bring into the world. Not clearly an it or a she, *chora* has neither existence nor becoming. *Not* to procreate or produce – this is the function of the father, the creator, god, the Forms – but to nurse, to support, surround, protect, incubate, to sort, or engender the worldly offspring of the Forms. Its function is a neutral, traceless production that leaves no trace of its contributions, and thus allows the product to speak indirectly of its creator without need for acknowledging its incubator. Plato explicitly compares the Forms to the role of the male, and *chora* to the role of the female according to Greek collective fantasies: in procreation, the father contributes all the specific characteristics to the nameless, formless incubation provided by the mother:

> We may indeed use the metaphor of birth and compare the receptacle to the mother, the model to the father, and what they produce between them to their offspring; and we may notice that, if an imprint is to present a very complex appearance, the material on which it is to be stamped will not have been properly prepared unless it is devoid of all the characters which it is to receive. For if it were like any of the things that enter it, it would badly distort any impression of a contrary or entirely different nature when it receives it, as its own features would shine through.
>
> (Plato, 1977:69)

Neither something nor yet nothing, *chora* is the condition for the genesis of the material world, the screen onto which is projected the image of the changeless Forms, the space onto which the Form's duplicate or copy is cast, providing the point of entry, as it were, into material existence. The material object is not simply produced by the Form(s), but also resembles the original, a copy whose powers of verisimilitude depend upon the neutrality, the blandness, the lack of specific attributes of its 'nursemaid.'

This peculiar receptacle that is *chora* functions to receive, to take in, to possess without in turn leaving any correlative impression. She takes in without holding onto: she is unable to possess for she has no self-possession, no self-identity. She supports all material existence with nothing to support her own.

Though she brings being into becoming she has neither being nor the possibilities of becoming; both the mother of all things and yet without ontological status, she designates less a positivity than an abyss, a crease, perhaps a pure difference, between being and becoming, the space which produces their separation and thus enables their co-existence and interchange.

Plato slips into a designation of *chora* as space itself, the condition for the very existence of material objects. (It is no accident that Descartes takes the ability to occupy space as the singular defining characteristic of material objects.) Space is a third kind of 'entity' that is neither apprehended by the senses nor by reason alone, being understood only with difficulty, in terms of a 'spurious reason,' 'in a kind of a dream,' in a modality that today, following Kant, may be described as apperception. Plato describes a space

> which is eternal and indestructible, which provides a position for everything that comes to be, and which is apprehended without the senses by a sort of spurious reasoning and so is hard to believe in – we look at it indeed in a kind of dream and say that everything that exists must be somewhere and occupy some space, and that what is nowhere in heaven or earth is nothing at all.
>
> (Plato, 1977:71–2)

Chora, then, is the space in which place is made possible, the chasm for the passage of spaceless Forms into a spatialized reality, a dimensionless tunnel opening itself to spatialization, obliterating itself to make others possible and actual. It is the space that engenders without possessing, that nurtures without requirements of its own, that receives without giving, and that gives without receiving, a space that evades all characterizations including the disconcerting logic of identity, of hierarchy, of being, the regulation of order. It is no wonder that *chora* resembles the characteristics the Greeks, and all those who follow them, have long attributed to femininity, or rather, have expelled from their own masculine self-representations and accounts of being and knowing (and have thus *de facto* attributed to the feminine). Moreover, this femininity is not itself merely an abstract representation of generic features (softness, nurturance, etc.), but is derived from the attributes culturally bestowed on women themselves, and in this case, particularly the biological function of gestation. While *chora* cannot be directly identified with the womb – to do so would be to naïvely pin it down to something specific, convert it into an object rather than as the condition of existence of objects – nonetheless, it does seem to borrow many of the paradoxical attributes of pregnancy and maternity.

DERRIDA: BETWEEN WRITING AND ARCHITECTURE

Derrida has written a good deal on Greek philosophy and has devoted considerable attention to unravelling the texts of Plato. He has done so not only because Plato's work functions at the cultural horizon of the inauguration of Western philosophy (such an approach would remain tied to the history of ideas), but also because the

Platonic tradition has established basic frameworks, assumptions, and methods that have guided philosophy, and Western reason, ever since. It is thus not entirely surprising that for his two contributions written explicitly with an architecturally literate public, Derrida has again chosen to write on, with, or around Plato and the *Timaeus*. As I understand him, Derrida's work is neither architectural in itself (although no doubt it possesses its own 'architectonic') nor is it devoid of architectural relevance. He challenges, not architecture itself, but a series of assumptions, categories, and terms *by which architecture is*, as are all *writing* practices – and architecture is clearly a mode of writing in the Derridean sense – implicated in and governed by metaphysics. He challenges architecture with its own irreducibly written traces, its own self-undoing, just as his work in turn is challenged with its own modes of textuality, its obliteration of spatiality and materiality.

Derrida's reading of *chora* is ingenious: he shows how the counterlogic or a logic of the *chora* as concept-term in Plato's writings, infects the other apparently unrelated claims of the *Timaeus*, its explanation of the origins of the universe, and the ways in which political, physical, and biological factors are rendered explicable. Moreover, it also seeps into Plato's self-conception, that is, the position he accords to Socrates in his texts. The peculiar functioning of *chora* cannot be readily contained in a self-identical place for it seeps into all that it contains, into all the oppositions and metaphysical assumptions that depend on it for their existence: the Forms, the material world, and their interrelations remain inexplicable except in terms of the mediation produced by *chora*. The world of objects, material reality in all its complexity, is in fact infiltrated by the very term whose function is to leave no imprint, no trace. *Chora* is interwoven throughout the fabric of Plato's writing. It effectively intervenes into Plato's accounts of ontology, political rulership, the relations between heavenly bodies (his cosmology), and the organization of the human body – of all that makes up the world. These other relations all exhibit an 'abyssal and analogous reflexivity,' with what Plato says about *chora*. Moreover and more importantly for the purposes of this argument, it is interwoven into the very *economy* of the architectural project itself.

It is significant that 'economy' is derived from the Greek term, *oikos*, meaning home or house, residence or dwelling. An economy is the distribution of material (cultural, social, economic, representational, libidinal) goods in a system of production, circulation, and consumption. An architectural economy consists in the distribution, not only of bricks, stone, steel, and glass, but also in the production and distribution of discourses, writings (including the bodily traces of a building's occupants), and its divisions of space, time and movement, as well as the architectural plans, treatises, and textbooks that surround and infuse building. Derrida's goal seems not to be to destroy, to deconstruct (in a more pedestrian sense), to problematize and render architecture's assumptions unworkable, but rather to see whether it is possible to build/write according to a different economy, to reroute and transform the logic that distinguishes between space and time, form and matter, the intelligible and the sensible, theory and practice, so that it functions in different ways, with unexpected and unpredictable results, innovating different modalities of construction, both conceptual and material. His goal has always been to upset pregiven categories, to demonstrate the textual contortions that they entail, to show their cost and to effect some sort of rupture or transformation in their operations. His contributions to architecture remain of the same order: to open other possibilities for rethinking space, time, dwelling, the built environment, and the operative distinctions with which such concepts function.

Derrida does not intervene *as such* into architectural practice. He reserves a different role for himself: in effect, providing some kind of validation of the writing and building experiments of others (most notably, Eisenman and Tschumi), who themselves challenge the prevailing assumptions of functionalism, form, and measure in their attempts to think and produce what might be considered a 'radical architecture,' an architecture of transgression. In this sense, *chora*, and the reconceptualization of space that a deconstructive reading of this concept entails, begs rethinking the requirements of those oppositions that have structured architecture to the present: figure and ground, form and function, ornament and structure, theory and practice; and most particularly, both architectural consumerism (whose function is to subordinate materiality to the consumer's will or desire – a fundamentally impossible project, given the inherent open-endedness of desire, its fundamentally volatile and ever-changing nature) and architectural functionalism (whose goal is to subordinate subjects' desires to the exigencies of function, an increasingly impossible project, particularly in an era of rapid transformations in technological and corporate functions). One of his goals remains to contest the intervention into architectural practices of the exigencies of either aestheticism (the demands of beauty) or functionalism (the requirements of dwelling). Not that these requirements can be dispensed with, nor must they be abandoned; rather, they need to be rethought in terms of their role as internal or constitutive factors that function according to a different economy:

> you have to reinscribe these motifs [the hegemony of the aesthetic and the useful] within the work. You can't (or you shouldn't) simply dismiss those values of dwelling, functionality, beauty and so on. You have to construct, so to speak, a new space and a new form, to shape a new way of building in which those motifs or values are reinscribed, having meanwhile lost their external hegemony.
>
> (Derrida and Norris:73)

This reconceptualization of space and spatiality that Derrida signals without specifying and that he indicates is at the heart of both philosophical and architectural reflection is, I believe, a concern he shares with feminist theory, particularly with feminists involved in architectural theory and practice. It is also one of the major areas of concern in the writings of Irigaray, who, like Derrida, concentrates primarily on philosophical texts, but particularly on those that also have some direct relevance to understanding the built environment.

I do not want to suggest that Derrida's work is directly compatible with the interests of feminist theory, quite the contrary. Whatever relations may exist between Derridean deconstruction and feminist theory have yet to be forged and explored in thorough detail, although it is today clear that a number of feminist theorists, with whatever reservations they may individually have regarding the feminist utility of Derrida's work, nonetheless are interested in and have worked with Derridean texts and concepts for various feminist projects. It seems clear to me that while Derrida's work is neither feminist nor anti-feminist, it retains elements of both. His work is fundamentally ambivalent. Making it relevant to feminist concerns is a matter of considerable negotiation: his writings always contain an unassimilable residue that is not only problematic in feminist terms, but which always tilts his writings into an uneasy and ambiguous alliance with other complex and undecidable interests and issues.

FEMINIST REOCCUPATIONS OF SPACE

Conceptions of spatiality and temporality have rarely been the explicit object of feminist reflection: they have always appeared somehow above the more mundane concerns of day-by-day politics, too abstract, too neutral and self-evident to take as an object of critical feminist analysis (although this is now increasingly being revised in the work of some feminists working in the area of architecture, for example, Bergren, Bloomer, and Colomina). It has, however, become increasingly clear that the organization and management of space – the project of architecture and regional planning, among others – has very serious political, social, and cultural impact, and in a sense cannot but be of concern to feminists. Among the more interesting writings on (philosophical notions of) space and spatiality are Irigaray's, whose works, while perhaps less well known in the area of architectural theory, have had considerable impact on Anglo-American feminist theory and philosophy and, through them, on the ways in which space, time, subjectivity, and corporeality are currently considered.

While I cannot here outline her claims regarding the opposition between space and time – which she discusses with reference to Kant in *An Ethics of Sexual Difference* (1993) – I would like to use elements of her work to counterpoise to the Derridean reading and use of the Platonic *chora* and to show the ways in which a feminist reading of *chora* may be able to reappropriate the maternal dimension implied by the term, and thus to reorient the ways in which spatiality is conceived, lived, and used.

Irigaray's writings on the dwelling are based largely on her readings of a number of philosophical texts, most particularly those of Kant, Heidegger, and Levinas. But more particularly, like Derrida, and a whole history of Western philosophers, she relies heavily on metaphors of dwelling, inhabitation, building, unearthing, tombs, ruins, temples, homes, caves, and prisons. Like Derrida, her work remains indirect in its relation to architectural practice, but her writing, like his, may be readily appropriated by architectural practices in the hope of transforming men's and women's relations to space. Her concerns are directed towards the establishment of a *viable* space and time for women to inhabit as women. The ways in which space has been historically conceived have always functioned to either contain women or to obliterate them. She makes it clear that a reconceptualization of the relations between men and women – as is required for an autonomous and independent self-representation for women and femininity – entails the reconceptualization of the representations of space and time.

> In order to make it possible to think through and live [sexual] difference, we must reconsider the whole problematic of space and time. . . . The transition to a new age requires a change in our perception and conception of space-time, the inhabiting of places and of containers, or envelopes of identity.
>
> (Irigaray, 1993:7)

Irigaray claims that masculine modes of thought have performed a devastating sleight-of-hand: they have obliterated the debt they owe to the most primordial of all spaces, the maternal space from which all subjects emerge, and which they ceaselessly attempt to usurp. Here Irigaray is not talking about specific men, nor even a general tendency in men (although this may in fact be appropriate), but rather, a tendency in phallocentric thought to deny and cover over the debt of life and existence that all subjects, and indeed all theoretical frameworks, owe to the maternal body, their elaborate attempts to foreclose and build over this space with their own (sexually specific) fantasmatic and paranoid projections. The production of a (male) world – the construction of an 'artificial' or cultural environment, the production of an intelligible universe, religion, philosophy, the creation of true knowledges and valid practices of and in that universe – is implicated in the systematic and violent erasure of the contributions of women, femininity, and the maternal. This erasure is the foundation or ground on which a thoroughly masculine universe is built:

> He can only touch himself from the outside. In order to recapture that whole sensation of the inside of a body, he will invent a world. But the world's circular horizon always conceals the inner movement of the womb. The imposition of distinctions is the mourning which their bodies always wear.
>
> (Irigaray, 1992:15)

Men produce a universe built upon the erasure of the bodies and contributions of women/mothers and the refusal to acknowledge the debt to the maternal body that they owe. They hollow out their own interiors and project them outward, and then require women as supports for this hollowed space. Women become the guardians of the private and the interpersonal, while men build conceptual and material worlds. This appropriation of the right to a place or space correlates with men's seizure of the right to define and utilize a spatiality that reflects their own self-representations. Men have conceived of themselves as self-made, and in disavowing this maternal debt, have left themselves, and women, in dereliction, homelessness. The question of dwelling, of where, and how, to live, is thus a crucial one in both the production of the male domination of women's bodies and in women's struggles to acquire an autonomous space they can occupy and live as women. In seeking to take up all (social) space themselves, in aspiring to occupy not only the territory of the earth, but also that of the heavens, in seeking a dominion from the earth to the sky, men have contained women in a death-like tomb, which she sometimes refers to as a 'sepulchre' (Irigaray, 1985a: 143–4). In a rigid containment or mortification of women's explorations of their own notions of spatiality (and temporality), men place women in the position of being 'guardians' of their bodies and their spaces, the conditions of both bodies and space without body or space of their own: they become the living representatives of corporeality, of domesticity, of the natural order that men have had to expel from their own self-representations in order to construct themselves as above-the-mundane, beyond the merely material. To sustain this fantasy of auto-production and pure self-determination in a systematic way, men have had to use women as the delegates of men's materiality. This containment within the (negative) mirror of men's self-reflections strips women of an existence either autonomous from or symmetrical with men's: it relegates women to the position of support or precondition of the masculine – precisely the status of *chora* in the Platonic tradition:

> I was your house. And, when you leave, abandoning this dwelling place, I do not know what to do with these walls of mine. Have I ever had a body other than the one which you constructed according to your idea of it? Have I ever experienced a skin other than the one which you wanted me to dwell within?
>
> (Irigaray, 1992:49)

The containment of women within a dwelling that they did not build, nor was even built *for* them, can only amount to a homelessness within the very home itself: it becomes the space of duty, of endless and infinitely repeatable chores that have no social value or recognition, the space of the affirmation and replenishment of others at the expense and erasure of the self, the space of domestic violence and abuse, the space that harms as much as it isolates women. It is as if men are unable to resist the temptation to colonize, to appropriate, to measure, to control, to instrumentalize all that they survey, reducing the horizon (the horizon of becoming, the measure and reflection of positionality) into the dwelling, as Irigaray claims in the quotation opening this chapter. But this manipulation and containment of women and space always has its costs: in appropriating the body of the other, he must lose access to his own. In succumbing to the inducements of the phallus, and the paternal privilege it entails, he gives up the rest of his body. In exchange for the body he has had to sacrifice (the polymorphous pleasures of the pre-oedipal period) he is granted access to the bodies of women whose bodies replace the place from whence he came (the maternal womb). Women's bodies are the socially guaranteed compensation for men's acquisition of phallic status, the repositories of men's own lost corporeality, and the guardians of men's mortality. It is not surprising, given the massive disavowal necessary to sustain men's vicarious containment of and living from women's energies, that it is steeped in hostility, resentment, and aggression. Dwelling becomes the domain of hatred and murderous control:

He passes from the formlessness of his relationship with his mother to the measureless excess of his male power. . . . He enters into paternal power, to keep within him the life he drinks from the other. But enclosed within that form, she dies.

(Irigaray, 1992:53–4)

This enclosure of women in men's physical space is not entirely different from the containment of women in men's conceptual universe either: theory, in the terms in which we know it today, is also the consequence of a refusal to acknowledge that other perspectives, other modes of reason, other modes of construction and constitution are possible. Its singularity and status as true and objective depends on this disavowal.

For women to be able to occupy another space, or to be able somehow to occupy this space in a different way, it is clear for Irigaray that several major transformations need to be effected. Most particularly, a series of upheavals in the organization of personal life (transformations in the way the mother–daughter relation is both conceived and mediated, changes in the ways in which female subjectivity and sexuality are structured according to the privileges of phallic subjectivity and sexuality, changes in the ways in which the two sexes relate to and exchange with each other), in the ways in which women's relations to what is larger than them (the divine, the environment, nature) are conceived, and in the ways in which theory, and cultural production more generally, are regarded. This interconnected cluster of issues cannot be readily untangled or easily resolved: these are more directions to which feminists must now turn rather than issues to be solved and eliminated. One thing remains clear, though: unless men can invent other ways to occupy space; unless space (as territory which is mappable, explorable) gives way to place (occupation, dwelling, being lived in); until space is conceived in terms other than according to the logic of penetration, colonization, and domination; unless they can accord women their own space, and negotiate the occupation of shared spaces; unless they no longer regard space as the provenance of their own self-expression and self-creation; unless they respect spaces and places which are not theirs, entering only when invited, and accepting this as a gift, can they share in the contributions that women may have to offer in reconceiving space and place.

Irigaray's work seems to confirm that its disruptive 'logic' is everywhere at work, even today, in the production of phallocentric discourses and patriarchal modes of domination. *Chora* emblematize a common maneuvre used to maintain this domination: the silencing and endless metaphorizaton of femininity as the condition for men's self-representation and cultural production. This is no less true of Derrida than it is of Plato: their various philosophical models and frameworks depend on the resources and characteristics of a femininity disinvested of its connections with the female, and especially the maternal, body made to carry the burden of what it is that men cannot explain, cannot articulate or know, that unnameable recalcitrance that men continue to represent as an abyss, as unfathomable, lacking, enigmatic, veiled, seductive, voracious, dangerous, disruptive, but without name or place may well serve as one of the earliest models of this appropriation and disenfranchisement of femininity.

The project ahead, or one of them, is to return women to those places from which they have been dis- or re-placed or expelled, to occupy those positions – especially those which are not acknowledged as positions – partly in order to show men's invasion and occupancy of the whole of space, of space as their own and thus the constriction of spaces available to women, and partly in order to be able to experiment with and produce the possibility of occupying, dwelling, or living in new spaces, which in their turn help generate new perspectives, new bodies, new ways of inhabiting.

REFERENCES

Derrida, Jacques, 'Chora' in *Choral Works. A Collaboration between Peter Eisenman and Jacques Derrida*, ed. Jeffrey Kipnis (New York, 1993).

Irigaray, Luce, *Speculum of the Other Woman*, trans. Gillian C. Gill (Ithaca, NY: Cornell University Press, 1985).

——, *Elemental Passions* (New York: Routledge, 1992).

——, *Je, Tu, Nous: Toward a Culture of Difference* (New York: Routledge, 1993).

Plato, *Timaeus and Critias*, trans. D. Lee (Harmondsworth: Penguin, 1977).

Part 3

Gender, Space, Architecture

26 Jane Rendell

Introduction: 'Gender, Space, Architecture'

Do women practise architecture differently? How are such differences manifest? Do women have a different sense of aesthetics, sense of space and time? Do women use materials differently, organise practice differently, prefer certain kinds of design methodology? Further, how do we explain such differences? Do they derive from biology or society? For example, is the connection of women with inside spaces due to biology – to the specific shape of their bodies or society – to social and cultural associations of women with the private space of the home and children?

If we are to believe that women approach design in a different way, a more holistic way, for example, is it because women have different psychical structures from men, ones which result in different creative processes, different aspirations in relation to the production of objects and spaces and different sensitivities towards materials? Where do we locate these differences in architecture, in the building façade or the ground plan, in the construction detailing or the interior finishes, or in the occupation of the building?

The list of questions above only barely touches the issues at stake for women in architectural practice. It is very difficult to provide a clear and coherent frame-work in which to organise all the differing aspects of the various relations which exist between feminism, gender theory and architectural practice, without prioritising one view over another. Most recent books on gender and architecture have side-stepped this problem by not subdividing the chapters into sections, arguing that such a formal structure is divisive and alien to the multi-disciplinary nature of feminist work. One exception to these precedents is Sherry Ahrentzen's comprehensive article which introduces readers to the subject area, through headings such as 'an equal rights architecture', 'architecture of the "other"', 'an architecture of context', 'textual/contextual' and 'transformative/contextual'.[1] My feeling is that, despite the limitations and biases inherent in putting forward any conceptual framework, it is vital at this moment in the development of the field of gender, space and architecture to give some account of the relationship between the various contributions made by feminists in architecture over the last twenty years.

One of the problems in organising the material is the tracing of a number of different historical trajectories: the development of feminism over time, the shifting role of feminists in architectural history and the changes taking place in women's role as architects, while at the same time aiming to clarify the key conceptual points and theoretical concerns which define the paths of each trajectory and form the areas of their overlap. Another difficulty has been to create a framework which is simple yet complex enough to relate the different forms of architectural practice – history, theory and design.

Over the last twenty years the disciplines of architectural history and design have changed dramatically, both internally and in relation to one another. On the one hand, feminist architectural history has developed from a recovery of evidence of women architects to embrace the role of theory, specifically critical and gender theory in interpreting architectural representations historically. On the other hand, women in architectural practice continue to fall between those who wish to remain gender neutral and those who aim to make explicit their feminist intentions. Along with interventions from other areas of cultural studies, gender theories have opened up definitions of architectural practice to include process as well as product, drawing and writing as well as building, so that the distinctions between design, history and theory are now, more than ever, less than clear-cut.

In order to respond to the issues raised above, this introduction is divided into four sections, each of which corresponds to a number of chapters contained in Part 3, 'Gender, Space, Architecture'. The division is both chronological, charting the influence of feminism on architectural practice over the past twenty years, and disciplinary. The first section, '"Herstory": Women in Architectural History', which comprises Chapters 28–29, and the second section, '"Drawing on Diversity": Women in Architectural Design', which includes Chapters 30–33, deal in general with feminist projects from the 1970s and early 1980s. The third section, '"Sexuality and Space": Rethinking Architectural History' – Chapters 34–38, and the fourth section, '"Desiring Practices": Rethinking Architectural Design' – Chapters 39–41, comprise feminist work produced in the late 1980s and 1990s. The first and third parts emphasise the concerns of writers and historians; while the second and fourth parts focus on issues more pertinent to those designing architectural spaces.

Over the past thirty years, there has been a quite dramatic change in the focus of feminist architectural criticism and practice, one which might be described as a shift from modern to postmodern. The essays selected here illustrate the direction this change has taken – for example, we might consider the difference between the work of Matrix, originally an architectural feminist co-operative, in Chapter 31 and the writings of Jennifer Bloomer, a professor of architecture, at Iowa State University, in Chapter 40. Although the decade that marks the time between them chronologically is relatively short, it is important in marking a definite change in approach to feminist architectural practice. These two practices highlight quite clearly the scope of the ideas that have been developed in relation to feminism and architecture, from those that concentrate on the practice of architecture as the design of buildings, without a critique of architectural language, to those that concentrate on re-defining what the practice of a feminist architect might be.

'HERSTORY': WOMEN IN ARCHITECTURAL HISTORY

Some feminist historians, following reformist or liberal tactics aimed at establishing conditions of equality for women, have been concerned with women's exclusion from architecture, and have sought to produce an alternative history of architecture by uncovering evidence of women's contributions to architecture.[2] An interesting study here is Sara Boutelle's, outlined in Chapter 27, of the architect Julia Morgan who was so keen not to develop a cult status, or to inculcate an area of 'genius', that she intentionally wiped out traces of her identity. Research on her is consequently extremely difficult, since she arranged for all the office records to be burnt after her death, while the buildings she designed were built in such a wide range of styles that her work cannot be easily identified from its appearance alone.

The work of feminist architectural historians has been vital in providing research and documentation of women's different kinds of contribution to architecture historically; either as architects of large institutional buildings in the public realm, or within the building industry and also through their roles as patrons.[3] The issue of female patronage is a subject which has been extensively explored by Alice T. Friedman in Chapter 36.[4] The work of Lynne Walker in the United Kingdom, included here in Chapter 28, and Gwendolyn Wright in the United States, emphasises an important aspect of the historical recovery of the contribution of women to architecture. Both historians have highlighted the ways in which women have had to fight for inclusion in the predominantly male profession, from their acceptance in institutions of architectural education, to establishing themselves in offices as professional architects.[5]

Other feminists have followed a more radical line in focusing their critique on the gendered nature of architectural history itself. Feminists have argued that only the buildings of the great male masters have been categorised as 'architecture' and included in architectural history. By reclaiming the history of low-key buildings, everyday housing, domestic, interior and textile design, spaces or practices typically associated with women and regarded as trivial, such feminists show that it is not only the buildings of the public realm, financed by wealthy patrons, the nobility and merchants of the past and the wealthy capitalists of today, that are worthy of being historical writing. They simultaneously challenge the biases at work in traditional architectural history, especially with respect to what constitutes architecture, and correct its oversights, painting a fuller picture of architectural practice.

Pioneering work in this area has been developed in interior and design history,[6] and planning and urban history.[7] Such work suggests a view of architecture as part of a continuum of space which extends from a consideration of objects and interiors at the micro scale to regional and local planning processes at the macro level. Historical work in vernacular studies, local history and the history of housing has also contributed valuable material to this debate.[8]

'DRAWING ON DIVERSITY': WOMEN IN ARCHITECTURAL DESIGN[9]

Women's exclusion from the architectural profession and education is not only a historical problem but also one critical to the role of women architects practising today. For example, in the United Kingdom, although many women start architectural courses – an average of 27 per cent of all architectural students are women – only 9 per cent of women complete their studies and practise architecture. In the profession, although there has been an increase in the number of women registered as architects, from 5 per cent in 1975 to 11 per cent in 1997, the figure still shows that only one in ten of practising architects is female.[10]

One of the most important aspects emphasised in relation to women's role as architects has been the diverse nature of women's practice. Some could be considered to follow principles of 'equality', while others prefer principles of 'difference'. First we will consider those women who have sought to advance their recruitment and status within the ranks of the architecture profession as it exists. Second we will discuss those women who have questioned the nature of architectural practice and instead redefined their architectural design practice in ways that differ radically from existing models.

In architectural practice, many women architects have chosen, and still choose, to remain invisible, preferring to operate as 'architects' and not to emphasise their female status. Such women have worked both as prominent female professionals and as sole practitioners or as the main architect in their own firms. Historically we have the examples of Eileen Gray, Lilly Reich, Truus Schröder, Charlotte Perriand, and more recently, Zaha Hadid, Itsuko Hasegawa, Eva Jiricna, Judith Scheine and Margaret Duinker. Women also are key architects in firms like Architectonica, D/PZ, Future Systems, Koning Eizenberg and Werkfabrik. These female architects do not raise issues of gender in relation to their design work, except in the case of sex discrimination in relation to the nature and size of their commissions or their role in the office.

Taking a role as the female architect in a male–female architectural partnership has long been a chosen form of architectural practice for women. There is a long tradition of this mode of practice, in couples such as Jane Drew and Maxwell Fry, Alison and Peter Smithson, Charles and Ray Eames, Diane Agrest and Mario Gandelsonas, Patti and Michael Hopkins, Elizabeth Diller and Ricardo Scofidio. Certainly for many women this model has provided them with a stable and often high-profile form of practice. Arguably, the male partner eases routes of access to a male professional elite and provides the continuity required to sustain practice while raising children. But quite often, working alongside a man may prove disadvantageous. In seeking to delineate the nature of each person's contribution to the architectural outputs, many assume the woman's role to be connected to the interior and decorative aspects of the design or to the implementation of schemes designed by their male partner, either as draughtsperson or administrator. This raises the important issue of authorship, which has been critiqued by certain feminists who instead emphasise the collaborative nature of architectural design.

Few practising architects have written extensively about this kind of experience from a feminist perspective, but Denise Scott Brown's account in Chapter 29 is exemplary. Scott Brown discusses candidly the sexism she was subjected to as the female partner of the prominent male architect Robert Venturi, and the ways in which critics and journalists frequently assumed her role in the creation of design ideas and projects to be minimal. The tendency was to exclude her as author in representations of their joint architectural practice: design and writing.[11] The experience of Denise Scott Brown raises the question of the dissemination of architecture. The role of feminist critics in promoting the work of women and in raising issues of gender and sexism in architectural design is an important one. There is a strong historical tradition of female architectural critics, such as Ada Louise Huxtable and Jane Jacobs commentating on the problems of urban and architectural design, as well as women such as Margaret Schütte-Lihotzky and Charlotte Perkins Gilman involving themselves as the promoters and champions of design reforms to benefit women as users.

In dealing with issues of difference, there have been several approaches to looking at the ways in which gender difference impacts on the practice of architecture. One has been to critique architectural value systems as implicitly patriarchal and to suggest that, since women are different from men, they have different priorities in organising and designing the production of architecture. This approach focuses on the problems inherent for women as users in 'man-made' environments and the ways in which patriarchal ideology is inscribed in space. This particular agenda can be aligned with the approach of radical feminism outlined in the first part of this book.[12]

Essentalist radical feminists see femaleness and femininity as encompassing a set of qualities which are quite different from maleness and masculinity.[13] According to this argument, contemporary societies which are patriarchal – which organise and monopolise private property to the benefit of the male head of the family – reflect such values in the often phallic building forms that they produce, the quintessential example being the skyscraper. Conversely, cultures that revere the feminine principle and treat women as equals produce built forms related to the morphology of the female body.[14] The most obvious manifestation of sex difference in architectural practice has traditionally been in connection to formal differences, where feminist intentions are believed to be best communicated through biological symbolism. A number of feminist designers have drawn architectural inspiration from the female body, designing womb-like and curvaceous forms rather than phallic towers, spaces which focus on aspects of enclosure (shelters and prisons), exploring the relationship between inside and outside (openings, hollows and gaps).

Socialist and Marxist feminists have also been involved in critiquing the 'man-made' environment and promoting different kinds of architectural design.[15] In the late 1970s and early 1980s, feminists in planning and architecture in the United States and in Europe were primarily concerned with the ways in which gender differences impacted on the production and use of built space, focusing on the predominance of men as producers of a man-made environment and of women's experiences as users of these spaces. The work of the American feminist planner and historian Dolores Hayden, for instance, outlined in Chapter 30, identifies how certain features of the man-made environment discriminate against women, such as inhospitable streets, sexist symbolism in advertising and pornographic outlets. Hayden proposes removing these sexist features and replacing them instead with child-care facilities, safe houses and better public transport to ensure a more equitable society.

The work of Matrix , a London-based feminist architectural co-op set up in the early 1980s, takes a slightly different approach, as discussed in Chapter 31. Matrix , like Hayden, was also concerned with the problems experienced by women users in the man-made environment, as well as designing spaces for women users which improved upon aspects of safety and accessibility in the public and domestic realms. Matrix also critiqued the organisation of the building industry and the architectural profession. By organising the office as a co-operative where each worker, regardless of experience and job description, was paid the same wage, Matrix sought to work in an egalitarian manner in their internal office structure. In encouraging women to become involved in the building professions, particularly women from ethnic minorities who were often doubly discriminated against in the building profession through gender and race, Matrix were involved in educational work and the promotion of alternative role models in architectural practice.

The co-operative also advocated a different design process, one where users were involved in the design from the outset, and architects, rather than imposing their designs, acted as enablers, helping future occupants realise their own spatial needs and desires. This interest in a different design process was reflected in the ways in which ideas about buildings were communicated – attempts were made to ensure that architectural drawings and models prioritised the communication of spatial ideas rather than aesthetic preoccupations.[16]

Implicit within this work is a critique of architectural value systems and a suggestion that women have different priorities in the design of built spaces and the organisation of their production.[17] These kinds of projects raise important issues for the practitioner and the critic concerning the role of the architect and the definition of architecture. Such work tends to use the more inclusive, less hier-archical term 'built environment', rather than 'architecture.' It defines the role of the architect as an enabler, rather than a genius, a figure who facilitates and allows clients and users to participate in the development of their own spaces. By revaluing process, the people involved in building production are then as interest-ing and important to architectural history as those who finance or design buildings.

Feminists have suggested that it is precisely in the area of design process that female difference might be expressed. The emphasis varies. On the one hand, as discussed with respect to Matrix, for some practitioners the intention has been to organise the design process in such a way that it benefits users and clients.[18] On the other hand, American critic Karen Franck, following Nancy Chodorow in Chapter 8, argues in Chapter 32 that women's socialisation fosters a different value system, emphasising certain qualities such as connectedness, inclusiveness, an ethics of care, everyday life, subjectivity, feelings, complexity and flexibility in design. In Chapter 32, Franck sites the work of women architects such as Eileen Gray and Lilly Reich, and Susana Torre's projects such as 'House of Meaning' and 'Space as Matrix' as exemplary of this approach.[19] Promoting the idea that women designers and users value different kinds of spaces – ones which foster the flexibility required by women's social roles – also suggests analogies between spatial matrices and the fluid spatiality of the female body.[20]

Anthropologist Labelle Prussin's account of the architecture produced by nomads in Africa in Chapter 33 raises a critique of normative architectural practice from a different cultural perspective. Prussin's descriptions of the design processes adopted by moving peoples emphasise the importance of specific kinds of built structures traditionally perceived as 'outside' the domain of architecture, such as transitional places and nomadic spaces. But it is important in this case not to collapse the creative processes of specific groups of black African women with the design work of black women practising architecture in other cultures. The influences of cultural and economic differences regarding land ownership and social relations of production produce forms of architectural practice which differ significantly from those in developed capitalist western countries. Like sex and gender, differences of race and ethnicity are contingent on geographical locations and other forms of social relations.[21]

'SEXUALITY AND SPACE': RETHINKING ARCHITECTURAL HISTORY[22]

Drawing on gender theory, from fields such as psychoanalysis, philosophy, cultural studies, film theory and art history, has increasingly developed the work of feminists in architectural studies, particularly architectural history, theory and criticism. The latter section of Part 3, 'Gender, Space, Architecture', comprising Chapters 34–41 includes a selection of essays which specifically use interdisciplinary feminist criticism to extend the field of architectural discourse, blurring the boundaries between theory and history and between criticism and practice.

The focus in Chapters 34–38 is on the ways in which feminist and critical theory have influenced the writing of architectural history. It is worth therefore noting the academic context in which feminist architectural history is located and which it radically critiques. Architectural history can be broadly described as a practice which studies the history of buildings. Although approaches vary, traditionally architectural historians have tended to concentrate on defining 'architecture' as those buildings financed by wealthy and influential patrons and designed by prestigious architects. They have analysed this architecture in terms of form, style, type and aesthetics. Critical approaches to architectural history have been made by those concerned with the politics of architecture, specifically with issues of class. So-called 'Marxist' architectural history entails seeing buildings as the products of the processes of capitalism and, as such, to be implicated in the political, social and cultural values of dominant classes and elite social groupings.[23] But although Marxist architectural historians have considered the social production of architecture, and also its reproduction through image and text, seldom has this work been from a feminist perspective.[24]

The early work of feminists engaged with issues concerning the practice of architectural history ranged from articles reclaiming the work of women architects to discussions of women's fight for equal access within architectural education and the profession. Although vital in providing new material, this work does not seek to question conventional architectural historical models or raise methodological issues concerning, for example, the status of the architectural object, the role of the architect and kind of analysis relevant to the objects of study.

The implications of feminist work on representation and gender in other fields – namely, psychoanalysis, philosophy, cultural studies, film theory and art history – have raised two main issues for the practice of architectural history: first, new objects of study – the actual material which historians choose to look at; and second, the intellectual criteria by which historians interpret those objects of study. An important body of work coming out of US scholarship, specifically East Coast universities such as Princeton, and publications such as *Assemblage* and *ANY*, highlights the relevance of such methodological issues. Critics such as Beatriz Colomina in Chapter 34, Zeynep Çelik in Chapter 35 and Mabel Wilson have focused on developing sustained feminist critiques of the traditional male canon. Using feminist interpretative techniques, they place issues of gender, race and ethnicity at the heart of the architectural practice of such male masters as Adolf Loos and Le Corbusier.[25]

Simultaneous to the emergence of differing feminist positions concerning class, race and sexuality, architectural history has become more critical of how patriarchy, capitalism, heterosexism and racism operate in the production of architecture. Alice T. Friedman's essay in Chapter 36 looks at an object of study common among feminist architectural historians – the contribution of female patrons to architecture – but attempts to complexify earlier versions of 'herstory', drawing on psychoanalytic theory to examine the relations of power played out through vision in certain architectural designs.[26]

Theoretical approaches suggest new aspects of architecture to explore; equally, new architectural objects provide new sites through which to explore theory and suggest new kinds of interpretative modes. Feminist theory as a critical theory informs architectural history. Drawing on the work by queer theorists such as Judith Butler and Eve Kosofsky Sedgwick, whose notions of 'performativity' have provoked those in spatial disciplines to look at 'place' as a critical location for 'performing' gender, Henry Urbach's essay in Chapter 37 is another example of a piece of architectural history which draws on critical theory, in this case queer theory, in relation to the spatial practice of 'coming out'. In order to develop an argument concerning secrecy and display with relation to homosexuality, Urbach focuses on an unusual object of study, the design of the closet.[27]

Drawing on poststructuralism, psychoanalysis and gender theory has also allowed a body of work to develop which problematises such seemingly stable terms as 'architecture', 'male' and 'female'. Architecture and masculinity are examined as mutually reinforcing ideologies. In a profession where masculinity is collapsed into the neutral figure of the 'architect' and sites of current architectural education and discourse – the office, the media, the institution and the profession – are also considered to be gender neutral, the importance of recognising gender as a social construction in order to critique the heterosexual, patriarchal bastion of architectural practice is emphasised. In Chapter 38 Joel Sanders critiques a project by architectural practice SOM, Cadet Quarters, US Air Force Academy, Colorado Springs, showing how representations of masculinity are central to the work of these contemporary architects.[28] Joel Sanders' edited collection *Stud: Architectures of Masculinity*, is the first text to deal specifically with issues of masculinity and architecture, but rather than providing a study of the work of male architects, the texts are firmly positioned within multi-disciplinary discourse and the book consists of chapters of history, theory and practice.

'DESIRING PRACTICES': RETHINKING ARCHITECTURAL DESIGN[29]

The final three chapters in Part 3, 'Gender, Space, Architecture', quite clearly highlight the scope of work and new directions for feminist architectural practice. Feminist criticism has allowed a scrutiny of the aims and ambitions of architectural designers and the value given to the end product over process. More recent feminist work, however, suggests that radical practice should not only concentrate on solving problems in a practical way but also critique architecture as a form of representation consisting of images and writing. Such a shift, which involves thinking about architectural practice as text as well as building, may be characterised as postmodern and opens up possibilities for many different approaches to the feminist practice of architecture. Feminist criticism in shifting the location of theory from within architecture, as a description of architectural design and a way of prescribing practice, to outside architectural discourse, has changed definitions of the practice of architecture. Architecture is no longer considered only in relation to the mode of production, but rather in relation to its reproduction through cultural representations, through consumption, appropriation and occupation.

As historians have shown, representations of architecture – drawings, plans, sections and photographs – are gendered, but the language used to describe architectural form is also gendered, such as the classical orders of architecture, where Doric is masculine and Ionic and Corinthian feminine, or the binary of masculine-structure/feminine-decoration. In traditional architectural discourse, in theory, history and design, architecture which contains undesirable qualities, such as weakness, has traditionally been defined as 'feminine', whereas the term 'masculine' is applied to buildings considered more successful.

The language of architectural professional practice is also gendered, as Diane Agrest shows in Chapter 39. The procedures and methodologies of architecture, laid out in treatises, to be adopted by those practising architecture, contain representations of male and female. Using examples from the drawing and writing of Renaissance architects who advocated the use of particular proportion systems for setting out the formal geometries of buildings, Agrest argues that it is the male which is used to represent the ideal set of proportions, whereas the female body is either rejected from the practice of architecture or suppressed within it.[30] Since the activity of architecture is also considered gendered – a male creative genius inspired by a female muse – for women to be considered active practitioners has proved difficult.

American architect and critic Jennifer Bloomer also raises a number of questions concerning the professional practice of architecture through her drawn and written projects, in Chapter 40. In Bloomer's writing, text has a materiality and is carefully constructed and spatially structured, operating as a metaphoric site through which imaginative narratives are explored. For Bloomer, different modes of writing express different ways of understanding architecture through the intimate and personal, the subjective rather than objective, through sensual rather purely visual stimulation. Bloomer's text is her architecture, her textual strategies are used to interpret architectural drawings and spaces but also to create new notions of space and creativity, allowing links to be made between architectural design to history and theory.[31] This type of work focuses on the complicated issue of architectural representation, considering cultural definitions of architecture and the feminine, both in scripted texts and architectural drawings.

Bloomer's work follows Derridean deconstruction, aiming to reveal the insufficiency of logical and rational structures such as spoken language to explain the world. Instead she brings into operation the irrational and subversive elements in written texts – the feminine. Bloomer's work demonstrates that the feminine can be a radical element in architectural practice. Drawing parallels between the creation of a building, assumed to be a clean act of control and precision, and the mess of childbirth, Bloomer questions the gender of creativity. Through her dirty drawings and her incorporation of parts of the female anatomy – breasts, milk, fluids, blood, hatching, udders – into architecture, Bloomer generates a critique of the sterility of the architectural drawing process. The feminine is found in the so-called slippage of words in Bloomer's work; for example, the words 'big jugs' placed within an architectural context may suggest many things, such as large breasts. But can the role of the feminine and female body as a container or empty signifier be used to represent patriarchal ideologies?

A number of architectural design projects have followed a similar kind of approach, drawing on theoretical concerns to stimulate a different way of considering the process of design, from the choosing of site to the articulation of services. In the work of Clare Robinson, this is clearly formulated in a project which redefines site as *chora* or female container. For Michelle Kauffman, the gaps between buildings and occupied by women in patriarchy gave rise to a design project based on a lacuna wall.[32] The work of other so-called feminist architectural practices such as muf in the United Kingdom and Liquid Incorporated in the

United States, is more ambiguous. The relation of feminist theory to architectural design in projects which link built practice to written text, deal with issues of femininity and decoration, relations of looking and the materiality of fluids may be a matter of critical interpretation rather than intention.[33] Also emerging are connections to be made with other kinds of spatial practices, such as those of artists operating in the public spaces of the city – for example, Niki Sant Phalle, Maya Lin and Suzanne Lacy.[34]

Chapters in Part 2, 'Gender, Space', argue convincingly that culturally produced space is necessarily gendered, but this argument is more difficult to make in relation to the explicit gendering of space through design intention. This issue is always clouded by the question of whether architecture can communicate meaning, let alone politicised meaning.[35] For architecture,[36] and for feminists, there is another layer of difficulty; for if women are not speaking subjects in the existing symbolic order, then the only way for women to represent themselves is through an acknowledgement of this condition – through mimicking or parodying their objectified position.[37]

Luce Irigaray's theory of 'mimicry' has been used to show how, when working within a symbolic system with predetermined notions of feminine and masculine, where there is no theory of the female subject, women can seek to represent themselves through mimicking the system itself.[38] The last chapter in Part 3, 'Gender, Space, Architecture', by Elizabeth Diller, addresses this issue through a project which demonstrates how a feminist critique of women's role as domestic labourers can be used to inspire creativity. Diller's architectural project involves a complex choreography where, by performing a series of folding movements similar to origami, a number of shirts are ironed into perfectly useless forms. This can be read as a parody of the precision of housework and a reworking of the skills for a new function, as a critical architectural practice.

Studying the work of architects who focus on issues of gender and representation provides us with some examples of possible feminist architectural tactics and strategies; so too can work in other spatial practices – for example, in dance, film, art and writing. Clearly, as well as the makers of works (the architectural practitioners, designers, historians, theorists) the roles of audience, user and critic are vital to the construction of the meaning of feminist practices. Can users agree on what constitutes a feminist response to architectural practice and can such qualities, be they functional, material or aesthetic, be communicated through architectural experience? Is consensus necessary? How do critics interpret gendered meanings in architectural discourse? Is architecture gendered only through criticism? Or as one feminist critic has suggested, should the role of females in producing architectural space be examined without recourse to the 'feminine'?[39]

Finally, it is clear that common to the development of all architectural practices attentive to gender difference is a commitment to diversity and the production of work which bridges theory, history and design. But we must not lose sight of the continuing discrimination against women in the architectural profession. While societies continue to expect that women bear children, and while women still bear the responsibility of being the primary child-carers, female architects will face problems of negotiating the twin demands of home and work. As feminists, we must continue to be attentive to the relation of theory and practice. As bell hooks points out so eloquently in the epilogue, 'it is our capacity to imagine that lets us move beyond boundaries'.[40] Theoretical insights provide new possibilities for considering the relation of women to architectural practice, while the experience of female practitioners sustains and enriches the work of theoreticians. This is feminist architectural praxis.

NOTES

1 Sherry Ahrentzen, 'The F Word in Architecture: Feminist Analyses in/of/for Architecture', Thomas A. Dutton and Lian Hurst Mann (eds), *Reconstructing Architecture: Critical Discourses and Social Practices* (Minneapolis: University of Minnesota Press, 1996), pp. 71–118.

2 See, for example, Sara Boutelle, 'Julia Morgan', Susana Torre (ed.), *Women in American Architecture: A Historic and Contemporary Perspective* (New York: Whitney Library of Design, 1977), pp. 79–87; Sara Boutelle, *Julia Morgan: Architect* (New York: Abbeville Press, 1988).

3 See, for example, Lynne Walker, *British Women in Architecture 1671–1951* (London: Sorello Press, 1984).

4 See Alice Friedman, *House and Household in Elizabethan England* (London and Chicago: University of Chicago Press, 1989); Alice Friedman, *Women and the Making of the Modern House* (New York, Harry N. Abrams, 1997).

5 See, for example, Lynne Walker, 'Women and Architecture', Judy Attfield and Pat Kirkham (eds), *A View from the Interior: Feminism, Women and Design* (London: The Women's Press, 1989), pp. 90–110; and Gwendolyn Wright, 'On the Fringe of the Profession: Women in American Architecture', Spiro Kostof (ed.), *The Architect: Chapters in the History of the Profession* (Oxford: Oxford University Press, 1977), pp. 280–309.

6 See, for example, Isabelle Anscombe, *A Woman's Touch: Women in Design from 1860 to the Present Day* (London: Virago, 1984); Judy Attfield and Pat Kirkham (eds), *A View from the Interior: Feminism, Women and Design* (London: The Women's Press, 1989); Ellen Lupton and J. Abbott Miller, *The Bathroom, the Kitchen and the Aesthetics of Waste: A Process of Elimination* (MIT List Visual Arts Centre, Cambridge MA, 1992); Ellen Lupton, *Mechanical Brides: Women and Machines from Home to Office* (New York: Cooper Hewitt National Museum of Design and Princeton Architectural Presss, 1993); and Jude Burkhauser, *Glasgow Girls: Women in Art and Design 1880–1920* (Edinburgh: Canongate, 1993).

7 See, for example, L. Ottes, E. Poventud, M. van Schendelen and G. Segond von Banchet (eds), *Gender and the Built Environment: Emancipation in Planning, Housing and Mobility in Europe* (Assen, The Netherlands: Van Gorcum, 1995).

8 See, for example, Caroline O. N. Moser and Linda Peake (eds), *Women, Human Settlements and Housing* (London: Tavistock, 1987); and Elizabeth Collins Cromley

and Carter L. Hudgins (eds), *Gender, Class and Shelter: Perspectives in Vernacular Architecture* (Knoxville: The University of Tennessee Press, 1995).

9 This phrase has been borrowed from the title of an exhibition of 1997. See Lynne Walker, *Drawing on Diversity: Women, Architecture and Practice* (exhibition catalogue, London: RIBA, Heinz Gallery, 1997).

10 *Architects' Employment and Earnings 1997* (London: Royal Institute of British Architects, June 1997), p. 9.

11 See, for example, Denise Scott Brown, 'Room at the Top? Sexism and the Star System in Architecture', Ellen Perry Berkeley (ed.), *Architecture: A Place for Women* (London and Washington, DC: Smithsonian Institution Press, 1989), pp. 237–46.

12 See, for example, Leslie Kanes Weisman, *Discrimination by Design* (Chicago: University of Illinois Press, 1992).

13 See, for example, Magrit Kennedy, 'Seven Hypotheses on Male and Female Principles', 'Making Room: Women and Architecture', *Heresies: A Feminist Publication on Art and Politics* (New York: Heresies Collective Inc., 1981), vol. 3, no. 3, issue 11, pp. 12–13.

14 See, for example, Mimi Lobell, 'The Buried Treasure', Berkeley (ed.), *Architecture*, pp. 139–57.

15 See, for example, Dolores Hayden, *Redesigning the American Dream* (New York and London: W. W. Norton and Company, 1986); Matrix, *Making Space: Women and the Man Made Environment* (London: Pluto Press, 1984); J. Little, L. Peake and P. Richardson (eds), *Women in Cities: Gender and the Urban Environment* (London: Macmillan, 1988); and Marion Roberts, *Living in Man-made World: Gender Assumptions in Modern Housing Design* (London: Routledge, 1991).

16 See, for example, Frances Bradshaw, 'Working with Women', Matrix, *Making Space* (London: Pluto Press, 1984), pp. 89–105.

17 See Frances Bradshaw, 'Working with Women', Matrix, *Making Space*, pp. 89–105; and Karen A. Franck, 'A Feminist Approach to Architecture: Acknowledging Women's Ways of Knowing', Berkeley (ed.), *Architecture*, pp. 201–16.

18 See Frances Bradshaw, 'Working with Women', Matrix, *Making Space*, pp. 89–105.

19 See Karen A. Franck, 'A Feminist Approach', Berkeley (ed.), *Architecture*, pp. 201–16.

20 See Susana Torre, 'The Pyramid and Labyrinth', Susana Torre (ed.), *Women in American Architecture*, pp. 186–202; and Susana Torre, 'Space as Matrix', *Heresies*, pp. 51–2.

21 Labelle Prussin, 'Labour Value, Productivity, and Women's Work' to 'Mnemonics, the Acquisition of Skills, and Play as Children's Work' inclusive, 'The Creative Process', *African Nomadic Architecture: Space, Place and Gender* (Washington, DC: Smithsonian Institution Press, 1995), pp. 58–63.

22 This title is taken from the book of the same name. See Beatriz Colomina (ed.), *Sexuality and Space* (New York: Princeton Architectural Press, 1992).

23 See, for example, Linda Clarke, *Building Capitalism* (London: Routledge, 1992); Anthony D. King (ed.), *Buildings and Society: Essays on the Social Development of the Built Environment* (London: Routledge and Kegan Paul, 1980) and Thomas A. Markus, *Buildings and Power* (London: Routledge, 1993).

24 See, for example, Beatriz Colomina (ed.), *ArchitectureProduction* (New York: Princeton Architectural Press, 1988).

25 Beatriz Colomina, 'The Split Wall: Domestic Voyeurism', Beatriz Colomina (ed.), *Sexuality and Space* (New York: Princeton Architectural Press, 1992), pp. 73–98; and Zeynep Çelik, 'Gendered Spaces in Colonial Algiers', Diane Agrest, Patricia Conway and Leslie Kanes Weisman (eds), *The Sex of Architecture* (New York: Harry N. Abrams Publisher, 1997), pp. 127-40, originally published as 'Le Corbusier, Orientalism, Colonialism', in *Assemblage* (April 1992), 17, pp. 66–77; and Mabel O. Wilson, 'Black Bodies/White Cities: Le Corbusier in Harlem', *ANY* (1996), no. 16, pp. 35–9.

26 See, for example, Agrest, Conway and Weisman (eds), *The Sex*; Debra Coleman, Elizabeth Danze and Carol Henderson (eds), *Architecture and Feminism* (New York: Princeton Architectural Press, 1996); Francesca Hughes (ed.), *The Architect: Reconstructing Her Practice* (Cambridge, Mass.: MIT Press, 1996); Duncan McCorquodale, Katerina Rüedi and Sarah Wigglesworth (eds), *Desiring Practices* (London: Black Dog Publishing Ltd, 1996); and Joel Sanders (ed.), *Stud: Architectures of Masculinity* (New York: Princeton Architectural Press, 1996).

27 McCorquodale, Rüedi and Wigglesworth (eds), *Desiring Practices*; and Sanders (ed.), *Stud*.

28 Joel Sanders, 'SOM, *Cadet Quarters*, US Air Force Academy, Colorado Springs', Sanders (ed.), *Stud*, pp. 68–78.

29 This title is taken from a multi-discipinary book, conference and exhibition of the same name held at the Royal Institute of British Architects, London, October 1995. McCorquodale, Rüedi and Wigglesworth (eds), *Desiring Practices*.

30 See, for example, Diane Agrest, *Architecture from Without: Theoretical Framings for a Critical Practice* (Cambridge, Mass.: MIT Press, 1993).

31 Jennifer Bloomer, 'Big Jugs', Arthur Kroker and Marilouise Kroker (eds), *The Hysterical Male: New Feminist Theory* (London: Macmillan Education 1991), pp. 13–27; and Jennifer Bloomer, *Architecture and the Text: The (S)crypts of Joyce and Piranesi* (New Haven and London: Yale University Press, 1993).

32 See Claire Robinson, 'Chora Work', 'Dear Jennifer', *ANY* (January/February 1994), no. 4, pp. 34–7; and Michelle Kaufman 'Liquidation, Amalgamation', Dear Jennifer', *ANY*, (January/February 1994), no. 4, pp. 38–9.

33 See Muf, *Architectural Design* (August 1996), vol. 66, nos 7–8, pp. 80–3; and Amy Landesberg and Lisa Quatrale, 'See Angel Touch', Debra Coleman, Elizabeth Danze and Carol Henderson (eds), *Architecture and Feminism* (New York: Princeton Architectural Press, 1996), pp. 60–71.

34 See, for example, Jeff Kelley, 'The Body Politics of Suzanne Lacy', Nina Felshin, *But is it Art? The Spirit of Art as Activism* (Seattle: Bay Press, 1995); Suzanne Lacy (ed.), *Mapping the Terrain: New Genre Public Art* (Seattle, Bay Press, 1995); and Molly Hankwitz, 'The Story of Hon-Katedral: A Fantastic Female', Coleman, Danze and Henderson (eds), *Architecture and Feminism*, pp. 161–82.

35 See, for example; Frederick Jameson, 'Is Space Political?', *Any Place* (Cambridge, Mass.: MIT Press), pp. 192–204.

36 See Bernard Tschumi, *Architecture and Disjunction* (Cambridge, Mass.: MIT Press, 1996). For a feminist reference, see Christiane Erlemann, 'What is feminist architecture?' Grisela Ecker (ed.), *Feminist Aesthetics* (Boston: Beacon Press, 1986), pp. 125–34.

37 See, for example, Bloomer, 'Big Jugs'.

38 See Luce Irigaray, 'Any Theory of the "Subject" has Always been Appropriated by the "Masculine"', *Speculum of the Other Woman* (Ithaca, NY: Cornell University Press, 1985), pp. 133–46.

39 Ann Bergren, 'Dear Jennifer', *ANY* (January/February 1994), no. 4, pp. 12–15.

40 bell hooks, Julie Eizenberg and Hank Koning, 'House, 20 June 1994', *Assemblage* (1995), 24, pp. 22–9. p. 29.

27 Sara Boutelle

'Julia Morgan'

from Susana Torre (ed.) *Women in American Architecture: A Historic and Contemporary Perspective* (1977)

Julia Morgan (1872–1957), our most prolific pioneer woman architect, emerged on the American scene at the turn of the century. She designed more than 800 buildings in a career that spanned half a century.

A native of San Francisco, but longtime Oakland resident, she was accepted into the rigorous Engineering School at the University of California at Berkeley, the only woman student at the time. She received an engineering degree in 1894. During her 4-year study she attended informal discussion seminars on architecture at the home of Bernard Maybeck. With his encouragement and that of her family – especially her architect-cousin Pierre Lebrun of New York – she firmly resolved to pursue an architectural career.

After a year's work experience building with Maybeck, Morgan decided to further her training at the École des Beaux-Arts in Paris, then the center of architectural education. Women, however, were not eligible for entrance into the school. Nevertheless, Morgan set out for Paris and the atelier of Marcel de Monclos,[1] where she endured 2 years of grueling tests and competition before being accepted at the École, the first woman in the world to study there. For the next 4 years she studied at the Atelier Chaussemiche, where she won many awards and medals. In 1902 she received her Certificat d'Étude.[2]

Morgan returned to the San Francisco Bay Area in 1902 and became a licensed architect – probably the first woman in California history to do so.[3] She joined the office of John Galen Howard, who was then developing a master plan for the University of California at Berkeley. Morgan worked with him on the Hearst Memorial Mining Building and is said to have designed the campus's Greek Theatre.[4] Howard is said to have boasted of possessing 'the best and most talented designer, whom I have to pay almost nothing, as it is a woman.'[5]

Late in 1904, 'JM,' as she was known to her staff, started a firm of her own in San Francisco. Between 1907 and 1910 she had a partnership with a former Howard draftsman, Ira Hoover, but she re-established her office as an independent practice late in 1910.[6] Her first commissions included numerous informal

Figure 27.1
Julia Morgan, 'Hearst Castle', San Simeon, California

residences for private clients like her sister Emma North in Berkeley in 1909, as well as college buildings like the Mission Revival Campanile of 1904 and library of 1906 at Mills College, a women's college in Oakland. Possibly because the reinforced concrete Mills Campanile withstood the 1906 earthquake, JM was given the commission to rebuild the structurally damaged Fairmont Hotel in San Francisco. From this point on her reputation was made.

Perhaps the most important Morgan client was Phoebe Apperson Hearst, the arbiter of Bay Area taste, whom Morgan had known during her Paris school days.[7]

Soon after establishing her own practice, JM was given the job of building an addition to the Hearst Hacienda in Pleasonton. It was considered a success and led to further commissions from the Hearst family, culminating in the famous San Simeon (begun in 1919, with work continuing through the 1930s) for William Randolph Hearst.

The importance of Phoebe Apperson Hearst to Julia Morgan's career has been variously argued. Although Asilomar, the great seaside conference center begun by Morgan in 1913 for the YWCA, was a pet project of Hearst's, there is evidence that the YWCA in Oakland of 1915, the first of a national chain of commissions built by Morgan for the women's social service organization, had been planned with Grace Merriam Fisher, a Berkeley sorority sister of Morgan's, who became an important board member of the YWCA in 1910.[8]

Institutions – especially for women's use – played a major role in Morgan's practice. Aside from the previously mentioned YWCA buildings, Morgan served as consulting architect for the organization's hospitality houses built during World War I. A surge of interest in women's clubs gave JM the opportunity to build both the simple redwood Saratoga Foothill Club in 1915 and the very elaborate Romanesque-Gothic reinforced concrete Berkeley Women's City Club in 1929. Work also came from women's hospitals and retirement homes.

Julia Morgan's buildings reveal an eclectic approach to design. Although the larger share of her work suggests a loose historicism influenced by her École training in Paris, her architectural practice among the so-called California School familiarized JM with the avant-garde interest in structural honesty and the use of indigenous materials. Her most notable early commission of 1908–10, the St John's Presbyterian Church in Berkeley, used the Craftsman style, which allowed the structural materials to become part of the design by leaving the interior wooden studs and trusses exposed. If Morgan's side-entranced house designs in city and suburb seem derived from the same general plan, it is not obvious in the finished product.[9] The interiors, consisting downstairs of entry hall and staircase placed between living and dining rooms with a kitchen and pantry placed behind them, were varied in size and character so as to accommodate both the Piedmont tycoon and the middle-class Berkeley or Oakland professional.

Julia Morgan's role as patron or director of her office's architectural commissions was never in question. Her suite of offices, located in the Merchants Exchange Building in San Francisco from 1906 to 1952, contained a complete library of rare books and periodicals and operated as an atelier or workshop.[10] Morgan was the one who saw or dealt with clients, and all her engineers and designers carried out her projects without deviation from her small sketches. The staff became her family, shared in her successes, and were always carried during illness or slow times. Thadeus Joy, Walter Steilberg, James LeFeaver, Bjarne Dahl, Ed Hussey, Camille Solon, and others were with her for years. At least two women who worked for Morgan became certified architects: Dorothy Wormser and Elizabeth Boyter.[11] In fact, by 1927 there were 6 women among an office staff of 14, an unusual ratio for that time, as well as for the present.[12]

Julia Morgan's architectural career was a full-time, lifelong endeavor. Her last major project, in the 1940s, was a Museum of Medieval Art for San Francisco. William Randolph Hearst had bought the abandoned Spanish monastery of Santa Maria de Ovila in 1931 with the idea of reassembling the structure in his northern California mountain retreat. Because of the costly nature of the project, he donated the monastery instead to the city of San Francisco, stipulating that the structure be incorporated into a Julia Morgan design for a medieval art museum. Ultimately much of the disassembled structure was destroyed in a fire, and the project was never completed. Nevertheless, despite this last fiasco, as well as her wilful destruction of nearly all her office's records in 1952, Julia Morgan's legacy – in redwood, concrete, and brick – survives.

NOTES

1 Letters to Pierre Le Brun, Morgan Estate, Berkeley, Calif.

2 *Who's Who in California 1928–29*; material submitted by Morgan.

3 California Architect Certificate B-344–1903; letter from Board of Examiners, Sacramento, Calif., January 1976.

4 Walter Steilberg (engineer-architect who worked for her for many years), oral communication, October 1974.

5 Ibid.

6 Ibid.

7 In Paris Julia Morgan lived in the same house with the Maybecks, who were there to further the International Competition for the Phoebe Apperson Hearst Architectural Plan for the University of California. Letter from JM to Mrs Hearst in the Bancroft Library at the University of California at Berkeley is dated February 1899, but it is possible that Hearst and Morgan met as early as 1893 in Berkeley.

8 *YWCA News, Oakland and Alameda County Branch* 2, no. 6 (November 1975), p. 4.

9 Unpublished paper by Richard Longstreth and Robin Clements, in the records of the Archive of Women in Architecture, the Architectural League of New York.

10 Otto Haake (who helped JM close up in 1952), oral communication, January 1976.

11 Dorothy Wormser Coblentz, oral communication; *San Francisco Chronicle*, April 1937; article said that Boyter was the first woman to receive the certificate in Northern California since 1927 and that she trained in the offices of Julia Morgan. Boyter certificate no. C-215; letter from State Association of California Architects, Northern Section, April 1937.

12 Walter Steilberg, oral communication, October 1974.

28 Lynne Walker

'Women and Architecture'

from Judy Attfield and Pat Kirkham (eds), *A View from the Interior: Feminism, Women and Design* (1989)

Many women in Britain today are actively involved in a range of activities and positive initiatives related to architecture. They participate in the creation of the built environment through the design process as architects, planners, engineers and designers and contribute to its production as builders, quantity surveyors, construction workers and, most numerously, as consumers of architecture, users of buildings and the spaces around them.

The work of women architects represents the full range of contemporary professional practice and includes the public sector, private practice and housing associations, while feminist architects concentrate on projects which give priority to women's needs. Although architecture remains a male-dominated activity with 2,502 women currently registered as architects to 25,298 men (about 9 per cent), women in professional practice have made major contributions to some of the best-known contemporary buildings: the Open University (Jane Drew, completed 1977); the Joseph shops in West London (Eva Jiricna, 1984 and 1986); Heathrow Airport Terminal 4 (Ann Gibson of Scott, Brownrigg & Turner, 1985); the Manchester Crafts Village (Gillian Brown of the Manchester City Architects Department, 1982); the Thames Barrier (Jean Clapham, GLC Architects Department, 1972–78); and the pedestrianisation of South Molton Street (Iona Gibson, 1977). And there are feminist architects, or, more precisely, women who are architects and feminists and who emphasise 'the primary importance of changing the existing design process so that women are involved in decision-making at every stage',[1] who choose to work with women whose interests are not normally represented in the design process – ethnic minorities, disabled and working-class groups – to provide building types which are intended specifically to serve these groups' needs – for instance, health centres, nurseries and women's training centres. Feminist cooperatives, such as Matrix and Mitra and the Women's Design Service (WDS), an information and resource centre, work collectively and challenge conventional design philosophy, which they see as overlooking women's interests in the built environment.

Matrix's architecture is grounded in their study of architectural history and their research into women's past role and position in architecture, which they wrote about in *Making Space: Women and the Man-made Environment*, 1984. But they wear this learning lightly, designing low-key, well-planned and comfortable environments, working together with the client group. Often under-resourced, one of Matrix's best-known buildings, the Jagonari Women's Educational Resource Centre, designed with the Asian women's group Jagonari, was well-funded by a grant of £600,000 from the GLC and brings to a larger scale the best qualities of their earlier projects and buildings. Conscious of its context, which is next to a listed historic building, and with security a major consideration, this substantial four-storey brick building with a two-storey crèche across the courtyard at the rear was designed 'to have an Asian feel about it but . . . to avoid the symbolism of any particular religion'.[2] The dignified and eclectic Whitechapel Road front has a shaped gable, onion-domed flèche and is metal-grilled, for decoration and security, while the carefully planned interior is light and spacious with a reassuring atmosphere of comfort and safety, essential to an Asian women's building in a neighbourhood where racist attacks are commonplace.

With contemporary practice as the starting-point, I want to look back to the late nineteenth and early twentieth centuries at the role and position of women who, as architects and designers of buildings, were active agents in challenging patriarchy, which limited women's activities to the home and unpaid domestic duties. In fact, many of the women who took part in architecture as designers during this period – Harriet Martineau, Agnes and Rhoda Garrett, Ethel and Bessie Charles and Elisabeth Scott – identified themselves with the Women's Movement. The contemporary corollary of this precedent is that women's present under-representation in the design process can only be altered by similar resistance and struggle.

After a brief introduction, I shall first examine the relationship between architecture and patriarchal assumptions about women's role and position in society, from the emergence of the organised Women's Movement around 1850 to the design of the first major public building by a woman in this country, in 1927. Important debates about the nature and value of a woman's role in this period in the context of architecture centred around the campaign for married women's property rights, women's access to professional training and the entry of women into the Royal Institute of British Architects (RIBA). These issues are significant because they generated overt expressions of cultural assumptions and norms which reveal the socially constructed nature of attitudes to women.

THE AMATEUR TRADITION

Before the nineteenth century there were two routes to becoming an architect: through the building trades or through an amateur interest in architecture. From the seventeenth century until the end of the nineteenth century, women worked mainly in the amateur tradition, which until the nineteenth century was associated with the aristocracy and upper classes, without having its later pejorative, feminine connotations.

Although it was exceptional for unmarried women to be apprenticed to the guilds which were allied to building, such as carpentry and masonry, married women in the seventeenth century did sometimes receive their husbands' rights and privileges, and widows of carpenters could take apprentices and have 'practical control'[3] of the business. As in carpentry, in architecture some women also practised in succession to their husbands. After the death of her architect husband Elizabeth Deane (1760–1828), for instance, completed the Naval Dock-yards and Works on Haulbowline Island, Cork (1822), efficiently carrying on the family firm, which was joined in 1806 by Thomas Deane, her eldest son, who was 'aided by his mother's great ability'.[4]

However, in the seventeenth and eighteenth centuries architectural design by women was, it seems, exclusively associated with the upper class, which had the time, money and leisure for essentially amateur pursuits. For the sufficiently well-off, architecture was a domestic activity and was therefore appropriate to women, because it could be practised completely within the confines of the family estate, which might provide not only the site but also the building materials and workers. Lady Wilbraham, who designed Weston Park (1671), a country house in Staffordshire, guided by Palladio's *First Book of Architecture*, is an early but typical example of a woman architect working in the amateur tradition.[5]

During the Enlightenment, educated women were taught drawing, mathe-matics and surveying, which gave them an excellent preparation for architecture. For aristocratic women, the design of buildings was seen as an extension of these approved ladies' accomplishments, which in the eighteenth century were often expressed in shellwork rooms and grottoes done in the company of women friends and female members of the family. For instance, in the 1740s the Duchess of Richmond and her daughters devised and executed the decoration of the Goodwood Shell House, which was the result of their serious and expensive avocation.[6]

Upper- and middle-class women in the nineteenth century combined their interest in architecture with a desire to improve the condition of their estate workers. This, in addition to the benevolent end of providing better accommoda-tion, contributed to the consolidation of the position of the landowning classes. George Eliot's Dorothea in *Middlemarch*, who built 'good cottages' for farm labourers to the architect J.C. Loudon's designs, may have been inspired by Louise, Marchioness of Waterford, artist, friend of Ruskin and founder of the model village of Ford in Northumberland.[7]

This combination of philanthropy and building within the amateur tradition was significant for women architects. Estate improvements, in one instance, led to projects for large-scale public works – an entrance to Hyde Park Corner and a Thames Embankment promoted by Elizabeth, Duchess of Rutland.[8] Nevertheless, more typically, women of education and means practised the twin motives of philanthropy and building exclusively in the domestic sphere. After studying architecture while travelling on the Continent for ten years, the cousins Jane

(d. 1811) and Mary (d. 1841) Parminter built a chapel, school and almshouses in Exmouth for their foundation to promote the conversion of Jews to Christianity. This complex of buildings was joined to a thatched polygonal stone house, A-la-Ronde (1794), by a garden, all designed by the Parminters.[9] In their house, much of the Regency-style furniture and the interior decoration in patterns of shells and feathers was also designed and executed by them in the eighteenth-century mosaic fashion favoured by lady amateurs.

By 1850 the enormous pool of untrained, single women was recognised as a social and economic problem. Suitable employment had to be found that would be appropriate for what were perceived as women's special feminine qualities, which were not to be polluted by the commercial world and, as Anthea Callen has pointed out, would not weaken male dominance or threaten to undermine the patriarchal order of Victorian society.[10] Married women whose position was particularly invidious often also undertook useful but unpaid employment to preserve their respectability as 'ladies'. In the mid-Victorian period, the approval of middle-class women's mission to the poor gave many of them experience beyond the home, and architecture, although it remained an exclusively male profession until the 1880s, became an area of acceptable activity for middle-class women if it was combined with philanthropy.[11]

One of the earliest and most prominent campaigners for women's rights in Victorian Britain, Harriet Martineau, designed her own house, with a concern for philanthropy which was typical of the nineteenth century but highly uncharacteristic of most private house-builders in that period. She wrote in her *Autobiography* about her efforts to reform the payment of building workers. She was strongly opposed to 'the pernicious custom of the district to give very long credit, even in the case of workmen's wages', and one of her intentions in building her own house 'was to discountenance this and to break through the custom in my own person'.[12]

The other building type which, with domestic architecture, was thought appropriate for women to design was a church or chapel, especially if built as a memorial to a family member. This activity reinforced the idea of women's supposedly superior moral and spiritual nature; their traditional caring role could be expressed in the design of memorial churches and these, like most domestic architecture designed by women before the end of the nineteenth century, were first and foremost monuments to the family. They were for the family's use, designed as an unpaid private pursuit, thought to be comfortably within the domestic sphere, but they nevertheless gave women opportunities to design buildings and established precedents for participation in professional practice. Sara Losh, for example, designed the highly individual and imaginative St Mary at Wrey, in the Lake District, as a memorial to her sister, Katherine (consecrated in 1842).[13] Like the eighteenth-century Parminters, her travels on the Continent led her to an appreciation of architecture (in her case, early German and Italian Romanesque), which she treated in a completely personal way, untrammelled by architectural fashion.

The memorial motive and benevolence were combined by Mary Watts in the Mortuary Chapel which she designed for the remains of her husband, the painter

G. F. Watts, and executed with her class of the Compton Home Arts and Industries Association, which she had established for the improvement of local young men and women. This provided meaningful, paid employment in the craft-based terra-cotta industry. The Watts Chapel was a focus of Arts and Crafts philanthropy and design, and, as Mary Watts described in her book *The Word in the Pattern*, the local villagers joined her in the construction and decoration of this Chapel of Rest, which she had planned in a complex symbolic system. The round-headed Norman doorway, for example, 'is decorated with a terra-cotta choir of *Art nouveau* heads of angels – not cast from a single mould but each a labour of love of a single villager following, to the best of his or her ability, models provided by Mary Watts.'[14]

In addition to architectural design, the philanthropic motive led many Victorian women, such as Angela Burdett-Coutts, Adeline Cooper, Octavia Hill and Henrietta Barnett, to formulate policies and housing experiments which prepared the way for the involvement of professional women architects in the public sector in Britain in the twentieth century.[15] Also under the philanthropic umbrella, many impoverished middle-class women found employment relating to architecture by tracing plans and writing specifications. The tasks assigned to women in architects' offices in the second half of the nineteenth century represent the aspirations of women for personal and financial independence through architecture, but they also stand for the limitations of their role and position both in society and in the profession. The copying of architectural plans by tracing, for example, was an essential element of Victorian architectural practice, but it was the least prestigious and most boring job for the most junior member of the firm. It was demanding and required the attention to detail and the neat, repetitive work which were seen as a natural extension of those feminine qualities which were so apt for women's domestic activities, most notably embroidery. Even when women joined together as they did in the Ladies Tracing Society, their marginal position was exploited, since, as a delighted Halsey Ricardo reported to a client, they worked 'at a very cheap rate'.[16]

Women as a source of cheap, often occasional or part-time labour whose presence is a threat as well as an assistance to the male workforce is a theme which recurs in architecture, as in other professions and trades, throughout the nineteenth and twentieth centuries. But in the 1850s and 1860s the liberal reformers of the Women's Movement, led by Barbara Leigh Smith, an artist and founder of a Cambridge college, who set up the Association for the Promotion of the Employment of Women, were more concerned with women's access to paid work in an expanding free market than with the implications of the capitalist system for employed working-class women.[17]

The debates about women's involvement in architecture often centred on their physical limitations. Yet the participation in the building industry of thousands of working-class women in the much more physically demanding work of nail- and brick-making was not seen as problematic or threatening to women's role, because this, in the context of architecture, was defined in middle-class or upper-middle-class terms. The class bias of the nineteenth-century debates ignored the plight of working-class women in the building industry and produced a myopic view of women's capabilities and their potential as architects, blocking women from full participation in the profession, limiting them to decorative or auxiliary tasks.

In the second half of the nineteenth century the continuum of feminist concerns which included the employment of middle-class women also covered women's education, their entry into the professions and the campaign for married women's rights and female suffrage. Of crucial importance from the mid-century was the commitment of English feminists to reform the married women's property law. Inspired by Harriet Taylor's 1851 article on the first women's rights convention in the United States, a nationwide committee was organised and their work culminated in the Married Women's Property Acts, which went through Parliament in diluted form in 1870 and in the full and final version in 1882. Before this date, under common law married women's property, earnings and inheritances belonged to their husbands. As the distinguished jurist Sir William Blackstone explained: 'By marriage the very being or legal existence of women is suspended, or at least incorporated or consolidated into that of her husband.'[18] This 'virtual slavery',[19] which denied full rights and status to women, was the linchpin of patriarchy and the iron fist in the velvet glove of the doctrine of separate spheres that designated a woman's place as in the home rather than in the commercial world, where she could compete with men for jobs and income.

Architecture, unlike painting, sculpture or the decorative arts, was more clearly a 'profession', practised in offices, often organised by partnerships and in firms, with legal obligations to apprentices, clients and builders through legally binding contracts and under the control of local government boards and bylaws. Architects were sued, often in connection with these contracts, and were bound by local ordinances. Since, under common law, married women were not allowed to make contracts or be sued in their own right, they were thereby precluded from many of the professional responsibilities of architecture. These legal restrictions reinforced and heightened the set of underlying negative assumptions about women's role and value that supporters of the reform of the property laws had organised to oppose. As long as women were the virtual property of their husbands, they did not, and could not, act in a professional capacity as the designers of property – property cannot design property. The removal of the legal, ideological and psychological impedimenta by the Married Women's Property Acts, therefore, had great significance for all women, and it had particular importance for the entry of women into the architectural profession.

In the early 1890s leading architects, such as Norman Shaw and W.R. Lethaby, argued that architecture was an art, not a business or profession, and indeed, between the census of 1887 and that of 1891, the classification and status of the architect altered from 'Industrial Class' in 1881 to 'Professional Class' under 'Artist' in 1891. The implication for women of these new perceptions was that if architecture was an art, and art was an area appropriate for women's participation, then architecture was also a suitable activity for women.

The question remained, however, whether women should be allowed full participation in the profession on an equal footing with men or be restricted to those aspects of practice which were seen as expressions of their femininity. Here male supporters from within the ranks of architects, E.W. Godwin, C.H. Townsend and R. Weir Schultz, often did as much harm as good. For example, the Arts and Crafts architect C.H. Townsend's view was superficially sympathetic but exasperatingly double-edged. Citing the divided skirt and the precedent of women decorators who 'have been known to work for days on scaffolds' to counter the often quoted 'difficulty women would experience as regards the inspection of the buildings and the necessary mounting of scaffolding', Townsend concluded quite illogically that 'women's work in an architect's office should be "drawing board work", such as ornamental and other detail drawings, competition sets of plans, schemes of colour decoration, and perspective drawings'.[20]

The extension of the ladies' accomplishment of sketching to architectural drafting was part of a process that was gradualist to the point of being counterproductive. Male gatekeepers allowed women out of their domestic sphere and into architects' offices with the ultimate possibility of becoming architects, but it was felt by C.H. Townsend and others that their femininity created problems from which they had to be protected. In fact, this chivalrous view, which dominated thinking about women's role in architecture in this period, circumscribed their architectural activities and blocked them from becoming designers, the most prestigious role in architectural practice. As women's presence would threaten propriety, the dreaded 'commingling of the sexes' could only be avoided by a system of architectural apartheid which physically separated women from men in their own room, and reduced their status and therefore their threat to the established order. In a separate '"women-clerks" room' she could be set to work as 'a "draughtswoman"' which was, Townsend wrote, 'an occupation . . . requiring neatness and delicacy of touch, attention to detail, patience and care, [and] is one which would seem at first blush more likely to find its proficients among women than men'. This patriarchal view saw these characteristics as springing from women's femininity and fitting them most naturally and comfortably on to the lower rungs of the architectural ladder.

Today, when women have become professional architects, a similar pattern of discrimination, implemented through the mechanism of sexual division of labour, remains, according to a recent RIBA survey, which showed that women architects can expect to hold fewer positions of power and influence in architectural practices and that they are more likely to earn less than men throughout their careers.[21]

In addition to the more mundane office jobs, the other area to which women were assigned in the late nineteenth century was design for the decorative arts associated with architecture. In *Women and Work*, edited by one of the founding mothers of the Women's Movement, Emily Faithfull, E.W. Godwin argued convincingly that women should be trained as architects who could design for the applied arts as well as building, and that furniture and decoration were particularly profitable areas for women architect-designers, as they had been for him.[22] However, Godwin's public position was in fact eroded in practice. The work of Beatrice

Philip, Godwin's architectural pupil, and later his wife, shows that his argument was applied in his own office, as it was in the profession generally, in its narrowest sense, with Philip painting the decorative panels for Godwin-designed furniture, such as the satinwood cabinet with four painted panels depicting the seasons, 1877, which is today in the Victoria and Albert Museum. There is no evidence that Beatrice Philip designed buildings, and even at a time when the status of the applied and decorative arts was rising and there was much talk of 'the democracy of the arts', the hierarchy of the arts which privileged architecture over decoration made architecture more prestigious, and more financially rewarding, than decoration. Thus, through the repressive mechanism of the sexual division of labour, women were assigned to the 'lesser arts', without the option that male architect-designers had of architectural design.

In addition to decoration, women's experience in the home and their higher moral sense particularly fitted them, it was reasoned, to interior design. Thus the Domestic Revival and the 'Queen Anne' and Arts and Crafts Movements in the late nineteenth and early twentieth centuries helped promote women's participation in the decorative arts and in interior design, as well as, to a more limited extent, in the architectural profession, at the same time reinforcing the cultural stereotype. As interior designers, architectural theorists and writers, women helped develop the late-Victorian cult of the 'House Beautiful'. Books by women proliferated: for example, *The Drawing Room* (1878) by Lucy Faulkner, *The Dining Room* (1876) by Mrs Loftie, *Beautiful Houses* (1882) by Mrs H. R. Haweis and *Suggestions on House Decoration in Painting, Woodwork and Furniture* (1876) by Agnes and Rhoda Garrett.

The Garretts were not only the best-known women designers and decorators of the period but they were also active feminists, campaigning tirelessly for women's rights and 'the struggle "for the successful removal of intolerable grievances"',[23] as Rhoda's sister, Millicent Garrett Fawcett, called it. For Rhoda, joined by her cousin Agnes, architecture was the original goal, but at first they found it impossible to get taken on in an architect's office. Undaunted, they occupied rooms in a glass-stainer's office and then were formally apprenticed for 18 months to the architect J. M. Brydon, although they were not given any building work there. Their decoration of a house for Agnes' sister, the pioneer doctor Elizabeth Garrett Anderson, and other projects, including much of the drawing-room furniture at Philip Webb's country house, Standen, established them as leaders in the field.[24]

THE ENTRY INTO THE PROFESSION

Like medicine and the law, architecture achieved professional status in the nineteenth century, most notably through the founding in 1834 of the professional body, the Royal Institute of British Architects. Although women were not admitted for more than 60 years after its establishment, women, as we have seen, worked as architects without RIBA membership or approval. The 1891 census records 19 women architects in England and Wales and five in Scotland, in addition to the women who designed buildings within the 'amateur tradition', who would not have shown up in the census.

In 1898, Ethel Mary Charles (1871–1962) became the first woman to enter the RIBA. Ethel Charles and her sister, Bessie Ada Charles, who became the second woman member of the Institute in 1900, were articled for three years to George and Peto, after being barred from entering the Architectural Association (AA) in 1893. Ethel Charles supplemented her training by doing university extension courses – in which she received distinctions. After completing her time with Ernest George, she worked as an assistant to the Arts and Crafts architect Walter Cave, and travelled in England, studying gothic and domestic architecture. In June 1898 she sat the RIBA examinations, almost unnoticed, and her name went forward for Associate membership.[25]

A last-ditch stand was made by Fellows who wished the RIBA to continue as an all-male organisation. W. Hilton Nash circulated a paper, which was signed by other architects who believed that 'it would be prejudical [sic] to the interests of the Institute to elect a lady member'.[26] Ernest George nominated Ethel Charles and vouched for her ability and seriousness of purpose. A motion to adopt all proposed new members was put and the vote stood 51 for and 16 against. A few months later the RIBA came within one vote of reversing this decision to admit women.[27]

Ethel Charles practised with her sister, Bessie Ada, and specialised in domestic work, entering a competition for labourers' cottages and designing houses, especially in Falmouth, such as Gyllyngvase Terrace, 1907.[28] In 1909 she won first prize for a church design from among 200 competitors in Germany,[29] but her knowledge of London architecture directed her attention to the City and commercial building. However, domestic architecture remained the socially sanctioned sphere for women architects and, ironically, the volume of domestic building was beginning to dwindle just as they started to enter the profession. Edwardian England was characterised by a concentration of wealth, population and building commissions in the cities, and large public commissions were jealously guarded by male architects. Alas, Ethel Charles, the first woman member of the RIBA, holder of its Silver Medal (1905), international competition winner and the first woman to address an architectural society in Great Britain, built, with few exceptions, simple, quiet houses, often for women clients, instead of the experimental large-scale projects which she admired. This 'domestic ghetto', in which the Charles sisters and many women architects have since found themselves, limited women's opportunities and reinforced sexual stereotypes; however, it also directed women architects to the most socially useful area of architecture – housing. It is a measure of the different perspectives in the debates surrounding architectural practice today that while many women of the older generation reject domestic architecture for fear of being typecast, and many professional women architects strive for conventional success through the design of public and commercial buildings, feminist architects, with their commitment to women's needs, consciously embrace the stereotype of women as having a special concern for the family and house design.

Although Ethel and Bessie Charles had made a breakthrough into the male domain of professional architecture, few women followed. It made little immediate difference for other women and few joined them in the ranks of the architectural profession. The Charles sisters' struggle shows that at the precise time women were making their entry into the architectural profession, the pressure to maintain the traditional role and position of women intensified: they were refused admission to the Architectural Association (1893), embroiled in battles at the RIBA over entry (1898 and 1899) and involved in confrontations at the AA (1902). All these specific instances of overt discrimination were combined with the daily strain of being outside established practice, swimming against cultural assumptions in a male-dominated profession.

The idea that women were interlopers in the male workplace held sway long after the institutional barriers had been breached at the RIBA. Ideologically, there was only the merest chink in the rigid sexual division of labour which assigned the practice of architecture to men until the conditions of the First World War and the militant suffragist movement combined to force a reappraisal of women's role. Numerically, little impression was made on the profession until the 1930s. The architect Arnold Mitchell expressed the entrenched nature of these attitudes which circumscribed women's activities when he spoke of the 'very serious problem . . . this problem of sex and the woman taking up work which the man up to the present had been accustomed to consider his own separate province'.[30] Fear that women would take jobs, and lucrative ones at that, which had traditionally belonged to men was often heightened by fears of unemployment – male unemployment. 'Architecture, like all professions, is very much over-stocked,'[31] R. Weir Schultz reminded his audience at a conference on employment for women at Caxton Hall, London. Looking back on the previous years of her experience, a young woman architect who was optimistic that women would succeed as architects registered the feeling of otherness and the difficulties of getting work in the 1920s.

> There is a certain prejudice against taking women into architects' offices not because they cannot do the work, but because a tendency to jealousy on the part of men is feared. Accordingly the few girl students who start looking for positions have up to now found it rather difficult to get and to keep them.[32]

After the First World War, a new generation of professional women architects emerged in Britain. Although most architectural schools have no records of when they first admitted women, the Glasgow School of Art (c. 1905) and the University of Manchester (1909) are the earliest now known to have accepted women students.[33] Scotland seems to have been more advanced than England in architectural education for women; Edith M. Burnet Hughes was awarded the Diploma in Architecture in 1914 from the Aberdeen Art School, where she later taught (1915–18). The Architectural Association, which eventually produced the most successful group of women graduates, did not open its doors to women until 1917.

In the 1920s less than a handful of women were taken into the RIBA as Associates: Gillian Harrison (née Cooke), Eleanor K. D. Hughes, Winifred Ryle (later Maddock) and Gertrude W. M. Leverkus. It was not until 1931 that Gillian Harrison (1898–1974) became the first full woman member of the RIBA.[34]

In 1928 Elisabeth Whitworth Scott (1898–1972), a recent graduate of the Architectural Association, won the competition for the Shakespeare Memorial Theatre, Stratford-upon-Avon. Scott's theatre galvanised British women architects, as Sophia Hayden's Women's Pavilion at the Chicago World's Fair had done for American women in 1893. The Stratford Theatre, apart from its obvious importance as the home for Shakespearean productions, was seen as a victory for all women and as evidence of their ability to win and complete large-scale public commissions. Professor A. E. Richardson praised it as 'the first important work erected in this country from the designs of a woman architect'.[35]

Chosen out of 72 entries by a distinguished jury, Scott's design of 1927 looked to new architectural developments on the Continent and in Scandinavia and was put up with the greatest care for craftsmanship and materials by the firm that she formed, Scott, Chesterton and Sheperd. The theatre was completed in 1932. Maurice Chesterton disclaimed 'any personal share whatever in the successful design'.[36]

Elisabeth Scott was representative of women architects of her generation. They tended to be eldest daughters or only children, from a professional background, with an architect relative and often building for women clients. She was conscious that she would encounter discrimination.

After the Second World War, like many other women architects, she moved into the public sector, and in the 1960s she worked for the Bournemouth Borough Architects Department on projects such as the rebuilding of the Bournemouth Pier Pavilion Theatre and Restaurant and the Entertainment Hall of the Boscombe Pier Pavilion.[37]

The sexual division of labour, which Anthea Callen describes in her essay, is the repressive mechanism through which architecture is made gender-specific. Architecture in our society is still thought to be an activity more appropriate for men than women, and in spite of improvements in the law and in access to professional bodies and in spite of better educational opportunities for women, women do not have the same options to participate in architecture that men do.

Women's exclusion from architectural practice is a case study in patriarchal control and economic hegemony. The debates which surround women's participation in architecture are highly charged both emotionally and politically, because architecture physically defines the public and private spheres: to allow women access to the design of architecture therefore threatens patriarchal control of spatial definitions, which are essential to maintain the social, economic and cultural *status quo*.

Although the proportion of women entering schools of architecture is rising, women students are met with a set of pressures which induce feelings of inadequacy and isolation. Architectural schools are male-dominated institutions with their overwhelmingly male student bodies and virtually all-male teaching staff (97 per cent). Without female role-models and with an architectural history constructed of male cult-figures, past and present, a precedent for women's architectural practice is still a very real need of women students and architects alike.

This paper has shown that for hundreds of years women have worked as architects in the 'amateur tradition', as conventional, professional architects and more recently feminist architectural cooperatives have developed a radical client-centred practice.[38] However, the relationship of women to architecture remains highly problematic; at one end of the design continuum, the image of the architect remains firmly male, and at the other, the women who use buildings have little control over or understanding of their production. The art historical values of innovation and quality which exist in relation to an aesthetic currently known as 'the mainstream' place women's issues and achievements in a nether-world of 'other', while British cities are planned and designed with scant attention paid to the needs of women, especially those in communities where mobility and spending power are restricted.[39]

Women are not, however, inert or powerless. Struggle and the daily life of architectural practice come together. In dealing with clients, for example, issues of race, class and sex are confronted. As the architect Elsie Owusu has pointed out, the expectation that buildings are designed by white middle-class men for white middle-class male clients 'is challenged every time a black woman [architect] walks on site'.[40]

NOTES

1 Boys, Jos, 'Architecture', in *A Resource Book on Women Working in Design*, ed. Tag Gronberg and Judy Attfield, London Institute, Central School of Art and Design, 1986, p. 11.

2 'Jagonari Women's Educational Resource Centre', Matrix, 1987. Both Matrix and the Women's Design Service produce information publications, which I have relied on heavily.

3 Fraser, Antonia, *The Weaker Vessel: Woman's Lot in Seventeenth-century England*, Methuen, London, 1984, p. 108.

4 Deane, Sir Thomas Manley, 'Sir Thomas Deane PRHA', *Cork Historical and Archaeological Society Journal*, 1901, p. 152; in the possession of the Deane family.

5 Hussey, Christopher, 'Weston Park, Staffordshire – I', *Country Life*, 9 November 1945, vol. 98, p. 819.

6 Jourdain, M., 'Shellwork and grottoes', *Country Life*, 11 February 1944, vol. 95, pp. 242–3.

7 Darley, Gillian, *Villages of Vision*, Architectural Press, London, 1975, p. 47.

8 Hussey, Christopher, *English Country Houses: Late Georgian 1800–1840*, Country Life, 1958, pp. 122–3.

9 'Some points of view we all pursue', n.d., and other archival material, National Monuments Record Office.

10 Callen, Anthea, *Angel in the Studio: Women in the Arts and Crafts Movement 1870–1914*, Astragal Books, London, 1979, p. 22.

11 See, for example, 'Employment for educated women', *Builder*, 30 November 1861; ibid., 2 November 1883, vol. 44, p. 622; Walker, Lynne, ed., *Women Architects: Their Work*, Sorella Press, London, 1984, especially pp. 19 and 37.

12 Martineau, Harriet, *Autobiography*, vol. 2, Virago, London, 1983, p. 231 (originally published 1877).

13 Wood, M. A., 'Memorial to two sisters: Sara Losh's church of St Mary, Wrey', *Country Life*, 4 November 1971, vol. 150, pp. 1230–1.

14 Blunt, W. S. 'Guide to the Watts Gallery', n.d. Mary Watts detailed the symbolism of her work in *The Word in the Pattern: A Key to the Symbols on the Chapel at Compton*, W. H. Ward & Co., London, n.d. (1905?).

15 Darley, Gillian, 'Women in the public sector', in Walker, op. cit., pp. 37–40. See also, Pearson, Lynn F., *The Architectural and Social History of Cooperative Living*, Macmillan, London, 1988.

16 Letter from Halsey Ricardo to a client, 1883, British Architectural Library.

17 Taylor, Barbara, *Eve and the New Jerusalem: Socialism and Feminism in Nineteenth-century England*, Virago, London, 1983, p. 279.

18 Quoted by Holcombe, Lee, in *Wives and Property: Reform of the Married Women's Property Law in Nineteenth-century England*, Martin Robertson, Oxford, 1983, p. 25. Before 1882, married women could go to law to obtain their property rights in Equity, but it was an expensive process, thus limiting it to the wealthy. Transactions afterwards were through a trustee, making dealings protracted and cumbersome.

19 Eliza Lynn Linton, quoted ibid., p. 18.

20 Townsend, C.H., 'Women as Architects', *British Architect*, 31 December 1886, vol. 26, p. viii.

21 'Report from the Women in Architecture Sub-Group', RIBA, January 1985.

22 Reprinted in *British Architect*, 12 June 1874, vol. 1, p. 378.

23 Quoted in Taylor, op. cit., p. 279.

24 Moncure, Daniel Conway, *Travels in South Kensington*, Trübner & Co., London, 1882, pp. 166–71.

25 RIBA Nomination Papers for Associate Membership, 1898, British Architectural Library.

26 'The admission of lady Associates,' *RIBA Journal*, 10 December 1898, vol. VI, p. 78.

27 *RIBA Journal*, 11 March 1899, vol. VI, p. 278.

28. Drawings by Ethel and Bessie Charles, held by the British Architectural Library, are listed in *Catalogue of the Royal Institute of British Architects C–F*, Gregg Press, Farnborough, 1972, pp. 22–3. The Charles sisters' London address was 49 York Chambers, a block of flats for professional women with communal facilities, designed by Balfour & Turner in 1892 (illustrated in *Architectural Design*, 1978, vol. 48, p. 357).

29 Postcard from Berlin organisers to Ethel Charles, 8 May 1909, in the possession of the family.

30 Mitchell, Arnold, *Builder*, 22 February 1902, vol. 82, p. 181. This statement was

made after a talk by Ethel Charles at the Architectural Association which is extensively reported in this article.

31 Schultz, R. Weir, 'Architecture for women', *Architectural Review*, September 1908, vol. 24, p. 154.

32 *Birmingham Dispatch*, 5 January 1928.

33 Surveys of Schools of Architecture, Beeban Morris and Lynne Walker, 1984.

34 *Architects: Women, Biography File*, British Architectural Library.

35 Richardson, A. E., *Builder*, 22 April 1932, vol. 142, p. 718.

36 *Daily Telegraph*, 6 January 1928.

37 Letter from Bernard Ward, former Chief Architect, City of Bournemouth, to Nadine Beddington, 9 May 1984.

38 See especially, Matrix, *Making Space: Women and the Man-made Environment*, Pluto Press, London, 1984; *Building for Childcare: Making Better Buildings for the Under-5's*, produced and published jointly by Matrix and the GLC Women's Committee, London, 1986.

39 For the radical role that working-class women played in making and assessing housing policy, see, for instance, Swenarton, Mark, *Homes Fit for Heroes: The Policy and Architecture of Early State Housing*, Heinemann, London, 1981, pp. 62, 91–2 and 97–9.

40 Elsie Owusu, talk on design practice at the ICA, 'The design world: women on the cutting edge', 21 May 1988.

29 Denise Scott Brown

'Room at the Top? Sexism and the Star System in Architecture'

from Ellen Perry Berkeley (ed.) *Architecture: A Place for Women* (1989)

Most professional women can recount 'horror stories' about discrimination they have suffered during their careers. My stories include social trivia as well as grand trauma. But some less common forms of discrimination came my way when, in mid-career, I married a colleague and we joined our professional lives just as fame (though not fortune) hit him. I watched as he was manufactured into an architectural guru before my eyes and, to some extent, on the basis of our joint work and the work of our firm.

When Bob and I married, in 1967, I was an associate professor. I had taught at the Universities of Pennsylvania and Berkeley, and had initiated the first program in the new school of architecture at UCLA. I had tenure. My publication record was respectable; my students, enthusiastic. My colleagues, mostly older than I, accorded me the same respect they showed each other, and I had walked the same corridors of power they had (or thought I had).

The first indication of my new status came when an architect whose work I had reviewed said, 'We at the office think it was Bob writing, using your name.' By the time we wrote *Learning from Las Vegas*, our growing experience with incorrect attributions prompted Bob to include a note at the beginning of the book asking that the work and ideas not be attributed to him alone and describing the nature of our collaboration and the roles played by individuals in our firm. His request was almost totally ignored. A body of theory and design in architecture apparently must be associated by architecture critics with an individual; the more emotional their criticism, the stronger is its focus on one person.

To avoid misattributions, our office provides an information sheet describing our preferred forms of attribution – the work to our firm, the writing to the person who signed the article or book. The result is that some critics now make a pro forma attribution in an inconspicuous place; then, in the body of the text, the *design* of the work and the *ideas* in the writing are attributed to Robert Venturi.

In the Japanese journal *Architecture and Urbanism*, for example, Hideki Shimizu wrote:

A review of his plan for the Crosstown Community suggests that Venturi is not so much affording his theory new development as giving the source of his architectural approach clear form in a fundamental attitude toward city planning. . . . Venturi's position in relation to city planning is the thing that enables him to develop his basic posture in relation to architecture. The Crosstown Community reveals a profound mood of affectionate emotion.[1]

This would be fine except that the Crosstown Community was my work and was attributed as such in our book; I doubt whether, over a period of three years, Bob spent two afternoons on it.

When Praeger published a series of interviews with architects,[2] my name was omitted from the dust jacket. We complained and Praeger added my name, although objecting that this would spoil the cover design. On the inside flap, however, 'eight architects' and 'the men behind' modern architecture were mentioned. As nine were listed on the front, I gather I am still left out.[3]

There have been exceptions. Ada Louise Huxtable has never put a foot wrong with me. She works hard at reporting our ideas correctly too. A few critics have changed their methods of attribution in response to our requests, but at least one, in 1971, was on the warpath in the opposite direction, out to prove that Great Art can only be made by one Man, and that Robert Venturi (read Howard Roark) is led astray when 'he joins his wife Denise Scott Brown in praising certain suburban practices.' And the consort and collaborator of a famous architect wrote to me that, although she sees herself in his work, the work owes its quality to his individual talents and not to her collaboration. When real artists collaborate, she claimed, their separate identities remain; she gave as an example the *lieder* of Schubert and Goethe. We countered with the Beatles.

The social trivia (what Africans call *petty apartheid*) continue too: 'wives' dinners' ('We'll just let the architects meet together, my dear'); job interviews where the presence of 'the architect's wife' distressed the board; dinners I must not attend because an influential member of the client group wants 'the architect' as her date; Italian journalists who ignore Bob's request that they address me because I understand more Italian than he does; the tunnel vision of students toward Bob; the 'so you're the architect!' to Bob, and the well-meant 'so you're an architect too?' to me.[4]

These experiences have caused me to fight, suffer doubt and confusion, and expend too much energy. 'I would be *pleased* if my work were attributed to my husband,' says the designer wife of an architect. And a colleague asks, 'Why do you worry about these things? We know you're good. You know your real role in the office and in teaching. Isn't that enough?' I doubt whether it would be enough for my male colleagues. What would Peter Eisenman do if his latest article were attributed to his co-editor, Kenneth Frampton? Or Vincent Scully, if the book on Newport houses were attributed to his co-author, Antoinette Downing – with perhaps a parenthesis to the effect that this was not intended to slight the contribution of others?

So I complain to the editor who refers to 'Venturi's ducks,' informing him that I invented the 'duck.' (He prints my letter under the title 'Less is a Bore,' a quotation from my husband.) But my complaints makes critics angry, and some have formed lasting hostilities against both of us on this score. Architects cannot afford hostile critics. And anyway I begin to dislike my own hostile persona.

That is when self-doubt and confusion arise. 'My husband is a better designer than I am. And I'm a pretty dull thinker.' The first is true, the second probably not. I try to counter with further questions: 'How come, then, we work so well together, capping each other's ideas? If my ideas are no good, why are they quoted by the critics (even though attributed to Bob)?'

We ourselves cannot tease our contributions apart. Since 1960 we have collaborated in the development of ideas and since 1967 we have collaborated in architectural practice. As chief designer, Bob takes final design responsibility. On some projects, I am closely involved and see many of my ideas in the final design; on others, hardly at all. In a few, the basic idea (what Lou Kahn called the What) was mine. All of our firm's urban planning work, and the urban design related to it, is my responsibility; Bob is virtually not involved with it, although other architects in the firm are.[5]

As in all firms, our ideas are translated and added to by our co-workers, particularly our associates of long standing. Principals and assistants may alternate in the roles of creator and critic. The star system, which sees the firm as a pyramid with a Designer on top, has little to do with today's complex relations in architecture and construction. But as sexism defines me as a scribe, typist, and photographer to my husband, so the star system defines our associates as 'second bananas' and our staff as pencils.

Short of sitting under the drawing board while we are around it, there is no way for the critics to separate us out. Those who do, hurt me in particular but others in the firm, too, and by ignoring as unimportant those aspects of our work where Bob has interfaced with others, they narrow his span to meet the limits of their perception.

Although I had been concerned with my role as a woman years before the rebirth of the movement, I was not pushed to action until my experience as an architect's wife. In 1973 I gave a talk on sexism and the star system to the Alliance of Women in Architecture, in New York City. I requested that the meeting be open to women only, probably incorrectly, but for the same emotional reasons (including hurt pride) that make national movements initially stress separatism. Nevertheless, about six men came. They hid in the back and sides of the audience. The hundred or so women identified strongly with my experience; 'Me too!' 'My God, you too?' echoed everywhere. We were soon high on our shared woe and on the support we felt for and from each other. Later, it struck me that the males had grown glummer as we grew more enthusiastic. They seemed unable to understand what was exercising us.

Since then I have spoken at several conferences on women in architecture. I now receive inquiries of interest for deanships and departmental chairs several times a year. I find myself on committees where I am the only woman and there is one black man. We two tokens greet each other wryly. I am frequently invited to lecture at architecture schools, 'to be a role model for our girls.' I am happy to do this for their young women but I would rather be asked purely because my work is interesting.

Finally, I essayed my own interpretation of sexism and the star system in architecture. Budd Schulberg defines 'Star Quality' as a 'mysterious amalgam of self-love, vivacity, style and sexual promise.'[6] Though his definition catches the spirit of architectural stardom, it omits the fact that stardom is something done to a star by others. Stars cannot create themselves. Why do architects need to create stars? Because, I think, architecture deals with unmeasurables. Although architecture is both science and art, architects stand or fall in their own estimation and in that of their peers by whether they are 'good designers,' and the criteria for this are ill-defined and undefinable.

Faced with unmeasurables, people steer their way by magic. Before the invention of navigational instruments, a lady was carved on the prow of the boat to help sailors cross the ocean; and architects, grappling with the intangibles of design, select a guru whose work gives them personal help in areas where there are few rules to follow. The guru, as architectural father figure, is subject to intense hate and love; either way, the relationship is personal, it can only be a one-to-one affair. This accounts for the intensely *ad hominem* stance of some of 'Venturi's' critics. If the attribution were correct the tone would be more even, as one cannot easily wax emotional over several people. I suspect, too, that for male architects the guru must be male. There can be no Mom and Pop gurus in architecture. The architectural prima donnas are all male.

Next, a colleague having her own difficulties in an American Studies department brought the work of Lionel Tiger to my attention. In *Men in Groups*, he writes that men run in male packs and ambitious women must understand this.[7] I recalled, as well, the exclamation of the French architect Ionel Schein, writing in *Le Carré Bleu* in the 1950s: 'The so-called studio spirit is merely the spirit of a caste.' This brings to mind the upper-class origins of the American architecture profession, the differences between upper-class and middle-class attitudes to women, and the strong similarities that still exist today between the architecture profession and a men's club.

American architectural education was modeled on the turn-of-the-century, French Ecole des Beaux-Arts. It was a rip-roaring place and loads of fun, but its organization was strongly authoritarian, especially in its system for judging student work. The authoritarian personalities and the we-happy-few culture engendered by the Beaux-Arts stayed on in Modern architecture long after the Beaux-Arts architectural philosophy had been abandoned; the architecture club still excludes women.

The heroically original, Modern architectural revolutionary with his avant-garde technology, out to save the masses through mass production, is a macho image if ever there was one. It sits strangely on the middle-aged reactionaries who bear its mantle today. A more conserving and nurturing (female?) outlook is being recommended to the profession by urban planners and ecologists, in the name of social justice and to save the planet. Women may yet ride in on this trend.

The critic in architecture is often the scribe, historian, and kingmaker for a particular group. These activities entitle him to join the 'few,' even though he pokes them a little. His other satisfaction comes from making history in his and their image. The kingmaker-critic is, of course, male; though he may write of the group as a group, he would be a poor fool in his eyes and theirs if he tried to crown the whole group king. There is even less psychic reward in crowning a female king.

In these deductions, my thinking parallels that of Cynthia F. Epstein, who writes that elevation within the professions is denied women for reasons that include 'the colleague system,' which she describes as a men's club, and 'the sponsor–protégé relationship, which determines access to the highest levels of most professions.' Epstein suggests that the high-level sponsor would, like the kingmaker-critic, look foolish if he sponsored a female and, in any case, his wife would object.[8]

You would think that the last element of Schulberg's definition of a star, 'sexual promise,' would have nothing to do with architecture. But I wondered why there was a familiar ring to the tone – hostile, lugubriously self-righteous, yet somehow envious – of letters to the editor that follow anything our firm publishes, until I recognized it as the tone middle America employs in letters to the editor in pornography. Architects who write angry letters about our work apparently feel we are architectural panderers, or at least we permit ourselves liberties they would not take, but possibly envy. Here is one, by an English architecture instructor: 'Venturi has a niche, all right, but it's down there with the flagellant, the rubber-fetishist and the Blagdon Nude Amateur Rapist.' These are written by men, and they are written to or of Bob alone.

I have suggested that the star system, which is unfair to many architects, is doubly hard on women in a sexist environment, and that, at the upper levels of the profession, the female architect who works with her husband will be submerged in his reputation. My interpretations are speculative. We have no sociology of architecture. Architects are unaccustomed to social analysis and mistrust it; sociologists have fatter fish to fry. But I do get support for my thesis from some social scientists, from ironists in architecture, from many women architects, from some members of my firm, and from my husband.

Should there be a star system? It is unavoidable, I think, owing to the prestige we give design in architecture. But the schools can and should reduce the importance of the star system by broadening the student's view of the profession to show value in its other aspects. Heaven knows, skills other than design are important to the survival of architecture firms. The schools should also combat the student's sense of inadequacy about design, rather than, as now, augmenting it through wrongly authoritarian and judgmental educational techniques. With these changes, architects would feel less need for gurus, and those they would need would be different – more responsible and humane than gurus are asked to be today.

To the extent that gurus are unavoidable and sexism is rampant in the architecture profession, my personal problem of submersion through the star system is insoluble. I could improve my chances for recognition as an individual if I returned to teaching or if I abandoned collaboration with my husband. The latter has happened to some extent as our office has grown and our individual responsibilities within it take more of our time. We certainly spend less time at the drawing board together and, in general, less time writing. But this is a pity, as our joint work feeds us both.

On the larger scene, all is not lost. Not all architects belong to the men's club; more architects than before are women; some critics are learning; the AIA actively wants to help; and most architects, in theory at least, would rather not practice discrimination if someone will prove to them that they have been and will show them how to stop.

The foregoing is an abridgment of an article I wrote in 1975. I decided not to publish it at the time, because I judged that strong sentiments on feminism in the world of architecture would ensure my ideas a hostile reception, which could hurt my career and the prospects of my firm. However, I did share the manuscript with friends and, in *samizdat*, it achieved a following of sorts. Over the years I have received letters asking for copies.

In 1975, I recounted my first experience of the new surge of women in architecture. The ratio of men to women is now 1 : 1 in many schools. The talent and enthusiasm of these young women has burst creatively into the profession. At conferences today I find many women participants; some have ten years or more in the field.

Architecture, too, has changed since I wrote. My hope that architects would heed the social planners' dicta did not pan out, and women did not ride in on that trend. Postmodernism did change the views of architects but not in the way I had hoped. Architects lost their social concern; the architect as macho revolutionary was succeeded by the architect as *dernier cri* of the art world; the cult of personality increased. This made things worse for women because, in architecture, the *dernier cri* is as male as the prima donna.

The rise in female admissions and the move to the right in architecture appear to be trends in opposite directions, but they are, in fact, unrelated because they occur at either end of the seniority spectrum. The women entrants are young; the cult of personality occurs at the top. The two trends have yet to meet. When they do, it will be fascinating to see what happens. Meanwhile, affirmative action programs have helped small female-owned firms get started but may have hindered the absorption of women into the mainstream of the profession, because women who integrate large existing practices gain no affirmative action standing unless they own 51 per cent of the firm.

During the eighties there has been a gradual increase of women architects in academe. (I suspect that the growth has been slower than in other professions.)

I now receive fewer offers of deanships, probably because there are more female candidates than before and because word is out that I am too busy to accept. I have little time to lecture. As our office has grown, Bob and I have found more, rather than less, opportunity to work together, since some of our responsibilities have been delegated to the senior associates and project directors who form the core of our firm.

During this period, we have ceased to be regarded as young turks and have seen a greater acceptance of our ideas than we would have dreamed possible. Ironically, a citation honoring Bob for his 'discovery of the everyday American environment' was written in 1979 by the same critic who, in 1971, judged Bob lacking for sharing my interest in everyday landscape.

For me, things are much the same at the top as they were. The discrimination continues at the rate of about one incident a day. Journalists who approach our firm seem to feel that they will not be worth their salt if they do not 'deliver Venturi.' The battle for turf and the race for status among critics still require the beating-off of women. In the last twenty years, I cannot recall one major article by a high-priest critic about a woman architect. Young women critics, as they enter the fray, become as macho as the men and for the same reasons – to survive and win in the competitive world of critics.

For a few years, writers on architecture were interested in sexism and the feminist movement and wanted to discuss them with me. In a joint interview, they would ask Bob about work and question me about my 'woman's problem.' 'Write about my work!' I would plead, but they seldom did.

Some young women in architecture question the need for the feminist movement, claiming to have experienced no discrimination. My concern is that, although school is not a nondiscriminatory environment, it is probably the least discriminatory one they will encounter in their careers. By the same token, the early years in practice bring little differentiation between men and women. It is as they advance that difficulties arise, when firms and clients shy away from entrusting high-level responsibility to women. On seeing their male colleagues draw out in front of them, women who lack a feminist awareness are likely to feel that their failure to achieve is their own fault.

Over the years, it has slowly dawned on me that the people who cause my painful experiences are ignorant and crude. They are the critics who have not read enough and the clients who do not know why they have come to us. I have been helped to realise this by noticing that the scholars whose work we most respect, the clients whose projects intrigue us, and the patrons whose friendship inspires us, have no problem understanding my role. They are the sophisticates. Partly through them I gain heart and realise that, over the last twenty years, I have managed to do my work and, despite some sliding, to achieve my own self-respect.

NOTES

1   Hideki Shimizu, 'Criticism,' *A + U (Architecture and Urbanism)* 47 (November 1974): 3.
2   John W. Cook and Heinrich Klotz, *Conversations with Architects* (New York: Praeger Publishers, Inc., 1973).

3 The architects originally listed were Philip Johnson, Kevin Roche, Paul Rudolph, Bertrand Goldberg, Morris Lapidus, Louis Kahn, Charles Moore, and Robert Venturi. Also omitted from the dust jacket was the architect Alan Lapidus, interviewed with his father, Morris. Alan did not complain; at least he's up there with those men behind the architecture.

4 The head of a New York architecture school reached me on the phone because Bob was unavailable: 'Denise, I'm embarrassed to be speaking to you because we're giving a party for QP [a well-known local architect] and we're asking Bob but not you. You see, you *are* a friend of QP and you *are* an architect, but you're also a wife, and we're not asking wives.'

5 Bob's intellectual focus comes mainly from the arts and from the history of architecture. He is more of a specialist than I am. My artistic and intellectual concerns were formed before I met Bob (and indeed before I came to America), but they were the base of our friendship as academic colleagues. As a planner, my professional span includes the social sciences and other planning-related disciplines that I have tried to meld into our critique and theory of architecture. As an architect, my interests range widely but I am probably most useful at the initial stages of a design as we work to develop the *parti*.

6 Budd Schulberg, 'What Price Glory?,' *New Republic* 168 (6 and 13 January 1973): 27–31.

7 Lionel Tiger, *Men in Groups* (New York: Random House, 1969).

8 Cynthia F. Epstein, 'Encountering the Male Establishment: Sex-Status Limits on Women's Careers in the Profession,' *American Journal of Sociology* 75 (May 1970): 965–82.

30 Dolores Hayden

'What Would a Non-sexist City Be Like? Speculations on Housing, Urban Design and Human Work'*

from Catharine R. Stimpson, Elsa Dixler, Martha J. Nelson and Kathryn B. Yatrakis (eds), *Women and the American City* (1981)

America's cities and housing have not kept pace with the changing needs of households. Women have been entering the paid labor force in larger and larger numbers. Yet housing, neighborhoods, and cities continue to be designed for homebound women. This situation constrains women physically, socially, and economically, and reinforces their dependence. Some models of alternative housing and neighborhood designs that better meet women's needs are proposed in this chapter.[1]

'A woman's place is in the home' has been one of the most important principles of architectural design and urban planning in the United States for the last century. An implicit rather than explicit principle for the conservative and male-dominated design professions, it will not be found stated in large type in textbooks on land use. It has generated much less debate than the other organizing principles of the contemporary American city in an era of monopoly capitalism, which include the ravaging pressure of private land development, the fetishistic dependence on millions of private automobiles, and the wasteful use of energy.[2] However, women have rejected this dogma and entered the paid labor force in larger and larger numbers. Dwellings, neighborhoods, and cities designed for homebound women constrain women physically, socially, and economically. Acute frustration occurs when women defy these constraints to spend all or part of the workday in the paid labor force. I contend that the only remedy for this situation is to develop a new paradigm of the home, the neighborhood, and the city; to begin to describe the physical, social, and economic design of a human settlement that would support, rather than restrict, the activities of employed women and their families. It is essential to recognize such needs in order to begin both the rehabilitation of the existing housing stock and the construction of new housing to meet the needs of a new and growing majority of Americans – working women and their families.

When speaking of the American city in the last quarter of the twentieth century, a false distinction between 'city' and 'suburb' must be avoided. The urban region, organised to separate homes and workplaces, must be seen as a whole. In such urban regions, more than half of the population resides in the sprawling suburban areas, or 'bedroom communities.' The greatest part of the built environment in the United States consists of 'suburban sprawl': single-family homes grouped in class-segregated areas, crisscrossed by freeways and served by shopping malls and commercial strip developments. Over 50 million small homes are on the ground. About two-thirds of American families 'own' their homes on long mortgages; this includes over 77 percent of all AFL-CIO members (*Survey of AFL-CIO Members' Housing*, 1975, 16).[3] White, male skilled workers are far more likely to be homeowners than members of minority groups and women, long denied equal credit or equal access to housing. Workers commute to jobs either in the center or elsewhere in the suburban ring. In metropolitan areas studied in 1975 and 1976, the journey to work, by public transit or private car, averaged about 9 miles each way. Over 100 million privately owned cars filled two- and three-car garages (which would be considered magnificent housing by themselves in many developing countries). . . .

The roots of this American settlement form lie in the environmental and economic policies of the past. In the late nineteenth century, millions of immigrant families lived in the crowded, filthy slums of American industrial cities and despaired of achieving reasonable living conditions. However, many militant strikes and demonstrations between the 1890s and 1920s made some employers reconsider plant locations and housing issues in their search for industrial order.[4] 'Good homes make contented workers' was the slogan of the Industrial Housing Associates in 1919. These consultants and many others helped major corporations plan better housing for white, male skilled workers and their families in order to eliminate industrial conflict. 'Happy workers invariably mean bigger profits, while unhappy workers are never a good investment,' they chirruped.[5] Men were to receive 'family wages' and become home 'owners' responsible for regular mortgage payments, while their wives became home 'managers' taking care of spouse and children. The male worker would return from his day in the factory or office to a private domestic environment, secluded from the tense world of work in an industrial city characterized by environmental pollution, social degradation, and personal alienation. He would enter a serene dwelling whose physical and emotional maintenance would be the duty of his wife. Thus the private suburban house was the stage set for the effective sexual division of labor. It was the commodity *par excellence*, a spur for male paid labor and a container for female unpaid labor. It made gender appear a more important self-definition than class, and consumption more involving than production. In a brilliant discussion of the 'patriarch as wage slave,' Stuart Ewen has shown how capitalism and antifeminism fused in campaigns for homeownership and mass consumption: The patriarch whose home was his 'castle' was to work year in and year out to provide the wages to support this private environment (Ewen, 1976).

Although this strategy was first boosted by corporations interested in a docile labor force, it soon appealed to corporations that wished to move from World War

I defense industries into peacetime production of domestic appliances for millions of families. The development of the advertising industry, documented by Ewen, supported this ideal of mass consumption and promoted the private suburban dwelling, which maximized appliance purchases (Walker, 1977). The occupants of the isolated household were suggestible. They bought the house itself, a car, stove, refrigerator, vacuum cleaner, washer, carpets. Christine Frederick, explaining it in 1929 as *Selling Mrs Consumer*, promoted homeownership and easier consumer credit and advised marketing managers on how to manipulate American women (Frederick, 1929). By 1931 the Hoover Commission on Home Ownership and Home Building established the private, single-family home as a national goal, but a decade and a half of depression and war postponed its achievement. Architects designed houses for Mr and Mrs Bliss in a competition sponsored by General Electric in 1935; winners accommodated dozens of electrical appliances in their designs with no critique of the energy costs involved.[6] In the late 1940s the single-family home was boosted by FHA and VA mortgages, and the construction of isolated, overprivatized, energy-consuming dwellings became commonplace. 'I'll Buy that Dream' made the postwar hit parade (Filene, 1974: 189).

Mrs Consumer moved the economy to new heights in the 1950s. Women who stayed at home experienced what Betty Friedan called the 'feminine mystique' and Peter Filene renamed the 'domestic mystique.'[7] While the family occupied its private physical space, the mass media and social science experts invaded its psychological space more effectively than ever before.[8] With the increase in spatial privacy came pressure for conformity in consumption. Consumption was expensive. More and more married women joined the paid labor force, as the suggestible housewife needed to be both a frantic consumer and a paid worker to keep up with the family's bills. Just as the mass of white male workers had achieved the 'dream houses' in suburbia where fantasies of patriarchal authority and consumption could be acted out, their spouses entered the world of paid employment. By 1975, the two-worker family accounted for 39 percent of American households. Another 13 percent were single-parent families, usually headed by women. Seven out of 10 employed women were in the work force because of financial need. Over 50 percent of all children between the ages of 1 and 17 had employed mothers (Baxandall *et al.*, 1976).[9]

How does a conventional home serve the employed woman and her family? Badly. Whether it is in a suburban, exurban, or inner-city neighborhood, whether it is a split-level ranch house, a modern masterpiece of concrete and glass, or an old brick tenement, the house or apartment is almost invariably organized around the same set of spaces: kitchen, dining room, living rom, bedrooms, garage, or parking area. These spaces require someone to undertake private cooking, cleaning, child care, and usually private transportation if adults and children are to exist within it. Because of residential zoning practices, the typical dwelling will usually be physically removed from any shared community space – no commercial or communal day-care facilities, or laundry facilities, for example, are likely to be part of the dwelling's spatial domain. In many cases these facilities would be illegal if placed across property lines. They could also be illegal if located on residentially zoned sites. In some cases sharing such a private dwelling with other individuals (either relatives or those unrelated by blood) is also against the law.[10]

Within the private spaces of the dwelling, material culture works against the needs of the employed woman as much as zoning does, because the home is a box to be filled with commodities. Appliances are usually single-purpose, and often inefficient, energy-consuming machines, lined up in a room where the domestic work is done in isolation from the rest of the family. Rugs and carpets that need vacuuming, curtains that need laundering, and miscellaneous goods that need maintenance fill up the domestic spaces, often decorated in 'colonial,' 'Mediterranean,' 'French Provincial,' or other eclectic styles purveyed by discount and department stores to cheer up that bare box of an isolated house. Employed mothers usually are expected to, and almost invariably do, spend more time in private housework and child care than employed men; often they are expected to, and usually do, spend more time on commuting per mile traveled than men, because of their reliance on public transportation. One study found that 70 percent of adults without access to cars are female.[11] Their residential neighborhoods are not likely to provide much support for their work activities. A 'good' neighbourhood is usually defined in terms of conventional shopping, schools, and perhaps public transit, rather than additional social services for the working parent, such as day care or evening clinics.

While two-worker families with both parents energetically cooperating can overcome some of the problems of existing housing patterns, households in crisis, such as subjects of wife and child battering, for example, are particularly vulnerable to housing's inadequacies. According to Colleen McGrath, every 30 seconds a woman is being battered somewhere in the United States. Most of these batterings occur in kitchens and bedrooms. The relationship between household isolation and battering, or between unpaid domestic labor and battering, can only be guessed, at this time, but there is no doubt that America's houses and households are literally shaking with domestic violence (McGrath, 1979: 12, 23). In addition, millions of angry and upset women are treated with tranquilizers in the private home – one drug company advertises to doctors: 'You can't change her environment but you can change her mood.'[12]

The woman who does leave the isolated, single-family house or apartment finds very few real housing alternatives available to her.[13] The typical divorced or battered woman currently seeks housing, employment, and childcare simultaneously. She finds that matching her complex family requirements with the various available offerings by landlords, employers, and social services is impossible. One environment that unites housing, services, and jobs could resolve many difficulties, but the existing system of government services, intended to stabilize households and neighborhoods by insuring the minimum conditions for a decent home life to all Americans, almost always assumes that the traditional household with a male worker and an unpaid homemaker is the goal to be achieved or simulated. In the face of massive demographic changes, programs such as public housing, AFDC, and food stamps still attempt to support an ideal family living in an isolated house or apartment, with a full-time homemaker cooking meals and minding children many hours of the day.

By recognizing the need for a different kind of environment, far more efficient use can be made of funds now used for subsidies to individual households. Even for women with greater financial resources, the need for better housing and services is obvious. Currently, more affluent women's problems as workers have been considered 'private' problems – the lack of good day care, their lack of time. The aids to overcome an environment without child care, public transportation, or food service have been 'private,' commercially profitable solutions: maids and babysitters by the hour; franchise day care or extended television viewing; fast-food service; easier credit for purchasing an automobile, a washer, or a microwave oven. Not only do these commercial solutions obscure the failure of American housing policies; they also generate bad conditions for other working women. Commercial day-care and fast-food franchises are the source of low-paying non-union jobs without security. In this respect they resemble the use of private household workers by bourgeois women, who may never ask how their private maid or child-care worker arranges care for her own children. They also resemble the insidious effects of the use of television in the home as a substitute for developmental child care in the neighborhood. The logistical problems that all employed women face are not private problems and they do not succumb to market solutions.

The problem is paradoxical: Women cannot improve their status in the home unless their overall economic position in society is altered; women cannot improve their status in the paid labor force unless their domestic responsibilities are altered. Therefore, a program to achieve economic and environmental justice for women requires, by definition, a solution that overcomes the traditional divisions between the household and the market economy, the private dwelling and the workplace. One must transform the economic situation of the traditional homemaker, whose skilled labor has been unpaid but economically and socially necessary to society; one must also transform the domestic situation of the employed woman. If architects and urban designers were to recognize all employed women and their families as a constituency for new approaches to planning and design and were to reject all previous assumptions about 'woman's place' in the home, what could we do? Is it possible to build non-sexist neighborhoods and design non-sexist cities? What would they be like?

Some countries have begun to develop new approaches to the needs of employed women. The Cuban Family Code of 1974 requires men to share housework and child care within the private home. The degree of its enforcement is uncertain, but in principle it aims at men's sharing what was formerly 'women's work,' which is essential to equality. The Family Code, however, does not remove work from the house, and relies upon private negotiation between husband and wife for its day-to-day enforcement. Men feign incompetence, especially in the area of cooking, with tactics familiar to any reader of Patricia Mainardi's essay 'The Politics of Housework,' and the sexual stereotyping of paid jobs for women outside the home, in day-care centers for example, has not been successfully challenged (Mainardi, 1970).[14]

Another experimental approach involves the development of special housing facilities for employed women and their families. The builder Otto Fick first introduced such a program in Copenhagen in 1903. In later years it was encouraged in Sweden by Alva Myrdal and by the architects Sven Ivar Lind and Sven Markelius. Called 'service houses' or 'collective houses,' such projects provide child care and cooked food along with housing for employed women and their families (Muhlestein, 1975). Like a few similar projects in the USSR in the 1920s, they aim at offering services, either on a commercial basis or subsidized by the state, to replace formerly private 'women's work' performed in the household. The Scandinavian solution does not sufficiently challenge male exclusion from domestic work, nor does it deal with households' changing needs over the life cycle, but it recognizes that it is important for environmental design to change.

Some additional projects in Europe extend the scope of the service house to include the provision of services for the larger community or society. In the Steilshoop Project, in Hamburg, Germany, in the early 1970s, a group of parents and single people designed public housing with supporting services.[15] The project included a number of former mental patients as residents and therefore served as a halfway house for them, in addition to providing support services for the public housing tenants who organized it. It suggests the extent to which current American residential stereotypes can be broken down – the sick, the aged, and the unmarried can be integrated into new types of households and housing complexes, rather than segregated in separate projects.

Another recent project was created in London by Nina West Homes, a development group established in 1972, which has built or renovated over 63 units of housing on six sites for single parents. Children's play areas or day-care centers are integrated with the dwellings; in their Fiona House project the housing is designed to facilitate shared babysitting, and the day-care center is open to the neighborhood residents for a fee. Thus the single parents can find jobs as day-care workers and help the neighborhood's working parents as well (*Architects' Journal*, 27 Sept. 1972, 680–84).[16] What is most exciting here is the hint that home and work can be reunited on one site for some of the residents, and home and child-care services are reunited on one site for all of them.

In the United States, we have an even longer history of agitation for housing to reflect women's needs. In the late nineteenth century and early twentieth century there were dozens of projects by feminists, domestic scientists, and architects attempting to develop community services for private homes. By the late 1920s, few such experiments were still functioning.[17] In general, feminists of that era failed to recognize the problem of exploiting other women workers when providing services for those who could afford them. They also often failed to see men as responsible parents and workers in their attempts to socialize 'women's' work. But feminist leaders had a very strong sense of the possibilities of neighborly cooperation among families and of the economic importance of 'women's' work.

In addition, the United States has a long tradition of experimental utopian socialist communities building model towns, as well as the example of many communes and collectives established in the 1960s and 1970s, which attempted to broaden conventional definitions of household and family.[18] While some communal groups, especially religious ones, have often demanded acceptance of a traditional sexual division of labour, others have attempted to make nurturing activities a responsibility of both women and men. It is important to draw on the examples of successful projects of all kinds in seeking an image of a nonsexist settlement. Most employed women are not interested in taking themselves and their families to live in communal families, nor are they interested in having state bureaucracies run family life. They desire, not an end to private life altogether, but community services to support the private household. They also desire solutions that reinforce their economic independence and maximise their personal choices about child rearing and sociability.

What, then, would be the outline of a program for change in the United States? The task of reorganizing both home and work can be accomplished only by organizations of homemakers, women and men dedicated to making changes in the ways that Americans deal with private life and public responsibilities. They must be small, participatory organizations with members who can work together effectively. I propose calling such groups HOMES (Homemakers Organization for a More Egalitarian Society). Existing feminist groups, especially those providing shelters for battered wives and children, may wish to form HOMES to take over existing housing projects and develop services for residents as an extension of those offered by feminist counselors in the shelter. Existing organizations supporting cooperative ownership of housing may wish to form HOMES to extend their housing efforts in a feminist direction. A program broad enough to transform housework, housing, and residential neighborhoods must (1) involve both men and women in the unpaid labor associated with housekeeping and child care on an equal basis; (2) involve both men and women in the paid labor force on an equal basis; (3) eliminate residential segregation by class, race, and age; (4) eliminate all federal, state, and local programs and laws that offer implicit or explicit reinforcement of the unpaid role of the female homemaker; (5) minimize unpaid domestic labor and wasteful energy consumption; (6) maximize real choices for households concerning recreation and sociability. While many partial reforms can support these goals, an incremental strategy cannot achieve them. I believe that the establishment of experimental residential centers, which in their architectural design and economic organization transcend traditional definitions of home, neighborhood, city and workplace, will be necessary to make changes on this scale. These centers could be created through renovation of existing neighborhoods or through new construction.

Suppose 40 households in a US metropolitan area formed a HOMES group and that those households, in their composition, represented the social structure of the American population as a whole. Those 40 households would include 7 single parents and their 14 children (15 percent); 16 two-worker couples and their 24 children (40 percent); 13 one-worker couples and their 26 children (35 percent);

and 4 single residents, some of them 'displaced homemakers' (10 percent). The residents would include 69 adults and 64 children. There would need to be 40 private dwelling units, ranging in size from efficiency to three bedrooms, all with private, fenced outdoor space. In addition to the private housing, the group would provide the following collective spaces and activities: (1) a day-care center with landscaped outdoor space, providing day care for 40 children and after-school activities for 64 children; (2) a laundromat providing laundry service; (3) a kitchen providing lunches for the day-care center, take-out evening meals, and 'meals-on-wheels' for elderly people in the neighborhood; (4) a grocery depot, connected to a local food cooperative; (5) a garage with two vans providing dial-a-ride service and meals-on-wheels; (6) a garden (or allotments) where some food can be grown; (7) a home-help office providing helpers for the elderly, the sick, and employed parents whose children are sick. The use of all these collective services should be voluntary; they would exist in addition to private dwelling units and private gardens.

To provide all of the above services, 37 workers would be necessary: 20 day-care workers; 3 food-service workers; 1 grocery-depot worker; 5 home helpers; 2 drivers of service vehicles; 2 laundry workers; 1 maintenance worker; 1 gardener; 2 administrative staff. Some of these may be part-time workers, some full-time. Day care, food services, and elderly services could be organized as producers' co-operatives, and other workers could be employed by the housing cooperative as discussed below.

Because HOMES is not intended as an experiment in isolated community buildings but as an experiment in meeting employed women's needs in an urban area, its services should be available to the neighborhood in which the experiment is located. This will increase demand for the services and insure that the jobs are real ones. In addition, although residents of HOMES should have priority for the jobs, there will be many who choose outside work. So some local residents may take jobs within the experiment.

In creating and filling these jobs it will be important to avoid traditional sex stereotyping that would result from hiring only men as drivers, for example, or only women as food-service workers. Every effort should be made to break down separate categories of paid work for women and men, just as efforts should be made to recruit men who accept an equal share of domestic responsibilities as residents. A version of the Cuban Family Code should become part of the organization's platform.

Similarly, HOMES must not create a two-class society with residents outside the project making more money than residents in HOMES jobs that utilize some of their existing domestic skills. The HOMES jobs should be paid according to egalitarian rather than sex-stereotyped attitudes about skills and hours. These jobs must be all classified as skilled work rather than as unskilled or semiskilled at present, and offer full social security and health benefits, including adequate maternity leave, whether workers are part-time or full-time. . . .

A limited-equity housing cooperative offers the best basis for economic organization and control of both physical design and social policy by the residents.

Many knowledgeable nonprofit developers could aid community groups wishing to organize such projects, as could architects experienced in the design of housing cooperatives. What has not been attempted is the reintegration of work activities and collective services into housing cooperatives on a large enough scale to make a real difference to employed women. Feminists in trade unions where a majority of members are women may wish to consider building cooperative housing with services for their members. Other trade unions may wish to consider investing in such projects. Feminists in the coop movement must make strong, clear demands to get such services from existing housing cooperatives, rather than simply go along with plans for conventional housing organized on a cooperative economic basis. Feminists outside the cooperative movement will find that cooperative organizational forms offer many possibilities for supporting their housing activities and other services to women. In addition, the National Cooperative Bank has funds to support projects of all kinds that can be tied to cooperative housing.

In many areas, the rehabilitation of existing housing may be more desirable than new construction. The suburban housing stock in the United States must be dealt with effectively. A little bit of it is of architectural quality sufficient to deserve preservation; most of it can be aesthetically improved by the physical evidence of more intense social activity. To replace empty front lawns without sidewalks, neighbors can create blocks where single units are converted to multiple units; interior land is pooled to create a parklike setting at the center of the block; front and side lawns are fenced to make private outdoor spaces; pedestrian paths and sidewalks are created to link all units with the central open space; and some private porches, garages, tool sheds, utility rooms, and family rooms are converted to community facilities such as children's play areas, dial-a-ride garages, and laundries.

Consider a typical suburban block of 13 houses, constructed by speculators at different times, where about 4 acres are divided into plots of one-fourth to one-half acre each. The 13 driveways are used by 26 cars; 10 garden sheds, 10 swings, 13 lawn mowers, and 13 outdoor dining tables begin to suggest the wasteful duplication of existing amenities. Yet despite the available land there are no transitions between public streets and these private homes. Space is either strictly private or strictly public. A typical one-family house of 1,400 square feet on this block would have three bedrooms and den, two-and-a-half baths, laundry room, two porches, and a two-car garage, and would have been constructed in the 1950s at the height of the 'feminine mystique.'

To convert this kind of whole block and the housing on it to more efficient and sociable uses, one has to define a zone of greater activity at the heart of the block, taking a total of 1½ to 2 acres for collective use. Essentially, this means turning the block inside out (compare with Fig. 30.1). The Radburn plan, developed by Henry Wright and Clarence Stein in the late 1920s, delineated this principle very clearly as correct land use in 'the motor age,' with cars segregated from residents' green spaces, especially spaces for children. In Radburn, New Jersey, and in the Baldwin Hills district of Los Angeles, California, Wright and Stein achieved remarkably luxurious results (at a density of about seven units to the acre) by this

Figure 30.1
Diagrams showing some of the
possibilities of reorganizing a
typical suburban block through
rezoning, rebuilding, and
landscaping
(a) Ten single-family houses
(1) on ten private lots

(b) The same houses
(1) with smaller private lots
(2) after a backyard rehabilitation
program has created a new village
green
(3) at the heart of the block

(c) The same houses
(1) and many small private gardens
(2) with a new village green
(3) surrounded by a zone for new
services and accessory apartments
(4) connected by a new sidewalk
(5) and surrounded by a new border
of street trees
In this diagram (4) could include
space for such activities as day care,
elderly care, laundry, and food
service as well as housing, while (3)
could accommodate a children's play
area, vegetable or flower gardens,
and outdoor seating. (5) may be a
sidewalk, a vine-covered trellis, or a
formal arcade. The narrow ends of
the block can be emphasized as
collective entrances with gates (to
which residents have keys), leading
to new accessory apartments
entered from the arcade or sidewalk.
In the densest possible situations (3)
may be alley and parking lot if
existing street parking and public
transit are not adequate.

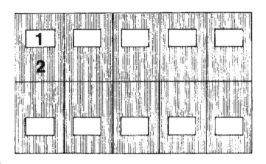

a)

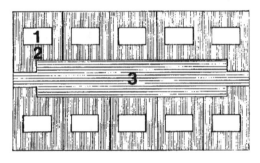

b)

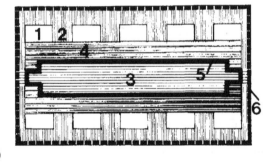

c)

method, since their multiple-unit housing always bordered a lush parkland without any automobile traffic. The Baldwin Hills project demonstrates this success most dramatically, but a revitalized suburban block with lots as small as ¼ acre can be reorganized to yield something of this same effect.[19] In this case, social amenities are added to aesthetic ones, as the interior park is designed to accommodate community day care, a garden for growing vegetables, some picnic tables, a playground where swings and slides are grouped, a grocery depot connected to a larger neighborhood food cooperative, and a dial-a-ride garage.

Large single-family houses can be remodeled quite easily to become duplexes and triplexes, despite the 'open plans' of the 1950s and 1960s popularized by many developers. The house in Figure 30.2 becomes, in Figure 30.3, a triplex, with a two-bedroom unit (linked to a community garage); a one-bedroom unit; and an efficiency unit (for a single person or elderly person). All three units are shown with private enclosed gardens. The three units share a front porch and entry hall. There is still enough land to give about two-fifths of the original lot to the community. Particularly striking is the way in which existing spaces such as back porches or garages

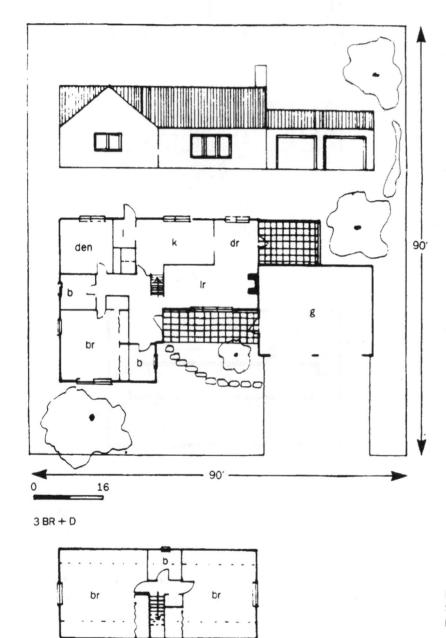

3 BR + D

Figure 30.2
Suburban single-family house,
plan, three bedrooms plus den

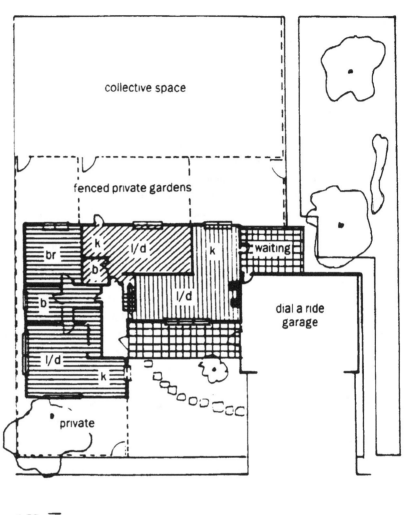

1 BR ≡
2 BR ||||
EFF ⁄⁄

Figure 30.3
Proposed HOMES revitalization,
same house converted to three
units (two bedroom, one bedroom,
and efficiency), plus dial-a-ride
garage and collective outdoor
space.

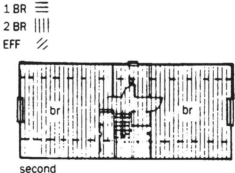

second

lend themselves to conversion to social areas or community services. Three former private garages out of 13 might be given over to collective uses – one as a central office for the whole block, one as a grocery depot, and one as a dial-a-ride garage. Is it possible to have only 20 cars (in 10 garages) and 2 vans for 26 units in a rehabilitated block? Assuming that some residents switch from outside employment to working within the block, and that for all residents, neighborhood shopping trips are cut in half by the presence of day care, groceries, laundry, and cooked food on the block, as well as aided by the presence of some new collective transportation, this might be done.

What about neighbours who are not interested in such a scheme? Depending on the configuration of lots, it is possible to begin such a plan with as few as three or four houses. In Berkeley, California, where neighbors on Derby Street joined their backyards and created a cooperative day-care center, one absentee landlord refused to join – his entire property is fenced in and the community space flows around it without difficulty. Of course, present zoning laws must be changed, or variances obtained, for the conversion of single-family houses into duplexes and triplexes and the introduction of any sort of commercial activities into a residential block. However, a community group that is able to organize or acquire at least five units could become a HUD housing cooperative, with a nonprofit corporation owning all land and with producers' cooperatives running the small community services. With a coherent plan for an entire block, variances could be obtained much more easily than on a lot-by-lot basis. One can also imagine organizations that run halfway houses – for ex-mental patients or runaway teenagers or battered women – integrating their activities into such a block plan, with an entire building for their activities. Such groups often find it difficult to achieve the supportive neighborhood context such a block organization would offer.

I believe that attacking the conventional division between public and private space should become a socialist and feminist priority in the 1980s. Women must transform the sexual division of domestic labor, the privatized economic basis of domestic work, and the spatial separation of homes and workplaces in the built environment if they are to be equal members of society. The experiments I propose are an attempt to unite the best features of past and present reforms in our own society and others, with some of the existing social services available in the United States today. I would like to see several demonstration HOMES begun, some involving new construction following the program I have laid out, others involving the rehabilitation of suburban blocks. If the first few experimental projects are successful, homemakers across the United States will want to obtain day-care, food, and laundry services at a reasonable price, as well as better wages, more flexible working conditions, and more suitable housing. When all homemakers recognize that they are struggling against both gender stereotypes and wage discrimination, when they see that social, economic, and environmental changes are necessary to overcome these conditions, they will no longer tolerate housing and cities, designed around the principles of another era, that proclaim that 'a woman's place is in the home.'

ACKNOWLEDGMENTS

I would like to thank Catharine Stimpson, Peter Marris, S.M. Miller, Kevin Lynch, Jeremy Brecher, and David Thompson for extensive written comments on drafts of this paper.

NOTES

1 This chapter was originally part of the text of a talk for the conference 'Planning and Designing a Non-Sexist Society,' University of California, Los Angeles, 21 April 1979. It also appeared under the title 'What Would a Non-Sexist City Be Like? Speculations on Housing, Urban Design and Human Work,' in *SIGNS* 5, no. 3 supplement (Spring 1980): 167–84.

2 There is an extensive Marxist literature on the importance of spatial design to the economic development of the capitalist city, including Castells, 1977; Lefebre, 1974; Gordon, 1978; Harvey, 1974. None of this work deals adequately with the situation of women as workers and homemakers, nor with the unique spatial inequalities they experience. Nevertheless, it is important to combine the economic and historical analysis of these scholars with the empirical research of non-Marxist feminist urban critics and sociologists who have examined women's experience of conventional housing, such as Wekerle, 1978; and Keller, 1978. Only then can one begin to provide a socialist–feminist critique of the spatial design of the American city. It is also essential to develop research on housing similar to Kamerman, 1979: 632–50, which reviews patterns of women's employment, maternity provisions, and child-care policies in Hungary, East Germany, West Germany, France, Sweden, and the United States. A comparable study of housing and related services for employed women could be the basis for more elaborate proposals for change. Many attempts to refine socialist and feminist economic theory concerning housework are discussed in an excellent article by Malos, 1978. A most significant theoretical piece is Movimento di Lotta Femminile, 1972.

3 I am indebted to Allan Heskin for this reference.

4 Gordon, 1978: 48–50, discusses suburban relocation of plants and housing.

5 Industrial Housing Associates, 1919. Also see Ehrenreich and English, 1975: 16. They quote an unidentified corporate official (ca. 1920): 'Get them to invest their savings in homes and own them. Then they won't leave and they won't strike. It ties them down so they have a stake in our prosperity.'

6 Barkin (1979: 120–4) gives the details of this competition; Ruth Schwartz Cowan, in an unpublished lecture at MIT in 1977, explained GE's choice of an energy-consuming design for its refrigerator in the 1920s, because this would increase demand for its generating equipment by municipalities.

7 Friedan (1974: 307) somewhat hysterically calls the home a 'comfortable concentration camp'; Filene (1974: 194) suggests that men are victimized by ideal homes too, thus 'domestic' mystique.

8 Zaretsky (1976) develops Friedan's earlier argument in a more systematic way. This phenomenon is misunderstood by Lasch (1977), who seems to favor a return to the sanctity of the patriarchal home.

9 For more detail, see Howe, 1977.

10 Recent zoning fights on the commune issue have occurred in Santa Monica, Calif.; Wendy Schuman, 'The Return of Togetherness,' *New York Times*, 20 Mar. 1977,

reports frequent illegal downzoning by two-family groups in one-family residences in the New York area.

11 Study by D. Foley, cited in Wekerle, 1978.

12 Research by Malcolm MacEwen, cited in *Associate Collegiate Schools of Architecture Newsletter*, Mach 1973: 6.

13 See, for example, Brown, 1978; Anderson-Khleif (1979: 3–4), research report for HUD on single-parent families and their housing.

14 My discussion of the Cuban Family Code is based on a visit to Cuba in 1978; a general review is Bengelsdorf and Hageman, 1979. Also see Fox, 1973.

15 This project relies on the 'support structures' concept of John Habraken to provide flexible interior partitions and fixed mechanical core and structure.

16 Personal interview with Nina West, 1978.

17 See Hayden, 1977, 1978, 1979, 1979–80, 1981.

18 Hayden (1976) discusses historical examples and includes a discussion of communes of the 1960s and 1970s.

19 See also the successful experience of Zurich, described in Hans Wirz, 1979.

REFERENCES

Susan Anderson-Khlief, *Research Report*, MIT-Harvard Joint Center for Urban Studies (April 1979): 3–4.

Carol Barkin, 'Home, Mom and pie-in-the-sky', M.Arch. thesis, University of California, 1979, pp. 120–4.

R. Baxandall, L. Gordon and S. Reverby (eds), *America's Working Women: A Documentary History, 1600 to the Present* (New York: Vintage Books, 1976).

Carollee Bengelsdorf and Alice Hagerman, 'Emerging from under-development: women and work in Cuba', *Capitalist Patriarchy and the Case for Socialist Feminism*, ed. Z. Eisenstein (New York: Monthly Review Press, 1979).

'Bridge over trouble water', *Architects' Journal* (27 September 1972): 680–4.

Carol A. Brown, 'Spatial inequalities and divorced mothers', Paper delivered at the annual meeting of the American Sociological Association, San Francisco, 1978.

Manuel Castells, *The Urban Question* (Cambridge, Mass.: MIT Press, 1977).

Barbara Ehrenreich and Deirdre English, 'The manufacture of housework', *Socialist Revolution* 5 (1975): 16.

S. Ewen, *Captains of Consciousness: Advertising and the Social Roots of the Consumer Culture* (New York: McGraw-Hill, 1976).

P. Filene, *Him/Her/Self: Sex Roles in Modern America* (New York: Harcourt Brace Jovanovich, 1974).

Geoffrey E. Fox, 'Honor, shame, and women's liberation in Cuba: views of working-class émigré men', in *Female and Male in Latin America*, ed. A. Pescatello (Pittsburgh: University of Pittsburgh Press, 1973).

C. Frederick, *Selling Mrs Consumer* (New York: Business Burse, 1929).

Betty Friedan, *The Feminine Mystique* (1963; New York: W. W. Norton, 1974).

David Gordon, 'Capitalist development and the history of American cities', in *Marxism and the Metropolis*, ed. W. K. Tabb and L. Sawyers (New York: Oxford University Press, 1978).

David Harvey, *Social Justice and the City* (London: Edward Arnold, 1974).

Louise Kapp Howe, *Pink Collar Workers: Inside the World of Women's Work* (New York: Avon Books, 1977).

Industrial Housing Associates, 'Good homes make contented workers', 1919, Edith Elmer Wood Papers, Avery Library, Columbia University.

Dolores Hayden, *Seven American Utopias: The Architecture of Communitarian Socialism, 1790–1975* (Cambridge, Mass.: MIT Press, 1976).

————, 'Catherine Beecher and the politics of housework', in *Women in American Architecture*, ed. S. Torre (New York: Whitney Library of Design, 1977).

————, 'Melusina Fay Peirce and cooperative housekeeping', *International Journal of Urban and Regional Research* 2 (1978).

————, 'Two utopian feminists and their campaigns for kitchenless houses', *Signs: Journal of Women in Culture and Society* 4, no. 2 (Winter 1979).

————, 'Charlotte Perkins Gilman: domestic evolution or domestic revolution?', *Radical History Review*, 21 (Winter 1979–80).

————, *A 'Grand Domestic Revolution': Feminism, Socialism and the American Home, 1870–1930* (Cambridge, Mass.: MIT Press, 1980).

Sheila B. Kamerman, 'Work and the family in industrialised societies', *Signs: Journal of Women in Culture and Society* 4, no. 4 (Summer 1979).

Suzanne Keller, 'Women in a planned community', Paper for the Lincoln Institute of Land Policy (Cambridge, Mass., 1978).

Christopher Lasch, *Haven in a Heartless World* (New York: Alfred A. Knopf, 1977).

Henri Lefebre, *La Production de l'espace* (Paris: Editions Anthropos, 1974).

Colleen McGrath, 'The crisis of domestic order', *Socialist Review* (January–February 1979), 9: 12 and 23.

Patricia Mainardi, 'The politics of housework', Robin Morgan (ed.), *Sisterhood is Powerful* (New York: Vintage Books, 1970).

Ellen Malos, 'Housework and the politics of women's liberation', *Socialist Review* 37 (January–February 1978).

Movimento di Lotta Femminile, 'Programmatic manifesto for the struggle of housewives in the neighborhood', *Socialist Revolution* 9 (May–June 1972).

Erwin Muhlestein, 'Kollektives Wohnen: Gestern und Heute', *Architese* 14 (1975): 3–23.

Wendy Schuman, 'The return of togetherness', *New York Times*, 20 March 1977.

Survey of AFL-CIO Members' Housing (Washington, DC: AFL-CIO, 1975).

R. Walker, *'Suburbanization in passage'*, Unpublished draft paper (University of California, Berkeley, Department of Geography, 1977).

Gerda Wekerle, 'A woman's place is in the city', Paper for the Lincoln Institute of Land Policy (Cambridge, Mass.: 1978).

Hans Wirz, 'Back yard rehab: urban microcosm rediscovered', *Urban Innovation Abroad* 3 (July 1979).

Eli Zaretsky, *Capitalism, the Family, and Personal Life* (New York: Harper & Row, 1976).

31 Frances Bradshaw (Matrix)

'Working with Women'

from Matrix, *Making Space: Women and the Man-made Environment* (1984)

In 1978 the Feminist Design Collective was formed. Its purpose, loosely defined, was to understand and develop a feminist approach to architecture through discussion and architectural work. Two of the projects I am going to describe were undertaken by this group. In 1980 the Feminist Design Collective split and Matrix was formed. Groups within Matrix formed to undertake different projects: an exhibition on housing design called 'Home Truths', this book, and architectural work for women's community groups. The ideas outlined in this chapter are based on lots of discussion. This is my interpretation of our shared experience.

Women working in Matrix (and in the Feminist Design Collective between 1978 and 1980) have been attempting to develop a way of designing buildings together, which values women's involvement in all the stages of the evolution of a building. The stages include recognizing the need for a building, obtaining finance for it, organizing it, designing, building and finally using it. Working together as a group, and working with other women's groups, have been among our most important experiences. Working and making decisions collectively has developed our confidence and ability to pursue and articulate elusive ideas.

We have all been trained conventionally by and with men, who have often devalued or ignored our work, describing it as 'emotional' or 'confused'. As practising architects we have often felt alienated and marginalized. In order to revalue our ideas and feelings, we have always tried to do work together, to go to meetings and give talks in pairs and to discuss work in progress with a larger group. We have learnt from working with women who have not been trained as architects. They have questioned conventional assumptions about design and have been excited by the possibilities of creating buildings that suit their needs.

The re-emergence of the women's movement over the last 15 years has meant that women have seen the need for, and started to make, new kinds of buildings. Places to live in together, refuges where women can be safe from men's violence, women's centres that are both meeting places and advice centres, places for teaching and learning skills previously inaccessible to women. Women have also been involved in creating places for children which are not formal state institutions, but which respond to the differing needs of children and grown-ups. New buildings need to be evolved which are appropriate for these new ways of organizing and living our lives. At present most women's centres and refuges, for instance, are housed in old and badly repaired buildings. Yet buildings help or hinder the development of new ideas in all sorts of subtle ways. The projects described in this chapter are not ideal women's buildings but they are a beginning. Except for Stockwell Health Centre in South London, they were all conversions of existing buildings.

People often ask us, 'If women design buildings, will the buildings be different or better?' If women collectively organize, design and make buildings that suit their needs rather than having to fit into what exists already (buildings created by a patriarchal culture) then the buildings are bound to look and feel different. We have to begin by being clear about our needs and not just wanting buildings to *look* different. Conventionally, great stress is put on the external appearance of buildings; this especially undervalues the experience and knowledge of women who use them. Buildings are for the most part just background, not important for what they look like but for how people can live and work in them.

We are trying to enable women to make buildings that are like good clothes. They should do the job they are there for, be useful, comfortable, likeable, and then every now and again they should be just a little bit special.

DESIGNING WITH WOMEN'S GROUPS

A new health centre was to be built in Stockwell, an area desperately lacking health facilities, and Stockwell Health Centre group came together through a meeting of community representatives. The group was concerned with the sort of health care the community needed, placing emphasis on preventive medicine, community use and self-help. Drawings had been made long ago by the local authority architect for the Area Health Authority, and the health centre group very quickly realized that they needed a different kind of building. 'When we were thinking about it, we kept having to look at this horrible plan and feeling irritated with it, so we thought. "Let's have one of our own."'

The Feminist Design Collective became involved at this point. For the health centre group it was important that we were a group of women, rather than one individual, so that we would understand the process of working in groups. They did not want 'an expert coming in and taking over' but wanted to retain control of the ideas for the building as it developed. 'We were feeling insecure enough already. We wanted help expressing our own ideas. Having people around showing how our ideas could be translated into a building made us more confident.'

The group had written a report for the health authority describing the kind of centre they wanted. They saw clearly that the type of building would strongly influence the possibility of implementing their ideas. They knew from experience in local community campaigns that the design of buildings affects women's lives in all sorts of ways. They had also learnt that loose and informal ways of organizing the health centre could be just as effective as the rigid ones imposed by the health authority; their ways of organizing would enable the community to have control of the building.

We all found it extremely difficult to define what a radically different kind of health centre would be like. Two principles emerged, reiterated in endless meetings with the health authority: that the centre should fulfil the needs of the community as a resource, and that it should feel open, inviting and easy to use. These principles were to be demonstrated clearly and simply by a building.

We worked out a design with the health centre group by imagining how the building could be used, discussing which activities could overlap, how the space would affect the way people relate to each other. These discussions suggested various arrangements and we made several different sketch designs. For instance, in one suggestion there was a café at the centre of everything, and all other spaces were arranged around it. In another the building was to have a street running through its centre, with all the drop-in facilities along both sides. Both of these ideas had disadvantages, but they were useful because each one expressed spatially an idea we had discussed about how the building could be used.

The health centre group discussed these sketches with other local groups and at a public meeting. As well as involving people not centrally working on the campaign, this consultation process also meant that women in the health group explained and discussed the various possibilities and in that process clarified and extended their own ideas.

The final design was L-shaped, with a café/meeting place on the corner, and crèche and community health worker's office (who is the centre's co-ordinator) behind. The crèche opened onto the garden enclosed by the 'L'. One arm of the 'L' along the existing main street housed the 'drop-in' facilities where people could get information and the services related to health care. These were to include chiropody, childcare clinics, osteopathy, as well as rooms for a dentist and optician. The other arm was to contain the more private offices and consulting rooms. The café and related spaces were intended for use in the evening as a more general community resource.

The alternative design for Stockwell Health Centre (Figure 31.1) was part of the ammunition the health centre group needed in the struggle for a locally controlled health centre. It was never actually built although some suggestions were incorporated into the local authority designed building. Our job was to discover *with* the group how a health centre, democratically run and open to the community, could be designed, and to help the group convince the Area Health Authority that the community's ideas were realizable.

Lambeth Women's Workshop is a carpentry and joinery teaching workshop in South London. It runs beginners' courses aimed especially at women with children, black, and working-class women. It came into existence through discussions in a Women's Aid group about women's employment. It was organized, designed, and converted by women, and is run by women now. We looked at possible spaces with the Workshop group. The place that finally seemed most appropriate was a unit in

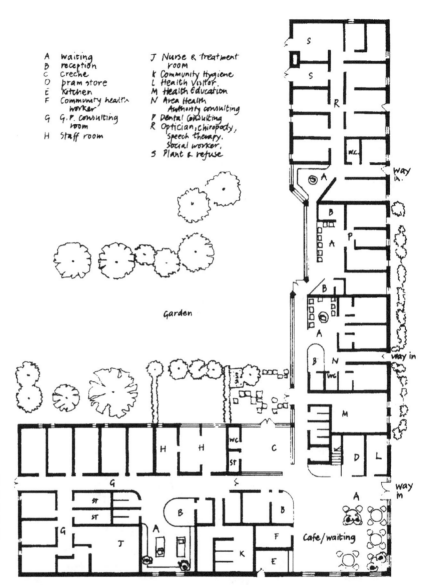

A waiting
B reception
C creche
D pram store
E kitchen
F Community health
   worker
G G.P. consulting
   room
H Staff room

J Nurse & treatment
   room
K Community hygiene
L Health Visitor.
M Health Education
N Area Health
   Authority consulting
P Dental Consulting
R Optician, chiropody,
   speech therapy.
   Social worker.
S Plant & refuse

Garden

Figure 31.1
Plan for the Stockwell Health
Centre, South London – a
proposed design based on
community needs

a large industrial building. The space chosen had the advantage of being already weatherproof, with good natural lighting and adequate service lifts for bringing up materials; however, it had an inhospitable atmosphere, reminding one of harsh working conditions.

The women on the management committee wanted the workshop space to assert a friendly working atmosphere. One way to do this was to make curving walls, to contrast directly with the straight lines and right angles of the factory. But we found this did not make economic use of the space. Finally it was broken into more intimate areas by, for instance, raising the floor of the sitting and kitchen space to give low window sills and ceiling height.

In making decisions about the way the workshop was designed, we talked about aesthetics, about the proportions of the space, and the relationship between windows, light and columns. Architects are trained to discuss and think about such ideas in an abstract way, which was obviously inappropriate, distancing the world from our experience and making it less part of ourselves and our everyday lives. We realized we had to find ways of talking about the qualities of the space; how light or dark, soft or hard, high or wide the space should be. We needed to find a language accessible to everyone involved. We have continued thinking about this. It means starting from feelings about the spaces women know and their everyday experiences in them, and using that information to gradually build up a picture of the new space.

Dalston Children's Centre was set up by a group of women in Hackney, North London, and provides facilities for women and children which are not normally

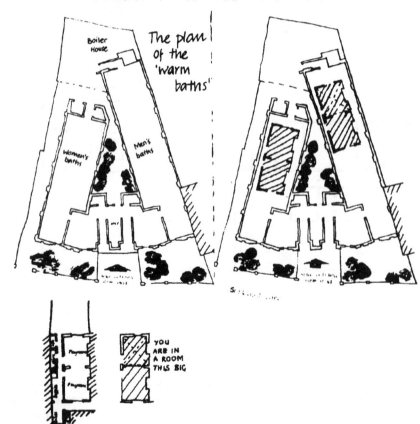

THE SIZE OF THE WARM BATHS
COMPARED TO 112 GREENWOOD ROAD.

The plan of the 'warm baths'

Boiler House

Women's baths

Men's baths

YOU ARE IN A ROOM THIS BIG

Plan of present Childrens' Centre building

Figure 31.2
Drawings that compare the building used by the East London Dalston Children's Centre with its new premises, a former warm bath house

available. Women with pre-school children can 'drop in' and either be with or leave their children for a few hours. It runs daytime classes for women, and children of school age can go there before and after school, to specific classes like music, theatre, swimming, or just to play. The centre also runs classes and play schemes at weekends and in the school holidays. The centre had been housed in various temporary premises for three years. Matrix was involved both in making the present temporary premises usable (they moved in September 1982) and in finding permanent premises and doing the architectural work necessary. The building that will be their permanent premises is an old bath-house, very different from the house the Children's Centre is in at present.

Imagining how a bath-house can be changed into a children's centre is not easy. We tried comparing the new building with their existing building. We drew pictures of how we thought the building could be, and worked with the various groups who use the centre to get their ideas. Matrix also ran a short course for the women who were to be particularly responsible for making design decisions. The course included sessions about the building programme, discussing which decisions have to be made at different times, and about drawings. For instance, the women measured the room we were in and drew it to get an idea of how scale drawings relate to real spaces.

In each of these jobs we have wanted to spend far more time designing the building than is conventionally allowed for: talking, trying out possibilities and finding ways women can become more confident about expressing their ideas about buildings. The more people are involved in the process the more time is needed for everyone's ideas to be expressed and considered seriously.

DRAWINGS AND OTHER DESIGN TOOLS

We learnt a lot about using drawings through working on Lambeth Women's Workshop. At first we did not realize how difficult it was for women on the management committee to get a feel of the building from the plans, of where the windows and doors and walls were, how big or small the space was. Next we tried drawing proposals with work benches and people in them, which seemed to be even more confusing.

The management committee felt that we were presenting 'fait accompli' choices, 'TV dinner drawings', for instant consumption or rejection. At that point we all started again. This time we used cut-out bits of paper for all the work benches and machinery and walls and windows. Everybody moved the bits of paper around trying out different arrangements and seeing how big things were in relation to each other. This really seemed to work. Women's experiences in different workplaces became relevant and useful and each woman felt involved in the process. We did not necessarily come to conclusions about the design, but everyone understood the problem.

With Stockwell Health Centre the first thing we did was to write on existing plans with big arrows pointing out all the criticisms different women had made. The group involved women with different experiences of health care, as 'patients' and as health workers. The comments varied from descriptions of what it is like being in a waiting room using an electronic call system if you are deaf or blind, to what sort of atmosphere is needed for giving family planning advice to women who are nervous.

Next, we did bubble diagrams showing the relationships between different activities. It was in general discussion that the idea evolved for a café around which the building could informally focus. This proved to be a key idea for the alternative scheme. On this first relationship diagram the café was drawn in a circle, relating to the other activity places in circles with arrows to them. Immediately the café became circular in people's minds. While we had made a distinction between diagram and building shape, others had not. When we later drew a square café on a plan, several women were disappointed and we were then able to discuss our different mental pictures. This seems quite a good example of accidental miscommunication which provoked useful ideas by chance, rather than carefully thought-out use of drawings. We were trying to find ways the group could get a feel of manipulating the spaces and take an active part in the process. We found we needed to do drawings that looked as throwaway as possible. We used scrap paper, and unruled lines – anything to overcome the feeling that once something was drawn it could not be changed.

A different experience of using drawings came from working with Balham Food and Book Co-operative, to redesign and build their new shop, an old four-storey house and shop in Balham High Street, South London. They had already been in existence for a year, and wanted to move to a more public shop, and to be able to open a café, provide meeting rooms, etc. They wanted to work with another co-operative.

Two women from Matrix were working with the Women's Building Co-op, so we were able to function as a 'design and build' group. The design was evolved with the Balham Food and Book Co-op; drawings and 'a specification of works' (that is, the description of work to be done) were done by a combination of designers and builders. Particularly successful were drawings of how the shop would look. These were colour sketches done by women trained in building, not architecture. We wanted to challenge the idea that only designers can imagine what spaces will be like. Builders are used to working three-dimensionally and understand how spaces relate to each other through specific and detailed experience. The drawings did not use complicated or formal drawing techniques and so were very immediate. They made the Balham Food and Book Co-op enthusiastic about the building and it was then much easier to discuss details of the proposal.

When working on Dalston Children's Centre, we started making models which could be taken to pieces and reassembled differently. Lots of different groups use the centre and so we had to find ways of involving as many women as possible in imagining what the building would be like. As well as doing sketches of different parts of the building converted in different ways, we made a rough cardboard model in which all the parts of the building that could not be changed were fixed and all the rest could be moved around. We found this model very useful during discussions. The relative size and position of spaces could be judged and women could immediately show what they meant when suggesting how the space could be used.

THE BUILDINGS

Dalston Children's Centre has from the first had a comfortable friendly atmosphere because creating that feeling has been a priority for the group. In discussions about the bath-house conversion, the group expressed concern that a newly converted building with large spaces, although more flexible in use, could feel cold and institutional. It has been important to find ways of making sure that does not happen.

The same issue has been confronted over all the buildings or proposed buildings I have described. They are all in different ways places where people, women especially, can meet and share experiences. This is not their primary function, but the 'client' group in each case emphasized that the place should be welcoming, comfortable and easy to find your way around. Each building involved a quite complex picture of activities and functions that were to remain closely interconnected. For instance, spaces where women could sit and talk had some link with the other activities going on in the building.

The health centre group wanted a café instead of a large waiting room, so that people could go to the health centre informally. Also a woman might get reassurance about a child's health, for instance, simply by talking to others in this space.

The entrance to the Lambeth Women's Workshop is an informal space, which includes a sitting area, a kitchen and an office. Each area is distinct but not separated by walls. The group did not want the workshop space to be completely cut off, but it is noisy and has potentially dangerous machinery in it. Two large windows allow you to see who is in the workshop and watch what they are doing. Without getting in the way, women who are new to the workshop can get a feel of the work that goes on there.

To say that buildings should feel friendly and be able to accommodate different sorts of social exchange may sound curious. It is obvious that they should. Yet if you think of the public buildings you know, from hospitals to workplaces, you will find there are few you could describe as either friendly or accommodating. They are intimidating to all except those who control them.

Making buildings where most people can feel at home involves changing who controls buildings. It also involves thinking about qualities that are hard to define and would be considered soppy on an architectural brief but are nonetheless important.

BEING AN ARCHITECT

We have learnt that it is important to explain on each job what an architect does, because so much of her work is invisible, unlike the builder's work, for instance. Conventionally, an architect's role is to find out what kind of building is wanted, what money is available and how it can best be used, then what spaces are needed in the building, how people are going to use the building and what it should feel like.

Listening to what people want can be complex, depending on how many people are involved in making decisions about the building. The accumulated information will come in various forms – and it has got to be made into usable information related to the proposed building. This means architects need to know how to organize information. They are taught techniques for doing this which are assumed to be universally applicable.

'Designing' is used to describe thinking out the possible ways of organizing and shaping the building according to all the gathered information. This process is more or less creative depending on the job; often the design decisions being made are quite small in themselves, especially in conversions, and may be limited by all sorts of regulations so that 'designing' may be rather like doing a jig-saw puzzle.

Once the design for the building is agreed, it has to be checked with *all* the authorities who control drainage, fire regulations, structural details, etc. The architect has to produce 'working drawings', rather like maps, which tell the builder where doors and windows and walls are to be. Also there is a written document (either a 'specification of works' or a 'bill of quantities', depending on the size of the job) that describes which materials to use, and other details that cannot be drawn. The builder will use this information to work out the cost of the building. When building work finally starts this information tells the builder exactly what to do. However, there are always some details that change, or cannot be decided beforehand. The architect is there to make sure the builder has all the necessary information, to ensure that the work is done as specified and to a 'reasonable' standard, and to mediate between the builder and the client. Arguments between them will be either about money or the standard of work, and until such a dispute gets so bad that it is taken to law, the architect's professional role is to say what is a 'reasonable' standard, and to act as a kind of adjudicator between the two parties. It is an ambiguous role because the architect is paid by the client, not the builder.

The whole process of designing and getting a building built is conventionally described as only a technical process. The ideology underlying how information is organized, whom you listen to, what questions you ask, which parts of the process could be open to group involvement – these are not generally discussed by architects or by those who employ them.

Nonetheless, a large part of the architect's job is a technical job and this means the architect does have technical skills. These skills are:

- obtaining information;
- organizing information, being able to juggle spaces and their relation-

ship to each other; either within an existing building or by creating a
new one;

- understanding the consequences of practical decisions, the effect on
the drainage layout of where the bathroom is positioned, or whether it
is possible to knock a wall down without the building collapsing, etc.;
- being able to make assessments about what a building will feel and
look like, before it exists;
- knowing what is feasible – financially (how much will it cost?),
structurally (will it fall down?), functionally (how big does a bathroom
have to be?), constructionally (keeping the rain out), environmentally
(keeping the heat in);
- knowing enough about building materials and services like plumbing
to know what works and how;
- knowing and being able to deal with the building, planning and
environmental health regulations;
- providing information (drawings, writing) for the builders;
- organizing and running the contract between builder and client.

The question for us as feminist architects is, how do we use these skills to further
the liberation of women?

ARCHITECTS, BUILDERS AND 'CLIENTS'

I want to describe our experience of the relationships between architect, 'client'
and builders. I am not trying to write a radical critique of the building industry, or to
suggest a blueprint for architectural practice. The experiences I am describing have
come not from a conscious plan to work in a predetermined way, but from a
personal sense of unease about how architects are supposed to work. For me and
for others in Matrix this attempt to find a more appropriate way of working had led
us to learn a building skill, and to work on site as builders or on design-and-build
projects. This has given us an understanding of the realities of day-to-day building,
but also has made us conscious in very practical ways of how divided the building
industry is.

The relationship between architect, client and builder has always been a class
relationship. The client has the money, the builder the craft skills, and the architect
(from an educated middle-class background) is paid by the client to provide the
design and to manage the job. Nowadays the building industry is extremely
complex, and management at different levels, from 'foreman' to contract manager,
has been created in response to the increased size of building projects, but the
fundamental relationships are the same. There is a hierarchy of status within the
building industry, with building workers (I have usually called them builders) at the
bottom.

The architect (still from a predominantly middle-class background) works
either for a private architectural practice or private building firm, or is a salaried

employee of the state. It is only on fairly small-scale work that architect and building worker come into direct contact. Nonetheless, when they do, as on the projects I have described, the class and status differences are obvious.

The architectural profession (like other professions) has attempted to define an area of work and gain control of it. It has been aided in this by the growing complexity of legislation, regulations and bureaucracy around building, which have developed as buildings have become technically more complex. Architects and builders are mutually dependent on each other in the production of buildings, while both are dependent on the client for finance. Examining the relationship between architect, builder and client also involves questioning the way their individual roles are defined. Is it appropriate that we should automatically adopt the profession's idea of the architect as I have described it above? For, while the builder's skills are at least as essential as the architect's, they are not valued in the same way. Architects are paid more than building workers, and they usually have more control over how they do their work.

Our attempts to create a more equal relationship between builder, 'client' and architect are by no means the first. Both women and men have discussed and explored these possibilities in the past and are doing so now. The jobs I have described, however, were thought-provoking because they allowed a group of women designers to work with women on women-centred buildings. They all involved working with sympathetic women 'clients', not all with women builders. Projects have been funded by the state and/or a local authority, rather than directly by the 'client' group. This has made it easier to establish an egalitarian relationship between architects and 'client' group than between architects and women builders. It is our shared politics and feminist intentions that make an equal relationship possible, but this can be very easily undermined when one group assesses the quality and value of the other group's work, and pays them. Relationships between women architects and women builders are much more difficult because to some extent the architect's job always includes supervising the builder's work, and authorizing payment for work completed.

The conventional relationship between architect and builder, where the builders are all men, is an uncomfortable one for most women architects. Whereas middle-class men are socialized to use the rational detachment required of their assigned role as adjudicator between client and builder, women's socialized role is to sympathize with people and to understand and be supportive to the problems of others.

This may mean that women tend to give everybody concerned more thought and the job more care. Women tend to consult and ask for participation in decision-making more than men. However, the architect's role is more stressful for women since it is usually difficult to please both client and builder. It is also a contradictory role. Women architects are in an authoritative role, which class differences reinforce, yet as women they do not normally have authority over men. Male architects and builders can overcome class differences to some extent by sharing male camaraderie, but women cannot do this. Thus women architects are isolated by both sex and class. Because of this it has been particularly important for us to be able to work with women builders. The building work for Lambeth Women's Workshop, the temporary premises for Dalston Children's Centre and the shop for Balham Food and Book Co-operative were done by women builders. These projects have brought up more questions than they have answered; however, I think it is worth outlining the questions.

Because of differences in status, class and decision-making roles, and because the contract normally used between client and builder assumes no trust between them, there is usually some degree of tension between architect and builder. If women architects work with women builders within the conventional framework, this tension is in direct conflict with the expectations of working in a sisterly way, that is, supportively and co-operatively. How do we find a framework for working together which is based on mutual trust in order to resolve these contradictions?

What do we expect from skill-sharing? Four of us in Matrix have learnt building skills in order to work on site. It is far easier to us to do that than it is for builders to learn design skills, because builders are trained in a more *ad hoc* way than architects, and the training is shorter. It is obviously not possible or desirable that everyone should be able to do everyone else's job, but it is necessary to understand and be able to relate to others' skills. Because architects' skills are less visible than builders', it is even more important that architects' skills should be de-mystified and made clear and accessible. How do we do that?

Because women do not have a history of being builders or architects, every project is like pioneering. Women want it to be really good because they do not have mothers and grandmothers who have done it before, and who prove they will be able to do it too. This question of confidence affects day-to-day work. In many ways women expect more of each other than they do of men, and worry lest others should think they are not doing a good enough job. How do we establish standards of our own, ways that suit our skills and expectations?

The constraints of money and time mean that on site there is continual pressure to keep working. Finding ways of working more equally involves making time to discuss ideas and work out problems. While architects are paid enough to be able to choose to some extent how to spend their time, this is not the case for builders.

There are no obvious answers to these questions. Exploring ways of working together takes place within a divided and exploitative building industry. We tried one way of working more closely together when two women architects worked on site with the Women's Building Co-op. The advantages of this design-and-build process are usually described functionally – it is more efficient to have designers and builders working closely together. Everyone knows more about what is going on, fewer mistakes are made of the kind that happen on conventional sites due to bad communication. These *are* advantages. But it is also important that the status differences between designing and building work are broken down.

The assumptions that go with conventional roles within the building industry are powerful. The definition of jobs, which skills are considered necessary in the creation of buildings and how they are relatively valued and paid for – these are all issues of vital importance. We cannot expect to avoid these hierarchies, except perhaps on particular projects, but neither can we accept them. How women are involved in the building process affects the buildings we create as much as involvement in the design does.

During the time we have been working together as Matrix we have continued to feel that more and more women are exploring the same ideas, wanting to learn how we can mould the physical environment around us.

I have been trying to describe ideas and feelings about women and buildings which I think we are only beginning to understand clearly. It is a process of unravelling all the ways we are conditioned to think about the places around us, and then creating our own ways, our own spaces. It is a tentative, lurching process, sometimes making us feel trapped by endless trivial matters, sometimes giving us feelings of great excitement and discovery. What we have learnt is how much there is to discover, and that it is possible to make spaces that respond to women's needs. If we can become more aware of how the buildings we live and work in relate to how we live, then we can create buildings that work with women's struggle for liberation rather than against it.

32 Karen A. Franck

'A Feminist Approach to Architecture: Acknowledging Women's Ways of Knowing'

from Ellen Perry Berkeley, *Architecture: A Place for Women* (1989)

The qualities that seem to characterize women's ways of knowing and analyzing appear variously in social-architectural research conducted by women, in alternative communities proposed by women, and in projects designed by women.[1] Evidence that such qualities exist or that they distinguish women from men is suggestive at best. The test for this essay, however, is not in the scientific persuasiveness of the evidence but in the degree to which the descriptions resonate with women's own experiences in architecture and in everyday life. One goal is to help women in architecture to identify qualities and concerns in themselves that are often unrecognized or suppressed in architectural education, research, and practice. A second goal is to celebrate these qualities and concerns; a third is to work toward a profession that is more hospitable to feminist practitioners and that produces an environment more attuned to people's needs.[2]

'Knowing' is discussed here as an act of creating. We construct what we know, and these constructions are deeply influenced by our early experiences and by the nature of our underlying relationship to the world. As the early experiences of women and men and their relationship to the world differ in significant ways, so too will their characteristic ways of knowing and analyzing. Many writers in the past decade have pointed out that women's underlying relationship to the world is one of connection while men's is one of separation.[3] This fundamental tenet of much feminist thought is based on object relations theory (as expounded by Nancy Chodorow in *The Reproduction of Mothering*). Chodorow holds that since the daughter is of the same gender as the mother, development of the daughter's self-identity centers on attachment to the main parenting figure and thereby to the generalized 'other' and the world. In contrast, development of the son's self-identity requires differentiation and separation from the mother, leading to separation from the 'other' and the world.

That masculinity is defined in terms of the denial of connection, and that femininity is defined as self-in-relationship, has important implications for cognitive activities and hence for western science, philosophy, and architecture. Evelyn Fox

Keller suggests in *Reflections on Gender and Science* that the nature of science mirrors the nature of masculinity; the scientific method requires the scientist's separation from, and domination of, the objects of research. Emotion and subjectivity, as qualities of connectedness, are demarcated from reason and objectivity, with the former given little credence in scientific endeavors. As an alternative to this 'static objectivity,' Keller describes 'dynamic objectivity.' This approach acknowledges and relies on the connectedness between researcher and observed world, and is demonstrated in the work of the geneticist Barbara McClintlock; her premise for research was to 'listen to what the material has to tell you' rather than to impose an answer on it.[4]

In provocative works, Carol Gilligan has used the definition of the feminine identity as self-in-relationship to interpret observed differences between women and men in resolving moral dilemmas.[5] She finds that women and girls draw upon a 'reflective understanding of care' requiring that no one be hurt and that one respond to the needs of others, whereas men and boys are concerned that everyone be treated fairly. Gilligan calls the first, women's 'ethic of care' and the second, men's 'ethic of justice.'

Nancy Hartsock, in her article 'The Feminist Standpoint,' relates the development of male self-identity to the masculinist tendency to degrade everyday life and to value abstraction. The masculinity that boys must achieve is an ideal not directly experienced in the home and family but reached only by escaping into the masculine world of public life, which remains distant from the child's experience. Boys thus see two worlds: one 'valuable, if abstract and deeply unattainable, the other useful and demeaning, if concrete and necessary.'[6] In contrast, the female sense of self is achieved within the context of home and family, and hence embraces and values everyday life and experience.

Connectedness applies to analyzing as well as to knowing. Since analyzing is the activity of distinguishing between elements, it can easily lead to seeing distinctions as being divisions – to seeing elements that are different as being separate, distant, and disconnected. In the masculinist world view, based on separations, this is particularly true.[7]

The tendency to see only division and separation takes its most extreme form in dualistic thinking, where only two categories are posited in opposition to each other, and where one category is often valued more highly than the other. Nancy Hartsock suggests that the masculinist dualism between the abstract and the concrete is replicated in many other combative and hierarchical dualisms: ideal/real, stasis/change, culture/nature, man/woman. In her feminist materialism she sees variety, connectedness, continuity, and unity between manual and mental work as marking a new social synthesis. Sandra Harding similarly questions the dichotomous structures of culture/nature, mental/manual, and abstract/concrete. She sees an opportunity in feminist thinking to integrate what are traditionally seen as separate categories. She posits a feminist way of living and understanding that will unify the labor of hand, head, and heart. In addition, Harding advocates the valuation of change in her proposal for a feminist materialism, and she praises the instability of categories in feminist theory.[8]

These writings from recent feminist literature in psychoanalysis, psychology, philosophy, and philosophy of science suggest seven qualities that characterize feminine or feminist ways of knowing and analyzing: (1) an underlying connectedness to others, to objects of knowledge, and to the world, and a sensitivity to the connectedness of categories; (2) a desire for inclusiveness, and a desire to overcome opposing dualities; (3) a responsibility to respond to the needs of others, represented by an 'ethic of care'; (4) an acknowledgment of the value of everyday life and experience; (5) an acceptance of subjectivity as a strategy for knowing, and of feelings as part of knowing; (6) an acceptance and desire for complexity; and (7) an acceptance of change and a desire for flexibility. These same characteristics appear in social/architectural research conducted by women, in utopian and alternative communities proposed by women, and in architectural projects designed by women.

Connectedness and Inclusiveness

Synthesism, or the integration of categories, is one alternative to dualistic thinking.[9] Another, perhaps a prerequisite for greater connectedness, is to recognize the dualisms and other forms of categorization that exist and to study their origins, their status, and the consequences they have for everyday life, for research, and for design. Researchers in the field of environment and behavior are beginning to do this and to indicate how an unreflective categorization precludes the recognition of variety, complexity, and change.[10] One eventual consequence of such research should be the spurning of oppositional and hierarchical dualisms and the development of more inclusive, more complex, and more changeable categories.

Analysis of the categories used in urban theory, planning, and design is the hallmark of recent feminist analysis of the contemporary, designed environment in Great Britain and the United States. The writings of Susan Saegert, Ann Markusen, Linda McDowell, Suzanne MacKenzie, and Damaris Rose reveal the pervasive influence of the dualisms of public/private, city/suburb, work/home, and production/reproduction, which are habitually and unthinkingly aligned with each other and with men/women in urban theory and design.[11]

These dichotomies are applied in theory and in practice as if they were separate and unrelated; in fact, in each case, they are interdependent and overlapping. Industrial capitalism depends on the home/work, reproduction/production, and women/men divisions for the large-scale consumption of goods generated by the needs of separate households in suburban locations[12] and for the biological and psychological renewal of the wage labor force in the home setting.[13] Industrial capitalism helped to create and continues to enforce the spatial separations that accompany these categories in contemporary communities in the United States.

By examining the daily lives of women, it is possible to see that the simple dichotomies are not an accurate reflection of women's experience. The home has always been a place of work for women; women habitually frequent public settings; and the quality of idyllic retreat romantically associated with the suburban home is more myth than reality.[14] The ideology of separation between the spheres of public/private, men/women, and work/home makes everyday activities more difficult to pursue precisely because of the spatial distances that the ideology has generated.[15] In addition to revealing the existence and consequences of these dualisms, commentators have called for a greater degree of analytic synthesis between the categories and for a greater degree of overlap between the spatial domains that this dualistic thinking has generated in the built environment.

The desire for greater connectedness between different types of activities and the spaces to support them appears in many feminist visions of utopian or alternative communities. In Marge Piercy's utopian novel *Woman on the Edge of Time*, work takes place within walking distance of people's cottages and of all other centers of activity. Dolores Hayden, in her proposal for the redesign of forty suburban houses into a community, connects social activities, wage work, and home life through the provision of on-site jobs, good public transportation, and shared services and facilities. Suzanne MacKenzie imagines a future where women themselves have integrated home and work by redesigning their homes into a combination of dwelling and workshop and by substituting the exchange of services for money.[16]

A closer spatial connection between activities currently separated is one way of reducing the extreme dichotomy between private and public domains. This dichotomy enforces the traditional sexual division of labor. Thus at the heart of any feminist alternative must be the goal of lessening the separation between public and private, and between wage work and home life. Piercy lessens the private/public split by envisioning small and highly localized communities where all residents know each other; there is no anonymous public realm. MacKenzie's vision also does away with the anonymous realm: home and local community become the domain for all daily activities. In Hayden's proposal, private yards are redesigned to be shared, and many services and some sources of employment are placed within the residential setting. The integration of services with housing, as a way of reducing the current distance between activities and between the private and public domains, is also advocated by Gerda Wekerle, Susan Saegert, and Jacqueline Leavitt.[17]

In designing, connectedness takes several forms. One form is a close relationship between designer and client or designer and user.[18] Designing from a feminist perspective is likely to blur role distinctions between designer and client and designer and user. This is the approach taken by Matrix, a group of feminist architects in England.[19]

A second form of connectedness is the desire for closer spatial or visual connections between spaces. The Matrix group has identified among its women clients an interest in connecting spaces and activities in buildings and in connecting the people who use the building. Thus, a waiting room in a community health center becomes a café so that women can meet and share experiences; in a community center, large windows in an interior wall allow people to see activities inside a workshop. The clients for Susana Torre's House of Meanings were also women. Each version of the house she designed for them creates a spatial continuity between spaces conventionally kept separate and distinct. Moreover, the house allows opposites (including private/public, individual/shared, outside/inside) to inter-act rather than to remain in opposition.[20] Thus a third form of connectedness in designing is the integration of opposite types of spaces. A fourth type of connected-ness is the integration of what are usually seen as opposing design approaches. Julia Robinson proposes a design process, called 'design as exploration,' that will create 'a dialogue between the subjective and the objective, the intuitive and the rational.'[21]

Ethic of Care and Value of Everyday Life

These are prominent characteristics of the alternative communities proposed by women, and they appear in social and architectural research by women as early as the housing reforms of Catherine Bauer and Edith Elmer Wood. The attention given to issues of family life in early public housing is attributed to these reformers.[22] Similarly, Elisabeth Coit was paramountly concerned with the daily lives of families in her surveys and observations of conditions in New York public housing between 1938 and 1940.[23]

Subsequently, Jane Jacobs showed how people's everyday activities and needs were being ignored or frustrated by the large scale, single-use, superblock develop-ments so popular in urban renewal. Her concern was daily experience and the ways in which the designed environment could support and enhance that experience – a far cry from the abstract concepts and geometric site planning of urban renewal plans. More recently, researchers such as Clare Cooper have taken a similar approach: focusing on the everyday lives and perceptions of residents and com-paring these with the intentions and expectations of architects.[24] Hayden's *Redesigning the American Dream* demonstrates a similar sensitivity, to daily life, particularly that of women and children and the elderly whose needs have long been ignored or misunderstood by planners and architects.

Attention to everyday activities and the ethic of care appear in women's design work as well. The winning entry in the recent New American House Competition, designed by Troy West and Jacqueline Leavitt, demonstrates a strong concern for the special needs of different kinds of parents and children, as well as a desire to bring neighbors together. Architects in the Matrix group draw upon their own experience and that of their clients so that daily experiences rather than abstract concepts become the source material for design. Eileen Gray and Lilly Reich designed furniture and spaces that were especially sensitive to mundane needs. Gray's acknowledgment of unmade beds, and eating or reading in bed, led her to design the first colored sheets! And her awareness of the ever-present need for storage generated ingenious designs, including drawers that pivot.[25]

The furniture of Lilly Reich, who collaborated with Mies van der Rohe, showed a similar attentiveness to human comfort; Reich's chairs featured backs contoured to the body while Mies's took idealized lines.[26] Margrit Kennedy lists as a female principle in architecture a greater emphasis on functional issues and a lesser

299 □

emphasis on formal ones, and Jane Thompson makes the concern for human comfort and growth a goal of feminist architecture.

Value of Subjectivity and Feelings

The acceptance of subjectivity as a strategy for knowing allows personal experience and knowledge to be sources of information and design. Many of Jane Jacobs' insights were drawn from her own experience of living on Hudson Street in Greenwich Village. In other instances, environmental autobiographies are used as a way for individuals, including architects, to become aware of their own preferences as these derive from life experiences. Cooper Marcus explores the deep-seated meanings of house and home by using Gestalt techniques whereby respondents role-play their own homes, speaking as their homes might speak.[27] In a recent course on architecture for utopia, I asked students to list their own complaints about current social and physical arrangements, to imagine more desirable arrangements, and to develop them in an illustrated narrative.[28] Robinson, in her proposed design process, presents a more systematic way of using personal experience in design – through making one's preconceptions conscious and using these preconceptions, and revisions to them, as sources for design ideas.

The importance of feelings (and, relatedly, of intimate relationships) is recognized in women's proposals for alternative communities. The attitudes commonly associated with mothering – expressiveness, caring, affection, attachment – are part of all relationships in Piercy's utopian community. Happiness, love, anger, conflict, and depression are all dealt with as openly and as considerately as possible. Many writers acknowledge the importance of informal, intimate, and caring relationships between people and favor designed settings and programs that reinforce such relationships.[29]

And it is the lack of emotion and lack of intimacy that Eileen Gray decried in modernism in 1929: 'Modern designers have exaggerated the technological side. . . . Intimacy is gone, atmosphere is gone. . . . Formulas are nothing; life is everything. And life is mind and heart at the same time.'[30]

Value of Complexity and Flexibility

Eileen Gray attributed this lack of intimacy to the substitution of simplification for simplicity. Women architects since then have voiced their desire for greater complexity. Margrit Kennedy lists complexity among her female principles in architecture; Sheila de Bretteville sees complexity and ambiguity as desirable design qualities because they undermine control and invite user participation.[31] And Jane Thompson calls for an architecture that embraces both the aesthetic of the industrial age (valuing simplification) and the earlier aesthetic embodied in religion and magic (valuing complexity).

The desire for complexity is allied with an attention to multiple use, and more generally with awareness of change and the need for flexibility and transformation. Eileen Gray's understanding of the use of an object over time allowed her to design a table that could be used as coffee table, side table, or bed table. Flexibility or the anticipation of change also guided Lilly Reich's design of an open-plan apartment where she divided the apartment across the narrow dimension to give areas for rest, study, and meals; the furniture could be rearranged to change divisions or to unite the entire room. In contrast, Mies's open plan generated a hierarchial set of spaces, main and subsidiary spaces, for fixed functions: the living space could not serve as a minor space because of its central placement in the formal composition.[32] Multiple use of space and transformation of space were guiding principles in Torre's House of Meanings and in West and Leavitt's New American House.

These qualities of connectedness, multiple use, flexibility, and complexity find expression in designing space as a matrix. The idea of the matrix fulfilling women's design proclivities is implied by several authors. De Bretteville identifies quilts and blankets as examples of women's work that grow over time, are organized with many centers, and do not have beginnings or ends. They are examples of designing a matrix.[33] Designing her House of Meanings as 'matrix space' allowed Torre to achieve her objectives of overcoming opposing dualisms, of creating multi-functional spaces, and of combining completeness with the opportunity for trans-formation. Given the potential usefulness of the idea of matrix for women's concerns in architecture, it is fitting that the original meaning was uterus or womb, coming from the Latin word 'mater' or mother. (Later it came to mean a place or medium in which something is produced or bred; most recently, the rectangular arrangement of qualities.)

Although this essay follows earlier feminist thinking in architecture and other fields, it is still only part of a fledgling effort to outline a feminist approach to architecture. Some of the qualities that a feminist approach to architecture might well encourage have been discussed in this essay. Other qualities that could be explored are cooperation and collaboration, organic systems of spatial organization and form-making, and metaphors based on hearing and touching (this last, to balance the exclusive reliance on the metaphor of vision in western philosophy and archi-tecture).[34] Similarly, the activities of analyzing, proposing alternative communities, and designing are only some of the activities of architecture; others would include teaching and professional practice, and advocacy. At first glance, the qualities discussed here seem to apply to these other activities as well. I have noticed that my teaching has come to possess some of them and I see some of them reflected in the work of early women architects such as Eleanor Raymond and Mary Jane Colter, as well in the concerns of more recent ones including Dolores Hayden and Joan Forrester Sprague.[35]

Finally, this essay has drawn entirely upon literature from and about western industrialized capitalist society. The qualities and concerns described may only be true of women in this society and of a limited segment of those women (those with economic and educational resources). One way for women to express their desire for greater and different forms of connectedness is to explore the qualities and concerns of women in other societies and in other circumstances.[36] If it is true that women in architecture in this society are less likely than men to be distanced from other people by perceived differences, and if it is true that we wish to overcome opposing dualities, then there is less to stop us from discovering both our similarities and our differences with women elsewhere in the world.[37]

NOTES

1 Research for this essay was supported in part by a grant from the New Jersey Department of Higher Education, award number 87–990780-2494. I would like to thank my research assistant Nancy Bartlett for her help and Cathie Comerford for her encouragement. This essay is dedicated to these two young women in architecture and to others like them.

2 The spirit of this essay follows earlier proposals of female principles in architecture. See: Jane Thompson, 'The World of Double Win,' *Feminist Art Journal* (Fall 1976): 16–20, and Margrit Kennedy. 'Toward a Rediscovery of Feminine Principles in Architecture and Planning,' *Women's Studies International Quarterly* 4 (1981): 75–81. Other feminist approaches to architecture focus on the importance of understanding how the designed environment oppresses women and the need for environments that respond to women's needs. See Leslie Kanes Weisman, 'Women's Environmental Rights,' *Heresies* 3 (1981): 6–8; Nunzia Rondanini, 'Architecture and Social Change,' *Heresies* 3 (1981): 3–5; and Jos Boys, 'Is There a Feminist Analysis of Architecture?' *Built Environment* 10 (1984): 25–34. The framework described in the present essay complements and can encompass these other approaches. Discussions of feminine or feminist aesthetics in other fields may have implications for architecture. See, for example: Gisela Ecker, ed., *Feminist Aesthetics*, trans., Harriet Anderson (Boston: Beacon Press, 1985); Naomi Schor, *Reading in Detail* (New York: Methuen, 1987).

3 Dorothy Dinnerstein, *The Mermaid and the Minotaur* (New York: Harper and Row, 1976); Nancy Chodorow, *The Reproduction of Mothering* (Berkeley: University of California Press: 1978); Carol Gilligan, 'Women's Place in Man's Life Cycle,' *Harvard Educational Review* 49 (November 1979): 431–46; Evelyn Fox Keller, *Reflections on Gender and Science* (New Haven: Yale University Press, 1985); Nancy Hartsock, 'The Feminist Standpoint' in *Discovering Reality*, eds, Sandra Harding and Merrill B. Hintikka (Dordrecht, Holland: D. Reidel, 1983).

4 Keller, *Gender and Science*, 138. Others have proposed that connectedness with the object to be known is the most developed form of 'women's knowing.' See Mary F. Belenky, Blythe Clincy, Nancy Goldberger, and Jill Tarnle, *Women's Ways of Knowing* (New York: Basic Books, 1986).

5 Gilligan, 'Women's Place.' See also Carol Gilligan, *In a Different Voice* (Cambridge: Harvard University Press, 1982).

6 Hartsock, 297.

7 Keller contrasts this propensity with the approach of Barbara McClintlock who was willing to accept complexity and connectedness and who saw anomalous evidence as indicative not of disorder but of a larger and more complex pattern.

8 Sandra Harding, 'The Instability of the Analytical Categories of Feminist Theory,' *'Signs* 11 (1986): 645–64. See also: Hilary Rose, 'Hand, Brain and Heart: A Feminist Epistemology for the Natural Sciences,' *Signs* 9 (1983): 73–90.

9 Lynda Glennon, 'Synthesism: A Case of Feminism Methodology,' in *Beyond Method*, ed. Gareth Morgan (Beverly Hills: Sage Publications, 1983).

10 Karen A. Franck, 'A Call for Examining Categories in Environmental Design Research,' in *The Costs of Not Knowing*, eds Jean Wineman, Richard Barnes, and Craig Zimring (Washington, DC: Environmental Design Research Association, 1986); Karen A. Franck, 'When Type is Stereotype (and What to Do about It)' (Paper presented at University of Minnesota conference 'Type and the Possibilities of Convention, 'May 1987 in Minneapolis); Eileen Bradley and Maxine Wolfe, 'Where do the 65-year-old Latina Jewish Lesbians Live?' in *Public Environments*, eds Joan Harvey and Don Henning (Washington, DC: Environmental Design Research Association, 1987).

11 Susan Saegert, 'Masculine Cities and Feminine Suburbs,' in *Women and the American City*, eds, C.R. Stimpson, F. Dixler, M.J. Nelson, and K.B. Yatrakis (Chicago: University of Chicago Press, 1981); Ann Markusen, 'City Spatial Structure, Women's Household Work and National Policy,' in *Women and the American City*, eds, C.R. Stimpson *et al.* (Chicago: University of Chicago Press, 1981); L. McDowell, 'Towards an Understanding of the Gender Division of Urban Space,' *Environment and Planning D* 1 (1983): 59–72; Suzanne MacKenzie and Damaris Rose, 'Industrial Change, the Domestic Economy and Home Life,' in *Redundant Spaces in Cities and Regions*, eds J. Anderson, S. Duncan, and R. Hudson (London: Academic Press, 1983).

12 R. Miller, 'The Hoover in the Garden,' *Environment and Planning D*, 1 (1983): 73–87.

13 McDowell, 'Towards an Understanding'; MacKenzie and Rose, 'Industrial Change.'

14 Leonore Davidoff, Jean L'Esperance and Howard Newby, 'Landscape with Figures,' in *The Rights and Wrongs of Women*, eds Juliet Mitchell and Ann Oakley (New York: Penguin, 1976); Saegert, 'Masculine Cities and Feminine Suburbs.'

15 Dolores Hayden, 'What Would a Non-sexist City be Like?' in *Women and the American City*; Dolores Hayden, *Redesigning the American Dream* (New York: Norton, 1984); Karen A. Franck, 'Social Construction of the Physical Environment: The Case of Gender,' *Sociological Focus* 18 (1985): 143–70.

16 Marge Piercy, *Women on the Edge of Time* (New York: Fawcett, 1976); Hayden, 'What Would a Non-sexist City be Like?', Suzanne MacKenzie, 'No One Seems to Go to Work Anymore,' *Canadian Women's Studies* 5 (1985): 5–8.

17 Jacqueline Levitt, 'The Shelter Service Crisis and Single Parents,' in *The Unsheltered Woman*, ed. F.L. Birch (New Brunswick, NJ: Center for Urban Policy Research, 1985); Gerda Wekerle, 'Neighborhoods that Support Women,' *Sociological Focus* 18 (1985): 79–95; Susan Saegert 'The Androgenous City,' *Sociological Focus* 18 (1985): 79–95.

18 Jane Thompson ('The World of Double Win') refers to women designers' empathy with the user; Margrit Kennedy ('Toward a Rediscovery of Feminine Principles') suggests that one female principle in architecture is to be more user-oriented than designer-oriented.

19 Frances Bradshaw, 'Working with Women,' in *Making Space*, ed. Matrix (London: Pluto Press, 1984).

20 Susana Torre, 'Space as Matrix,' *Heresies* 3 (1981): 51–2. Elsewhere, Torre contrasts this view of opposites-as-complementary with the more prevailing belief in their irreconcilability. See: Susana Torre, 'The Pyramid and the Labyrinth,' in *Women in American Architecture: A Historic and Contemporary Perspective*, ed. Susana Torre (New York: Whitney Library of Design, 1977).

21 Julia Robinson, 'Design as Exploration,' *Design Studies* 7 (April 1986): 67–78. See also Julia Robinson and Stephen Weeks, *Programming as Design* (Minneapolis: School of Architecture and Landscape Architecture, University of Minesota, 1983).

22 Eugenie Birch, 'Women-made America,' in *The American Planner*, ed. D. Krueckberg (New York: Methuen, 1983).

23 Mary Otis Stevens, 'Struggle for Place,' in *Women in American Architecture*.

24 Jane Jacobs, *The Death and Life of Great American Cities* (New York: Random House, 1961); Clare Cooper, *Easter Hill Village* (New York: Free Press, 1975). While Cooper's approach is now fairly common in environment behavior research, her book was an early and influential example.

25 Jacqueline Leavitt, 'A New American House,' *Women and Environments* 7 (1985): 14–16; Deborah Nevins, 'Eileen Gray' *Heresies* 3 (1981): 67–71; J. Stewart Johnson, *Eileen Gray* (London: Debrett's Peerage Ltd and The Museum of Modern Art, 1979). Johnson points out the close resemblance between Joe Colombo's 1968 design of pivoting drawers and Gray's small chest, published in 1939. See also: Peter Adams, *Eileen Gray: Architect/Designer* (New York: Harry N. Abrahams, 1987).

26 Deborah Dietsch, 'Lilly Reich,' *Heresies* 3 (1981): 73–6.

27 Clare Cooper Marcus, 'Home-as-Haven, Home-as-Trap,' in *The Spirit of Home*, eds Patrick Quinn and Robert Benson (Washington, DC: Association of Collegiate Schools of Architecture, 1986). Cooper Marcus is currently writing a book based on this research.

28 Elsewhere in the field of architecture, the personal narrative is being used as a way to generate design. See, for example: John Hejduk, *Mask of Medusa* (New York: Rizzoli, 1985). Misuse of this approach can become purely narcissistic, especially when it is not coupled with an ethic of care (and the empathy that this entails).

29 Hayden, 'What Would a Non-sexist City be Like?'; Wekerle, 'Neighborhoods that Support Women'; MacKenzie, 'No One Seems to Go to Work Anymore'; Saegert, 'The Androgenous City'; Leavitt, 'A New American House.'

30 Deborah Nevins, trans., 'From Eclecticism to Doubt.' *Heresies* 3 (1981): 72.

31 Sheila de Bretteville. 'A Reexamination of the Design Arts from the Perspective of a Woman Designer,' *Women and the Arts* 11 (1974): 115–23.

32 Dietsch, 'Lilly Reich.'

33 See also: Lucy Lippard, 'Centers and Fragments,' in *Women in American Architecture*.

34 Evelyn Fox Keller and Christine Gronthowski, 'The Mind's Eye,' in *Discovering Reality*.

35 Doris Cole, *Eleanor Raymond* (Cranbury, NJ: Associated University Presses, 1981);

Virginia L. Grattan, *Mary Colter: Builder upon the Red Earth* (Flagstaff, Ariz.: Northland Press, 1980): Dolores Hayden, Gail Dubrow, and Carolyn Flynn, *The Power of Place: Los Angeles* (Los Angeles: The Power of Place, 1985), available from Graduate School of Architecture and Urban Planning, University of California; Joan Forrester Sprague, *A Manual on Transitional Housing* (Boston: Women's Institute for Housing and Economic Development, 1986).

36 The idea that women have a desire for greater connectedness to ideas, people, and nature is developed by Catherine Keller, *From a Broken Web* (Boston: Beacon Press, 1986). A more global view of feminism is emerging, as evidenced by recent comparisons between different cultures. See Susan Bassnett, *Feminist Experiences* (Winchester, Mass.: Allen and Unwin, 1986), and Kumari Jayawrdena, *Feminism and Nationalism in the Third World* (London: Zed Brooks/Kali for Women, 1986).

37 I appreciate comments from Setha Low and Jody Gibbs that inspired this conclusion.

33 Labelle Prussin

Excerpts from 'The Creative Process'

from *African Nomadic Architecture: Space, Place and Gender* (1995)

LABOR VALUE, PRODUCTIVITY, AND WOMEN'S WORK

Most, if not all, of my years of fieldwork in Africa had been spent in the company of men. Men were the guardians, the custodians of both the social structure and the acceptable livelihoods; they were the knowledgeable bearers of the history, the oral traditions, the literature. It was they who granted permission to ask questions, to photograph, to record information. The building traditions I was recording seemed to be primarily in their hands.

Subsequently, in the course of combing through the rather elusive but vast literature on African nomads, I was struck by how many early observers commented on women's building roles, in the course of their travels, in contrast to the paucity of such commentary in more recent accounts. The earliest European account of the Mauretanian nomads in the environs of Isle d'Arguin (near Nouadibou, Mauretania) already mentioned the fact that tents are women's work.[1] A century later the work done by Zenaghe women equally evoked comment.[2] Closer to us in time, Douls wrote (1888: 204): 'Immediately after morning prayers . . . the women and young girls occupied themselves with striking the tent and loading the camels. The men surveyed the operation.'

Duveyrier, the first European to give a scholarly account of the Kel Ahaggar Tuareg, was equally impressed with the extent of Tuareg women's work.[3] Even earlier, Pallme, traveling in the region of Kordofan in the Sudan, had commented on how much more industrious women were than men.[4] Further east on the continent, the Somalis evoked the same reaction (Guillain 1856, 2: 427): 'Among the Somali, all the work rests on the women: the care and education of the infants, the maintenance of the house, the preparation of food, the cutting of wood, the supply of water, up to the construction of the house are in her department.'

In general, with few exceptions, economists tend to dismiss domestic production and home industries as marginal. In the case of nomadic societies, economic studies, and by extension political studies, focus on herding economies and their management by men. Herding is a male occupation. For the most part, women's labor time is part of the reproductive cycle rather than the productive cycle of labor time. The creation of a marriage house, women's work, is culturally perceived as part of the woman's reproductive process, not as a technologically productive process. In general, those parts of the built environment created by women are often considered expendable, perishable, and less valuable. When a door is fabricated by a woodworker out of carved wooden elements, it is recognized as having value, whereas when the door is made of plaited rope by a basket-maker, it carries little architectural value. Yet almost all the labor necessary for the creation, maintenance, and transport of the architecture and its related artifacts continues, to this day, to be in the hands of women.

Neglecting the gender-based allocation of labor is a reflection (or a result) of the cultural value system that accrues to the work: it is equally a reflection of the social and political position of the gender involved in its creation. The Gabra said to me: 'Standing is work, sitting is resting.' The implication is that whatever is done while sitting is not work. So herding, of course, is work, hard work, because one stands all day, and perhaps house pitching and striking, camel loading and unloading, are also work. But when the manufacture of every furnishing or the transformation of every raw material into a finished-artifactual or architectural component is done by women while they are 'sitting down,' then the perception of women's work carries with it a negative connotation: women do not work.

DOWRIES AND ENGENDERED ARCHITECTURE

The creation of a house and its furnishings in nomadic society is part of the dowry institution: it occurs in the context of marriage. Considered by many as simply a means of insuring a woman's right to inherit a share of the patrimonial property, the institution requires considerable rethinking in light of the nomadic condition where such a major part of women's work enters into its creation. The important distinction to be considered lies in the nature of the inheritance. While animals that are inherited reproduce and herds increase, the house and its furnishings, inherited from mother to daughter, tend to dissipate and disintegrate over time. Is then the nomadic dowry, properly speaking, an inheritance? To the extent that it does give women power and control over the domicile, it is. The key issue, as Moore (1988: 52–3) has pointed out, is the relationship between women's productive and repro-ductive roles. Since the productive role, that is, the production of the domicile, is integral with the reproductive role in domestic, women's work, the architectural and artifactual creative role it involves tends to be ignored or neglected.

The first time I arrived in a nomadic camp, I was startled to discover that there were almost no men about other than the venerable elders lolling under the single shade tree in the distance. Adult men and adolescent boys were absent. Men and boys spend their days largely outside the camp; women and girls stay within it, even though the 'work' of each gender may be equally necessary to the product-ivity and to the maintenance of the social structure.

The daily tasks involved in productive labor are equally divided into masculine and feminine realms, as is the case in much of rural Africa – and the world at large. The work is carried out separately, and skills are transmitted within the tightly defined gender-discrete social interaction. The division of labor by sex and the nature of gender-discrete labor, productivity, and creativity in nomadic society are somehow far more evident and obvious than in sedentary agricultural societies. The responsibilities are more specifically defined along gender lines: who does what, who is responsible for providing what, who speaks to whom, and which gender occupies which space in the course of the day. The very division of the spaces within a tent reflect and echo, as already pointed out, this division of social labor.

But there are two parts to productive labor: the production of raw materials (i.e., their collection) and the processing of these materials. Here, too, the 'produc-tion' of materials themselves sometimes defines the gender responsibility vis-à-vis processing responsibilities. For example, metalworking is exclusively in the masculine domain, and by extension woodworking with specialized metal tools is equally men's work. But wood and its products (e.g., bark, fiber, leaves) are utilized in many other ways. As a result, the cutting down of heavy timber and the carving of wood, which are in men's hands, and the bending of wood, which relates to stems and roots and is in women's hands, are equally processing responsibilities, but they are defined by collection. One of the striking phenomena that emerged so clearly from the overview of building and transport technology is that wood which is gathered or harvested, particularly roots below ground, is in the realm of women's responsibility; it is part of the more general gathering and harvesting activities that women's parties engage in.

The process of leatherworking (i.e., sewing and tailoring) is equally a function of its production. Tanning is related to herding: women tan goat and sheepskins, while men tan camel and wild animal skins (antelope and giraffe). At the same time, tanning itself is related to the collection of acacia bark (obtained by women) from which tannin is obtained. The various kinds of tanning processes that result from this division of labor have a direct impact on the finished materials used in creating the nomadic architecture, as well as on their 'style.'

By distinguishing the process of leatherworking from its production, the historical record becomes easier to unravel. Centuries ago, Ibn Khaldun (1958, 2:366) made the distinction between spinning, weaving, and tailoring when he enumerated the 'necessary and noble crafts of civilization.' While spinning and weaving is necessary to all, tailoring (and embroidery) is a function of sedentary 'civilization.'[5] Thus embroidery on leather, which is equivalent to silk embroidery and involves 'tailoring,' is quite distinct from merely tanning it, and traditionally in the Near East embroidery was always in the hands of men. But when 'nobility,' the written word, and inheritance were functions of matrilineality, gender roles in both process and production assumed a different dimension.

The production of spun fiber and the process of weaving are another case in point which, if analyzed in detail, would surely shed historic light on the prefer-ential use, as well as the changing availability of woven in preference to leather velums among particular nomadic populations. It would give added relevance to the clear distinction made by the 'ancestor of the Arabs of the desert' when he gave one of his sons a black tent of animal hair and the other a round tent (*kubba*) of red leather (Feilberg 1944:197, citing al-Mas'udi, AD 943).

Ultimately the distinction can be applied to building and transport technologies. The substitution of bent arches for straight poles involves more than a simple structural alternative, more than the mere availability of natural resources; it involves a gender-discrete differentiation between production and process. The substitution of pliable roots gathered, bent, and shaped by women for the straight poles cut and carved by blacksmiths and woodworkers is an equally strong explanation for transitional styles among the Tuareg as the substitution of mats for leather velums. Technological style has more to do with shifts in gender-discrete responsibilities during cultural interaction than with simple 'diffusion.'

Equally related to the distinction between production and process is the collective nature of one in contrast to the other. The gathering of plants and wild grains, of roots and branches – the processing of materials – involves veritable expeditions by nomadic women. The subsequent production of artifacts, as well as the creation of house and furnishings, also involve collective labor. The labor of maintaining and transporting the entire built environment is likewise a collective process.

In the nomadic world, herding and domesticity, ritual and creativity, are separate and discrete in space. Hence labor prescriptions and practices in each of the two separate, gendered worlds should also be considered in terms of space. Access to resources, the conditions of work, and the distribution of the products of work, all of which reflect this discrete, engendered occupancy pattern, have a spatial as well as a temporal component. Consideration of the relationship of production and processing to space of the 'workplace' (i.e., the bush, the camp) suggests that the domicile is as important as the collective nature of the creative process because it represents 'control' over space. It follows logically that since so much of the woman's creativity is directed toward setting up the physical requirements for a household, and since the domicile is the scene of both her creativity and control, much of the work involved in transforming the natural environment into a built environment is in her hands.

RITUAL AND CELEBRATION

African nomadic architecture comes into being in the context of the marriage ritual: the architectural process is experienced by the society of women; men look on. The building process is a ritual process, a female ritual process that rigorously excludes male kith and kin, a ritual that patterns women's lives from birth to death. By looking at the marriage ritual, we can focus on the discovery of women's experiences as distinct from men's perception of women's experience. We can discover that world of intimacy, love, and uniquely female bonding which draws women together during every stage of their lives, from childhood through adolescence through courtship, marriage, childbirth and child rearing, death and mourning. It is during the marriage ritual that women reveal their deepest feelings to each other. Most importantly, it is this component of the nomadic marriage ceremony that grants women control.

Historians rarely consider architecture as a handmaiden of ceremony and spectacle, except in very highly charged religious or emotional situations such as the Gothic cathedral, in which the ritual related to the Stations of the Cross establishes the plan, or the Kaaba in which the seven circumambulations around it establish the ideal of the square. In ritual, movement is highly ordered and structured. For example, it is only by pacing and touching the surfaces that articulate space (e.g., the Kaaba at Mecca), by inhaling its good and bad smells, that we come to terms with it, come to know and possess it, make it ours.

The nomadic tent is equally a handmaiden of ceremony and spectacle, and movement in space is inherent in the marriage ritual: the movement of people, of its key actors, and of their entire built world. The creation of the tent is a moving spectacle. There is no better illustration in response to Turner's plea for the need to view celebratory symbols in action, in movement, in becoming, as essentially involved in process (1982: 20) than the nomad's tent.

Not only are movements *per se* tightly prescribed; locations and positions in space are prescribed for particular sequences of the ritual so that it is possible to conceive of the marriage ritual as a pilgrimage, particularly when one recalls the role of the litter-palanquin in it (Turner 1974). If, as Turner suggests, the pilgrimage is a liminal phenomenon with heightened intensity, there are thus vital spatial aspects to the liminality of the marriage-cum-pilgrimage process.

Gabra marriage ritual provides a poignant illustration of what characterizes, in one way or another, all nomadic marriages. Rather than occurring as a single, ceremonial, climactic event, the marriage is enacted in slow, progressive stages over various places and spaces. No marriage tent, initially put up, remains so. In the first stage of the marriage, the arrival of the groom's family in the bride's camp initially involved spatial displacement. The exchange of dowry components and bridewealth, which is the overture to the four-day ceremony, also involves movement between families and through the open space and camel kraals of each, as do the other obligatory exchanges in the course of the ceremony related to the creation of the marriage tent and a new kraal. But the ritual does not end with the four-day ceremony or the consummation of the marriage; it extends over a lunar month. Every seven days the marriage tent is struck and loaded onto the camels, and the bride plus her tent-cum-palanquin are led in a circle around the campsite. Returning to the kraal, the tent is pitched again within it, but not in the same location. The location itself revolves within the circle of the kraal. The liminality of the marriage ritual, expressed in the spatial displacement of the marriage tent, ends only after a lunar month, when the newly constituted family breaks camp and returns to the groom's encampment.

The gender-discrete aspect of ritual movement in space, so evident in the marriage-cum-pilgrimage process of the Gabra wedding ceremony, is present in the environments of all Gabra ritual, those involving men *and* women, as one of their transition feasts (*kolompte*) clearly reveals. The feast, which accompanies the transition of male generation-sets (*luba*), is held in the camp that holds the religious and political powers of the Gabra phratry. These villages always contain a special enclosure (*nabo*) where a fire and the sacred symbols (the drum, the horn, and the fire-sticks) are always kept, and in which the solemn ceremonies are performed (Tablino 1985).

This particular feast was celebrated in two special thornbush enclosures (*nabo*) aligned along a north–south axis. The houses and camel kraals of the two moieties that comprise this phratry were aligned parallel to the elongated enclosures, their entrances all facing west. An analysis of the complex details of the ceremony would surely yield additional insights, but what is particularly relevant to the subject of pilgrimage was the spatial, directional, and gender-discrete nature of the processionals enacted in and around these two enclosures.

The enclosure on the north was the 'virile' enclosure; young men sang at the northern openings, and women sang at the southern ones. The sacrifice (*sorio*) of male animals took place at the northern opening of the young men's enclosure, while the sacrifice of female animals was performed south of it (actually north of the elders' [who are 'becoming women'] enclosure). The processional movements (all involving men) occurred along the cardinal axes: that of the young men moving into a new generation set from south to north, that of the elders east to west. The north is masculine, and the south is feminine.

The participants in the ritual (all men) who occupy the space *within* the *nabo* are in a transitional state; they are 'becoming,' just as the bride in her marriage tent is. In spatial terms, the movement of each gender in the marriage ritual parallels their movements in this male generation-set ritual. As a consequence, if one compares the interior space of a Gabra tent, the processionals of people, tent, and wedding camels involved in the marriage ceremony, and the spatial configuration of the *kolompte* feast, movement and the occupancy of space by both genders are conjoined.

Another aspect of ritual behavior that has bearing on its architectural quality is that it persists over time in ways that other customs and behaviors do not. Which of us cannot recall the age-old retention of particular customs for ceremony, far beyond their comparable but profane day-to-day habits? This conservative dimension of ritual has particular implications for nomadic architecture created in the context of a marriage ritual. Resistance to change adds a dimension of 'permanence' to what would normally be an easily disassembled structure, more responsive to altering conditions by virtue of its processual quality. The architectural permanence achieved through ritual behavior enhances and reifies the abstract process of renewal, birth, and rebirth that a woman experiences with each move.

MNEMONICS, THE ACQUISITION OF SKILLS, AND PLAY AS CHILDREN'S WORK

The enveloping polyvalence that we in the Western world have attributed to architecture takes on as much new meaning in the nomadic context as does memory itself. Of all the faculties, Rykwert wrote (1982), 'memory has most to do with architecture: memory, whom the Greeks personified as Mnemosyne, mother of all the muses is her true patron.' Nomadic women use their bodies as a primary measure for the creation of its bounded, enclosed space. As individuals they come to know and appropriate their environment through sensory habit, but habit requires repetition, and rhythmic repetition is the handmaiden of a mnemonic that serves in lieu of blueprint and the written instruction or guideline for reconstruction. The marriage tent is a mnemonic par excellence because it is also a mnemonic enveloped in emotion and impregnated with emotional content. Dwellings without memory are dwellings without inhabitants.

Scientists have long known that play is widespread in the animal kingdom, but only lately have they appreciated just how profoundly important play must be to an animal's physical, mental, and social growth. Scientists believe that the intense sensory and physical stimulation that comes with playing is critical for proper motor development; some biologists have found that the vigorous movements of play help in the maturation of muscle tissue.

Through play, animals can rehearse many of the moves they will need as adults, and play serves to ease the transition into community. Play socializes an individual, and play is sexually segregated, as Erikson (1968) pointed out in his early study of gender-related spatial and architectural preferences in children's play.

From culture to culture, girls often rehearse elements of motherhood: among the nomads, playing with dolls is subsumed by playing house and how to move. The acquisition of skills related to domestic tasks is not limited to those we usually associate with domesticity, such as basketry, tending a fire, carrying firewood, sweeping, and raising children. Playing house for young nomadic girls involves the skills of tent building as well as tent transport.

Games of pretense are not pretense at all. When little girls build their miniature tents with branches and twigs, using leaves for mats, they are developing a heightened perception of their environment as well as acquiring and developing the construction skills that will be essential for their success as adult women.

Finally, when mnemonic is enveloped in emotion yet another facet of play and the transmission of knowledge is revealed. If the process of acquiring the skills of construction is enveloped in the anticipation of emotion, in the course of play during which voluntarily controlled movements are superseded by automatic, habitual ones, then the stage is set for the close accord of the imaginative and emotional faculties that underlie architectural creativity and achievement in the nomadic world and that turn the nomadic architectural styles into metaphors.

NOTES

1   Labat wrote (1728, 1: 262): 'it is the work of the women; they spin the hair and the wool which makes up this cloth, they work it on the loom and do all the other work of the house including the currying of horses, searching for wood and water, preparing bread and meat.' He subsequently added that 'all the women in general work very much . . . in a word, they are charged with all the work of the house' (vol. 2: 301). See Père Jean-Baptiste Labat, 1728, *Nouvelle relation d'Afrique*

Occidentale, 5 vols. Paris: Cavelier.

2   Caillié (1830, 1: 154) wrote: 'The Zenague women, laborious through necessity, spin and weave the hair of the sheep and camels, to form covering for their tents; they also sew them together; tan leather, make the *varrois* [the large leather velums of tanned sheepskins which are used during the winter season] and everything, except iron work.' See René Caillié, 1830, *Journal d'un Voyage à Tembouctou et à Senné dans L'Afrique Centrale pendant les années 1824–8*, 4 vols. Reprint 1965, Paris Editions Anthropos.

3   Duveyrier noted (1864: 187): 'The women . . . occupy themselves weaving burnous, and during the great heat of the day, at the time men are taking their siestas, one hears, in almost all the houses, the noise of moving shuttles.' See Henri Duveyrier, 1864, *Les Touareg du Nord*. Paris: Chattamel Ainé.

4   According to Pallme (1844: 63): As a general rule, the women are far more industrious than the men: for, besides attending to their domestic occupations, they employ themselves more especially with plaiting straw mats, making baskets to hold milk, and funnels for filtering *merissa*. They perform, moreover, other business, which should more properly be considered as the duty of the men. I have even seen them tanning leather, whilst their husbands were quietly looking on, smoking their pipes, and indulging in idleness. See Ignatius Pallme, 1844, *Travels in Kordofan*, London: J. Madden and Co.

5   Rio (1961) makes the same point in his discussion of the leatherworkers in the oasis of Tamentit, southern Algeria, a historic capital of the Touat region. The few men leatherworkers there, in comparison to the many found among the nomads, are almost exclusively engaged in embroidery on leather. The term by which they are known derives from the word for silk. See Capitaine Rio, 1961, 'L'Artisanat à Tamentit; Trav. IRS 20: 135–83.

REFERENCES

Camille Douls, 'Cinq mois chez les Maures nomades du Sahara occidental', *Le Tour du Monde*, 55 (1888): 177–224.

E.H. Erikson, *Identity, Youth and Crisis* (New York: W.W. Norton, 1968).

C.G. Feilburg, *La Tente noire* (Copenhagen: Glydendalske Boghandel, 1944).

M. Guillan, *Documents sur l'histoire, la géographie et le commerce de l'Afrique Orientale* (Paris: Arthur Bertrand, 1856), 3 vols + folio.

Ibn Khaldun, *Histoires des Berbères*, trans. Baron de Slane, 4 vols (Paris: Imprimerie Nationale, 1927).

Henrietta L. Moore. *Feminism and Anthropology* (Oxford: Polity Press, 1988).

Joseph Rykwert, *The Necessity of Artifice* (New York: Rizzoli, 1982).

Paolo Tablino, 'The Traditional Celebration of Marriage among the Gabbra of Northern Kenya', *Africa* (Rome, 1985), 33 (4): 568–78.

Victor Turner, *Drama, Fields and Metaphors* (Ithaca, NY, and London: Cornell University Press, 1974).

———, *Celebration* (Washington, DC: Smithsonian Institution Press, 1982).

34 Beatriz Colomina

Excerpts from 'The Split Wall: Domestic Voyeurism'

from Beatriz Colomina (ed.) *Sexuality and Space* (1992)

'To live is to leave traces,' writes Walter Benjamin, in discussing the birth of the interior. 'In the interior these are emphasized. An abundance of covers and protectors, liners and cases is devised, on which the traces of objects of everyday use are imprinted. The traces of the occupant also leave their impression on the interior. The detective story that follows these traces comes into being. . . . The criminals of the first detective novels are neither gentlemen nor apaches, but private members of the bourgeoisie.'[1]

There is an interior in the detective novel. But can there be a detective story of the interior itself, of the hidden mechanisms by which space is constructed as interior? Which may be to say, a detective story of detection itself, of the controlling look, the look of control, the controlled look. But where would the traces of the look be imprinted? What do we have to go on? What clues?

There is an unknown passage of a well-known book. Le Corbusier's *Urbanisme* (1925), which reads: 'Loos told me one day: "A cultivated man does not look out of the window; his window is a ground glass; it is there only to let the light in, not to let the gaze pass through."'[2] It points to a conspicuous yet conspicuously ignored feature of Loos' houses: not only are the windows either opaque or covered with sheer curtains, but the organization of the spaces and the disposition of the built-in furniture (the *immeuble*) seems to hinder access to them. A sofa is often placed at the foot of a window so as to position the occupants with their back to it, facing the room. This even happens with the windows that look into other interior space – as in the sitting area of the ladies' lounge of the Müller house (Prague, 1930) (Figure 34.1). Moreover, upon entering a Loos interior one's body is continually turned around to face the space one just moved through, rather than the upcoming space or the space outside. With each turn, each return look, the body is arrested. Looking at the photographs, it is easy to imagine oneself in these precise, static positions, usually indicated by the unoccupied furniture. The photographs suggest that it is intended that these spaces be comprehended by occupation, by using this furniture, by 'entering' the photograph, by inhabiting it.[3]

Figure 34.1
Adolf Loos, Müller House, Prague

In the Moller house (Vienna, 1928) there is a raised sitting area off the living room with a sofa set against the window. Although one cannot see out the window, its presence is strongly felt. The bookshelves surrounding the sofa and the light coming from behind it suggest a comfortable nook for reading. But comfort in this space is more than just sensual, for there is also a psychological dimension. A sense of security is produced by the position of the couch, the placement of its occupants, against the light. Anyone who, ascending the stairs from the entrance (itself a rather dark passage), enters the living room, would take a few moments to recognize a person sitting in the couch. Conversely, any intrusion would soon be detected by a person occupying this area, just as an actor entering the stage is immediately seen by a spectator in a theater box.

Loos refers to the idea of the theater box in noting that 'the smallness of a theater box would be unbearable if one could not look out into the large space beyond.'[4] While Kulka, and later Münz, read this comment in terms of the economy of space provided by the *Raumplan*, they overlook its psychological dimension. For Loos, the theater box exists at the intersection between claustrophobia and agoraphobia.[5] This spatial-psychological device could also be read in terms of power, regimes of control inside the house. The raised sitting area of the Moller house provides the occupant with a vantage point overlooking the interior. Comfort in this space is related to both intimacy and control.

This area is the most intimate of the sequence of living spaces, yet, paradoxically, rather than being at the heart of the house, it is placed at the periphery, pushing a volume out of the street façade, just above the front entrance. Moreover, it corresponds with the largest window on this elevation (almost a horizontal window). The occupant of this space can both detect anyone crossing-trespassing the threshold of the house (while screened by the curtain) and monitor any movement in the interior (while 'screened' by the backlighting).

In this space, the window is only a source of light (not a frame for a view). The eye is turned towards the interior. The only exterior view that would be possible from this position requires that the gaze travel the whole depth of the house, from the alcove to the living room to the music room, which opens onto the back garden. Thus, the exterior view depends upon a view of the interior.

The look folded inward upon itself can be traced in other Loos interiors. In the Müller house, for instance, the sequence of spaces, articulated around the staircase, follows an increasing sense of privacy from the drawing room, to the dining room and study, to the 'lady's room' (*Zimmer der Dame*) with its raised sitting area, which occupies the center, or 'heart,' of the house.[6] But the window of this space looks onto the living space. Here, too, the most intimate room is like a theater box, placed just over the entrance to the social spaces in this house, so that any intruder could easily be seen. Likewise, the view of the exterior, towards the city, from this 'theater box,' is contained within a view of the interior. Suspended in the middle of the house, this space assumes both the character of a 'sacred' space and of a point of control. Comfort is paradoxically produced by two seemingly opposing conditions, intimacy and control.

This is hardly the idea of comfort which is associated with the nineteenth-century interior as described by Walter Benjamin in 'Louis-Philippe, or the Interior.'[7] In Loos' interiors the sense of security is not achieved by simply turning one's back on the exterior and immersing oneself in a private universe – 'a box in the world theater,' to use Benjamin's metaphor. It is no longer the house that is a theater box: there is a theater box inside the house, overlooking the internal social spaces. The inhabitants of Loos' houses are both actors in and spectators of the family scene – involved in, yet detached from, their own space.[8] The classical distinction between inside and outside, private and public, object and subject, becomes convoluted.

The theater boxes in the Moller and Müller houses are spaces marked as 'female,' the domestic character of the furniture contrasting with that of the adjacent 'male' space, the libraries. In these, the leather sofas, the desks, the chimney, the mirrors, represent a 'public space' within the house – the office and the club invading the interior. But it is an invasion which is confined to an enclosed room – a space which belongs to the sequence of social spaces within the house, yet does not engage with them. As Münz notes, the library is a 'reservoir of quietness,' 'set apart from the household traffic.' The raised alcove of the Moller house and the *Zimmer der Dame* of the Müller house, on the other hand, not only overlook the social spaces but are exactly positioned at the end of the sequence, on the threshold of the private, the secret, the upper rooms where sexuality is hidden away. At the intersection of the visible and the invisible, women are placed as the guardians of the unspeakable.[9]

But the theater box is a device which both provides protection and draws attention to itself. Thus, when Münz describes the entrance to the social spaces of the Moller house, he writes: 'Within, entering from one side, one's gaze travels in the opposite direction till it rests in the light, pleasant alcove, raised above the living room floor. Now we are really inside the house.'[10] That is, the intruder is 'inside,' has penetrated the house, only when his/her gaze strikes this most intimate space, turning the occupant into a silhouette against the light.[11] The 'voyeur' in the 'theater box' has become the object of another's gaze; she is caught in the act of seeing, entrapped in the very moment of control.[12] In framing a view, the theater box also frames the viewer. It is impossible to abandon the space, let alone leave the house, without being seen by those over whom control is being exerted. Object and subject exchange places. Whether there is actually a person behind either gaze is irrelevant:

> I can feel myself under the gaze of someone whose eyes I do not even see, not even discern. All that is necessary is for something to signify to me that there may be others there. The window if it gets a bit dark and if I have reasons for thinking that there is someone behind it, is straightway a gaze. From the moment this gaze exists, I am already something other, in that I feel myself becoming an object for the gaze of others. But in this position, which is a reciprocal one, others also know that I am an object who knows himself to be seen.[13]

Architecture is not simply a platform that accommodates the viewing subject. It is a viewing mechanism that produces the subject. It precedes and frames its occupant.

The theatricality of Loos' interiors is constructed by many forms of representation (of which built space is not necessarily the most important). Many of the photographs, for instance, tend to give the impression that someone is just about to enter the room, that a piece of domestic drama is about to be enacted. The characters absent from the stage, from the scenery and from its props – the conspicuously placed pieces of furniture – are conjured up.[14] The only published photograph of a Loos interior which includes a human figure is a view of the entrance to the drawing room of the Rufer house (Vienna, 1922). A male figure, barely visible, is about to cross the threshold through a peculiar opening in the wall.[15] But it is precisely at this threshold, slightly off stage, that the actor/intruder is most vulnerable, for a small window in the reading room looks down onto the back of his neck. This house, traditionally considered to be the prototype of the *Raumplan*, also contains the prototype of the theater box.

In his writing on the question of the house, Loos describes a number of domestic melodramas. In *Das Andere*, for example, he writes:

> Try to describe how birth and death, the screams of pain for an aborted son, the death rattle of a dying mother, the last thoughts of a young woman who wishes to die . . . unfold and unravel in a room by Olbrich! Just an image: the young woman who has put herself to death. She is lying on the wooden floor. One of her hands still holds the smoking revolver. On the table a letter, the farewell letter. Is the room in which this is happening of good taste? Who will ask that? It is just a room.[16]

One could as well ask why it is only the women who die and cry and commit suicide. But leaving aside this question for the moment, Loos is saying that the house must not be conceived of as a work of art, that there is a difference between a house and a 'series of decorated rooms.' The house is the stage for the theater of the family, a place where people are born and live and die. Whereas a work of art, a painting, presents itself to ritual attention as an object, the house is received as an environment, as a stage.

To set the scene, Loos breaks down the condition of the house as an object by radically convoluting the relation between inside and outside. One of the devices he uses is mirrors which, as Kenneth Frampton has pointed out, appear to be openings, and openings which can be mistaken for mirrors.[17] Even more enigmatic is the placement, in the dining room of the Steiner house (Vienna, 1910) of a mirror just beneath an opaque window.[18] Here, again, the window is only a source of light. The mirror, placed at eye level, returns the gaze to the interior, to the lamp above the dining table and the objects on the sideboard, recalling Freud's studio in Berggasse 19, where a small framed mirror hanging against the window reflects the lamp on his work table. In Freudian theory the mirror represents the psyche. The reflection in the mirror is also a self-portrait projected onto the outside world. The placement of Freud's mirror on the boundary between interior and exterior undermines the status of the boundary as a fixed limit. Inside and outside cannot simply be separated. Similarly, Loos' mirrors promote the interplay between reality and illusion, between the actual and virtual, undermining the status of the boundary between inside and outside.

This ambiguity between inside and outside is intensified by the separation of sight from the other senses. Physical and visual connections between the spaces in Loos' houses are often separated. In the Rufer house, a wide opening establishes between the raised dining room and the music room a visual connection which does not correspond to the physical connection. Similarly, in the Moller house there appears to be no way of entering the dining room from the music room, which is 70 centimeters below; the only means of access is by unfolding steps which are hidden in the timber base of the dining room.[19] This strategy of physical separation and visual connection, of 'framing,' is repeated in many other Loos interiors. Openings are often screened by curtains, enhancing the stagelike effect. It should also be noted that it is usually the dining room which acts as the stage, and the music room as the space for the spectators. What is being framed is the traditional scene of everyday domestic life.

NOTES

1 Walter Benjamin, 'Paris, Capital of the Nineteenth Century,' in *Reflections*, trans. Edmund Jephcott (New York: Schocken Books, 1986), pp. 155–6.

2 'Loos m'affirmait un jour: "Un homme cultivé ne regarde pas par la fenêtre; sa fenêtre est en verre dépoli; elle n'est là que pour donner de la lumière, non pour laisser passer le regard." ' Le Corbusier, *Urbanisme* (Paris, 1925), p. 174. When this book is published in English under the title *The City of Tomorrow and its Planning*, trans. Frederick Etchells (New York, 1929), the sentence reads: 'A friend once said to me: No intelligent man ever looks out of his window: his window is made of ground

glass; its only function is to let in light, not to look out of (pp. 185–6). In this translation, Loos' name has been replaced by 'a friend.' Was Loos 'nobody' for Etchells, or is this just another example of the kind of misunderstanding that led to the mistranslation of the title of the book? Perhaps it was Le Corbusier himself who decided to erase Loos' name. Of a different order, but no less symptomatic, is the mistranslation of 'laisser passer le regard' (to let the gaze pass through) as 'to look out of,' as if to resist the idea that the gaze might take on, as it were, a life of its own, independent of the beholder. This could only happen in France!

3 The perception of space is not what space *is* but one of its representations; in this sense built space has no more authority than drawings, photographs, or descriptions.

4 Ludwig Münz and Gustav Künstler, *Der Architekt, Adolf Loos* (Vienna and Munich, 1964), pp. 130–1. English translation *Adolf Loos, Pioneer of Modern Architecture* (London, 1966), p. 148: 'We may call to mind an observation by Adolf Loos, handed down to us by Heinrich Kulka, that the smallness of a theatre box would be unbearable if one could not look out into the large space beyond: hence it was possible to save space, even in the design of small houses, by linking a high main room with a low annexe.'

5 Georges Teyssot has noted that 'The Bergsonian ideas of the room as a refuge from the world are meant to be conceived as the "juxtaposition" between claustrophobia and agoraphobia. This dialectic is already found in Rilke.' Teyssot, 'The Disease of the Domicile,' *Assemblage* 6 (1988): 95.

6 There is also a more direct and more private route to the sitting area, a staircase rising from the entrance of the drawing room.

7 'Under Louis-Philippe the private citizen enters the stages of history. . . . For the private person, living space becomes, for the first time, antithetical to the place of work. The former is constituted by the interior; the office is its complement. The private person who squares his account with reality in his office demands that the interior be maintained in his illusions. This need is all the more pressing since he has no intention of extending his commercial considerations into social ones. In shaping his private environment he represses both. From this spring the phantasmagorias of the interior. For the private individual the private environment represents the universe. In it he gathers remote places and the past. His drawing room is a box in the world theater'. Walter Benjamin, 'Paris, Capital of the Nineteenth Century,' in *Reflections*, p. 154.

8 This calls to mind Freud's paper 'A Child Is Being Beaten' (1919) where, as Victor Burgin has written, 'the subject is positioned both in the audience *and* on stage – where it is both aggressor *and* aggressed. Victor Burgin. 'Geometry and Abjection,' *AA Files*, no. 15 (Summer 1987): 38. The *mise-en-scène* of Loos' interiors appears to coincide with that of Freud's unconscious. Sigmund Freud, 'A Child Is Being Beaten: A Contribution to the Study of the Origin of Sexual Perversions,' in *The Standard Edition of the Complete Psychological Works of Sigmund Freud*, vol. 17, pp. 175–204. In relation to Freud's paper, see also: Jacqueline Rose, *Sexuality in the Field of Vision* (London, 1986), pp. 209–10.

9 In a criticism of Benjamin's account of the bourgeois interior, Laura Mulvey writes:

'Benjamin does not mention the fact that the private sphere, the domestic, is an essential adjunct to the bourgeois marriage and is thus associated with woman, not simply as female, but as wife and mother. It is the mother who guarantees the privacy of the home by maintaining its respectability, as essential a defence against incursion or curiosity as the encompassing walls of the home itself.' Laura Mulvey, 'Melodrama Inside and Outside the Home,' *Visual and Other Pleasures* (London, 1989).

10 Münz and Künstler, *Adolf Loos*, p. 149.

11 Upon reading an earlier version of this manuscript, Jane Weinstock pointed out that this silhouette against the light can be understood as a screened woman, a veiled woman, and therefore as the traditional object of desire.

12 In her response to an earlier version of this paper, Silvia Kolbowski pointed out that the woman in the raised sitting area of the Moller house could also be seen from behind, through the window to the street, and that therefore she is also vulnerable in her moment of control.

13 Jacques Lacan, *The Seminar of Jacques Lacan: Book 1, Freud's Papers on Technique 1953–1954*, ed. Jacques-Alain Miller, trans. John Forrester (New York and London: W.W. Norton and Co., 1988), p. 215. In this passage Lacan is referring to Jean-Paul Sartre's *Being and Nothingness*.

14 There is an instance of such personification of furniture in one of Loos' most auto-biographical texts, 'Interiors in the Rotunda' (1898), where he writes: 'Every piece of furniture, every thing, every object had a story to tell, a family story.' *Spoken into the Void: Collected Essays 1897–1900*, trans. Jane O. Newman and John H. Smith (Cambridge, Mass. and London: MIT Press, 1982), p. 24.

15 This photograph has only been published recently. Kulka's monograph (a work in which Loos was involved) presents exactly the same view, the same photograph, but without a human figure. The strange opening in the wall pulls the viewer toward the void, toward the missing actor (a tension which the photographer no doubt felt the need to cover). This tension constructs the subject, as it does in the built-in couch of the raised area of the Moller house, or the window of the *Zimmer der Dame* overlooking the drawing room of the Müller house.

16 Adolf Loos, *Das Andere*, no. 1 (1903): 9.

17 Kenneth Frampton, unpublished lecture, Columbia University, Fall 1986.

18 It should also be noted that this window is an exterior window, as opposed to the other window, which opens into a threshold space.

19 The reflective surface in the rear of the dining room of the Moller house (halfway between an opaque window and a mirror) and the window on the rear of the music room 'mirror' each other, not only in their locations and their proportions, but even in the way the plants are disposed in two tiers. All of this produces the illusion, in the photograph, that the threshold between these two spaces is virtual – impassable, impenetrable.

35 Zeynep Çelik

Excerpts from 'Le Corbusier, Orientalism, Colonialism'

from *Assemblage*, 17 (April 1992)

Le Corbusier's fascination with Islamic architecture and urbanism forms a continuing thread throughout his lengthy career. The first, powerful manifestation of this lifelong interest is recorded in his 1911 travel notes and sketches from the 'Orient' – an ambiguous place, loosely alluding in nineteenth- and early twentieth-century discourse to the lands of Islam in the Middle East and North Africa, and in Corbu's case, solely to Istanbul and western Asia Minor.[1]

The formative role of this *voyage d'Orient* for Le Corbusier is evident in his theoretical work and practice thereafter.[2] References to Islamic architecture and urban forms appear in his writings as early as 1915 and span his numerous publications, among them *L'Art décoratif d'aujourd'hui* (1925), *La Ville radieuse* (1933), *Quand les cathédrales étaient blanches* (1937), and *Le Modulor* (1949).[3] A number of his early villas, such as the Villa Jeanneret-Perret (1912), Villa Favre-Jacot (1912), and Villa Schwob (1916), are inspired by the Ottoman houses in terms of their interior organization around a central hall, their simple spaces, massing, and blank street façades. The Mediterranean vernacular with an Islamic touch surfaces sporadically in his built work – for example, in the Weekend House (1935), the Roq and Rob project (1949), and the Maison Jaoul (1956) – recording its most memorable moment with the Notre Dame de Ronchamp (1950–55), inspired by the sculptural mass of the Sidi Ibrahim Mosque near El Ateuf in the Algerian countryside.

In one episode of Le Corbusier's career, however, Islam no longer only serves as a source of inspiration and reference, but becomes a living challenge: his projects for Algiers, developed between 1931 and 1942, attempt to establish an ambitious dialogue with Islamic culture, albeit within a confrontational colonial framework. The most lyrical of Le Corbusier's urban design schemes, these projects have been discussed at length by architectural historians of modernism. Yet, aside from brief references, their colonial context and ideological implications for French policies in Algeria have remained uninvestigated – a surprising oversight given their *raison d'être*: the decision to renovate the city in celebration of the centennial of

French occupation and in preparation for its becoming the capital of French Africa.[4] They have been explained as a parable of European modernism, as a poetic response to the machine age, to syndicalism, and so forth, and thus abstracted from the 'political geography' of colonial Algeria.[5] Neither have the Algiers projects been analyzed as part of Le Corbusier's infatuation with Islamic culture, on one side, shaped by the legacy of nineteenth-century French discourse on the 'Orient,' and on another, informed by the Parisian avant-garde's preoccupation with the non-Western Other in the 1920s and 1930s.[6] To fill this lacuna in the extensive literature on Le Corbusier, I will attempt to read the work of perhaps the most controversial figure of modernism from a shifted perspective informed by recent postcolonial discourse.

Not surprisingly, architecture and urban forms constituted the overrriding theme in Le Corbusier's observations of other cultures. Nevertheless, they were accompanied by an inquiry into the social norms, in particular, religious and sexual one – two of the three realms historian Norman Daniel defines as having characterized Islam for centuries in European discourse.[7] It is my hope that an interconnected analysis of Le Corbusier's ideas on these issues will provide a comprehensive understanding of the architect's vision of Islam as the Other and reveal a new level of ideological complexity within the Algiers projects. [. . .]

Given Le Corbusier's loyalty to the idea of *la grande France* and to French rule in Algeria, it makes sense to analyze his projects within the framework of colonial planning traditions in the earlier part of the century. In the history of French colonial urbanism, the name of Hubert Lyautey, governor-general of Morocco from 1912 to 1925, stands out. Under the rule of Marshal Lyautey and the supervision of the architect Henri Prost, France had undertaken extensive experiments in urban planning that expanded Rabat, Fez, and Casablanca according to a well-developed social strategy. Certain ideas and passions connected Lyautey and Prost to Le Corbusier. Like Corbu, Prost had visited Istanbul as a young man while studying at the academy in Rome, which he had convinced to finance a study of Hagia Sophia – not as a monument in isolation, but in its urban context. The historical and cultural richness of the Ottoman capital as well as its formal structure had indeed appealed to Prost and underlined his proposal for a restitution project of the neighborhood around Hagia Sophia.[8]

Lyautey and Le Corbusier shared an admiration for the vernacular architecture of the Islamic Mediterranean, which reflected on their implementations and proposals in the historic fabrics of the Arab cities they were involved in, as well as on their preference for modernist aesthetics. Lyautey confirmed the latter point clearly: 'Islam gave me,' he declared in 1931, 'a taste for great white walls and I could almost claim to be one of the forerunners of Le Corbusier.'[9] Furthermore, Lyautey and Le Corbusier both believed in the central role urbanism played in changing people's lives. Lyautey's urbanism aimed to accommodate his new colonial order, based on diversity, where people of different social and cultural circumstances would coexist. His widely quoted statement, 'A construction site is worth a battalion,' meant that city planning would replace the older colonial policies based on military force.[10] The strong social engineering agenda in Le Corbusier's urbanism, especially in reference to the new man of the machine age, is well known. Yet his understanding of diversity, which also seems to imply regionalism and enables us to understand the Algiers projects better, has remained more obscure. On the title page of *La Ville radieuse*, Le Corbusier defined urban plans as 'the rational and poetic monuments set up in the midst of contingencies,' 'places, peoples, cultures, topographies, climates . . . only to be judged as they relate to the entity – "man." ' The specificity of some of these contingencies in Algiers – the place, the topography, the climate – surfaces in the unprecedented lyricism of Le Corbusier's Algiers projects. The other contingencies – different peoples and cultures – help to explain the parallels between Le Corbusier's and Lyautey's urbanism in the colonies.

The two principles that Lyautey had outlined for Prost at the outset of the latter's arrival in Morocco in 1913 were, according to legend, to preserve the medinas in respect to the local culture and aesthetics and to build new, modern cities for the European populations.[11] Both of these principles underlie the structure of Le Corbusier's plans for Algiers, leading to the separation of the French from the indigenous people, a phenomenon Janet Abu-Lughod has labeled 'urban apartheid' in reference to Moroccan cities.[12]

For Lyautey, the preservation of the Arab town held several meanings, some emotional, some practical. Above all, he savored the aesthetic qualities of the Arab town, its 'charm and poetry,' which he attributed to the sophistication of the culture.[13] To understand the *difference* between this culture and the European one was essential to building a colonial policy that would endure:

> The secret . . . is the extended hand, and not the condescending hand, but the loyal handshake between man and man – in order to understand each other . . . This [Arab] race is not inferior, it is different. Let us learn how to understand their difference just like they will understand them from their own side.[14]

This major difference between the two cultures required the separation of the indigenous from the European populations in the city:

> Large cities, boulevards, tall façades for stores and homes, installation of water and electricity are necessary, [all of] which upset the indigenous city completely, making the customary way of life impossible. You know how jealous the Muslim is of the integrity of his private life; you are familiar with the narrow streets, the façades without opening behind which hides the whole of life, the terraces upon which the life of the family spreads out and which must therefore remain sheltered from indiscreet looks.[15]

Consequently, Lyautey made the conservation of the Moroccan medinas one of his priorities in urban planning. He announced proudly. 'Yes, in Morocco, and it is to our honor, we conserve. I would go a step further, we rescue. We wish to conserve in Morocco Beauty – and it is not a negligible thing.'[16] Behind these compassionate words, nevertheless, lay an economic goal; the medinas were essential for the development of tourism, especially for the romantic travelers and artists who would be eternally thankful to Lyautey.[17]

The International Congress on Urbanism in the Colonies, held during the 1931 Colonial Exposition in Paris, recorded the powerful influence of Lyautey's ideas and practice on the new rules of planning in the French colonies. Among the goals of the congress, as listed by Prost, were 'tourism and conservation of old cities' and 'protection of landscapes and historic monuments'; the 'wish list' of the participants included a respect for the beliefs, habits, and traditions of various races and the creation of separate settlements.[18] By then, the implementation of such principles had already expanded to other colonial cities. In Algiers, for example, the casbah was placed under a special regime destined to conserve its picturesque character to promote tourism.[19]

Like Lyautey's Moroccan medinas, Le Corbusier's Algerian casbah was 'beautiful,' 'charming,' and 'adorable' and it 'never, no, never must be destroyed.'[20] Its historic significance as the 'place of European and Muslim life during centuries of picturesque struggles' was held to be of great interest for the entire world.[21] Therefore, its historical and aesthetic values, the vestiges of Arab urbanism and architecture, should be protected to enhance the 'gigantic' touristic potential of Algiers for western and central Europe.[22] The problem of the casbah was, however, an admittedly difficult one. This was mainly due to overpopulation caused by the influx of peasants escaping the miserable conditions in the countryside; the casbah sheltered four to six times more residents than it could contain, sometimes twenty persons in a single room, according to Le Corbusier's figures.[23] If Algiers was to become the capital of French Africa, the misery of its Muslim population had to be addressed, the casbah 'purified' and reorganized, its population reduced.[24]

Le Corbusier thus proposed to preserve the upper casbah in its integrity, while restricting the densities and intervening in the patterns of use, following the planning decisions made before him.[25] A number of buildings were to continue to function as residences, but others were to be converted into centers of arts and crafts in order to initiate an indigenous 'renaissance.' Indeed, an impressive number of new schools and workshops were established by the colonial authorities in the 1920s and 1930s to develop local crafts – embroidery, leatherwork, metalwork, copperwork, woodwork, carpentry, pottery, masonry, and decorative arts – with the goal of increasing their commercial value.[26] The lower casbah, on the other hand, would be expurgated of its slums; only the mansions would be preserved, converted into specialized museums for the indigenous arts. Parks and gardens would replace the areas cleared from the slums, but the existing street network would be maintained to link the high casbah to the Marine quarter and to the harbor.[27] Following the Moroccan precedent, the Muslim residents of Algiers would be strictly separated from the Europeans.

The policy of establishing separate cities was carried through to such an extent that written into the wish list of the participants in the 1931 urbanism congress was the creation of a 'green belt,' sometimes referred to as *cordon sanitaire* (a term that recalls the practice of evacuating Europeans from epidemic-ridden towns in the Algerian countryside and enforcing quarantine on local people).[28] Le Corbusier reinterpreted the idea of the green belt while wholeheartedly acknowledging its necessity. In his Obus plan of 1932, for example, a giant linear structure that connects the hillside residences for Europeans to the *cité d'affaires* in the Marine quarter forms a bridge over the casbah transforming the sanitary green belt into an air band and reversing the horizontality of the former into a vertical element. Repeating the concept in his later plans, Corbu himself emphasized the essential separation of the two settlements: 'This artery will be separated entirely from the indigenous town, by means of a level difference.'[29]

Le Corbusier's dramatic segregation of the casbah has been commonly interpreted by architectural historians as a symbolic gesture. Tafuri sees in Corbu's treatment of the casbah a 'timeless model . . . the metaphor of an ancient time,' which is 'foreign to time, foreign to the modern, indifferent to its destinies.'[30] These words from one of the most perceptive historians of our day belong, paradoxically, to the Orientalist tradition that attributes timelessness and a prehistorical existence to the Islamic city, denying it change and process and accentuating the difference between the dynamism of the European modern and the stasis of the ancient Muslim. No doubt, Le Corbusier's new Algiers would have stood in sharp contrast to the Muslim town, but his reading of the casbah was far more complex than Tafuri suggests. Emphasizing its cosmopolitan nature and its fascinating process of change, Le Corbusier praised the casbah for its houses that recorded the 'progress of styles, of periods, of history.'[31] Nevertheless, the implications of the project carry the colonial premises much farther than does Lyautey's work: Le Corbusier's plan establishes constant visual supervision over the local population and clearly marks the hierarchical social order onto the urban image, with the dominating above and the dominated below.[32]

The colonial planners envisioned the green belts as places where 'contact and collaboration' between races would not be prohibited: they were the potential sites for interaction.[33] Le Corbusier assigned this function to the starting point of his air belt, the Marine quarter, between the casbah and the streets of Bab Azoun and its eastern extension, Bab el Oued. Cleared and rebuilt with large *à redents* blocks over parks and gardens, harboring the 'business center' and 'civic center,' the quarter would provide the link between the European and the Arab cities. Certain Arab institutions, such as offices, shops, and meeting halls, would also be placed here.[34] The location was most convenient for overlapping functions, because of its proximity to the port, its centrality in terms of future growth, and its significance as a historical axis for Arabs.[35] At the time of Le Corbusier's involvement in Algiers, this crowded quarter, occupied by residents of diverse nationalities, was the most problematic area for the city administration due to a lack of 'material and moral hygiene.'[36] Provisions had already been made for its 'destruction and complete reconstruction.'[37] Le Corbusier's cleansing would be urban and social, at once providing for controlled activities for Arabs and racial contact in an ordered environment.

Le Corbusier's projects would thus endow the colonial administration in Algiers with a new apparatus for enhancing its political power by means of an urban order that facilitated supervision. In addition, a militaristic signal lies in the curving forms of the building complexes, emphasized by the architect himself in calling the plan 'Obus' in reference to the trajectory of an exploding shell. This is not a simple, light-hearted metaphor and should not be dissociated from its political context, from the violent confrontations between the French army and the local resistance forces during the one hundred years of occupation. Curiously enough, the curvilinear forms of Le Corbusier's project relate to another major aspect of French colonialism in Algeria: its obsession with Algerian women. Under colonial rule, the European fascination with Muslim women had led to controversial policies, among them penetrating the privacy of Muslim family life by 'liberating' the women. Women were, for example, strongly encouraged (and at times forced) to discard their veils – perhaps the most loaded symbol of Islam. The rationale was that if women were conquered, the core structure of this unyielding society would be destroyed, leading to its total surrender.[38]

Le Corbusier himself provoked the association between his projects and Algerian women by describing at length his enchantment with the women of the casbah and by likening the city of Algiers to a female body: 'Algiers drops out of sight,' he noted, viewing the city from a boat leaving for France in 1934, 'like a magnificent body, supple-hipped and full-breasted. . . . A body which could be revealed in all its magnificence, through the judicious influence of form and the bold use of mathematics to harmonize natural topography and human geometry.'[39] The cover sketch for *Poésie sur Alger* depicts a unicorn-headed (?), winged female body – supple-hipped and full-breasted – (the city/poem?) caressed gently by a hand (the architect's hand?) against the skyline of new Algiers. This type of analogy, which claims mastery over the feminized body of the colonized territory (in this case, claiming that its beauty can be reincarnated through the architect's intervention), is not unprecedented in the French discourse on Algeria. One author, writing at the turn of the century, called Algeria 'a wise and dangerous mistress,' but one who 'exudes a climate of caresses and torpor,' suggesting that control over her mind and body was essential.'[40] Although the feminization of the 'Orient' is a common theme in European descriptions and representations of Islam, the blatant use of the word *maîtresse* is specific to the colonies.

Le Corbusier was immersed in the discourse that attributed a lascivious sexuality to Islamic culture. This was one of the attractions that had drawn him to Istanbul in his youth. Re-enacting the scenes he had read of in books and had seen in paintings and repeating another favorite association between prison and palace, he fantasized about the life in the seraglio, which would be filled with 'divine, thrilling odalisques . . . [wearing] around their naked ankles and arms . . . solid gold rings . . . like serpents. Loaded with gold and their nails painted in vermillion, they suffocated from waiting so long in their magnificent cages.'[41] The houses on the quiet streets of Istanbul were 'perhaps . . . prisons of odalisques,' evoking in young Corbu feelings of 'a lightly painful, melancholic, beneficent poem.'[42]

The women of Istanbul, inaccessible to Le Corbusier, intrigued his sense of mystery further with their veils. He could barely make out their eyes through the pieces of cloth that enhanced their beauty: 'innocent eyes of gazelles,' he exclaimed, 'delicious.' He was more ambivalent about the long robes. At times he described the women in chadors as 'impressive bats, with the folds of their capes framing their heads and then fading away from their hips,' reminiscent of 'those friends at the towers of Notre Dame'; at others, as 'hidden treasures in burgundy, ebony silk . . . just as exquisite as Persian cats,' 'charming in their mysterious black veils, their disquieting anonymity of identical silks, their hidden treasures all alike.'[43]

The Muslim women of Algiers rekindled Corbu's memories of his youth, with all the associations. He now used the veil as a shorthand to denote the local culture. He included veiled women in his sketches to highlight the poetry and the duality of the city. But more, he also consistently represented the casbah as a veil in his diagrams, thus visually feminizing the colonized Muslim society. He was, of course, neither the first nor the last to do so; in 1933 Lucienne Favre, a French woman writer, had, for example, described the casbah as 'the vamp of North Africa,' bearing a 'capricious feminine charm' and a great 'sex appeal.'[44]

Le Corbusier's experience with the women of the casbah contrasted with the impenetrable distance he had encountered in Istanbul. Now as an older and more self-confident man, and one bearing the psychology of being French in a colony, he visited the brothels, sketched women in the nude, and claimed to have discovered here 'the nobility of the nude thanks to the plastic structure of certain females of the casbah under the intense but nuanced light of Algiers.'[45] Jean de Maisonseul, who later became the curator of the Museum of Modern Art in Algiers and who had accompanied Le Corbusier on his sight-seeing trips, witnessed to his astonishment the architect's purchase of popular postcards, 'horrible . . . in raw colors, pinks and greens, representing *indigènes nues* in an oriental decor.'[46] Such postcards, depicting women in the public realm, in prison settings that were homes, involved in 'typical' rituals and poses – all loaded with sexual innuendoes – have been studied by postcolonial critic Malek Alloula as expressions of the Frenchman's fantasies about the Algerian woman.[47] In the light of the previous discussion, Le Corbusier's appropriation of these public images bears some connection to his private life; nevertheless, he also relied on them for models, in addition to his own *in situ* sketches, in several paintings. One such painting from 1939, *Fathma*, displays two dominant themes of colonial representations of women in popular and 'high' art. Here, Fathma, the generic Algerian woman, sits on a roof terrace among the clutter of objects with an Islamic allure, revealing her double image: the veiled (the hidden, the mysterious) and the nude (the prostitute, the conquered).

Another painting by Le Corbusier, *Femmes d'Alger*, is the product of a similar process.[48] The story of *Femmes d'Alger*, which took its final form in 1938, has been told before, although little has been made of its colonialist implications. It is thus worthwhile to note again the close relationship of this work to the architect's Algiers projects and the appropriation of the Muslim woman as a metaphor. With *Femmes d'Alger*, Le Corbusier returns to the centennial celebrations of the French occupation one more time: he refers directly to Delacroix's *Femmes d'Alger* of 1833, a painting that had come to be regarded as a symbol of the conquest of Algeria.

I have tried to show here that Le Corbusier's Algiers projects were expressions of the French, 'colonial consensus,' which developed from the common French experience based on a shared perception of France's role in contemporary history, and which protected the French 'economic, moral and strategic' interests in Algeria.[49] As such, they must be situated in a broad time frame. They do not belong solely to the 1930s and to modernism's response to colonialism; they also 'speak' the idiom of other periods – nineteenth-century Orientalism as well as the colonial discourse of the first decades of the twentieth century. Furthermore, these projects epitomize a culmination of the long history of French interventions 'to represent, to inhabit, and to possess' a territory.[50] Had Le Corbusier's scheme been realized, it would have marked an appropriation of Algiers such as no colonial planner had elsewhere ever achieved. The comprehensive scale of the proposal and its aggressive seizure of the city's geography from the coastline to the mountains would have transformed the urban image radically – the now miniaturized casbah a symbol of the controlled existence of the colonized people and their 'different' culture, a constant reminder of the power of colonialism.

NOTES

I am grateful to the director and the staff of Fondation Le Corbusier for their assistance and to the National Endowment for the Humanities for a travel grant to Paris. Earlier versions of this paper were presented at the Fine Arts Department, Harvard University (March 1989), Society of Architectural Historians Annual Meeting in Montreal (April 1959) and the School of Architecture, Cornell University (April 1990). I would like to thank Howard Burns, Oleg Grabar, Michael Hays, Alicia Kennedy, Neil Levine, Mary McLeod, Gülru Necipoğlu-Kafadar, and Perry Winston for their comments and suggestions at various stages. The idea for the topic originated during a conversation with the late Spiro Kostof. I remember him with deep gratitude and affection.

1 See Le Corbusier, *Journey to the East*, trans. Ivan Zaknic with Nicole Pertuiset (Cambridge, Mass.: MIT Press, 1987). For an annotated edition in Italian, see Giuliano Gresleri, *Le Corbusier: Viaggio in Oriente* (Venice: Marsilio; Paris: Fondation Le Corbusier, 1984). The original notebooks have been printed in facsimile as *Le Voyage d'Orient* (Paris: Fondation Le Corbusier, 1988).

2 For a discussion of the impact of the Turkish house on Le Corbusier's work, see Pierre Pinon, 'La Maison turque,' in *Le Corbusier: Le Passé à réaction poétique*, exhibition catalogue (Paris: Hôtel de Sully, 1988), 165–73.

3 In his notes from 1915 for a book on city building, Le Corbusier cited the urban form of Istanbul to explain his concept of 'unity.' See *Le Corbusier Sketchbooks*, vol. 1, *1914–1948* (Cambridge, Mass.: MIT Press; New York: Architectural History Foundation, 1981), 6–7.

4 William Curtis, for example, mentions the 'blatant colonialism' of the project, but does not articulate it. See William Curtis, *Modern Architecture since 1900* (Englewood Cliffs, NJ: Prentice-Hall, 1990), 209. Mary McLeod provides a background to the 'assimilation' debate without situating Le Corbusier's projects within

the context of colonial urbanism. See Mary McLeod, 'Le Corbusier and Algiers,' Oppositions 16–17 (1980): 55–85. It is particularly striking that neo-Marxist historian Manfredo Tafuri does not once refer to colonialism in his analysis of the projects, which he calls 'still unsurpassed from the point of view of both ideology and form.' See Manfredo Tafuri, *Architecture and Utopia: Design and Captialist Development*, trans. Barbara Luigia La Penta (Cambridge, Mass.: MIT Press, 1976), 125–6.

5 I owe this interpretation to Said's critique of Albert Camus's critics. See Edward Said, 'Narrative, Geography, and Interpretation,' *New Left Review* 180 (1990): 88.

6 Giuliano Gresleri and Sibel Bozdoğan have written about Le Corbusier's dialogue with the East. Gresleri focuses on the impact of Corbu's journey on his professional growth. See Giuliano Gresleri, 'Home-Ties – Adrift Abroad: The Oriental Journey of CH. Jeanneret,' *Daidalos* 15 (March 1986): 102–11, and idem, 'Les Leçons du voyage d'Orient,' in *Le Corbusier et la Méditerranée* (Marseilles: Editions Parenthèses, Musée de Marseille, 1987), 37–49. Bozdoğan studies Corbu's sketches against the background of Orientalism: abstracting Le Corbusier from his cultural inheritance, she frees him from the legacy of Orientalism. See Sibel Bozdoğan. 'Journey to the East,' *Journal of Architectural Education* 41, no. 4 (1988): 38–45. Her position has been challenged by Richard Ingersoll, *Journal of Architectural Education* 42, no. 4 (1989): 61.

7 Daniel's third realm is power. See Norman Daniel, *Islam, Europe, and Empire* (Edinburgh, 1966), xvi.

8 While in Istanbul, Le Corbusier, too, had carefully studied Hagia Sophia. Yet he did not share Prost's enthusiasm for the Byzantine history of the city, which he considered 'imperially corrupt' and which he believed 'could not be brought to life' because 'its spirit [had] departed from the very few stones that remain[ed]' (Le Corbusier, *Journey to the East,* 89). Henri Prost returned to Istanbul in 1934, when the Turkish government commissioned him with the master plan for the city. He worked there from 1937 to 1951 and his plan was largely implemented. On Prost, see *L'Oeuvre d'Henri Prost: Architecte et urbaniste* (Paris: Académie d'architecture, 1960), and Jean Rover, 'Henri Prost: L'Urbanisation,' *Urbanisme* 88 (1965): 3–31. During approximately the same years, from 1939 to 1949, Le Corbusier was involved on and off in a rocky process of developing a master plan for the city of Izmir, which he completed in 1949, but which remained unimplemented. Originally, in 1928, Prost had designed a plan for Izmir, but Corbu was able to persuade the authorities to substitute Prost's plan with his own. See the correspondence between Le Corbusier and the French Ambassador to Ankara, 14 February 1939, 23 February 1939, 9 March 1939, and 30 January 1940, FLC. By this time, Le Corbusier was a strong critic of Prost's urbanism. Previously, he had fluctuated in his evaluation of Prost's work. As seen in his statement, quoted above, from *Quand les cathédrales étaient blanches*, he praised Prost (if indirectly) on the success of colonial urbanism in Morocco: however, in 1931, during his visit to Fez, he noted that 'Prost's city planning is nothing but confusion' ('Sketchbook: Espagne Route 31b//B7,' in *Le Corbusier Sketchbooks* 1:440).

9   Quoted in Jean-Claude Vigato, 'The Architecture of the Colonial Exhibitions in France.' *Daidalos* 15 (March 1986): 28–9.

10 On Lyautey in Morocco, see Paul Rabinow, *French Modern: Norms and Forms of the Social Environment* (Cambridge, Mass.: MIT Press, 1989), 177–319; Janet Abu-Lughod, *Rabat: Urban Apartheid in Morocco* (Princeton: Princeton University Press, 1980), 131–73, and Gwendolyn Wright, *The Politics of Urban Design in French Colonial Urbanism* (Chicago: University of Chicago Press, 1991), 85–160.

11 Rabinow, *French Modern*, 288.

12 See Abu-Lughod, *Rabat.*

13 Quoted in ibid., 141.

14 Quoted in Daniel, *Islam, Europe, and Empire*, 489.

15 Quoted in Abu-Lughod, *Rabat*, 143.

16 Ibid., 142.

17 Henri Prost. 'Le Développement de l'urbanisme dans le protectorat du Maroc, de 1914 à 1923,' in Jean Royer, ed., *L'Urbanisme aux colonies et dans les pays tropicaux*, vol. 1 (La Charité-sur-Loire: Delayance, 1932), 60, 68.

18 Henri Prost, 'Rapport général,' in ibid., 21–2.

19 M. Pasquier-Bronde, 'Alger, 'in ibid., 39, and Charles Montaland, 'L'Urbanisme en Algérie,' in ibid., 51–2.

20 Le Corbusier, *La Ville Radieuse,* 229.

21 Le Corbusier, letter to the Prefect of Algiers, 18 May 1942, FLC.

22 Le Corbusier, Questionnaire C, 1931–35, FLC; idem, note for M. Sabatier, 6 May 1941, FLC; and idem, *La Ville radieuse*, 244.

23 Le Corbusier, 'Le Folklore est l'expression fleurie des traditions,' 30.

24 Le Corbusier, note for M. Sabatier, and idem, 'Proposition d'un Plan Directeur.'

25 The conservation of the upper casbah and the transformation of the lower casbah into a 'museum quarter 'were matters decided by then. See René Lespês, 'Les Villes,' in *Les Arts et la technique moderne en Algérie 1937* (Algiers, 1937), 25–6.

26 See Montaland. 'L'Urbanisme en Algérie', 51, and *Pour le paysan et l'artisan indigènes* (Algiers: Gouvernement Général de l'Algérie, Direction Général des Affaires Indigènes et des Territoires du Sud. Service de l'Economic Sociale Indigène, 1939), 140–1. To hasten the pace and increase production and to provide more 'precision' to the work, these schools and workshops promoted the use of modern machinery.

27 Le Corbusier, 'Proposition d'un Plan Directeur.'

28 Prost, 'Rapport général,' 22. Also see Abu-Lughod, *Rabat*, 145.

29 Le Corbusier, 'Propositon d'un Plan Directeur.'

30 Manfredo Tafuri, 'Machine et mémoire: The City in the Work of Le Corbusier,' trans. Stephen Sartarelli, in *The Le Corbusier Archive*, ed. H. Allen Brooks, 32 vols (New York: Garland, 1982–84), vol. 10, xxxviii–xxxix.

31 Le Corbusier, 'Le folklore est l'expression fleurie des traditions,' 32.

32 In the light of this discussion I must refer once again to Tafuri's analysis that sees in Le Corbusier's megastructures into which residents could insert their choice of buildings 'the greatest liberty' allowed to the public (Tafuri, *Architecture and Utopia*, 131). While this observation is valid as far as the European public in Algiers is con-

cerned, it is disturbing that Tafuri dismisses the city's Muslim population as a nonentity.

33 Prost, 'Rapport général,' 22.

34 Le Corbusier, 'Note financière annexe au Projet C de l'urbanisation du Quartier de la Marine à Alger,' 1934, FLC.

35 Le Corbusier, Questionnaire B, 1931–35, FLC.

36 Joseph Sintes, 'Le Quartier de la Marine et la Casbah,' *Les Travaux nord-africains*, 31 December 1932.

37 Lespès, 'Les Villes,' 10–11.

38 One of the most memorable, if sentimental, essays on the topic was written by Frantz Fanon, who traced the origins of this policy to the early 1930s. See Frantz Fanon, 'Algeria Unveiled,' in *A Dying Colonialism*, trans. Haakon Chevalier (New York: Grove Press, 1965), 35–67 (first published in 1959 as *L'An cinq de la révolution algérienne*).

39 Le Corbusier, *La Ville radieuse*, 260.

40 J. Lorrain, *Heures d'Afrique* (1899), quoted in Yvonne Knibiehler and Régine Goutalier, *La Femme au temps des colonies* (Paris: Editions Stock, 1985), 40.

41 Le Corbusier, *Journey to the East*, 83.

42 Ibid., 94.

43 Ibid., 125, 128–30.

44 Fayre, *Tout l'inconnu de la casbah d'Alger*, 10 ('sex appeal' is in English in the original).

45 Quoted in Samir Rafi, 'Le Corbusier et "Les Femmes d'Alger,"' *Revenue d'histoire et de civilisation du Maghreb* (January 1968): 52. Prostitution was rampant in the casbah, a phenomenon attributed to French encouragement. See David Gordon, *Women of Algeria: An Essay on Change* (Cambridge, Mass.: Harvard University Press, 1968), 42. According to Favre, in the early 1930s there were five to six hundred 'girls . . . permanently active' in the casbah, especially in the lower casbah (Favre, *Tout l'inconnu de la casbah d'Alger*, 103). The presence of the brothels was so overwhelming that, not to be confused with them, many families residing in the quarter posted signs declaring 'honest home' [*maison honnête*]; others dressed their daughters *à la française* so that they would not be bothered on the streets of the casbah. See Sintes, 'Le Quartier de la Marine et la Casbah.'

46 De Maisonseul, letter to Rafem, 5 January 1968. This document was first discussed by Rafi himself in 'Le Corbusier et "Les Femmes d'Alger,"' 51–2, and then by Stanislaus von Moos, 'Le Corbusier as Painter,' trans. Jane O. Newman and John H. Smith, *Oppositions* 19–20 (Winter–Spring 1980): 89–91. The postcard collection is at the Fondation Le Corbusier.

47 See Malek Aloulla, *The Colonial Harem*, trans. Myrna Godzich and Wlad Godzich (Minneapolis: University of Minnesota Press, 1986).

48 Von Moos, 'Le Corbusier as Painter,' 92–3.

49 Tony Smith develops the notion of 'colonial consensus' in *The French Stake in Algeria 1945–1962* (Ithaca: Cornell University Press, 1978), 28–9.

50 I have borrowed these terms from Said's analysis of the appropriation of the geography of Algeria in Albert Camus's fiction. See Said, 'Narrative, Geography, and Interpretation,' 88–90.

36 Alice T. Friedman

Excerpts from 'Architecture, Authority and the Female Gaze: Planning and
Representation in the Early Modern Country House'

from *Assemblage*, 18 (August 1992)

In the history of English architecture, the period from 1590 to 1620 is characterized
by the gradual ascendance of Palladian planning over the conventions of medieval
English tradition. This shift in approach, which occurred in the plan of the English
country house more than two decades before it appeared in elevation, focused on
the handling of the great hall and its subsidiary spaces. In a number of prominent
new houses of the period, the traditional access of this double-height space along
a narrow screens passage and through a tripartite screen at one end – an arrangement still found, for example, at Longleat in the 1560s – gave way to an entrance
door on axis that opened directly into the great hall. While such historians as Sir
John Summerson and Mark Girouard have paid a great deal of attention to these
changes as stylistic and even socioeconomic developments, no significant analysis
has yet been proposed of the roles either of the patrons or of their programs
(broadly defined to include both conscious and unconscious goals) in the making of
these pivotal buildings.[1] This lack of attention is especially surprising given that
Hardwick Hall (1590–97), the earliest of them, was built for a woman whose status
as the head of her own household marked both her and it as unconventional and
whose very role as an architectural patron transgressed the values and gender
categories of her time. In this paper, I propose to reexamine these stylistic shifts
through the lens of convention and unconventionality in planning techniques,
gender relations, and household structure. Using household orders (written
descriptions of the tasks of all household members including family and servants),
letters, diaries, and handbooks of advice, I will trace the ideological context in
which domestic planning ordinarily took place and reconstruct the attitudes toward
the family, sexuality, and the female body – with particular attention to sight,
spectatorship, and display – that structured these conventions. This approach
suggests that gender played a subtle yet pronounced role in monumental domestic
architecture that surpassed the interests and tastes of the individual architect or
builder. Because design typology depends on conventional social relations, it is
evident from the cases presented here that the destabilizing of conventional patterns

that resulted from the presence of a female patron opened the way for the unexpected, including experiments in design that might not have been proposed in a more typical and thus more highly predetermined cultural and visual environment.[2]

Discussions of female spectatorship among feminist film critics over the last fifteen years have relentlessly pursued the elusive problem of gender and visual representation through various intriguing, but ultimately unsatisfactory, models in linguistic, psychoanalytic, and narrational convention. Early enthusiasm for a feminist critical method derived from Lacan and centred around his description of the role of the gaze in structuring both representation and identity – as outlined most notably in Laura Mulvey's 'Visual Pleasure and Narrative Cinema' of 1975 – inevitably reached an impasse due to the theory's inability to account satisfactorily for female spectatorship. Mulvey's reply to those critics who raised the problem of the female spectator fell back on an interpretive model drawn from post-structuralist literary criticism, the notion of oscillating identifications between the various roles offered by conventional narrative structure, thus diluting her original contention. Similarly, E. Ann Kaplan's 'Is the Gaze Male?' seemed to ask the right question but equivocated on the issue of female subjectivity; she tentatively proposed a model of maternal power drawn from work on object relations to theorize a parallel (yet, in the end, secondary and almost apologetic) role for the female spectator.[3] By adhering closely to psychoanalytic paradigms, these critical interventions failed to comprehend female agency, identity, and pleasure. Still more frustrating, particularly for the cultural historian, has been the apparent inadequacy of psychoanalytic and linguistic theory to account for the power of institutional and cultural systems in the past, despite the example (albeit not a feminist one) offered by Foucault.[4]

Nevertheless, some recent critical writing in feminist film theory does suggest certain points of departure for cultural, in particular architectural, analysis. Kaja Silverman's 'Fassbinder and Lacan: A Reconsideration of Gaze, Look and Image' takes the Lacanian model in a different direction.[5] Silverman shifts attention from the identity of the spectator to the constitution of the image, focusing on the processes through which identities are constructed and represented within visual culture. Her analysis, based on a close reading of Lacan's *Four Fundamental Concepts of Psychoanalysis*, rests on a key distinction between *look*, 'seeing' from the myriad viewpoints of individual subjects, and *gaze*, a more sustained, all-encompassing, and thus more menacing operation of vision that implies disembodied and transcendent authority, surveillance, and, ultimately, the creation of categories that distinguish between conformity and transgression.[6] Through Lacan, Silverman points to the role of convention in the formation of images and to the highly contested operations of vision and visuality that confer authority (and powerlessness). Her analysis calls attention to the role of the object in forming both its own image and that of the spectator. Moreover, by stressing the notion that seeing and being seen are reciprocal positions in the same operation, she returns us to the dual nature of representation: at once inscribing the image of the thing represented and revealing its own culturally constituted structure.[7]

Such a strategy has a number of potential applications for feminist architectural theory. The persistence of a naturalized social history of architecture, which
proposes that typical forms are an inevitable, logical response to natural conditions
and preexisting structures, has obscured the role that architecture – as representation and as convention – plays in the cultural system. Within a naturalized
architectural history and criticism, moreover, the representation (or, more
accurately, the marginalization) of women in the established order has come to
appear inevitable. Images of women as essentially recessive, nurturing, and domestic or as complicit, masquerading objects of narcissism and desire persist unchallenged. Here feminist film theory's emphasis on vision has a significant bearing on
architectural experience. Not only can architecture control, and limit, physical
movement (and inevitably, of course, control the faculty of sight as part of this
physical experience), it can also create an arena and a frame for those who inhabit
its spaces. Through screening, sight lines, contrasts of scale, lighting, and other
devices, architecture literally stages the value system of a culture, foregrounding
certain activities and persons and obscuring others. These attributes of built form
were briefly suggested by Griselda Pollock in 'Modernity and the Spaces of
Femininity,' a first step toward examining the role of the nineteenth-century city in
representing and controlling the status of women as spectators and as objects of
sight in the public arena.[8] My attempt here is to establish the outlines of an interpretive method in the area of domestic architecture, one that would account for
the persistence of convention in visual culture while also pointing to the destabilizing effects of cultural change, particularly in gender relations. Furthermore, by
emphasizing the constructed nature of spectatorship and spectacle in early modern
England, I hope to make a more general point about architecture as representation,
that is, as a medium in which function and imagery are viewed not as separate but
as overlaid aspects of a system through which meaning is constituted. [. . .]

Hardwick Hall must be read in this context.[9] Bess had begun restoring and
enlarging her ancestral manor house at Hardwick in the late 1580s (during a time
when she was officially separated from the earl); however, in 1590, after
Shrewsbury's death, she turned her attention to another project, commissioning an
enormous new house from the fashionable architect Robert Smythson, builder of
Longleat and Wollaton. Hardwick Hall represents a watershed in English architecture, not only because its patron was a woman, but because it radically altered
the typology of the English country house through its most distinctive feature, the
form and placement of the great hall. By situating the great hall at the center of a
symmetrical plan and providing a means of direct visual and physical access to it,
Smythson and his client openly defied tradition, constituting both a new form and
a new meaning for the country house.

Castles and fortified manor houses, distinguished by their imposing size and
defensibility, had existed in England since the Norman Conquest, and the roots of
their characteristic formal elements – the great hall and the tower – can be traced
to Roman precedents.[10] The form of the great hall had evolved over centuries to

serve the functional, ceremonial, and symbolic needs of the medieval household. The porch, passage, and screen limited access by establishing a series of barriers and checkpoints for visitors entering the household. Security was maintained less by surveillance over the house as a whole than by the disorienting effects of a mazelike path from one room or area of the estate to another. Visitors and residents alike moved through an environment in which they could never step back to survey the overall arrangement of space except in specific places devoted to spectacle: the courtyard, the great hall, and, later, the gallery and great chamber. In the hall, the ample light from the large windows, the raised dais, the unbroken sight lines, and the high vaulted ceiling created the ideal stage for the performance of rituals of service and hospitality, leaving the onlookers with a forceful impression of power and authority.

Although the need for active military defense of land and property subsided during the Tudor regime, the dominant military model and the disproportionate number of male servants in the great households continued well into the seventeenth century.[11] Yet with the gradual disappearance of the old feudal order, the large aristocratic household became obsolete and the focus of its activities had to be broadened to include a new range of social and economic pursuits. This necessitated changes in both the outward appearance of the great houses and in the size and variety of interior living spaces. Still more erosive of tradition, a new order of clients was commissioning large houses and for different reasons than had motivated the nobility or members of the court: the upper gentry and London-based professionals began to build country houses as places for leisure and as a form of display.[12] Yet despite their smaller households and their emphasis on entertainment and family privacy, these builders often replicated older ceremonial and symbolic forms such as the great hall and tower. The persistence of these emblems of authority is also noticeable in renovated family seats, such as Haddon Hall and Penshurst Castle, where great halls, turrets, and armories were preserved and valued well into the seventeenth century.

Tending an apparently antithetical direction, contemporary interest in Italian Renaissance architecture, especially northern Italian and specifically Palladian examples, ran high among architects, craftsmen, and educated patrons in court circles. Numerous sketches for country houses with distinctly un-English plans, derived from the works of Palladio and Serlio, appear in the portfolios of Smythson and other architects during this period.[13] Architectural treatises and handbooks on the topic fill the libraries of patrons and amateurs.[14] Yet while many builders had, since mid-century, incorporated isolated ornamental elements of Italianate classicism into their houses, none had gone so far as to replace the highly specialized form of the hall with the ordered symmetries and open spaces of the axial or central plan.[15] Loss of the aura of tradition associated with these conventional forms – an indispensable ingredient in the representation of power in this period – was apparently too great a risk. Wollaton Hall (1580–88), built by Smythson for Sir Francis Willoughby, is an important transitional example of this phenomenon. The house combines many aspects of the traditional ground-floor plan, including the

Figure 36.1
Hardwick Hall

screens passage, screen, and great hall, with a new compactness and axial planning in an upper-floor plan derived from Palladian models. Wollaton's exterior also integrates the two traditions, creating a characteristically late-Elizabethan mixture of superimposed medieval and classicizing images.

Turning from Wollaton back to Hardwick Hall – both the work of the same architect – we must ask whether it can be simple coincidence that the first break with traditional planning in England occurs in a country house built for a woman. To understand the design of Hardwick fully, we have to remember that in the spatial hierarchy of the country house only the master had access to all spaces; here the master was the mistress. Bess, as head of the household, oversaw the activities of her servants within her home and throughout her vast estates. She had learned the lessons of gender and power firsthand. In her earlier married life she had lived quite conventionally and, like others of her class, often felt the strain of conflicting expectations about money and power in her husbands' households. Caught more than once in a web of household intrigue – one former servant described her home as a 'hell' in which 'her ladyship had not one about her which faithfully love and honour in deed' – Bess resolved to keep a firm grip on the reins of power in her own home at Hardwick.[16] Like the queen (whose methods she knew well as a frequent petitioner at court and former lady-in-waiting), she understood that she could not rely solely on the traditional system of allegiances or on the inherited rituals of dominance to maintain control. Instead, she capitalized on her ability to see and be seen, flaunting her power and undermining the challenges of others. Moreover, Bess invented her own new imagery, employing a strategy similar to that of the queen, making subtle but fundamental shifts in design and household organization that altered the meaning of traditional forms.

At Hardwick, the hall – whose patriarchal significance Bess surely viewed in a different light than did her male counterparts – became an open room entered directly from the front door, with a waist-high screen and a vestigial, strictly

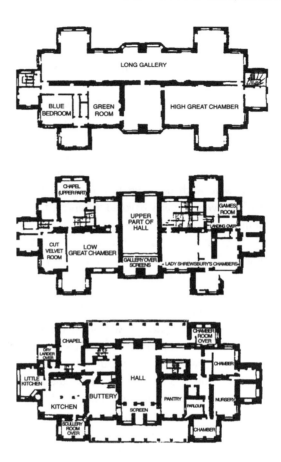

Figure 36.2
Hardwick Hall, plans of the
principal floors

symbolic, screens passage. Only the lower servants ate their meals here; the upper servants, whose number included more women than in other households, retired to dining rooms on the second floor, one for men and one for women, adjacent to Bess's own.[17] Thus, while the hall and its occupants remained at the center of the house, status shifted to the spaces above. The actual change in architectural effect, though visually striking, was functionally minor – indeed, in daily use its effects could be virtually ignored – but it nonetheless represented a radical break with the demands of both planning convention and representation.

This is a crucial point. I am not arguing here that Bess of Hardwick consciously saw her status as a female patron as an opportunity to alter the form of the hall nor that her household's use of the hall differed significantly from that of her contemporaries. No evidence exists for either assertion. On the contrary, Bess was much too cautious about her own status to cast off ritual and much too protective of the future of her children and descendants (notably, her son William Cavendish and her granddaughter Arabella Stuart) to propose a radical departure from convention. Bess built Hardwick with these descendants in mind and she no doubt anticipated its use by a more conventional household than her own. Nevertheless, it was Bess who was the client and Bess whose image (albeit an image strongly tied to both the past and the future) it represented. As such, the image of patriarchal and military power adhering to the hall could only have provided a very general outline into which Bess and her architect slipped the far more flexible and less gendered image of the powerful, perhaps androgynous courtly patron represented by the axial Palladian plan. In so doing, she undermined the conventional reading of the hall, suppressing gendered imagery while taking care to preserve all the traditional elements, both functional and symbolic, intact.[18]

Among Elizabethan and Jacobean country houses, Hardwick is distinguished by the rationality of its design.[19] As is clear even to the casual visitor, the three stories of the house were each designed to accommodate a different sort of activity: the ground floor was primarily devoted to service, the middle floor to the everyday needs of the mistress and her upper servants, and the top floor to formal entertainment, estate business, and state occasions. Unlike Wollaton, Hardwick has no basement; instead, the kitchen, buttery, and scullery occupy the north side of the ground floor adjacent to the hall. The so-called Low Great Chamber, dining chamber for the household, was reached by way of a back staircase on this side; the main stairs led from the nursery and small bed chambers on the south side of the ground floor to Bess's own chamber and withdrawing chamber above, whence it led to the High Great Chamber, the largest and most formal chamber of state, on the top floor. Here the Palladian plan structures the functional organization, imposing a discipline that forced Smythson to observe the axis and thus to make the house more compact and higher than his previous buildings.

Like others with ties to the court, Bess had a taste for Renaissance classicism and she knew which designers and craftsmen to hire for her jobs. Though hardly an intellectual, her long-standing interest in architecture had matured over decades. At Chatsworth, her nearby country house built some forty years earlier, she had used the best London-based craftsmen; at Hardwick she assembled a team of skilled artists and gave them an enormous budget and an imposing site to work on. She allowed her architect to try out new ideas while retaining the elements essential to the building's practical and symbolic operation. Bess welcomed the fusion of tradition and innovation that made her new house a fashionable showplace. At Hardwick, accordingly, ceremonial spaces are stacked up and elaborated in an unprecedented manner: the hall, the staircase, the great chambers, the gallery, and the roof terraces all present long vistas that far exceed the grandeur and spaciousness previously achieved by Smythson at Longleat or Wollaton. Moving through these spaces or sitting in her chair of state, Bess of Hardwick became part of the spectacle: each space was designed to present an image through which she assumed the central role in an orchestrated representation of power, a totalizing image composed of intricately patterned and highly colored architecture, painting, furnishings, and textiles. In this way, physical presence and architectural presence are uniquely elided at Hardwick, an elision that capitalizes on the notions of woman as spectacle and of widow as matriarch. It is, of course, through operations of vision that this chain of representational processes is put into motion.

Like other Elizabethan builders, Bess was careful to celebrate the sovereign under whose reign she prospered: the chimney-piece in the hall displays the Hardwick coat of arms, but the queen's arms dominate the High Great Chamber.[20] Yet clearly, the subject rather than the sovereign is the focus of attention in this house. Bess's own initials, ES, decorate the high parapets, in unambiguous terms marking the house as its builder's property and personal creation. Thus Hardwick is more than a stage; it is also an emblem that piles up and displays its imagery in a complex and rather disordered series of overlapping texts. Large rectangular windows, each signifying enormous expense, light up the opulent fabrics and furnishings in the expansive rooms; these windows foreground the gaze, calling attention to both display and surveillance. Similarly, the high towers provide not only a vantage point from which Bess could survey her property, but also a symbolic image of dominance. Instead of playing the shamefast wife, Bess created a new female role at Hardwick, becoming the master of her house and borrowing some of the attributes of the good housewife to augment her power. From her high towers she oversaw the running of her estate, in her great chamber and gallery she received visitors of every rank. The country house took on a new and unique meaning at Hardwick because the gaze of authority it embodied was female.[. . .]

NOTES

Earlier versions of this paper were presented at a conference on Women in Early Modern England at the University of Maryland (October 1990), at Northwestern University (November 1990), and at the Renaissance Studies Colloquium at Brown University (March 1991). I am grateful to Margaret Carroll, Ann Rosalind Jones, Katherine Park, Eve Blau, Shelley Tenenbaum, Jehan Kuhn, and John Rhodes for reading and commenting on various drafts of this essay. A Faculty Research Award from Wellesley College and a fellowship from the Bunting Institute, Radcliffe College, afforded me the opportunity to travel in England and to take part in a reading group on Gender and Representation at the Bunting in 1990–91.

1 See Mark Girouard, *Life in the English Country House: A Social and Architectural History* (New Haven: Yale University Press, 1978), and idem, *Richard Smythson and the Architecture of the Elizabethan Country House* (New Haven: Yale University Press, 1983); Sir John Summerson, *Architecture in Britain 1530–1830* (Harmondsworth: Penguin, 1969), and idem, ed., *The Book of Architecture of John Thorpe*, vol. 40 of *Walpole Society* (Glasgow: Walpole Society, 1966). My own *House and Household in Elizabethan England: Wollaton Hall and the Willoughby Family* (Chicago: University of Chicago Press, 1989), while primarily concerned with Wollaton, raises some of the questions with which this paper is concerned.

2 This paradigmatic approach forms the basis for my book-in-progress on houses built for women heads of households. These range from Ledoux's *hôtels* for Mlle Guimard and Mme Thélusson in the late eighteenth century to Frank Lloyd Wright's Barnsdall House (1916–21) and Mies van der Rohe's Farnsworth House (1946–51). Like Hardwick, these cases break with conventional typology and, in some

instances, represent stylistic turning points. They differ significantly from cases in which women acted as their husbands' surrogates or were otherwise seen as representatives of conventional social culture. These latter are treated by Trevor Lummis and Jan Marsh in *The Woman's Domain: Women and the English Country House* (New York and London: Viking, 1990).

3 For Mulvey, see Constance Penley, ed., *Feminism and Film Theory* (New York: Routledge, 1988), where the two essays are reprinted together with other key works of feminist film criticism. Penley's introductory essay, 'The Lady Doesn't Vanish: Feminism and Film Theory,' both points out the problems that this critical venture has encountered and suggests some ways of moving forward. For Kaplan, see her *Women and Film: Both Sides of the Camera* (New York: Methuen, 1983).

4 The essays of Mary Ann Doane in *The Desire to Desire: The Woman's Film of the 1940s* (Bloomington: Indiana University Press, 1987) and in *Femmes Fatales: Feminism, Film Theory and Psychoanalysis* (New York: Routledge, 1991) are the most insightful psychoanalytic studies of female spectatorship available. Doane's work, however, betrays an uneasy oscillation between historical interpretation and psychoanalytic structure, especially in her notion of the female spectator as consumer, which leaves significant questions unresolved. See also *Camera Obscura* 20–21 (May–September 1989), a double issue on 'The Spectatrix' that offers various responses to these questions.

5 See Kaja Silverman, 'Fassbinder and Lacan: A Reconsideration of Gaze, Look and Image,' *Camera Obscura* 19 (July 1991): 54–85.

6 This distinction was made earlier by Norman Bryson in *Vision and Painting: The Logic of the Gaze* (New Haven: Yale University Press, 1983), esp. chap. 5. Bryson's notion of 'the glance' as 'a furtive or sideways look whose attention is always elsewhere' (p. 94) is obviously related to Silverman's 'look,' though Silverman emphasizes the disempowering distinction between the individual and the broader culture (or the State), while Bryson only briefly alludes to this aspect of the system of signification.

7 Jill Dolan proposes a related strategy in *The Feminist Spectator as Critic* (Ann Arbor: UMI Research Press, 1988). Following Theresa De Lauretis (notably in *Technologies of Gender*), Dolan emphasizes the construction of cultural categories and the limitations imposed by available images within theater. Both spectator and spectacle participate in a deceptively 'natural' system; Dolan focuses on the mechanisms of representation and on the ways in which conventionalized images of gender and sexuality circumscribe identity by appealing to an approved spectator.

8 See Griselda Pollock, 'Modernity and the Spaces of Femininity,' in *Vision and Difference* (New York: Routledge, 1988), 50–90. See also Mary Ann Doane, 'Film and Masquerade: Theorizing the Female Spectator,' in *Femmes Fatales*, 17–32.

9 On Hardwick, see Girouard, *Robert Smythson*, chap. 4, and idem, *Hardwick Hall* (London: The National Trust, 1976).

10 Olive Cook, *The English Country House: An Art and a Way of Life* (London: Thames and Hudson, 1974), 8–26, discusses the roots of the manor house form. Girouard, *Life in the English Country House*, chap. 3, discusses the form of the medieval hall

and tower. See also M.W. Barley, 'Rural Housing in England,' in *Chapters from the Agrarian History of England and Wales,* vol. 4, *1500–1640,* ed. Joan Thirsk (Cambridge: Cambridge University Press, 1967).

11 The role of the housemaid is discussed in Cahn, *Industry of Devotion*, chap. 4, esp. 99–100. See also Girouard, *Life in the English Country House*, 27–8, 139, 142.

12 For literary reactions to these changes, such as Ben Jonson's 'To Penshurst,' see Don E. Wayne, *Penshurst: The Semiotics of Place and the Poetics of History* (Madison: University of Wisconsin Press, 1984).

13 See Friedman, *House and Household,* chap. 4, for an extended discussion of the type. Smythson's notebooks were published by Mark Girouard as 'The Smythson Collection of the Royal Institute of British Architects,' *Architectural History* 5 (1962).

14 See the appendix to Lucy Gent, *Picture and Poetry, 1560–1620: Relations between Literature and Visual Arts in the English Renaissance* (Leamington Spa: James Hall, 1981).

15 See Maurice Howard, *The Early Tudor Country House: Architecture and Politics, 1490–1550* (London: G. Philip, 1987).

16 *Manuscripts of Lord Middleton,* 153.

17 This was noted by David N. Durant in *Bess of Hardwick: Portrait of an Elizabethan Dynast* (London: Weidenfeld and Nicolson, 1977), 180–1.

18 Smythson and his son John worked with Charles and William Cavendish, sons of Bess of Hardwick and her second husband, on the rebuilding of Bolsover Castle (1608–40) as a medievalizing dream castle, which supports a gendered reading of these representations. On Bolsover, see P.A. Faulkner, *Bolsover Castle, Derbyshire* (London: HMSO, 1972).

19 On the use of rooms at Hardwick, see Lindsay Boynton, *The Hardwick Hall Inventories of 1601* (London: Furniture History Society, 1971).

20 Girouard, *Hardwick Hall*, 66.

37 Henry Urbach

'Closets, Clothes, disClosure'*

from Duncan McCorquodale, Katerina Rüedi and Sarah Wigglesworth (eds),
Desiring Practices: Architecture, Gender and the Interdisciplinary (1996)

The word 'closet' holds two distinct but related meanings. On the one hand, a closet is a space where things are stored. In this regard we might say, 'Your clothes are in the closet.' But when we observe, 'Joe has been in the closet for years,' we are not recounting his efforts to match trousers and tie. Instead, we are describing how he makes himself known to others. In this sense, the closet refers to a way that identity, and particularly gay identity, is concealed and disclosed. Concealed *and* disclosed because gay identity is not quite hidden by the closet, but not quite displayed either. Rather, it is represented through coded gestures that sustain uncertainty.

These two closets are not as different as they might appear. Taken together, they present a related way of defining and ascribing meaning to space. They both describe sites of storage that are separated from, and connected to, other room–like spaces, spaces of display. Each space – storage and display – excludes and defines, but also depends upon the other. The non–room, the closet, houses things that threaten to soil the room. Likewise, in a social order that ascribes normalcy to heterosexuality, the closet helps heterosexuality to present itself with certainty. The stability of these arrangements – a clean bedroom free of junk, and a normative heterosexuality free of homosexuality – depends on the architectural relation between closet and room.

The two closets resonate against one another within a linguistic and material network of representations that organise the relation between storage and display, secrecy and disclosure. The sexual closet refers, through an operation of metaphor, to the familiar architectural referent. The built-in closet, in turn, petrifies and disseminates, as architectural convention, the kind of subjectivity described by the homosexual closet. The built-in closet concretises the closet of identity, while the closet of identity literalises its architectural counterpart.

Despite their overlapping meanings in the present, the two closets bear histories that remain distinct and irreducible. We will take each of these in turn, beginning with the built-in closet, and focusing in particular on the clothes closet,

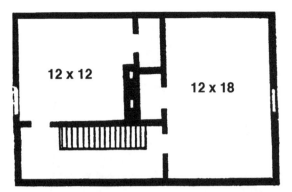

Figure 37.1
Second-floor plan for a labourer's
cottage showing closet hidden
within the wall cavity

even though closets have also been used for storing liners, cleaning supplies and other provisions. The closet we know today was invented as a new spatial type in mid-nineteenth-century America. For centuries, Europeans and Americans had stored clothing in furniture; sometimes it hung from wall pegs or hooks. Now, for the first time, a kind of wall cavity was produced for household storage. Briskly disseminated among all social classes, the closet effectively outmoded wardrobe, armoire and chest. These free-standing, mobile cabinets (which still exist, but without the same primacy) had encased clothing within the precinct of the room. Now, the place of storage was at, or more precisely *beyond*, the room's edge.

Armoires, chests and the like are volumetric objects with unambiguous spatial presence. By contrast, the closet presents itself more surreptitiously. Where the former are decorative objects, often lavished with paint, carving and inlay, the closet expresses itself only by a door plane, often smooth and unadorned. Unlike the closet, storage cabinets often display locks or key holes to indicate their concealed interior at the exterior surface. Free-standing, decorated, upright objects, armoires and the like are able to suggest, if not quite imitate, the clothed human body.

From about 1840 onwards, the closet offered, instead, diminished architectural expression. The storage of clothing had been respatialised as a kind of shameful secret. The closet not only concealed the things it contained but, significantly, it also promised *to hide itself*.

One of the most influential of the mid-nineteenth-century American 'pattern books', Andrew Jackson Downing's *Cottage Residences*, first published in 1842, describes the closet in the following, perfunctory way:

> The universally acknowledged utility of closets renders it unnecessary for us to say anything to direct attention to them under this head. In the principal story, a pantry or closets are a necessary accompaniment to the dining room or living room, but are scarcely required in connection with any of the other apartments. Bed-rooms always require at least one closet to each, and more will be found convenient.[1]

As spaces which merely *accompany* fully described rooms, closets are outlined in plan drawings but not otherwise elaborated. This is likewise the case with

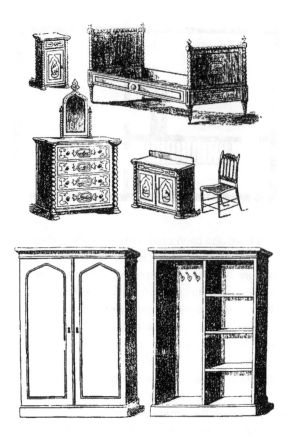

Figure 37.2 Free-standing mobile
cabinets
From *The Architecture of Country
Houses*

another pattern book of the period, Samuel Sloan's *The Model Architect* of 1852.
Although Sloan lavishes attention on a myriad aspects of house planning and
construction, he mentions closets only in passing to say that they must be 'fitted up
and fully shelved'.[2] Their height, ventilation, light, surface treatment and other
spatial qualities are not represented at all. In these mid-nineteenth-century texts, as
in constructed domestic space, the closet was rendered barely visible.

Concealing the storage of clothes and other possessions, the closet may have
served to address widespread ambivalence about material acquisition and the
accumulation of excess. This ambivalence appears clearly in an 1882 lecture by
Harriet Beecher:

> The good sense of the great majority of business men – and women – is in favour of
> enterprise, and of that frugality and economy which shall result in amassing
> property. . . . And yet there exists at the same time in the community . . . a vague sense
> of the unspirituality of the treasures of this life, and of the dangers that inhere in them,
> together with some sort of conscience – they know not what – or fear.[3]

For Americans of the period, encountering an expanding industrial economy
alongside the resurgence of Christian morality, wealth had come to represent both
virtue and decadence. It could be amassed but not comfortably shown. In this

context, it seems, Americans looked to the closet to moderate display while not interfering with actual possession.

The closet worked, along with other architectural strategies, to advance an extensive reform movement that aimed to invest the American home with signs of moral propriety. Increasingly strict codes of behaviour were given architectural form as, for instance, the stairway to second-floor bedrooms moved out of the entrance hall to a less visible part of the interior. Likewise, programmes and spaces once joined were separated into discrete rooms with distinct degrees of privacy. At a wide range of architectural scales, efforts mounted to moderate the visibility of spaces now deemed private. Downing proposed that the 'ideal' of domestic planning was to keep 'each department of the house . . . complete in itself, and intruding itself but little on the attention of the family or guests when not required to be visible.'[4] Consistent with other transformations of the American house, in a relatively small but powerful way, the closet provided concealment without eliminating access.

Holding clothes in abeyance, the closet not only hid 'excess' in general terms, but more specifically the sartorial multiplicity of the wardrobe. If a person's various garments offer a repertory for self-representation, the closet served to ensure, instead, that only those garments worn at any particular moment would be visible. In this way, what was worn could sustain a kind of singular legitimacy. The closet contained the overflow of garments and their meanings to heed Downing's maxim, a statement which neatly captures the spatial thrust of the era: 'The great secret of safe and comfortable living lies in keeping yourself and everything about you in the right place.'[5]

In the course of the last century and a half, the architecture of the closet has sustained a particularly strict relation between closet and room. Regardless of adjacent conditions, the closet usually opens to a single room – a room it is said to be 'in' – even though, in fact, it is *next* to this room, or between one room and another. In general, closets receive neither anterior nor lateral expression. Windows or doors rarely appear at the rear or side of the closet, even though they might serve to admit light and air as well as passage.[6] A monogamous relation thus emerges between the closet and its room, between the room and its closet. The room relies exclusively on its closet and the closet depends uniquely upon its room.

The threshold between closet and room mediates their relation, simultaneously connecting and dissociating the two spaces. Although the closet door may take many forms (among them, sliding, pocket and hinged single or double doors), the door always shuts to conceal the interior of the closet and opens to allow access. Moreover the door is usually articulated to minimise its own visibility, often set flush or painted to match the surrounding wall. As much as possible, the closet presents itself as an absence, a part of the (not-so) solid wall at the room's edge. According to a domestic planning manual from the 1940s: 'Closets should not interfere with main areas of activity in a house. They should be accessible but inconspicuous'.[7]

The tension between visual concealment and physical access has driven the architectural elaboration of the closet/room pair. But, despite its formidable architectural strength, it fails to contain the tension exerted by contrary imperatives: storage versus display, keeping things hidden versus keeping things handy. The closet, in the end, can only be so inconspicuous. The door cannot help but hint at the space beyond its planar surface. There is always some seam, gap, hinge, knob or pull that reveals the door as a mobile element. Moreover, the door displays the presence of the closet beyond by setting parameters for decorating and furnishing the room. One does not, for example, place furniture in front of a closet door as though it were part of the wall.

Holding things at the edge of the room, simultaneously concealing and revealing its interior, the closet becomes a carrier of abjection, a site of *interior* exclusion for that which has been deemed dirty. Julia Kristeva's psychoanalytic and socio-cultural analysis of abjection examines how things which are considered dirty and therefore subject to exclusion are never fully eliminated. Rather, they are deposited just beyond the space they simultaneously soil and cleanse. This partial, incomplete elimination keeps that which is dirty present so it can constitute, by contrast, the cleanliness of the clean.[8]

It is with this in mind that we can understand the peculiar architecture of the closet–room pair, along with its urgency for mid-nineteenth-century Americans and continuing presence. Closet and room work together to keep the room clean and the closet messy, to keep the contents of the room proper and those of the closet abject. They do not eliminate 'dirt', but reposition it across a boundary that is also a threshold. The closet door mediates imperatives of visual concealment and physical access, undermining the separation of closet and room while stabilising their difference.

The closet of sexual secrecy, named after the built-in closet, existed long before it was first called 'the closet' in the early 1960s. For at least a century, as David Miller, Eve Sedgwick, and others have demonstrated, the closet was a social and literary convention that narrated homosexuality as a spectacle of veiled disclosure.[9] The closet was the late-nineteenth-century device by which 'the love that dare not speak its name' could be spoken and vilified. It served a larger social project committed, as Michel Foucault has shown, to establishing homo- and hetero-sexuality as distinct and unequal categories of identity. Instead of polymorphic sexual practices, there was now a taxonomy of new sexual types. In Foucault's account: 'The sodomite had been a temporary aberration; the homosexual was now a species.'[10]

The closet organised homosexual identity as an open secret, a telling silence. Like the wall seams and door pulls that betray the closet, the absence of wedding bands and other positive assertions of heterosexuality would raise the spectre of gay identity even without forthright disclosure. One could neither be fully legible nor fully invisible; instead, dissemblance would serve to reveal a condition otherwise unstated.

'Heterosexuality' cast its abject other into the (yet unnamed) closet, at once nearby and far-off, hidden and accessible. Positioned in this way, the category of homosexuality accrued all the phantasmatic impropriety required by heterosexuality to secure its own proper domain, the sanctity of its own, tidy bedroom.[11] Excluded, but always just over there, homosexuality was identified with promiscuity and degeneracy. By contrast, heterosexuality was identified with procreation, fidelity and true love.

Despite its presence throughout the early part of this century, the homo-sexual closet was not named as such before the 1960s. The term 'closet', in this sense, arose in America during the period of political foment that produced, among other events, the Stonewall riots of June 1969. The nascent gay rights move-ments identified the closet as a tool of homophobic heterosexism and advanced a new battle cry: 'Out of the closets! Into the streets!'

From then on, 'coming out' has been understood as the origin of gay identity, the *sine qua non* of physical security, legal protection and social dignity. 'Coming out' is imagined, rather idealistically, as a way of rejecting the closet and its hold on gay self-representation. And, indeed, within a regime of (almost) compulsory heterosexuality, the personal and political value of coming out must not be underestimated. But, at the same time, its effects on the architecture of the closet should not be overstated. Where heterosexuality is presumed, coming out can never be accomplished once and for all. As Sedgwick has argued, the sustenance of gay identity (where straight identity is presumed) depends upon continuous acts of declaration.[12] To reveal gay identity in one situation does not obviate the need to reveal it again in the next. Every new acquaintance, every new situation demands a repetition of, or retreat from, disclosure.

For the past century, then, imagining an opposition of 'in' and 'out', gay identity has found itself in a double bind. Wherever one is, relative to the closet, one risks *both* exposure and erasure. But the binary logic of the closet/room pair, the rigid opposition of in and out, does not account for the dynamic entanglement of closet and room, the ways in which they constantly separate and reattach, the ways in which one is always *both* in and out, *neither* in nor out. This binary obses-sion has radically constricted the ways that gay people feel they can 'disclose', rather than perform, identity.[13]

To come out and declare 'I am gay' – whether to another person or to oneself – is to submit to a host of ideological imperatives: self-unity ('I'); immutability over time ('am'); and the given characterisation ('gay'). These are crude and brittle words, unable to capture the diachronicity and multivalence of identity as played out in social space. Performer k.d. lang seemed aware of this when, shortly after coming out in the national media, she appeared on the Radio City Music Hall stage, took the mike, and gingerly teased her audience: 'I . . . AM . . . (by now, soap bubbles had begun to fill the stage) . . . A . . . LLL . . . L . . . L . . . LL . . . LLLL . . . LLLLLLL . . . Lawrence Welk fan.'

Toying with the architecture of the closet and its codes of disclosure, k.d. points toward the possibility of manipulating language, verbal and sartorial codes alike, to elaborate 'identity' as a lively, ongoing process of resignification. This is something Mikhail Bakhtin theorised in his model of language as a site of social contest. The word, for Bakhtin, becomes 'one's own' only when the speaker populates it with his or her own accent and adapts it to his or her own semantic intention.[14] Consider, then, the reinvention of the once derogatory 'queer', 'fag' and 'dyke' as affirmative terms. Or the practice, common among gay men during the 1970s, of displaying a coloured handkerchief in the rear jeans pocket. Appropriated from the uniform of labourers, the handkerchief served not only to display sexual orientation, but also to indicate, with considerable nuance, particular sexual interests. Extending from the inside of the pocket to the outside of the trousers, the handkerchief also recapitulated, at the scale of the body, the larger spatial relation governing the storage and display of gay identity.

In recent years, gay people have learned to re-articulate other, more overtly homophobic codes of dress: (macho) tattoos, (Nazi) pink triangle, (gym teacher) hooded sweatshirt, (military) crew cut, (femme fatale) lipstick and (skinhead) Doc Martens. These gestures of *détournement* – when done well, and before they ossify into new norms – underscore the relation of homo- and hetero-sexualities without necessarily adopting the violence and inequity of their opposition. They are simultaneously effects of the closet and moments of its loosening.

Since the closet was invented alongside homo- and hetero-sexuality over a century ago, gay people have needed to work with and against it. Often the closet has served homophobic and heterosexist interests. At the same time, however, it has also provided for other, surprisingly articulate meanings.

The impressive architectural stability of the closet notwithstanding, it has not always – and need not necessarily – describe a spatiality so rigid. A wide range of spatial practices, including architectural scholarship and design, offer opportunities to redress, provoke and reconfigure the relation of closet and room. Working with and against the closure of the closet, it is possible to produce an expanded space between closet and room. Here, in this realm between storage and display, between the dirty and the clean, new opportunities for the representation of 'identity' emerge.

Long before the built-in closet was invented, there was another kind of closet, a very different kind of space. From the late-fourteenth to the nineteenth centuries, the closet referred, in terms both architectural and social, to an inhabitable room. In England and much of Continental Europe, the 'closet' (or its analogue, such as the French *grand cabinet*) described a place for retreat, prayer, study or speculation.[15] It served not only as a private sanctuary, but also as a special repository for the storage and display of books, paintings, and other treasured objects.

During the fifteenth century in England, a closet particular to royal residences emerged. Closely associated with the private apartments of the sovereign or other nobility, this closet referred to a chamber used for retreat, writing, contemplation, small receptions and religious activities.[16] At Hampton Court, 'holy-day closets' were added in 1536 to provide the King, Queen and their invited guests with semi-private spaces of worship apart from the court.[17] Eventually, the closet also came to refer to a pew in the chapel of a castle occupied by the lord and his family. Through its various incarnations, the royal closet allowed for gathering and interaction with others.

A private retreat, a small gathering space, a wall cavity for storage, a condition of gay secrecy: in what ways can the 'closet' continue to unfold, opening itself to other spatial forms, uses and meanings? Consider this: extending from the inside of the closet door frame to some distance in front of the closet, there is an interstitial space that appears, disappears and reappears again and again. Where the door slides or folds, the space is not so deep but, in the case of the ordinary hinged door, it is a space of considerable dimension. This is a space I call the *ante-closet*, the space before the closet. It is in the ante-closet where one selects clothes, where one dresses and undresses oneself, where one changes.

I recall my discovery of the ante-closet when I was a young boy. There, standing before a built-in closet, I discovered something about my own representational range. To be frank, this did not happen in front of my own closet, not the closet filled with the clothes little boys wore in New Jersey in the late 1960s. Instead, it was in my parents' room, in-between the hinged doors to my mother's closet, that I first found and learned to occupy this important little space.

On the inside surface of both doors was a tall mirror lit by delicate, vertically mounted fluorescent tubes. I remember pushing the switch as the lights flickered and hummed, then positioning the doors so the mirrors reflected space, and me, to infinity. Before removing my own clothing, I carefully selected an outfit from my mother's wardrobe – dress, shoes, necklace, handbag. The transformation was brief and private, as I never chose to display my new look to others. But it was a privacy that was profoundly limitless, a moment where selfhood and otherness became completely confounded. The paired mirrors redoubled every gesture to infinity as I saw myself, in a moment of narcissistic plenitude, transformed: grown-up, autonomous and lovely.

Nowadays, despite my more gender-consonant wardrobe, I continue to extend my representational range in the ante-closet. Between the closet and the room, in this ephemeral space, I explore the effects of sartorial gestures and imagine their significance to others. Respectable merino cardigan? Raw leather tunic? Mao jacket? Velour cigarette pants? Where the ante-closet contains a mirror, I am able to consider these modes of identification visually, as others might see them. Where there is no mirror, I rely instead on memory and imagination. Private and social realms interpenetrate as the line between what I hide and what I show breaks down, and I start to see myself as another.[18]

The ante-closet can be further elaborated with reference to Gilles Deleuze's notion of the *pli* or fold. The *pli* is a space that emerges, both within and against social relations, to constitute a space of self-representation at once connected to and free from social norms. In the *pli*, Deleuze writes:

> the relation to oneself assumes an independent status. It is as if the relations of the outside folded back to create a doubling, allow a relation to oneself to emerge, and constitute an inside which is hollowed out and develops its own unique dimension.[19]

The *pli* is not a secure idyll, a place of unobstructed selfhood. But it is, provisionally, an enclave. Social codes, inequities and violence penetrate the *pli* through and through, and yet it remains possible, in this space, to work with them. In the *pli*, the representational range of clothing, the multivalence of sexualities and identities, does not threaten and does not need to be foreclosed.

The ante-closet has a curious status in architectural drawings, conventionally rendered as a kind of graphic interruption. The notation for 'door swing' is an arc that traces the passage of the unhinged edge from open to shut. Whether drawn as a light solid line or a series of dashed segments, this arc does not indicate, as other lines do, 'cut' material. Instead, it registers the possibility of movement and spatial manipulation. At once conventional and abnormal, a moment of graphic folding, the door swing draws attention to the possibility of making and remaking space.

Like Doc Martens and hooded sweatshirts – worn by different people to diverse effects – the ante-closet is an effect of reappropriations and resignifications without end. It waits there, around the boundary between closet and room, for reactivation as the space of changing. It neither obliterates nor interferes with the spatial presence of closet or room, but brings them instead into a more complex and fluid adjacency. An expanded edge between closet and room, the ante-closet works with and against these spaces, dissolving their tired opposition to sustain the possibility of another arrangement.

We can imagine other kinds of ante-closets, other ways of elaborating the threshold between closet and room. A sliding rod that extends way beyond the closet; an inhabitable closet that is spatially continuous with its room; a closet that opens promiscuously to multiple spaces, even exposing itself to the exterior of the house: these are among the alternatives open to further architectural research. I have learned from my childhood encounter that the ante-closet is most exciting, most able to enrich the relation of storage and display when there is a play of scales from the bodily to the infinite and when the architectural elements can be manipulated – slid, swung, pushed or grabbed. Sometimes the ante-closet swells; at other times it recedes and disappears. It may be there if we desire it, if we need it, if we make it come between the closet and room.

ACKNOWLEDGEMENT

In addition to the organisers of Desiring Practices, I would like to thank the following people for helping me to advance the essay: Stephen Hartman, Catherine Ingraham, Mary McLeod, Joan Ockman, John Ricco, Brian Walker and Mark Wigley.

NOTES

1 A.J. Downing, *Cottage Residences*, New York: Wiley and Putnam, 1842, p. 7.
2 S. Sloan, *The Model Architect*, Philadelphia: E.S. Jones & Co., 1852, p. 14.
3 H.W. Beecher, 'The Moral Uses of Luxury and Beauty', *Outlook*, xxv, 16 March 1882, p. 257.

4 Downing, *Cottage*, p. 3.

5 E.C. Gardner, *The House that Jill Built, after Jack's had Proved a Failure*, New York: W.F. Adams Company, 1896, p. 166.

6 An American house planning guide from 1940 notes: '*Ventilation* of the clothes closet generally waits for the opening of the door into the bedroom . . . Daylight, particularly sunlight, is valuable as a steriliser, but we seldom manage to admit it to the closet.' W.B. Field, *House Planning*, New York: McGraw Hill, 1940, p. 149.

7 M. Wilson, *Closets and Storage Spaces*, Washington, DC: US Department of Agriculture Farmers' Bulletin no. 1865, 1940, p. 1.

8 J. Kristeva, *Pouvoirs de l'horreur*, L. S. Roudiez (trans.), Paris: Editions du Seuil, 1980, *Powers of Horror: An Essay on Abjection*, New York: Columbia University Press, 1982.

9 See D.A. Miller, *The Novel and the Police*, Berkeley and Los Angeles: University of California Press, 1988, especially chap. 6: 'Secret Subjects, Open Secrets'. Also see: E. Sedgwick, *Epistemology of the Closet*, Berkeley and Los Angeles: University of California Press, 1992.

10 M. Foucault, *La Volenté de savoir*, R. Hurley, (trans.), Paris: Gallimard, 1976, *The History of Sexuality*, vol. 1, New York: Random House, 1978, p. 43. Foucault writes, on pp. 42 and 43:

> 'This new persecution of the peripheral sexualities entailed an *incorporation of perversions* and a new *specification of individuals*. As defined by the ancient civil or canonical codes, sodomy was a category of forbidden acts; their perpetrator was nothing more than the juridical subject for them. The nineteenth century homosexual became a personage, a past, a case history, and a childhood, in addition to being a type of life, a life form, and a morphology, with an indiscreet anatomy and possibly a mysterious physiology. Nothing that went into his total composition was unaffected by his sexuality.'

11 Diana Fuss writes:

> Homosexuality, in a word, becomes the excluded; it stands in for, paradoxically, that which stands without. But the binary structure of sexual orientation, fundamentally a structure of exclusion and exteriorisation, nonetheless constructs that exclusion by prominently including the contaminated other in its oppositional logic. The homo in relation to the hetero, much like the feminine in relation to the masculine, operates as an indispensable interior exclusion – an outside which is inside interiority making the articulation of the latter possible, a transgression of the border which is necessary to constitute the border as such.

> D. Fuss, 'Inside/Out', in *Inside/Out*, D. Fuss, (ed.), New York: Routledge, 1991, p. 3.

12 Sedgwick writes:

> Furthermore, the deadly elasticity of heterosexist presumption means that, like Wendy in Peter Pan, people find new walls springing up around them even as they drowse: every encounter with a new classful of students, to say nothing of a new boss, social worker, loan officer, landlord, doctor, erects new closets whose fraught and characteristic laws of optics and physics exact from at least gay people new surveys, new calculations, new draughts and requisitions of secrecy or disclosure.

> Sedgwick, *Epistemology*, p. 68.

13 Judith Butler asks:

> Is the 'subject' who is 'out' free of its subjection and finally in the clear? Or could it be that the subjection that subjectivates the gay or lesbian subject in some ways continues to oppress, or oppresses most insidiously, once 'outness' is claimed? What or who is it that is 'out', made manifest and fully disclosed, when and if I reveal myself as lesbian? What is the very linguistic act that offers up the promise of a transparent revelation of sexuality? Can sexuality even remain sexuality once it submits to a criterion of transparency and disclosure, or does it perhaps cease to be sexuality precisely when the semblance of full explicitness is achieved?
>
> J. Butler, 'Imitation and Gender Subordination', in Fuss, *Inside/Out*, p. 15.

14 M. Holquist, (ed.), *The Dialogic Imagination, Four Essays by M. M. Bakhtin*, C. Emerson and M. Holquist, (trans.) Austin: University of Texas Press, 1981. On pp. 293 and 294 Bakhtin writes:

> As a living, socio-ideological concrete thing, as heteroglot opinion, language, for the individual consciousness, lies on the borderline between oneself and the other. The word in language is half someone else's. It becomes 'one's own' only when the speaker populates it with his own accent, when he appropriates the word, adapting it to his own semantic intention. Prior to this moment of appropriation . . . it exists in other people's mouths, in other people's contexts, serving other people's intentions: it is from there that one must take the word, and make it one's own.

15 According to the *Oxford English Dictionary*, a text from 1374 notes: 'in a closet for to avyse her bettre, she went alone'. A novel of 1566 states: 'we doe call the most secret place in the house appropriate unto our owne private studies . . . a Closet,' *Oxford English Dictionary*, 2nd edn., vol. III, Oxford: Clarendon Press, 1985, s.v. 'Closet', p. 349.

16 According to a text from 1625: 'If the Queens Closet where they now say masse were not large enough, let them have it in the Great Chamber'. *Oxford English Dictionary*, p. 349.

17 J. Bickereth and R.W. Dunning, (eds.), *Clerks of the Closet in the Royal Household: 500 years of Service to the Crown*, Phoenix Mill: Alan Sutton, 1991, pp. 5–6.

18 P. Ricoeur, *Soi-même comme un autre*, K. Blarney, (trans.) Paris: Editions du Seuil, 1990, *Oneself as Another*, Chicago: University of Chicago Press, 1992. On p. 3, Ricoeur writes: 'the selfhood of oneself implies otherness to such an intimate degree that one cannot be thought of without the other, that instead one passes into the other.'

19 Deleuze, G., *Foucault*, Paris: Editions de Minuit, 1986. S. Hand, (ed. and trans.), *Foucault*, Minneapolis: University of Minnesota Press, 1988, p. 100.

38 Joel Sanders

'Cadet Quarters, US Air Force Academy, Colorado Springs'

from Joel Sanders (ed.), *Stud: Architectures of Masculinity* (1996)

> Bring me men.
> (Motto at the Air Force Academy entry)

The words 'Bring me men' are incised in stone above the entrance ramp of Skidmore, Owings & Merrill's Air Force Academy. The inscription engendered a controversy when women were first admitted to this all-male academic institution; should the slogan remain or be removed? The decision of the female cadets to retain the motto demonstrates their recognition of the Academy as a site dedicated to the production of masculine subjects, irrespective of the soldier's biological sex. Within the campus, females as well as males train to become 'men.'

It comes as no surprise that the military would enlist architecture to shape and impart the masculine traits necessary to transform cadets into officers. Quite unexpected, however, was the military's decision in 1954 to deploy the language of modern architecture to achieve its goal.[1] The spirit of freedom associated with modernism's formal trademarks – spatial continuity and visual transparency – at first seemed antithetical to military values traditionally represented in classical styles. SOM's version of European modernism, refined in their commercial designs for American corporations, provided the appropriate medium for creating militaristic spaces of discipline and control.

From the disposition of buildings on the site to the layout of custom-designed aluminum-framed furniture within the dorm rooms, SOM's campus plan depends on the quintessential modernist instrument – the grid. But unlike the prototypical modernist open plan, where Cartesian coordinates provide the framework within which forms dynamically shift and slide, at the Academy the grid regulates the articulation and static placement of every architectural element. In short, the grid serves as an architectural manifestation of the order and regimentation the cadets are subject to during their four-year stay. According to the project architect, Walter Netsch, the project's governing modules (28", 14", 3' 6", and 1' 9") derive from the 7' 0" dimension of a cadet's bed – the scale of the receptacle of the male body at rest. However, in the hands of SOM, the grid accomplishes more than simply insuring an image of regularity and control; exceeding the architects' intentions, it determines not only the organization of spaces but the movement of

Figure 38.1
View of Vandenberg Hall, US Air
Force Academy, Colorado Springs

bodies within them. The scale of 1' 9" (a subdivision of 7' 0") stone pavers laid in a grid corresponds to the average shoulder width of a cadet. While designed by the architects to offer visual relief from the monotony of the vast plaza that organizes the campus, this geometric paving pattern has become institutionalized by the cadets, who now use it to mark the exterior pathways freshmen must adhere to when marching between buildings. Preventing direct diagonal movements, its formal structure enforces a rigid choreography of straight walks and 90-degree turns.

> We will not lie or cheat nor tolerate anyone amongst us who does
>> (Inscription on the arch above the ramp leading to the Administration Building)

The ground plane engenders virile behavior in other ways at the Air Force Academy. The collection of campus structures rests on an immense podium set against, and nearly indifferent to, its Rocky Mountain backdrop. This man-made base creates a relentless horizontal datum affording limitless views of the uninterrupted desert horizon framed between buildings. The plinth's excessive scale, panoramic views, and topographic indifference embodies in an exaggerated manner the Western conception of architecture as a vehicle for mankind's supremacy over nature. But if the campus's ground plane presents a legible world of truth and order against its immaculate surface, this membrane also functions as a mask. The Academy's 'fifth façade' hides the underside of masculinity; a vast network of underground tunnels hidden by the plinth shelter unauthorized 'spirit' activities – 'un-

Figure 38.2
View of closet, US Air Force
Academy, Colorado Springs

becoming' conduct that the military recognizes as essential for the production of men.[2]

Moving from exterior to interior, horizontal to vertical, Vandenberg Hall (1958) also employs surfaces that both reveal and conceal. Dark stained wood panelling lines the dormitory corridors, evoking the ambiance of a corporate men's club. Within each room, shared by two cadets, the same wall treatment forms the discrete doors of built-in drawers, cabinets, and closets. However, unlike conventional domestic settings where closets function to hide their contents from view, these are meant to be opened. During daily inspections they reveal custom-designed uniforms by Hollywood director and designer Cecil B. DeMille placed in precise arrangements dictated by military protocol. Drawers contain underwear, socks, and shirts carefully folded around cardboard to prominently display logos and insignias. Shoes are stored in neat rows on a two-tiered shelf and their laces are hidden from view. Demonstrating how the wall dressings that shape a building work analogously to the clothes that outfit a body, these uniforms, when seen framed within closets and drawers, reinforce the image of masculine regimentation, hierarchy, and control symbolized by the outfits themselves.

However, the clothes the cadets actually wear on a regular basis are stored not in these wardrobes but in cardboard boxes in small cupboards above the closets and in a vanity that houses the sink.[3] It is tacitly understood that these storage areas will be overlooked during inspection. Unbeknownst to their designer, Walter Dorwin Teague, the carefully designed dorm room wardrobes inculcate the unspoken but essential masculine values of the military: appearance and duplicity.

> Don't ask, don't tell, don't pursue
>
> (The Clinton administration's policy regarding homosexuals in the military)

NOTES

1   Impressed by the new university campus at Mexico City and Edward Durrell Stone's Hotel El Panama, Lieutenant General Hubert R. Harmon, in charge of planning for the Air Force Academy, was the first to suggest the viability of modernism for the new Academy's design. The Air Force ultimately awarded Skidmore, Owings & Merrill the commission in July 1954 after reviewing the qualifications of a number of large corporate applications including Eero Saarinen, Pietro Beluschi, and Harrison and Abramowitz. However, after SOM presented their preliminary design to members of Congress and to the press, a public controversy erupted with regard to the appropriateness of the modernist language for representing this American institution. For a detailed account of the architectural selection process, see Kristen Schaffer, 'Creating a National Monument,' in *Modernism at Mid-century: the Architecture of the Air Force Academy*, ed. Robert Bruegmann (Chicago: University of Chicago Press, 1994), pp. 16–54.

2   *Boyle*: You may not want this in the book but were there any kind of elements that made spirit missions (cadet activities that aren't supposed to happen but do) especially possible? *Hosmer*: Oh, the tunnels. The tunnels. . . . I was more interested in how you keep cadets out of the tunnels than how you get into them. *Boyle*: That probably wasn't an easy job. *Hosmer*: No, it was impossible. You couldn't keep cadets out of the tunnels. (Excerpt from an interview with Lieutenant Bradley Hosmer conducted by Academy Architect Duane Boyle, published in *Modernism at Mid Century*, 194).

3   Plumbing in the cadet rooms includes only a sink; SOM's original scheme to outfit

pairs of rooms with private bathrooms was rejected in favor of making cadets travel to ganged bathrooms located at the corner of each dormitory floor. This alternative represented a compromise between the architects' design and the military planner's intention of duplicating the facilities at West Point, where a common bathroom is located in the basement.

39 Diane Agrest

'Architecture from Without: Body, Logic and Sex'

from *Architecture from Without: Theoretical Framings for a Critical Practice* (1993)

Somewhere every culture has an imaginary zone for what it excludes, and it is this zone that we must try to remember today.[1]

For something to be excluded, two parts are necessary: something inside, some defined entity, and something outside. In our world of architectural ideology there is such an inside: the body of texts and rules developed in the Renaissance that, as a reading of the classics, established the foundations for Western architecture, which I call the 'system of architecture.' This inside has been transformed throughout history, at some times more profoundly than at others, and even through the apparent breaks of the first decades of this century it has remained at the very base of Western architectural thought.

Logocentrism and anthropomorphism, in particular male anthropomorphism, are underlying the system of architecture since Vitruvius, then read and rewritten in the Renaissance and through the modern movement.[2] This system is not only defined by what it includes, but also by what it excludes; inclusion and exclusion are parts of the same construct. That which is excluded, left out, is not really excluded but rather repressed; repression neither excludes nor repels an exterior force, for it contains within itself an interior of representation, a space of repression.[3] That repressed, that interior representation in the system of architecture that determines an outside (of repression) is woman and woman's body. The ideological construct of the architectural system determined by an idealistic logic and a concomitant system of repressions becomes apparent in the role sex plays within it. The logic in the system of architecture represses sex in two different ways: sex is thought of in both positive and negative terms; where woman is assigned the negative term (phallocentrism), and sex is neutralized or erased through the medium of the artist who, sexless, engenders by himself and gives birth to a work, the product of creation.[4]

Society established a certain kind of symbolic order where not everyone can equally fit. There are those who do fit and those who have to find their place between symbolic orders, in the interstices; they represent a certain symbolic instability. These are the people often called odd, abnormal, or perverse or who have been labeled neurotics, ecstatics, outsiders, witches, or hysterics.[5] In strange ways, woman has been placed in this category when she has tried to establish her presence rather than limit herself to finding a way of 'fitting' within the established symbolic order.

Woman has been allowed to surface from the space of her repression as a witch or a hysteric and thus has been burned or locked up, ultimately representing the abnormal.[6] Women, who are the bearers of the greatest norm, that of reproduction, paradoxically also embody the anomaly.[7] It is through her body and through the symbolic order that woman has been repressed in architecture, and in dealing with body and architecture the obvious question – what body? – is the key to the unveiling of many mysterious ideological fabrications. Asking 'what body?' is synonymous to asking 'which gender?' for a genderless body is an impossible body.

In many of the important texts of the Renaissance, the founding texts of Western architectural ideology, the subject of the body in architecture is not only essential but moreover is indissolubly linked to the question of gender and sex, a question that has generated the most extraordinary architectural metaphors in the elaboration of architectural ideology. The reading of those texts is an essential operation in the understanding of a complex ideological apparatus that has systematically excluded woman, an exclusion made possible by an elaborate mechanism of symbolic appropriation of the female body.

Two scenes will be presented here, two scenes of architecture: Scene I: The Book of the Renaissance; Scene II: The Text of the City.

SCENE I: THE BOOK OF THE RENAISSANCE

The Scene of the Repressed: Architecture from Within

Architecture in the Renaissance establishes a system of rules that is the basis of Western architecture. The texts of the Renaissance, which in turn read the classic texts from Vitruvius, develop a logocentric and anthropocentric discourse establishing the male body at the center of the unconscious of architectural rules and configurations. The body is inscribed in the system of architecture as a male body replacing the female body. The Renaissance operations of symbolization of the body are paradigmatic of the operations of repression and exclusion of woman by means of the replacement of her body. Woman not only has been displaced/replaced at a general social level throughout the history of architecture, but more specifically, at the level of body and architecture.

Architecture as a Representation of the Body

The texts of the Renaissance offer a certain clue to the mode in which the appropriation by man of woman's place and body in architecture has taken place in a complex process of symbolization that works at the level of architectural ideology, therefore at an almost unconscious level. Several texts are exemplary of this procedure in varying degrees, particularly Alberti's *Ten Books on Architecture*, Filarete's *Treatise on Architecture*, and Francesco Di Giorgio Martini's *Architettura Civile e Militare* and *Architettura Ingegneria e Arte Militare*, and of course we cannot forget Vitruvius, whose *Ten Books of Architecture* are at the base of every Renaissance text.

In the several steps in the operation of symbolic transference from the body to architecture, the first is the relationship established between man and nature through the notions of natural harmony and perfection.[8] Man is presented as having the attribute of perfect natural proportions. Thus the analogical relationship between architecture and the human body appears to ensure that the natural laws of beauty and nature are transferred into architecture. The body thus becomes a mediator, a form of 'shifter.'[9]

It is in Vitruvius that we first find the important notions that are to be re-elaborated in various ways in other later texts. His text clearly posits the issue of the human body as a model for architecture, particularly in his chapter 'On Symmetry in Temples and the Human Body,' where symmetry is related to proportion – symmetry being an essential feature in the design of temples and proportion being the correspondence among measures of an entire work.

> Without symmetry and proportion, that is, if there is no precise relation between the members as in 'a well-shaped man,' there can be no principles of design. Furthermore, the measurements for buildings are all to be derived from the members of the body. The design of a temple depends on symmetry, the principles of which must be carefully observed by the architect. They are due to proportion, in Greek 'avanoyia.' Proportion is a correspondence among measures of the members of an entire work, and of the whole to a certain part selected as standard. From this results the principles of symmetry. Without symmetry and proportion there can be no principles in the design of any temple; that is, if there is no precise relation between its members, as in the case of those of a well-shaped man. Further, it was from the members of the body that they derived the fundamental ideas of the measures which are obviously necessary in all works, as the finger, palm, foot and cubit.[10]

The relationship between architecture and the human body becomes particularly important at the moment in which the issue of the center, a preoccupation that filters throughout the history of art and architecture in its many symbolic roles, acquires a very specific meaning.

> Then again, in the human body the central point is naturally the navel. For if a man be placed flat on his back, with his hands and feet extended, and a pair of compasses centered at his navel, the fingers and toes of his two hands and feet will touch the circumference of a circle described therefrom. And just as the human body yields a circular outline, so too a square figure may be found from it. For if we measure the distance from the soles of the feet to the top of the head, and then apply measure to the outstretched arms, the breadth will be found to be the same as the height, as in the case of plane surfaces which are perfectly square.[11]

The center is represented by the navel, which becomes a metonymic object or a 'shifter' in relation to gender. It is a true shifter in that it transforms the body into geometry, nature into architecture, the 'I' of the subject into the 'I' of the discourse. The relationship between these two 'I's' is what allows the constant shifting of genders. This type of formal relationship between the body of man and architecture, developed by Vitruvius, will be ever-present in the Renaissance texts.

An analogical relationship between the body (of man) and architecture can also be found in Alberti's *Ten Books on Architecture*:

> The whole Force of the invention and all our skill and Knowledge in the Art of Building, it is required in the Compartition: Because the distinct Parts of the entire Building, and, to use such a Word, the Entireness of each of those parts and the Union and Agreement of all the lines and Angles in the Work, duly ordered for Convenience, Pleasure and Beauty are disposed and measured out by the Compartition alone: For if a City, according to the Opinion of Philosophers, be no more than a great House and, on the other hand, a House be a little City; why may it not be said that the Members of that House are so many little Houses . . . and as the Members of the Body are correspondent to each other, so it is fit that one part should answer to another in a Building; whence we say, that great Edifices require great Members.[12]

Alberti is never as direct in his analogies as Vitruvius or as other architects of the Renaissance. His text offers a far more elaborate system of metaphorical transformation by which he develops specific notions that allow for the development of an abstract system in a discourse that incorporates the 'laws of nature.'

> If what we have here laid down appears to be true, we may conclude Beauty to be such a Consent and Agreement of the Parts of the Whole in which it is found, as to Number, Finishing and Collocation, as Congruity, that is to say, the principal law of Nature requires. This is what Architecture chiefly aims at, and by this she obtains her Beauty, Dignity and Value. The Ancients knowing from the Nature of Things, that the Matter was in fact as I have stated it, and being convinced, that if they neglected this main Point they should never produce any Thing great or commendable, did in their Works propose to themselves chiefly the Imitation of Nature, as the greatest Artist at all Manner of Compositions. . . . Reflecting therefore upon the Practice of Nature as well with Relation to an entire Body, as to its several Parts, they found from the very first Principles of Things, that Bodies were not always composed of equal parts or Members; whence it happens, that of the Bodies produced by Nature, some are smaller, some are larger, and some middling.[13]

The process of symbolization takes place by relating the body as a system of proportion to other systems of proportion. The body, transformed into an abstract system of formalization, is thus incorporated into the architectural system as form, through the orders, hierarchies, and the general system of formal organization allowing for this anthropocentric discourse to function at the level of the unconscious.

Transsexual Operations in Architecture

Vitruvius and Alberti point the way to the incorporation of the body as an analogue, model, or referent, elaborating a system for its transformation into a system of architectural syntactic rules, elements, and meanings. In the work of Filarete and Francesco Di Giorgio Martini, the original ambiguity of the gender of the body in question is eliminated by making explicit the fact that human figure is synonymous with male figure. A different ambiguity will appear instead, the ambiguity of the gender or sex itself. In a rather complex set of metaphorical operations throughout these texts, the gender of the body and its sexual functions are exchanged in a move of cultural transsexuality whereby man's ever-present procreative fantasy is enacted.

Filarete starts by making sure that we understand not only that architecture is directly linked to the human figure but that when he refers to 'human' figure or body, it is the male figure:

> As I have said, the building is constructed as a simile for the human figure. You see that I have shown you by means of a simile that a building is derived from man, that is, from his form, members, and measure. . . . Now as I have told you above, I will show you how the building is given form and substance by analogy with the members and form of man. You know that all buildings need members and passages, that is, entrances and exits. They should all be formed and arranged according to their origins. The exterior and interior appearance of the building is arranged effectively in such a way that the members and passages are suitably located, just as the exterior and interior parts and members are correct for the body of man.[14]

The conditions are here for the development of a double analogy and for possible exchanges and combinations in the body considered as interior and/or exterior. In the most common and apparent analogical relationship between the body of man and architecture, we are faced with the exterior. In bringing about the interior, another set of metaphors will be possible, particularly those that allow for the permutation of the genders. To be able to elaborate on the question of the interior of man, Filarete does not stop at the formal analogy; his symbolic operations lead him to develop his most extraordinary metaphor, that of the building as living man:

> [When they are] measured, partitioned and placed as best you can, think about my statements and understand them clearly. I will [then] show you [that] the building is truly a living man. You will see it must eat in order to live, exactly as it is with man. It sickens or dies or sometimes is cured of its sickness by a good doctor.[15] . . . In the first book you have seen, as I have demonstrated to you, the origins of the building and its origins in my opinion, how it is proportioned to the human body of man, how it needs to be nourished and governed and through lack it sickens and dies like man.[16]

In this manner he slowly and steadily builds up a symbolic argument that unfolds from the building created as a formal analogue of the male body, from which even the orders are derived, to the building as a living body. If the building is a living man, the next necessary step in the argument is its conception and birth. It is at this critical point that another body will be incorporated: that of the architect himself.

> You perhaps could say, you have told me that the building is similar to man. Therefore, if this is so it needs to be conceived and then born. As [it is] with man himself, so [it is] with the Building. First it is conceived, using a simile such as you can understand, and then it is born. The mother delivers her child at the term of nine months or sometimes seven; by care and in good order she makes him grow. [17]

If the building is a living man, someone has to give birth to it. The figure of the architect becomes feminized in the act of procreation:

> The building is conceived in this manner. Since no one can conceive himself without a woman, by another simile, the building cannot be conceived by one man alone. As it cannot be done without woman, so he who wishes to build needs an architect. He conceives it with him and then the architect carries it. When the architect has given birth he becomes the mother of the building. Before the architect gives birth, he should dream about his conception, think about it, and turn it over in his mind in many ways for seven to nine months, just as a woman carries her child in her body for seven or nine months. He should also make various drawings of this conception that he has made with the patron, according to his own desires. As the woman can do nothing without the man, so the architect is the mother to carry this conception. When he has pondered and considered and thought [about it] in many ways, he ought to choose [according to his own desires], what seems most suitable and most beautiful to him according to the terms of the patron. When this birth is accomplished, that is when he has made, in wood, a small relief-design of its final form, measured and proportioned to the finished building, then he shows it to the father. [18]

Filarete takes this transsexual operation to its extreme by transforming the architect into a woman (or better, mother). He proceeds to state that, just like a mother, the architect also has to be a nurse, and 'with love and diligence' he will help the building grow to its completion. And just as a mother who loves her sons and with the help of the father tries to make them good and beautiful, the architect should make his buildings good and beautiful.

> As I have compared the architect to the mother, he also needs to be nurse. He is both mother and nurse. As the mother is full of love for her son, so he will rear it with love and diligence, cause it to grow, and bring it to completion if it is possible; if it is not, he will leave it ordered. [19]

Filarete will take this argument all the way in order to cover the various aspects involved in the building:

> A good mother loves her son and with the aid of the father strives to make him good and beautiful, and with a good master to make him valiant and praiseworthy. So the good architect should strive to make his buildings good and beautiful. [20]

Woman is excluded (repressed) in a first move by making architecture an image of man as an analogue to man's body and, as we have seen, to the point of making it a living organism. Woman is then replaced – her place usurped by man who as the architect has the female attributes necessary for the conception and reproduction – in an extraordinary operation that I call here architectural trans-sexuality, for which the repression of woman is essential.

Filarete's texts are greatly complemented by those of Franscesco Di Giorgio Martini. In his *Trattati: Architettura Civile e Militare* and *Architettura Ingegneria e Arte Militare*, Di Giorgio uses similar analogies between the human body and architecture, but in this case the analogy is proposed at the scale of the city.

> One should shape the city, fortress, and castle in the form of a human body, that the head and the attached members have a proportioned correspondence and that the head be the rocca, the arms its recessed walls, which, circling around, link the rest of the whole body, the vast city. . . . And thus it should be considered that just as the body has all its members and parts in perfect measurements and proportions, in the composition of temples, cities, fortresses, and castles the same principles should be observed.[21]

This argument is developed further by Di Giorgio in a more specific way, so that this ideology can be better translated into specific formal systems:

> Cities have the reasons, measurements, and form of the human body; I am going to describe precisely their perimeters and partitions. First, the human body stretched on the ground should be considered. Placing a string at the navel, the other end will create a circular form. This design will be squared and angles placed in similar fashion. . . . thus it should be considered just as the body has all the parts and members in perfect measurement and circumference, the center in the cities and other buildings should be observed. . . . The palms and the feet would constitute other temples and squares. And as the eyes, ears, nose and mouth, the veins, intestines, and other internal parts and members are organized inside and outside the body according to its needs, in the same way this should be observed in cities, as we shall show in some focus.[22]

The reading and reuse of Vitruvius takes a new dimension in Francesco Di Giorgio, for it is not only part of an analogical discourse between body (male) and the city, it is at the same time central in a representational discourse where the roles and places of male and female body in relation to architecture are swiftly exchanged. It is in shifting from the external appearance to the internal functions and order of the body that we will be faced once more with a transsexual operation:

> And so as it has been said that all the internal parts [of the human body] are organized and divided for its government and subsistence, in the same way that inside and outside parts of the body are necessary; it is that each member of the city should be distributed to serve its subsistence, harmony, and government.[23]
>
> I therefore say that first of all the main square [piazza] should be placed in the middle and the center of that city or as close as possible, just as the navel is to man's body; convenience should go second to this. The reason for this similitude could be the following; just as it is through his navel that human nature gets nutrition and perfection in its beginnings, in the same way by this common place the other particular places are served.[24]

This can only be an analogy after some operations of substitution are performed. In relation to the umbilical cord (the tie to the mother, the woman), Di Giorgio says, 'like the navel is to a man's body.' However, the relationship of the man's body to the umbilical cord is one of dependence. It is not he who is providing nourishment: rather, it is he who is being nourished by the mother at the beginning of life. Thus for the analogy to work for the city, the female body should be taken as the symbolic reference; instead the male body occupies its place. The female body is replaced by the male body, and man's navel is transformed into the city's 'womb.' Man's body is functionally transformed, feminized, in the production of this architectural analogy.

Although the sexual organs are never mentioned, they have an analogical presence in some of Di Giorgio's designs for cities, where the male sexual organ occupies the place and parts previously analogically assigned to the various parts of the body. That which has been taken must be negated; it is the denial that goes with repression.

I propose that there are three instances in this play of substitutions:

- The male body is projected, represented, and inscribed in the design of buildings and cities and in the texts that establish their ideology. The female body is suppressed or excluded.
- The architect himself is presented as a woman in relation to the reproductive creative functions, operating as a 'literal' sexual replacement.
- The male body becomes female body in its functions of giving nourishment – that is, life – to the city; man's navel becomes woman's womb.

It is remarkable that the replacement of the female body by the male body always occurs in relation to the maternal function, reproduction. It has been said that we live in a civilization in which the consecrated-religious or secular representation of femininity is subsumed by the maternal.[25] In this perspective, the whole operation appears to be a veiled representation of the myth of Mary.

In Filarete, the architect, a man, gives birth like a woman. In Di Giorgio, the center of the city, based on the configuration of man's body, gives subsistence through the umbilical cord from the womb, like a woman's body, to the rest of the city. In one case men's fantasies of conception and reproduction are placed in the figure of the architect, in the other they are set in the principles organizing the formal configuration of the city. Woman is thus suppressed, repressed, and replaced.

Suppressed, in the analogical relation between body and architecture. It is man's body – that is, according to the classic texts, the natural and perfectly proportioned body – from which architectural principles and measurements derive.

Repressed, in the model of the city. Woman's unique quality, that of motherhood, is projected onto the male body. Thus woman is not only suppressed, but indeed her whole sexual body is repressed.

Replaced, by the figure of the architect. The male, through what I have called before a transsexual operation, has usurped the female's reproductive qualities in the desire to fulfill the myth of creation.

It is motherhood that is taken more than woman, but motherhood has always been confused with womanhood as one and the same: the representation of femininity is subsumed by the maternal.[26]

In the art of the Renaissance, Mary, Queen of the Heavens and Mother of the Church, is an ever-present figure. Fantasies of conception by men could also be found in the texts by other men, including St Augustine. It is within the context of Christianism that the treatises of Alberti, Di Giorgio Martini, and Filarete were developed. The power of this religious ideology was evidenced in the mode of representation of religion and its concomitant myths. A most powerful one was that of the Virgin Mary. The nature of the mother/son relationship between Mary and Christ and the belief in immaculate conception leads toward the possibility of pregnancy without sex: woman, rather than being penetrated by a male, conceives with a nonperson, the spirit.[27] This conception without sex (sin) is the negation of sex as an essential part in the reproductive process, and ultimately, in the birth of Christ.

This religious ideology was all-encompassing. In a move of perfect ideological representation in a particular subregion of ideology, that of architecture, the architect can give birth to buildings or cities by usurping the female body, and just like Mary he can conceive without sex, only through spirit. Man is thus placed at the center of creation.

The treatises of architecture mentioned develop a system of rules elaborating an ideology that allows for the transformations in philosophy, Christianism, and the structure of power of the church to filter through the subregion of architecture.[28]

Woman (mother/Mary) is necessary as an imposing image within the system: woman outside that system, if not suppressed, had to be burned. Mary on one hand, heretics and witches on the other (those who pointed out the system of repressions and the possibility of a certain demystification). Men's mechanism of the assumption of the maternal role, through Christianism, may also be a mechanism of masculine sublimation.[29]

SCENE II: THE TEXT OF THE CITY

The Return of the Repressed: Architecture from Without

The system of architecture from within is characterized by an idealistic logic that can assume neither contradiction nor negation and therefore is based upon the suppression of either one of two opposite terms. This is best represented by the consistent repression of woman. Woman is excluded; she does not fit in the symbolic order. She is offside, in the cracks of symbolic systems; she has been called a witch, a hysteric, an outsider.[30]

It is in that outside that she stands. It is from that outside that she can project better than anyone the critical look. Woman can place herself from without the system of architecture by accepting heterogeneity and thus the positive inclusion of the negated, woman, the formerly repressed. In the ideological realm of architecture this implies a negation of the 'system of architecture' through a critical work, and the inclusion of the denied, the excluded, the hidden, the repressed.

This discourse from without incorporates heterogeneous matter, includes negation, and is psychoanalytical and historical. Woman, representing both heterogeneity of matter through her body and historical negation of her gender, is in the perfect position to develop such a discourse. Woman, a discourse of heterogeneity, 'represents the negative in the homogeneity of the community.'[31]

Taking a place from without the system is not only to include what has been negated, or excluded, or to surface the repressed; a more complex process takes place. The classic architectural project of the city (as a body) is a reflection in the mirror of a totally formed, closed, and unitary system. We are dealing now with the modern city instead, with a representation of a fragmented body.[32] The architect cannot recognize himself or his system of rules in the mirror of the city as did Di Giorgio or Filarete. The body as a metaphor of the fragmented architectural body, which cannot be recomposed within the system of architectural rules, will be that referential outside.

It is the explosion, the fragmented unconscious, where the 'architectural body' does not reflect the body of the subject, as it did in the Renaissance, but reflects instead the perception of the fragmented body as the built text, a set of fragments of languages and texts, the city. The body cannot be reconstructed, the subject – architect/man – does not recognize himself in architecture as an entity in front of the mirror. The system has been broken; architecture cannot be recognized again as a whole.

We will take that built social unconscious of architecture, the city, a text, for it is not the result of the creation of a subject/product of a logocentric, anthropomorphic system. There is no subject there. Here are only fragments of text and languages to be read, and in this reading they traverse the subject, in the position of reader-writer.

The Street: Streetwalkers

The city presents itself as a fragmentary text escaping the order of things and of language, a text to be 'exploded,' taken in pieces, in fragments, to be further decomposed in so many possible texts, open in a metonymy of desire.

To design is not to reclose but to affect the openings and be affected by them, to play an intersection between the two subjects, that of the reader and that of the writer, by an operation of shifting through the 'I.' The subject gets caught in the text and becomes part of the text.

This subject, woman, writes as she reads where the repression has failed, where the system is fragmented, and where she does not want to be reconstructed by finding in it the reflection of an enclosed homogeneous unitary system. She reads there and activates the absence of the repression/replacement of her body.

The street is the scene of her writing, with her body following the role that she is given in the evaluation of her body as merchandise. The street is the scene of architectural writing. The private realm is the scene of the institutions, where woman and her body have an assigned place: the house.

Wife in the kitchen. Whore in the street.

Rather than worshipping the monuments, we take the streets, we 'play house,' taking a critical view of the family as a hierarchical system and of the rules of architecture that go with it.

The city is the social scene where woman can publicly express her struggle. She was/is not accepted in the institutions of power, she is dispossessed (of her body) and is with the dispossessed. The public place is a no-man's-land ready to be appropriated. The scene of the city, of the street, of the public place, is that of the dispossessed; it is there where she is 'at home.'

A place outside the accepted institutions is taken and assumed through various texts and readings of an open and heterogeneous quality.

Reading from Without

I think of these projects. I have a vision, a realist image of unreal events. It flows without knowing like a mystic pad; the city like an unconscious of architecture unveils itself, three modes of time in three analogues of experience: permanence, succession, simultaneity.

A register of urban inscription, these three together – now I am reading, now I am writing – the boundaries are not clear. I can read the words, the unsaid, the hidden, there where no man wants to read, where there are no monuments to speak of an established and unitary system of architecture.

Like an optical illusion the grid becomes an object, then the fabric, then the object again. The apparent contradiction and undialectical opposition between object and fabric at the base of this process develops a text from the inclusions and juxtaposition of these opposite terms.

All of a sudden an erasure, the erasure necessary to remark, reinstates the obvious not seen, the *tabula rasa* that could become fabric, the object that would rather be a public place.

The 'refoulés' (repressed) of architecture, the public, the negation, all become the material of my fictional configuration. The (project) marks I make are organized through a contradiction – a negation through an affirmation. Negate the city to affirm the city. It is the affirmation of the erasure of the city in order to reinstate its trace. The critical reading is taking from the subject: I am spoken through the city, through architecture, and the city is read through me.

NOTES

This text originated in the fall of 1971 as a proposal for an article, 'Architecture from Without: Matter, Logic, and Sex,' to be published in an architectural journal. Although my interest was very strong at that time, I did not have the opportunity to develop it until 1986–87.

Although the original abstract was only four pages long, it contained all of the elements (arguments) necessary to develop this article. During the process of this development I realized that the first part, 'Architecture from Within,' could be expanded, whereas the second part, 'Architecture from Without,' could not be expanded in the same manner. The reason for this is that the latter posits a premise for critical work and a way of approaching it. I believe that this critical approach to architecture is present in my work produced throughout the years in practice, theory, criticism, and teaching.

I want to thank Judy O'Buck Gordon for her incentive and her persistent interest in the development of this essay.

1 Catherine Clément, 'La Coupable,' in *La Jeune Née* (Paris: Union Général d'Editions, 1975), p. 6.

2 Even the Modulor by Le Corbusier is entirely based on a male body.

3 Jacques Derrida, 'Freud et la scène de l'écriture,' in *L'écriture et la Différence* (Paris: Editions du Seuil, 1967).

4 Julia Kristeva, 'Stabat Mater,' in *Histoires d'amour* (Paris: Editions de Noël, 1983).

5 Clément, 'La Coupable,' p. 7.

6 Ibid.

7 Ibid., pp. 7–8, and Kristeva, 'Stabat Mater.'

8 François Choay, 'La ville et le domaine bâti comme corps,' in *Nouvelle Revue de Psychanalyse No. 9* (Paris: Editions Gallimard, 1974).

9 See D. Agrest, 'Design versus Non-Design,' *Architecture from Without: Theoretical Framings for a Critical Practice* (Cambridge, Mass.: MIT Press, 1993).

10 Vitruvius, *The Ten Books of Architecture*, trans. Morris Hicky Morgan (New York: Dover, 1960). Originally published by Harvard University Press, 1914.

11 Ibid.

12 Leon Battista Alberti, *Ten Books on Architecture* (1485). Reprint from the Leoni Edition of 1755, with the addition of the 'Life' from the 1734 edition. Ed. Joseph Rykwert (London: Alex Tiranti,1965), p. 13.

13 Ibid., p. 195.

14 'You have seen briefly the measures, understood their names and sources, their qualities and forms. I told you they were called by their Greek names, Doric, Ionic and Corinthian. The Doric I told you is the one of major quality; the Corinthian is in the middle, the Ionic is the smallest for the reasons alleged by the architect Vitruvius in his book, [where] he shows how they were in the times of the emperor Octavian. In these modes the Doric, Ionic and Corinthian correspond in measure to the form or, better, to the quality of the form to which they are proportioned. As the building is derived from man, his measures, qualities, form and proportions, so the column also derived from the nude man and fluted from that well-dressed young woman, as we have said. Both are derived from the form of man. Since this is so, they take their qualities, form and measure from man. The qualities, or better Ionic, Doric and Corinthian, are three, that is large, medium and small forms. They should be formed, proportioned and measured according to their quality. Since man is the measure of all, the column should be measured and proportioned to his form.' Filarete, *Treatise on Architecture* (1461–63). Translated and with an introduction and notes by John R. Spencer (New Haven: Yale University Press, 1965), p. 12.

15 Ibid.

16 Ibid., p. 15.

17 Ibid.

18 Ibid., pp. 15–16.
19 Ibid., p. 16.
20 Ibid.
21 Francesco Di Giorgio Martini, *Trattati: di Architettura Civile e Militare* and *Architettura Ingegneria e Arte Militare (1470–1492)*, compiled and edited by Corrado Maltese, transcribed by Livia Maltese Degrassi (Milan: Edizioni II Polifilo, 1967), p. 4.
22 Ibid., p. 20.
23 Ibid., p. 21.
24 Ibid., p. 363.
25 Kristeva, 'Stabat Mater.'
26 Ibid.
27 Ibid.
28 This question of the relationship between Christianism, the church, and humanism is an entire subject on its own and should be treated at length outside the context of this chapter.
29 Kristeva, 'Stabat Mater.'
30 Clément, 'La Coupable,' pp. 7–8.
31 Julia Kristeva, 'Matière, Sens, Dialectique,' in *Tel Quel 44* (Paris: Editions du Seuil, 1971).
32 Jean Jacques Lacan, 'Le stade du miroir comme formateur de la fonction du Je,' in *Ecrits I* (Paris: Editions du Seuil, 1966).

40 Jennifer Bloomer

'Big Jugs'[1]

from Arthur Kroker and Marilouise Kroker (eds) *The Hysterical Male: New Feminist Theory* (1991)

I have given this paper two parts, which we might call theoretical and practical (a construction), for the benefit of those who think that architects are incapable of thinking about what they do and even less capable of talking about it; and for those who believe that nobody needs to talk about architecture, one should just DO it. If you fall into one of these categories, you may choose to read only the appropriate part. Good luck in deciding which one is which.

PART ONE

Western architecture is, by its very nature, a phallocentric discourse: containing, ordering, and representing through firmness, commodity, and beauty; consisting of orders, entablature, and architrave; base, shaft, and capital; nave, choir, and apse; father, son and spirit, world without end. Amen.[2]

In the Garden of Eden there was no architecture. The necessity for architecture arose with the ordination of sin and shame, with dirty bodies. The fig leaf was a natural first impulse toward architecture, accustomed as it was to shading its vulvate fruit, its trunk and roots a complex woven construction of undulating forms. Was it the fig tree that was hacked up to build the primitive hut (that precursor of classical architecture)?

The primitive hut and all its begettings constitute a house of many mansions, a firm, commodious, and beautiful erection. The primitive hut is the house of my fathers. But there is the beginning of an intrusive presence in this house:

> She transforms, she acts: the old culture will soon be the new. She is mixed up in dirty things; she has no cleanliness phobia – the proper housecleaning attacks that hysterics sometimes suffer. She handles filth, manipulates wastes, buries placentas, and burns the cauls of new born babies for luck. She makes partial objects useful, puts them back in circulation – properly. *En voilà du propre!* What a fine mess![3]

Julia Kristeva has written:

> As capitalist society is being economically and politically choked to death, discourse is wearing thin and heading for collapse at a more rapid rate than ever before. Philosophical finds, various modes of 'teaching', scientific or aesthetic formalisms follow one upon another, compete, and disappear without leaving either a convinced audience or noteworthy disciples. Didacticism, rhetoric, dogmatism of any kind, in any 'field' whatsoever, no longer command attention. They have survived, and perhaps will continue to survive, in modified form, throughout Academia. Only one language grows more and more contemporary: the equivalent, beyond a span of thirty years, of the language of *Finnegans Wake*.[4]

Broadcast throughout the text of *Finnegans Wake* are thousands of seedy little t's, those bits of letter written, devoured, excreted, and pecked by the hen. They are little micturition sounds, tiny trabeation signs. To make those posts on beams properly classical, let us add the prescribed third part: the T becomes an I. The I, the ego, the I beam, the gaze, the image fixer, the instrument of fetish. When I was a child in church, I was told that the great golden 'I' embroidered on the altar cloth stood for 'INRI'. I wondered why the church didn't spell its Henry with an H. Hen *ri* – the hen laughs. Ha ha ha ha – the sound of H is pure expiration: laughter, sighing, and the way we breathe when we are giving birth to our children. BODY LANGUAGE. The sound of H is more than mere pronunciation of three marks on a page – two parallels, one bridge. It is a mark itself of invisible flows.

Much as David Byrne perhaps 'eggoarchicistically' burns down the house, James Joyce has enjoisted an other construction:

> The boxes, if I may break the subject gently, are worth about fourpence pourbox but I am inventing a more patent process, foolproof and pryperfect (I should like to ask that Shedlock Homes person who is out for removing the roofs of our criminal classics by what *deductio ad domunum* he hopes *de tacto* to detect anything unless he happens of himself, *movibile tectu*, to have a slade off) after which they can be reduced to a fragment of their true crust by even the youngest of Margees if she will take plase to be seated and smile if I please.[5]

Here is the hatchery. Let Us Deconstruct: Margee is the marginal one, taking her place, seated and smiling, faking, being woman as constituted by the symbolic order. *Movibile tectu*: homophonous to *horribile dictu* (horrible to tell, unspeakable). This is a passage from Virgil – repeated throughout the *Aeneid* much as the hen's letter is scattered throughout the text of *Finnegans Wake*. And *movibile tectu* is also moving touch: the moving finger writes, and, having writ, moves on. Architectural references abound: boxes, Shed, Lock (as in locked out of the house), Homes, roofs, classics, domunum, slade.

The hatchery is an apparatus of overlay of architecture, writing, and the body. The hatchery is a kind of architectural anti-type, i.e., it refers to a kind of built structure (the chicken house), but the structure to which it refers does not belong to the domain of the architect. It is a house, but not architecture, and its relationship to the primitive hut is mediated to the point of extreme tentativeness, primarily because the form of the hatchery is irrelevant. The hatchery is not bound or bounded by theory, but is a para-theoretical device. The hatchery is that which is not represented when the architecture-making is done. The hatchery is Work in Progress, a critical instrument, intrusive and elucidating. It refers to the place of the hatching of chickens from eggs, the place of the life flow, a dirty (soiled) cacaphonous place full of litter, the residue of life (eggshells, excrement, cast-off feathers, uneaten food). In this sense, it is a kind of alchemical vessel, a container of ingredients for the Philosopher's Stone (*un vaisseau de pierre*). Its floor is inscribed with the imprints of chicken feet (hatchings and cross-hatchings).

The hatchery is a writing machine. The biddies, the *chicks*, scratch marks in the dirt. These hieroglyphs constitute an historical document, a mapping and a marking of movement. This act of hatching resembles and belongs to the acts of etching, drawing, and writing. It is the act of the hatching of lines and the hatching of plots.

The body is, in a sense, a multiply-constituted hatchery, a messy assemblage of flows – blood, organic matter, libidinal, synaptic, psychic. The metaphor for the throat – the primary entrance portal – is the hatch, as in 'down the hatch.' This hatch is a door or passage. We describe our bodies and our constructions in terms of each other, with words as passages between one and the other. Writes of passage, hatcheries all.

Alice Jardine:

> [W]hat fiction has always done – the incorporation and rejection of that space [the space of schizophrenia, the libidinal economy, that which has begun to threaten authorship, that which is connoted as feminine – see Jardine, p. 88] as grounds for figurability – new theoretical discourses, with rapidly increasing frequency, have also been doing. Seeing themselves as no longer isolated in a system of loans and debts to former master truths, these new discourses in formation have foregrounded a *physis*, a space no longer passive but both active and passive, undulating, folded over upon itself, permeable: the self-contained space of eroticism.[6]

The hatchery is a bridge between the sacred and the voluptuous, between *physis* and *techne*.

In Frank Baum's *The Wizard of Oz*, Dorothy's house becomes disconnected at the point of the hatch (trap-door to the cellar underneath) and floats and rises gently in the center of the cyclone. When the house falls, it kills the wicked witch and Dorothy is construed as a sorceress in a country that is not civilized, and therefore retains a population of sorceresses, witches, and wizards.

Dorothy falls and Alice falls, but into other worlds – worlds of magic and strangeness. Adam, Lucifer, Humpty Dumpty, and Icarus fell to less desirable ends. The boys attempt to rise to power and fail, lose, fall from grace. The girls drop out, fall down the hatch, use the exits, find the dreamworld of condensation and displacement, of strangeness, of *délire*.[7] The position to take is perched at the rim of the hole, at the moment of the closing of the trap door, ready to fall, not to fall from, but INTO. The 'fall from' is hierarchical and you can hurt yourself. The 'fall into' is labyrinthine, dreamy, a dancing fall, a delirious fall.

'Her rising: is not erection. But diffusion. Not the shaft. The Vessel.'[8] The Hatchery is both vessel and erection (the topology of erection is vesicular flow, after all), but it is neither of these things in the formal sense. The form must remain undefined to escape co-optation. (The aestheticization of the political is a patriarchal sleight of hand power play against which Walter Benjamin warned us long ago.) We can, however, emblematize it with its initial letter. The H is an I in which the shaft has been allowed to rest horizontal for a moment, forming a vessel, a container, a bridge, a conduit.

The Hatchery might be, but cannot be, classified into categories. Political, unauthorized and unauthored, it is about acts, not images; transitory, it is move-ment, but is not *a* movement. Hacking at the edges of the architecture/state appar-atus, it is all these categories. It is political and collective and moving.

Barnacles, engulfings, underminings, intrusions: Minor Architecture.[9] Collec-tive, anonymous, authorless, scratched on the city and the landscape, they are hatched not birthed. (They are illegitimate – without father.) Bastard Constructions. In matriarchal societies, there is no concept of legitimacy. One is legitimate by virtue of existence. No-one knows a single father; all males are the nurturing fathers of all children. Children are born of the mother; they are legitimate by virtue of having made the passage from inside to out.

'Wee peeps'[10] appear locally upon the landscape of The Gaze. Wee peeps: we peeks, small chickens (chicks), brief glances, a hint of impropriety – micturition in public. Tattoos upon the symbolic order. They are the 'lens' that 'we need the loan of . . . to see as much as the hen saw.'[11] Like minor literature, or the little girls on Tintorelli's stair in *The Trial*, or the twenty-eight little girl shadows of Isabelle, or the rainbow girls in *Finnegans Wake*. Tattoos. T-t-t's.

'This battering babel allower the door and sideposts':[12] The hatchery, the place of babes and babble, both allows and lowers the supporting structure of the entrance to the House.

A biddy architecture (a surd and absurd[13] architecture): Around midnight, Atlanta, Georgia. Moving along Techwood Drive, the access road running parallel to Interstate 75-85, and accessing the House of Ted Turner. On the right: plantation image, tasteful, white sign with Chippendale frame – 'The Turner Broadcasting System.' On the left: parallax view of trees silhuetted against the glow of the here submerged interstate highway and, beyond, the city lights. Glimpsed among the trees: small constructions of sticks and draped membranes through which the lights osmose – so strange that you might be hallucinating. Against the membranes, blocking the glow with jarringly recognizable blackness: human figures here and there, existing for the moment between the lines.

PART TWO: JUGS

In Florida, as perhaps in other places, we are situated upon a most peculiar landscape. We stand upon a ground not of rock resting upon rock, but of the merest slice of solidity barely breaking the surface of the surrounding sea. Furthermore, the ground beneath our feet is not reliable, not the solid architecture of stone piled upon stone, carrying its loading in the proper compressive fashion, that we like our ground to be. It is in fact an architecture of holes and crypts, filling and emptying with fluids, an architecture delineated by suction and secretion, of solids, fluids, and gases, in such a complex and everchanging configuration that to pin it down with a word seems illogical. But it *is* named by a word: Alachua,[14] a word the previous residents of this place chose. Alachua: a vessel or jug. Alachua, a land of filling and emptying, of holes and crypts, a place where the superimposition of 'order' is ridiculous. A place where entire buildings are swallowed up, disappear into the surface of the ground, leaving behind only pock marks, that will eventually fill with fluid. The consideration of such an architecture is not about imbuing a mundane thing with pumped-up significance, nor about projecting an image of the place. It is about how it works. Not about what it means or what it looks like, but what it does. The following construction is a mapping of this territory. It is the landscape of Edgar Poe, a territory of significant voids.[15]

This construction consists of a collision of three texts: an essay by Martin Heidegger titled 'The Thing'; a character from Angela Carter's *Nights at the Circus*, Fanny Four-Eyes, who sports eyes on her breasts where nipples properly should be; and a third, the text of architecture, which in its over-Booked and boxed-in state, is pocked with more booby traps than those of us who practice it would like to think. It is possible that there is a fourth text, an oscillating text, quite 'rudely forc'd.'[16]

In a happenstance that gives me more pleasure than I can say, this text intersects with the conclusion of Catherine Ingraham's review, called 'Milking Deconstruction, or Cow Was the Show?',[17] of the 1988 Deconstructivism Show at the Museum of Modern Art. Here, Ingraham constructs a situation in which the contemporary architectural phenomenon of 'Deconstructivism' is allegorized in the contemporary corporate agricultural phenomenon of the 'necessity' to re-engineer the structure of the new hormone-injected, super milk-giving cows in order to support their mammoth udders.

> The idea of the cow as a thing – like the cow-thing [a jug] we fill with milk and set on our dinner table – is what makes the crude tampering with its bone structure possible. . . . Equally, the idea of deconstruction as a thing that can be built results in the crude surgeries of deconstructivism. It will ultimately be the shift in the idea of architectural structure – its dematerialization – that will interfere most substantially with the material surfaces of architecture, not so many jugs and pitchers cast in the shape of something called deconstructivism.[18]

Jugs and things are the objects of Heidegger's essay. If you will allow, I will recast this large and intricate vessel into a state that will accommodate an apprehension of a certain subtext. Despite the closure of space and time in the modern world, there is no nearness. We perceive that things are near to us, '[b]ut what is a thing?'[19] 'A jug is a thing. What is the jug? We say: a vessel, something of the kind that holds something else within it.'[20] 'As a vessel the jug stands on its own as self-supporting.'[21] When we put it into our field of perception either through immediacy or representation, it becomes an object, yet it remains a vessel. The jug as a thing holds something. It is a container that must be made. When we understand it as a constructed vessel, we apprehend it as a thing, not as an object. We can never learn how the jug is by looking at its outward appearance; '[t]he vessel's thingness does not lie at all in the material of which it consists, but in the void that holds.'[22] 'Only a vessel . . . can empty itself.'[23] 'How does the jug's void hold? It holds by taking what is poured in. It holds by keeping and retaining what it took in. The void holds in a twofold manner: taking and keeping. The word "hold" is therefore ambiguous.'[24] 'To pour from the jug is to give.'[25] 'But the gift of the outpouring is what makes a jug a jug.'[26] Even the empty jug suggests the gift by a 'nonadmission' of which 'a scythe . . . or a hammer is incapable.'[27] The thing is 'nestling, malleable, pliant, compliant. . . .'[28] The thing is 'modestly compliant.'[29] 'Inconspicuously compliant is the thing.'[30] 'Nestling' is the thing.

The logo of the Nestlé Corporation – known for its milk-like products – depicts a perfectly round nest – a domestic vessel – resting on a branch from which three leaves grow in trinitary symmetry. Nestled in the nest are two small birds with straining bodies and eager beaks. Perched on the rim is a large mother bird in the position of offering something to her young. But, look closely at this picture: the mother holds nothing in her beak. The logo is a hieroglyph that gives up a secret. The logo is a figuration of the corporation's activities in third world countries, where a small supply of infant formula, which carries with it the image of first world magic, is given 'free' to women who have just given birth. Inconspicuously – not readily noticeable, especially by 'eyes which do not see'[31] – the Nestlé Corporation makes empty vessels. The dry, petrified udder sells more man-made milk. This gift, mixed with promise and tainted water, is an outpouring of forced consumption, sickness, and death. The women are perhaps comforted by the 'gift' of breasts imbued with first-world aura: breasts which have not been sucked are privileged as objects. They are firm and erect; they stick out.

TWO WAYS OF LOOKING AT A JUG

Aesthetic: 'Stick 'em out just a little more. Yeah, now pull your tummy in all the way and let it out just a tad.' Lifted and separated from the wall, the things appear twice their actual size and full and round as if to bursting. 'Yeah. Now really push 'em up, hold your breath, keep your chin down and give me the look. Give it to me, baby, give it to me, yeah, yeah. Terrific!' Click!

Scientific: 'Now, you've got to get the whole thing up on the plate. It'll feel a little cold, but it'll be over in a minute.' The glass plate descends, pressing down, pressing, pressing the thing out to a horrifying, unrecognizable state: thin and flat, a broad, hideous slice of solidity criss-crossed with shocking blue lines. 'Yes, that's it. Now hold your breath. Good!' Click!

'"Well now that's done: and I'm glad it's over."'[32]

What is the secret that the firm, erect, sticking out thing holds? Unused, it is a frontier, where no man has gone before. What is the secret that lies beneath the power of this image, this object? What most desired and most feared thing is masked behind the desire to be the first, or the biggest? What does (M)other lack?

What is the secret that 'oozes from the box?' Deleuze and Guattari:

> The secret must sneak, insert, or introduce itself into the arena of public forms; it must pressure them and prod known subjects into action. . . . [S]omething must ooze from the box, something will be perceived through the box or in the half-opened box.[33]

Corporate architecture is a certain return of the repressed.

In Thomas Pynchon's novel V., a novel whose entire pages are devoted to a search for a figure which seems to be a woman, perhaps the mother of the protagonist, who exists only in traces and hints, V herself is masked by a seemingly infinite constellation of guises, forming the fetish construction that is the novel itself. Through the text there walks a figure known as the Bad Priest. Walks until, at a certain point of intersection, he falls down and falls apart, revealing himself to be a beautiful young woman who is in turn revealed, by the children and the imagination of the narrator who dismantle her body, as a machine assemblage of objects: glittering stones and precious metals, clocks, balloons, and lovely silks. The Bad Priest is a fetish construction mirroring the novel. As Alice Jardine has pointed out, it is 'an assemblage of the dead objects that have helped hold together the narrative thus far.'[34] The Bad Priest and V are reconstituted objects of desire, constructions of what is most desired and most feared. They are a rewriting of the urge to the aesthetic. (You will recall that Aesthetics begins with the assemblage of the most beautiful, most perfect – and malleable, modestly compliant – woman by cutting the most desirable parts off many women and gathering them to make one woman-thing.) Like Pandora, whose box was not a box, but a jar, or jug. When the Bad Priest falls, the children cry, 'It's a lady,' and then: 'She comes apart.'[35] Into '[a] heap of broken images.'[36]

'It's a Lady.' Consider the Statue of Liberty, a fetish construction: she is a thing placed on a pedestal – to 'lift and separate,' to put on display. She is a spectacle. She is the hyper-reification of Luce Irigaray's gold-plated (in this case, copper-clad) woman: woman's body covered with commodities (make-up, fashion, capital, gold).

> The cosmetics, the disguises of all kinds that women cover themselves with are intended to deceive, to promise more value than can be delivered. . . . Her body transformed into gold to satisfy his autoerotic, scopophiliac, and possessive instincts.[37]

This image of 'Liberty for All' contains a secret, a purloined letter ingeniously hidden because it is there, in plain sight, a secret that calls into question the concepts of 'Liberty' and 'All.' Beneath the surface of this woman's skin, beneath the implants which pump up the image, lies a 'creeping disaster,' [Irigaray] a crabby invasion, a crabgrass, a rhizome. The Statue of Liberty is an allegory of desire and fear. It is a container, 'a place where something is about to happen.'[38] It is structure and envelope, image and machine. A gift. A Lady. And she comes apart.

In the summer of 1987, a consortium of French institutions (including *L'Institut Français d'Architecture*) co-sponsored an international competition for the design of cultural artifacts commemorating the bicentenary of the French Revolution. The multidisciplinary and international intentions behind the competition were reinforced by the diversity of the jury, which ranged from the philosopher Jean Baudrillard to the structural engineer Peter Rice, and included writers, musicians, visual artists, and business people. The instructions for the production of the commemorative artifacts were vague, leaving site, event commemorated, media, and dimensions at the discretion of the authors. Attracted by the indeterminacy, two friends – Durham Crout, a former student presently teaching architecture at Clemson University and pursuing a PhD at the University of Pennsylvania, and Robert Segrest – and I decided to participate.

Our project began as a project of exchange. As citizens of the United States constructing a monument to the French Revolution, we began with the simple idea of returning the gesture of the gift given by the French to commemorate the American Revolution. This gift, the Statue of Liberty, immediately generated a series of correspondences to other concepts delineated by the idea of gift: woman as presentation (both in the sense of the allegorical figure of Liberty and in the sense of woman as spectacle, as object of the gaze), woman as currency (both in the sense of the medium of exchange and in the sense of a flow that must be controlled, woman as fetish construction to be bestowed upon the imagination). We were struck by the way in which several constructs of power coincided in this woman-thing: war, aesthetics, the monumental, the reification of the female, history, the symbolic. We chose to commemorate an event of the French Revolution that bore potential correspondences to this construction of constructs, an event described by Marilyn French in *Beyond Power*:

> When, on October 5 [1789], the market women discovered there was no bread in Paris,
> six thousand of them marched the twelve miles to Versailles to protest to the king
> personally. He promised to help them, and they marched triumphantly back to Paris with
> the royal family in tow.[39]

The itinerary that led to this choice is germane to an understanding of the project. Continuing along our line of the gift as generator, we selected nine sites on the body of woman/Liberty that are conventionally construed as (partial) objects of desire: eyes, lips, breasts, vulva, etc. These nine sites were made to correspond to nine sites of revolutionary points of intensity around the city of Paris through an operation involving sight lines, focal points, and the lens (a glassy instrument and the 'mechanical' apparatus of the objectifying gaze). We then made nine incisions upon the body of the Statue of Liberty, slicing through each of the nine sites to produce a generating section. The irony of the similarity of our operation to those of slasher films and pornography was not lost upon us. The commentary of our work upon the recent work of contemporary architects whose work is tethered to the 'aura' of mutilated and murdered women, we hope is not lost upon you. The nine sections were then to produce nine objects, to form a constellation of partial objects which, in their assemblage, would form a certain 'gift' to the French. As is the way with well-laid plans, for a host of reasons including both fatigue and the powerful correspondence of the section through the eye and the site at the Palace at Versailles upon which it fell, we diverged from our original intentions and chose to operate only upon the eye and the march of the six thousand market women upon Versailles. The eye of the woman bears with it, after all, the potential to return the gaze; to return not merely in a sense of the conventional female acquiescence in sexual discourse, but also to re-turn, to deflect the power of the male gaze through a re-turn of the repressed, through the exorbitance of the female gaze. There is then in the project something of a reversal of the mechanics of the fascinus, a phallus-shaped amulet for warding off the 'evil eye' of the fascinating woman. The evil eye, and to whom it belongs, is called into question.

It is the *unseen* in the body which is critical here. The sectioning of the statue is an act of incision and release. The incision marks the temporal and geographical point at which the image of the body gives way to the possibilities of the body. It becomes a gift of another kind, an insidious gift, with unseen agents hiding within, like the Trojan Horse. This hollow vessel, this monument, this gift to the state, holds within it the potential of undermining the state. In the Trojan Horse, the body masks the body politic. The Trojan Horse is a viral architecture: a sleek protein coat with invasive content.

The incision marking the initiation of generation is repeated as an incising inscription. A slash three hundred meters long and a meter square in section is made on the Palace grounds. This repetition is simultaneously a reflection (an other kind of repetition) of an already-there gash in the earth: the Grand Canal, a commanding axis of inscription terminating in a statue. Thus, that which marks the termination of the grand axis is the same (vessel, statue) as that which marks the initiation of our project. And again, this identity is marked in reverse, setting the project into interminable reflexivity: the western end of the trench stops abruptly at the base of an other statue: that of Louis Quatorze atop a, perhaps now suspicious, horse. The new incision is a reflection of the old; the radical project is a mimicry of the State project. Furthermore, it is a rational response to the existing topography: our trench is a physically inscribed reflection of that which is marked by the relationship of the incision of the Grand Canal and the vertical slicing plane of the west (mirrored) wall of the Hall of Mirrors. In other words, we have taken the image of what one would see if one could see through the mirror and projected it back into the world before the mirror, reversing the customary relationship of 'reality' and 'image' in the mirror. In this geography of the imagination,[40] the idea that the mirror is utterly contained within its grandiose vessel – the Palace – is simultaneously negligible and crucial.

The reflection works at another level as well. If one renders malleable the word for our gift, *un cadeau*, into a Franco-Italian hybrid of *ca d'eau*, there is here a house of water (a body), which parodies the wateriness, the flow, of the Grand Canal. A *ca d'eau* is a house of currency. The trench functions as a monumental *pissoir*, open to the public in a public place. But being pissed off, here, is a redundant gesture. Nestled (modestly and compliantly) in the floor of the trench are six thousand vessels, with pear-like shapes and copper skins. Each is lined with mirror tain and glass and each is full to bursting with body fluids. Their bodily secrets allow them to laugh away or write off the oppression of being pissed on. These reproducing cells (vessels, fluid-filled uteri) mirror a something disastrous going on beneath the surface of the court of history, of power. It is the injection into a Revolution of 'Feed Our Children.' An injection of what is more 'powerful than' (beyond) power. A giving suck, an other, although not *the* other, side of a suck taken. A gift.

Its borders incised with alchemical glyphs signifying moons and months and body fluids, and marked by criss-crossing sutures of iron rods, this slice of void barely breaking the surface tension of the surrounding sea gives up its secret, a secret marked, as things which must remain properly hidden often are, with an X. The X is an emblem of Heidegger's fourfold, in which 'each of the four mirrors in its own way the presence of the others.'[41] X is a generic substitute for a thing. The thing is 'nestling, malleable, pliant, compliant, nimble.' Heidegger suggests circularity (O), but there is an X hidden here, an unknown, a secret. Heidegger's thing folds the fourfold along a hinge, which he suggests is a mirroring. An X hinged is two Vs folded at the point of intersection, the place where the secret is both enfolded and released. X is the doubled perspective on two canals intersecting in a mirror. It is a vanishing point. To X is 'to delete, cancel, or obliterate with a series of x's.'[42] X marks the (blind) spot(s) of history. 'Cross your heart' – and hope to die and stick your finger in your eye. X is a cartoon convention marking 'lidless eyes'[43] blinded by a surprise or blow to the head. As Catherine Ingraham has pointed out, the criss-cross of heavy mascara marks 'eyes which do not see' – eyes which do not look beyond the look. X is a mark of non-identity, a non-identifying signature, like that of a person who is identified by the name of her father which, in a mirroring, is replaced by the name of her husband. Yet X is a chiasmus, signifying the alchemical androgyne – 'blind, throbbing between two lives. . . .'[44] X is the mark of Xantippe, who dumped a pot of piss on the head of her husband, Socrates. X is a kiss, both a 'patronising'[45] and a nurturing gesture. A puckering, a sucking, an undulating architecture of solids, liquids, and gases.

A reverse *fascinus*, warding off the evil eye represented by the eye of the 'one-eyed trouser snake' of Joyce, the Cyclopean eye of power invested in the Palace – the project is a defetishizing move, inviting the (male) body, refusing the power structure of the phallus that represses and corrupts the male body, and displaying the profound return of the repressed of the female body through an obscuring, a darkening, of the image, and a display of the generative – the jug is not a thing, but a magical machine – an interwoven system of apparatuses, a text.

> And Schreck would say: 'Look at him, Fanny.' So Fanny would take off her blindfold and give him a beaming smile.

Then Madame Schreck would say: 'I said, *look* at him, Fanny.' At which she'd pull up her shift.

For, where she should have had nipples, she had eyes.

Then Madame Schreck would say: 'Look at him properly, Fanny.' Then those two other eyes of hers would open.

They were a shepherd's blue, same as the eyes in her head; not big, but very bright.

I asked her once, what did she see with those mammillary eyes, and she says: 'Why, same as with the top ones but lower down.'[46]

NOTES

1 This is the expanded (or augmented) text of a lecture called 'Jugs' that I gave for the 'Body/Space/Machine' Symposium held at the University of Florida in March 1989. The expanded version, called 'Big Jugs,' was delivered as a lecture at Princeton University in October 1989. A substantial portion of the implant comes from a paper, 'Architecture, Writing, the Body,' delivered in the session 'Forecasting the Direction of Architectural Theory,' at the Annual Meeting of the Association of Collegiate Schools of Architecture in Miami 1987.

2 In the pages of an alumni newsletter from the University of Virginia's School of Architecture, there appeared recently a stinging critique of the current state of the grove of academe: that the students are engaged in producing 'flaccid classicism.' *Webster's Third* tells us that 'flaccid' suggests a lack of firmness and stiffness or vigor and force. So, we might deduce that the architectural projects being produced at Virginia are, to the alumnus' eye, ones in which the first Vitruvian requisite is missing. An architecture, then, of *commoditas* and *venustas*, but no *firmitas*. But is there any other reading of this clearly pejorative phrase?

3 Hélène Cixous and Catherine Clément, *The Newly Born Woman*, trans. Betsy Wing, (Manchester: Manchester University Press, 1986 [1975]), p. 167. The translator points out that the phrase '*En voilà du propre!*' (the English equivalent of which is 'What a fine mess!') is used in the text in places where that which is considered 'appropriate' is called into question.

4 Julia Kristeva, *Desire in Language: A Semiotic Approach to Art and Literature*, ed. Leon Roudiez (New York: Columbia University Press, 1980), p. 92.

5 James Joyce, *Finnegans Wake* (New York: Viking Press, 1965 [1939]), 165.30-166.02.

6 Alice Jardine, *Gynesis: Configurations of Women and Modernity* (Ithaca: Cornell University Press, 1985), p. 100.

7 See Jean-Jacques Lecercle, *Philosophy Through the Looking Glass: Language, Nonsense, Desire* (London: Hutchinson and Co., 1985). Lecercle locates *délire*: '*Délire*, then, is at the frontier between two languages, the embodiment of the contradiction between them. Abstract language is systematic; it transcends the individual speaker, separated from any physical or material origin, it is an instrument of control, mastered by a regulating subject. Material language, on the other hand, is

unsystematic, a series of noises, private to individual speakers, not meant to promote communication, and therefore self-contradictory, 'impossible' like all 'private languages.' . . . Language which has reverted to its origin in the human body, where the primary order reigns.' (pp. 44–5).

8 Cixous and Clément, p. 88.

9 The term 'minor architecture' is both properly deducted from architectural historians' conventional use of the term 'major architecture' to refer to canonical buildings in the history of architecture, and is illegitimately appropriated from Gilles Deleuze's and Felix Guattari's concept of minor literature. See Deleuze and Guattari, *Kafka: Toward a Minor Literature*, trans. Dana Polan, (Minneapolis: University of Minnesota Press, 1986 [1975]).

Minor literature is writing that takes on the conventions of a major language and subverts it from the inside. Deleuze's and Guattari's subject is the work of Franz Kafka, a Jew writing in German in Prague in the early part of this century. Minor literature possesses three dominant characteristics: (1) It is that which a minority constructs within a major language, involving a deterritorialization of that language. Deleuze and Guattari compare Prague German to American Black English. (2) Minor literatures are intensely political: '[I]ts cramped space forces each individual intrigue to connect immediately to politics. The individual concern thus becomes all the more necessary, indispensable, magnified because a whole other story is vibrating within it' (p. 17). (3) Minor literatures are collective assemblages; everything in them takes on a collective value.

Deleuze and Guattari describe two paths of deterritorialization. One is to 'artifically enrich [the language], to swell it up through all the resources of symbolism, of oneirism, of esoteric sense, of a hidden signifier' (p. 19). This is a Joycean approach. The other is to take on the poverty of a language and take it further, 'to the point of sobriety' (p. 19). This is Kafka's approach. Deleuze and Guattari then reject the Joycean as a kind of closet reterritorialization which breaks from the people, and go all the way with Kafka.

In transferring such a concept to architecture, already much more intensely materially simple and with more complex relationships to 'the people' and to pragmatics, I believe it necessary to hang onto both possibilities, shuttling between them. This may begin to delineate a kind of line of scrimmage between making architectural objects and writing architectonic texts. What a minor architecture would be is a collection of practices that follow these conditions.

10 Joyce, 006.31-32.

11 Ibid., 112.01-2.

12 Ibid., 064.09.

13 That is, a voiceless, irrational construction characterized by a lack of agreement with accepted ideas (among other things). The relationships between the surd/absurd and architecture have been theorized by Jeffrey Kipnis. This represents the palest of allusions to his work.

14 My house is located a stone's throw from one of the numerous sinkholes in Alachua County, Florida. The architecture building at the University of Florida, where I

work, is located at the edge of another. 'Alachua' is a Seminole word meaning 'jug.'

15 See Edgar Allan Poe's *The Narrative of Arthur Gordon Pym*, for example

16 T.S. Eliot, 'The Waste Land,' *The Waste Land and Other Poems* (New York: Harcourt, Brace and World, 1962 [1922]), p. 37.

17 Catherine Ingraham, 'Milking Deconstruction, or Cow Was the Show?' *Inland Architect*, September/October, 1988.

18 Ibid., p. 65.

19 Martin Heidegger, 'The Thing,' *Poetry, Language, Thought*, trans. Albert Hofstadter (New York: Harper and Row, 1971), p. 166.

20 Ibid.

21 Ibid., p. 167.

22 Ibid., p. 169.

23 Ibid.

24 Ibid., p. 171.

25 Ibid., p. 172.

26 Ibid.

27 Ibid.

28 Ibid, p. 180.

29 Ibid, p. 182.

30 Ibid.

31 This phrase refers to the well-known chapter from Le Corbusier's *Vers une architecture* and to Catherine Ingraham's critique of it in 'The Burdens of Linearity,' a paper presented at the Chicago Institute for Architecture and Urbanism (Skidmore, Owings and Merrill Foundation) Working Session on Contemporary Architectural Theory, September 1988, as well as to its more transparent referent, the eye of power which sees only that which it chooses to see.

32 Eliot, p. 39.

33 Deleuze and Guattari, *A Thousand Plateaus (Capitalism and Schizophrenia)*, trans. Brian Massumi (Minneapolis: University of Minnesota, Press, 1987 [1980]), p. 287.

34 Jardine, p. 251.

35 Thomas Pynchon, *V.* (1963), (New York: Bantam Books, 1981), pp. 320–1.

36 Eliot, p. 30.

37 Luce Irigaray, *Speculum of the Other Woman*, trans. Gillian C. Gill (Ithaca: Cornell University Press, 1985 [1974]), p. 114.

38 These are the words of Aldo Rossi, whose obsession with the idea of architecture as vessel is well known and well documented. See *A Scientific Autobiography*, trans. Lawrence Venuti (Cambridge, Mass.: MIT Press, 1981).

39 Marilyn French, *Beyond Power: On Women, Men, and Morals* (New York: Ballantine Books, 1985), p. 191.

40 Many readers will recognize this allusion to the writing of Guy Davenport (*The Geography of the Imagination*, San Francisco: North Point Press, 1981), who has been an influential teacher to me.

41 Heidegger, p. 179.

42 From the *American Heritage Dictionary*.

43 Eliot, p. 34.

44 Eliot, p. 38. The androgyne here is Tiresias, blinded because his androgynous exper-
    ience led him to speak the unspeakable (that the female's pleasure – *jouissance* – is
    greater than that of the male). The complete phrase from Eliot is: 'At the violet hour,
    when the eyes and back/Turn upward from the desk, when the human engine waits/
    Like a taxi throbbing waiting/I Tiresias, though blind, throbbing between two lives,/
    Old man with wrinkled female breasts, can see/At the violet hour, the evening hour
    that strives/Homeward, and brings the sailor home from sea.'

45 Eliot, p. 39.

46 Angela Carter, *Nights at the Circus* (New York: Penguin Books, 1984), p. 69.

41 Elizabeth Diller

'Bad Press'

from Francesca Hughes (ed.), *The Architect: Reconstructing her Practice* (1996)

PRIVATE PROPERTY

To identify what falls under the category of indecent public exposure for recent antinudity legislation, the state of Florida produced a legal definition of the human buttocks:

> Extract: The area at the rear of the human body which lies between two imaginary lines running parallel to the ground when a person is standing – the first or top of such line drawn at the top of the cleavage of the nates (i.e. the prominence formed by the muscles running from the back of the hip to the back of the leg) and the second or bottom line drawn at the lowest visible point of this cleavage or the lowest point of the curvature of the fleshy protuberance, whichever is lower, and – between two imaginary lines on each side of the body, which run perpendicular to the ground and to the horizontal lines described above, and which perpendicular lines are drawn through the point at which each nate meets the outer side of each leg.[1]

Any exposure of flesh within this rectangular boundary would constitute a legal infraction. Unlike land law where property lines protect the space of the private from transgressions of the public, the property lines that define the socially 'decent' body defend public space from transgressions of the private(s). The play between *property* and *propriety* or the *proper*[2] is particularly intricate in considering the body as a legal site.

But the body has long been a site of uncertain jurisdiction, from Kafka's harrowing inscription of the crime against the state onto the body of the accused to William Buckley's proposal to legally mandate that all homosexuals testing HIV positive have their buttocks tattooed. More common are invisible markings onto social bodies – for example, the bodies produced by disciplinary technologies and techniques of power discussed by Michel Foucault. Here the body is inseparable from the institutional structure, as is the body of the soldier, 'instrumentally coded at the most minute levels. The articulation of his every gesture, from his marching posture to his penmanship was broken down into its component parts, each of which was assigned a duration and an order of appearance'[3] and invested with as much representational value as the uniform covering his skin. But bodies, as we know, are constructed by subtler mechanisms of control – like the fashionable body produced by popular media. This body is continually being reinscribed by a complex weave of discourses including health, beauty, economy, and geography.

HOMEBODIES

At the end of the nineteenth century, the body began to be understood as mechanical component of industrial productivity, an extension of the factory apparatus. Scientific management, or Taylorism, sought to rationalize and standardize the motions of this body, harnessing its dynamic energy and converting it to efficient labor power. According to Anson Rabinbach, 'the dynamic language of energy was central to many utopian social and political ideologies of the early twentieth century: Taylorism, Bolshevism, and fascism. All of these movements viewed the body both as a productive force and as a political instrument whose energies could be subjected to scientifically designed systems of organization.'[4]

It was not long before the practice of engineering bodies for the factory was introduced into the office, the school, and the hospital. By the first decade of the twentieth century, scientific management was brought into the home and applied to domestic housework. Time–motion studies developed to dissect every action of the factory laborer, with the intention of designing ideal shapes of movement and, ultimately, the ideal laborer, were imported into the home to scrutinize every movement exerted in housekeeping in order to produce the ideal housewife. (The term *housewife*, which had been in use since the thirteenth century in Europe, required reconceptualizing both 'wife' and 'house' in relation to the servantless, middle-class American household of the 1920s). Scientific management interpreted the body of this housewife as a dynamic force with unlimited capacity for work. Her only enemy was fatigue, and fatigue, in broader terms, undermined the moral imperative of the new social reform – the reclamation of all waste as usable potential.

When Frank Gilbreth raised the efficiency of bricklaying by reducing stooping, Christine Frederick, the earliest exponent of scientific efficiency in the home, asked, 'Didn't I with hundreds of women stoop unnecessarily over kitchen tables, sinks and ironing boards, as bricklayers stoop over bricks?'

> Extract: Pre-cooked foods, made possible by new packaging developments, are a major time-saver for housewives. Notice the difference in time and effort required in the preparation of a pre-cooked, pre-packaged goulash dinner and one fixed entirely from scratch. Lights attached to the cook's wrists show how many more movements she had to make in the 90 minutes it took the long way, compared with the pre-cooked way which took only 12 minutes.[5]

[Extract:] Reaching with the arms to heights of 46″, 56″, and 72″ above the floor, requires an increase of oxygen consumed per minute over simply standing of 12%, 24%, and 50%, respectively. The energy consumed is therefore in proportion to the height of the reach. Reaching up with the arms takes less energy than bending the body. Reaching by means of a trunk bend to 22″ and to 3″ above the floor, increases oxygen consumption above that required for standing to 57% and 131% of cubic centimeters of oxygen per minute. Reaching by using a knee bend to 3″ above the floor, requires 224% oxygen consumption. While this would indicate that a trunk bend requires less energy than a knee bend, the knee bend is believed to involve less muscular strain.[6]

The application of labor-saving techniques from scientific management, in conjunction with the introduction of household appliances, the new 'electric servants,' sought to conserve the physical expenditure of the 1920s housewife. The time and energy saved, according to the rhetoric of efficiency, would release the woman from the home and thus enable her to join the paid labor force.

The drive for efficiency, however, did not fulfill its liberating promise. Efficiency was often taken as an objective in itself. Ironically, it condemned the housewife to an increased workload as the expectations and standards of cleanliness in the home rose to compulsive levels. The discovery of the 'household germ' and the proliferation of germ theory galvanized a link between dirt and disease. Dirt soon became a moral construct yielding sexual, religious, and aesthetic distinctions. The fetishization of hygiene blurred the problem of cleanliness with beauty, chastity, piety, and modernity. As efficiency targeted domestic space as much as the domestic body, the design of the interior succumbed to this paranoid hygiene. The dust and germ-breeding intricacies of the nineteenth-century interior collapsed into pure surface – white, smooth, flat, nonporous, and seamless – under the continuous disciplinary watch of the housewife.

Although the application of scientific management to housework did not liberate the housewife, daily work in the home became increasingly rationalized by the women condemned to stay there. In order to remove the stigma from what was considered to be the service-oriented menial labor of the female, daily housework between the 1920s and 1940s was progressively masculinized and reconfigured into a more comprehensive economic management of the household.[7] The 'home economist' now combined the skills of nutritionist, doctor, accountant, child-care specialist, and informed consumer, among others.

Notwithstanding this new characterization, the actual physical labor involved in housework remained just as demanding and distasteful as it had ever been. The dirt previously absorbed by the body of the servant was now a direct concern to the woman of the house.[8] In the servantless household of the first half of the century, the maintenance of the idealized female body that exhibited no evidence of decay became a project of devotion equal to that of the maintenance of idealized domestic space. Both were dedicated to preventing the corrosions of age and to the daily restoration of an ideal order whose standards and values were produced and sustained in the popular media.

Today, home and body maintenance have found a new conjunction: household chores can be incorporated into a daily aerobic regimen and performed to the beat of a television fitness trainer. No longer socially isolated, the maintainer of the home can perform household tasks with countless other viewers. Even though housework is slowly becoming less gendered and the discrete sites of 'work' and 'leisure' exchangeable, most conventions of domestic maintenance remain un-challenged. Housework's primary activities of managing dirt and restoring daily order continue to be subjected to the economic ethos of industry, guided by motion-economy principles originally designed by efficiency engineers. Take, for example, the procedure for ironing a man's shirt outlined by a 1960s housekeeping manual:

> Extract: Center the back of the shirt on an ironing board with the yoke taut. Lifting the iron as little as possible, draw the iron, with its point facing the collar down the yoke to the rear tail hem and press the box pleat, using unhurried, well-directed, rhythmic motions. To avoid unnecessary manipulation of the garment, rotate the shirt in the following sequence: first, counterclockwise over the ironing surface to expose the left front panel. Press. Pause when pressing each button hole and pocket, allowing the steam to penetrate the fabric facing and inner band. Next, rotate the shirt clockwise to expose the right front panel and press, rotating the tip of the iron around every button. Slide the right shoulder yoke over the tip of the ironing board and press. Repeat with the left shoulder yoke. Lay out the right sleeve with the placket facing up and iron diagonally across the sleeve width from the underarm seam joint to the upper edge of the sleeve cuff, pressing in a sharp crease. Repeat this procedure for the left sleeve. With the rear yoke centered, press the undercollar and collar crease, working the sold plate towards the collar tips. Turn the shirt over with its front facing up and fasten the buttons. Using the Z-method to eliminate unnecessary movements of garment and arms, turn the shirt over. Fold the left rear facet in, toward the center, pressing in a sharp crease from the outer edge of the yoke shoulder, $2^1/_2$ inches out from the undercollar seam to the tail hem. Fold the left sleeve 45 degrees at the shoulder seam so that the length of the sleeve runs parallel along the length of the rear facet crease and press. Repeat this procedure for the right rear facet and right sleeve. Fold the shirt tail $^1/_3$ of the way toward the collar. Fold $^1/_3$ over again to the yoke, ensuring that all edges are aligned and form ninety degree corners. Using the Z-method, turn the shirt over with its front facing out and press lightly.

With the advent of the electric iron, the task of ironing became progressively governed by minimums, both aesthetic and economic. A minimum of effort is used to reshape the shirt through a minimum of flat facets into a two-dimensional, re-petitive unit that will consume a minimum of space. This shirt will exhibit a mini-mum of creases when worn, particularly in the exposed area between the lapels of the jacket. The standardized ironing pattern of a man's shirt habitually returns the shirt to a flat, rectangular shape that fits economically into orthogonal storage systems – at the site of manufacture, the factory-pressed shirt is stacked and packed into rectangular cartons that are loaded as cubic volumes onto trucks and transported to retain space where the shirt's rectangular form is reinforced in orthogonal display cases and then, after purchase, sustained in the home on closet shelves or in dresser drawers, and finally, on trips away from home, in suitcases. The shirt is disciplined at every stage to conform to an unspoken social contract.

When worn, the residue of the orthogonal logic of efficiency is registered on the surface of the body. The parallel creases and crisp, square corners of a clean, pressed shirt have become sought after emblems of refinement. The by-product of efficiency has become a new object of its desire.

But what if the task of ironing were to free itself from the aesthetics of efficiency altogether? Perhaps the effects of ironing could more aptly represent the postindustrial body by trading the image of the *functional* for that of the *dysfunctional*.

BAD PRESS (INSTRUCTIONS FOR A DISSIDENT IRONING)

Shirt 1
With the left front panel of the shirt over the ironing surface, pull the iron tip from the outer edge of the shoulder seam in a straight diagonal line down to the fifth or sixth buttonhole, depending on the inner lapel angle of the jacket to be worn. Repeat this procedure for the right panel and press only the area inside the *V*. Press the collar crease, working the sole plate toward the front collar tips. Press the exposed two inches of the shirt cuffs only. Button the front and lightly press a sharp crease into the left and right *V* edges.

> *The English dandies of the eighteenth and nineteenth centuries introduced the conception of personal cleanliness. The white shirt was introduced as a washable, socially accepted layer of covering between underwear and outer-wear. It represented a new sanitary order. Beau Brummel is said to be responsible for the startling innovation of wearing a clean shirt daily.*

> Extract: According to the social gentility of dandyism, the white layer covering the skin always extended beyond the edges of the overgarment at the wrists and neck, serving as a sanitary frame for the obsessively well-groomed hands and head. The detachable collar and cuffs were thus subjected to the most rigorous boiling, starching, ironing and polishing. What was initially meant to represent the new austerity in dress for the man, 'The Great Masculine Renunciation,' turned into a fascination with artifice which transformed the image of sobriety into the image of flamboyant efficiency.[9]

Shirt 2
Press the shirt according to ironing procedure but do not fold. With the shirt facing up, fasten the second button into the first buttonhole at the collar. Continue fastening the buttons in sequence, skipping the fourth buttonhole. The remaining buttons will fall into alignment. Turn the shirt over and press the left and right facets. Adjust for material discrepancy by skewing the shoulder ridge and mid-fold to seven degrees from the horizontal median.

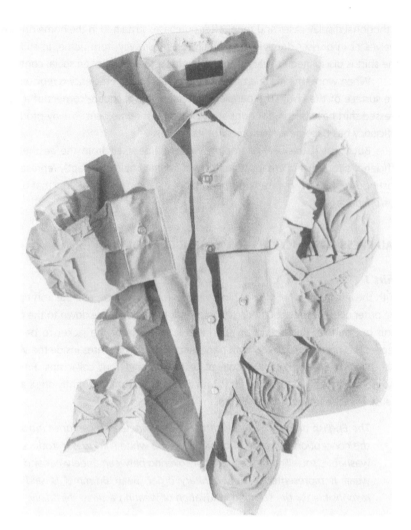

Figure 41.1–6
Elizabeth Diller, 'Shirts 1–6'
Figure 41.1: Shirt 1

Prisoners assigned laundering detail in a state correctional facility have invented a highly developed language articulated through the practice of ironing. Seemingly superfluous, decorative creases pressed into the clothing of other prisoners are invested with representational value understood only to the participants. Like the prison tattoo, another form of inscription on soft, pliable surfaces, the crease is a mark of resistance by the marginalized. Where the tattoo acts on the only possession left to the prisoner, the skin, the crease acts directly on the institutional skin of the prison uniform – a camouflaged defacing. The crease resists appropriation more so than the tattoo in that its abstract language is illegible to the uninitiated compared with the typically pictorial language of the tattoo.

Shirt 3

Press the shirt flat. Keeping the back panel facing up, use standard ironing procedure, folding the right sleeve over the right facet. Keeping the left sleeve free. Continue to press, folding the shirt along the axis of the right sleeve to reduce the shirt to the precise width of the front pocket. Fold the collar forward at a forty-five-degree angle to the shirt. Fold the right sleeve in half along its length and press. Cross-fold and bring the right sleeve up through the collar and, with a crease five inches from the cuff, tuck down into the pocket.

> Extract: When patient 'X' began ironing an article of clothing, she could not stop until she collapsed from exhaustion. The patient would meticulously, and without pause, press out the most imperceptible wrinkles in a shirt, for example, repeating the same areas over and over again. The wrinkles could never be completely removed, thus the job could never be properly finished according to her expectations – as new wrinkles would inevitably be introduced into the garment by the task of ironing itself.[10]

Shirt 4

Press the shirt without folding. Button the cuffs and front panels of the shirt. Push the collar into the shirt from the top and pull it out between the fourth and fifth buttons. Fold the cuffs back on themselves and iron flat. Pull the cuffs through the collar, keeping the crease axis at forty-five degrees. Fold the collar over and down.

Figure 41.2: Shirt 2

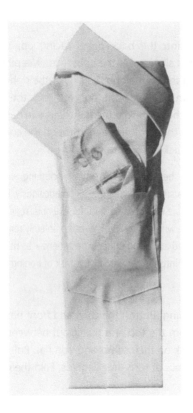

Figure 41.3: Shirt 3

Press the left and right facets and press perpendicular folds before the third button and after the sixth.

> Extract: Manufacturers are hailing the Japanese invention of a non-shrinking, durable press all-cotton shirt as the best new wrinkle in men's wear since the advent of permanent press shirts nearly three decades ago. Shirts represent the ultimate no-iron challenge because they are made of thin fabric compared with most other clothes. When cotton is worn and washed, the hydrogen bridges that connect the cellulose molecules in cotton can break. If bridges break, the molecular chains swell and shift upon washing and wrinkles form. However, when cotton is treated with resins and other reactive molecules, new bridges are formed between cotton molecules which stablize the fabric. Shirt scientists, as it turns out, have a scale for classifying wrinkles, with 1.0 being the equivalent of a withered prune and 5.0 being ideal. The new shirts have a rating between 3.5 and 4.0. In Japan, where domestic chores are still divided largely along traditional gender lines, the shirts are proving popular not only with housewives who hate to iron, but also with salary men, who on business trips can now wash a shirt in the sink, hang it up to dry and wear it the next day.[11]

Certainly the popularity of permanent press miracle fabrics among Japanese businessmen is maintaining the image of labor expended by their wives.

Figure 41.4: Shirt 4

From the popular game show *Family Feud*: Master of Ceremonies: 'Listen carefully to this question. We asked one hundred married men, "Name one of the first warning signs that a marriage is going on the rocks." The top six answers are on the board: Constant Arguing, No Communication, Stops Cooking, Lack of Sex, Stops Ironing, Infidelity.'

> *Perhaps with the advent of miracle fabrics, ironing will continue to linger as an expression of affection.*

Shirt 5

Press the right sleeve with a crisp crease down the center. Turn the left sleeve inside-out. Press and pull the sleeve through the buttoned collar. Extend one hand through the inside of the right sleeve at placket end and grasp the shirt bottom at the front bands. Gather the shirt completely into the right sleeve until the collar meets the underarm seam. Align the collar and cuff with the vertical crease of the sleeve.

Two speculations on the Deleuzian fold:

> Extract: John Rajchman: One cannot say that the 'fold' or 'pli,' is traditional to philosophy, though etymologically it is parent to many fold-words, words with -plic and -plex, like explication, implication, multiplicity and, perplexity, complexity or perplication and complication. The fold involves an 'affective' space. The modernist 'machines for living' sought to express a clean, efficient space for the new mechanical body; but who will invent a way to express the affective space for the new multiplicitous body?[12]
>
> Greg Lynn: Culinary theory has developed a definition for three types of mixtures. The first involves the manipulation of homogeneous elements. Beating, whisking and whipping change the volume but not the nature of a liquid through agitation. The

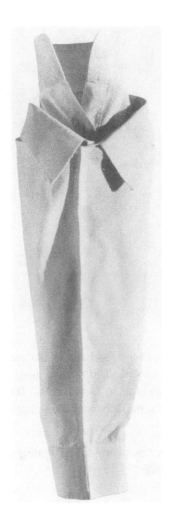

Figure 41.5: Shirt 5

second mixes two or more disparate elements. Chopping, dicing, grinding, grating, slicing, shredding and mincing eviscerate elements into fragments. The third, folding, creaming and blending mix smoothly multiple ingredients through repeated gentle overturnings in such a way that their individual characteristics are maintained. If there is a single effect produced in architecture by folding, it will be the ability to integrate unrelated elements within a new continuous mixture. A folded mixture is neither homogeneous like whipped cream, nor fragmented like chopped nuts, but smooth and heterogeneous.[13]

Shirt 6

Turn the shirt inside-out and center on the ironing surface pulling plackets taut. Evenly divide the back panel length into twenty sections. Fold each section over accordion fashion and firmly press. With the entire shirt back folded and pressed, roll it back into the collar, leaving left and right front panels extending from the

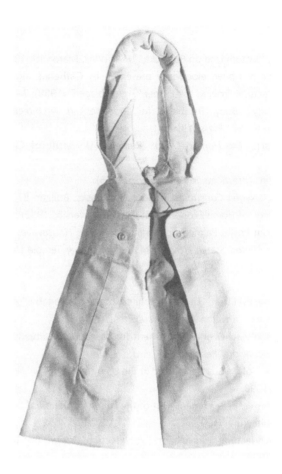

Figure 41.6: Shirt 6

collar tips. Fold the collar over compressed shirt back and fasten the collar buttons. Reverse the inside-out sleeves over remaining side panels. Fasten the cuffs and press.

> The fold has been a useful metaphor for the discourse of poststructuralist architecture, because it consolidates ambiguities, such as surface and structure, figure and organization. One of the prime attributes of the fold is that it is nonrepresentational. The fold also implies reversibility – if something can be folded, it can be unfolded and refolded.

> The crease is a more compelling metaphor because it presents a resistance to transformation. The crease has a longer memory than the fold and it has representational value, in the nature of an inscription. The crease is harder to get out. Its traces guide their continual confirmation – until a new order is inscribed, with the illusion of permanence.

Project assistants: Brendan Cotter, Heather Champ and John Bachus, Linda Chung, Paul Lewis, David Lindberg.

NOTES

1 Steve Marshall, 'Bottom Line on Buttocks,' *USA Today*, March 19, 1992.

2 This assemblage has been eloquently presented by Catherine Ingraham in 'The Faults of Architecture: Troping the Proper,' *Assemblage 7* (1988): 7–13.

3 Robert McAnulty, 'Body Troubles,' in *Strategies in Architectural Thinking* (Cambridge, Mass.: MIT Press, 1992).

4 Anson Rabinbach, *The Human Motor* (Berkeley: University of California Press, 1992).

5 Hazel Thompson, *Thresholds to Adult Living* (1955).

6 Esther Bratton, *Oxygen Consumed in Household Tasks*, Bulletin 873 (Ithaca: New York State College of Home Economics at Cornell University, 1952).

7 Paraphrased from Phyllis Palmer, *Domesticity and Dirt: Housewives and Domestic Servants in the United States, 1920–1945* (Philadelphia: Temple University Press, 1984).

8 Ibid.

9 Paraphrased from Zvi Effrat, 'The Unseemliness of the Fashionable,' *Architecture: In Fashion* (New York: Princeton Architectural Press, 1994).

10 Case citing schoolteacher under treatment for obsessional-compulsive disorder in the *Journal of Behavioral Research*.

11 'Low Iron 100% Cotton Shirts Expected in the US by Father's Day,' *New York Times*, December 30, 1993.

12 Paraphrased from John Rajchman, 'Out of the Fold,' *Architectural Design*, no. 102, 'Folding in Architecture' (1993): 61–3.

13 Greg Lynn, 'Architectural Curvilinearity,' *Architectural Design*, no. 102, 'Folding in Architecture' (1993): 9.

Epilogue: bell hooks, Julie Eizenberg and Hank Koning

Excerpts from 'House, 20 June 1994'

from *Assemblage*, 24 (1995)

dear julie e,

hearing your critique and dismissal of theory – of more abstract intellectual work that may not immediately, if ever, connect to a realm of concrete practice disturbed me. much of my work celebrates and affirms the primacy of theory as a guide to any critical project (even if that theory has not been overtly articulated). it is always much more constructive to identify the links between theory and practice rather than to further the conventional assumption that the links are not there. they are. when our minds and hearts are open we can recognize those links. our dialogue was difficult. when I look at my life and identify that factor that most prevented me from becoming a 'victim,' from allowing the very real limitations imposed by racism, sexism, and class elitism to block my path, i acknowledge the importance of critical literacy, of learning how to read and reflect. reading books created a revolution in my thinking and being that was liberatory – that gave me the courage to transgress boundaries. it was this spirit of action and reflection upon the world in order to change it that has led me to choose radical paths, to choose even to do this collaborative project with you. education for critical consciousness was taking place in our dialogue – we were each challenging the other – to transgress the boundaries. i felt i was the teacher in this dialogue. our dialogue should end here – at this point where we both have ideas to hold in our hearts – to critically reflect on – to use in the concrete circumstances of our lives and work. when i look at the buildings you have created i see expressed in them a love of living, the spirit of peace and freedom celebrated in these structures. our conversations remind me that just as there is theory that will never guide us to progressive concrete practice, there are individuals whose concrete cultural practice is progressive and enlightening even though those individuals may not use theoretical language to clarify and express the thinking and motivation that lies behind their work. these contradictions reveal the mystery and magic of life. they remind us that everything cannot be understood by pure reason – that the world of intuition, dreams, and folklore are all ways of knowing that shape and guide our work. to be open to those oppositional ways of knowing that teach us how to transgress we must free the imagination. it is our capacity to imagine that lets us move beyond boundaries – without imagination we cannot reinvent and recreate the world – the space we live in so that justice and freedom for all can be realized in our lives – everyday and always.

in sisterhood,
bell hooks

Bibliography

PART 1, GENDER

Selected bibliography

Michèle Barrett, *Women's Oppression Today: Problems in Marxist Feminist Analysis* (1980) (London: Version, 1988).

Simone de Beauvoir, *The Second Sex* (1949) (London: Vintage, 1997).

Harry Brod, 'The Case for Men's Studies', Harry Brod (ed.), *The Making of Masculinities: The New Men's Studies* (London: Routledge, 1987), pp. 39–47.

Judith Butler, *Gender Trouble: Feminism and the Subversion of Identity* (London: Routledge, 1990).

Nancy Chodorow, *The Reproduction of Mothering: Psychoanalysis and the Sociology of Gender* (Berkeley: University of California Press, 1978).

Betty Friedan, *The Feminine Mystique* (1963) (London: Penguin Books, 1992).

Luce Irigaray, *This Sex Which Is Not One* (Ithaca, NY: Cornell University Press, 1985).

Audre Lorde, *The Audre Lorde Compendium* (London: Pandora Press, 1996).

Chandra Talpade Mohanty, 'Under Western Eyes: Feminist Scholarship and Colonial Discourses' (1984), Chandra Talpade Mohanty, Ann Russo and Lourdes Torres (eds), *Third World Women and the Politics of Feminism* (Bloomington and Indianapolis: Indiana University Press, 1991), pp. 51–80.

Joan Wallach Scott, 'Gender: A Useful Category of Historical Analysis', Joan Wallach Scott (ed.), *Feminism and History* (Oxford: Oxford University Press, 1996), pp. 152–80.

Virginia Woolf, *A Room of One's Own* (1929) (London: Flamingo, 1994).

Further reading

Elizabeth Abel and Emily K. Abel (eds), *The Signs Reader: Women, Gender and Scholarship* (Chicago: University of Chicago Press, 1983).

Parveen Adams and Elizabeth Cowie (eds), *The Woman in Question* (London: Verso, 1990).

Bill Ashcroft, Gareth Griffiths and Helen Tiffin (eds), *The Post-Colonial Studies Reader* (London: Routledge, 1995).

Michèle Barrett and Anne Phillips (eds), *Destabilising Theory: Contemporary Feminist Debates* (Cambridge: Polity Press, 1992).

Sandra Lee Bartky, *Femininity and Domination: Studies in the Phenomenology of Oppression* (London: Routledge, 1990).

Mary Field Belenky, *Women's Ways of Knowing: The Development of Self, Voice and Mind* (New York: Basic Books, 1986).

Seyla Benhabib, *Situating the Self: Gender, Community and Postmodernism in Contemporary Ethics* (Cambridge: Polity Press, 1992).

Seyla Benhabib and Drucilla Cornell (eds), *Feminism as Critique: Essays on the Politics of Gender in Late-Capitalist Societies* (Cambridge: Polity Press, 1987).

Seyla Benhabib, Judith Butler, Drucilla Cornell and Nancy Fraser (eds), *Feminist Contentions: A Philosophic Exchange* (London: Routledge, 1995).

Jessica Benjamin, *The Bonds of Love: Psychoanalysis, Feminism and the Problem of Domination* (London: Virago, 1990).

Jessica Benjamin, *Shadow of the Other: Intersubjectivity and Gender in Psychoanalysis* (London: Routledge, 1998).

Maurice Berger, Brian Wallis and Simon Watson (eds), *Constructing Masculinity* (London: Routledge, 1996).

Susan Bordo, 'Postmodern Subjects, Postmodern Bodies', *Feminist Studies* (1992), 18(1), 176–90.

———, *Unbearable Weight: Feminism, Western Culture and the Body* (Berkeley: University of California Press, 1993).

Susan Bordo and Alison M. Jaggar (eds), *Gender/Body/Knowledge: Feminist Reconstructions of Being and Knowing* (New Brunswick, NJ: Rutgers University Press, 1989).

Rachel Bowlby, 'The Judgement of Paris (and the Choice of Kristeva)', *New Formations* (Winter 1989) 9: 51–60.

———, *Still Crazy after all these Years: Women, Writing and Psychoanalysis* (London: Routledge, 1992).

Rosi Braidotti, *Patterns of Dissonance: A Study of Women in Contemporary Philosophy* (Oxford: Polity, 1991).

Teresa Brennan, *Between Feminism and Psychoanalysis* (London: Routledge, 1989).

Harry Brod and Michael Kaufman (eds), *Theorizing Masculinities* (London: Sage Publications, 1994).

Rosemarie Buikema and Anneke Smelik (eds), *Women's Studies and Culture: A Feminist Introduction* (London: Zed Books, 1993).

Charlotte Bunch, *Passionate Politics: Feminist Theory in Action* (New York: St. Martin's Press, 1987).

Charlotte Bunch and S. Pollock (eds), *Learning our Way: Essays in Feminist Education* (New York: The Crossing Press, 1983).

Victor Burgin, James Donald and Cora Kaplan (eds), *Formations of Fantasy* (London: Methuen, 1986).

Judith Butler, *Bodies that Matter: On the Discursive Limits of 'Sex'* (London: Routledge, 1993).

Judith Butler, 'Gender as Performance', interviewed by Peter Osborne and Lynne Segal, October 1993, *Radical Philosophy* (Summer 1994), 67: 32–9.

———, *Excitable Speech: A Politics of the Performative* (London: Routledge, 1997).

Judith Butler and Joan W. Scott (eds), *Feminists Theorize the Political* (London: Routledge, 1992).

Kathleen Canning, 'Feminist History after the Linguistic Turn: Historicising Discourse and Experience', *Signs* (Winter 1994): 368–404.

Tina Chanter, *Ethics of Eros: Irigaray's Rewriting of the Philosophers* (London: Routledge, 1995).

Hélène Cixious, 'The Laugh of the Medusa', Elaine Marks and Isabelle de Courtivron (eds), *New French Feminisms: An Anthology* (London: Harvester, 1981), pp. 243–64.

Cynthia Cockburn and Jonathan Rutherford (eds), *Unwrapping Masculinity* (London: Lawrence and Wishart, 1988).

Patricia Hill Collins, *Black Feminist Thought* (London: Unwin Hyman, 1990).

The Combahee River Collective, 'A Black Feminist Statement', Gloria Hull, Patricia Bell Scott and Barbara Smith (eds), *All the Women are White, all the Blacks are Men, but some of us are Brave: Black Woman's Studies* (New York: The Feminist Press, 1982).

R. W. Connell, *Gender and Power: Society, the Person and Sexual Politics* (Cambridge: Polity Press, 1987).

Mary Daly, *Gyn/Ecology: The Metaphysics of Radical Feminism* (London: The Women's Press, 1979).

Angela Davis, *Women, Race and Class* (London: The Women's Press, 1982).

Jacques Derrida, *Of Grammatology* (Baltimore, Md, and London: Johns Hopkins University Press, 1976).

Jonathan Dilmore, *Sexual Dissidence* (Oxford: Clarendon Press, 1991).

Dorothy Dinnerstein, *The Mermaid and the Minotaur: The Rocking of the Cradle and the Ruling of the World* (London: The Women's Press, 1987).

Andrea Dworkin, *Intercourse* (London: Arrow Books, 1987).

Tim Edwards, *Erotic Politics* (London: Routledge, 1996).

Hester Eistenstein, *Contemporary Feminist Thought* (London: Unwin, 1986).

Diane Elam, *Feminism and Deconstruction* (London: Routledge, 1994).

Diane Elam and Robyn Wiegman (eds), *Feminism Beside Itself* (London: Routledge, 1995).

Shulamith Firestone, *The Dialectic of Sex* (New York: Bantam Books, 1971).

Jane Flax, *Thinking Fragments: Psychoanalysis, Feminism and Postmodernism in the Contemporary West* (Berkeley: University of California Press, 1991).

Michel Foucault, *The Order of Things* (London: Routledge, 1992).

———, *The Archaeology of Knowledge* (London: Routledge, 1994).

Diane Fuss, *Essentially Speaking: Feminism, Nature and Difference* (London: Routledge, 1989).

———, *Inside/out: Lesbian Theories, Gay Theories* (London: Routledge, 1991).

———, *Identification Papers* (London: Routledge, 1995).

Jane Gallop, *Feminism and Psychoanalysis: The Daughter's Seduction* (London: Macmillan, 1982).

Lorraine Gamman and Margaret Marshment (eds), *The Female Gaze: Women as Viewers of Popular Culture* (London: The Women's Press, 1988).

Lorraine Gamman and Merja Makinen (eds), *Female Fetishism: A New Look* (London: Lawrence and Wishart, 1994).

Moira Gatens, 'A Critique of the Sex/Gender Distinction', Sneja Gunew (ed.), *A Reader in Feminist Knowledge* (London: Routledge, 1991), pp. 139–60.

——, *Feminism and Philosophy: Perspectives on Difference and Equality* (Cambridge: Polity Press, 1992).

Carol Gilligan, *In a Different Voice: Psychological Theory and Women's Development* (Cambridge, Mass.: Harvard University Press, 1982).

Germaine Greer, *The Female Eunuch* (London: Grafton, 1986).

Jean Grimshaw, *Feminist Philosophers: Women's Perspectives on Philosophical Traditions* (Brighton: Wheatsheaf, 1986).

Elizabeth Grosz, *Sexual Subversions: Three French Feminists* (St Leonards, NSW: Allen and Unwin, 1989).

Elizabeth Grosz and Elspeth Probyn (eds), *Sexy Bodies: The Strange Carnalities of Feminism* (London: Routledge, 1995).

Sneja Gunew (ed.), *Feminist Knowledge: Critique and Construct* (London: Routledge, 1991).

—— (ed.), *A Reader in Feminist Knowledge* (London: Routledge, 1991).

Catherine Hall, *White, Male and Middle Class: Explorations in Feminism and History* (Cambridge: Polity Press, 1992).

Sarah Harasym (ed.), *Gayatri Chakravorty Spivak: Post Colonial Critic: Interviews, Strategies, Dialogues* (London: Routledge, 1990).

Donna Haraway, 'Situated Knowledges: The Science Question in Feminism and the Privilege of Partial Knowledge', *Feminist Studies* (Fall 1988), 14(3): 575–603.

——, *Primate Visions: Gender, Race and Nature in the World of Modern Science* (London: Routledge, 1989).

——, *Simians, Cyborgs and Women: The Reinvention of Nature* (London: Free Association, 1991).

——, *Modest.Witness @ Second Millennium.FemaleMan Meets OncoMouse, Feminism and Technoscience* (London: Routledge, 1997).

Sandra Harding, *The Science Questions in Feminism* (Ithaca, NY: Cornell University Press, 1986).

——, *Whose Science? Whose Knowledge? Thinking from Women's Lives* (Ithaca, NY: Cornell University Press, 1991).

Heidi Hartman, 'The Unhappy Marrriage of Marxism and Feminism', *Women and Revolution* (Boston: South End Press, 1981).

Jeff Hearn, *The Gender of Oppression: Men, Masculinity and the Critique of Marxism* (Brighton: Wheatsheaf, 1987).

——, *Men in the Public Eye* (London: Routledge, 1991).

Jeff Hearn and David Morgan (eds), *Men, Masculinities and Social Theory* (London:

Unwin Hyman, 1990).

Susan J. Hekman, *Gender and Knowledge: Elements of a Postmodern Feminism* (Cambridge: Polity Press, 1990).

Rosemary Hennessy, *Materialist Feminism and the Politics of Discourse* (London: Routledge, 1993).

Marianne Hirsch and Evelyn Fox Keller (eds), *Conflicts in Feminism* (London: Routledge, 1990).

Joan Hoff, 'Gender as a Postmodern Category of Paralysis', *Women's History Review* (1994), 3(2): 149–68.

Christine Holmlund, 'I love Luce: The Lesbian, Mimesis and Masquerade in Irigaray, Freud, and Mainstream Film', *New Formations* (Winter 1989), 9: 105–23.

bell hooks, *Ain't I a Woman: Black Women and Feminism* (London: Pluto, 1982).

——, *Feminist Theory from Margin to Center* (Boston: South End Press, 1984).

——, *Talking Back: Thinking Feminism, Thinking Black* (Boston: South End Press, 1989).

——, *Black Looks: Race and Representation* (Boston: South End Press, 1992).

——, *Teaching to Transgress: Education as the Practice of Freedom* (London: Routledge, 1994).

bell hooks and Cornell West, *Breaking Bread: Insurgent Black Intellectual Life* (Boston: South End Press, 1991).

Maggie Humm (ed.), *Feminisms: A Reader* (London: Harvester Wheatsheaf, 1992).

Luce Irigaray, *The Speculum of the Other Woman* (Ithaca, NY: Cornell University Press, 1985).

——, 'Women, the Sacred and Money', *Paragraph* (1986), 8: 6–18.

——, *Elemental Passions* (London: The Athlone Press, 1992).

——, *Thinking the Difference* (London: The Athlone Press, 1994).

——, *An Ethics of Sexual Difference* (London: The Athlone Press, 1993).

——, *Je, Tu, Nous: Towards a Culture of Difference* (London: Routledge, 1993).

Alice Jardine (ed.), *Men in Feminism* (London: Methuen, 1987).

Alice A. Jardine and Anne M. Menke (eds), *Shifting Scenes, Interviews on Women, Writing, and Politics in Post-68 France* (New York: Columbia University Press, 1991).

Joan Kelly, *Women, History and Theory: The Essays of Joan Kelly* (Chicago: University of Chicago Press, 1984).

Michael S. Kimmel (ed.), *Changing Men: New Directions in Research on Men and Masculinity* (Newbury Park, Cal.: Sage, 1987).

Julia Kristeva, *About Chinese Women* (London: Boyars, 1977).

——, *Desire in Language: A Semiotic Approach to Literature and Art* (Oxford: Blackwell, 1980).

——, *Powers of Horror: An Essay on Abjection* (New York: Columbia University Press, 1982).

——, *Tales of Love* (New York: Columbia University Press, 1987).

Barbara Kruger and Phil Mariani (eds), *Remaking History* (New York: DIA Art Foundation, 1989).

Toril Moi (ed.), *The Kristeva Reader* (Oxford: Blackwell, 1986).

Donna Landry and Gerald Maclean, *Materialist Feminisms* (Oxford: Blackwell, 1993).

———— (eds), *The Spivak Reader* (London: Routledge, 1996).

John Lechte, *Julia Kristeva* (London: Routledge, 1990).

Kathleen Lennon and Margaret Whitford (eds), *Knowing the Difference: Feminist Perspectives in Epistemology* (London: Routledge, 1994).

Genevieve Lloyd, *The Man of Reason: 'Male' and 'Female' in Western Philosophy* (London: Methuen, 1984).

Audre Lorde, *Sister Outsider: Essays and Speeches* (New York: The Crossing Press, 1984).

Nina Lykke and Rosi Braidotti (eds), *Between Monsters, Goddesses and Cyborgs: Feminist Confrontations with Science, Medicine and Cyberspace* (London: Zed Books, 1998).

Mairtin Mac an Ghaill (ed.), *Understanding Masculinities: Social Relations and Cultural Arenas* (Buckingham: Open University Press, 1996).

Elaine Marks and Isabelle de Courtivron (eds), *New French Feminisms: An Anthology* (Amherst: University of Massachusetts Press, 1980).

Rosalind Minsky, *Psychoanalysis and Gender* (London: Routledge, 1996).

Juliet Mitchell, *Psychoanalysis and Feminism* (Harmondsworth: Penguin, 1974).

————, *Women, the Longest Revolution: Essays on Feminism, Literature and Psychoanalysis* (London: Virago, 1984).

Tania Modleski, *Feminism without Women: Culture and Criticism in the Postfeminist Age* (London: Routledge, 1991).

Chandra Talpade Mohanty and M. Jacqui Alexander (eds), *Feminist Genealogies, Colonial Legacies, Democratic Futures* (London: Routledge, 1997).

Toril Moi, *Sexual/Textual Politics: Feminist Literary Theory* (London: Methuen, 1985).

Valentine M. Mooghadam (ed.), *Identity Politics and Women: Cultural Reassertions and Feminisms in International Perspective* (Boulder, Col.: Westview Press, 1994).

C. Moraga and G. Anzaldúa (eds), *This Bridge Called My Back: Writings by Radical Women of Color* (New York: Kitchen Table, 1983).

David H. J. Morgan, *Discovering Men* (London: Routledge, 1992).

Judith L. Newton, Mary P. Ryan and Judith R. Walkowitz (eds), *Sex and Class in Women's History* (London: Routledge and Kegan Paul, 1983).

Linda Nicholson (ed.), *Feminism/Postmodernism* (London: Routledge, 1990).

———— (ed.), *Second Wave Feminism* (London: Routledge, 1998).

Andrea Nye, *Feminist Theory and the Philosophy of Man* (New York: Croom Helm, 1989).

Judith Okely, *Simone de Beauvoir: A Re-Reading* (London: Virago, 1986).

Sherry Ortner, 'Is Female to Male as Nature is to Culture?' M. Rosaldo and L. Lamphere (eds), *Women, Culture and Society* (Stanford, Cal.: Stanford University Press, 1974).

Pratibha Parmar, 'Black Feminism: The Politics of Articulation', Jonathan Rutherford (ed.), *Identity: Community, Culture, Difference* (London: Lawrence and Wishart Ltd, 1990), pp. 101–26.

Carole Pateman, *The Sexual Contract* (Cambridge: Polity Press, 1988).

————, *The Disorder of Women* (Cambridge: Polity Press, 1989).

Michelle Perrot, *A History of Private Life: From the Fires of the Revolution to the Great War* (Cambridge, Mass.: The Belknap Press of Harvard University Press, 1990).

———— (ed.), *Writing Women's History* (Oxford: Blackwell, 1984).

Sadie Plant, ' "Bloody Woman": Review of Margaret Whitford, *Luce Irigaray: Philosphy in the Feminine*', *Radical Philosophy* (Spring 1992), 60: 47–8.

Kenneth Plummer, *Modern Homosexualities* (London: Routledge, 1992).

Val Plumwood, 'Do We Need a Sex/Gender Distinction?' *Radical Philosphy* (1989), 51: 2–11.

Mary Poovey, 'Feminism and Deconstruction', *Feminist Studies* (1988a), 14(1): 51–65.

———, *Uneven Developments: The Ideological Work of Gender in Mid-Victorian Britian* (Chicago: University of Chicago Press, 1988b).

Andrew Posner and Helaine Perchuk (eds), *The Masculine Masquerade* (Cambridge, Mass.: M.I.T. Press, 1995).

Eva Rathgeber, 'WID, WAD, GAD: Trends in Research and Practice', *Journal of Developing Areas* (1990), 24: 489–502.

Janice Raymond, *A Passion for Friends* (Boston: Beacon Press, 1986).

Rayna R. Reiter (ed.), *Toward an Anthropology of Women* (New York: Monthly Review Press, 1975).

Deborah L. Rhode (ed.), *Theoretical Perspectives on Sexual Difference* (New Haven, Conn.: Yale University Press, 1990).

Adrienne Rich, 'Compulsory Heterosexuality and Lesbian Existence', E. Abel and E.K. Abel (eds), *The Signs Reader: Women, Gender and Scholarship* (Chicago: University of Chicago Press, 1983).

———, *Blood, Bread and Poetry* (London: Virago, 1987).

Denise Riley, *Am I that Name? Feminism and the Category of 'Women' in History* (Minneapolis: University of Minnesota Press, 1988).

Joan Riviere, 'Womanliness as Masquerade', *International Journal of Psychoanalysis* (1929), 10: 303–13.

Michael Roper and John Tosh (eds), *Manful Assertions: Masculinities in Britain since 1800* (London: Routledge, 1991).

Michelle Rosaldo and Louise Lamphere, *Women, Culture and Society* (Stanford, Cal.: Stanford University Press, 1974).

Jacqueline Rose, *Sexuality in the Field of Vision* (London: Verso, 1986).

Sheila Rowbotham, *Woman's Consciousness, Man's World* (Harmondsworth: Penguin, 1973).

Jonathan Rutherford (ed.), *Identity: Community, Culture, Difference* (London: Lawrence and Wishart Ltd, 1990).

Edward Said, *Orientalism* (New York: Vintage, 1979).

Morag Schiach, *Hélène Cixious: A Politics of Writing* (London: Routledge, 1991).

Joan W. Scott, 'Deconstructing Equality versus Difference: or, The Uses of Post-structuralist Theory for Feminists', *Feminist Studies* (Spring 1981), 14(1): 33–50.

———, *Gender and the Politics of History* (New York: Columbia University Press, 1988).

———, 'The Evidence of Experience', *Critical Enquiry* (Summer 1991), 17: 773–99.

——— (ed.), *Feminism and History* (Oxford: Oxford University Press, 1996).

Eve Kosofsky Sedgwick, *Between Men: English Literature and Male Homosexual Desire* (New York: Columbia University Press, 1985).

———, *The Epistemology of the Closet* (New York: Harvester Wheatsheaf, 1991).

——, *Tendencies* (London: Routledge, 1994).

Lynne Segal, *Slow Motion: Changing Masculinities, Changing Men* (London: Virago, 1990).

Victor Seidler, *Rediscovering Masculinity: Reason, Language and Sexuality* (London: Routledge, 1989).

Susan Sellers (ed.), *The Hélène Cixious Reader* (London: Routledge, 1994).

Gayatri Chakovorty Spivak, *In Other Worlds: Essays in Cultural Politics* (London: Methuen, 1987).

——, 'In a Word', Interview with Ellen Rooney, *Differences: A Journal of Feminist Cultural Studies* (Fall 1989), 1: 124–55.

——, *Outside the Teaching Machine* (London: Routledge, 1993).

Rosemary Tong, *Feminist Thought: A Comprehensive Introduction* (London: Routledge, 1992).

Nancy Tuana and Rosemary Tong (eds), *Feminism and Philosophy: Essential Readings in Theory, Reinterpretation and Application* (San Francisco: Westview Press, 1995).

Amanda Vickery, 'Historiographical Review: Golden Age to Separate Spheres? A Review of the Categories and Chronology of English Women's History', *The Historical Journal* (1992), 36(2): 383–414.

Sylvia Walby, *Theorising Patriarchy* (Oxford: Blackwell, 1990).

Alice Walker, *In Search of our Mothers' Gardens* (London: The Women's Press, 1984).

Vron Ware, *Beyond the Pale: White Women, Racism and History* (London: Verso, 1992).

Jeffrey Weeks, *Coming Out: Homosexual Politics in Britain from the Nineteenth Century to the Present* (London: Quartet, 1977).

——, *Sex, Politics and Society* (London: Longman, 1989).

Margaret Whitford, *The Irigarary Reader* (Oxford: Blackwell, 1991a).

——, *Luce Irigaray: Philosophy in the Feminine* (London: Routledge, 1991b).

Mary Wollstonecraft, *A Vindication of the Rights of Woman* (1792) (London: Penguin, 1992).

Elizabeth Wright (ed.), *Feminism and Psychoanalysis: A Critical Dictionary* (Oxford: Blackwell, 1992).

PART 2, GENDER, SPACE

Selected bibliography

Shirley Ardener (ed.), *Women and Space: Ground Rules and Social Maps* (Oxford: Berg, 1993).

Rosalyn Deutsche, 'Men in Space', *Evictions: Art and Spatial Politics* (Cambridge, Mass.: MIT Press, 1996), originally published in *Strategies* (1990) 3: 130–7.

Elizabeth Grosz, *Space, Time and Perversion* (London: Routledge, 1996).

bell hooks, *Yearnings: Race, Gender and Cultural Politics* (London: Turnaround Press, 1989).

Mary McLeod, 'Everyday and "Other" Spaces', Debra L. Coleman, Elizabeth Ann Danze and Carol Jane Henderson (eds), *Feminism and Architecture* (New York: Princeton Architectural Press, 1996), pp. 3–37.

Doreen Massey, *Space, Place and Gender* (Cambridge: Polity Press, 1994).

Meaghan Morris, 'Things to Do with Shopping Centres', Susan Sheridan (ed.), *Grafts: Feminist Cultural Criticism* (London: Verso, 1988), pp. 193-208.

Griselda Pollock, *Vision and Difference: Femininity, Feminism and Histories of Art* (London: Routledge, 1992).

Daphne Spain, *Gendered Space* (Chapel Hill, NC: University of North Carolina Press, 1985).

Susana Torre, 'Claiming the Public Space: The Mothers of Plaza de Mayo', Diana Agrest, Patricia Conway and Leslie Kanes Weisman (eds), *The Sex of Architecture* (New York: Harry N. Abrams, Inc., Publishers, 1996), pp. 241–50.

Elizabeth Wilson, *The Sphinx in the City: Urban Life, the Control of Disorder and Women* (London: Virago, 1991).

Further reading

Kathleen Adler, 'The Suburban, the Modern and une Dame de Paissy', *Oxford Art Journal* (1989), 12(1): 3–13.

Kathleen Adler and Marcia Pointon, *The Body Imaged: The Human Form and Visual Culture since the Renaissance* (Cambridge: Cambridge University Press, 1993).

Rosa Ainley (ed.), *New Frontiers of Space, Bodies and Gender* (London: Routledge, 1998).

John Allen and Doreen Massey (eds), *Geographical Worlds* (Milton Keynes: Open University Press, 1995).

John Allen, Doreen Massey and Allan Cochrane with Julie Charlesworth *et al.*, *Rethinking the Region* (London : Routledge, 1998).

Kay Anderson and Fay Gale (eds), *Inventing Places* (Australia: Longman Cheshire, 1992).

C. Andrew and B. Milroy, *Life Spaces: Gender, Household, Employment* (London: University of British Columbia Press, 1988).

Shirley Ardener, *Defining Females* (London: Croom Helm, 1978).

Beth I. Bailey, *From Front Porch to Back Seat: Courtship in Twentieth-century America* (Baltimore, Md: Johns Hopkins University Press, 1988).

Christine Battersby, *Gender and Genius: Towards a Feminist Aesthetics* (London: The Women's Press, 1989).

David Bell and Gill Valentine (eds), *Mapping Desires* (London: Routledge, 1995).

—————— (eds), *Consuming Geographies* (London: Routledge, 1997).

Liz Bondi, 'Feminism, Postmodernism and Geography: a Space for Women?', *Antipode* (August 1990), 22(2): 156–67.

——————, 'Gender and Dichotomy', *Progress in Human Geography* (1992), 16(1): 98–104.

——————, 'Gender Symbols and Urban Landscapes', *Progress in Human Geography* (1992), 16(2): 57–70.

——————, 'Locating Identity Politics', Michael Keith and Steve Pile (eds), *Place and the Politics of Identity* (London: Routledge, 1993a), pp. 84–101.

——————, 'Gender and Geography: Crossing Boundaries', *Progress in Human Geography* (1993b), 17(2): 241–46.

Liz Bondi and Mona Domosh, 'Other Figures in Other Places: On Feminism, Postmodernism and Geography', *Environment and Planning D: Space and Society* (1992), 10: 199–213.

F. Bonner *et al.* (eds), *Imagining Women: Cultural Representations and Gender* (Oxford: Polity Press, 1992).

Rachel Bowlby, *Just Looking: Consumer Culture in Dreiser, Gissing and Zola* (New York, London: Methuen, 1985).

——, *Shopping with Freud* (London: Routledge, 1993).

Jane Brettle and Sally Rice (eds), *Public Bodies – Private States: New Views on Photography, Representation and Gender* (Manchester: Manchester University Press, 1994).

Giuliana Bruno, 'Bodily Architecture', *Assemblage* (December 1992), 19: 106–11.

——, *Streetwalking on a Ruined Map: Cultural Theory and the City Films of Elvira Notari* (Princeton, NJ: Princeton University Press, 1993).

Michael de Certeau, *The Practice of Everyday Life* (Berkeley: University of California Press, 1988).

Whitney Chadwick and Isabelle de Courtivron, *Significant Creativity and Intimate Partnership* (London: Thames and Hudson, 1993).

Hollis Clayson, *Painted Love* (New Haven, Conn.: Yale University Press, 1991).

Stephanie Coontz and Peta Henderson, *Women's Work, Men's Property: The Origins of Class and Gender* (London: Verso, 1986).

Rosalind Coward, *Patriarchal Precedents: Sexuality and Social Relations* (London: Routledge and Kegan Paul, 1983).

Rosalind Coward and John Ellis, *Language and Materialism: Developments in Semiology and the Theory of the Subject* (London: Routledge and Kegan Paul, 1977).

Leonore Davidoff, *The Best Circles* (London: Croom Helm, 1986).

——, *Worlds Between: Historical Perspectives on Gender and Class* (Cambridge: Polity Press, 1995).

Leonore Davidoff and Catherine Hall, 'The Architecture of Public and Private Life', Derek Fraser and Anthony Sutcliffe (eds), *The Pursuit of Urban History* (London: Edward Arnold Publishers Ltd., 1983), pp. 327-45.

——, *Family Fortunes: Men and Women of the English Middle Class 1750–1850* (Chicago: University of Chicago Press, 1987).

Tracey C. Davis, *Actresses as Working Women: Their Social Identity in Victorian Culture* (London: Routledge, 1991).

Rosalyn Deutsche, 'Men in Space', *Strategies* (1990), 3: 130–7.

——, 'Boys Town', *Environment and Planning D: Space and Society* (1991), 9: 5–30.

Rosalyn Diprose and Robyn Ferrell, *Cartographies: Poststructuralism and the Mapping of Bodies and Spaces* (St. Leonards, NSW: Allen and Unwin, 1991).

Mary Ann Doane, 'Film and the Masquerade: Theorising the Female Spectator', *Screen*, (September–October 1982), 23(2–4): 74–87.

Mary Douglas, *Purity and Danger: An Analysis of Concepts of Pollution and Danger* (Harmondsworth: Penguin, 1966).

Robyn Dowling, 'Femininity, Place and Commodities: A Retail Case Study', *Antipode* (October 1993), 25(4): 295–319.

Gen Doy, *Seeing and Consciousness: Women, Class and Representation* (Oxford: Berg Publishers Ltd, 1995).

Nancy Duncan (ed.), *Body Space: Destablizing Geographies of Gender and Sexuality* (London: Routledge, 1997).

Pasi Falk, *The Consuming Body* (London: Sage, 1994).

Mike Featherstone, 'The Body in Consumer Culture', Mike Hepworth, Mike Featherstone and Bryan S. Turner (eds), *The Body: Social Process and Cultural Theory* (London: Sage, 1991), pp. 170–96.

Briony Fer, 'What's in a Line? Gender and Modernity', *Oxford Art Journal* (1990), 13(1): 77–88.

Nancy Fraser, *Unruly Practices: Power, Discourse and Gender in Contemporary Social Theory* (Minneapolis: University of Minnesota Press, 1989).

Marilyn French, 'Is there a Feminist Aesthetic? Hilda Hein and Carolyn Korsmeyer (eds), *Aesthetics in Feminist Perspective* (Bloomington: Indiana University Press, 1993).

Anne Friedberg, *Window Shopping* (Berkeley: University of California Press, 1993).

John Frow and Meaghan Morris (eds), *Australian Cultural Studies: A Reader* (Urbana : University of Illinois Press, 1993).

Eva Gamamikow *et al.* (eds), *The Public and the Private* (London: Heinemann, 1983).

Tamar Garb, 'Unpicking the Seams of her Disguise –Self-representation in the Case of Marie Bashkirtseff', *Block* (August 1987–8), 13: 79–85.

Victoria de Grazia (ed.) with Ellen Furlough, *The Sex of Things: Gender and Consumption in Historical Perspective* (Berkeley: University of California Press, 1996).

Clara H. Greed, *Women and Planning: Creating Gendered Realities* (London: Routledge, 1994).

Derek Gregory, *Geographical Imaginations* (Oxford: Blackwell, 1994).

Tag Gronberg, 'Speaking Volumes: The Pavillon d'Esprit Nouveau', *Oxford Art Journal* (1992), 15(2): 58–69.

Lawrence Grossberg *et al.* (eds), *Cultural Studies* (London: Routledge, 1992).

Elizabeth Grosz, *Sexual Subversions* (St Leonards, NSW: Allen and Unwin, 1989).

——, *Jacques Lacan: A Feminist Introduction* (London: Routledge, 1990).

——, 'Women, Chora, Dwelling', *ANY* (1994), 4: 22-7.

Elizabeth Grosz and Elspeth Probyn (eds), *Sexy Bodies: The Strange Carnalities of Feminism* (London: Routledge, 1995).

David Harvey, *The Condition of Postmodernity* (Oxford: Blackwell, 1989).

Liz Heron, *Streets of Desire: Women's Fiction of the Twentieth Century* (London: Routledge, 1993).

bell hooks, *Art on my Mind* (New York: The New Press, 1995).

Mary Jacobus, Evelyn Fox Keller and Sally Shuttleworth (eds), *Body/Politics: Women and the Discourses of Science* (London: Routledge, 1990).

Louise C. Johnson, 'What Future for Feminist Geography?' *Gender, Place and Culture* (1994), 1(1): 103–13.

Ann E. Kaplan, *Women and Film: Both Sides of the Camera* (New York: Methuen, 1983).

C. Katz and J. Monk, *Full Circles: Geographies of Women over the Life Course* (London: Routledge, 1993).

Michael Keith and Steve Pile (eds), *Place and the Politics of Identity* (London: Routledge, 1993).

Joan Kelly, 'The Doubled Vision of Feminist Theory', Judith L. Newton, Mary P. Ryan and Judith R. Walkowitz (eds), *Sex and Class in Women's History* (London: Routledge and Kegan Paul, 1983), pp. 259-70.

Richard Kendall and Griselda Pollock (eds), *Dealing with Degas: Representations of Women and the Politics of Vision* (London: Pandora Press, 1991).

Sarah Kent, *Domestic Architecture and the Use of Space: An Interdisciplinary Cross-cultural Study* (Cambridge: Cambridge University Press, 1990).

Anthony D. King (ed.), *Re-presenting the City: Ethnicity, Capital and Culture in the 21st Century Metropolis* (London: Macmillan and New York University Press, 1996).

Pat Kirkham (ed.), *The Gendered Object* (Manchester: Manchester University Press, 1996).

Linda Krumholz and Estella Lauter, 'Annoted Bibliography on Feminist Aesthetics in the Visual Arts', *Hypatia* (Summer 1990), 5: 158–72.

Annette Kuhn, *Women's Pictures; Feminism and Cinema* (London: Verso, 1994).

Thomas Laquer, *Making Sex: Body and Gender from the Greeks to Freud* (Cambridge Mass.: Harvard University Press, 1990).

Shirley Bradway Laska and Daphne Spain (eds), *Back to the City: Issues in Neighborhood Renovation* (New York: Pergamon Press, 1980).

Teresa de Lauretis, *Alice Doesn't: Feminism, Semiotics, Cinema* (London: Macmillan Press Ltd., 1984).

—— (ed.), *Feminist Studies/Critical Studies* (Bloomington: Indiana University Press, 1986).

——, *Technologies of Gender: Essays on Theory, Film and Fiction* (London: Macmillan Press Ltd., 1989).

Henri Lefebvre, *The Production of Space* (Oxford: Blackwell, 1991).

Richard T. LeGates and Frederic Stout (eds), *The City Reader* (London: Routledge, 1996).

Gerda Lerner, *The Creation of Patriarchy* (New York: Oxford University Press, 1986).

Claude Lévi-Strauss, *The Elementary Structures of Kinship* (Boston: Beacon Press, 1969).

Clare Lewis and Steve Pile, 'Woman, Body, Space: Rio Carnival and the Politics of Performance', *Gender, Place and Culture* (1996), 3(1): 23–41.

Robyn Longhurst, 'The Body and Geography', *Gender, Place and Culture* (1995), 2(1): 97–105.

Linda McDowell, 'Towards an Understanding of the Gender Division of Urban Space', *Environment and Planning D: Society and Space* (1983), (1): 59–72.

——, 'Space, Place and Gender Relations, Parts 1 and 2', *Progress in Human Geography* (1993), v17(2): 57–79 and 17(3): 305–18.

——, 'Performing Work: Bodily Representations in Merchant Banks', *Environment and Planning D: Society and Space* (1994), 12: 727–50.

Neil McKendrick, John Brewer and J. H. Plumb, *The Birth of a Consumer Society: The Commercialisation of Eighteenth Century England* (London: Europa Publications Ltd., 1982).

Suzanne Mackenzie, *Visible Histories: Women and Environments in a Post-war British City* (Montreal: McGill-Queen's University Press, 1989).

Philomena Mariani, *Critical Fictions: The Politics of Imaginative Writings* (Seattle, Wash.: Bay Press, 1991).

Doreen Massey, 'Flexible Sexism', *Environment and Planning D: Society and Space* (1991), 9: 31–57.

——, 'Masculinity, Dualisms and High Technology', *Transactions of the Institute of British Geographers* (1995a), 20.

——, *Spatial Divisions of Labour: Social Structures and the Geography of Production* (2nd edn) (Basingstoke: Macmillan Press, 1995b).

Doreen Massey and Pat Jess (eds), *A Place in the World? Places, Cultures and Globalization* (Oxford : Oxford University Press, 1995).

Marcel Mauss, *The Gift: Forms and Functions of Exchange in Archaic Societies* (New York: Harvester, 1967).

Andy Medhurst and Sally R. Munt (eds), *Lesbian and Gay Studies: A Critical Introduction* (London: Cassell, 1997).

Daniel Miller (ed.), *Acknowledging Consumption* (London: Routledge, 1995).

Trinh T. Minh-Ha, *When the Moon Waxes Red: Representation, Gender and Cultural Politics* (London: Routledge, 1991).

Henrietta L. Moore, *Space, Text and Gender* (Cambridge: Cambridge University Press, 1988).

Henrietta L. Moore, *Feminism and Anthropology* (Cambridge: Polity Press, 1988).

Meaghan Morris, *The Pirate's Fiancée: Feminism, Reading, Postmodernism* (London : Verso, 1988).

Frank Mort, *Cultures of Consumption* (London: Routledge, 1996).

Laura Mulvey (ed.), 'Visual Pleasure and Narrative Cinema', *Visual and Other Pleasures* (London: Macmillan, 1989).

——, 'Pandora: Topographies of the Mask and Curiosity', Beatriz Colomina (ed.), *Sexuality and Space* (New York: Princeton Architectural Press, 1992), pp. 53–72.

——, 'Cinematic Space: Desiring and Deciphering', Katerina Rüedi and Sarah Wigglesworth and Duncan McCorquodale (eds), *Desiring Practices: Architecture, Gender and the Interdisciplinary* (London: Black Dog Publishing Ltd, 1996a), pp. 206–15.

——, *Fetishism and Curiosity* (London: B.F.I. Publishing, 1996b).

Sally Munt, 'The Lesbian Flaneur', David Bell and Gill Valentine (eds), *Mapping Desire* (London: Routledge, 1995), pp. 114–25.

Heidi Nast and Steve Pile (eds), *Places through the Body* (London: Routledge, 1998).

Lynda Nead, *Myths of Sexuality: Representations of Women in Victorian Britain* (Oxford: Blackwell, 1988).

Molly Nesbit, 'In the Absence of the Parisienne', Beatriz Colomina (ed.), *Sexuality and Space* (New York: Princeton Architectural Press, 1992), pp. 307–25.

Judith L. Newton, M. P. Ryan and J. P. Walkowitz (eds), *Sex and Class in Women's History* (London: Routledge and Kegan Paul, 1983).

Linda Nochlin (ed.), *The Politics of Vision: Essays on Nineteenth-century Art and Society* (London: Thames and Hudson, 1991).

Ursula Paravicci, *Habitat au Féminin* (Presses Polytechniques et Universitaires Romandes, 1990).

Rozsika Parker and Griselda Pollock, *Old Mistresses: Women, Art and Ideology* (New York: Pantheon, 1981).

Rozsika Parker and Griselda Pollock (eds), *Framing Feminism: Art and the Women's Movement 1970–85* (London: Pandora, 1987).

Steve Pile, *The Body and the City* (London: Routledge, 1996).

Steve Pile and Gillian Rose, 'All or Nothing? Politics and Critique in the Modernism-Postmodernism Debate', *Environment and Planning D: Society and Space* (1992), 10: 123–36.

Steve Pile and Nigel Thrift (eds), *Mapping the Subject* (London: Routledge, 1995).

Griselda Pollock, *Vision and Difference: Femininity, Feminism and the Histories of Art* (London: Routledge, 1988).

———, 'Vicarious Excitements: London, a Pilgrimage by Gustave Doré and Blanchard Jerrold', *New Formations* (Spring 1988), 4: 25–50.

———, 'Trouble in the Archives: Introduction', *Differences: A Journal of Feminist Cultural Studies* (1992), 4(3): iii–xiv.

———, *Avant-garde Gambits, 1888–1893: Gender and the Colour of Art History* (London: Thames and Hudson, 1992).

——— (ed.), *Generations and Geographies in the Visual Arts: Feminist Readings* (London: Routledge, 1996).

———, *Mary Cassatt* (London: Thames and Hudson, 1998).

Patricia Price-Chalita, 'Spatial Metaphor and the Politics of Empowerment: Mapping a Place for Feminism and Postmodernism in Geography', *Antipode* (1994), 26(3): 236–54.

S. Radcliffe and S. Westwood (eds), *Viva: Women and Popular Protest in Latin America* (Andover, Hants: Routledge, 1993).

Hilary Radner, *Shopping Around: Feminine Culture and the Pursuit of Pleasure* (New York: Routledge, 1995).

Rayna R. Reiter (ed.), *Toward an Anthropology of Women* (New York: Monthly Review Press, 1975).

Adrain Rifkin, *Streèt Noises: Studies in Parisian Pleasure 1900–40* (Manchester: Manchester University Press, 1993).

Michelle Rosaldo and Louise Lamphere, *Women, Culture and Society* (Stanford, Cal.: Stanford University Press, 1974).

Gillian Rose, 'Review of Edward Soja, *Postmodern Geographies* and David Harvey, *The Condition of Postmodernity*', *Journal of Historical Geography* (January 1991), 17(1): 118–21.

———, *Feminism and Geography: The Limits of Geographical Knowledge* (Cambridge: Polity Press, 1993a).

———, 'Progress in Geography and Gender: Or Something Else?' *Progress in Human Geography* (1993b), 17(4); 531–7.

———, 'Distance, Surface, Elsewhere: A Feminist Critique of the Space of Phallocentric Self-knowledge', *Environment and Planning D: Society and Space* (1995), 13: 761–81.

———, 'Making Space for the Female Subject of Feminism', Steve Pile and Nigel Thrift (eds), *Mapping the Subject* (London: Routledge, 1996), pp. 332–54.

Gayle Rubin, 'The Traffic in Women: Notes on the "Political Economy" of Sex', Rayna Reiter (ed.), *Toward an Anthropology of Women* (New York: Monthly Review Press, 1975), pp. 157–210.

——, 'Sexual Traffic: Interview with Judith Butler', *Differences: A Journal of Feminist Cultural Studies* (1994), 6(2 and 3): 62–99.

—— 'The Traffic in Women: Notes on the "Political Economy" of Sex', Joan W. Scott (ed.), *Feminism and History* (Oxford: Oxford University Press, 1996), pp. 105–51.

Jenny Ryan, 'Women, Modernity and the City', *Theory, Culture and Society* (November 1994), 11(4): 35–64.

Mary P. Ryan, *Women in Public: Between Banners and Ballots 1825–80* (London: Johns Hopkins University Press, 1990).

Susan Saegart, 'Masculine Cities and Feminine Suburbs: Polarized Ideas, Contradictory Realities', *Signs*, 5(3): 93–108.

Renata Salecl and Slavoj Zizek (eds), *Gaze and Voice as Love Objects* (Durham, NC: Duke University Press, 1996).

Naomi Schor, *Reading in Detail: Aesthetics and the Feminine* (New York: Methuen, 1987).

Richard Sennett, *The Fall of Public Man* (New York: First Vintage Books Edition, 1978).

——, *Flesh and Stone* (London: Faber and Faber, 1994).

Rob Shields (ed.), *Lifestyle Shopping* (London: Routledge, 1992).

Debora L. Silverman, *Art Nouveau in Fin-de-Siècle France* (Berkeley: University of California Press, 1989).

Amita Sinha, 'Women's Local Space: Home and Neighbourhood in Northern India', *Women and Environment* (Winter 1989), pp. 15–18.

Edward Soja, *Postmodern Geographies: The Reassertion of Space in Social Theory* (London: Verso, 1989).

Abigail Solomon-Godeau, 'The Legs of the Countess', *October* (Winter 1986): 65–108.

——, *Male Trouble: A Crisis in Representation* (London: Thames and Hudson, 1997).

Daphne Spain and Suzanne M. Bianchi (eds), *Balancing Act: Motherhood, Marriage and Employment among American Women* (New York: Russell Sage Foundation, 1996).

Judith Squires, 'Private Lives, Secluded Places: Privacy as Political Possibility', *Environment and Planning D: Society and Space* (1994), 12: 387–410.

Peter Stallybrass and Allon White, *The Politics and Poetics of Transgression* (London: Methuen, 1986).

Gillian Swanson, 'Drunk with the Glitter: Consuming Spaces and Sexual Geographies', Sophie Watson and Katherine Gibson (eds), *Postmodern Cities and Spaces* (Oxford: Blackwell, 1995), pp. 80–99.

Keith Tester (ed.), *The Flâneur* (London: Routledge, 1994).

John Tosh, 'Domesticity and Manliness in the Victorian Middle-class', Michael Roper and John Tosh (eds), *Manful Assertions: Masculinities in Britain since 1800* (London: Routledge, 1991), pp. 43–73.

Efrat Tseelon, *The Masque of Femininity: The Presentation of Woman in Everyday Life* (London: Sage, 1995).

John Urry, *Consuming Places* (London: Routledge, 1995).

Gill Valentine, '(Hetero)sexing Space: Lesbian Perceptions and Experiences of Everyday Spaces', *Environment and Planning D: Society and Space* (1993), 11: 395–413.

Thorstein Veblen, *The Theory of the Leisure Class* (London: Penguin, 1979).

Judith Walkowitz, *Prostitution and Victorian Society: Women, Class and the State* (Cambridge: Cambridge University Press, 1980).

———, *City of Dreadful Delight: Narratives of Sexual Danger in Late Victorian London* (London: Virago Press, 1992).

Marina Warner, *Monuments and Maidens: The Allegory of the Female Form* (London: Picador, 1988).

Sophie Watson and Katherine Gibson (eds), *Postmodern Cities and Spaces* (Oxford: Blackwell, 1995).

Jeffrey Weeks, *Sex, Politics and Society: The Regulation of Sexuality since 1800* (London: Longman, 1989).

Andrea Weiss, *Paris was a Woman: Portraits from the Left Bank* (London: HarperCollins Publishers, 1995).

Judith Williamson, *Consuming Passions: The Dynamics of Popular Culture* (London: Marion Boyars, 1986).

Elizabeth Wilson, *Adorned in Dreams* (London: Virago Press, 1985).

———, 'The Invisible Flaneur', *The New Left Review* (1992), 191: 90–110.

———, 'The Rhetoric of Urban Space', *New Left Review* (1995), 209: 146–60.

Hilary Winchester, 'The Construction and Deconstruction of Women's Roles in the Urban Landscape', Kay Anderson and Fay Gale (eds), *Inventing Places* (Australia: Longman Cheshire, 1992), pp. 139–55.

Janet Wolff, 'The Invisible Flaneuse', *Theory, Culture and Society* (1985), 2(3): 37–46.

———, *Feminine Sentences: Essays on Women and Culture* (Cambridge: Polity Press, 1990).

———, 'Memoirs and Micrologies: Walter Benjamin, Feminism and Cultural Analysis', *New Formations: The Actuality of Walter Benjamin* (Summer 1993), 20: 113–22.

Women and Geography Study Group of the IBG, *Geography and Gender: An Introduction to Feminist Geography* (London: Hutchinson, 1984).

Lola Young, 'A Nasty Piece of Work: A Psychoanalytical Study of Sexual and Racial Difference in "Mona Lisa"', Jonathan Rutherford (ed.), *Identity: Community, Culture, Difference* (London: Lawrence and Wishart, 990), pp. 188–206.

———, *Fear of the Dark: 'Race', Gender and Sexuality in the Cinema* (London: Routledge, 1996).

PART 3: GENDER, SPACE, ARCHITECTURE

Selected bibliography

Diane Agrest, *Architecture from Without: Theoretical Framings for a Critical Practice* (Cambridge, Mass.: MIT Press, 1993).

Jennifer Bloomer,'Big Jugs', Arthur Kroker and Marilouise Kroker (eds), *The Hysterical Male: New Feminist Theory* (London: Macmillan, 1991), pp. 13–27.

Sara Boutelle, 'Julia Morgan', Susana Torre (eds), *Women in American Architecture: An*

Historic and Contemporary Perspective (New York: Whitney Library of Design, 1977), pp. 79–87.

Frances Bradshaw, 'Working with Women', Matrix, *Making Space: Women and the Man-made Environment* (London: Pluto Press, 1984), pp. 89–105.

Denise Scott Brown, 'Room at the Top? Sexism and the Star System in Architecture', Ellen Perry Berkeley (ed.), *Architecture: A Place for Women* (Washington, DC: Smithsonian Institution Press, 1989), pp. 237–46.

Zeynep Çelik, 'Le Corbusier, Orientalism, Colonialism', *Assemblage* (April 1992), 17: 66–77.

Beatriz Colomina, 'The Split Wall: Domestic Voyeurism', Beatriz Colomina (ed.), *Sexuality and Space* (New York: Princeton Architectural Press, 1992), pp. 73–98.

Elizabeth Diller, 'Bad Press', Francesca Hughes (ed.), *The Architect: Reconstructing her Practice* (Cambridge, Mass.: The MIT Press, 1996), pp. 74–94.

Karen A. Franck, 'A Feminist Approach to Architecture: Acknowledging Women's Ways of Knowing', Ellen Perry Berkeley (ed.), *Architecture: A Place for Women* (Washington: Smithsonian Institution Press, 1989), pp. 201–16.

Alice Friedman, 'Architecture, Authority and the Female Gaze: Planning and Representation in the Early Modern Country House', *Assemblage* (August 1992), 18, pp. 40–61.

Dolores Hayden, 'What Would a Non-sexist City Be Like? Speculations on Housing, Urban Design and Human Work', Catharine R. Stimpson, Elsa Dixler, Martha J. Nelson and Kathryn B. Yatrakis (eds), *Women and the American City* (Chicago: University of Chicago Press, 1981).

bell hooks, Julie Eizenberg and Hank Koning, 'House, 20 June 1994', *Assemblage* (1995), 24: 22–9.

Labelle Prussin, *African Nomadic Architecture: Space, Place and Gender* (Washington, DC: Smithsonian Institution Press, 1995).

Joel Sanders (ed.), *Stud: Architectures of Masculinity* (Princeton, NJ: Princeton Architectural Press, 1996), pp. 68–78.

Henry Urbach, 'Closets, Clothes, disClosure', Duncan McCorquodale, Katerina Rüedi and Sarah Wigglesworth (eds), *Desiring Practices: Architecture, Gender and the Interdisciplinary* (London: Black-Dog, 1996), pp. 246–63.

Lynne Walker, 'Women and Architecture', Judy Attfield and Pat Kirkham (eds), *A View from the Interior: Feminism, Women and Design* (London: The Women's Press, 1989), pp. 90–105.

Further reading

Peter Adam, *Eileen Gray: Architect/Designer: A Biography* (New York: Harry N. Abrams, 1987).

Diane Agrest, 'Architecture from Without: Body, Logic, and Sex', *Assemblage* (October 1988), 7: 28–41.

Diane Agrest, Patricia Conway and Leslie Kanes Weisman (eds), *The Sex of Architecture* (New York: Harry N. Abrams, 1997).

Sherry Ahrentzen, 'The F Word in Architecture: Feminist Analyses in/of/for Architecture', Thomas A. Dutton and Lian Hurst Mann (eds), *Reconstructing Architecture:*

Critical Discourses and Social Practices (Minneapolis: University of Minnesota Press, 1996), pp. 71–118.

Polly Wynn Allen, *Building Domestic Liberty: Charlotte Perkins Gilman's Architectural Feminism* (Amherst: University of Massachusetts Press, 1988).

Irwin Altman and Arza Churchman (eds), *Women and the Environment* (New York: Plenum Press, 1994).

Isabelle Anscombe, *A Woman's Touch: Women in Design from 1860 to the Present Day* (London: Virago, 1984).

Emily Apter, 'Cabinet Secret: Fetishism, Prostitution and the Fin de Siècle Interior', *Assemblage* (June 1989), 9: 7–19.

'Architecture and Gender', *Design Book Review* (Summer 1992), 25.

'Architecture and the Feminine: Mop-up Work', *ANY* (January–February 1994), 4.

'Architecture: A Place for Women', *Architectural Design* (1990), 60(1–2): ix–xiii.

Judy Attfield and Pat Kirkham (eds), *A View from the Interior: Feminism, Women and Design* (London: The Women's Press, 1989).

Christine Battersby, 'Hermaphrodites of Art and Vampires of Practice: Architectural Theory and Feminist Theory', *Journal of Philosophy and the Visual Arts* (1992), 3.

Catherine E. Beecher and Harriet Beecher Stowe, *The American Woman's Home* (1869) (Hartford, Conn: Stowe-Day Foundation, 1975).

Ann Bergren, 'Architecture Gender Philosophy', John Whiteman, Jeffrey Kipnis and Richard Burdett (eds), *Strategies in Architectural Thinking* (Cambridge, Mass.: The MIT Press, 1992).

———, 'Dear Jennifer', *ANY* (January–February 1994), 4: 12–15.

———, 'Gold's Gym in Venice, California', *Assemblage*: (December 1998) 37: 8–35.

Ellen Perry Berkeley (ed.), *Architecture: A Place for Women* (Washington, DC: Smithsonian Institution Press, 1989).

Aaron Betsky, *Building Sex: Men, Women, Architecture and the Construction of Sexuality* (New York: William Morrow and Company, 1995).

Jennifer Bloomer, *Architecture and the Text: the (S)crypts of Joyce and Piranesi* (New Haven, Conn: Yale University Press, 1993).

———, *A Longing for Gravity* (London: Academy Editions, 1997).

Iain Borden, 'Gender and the City', Iain Borden and David Dunster (eds), *Architecture and the Sites of History* (Oxford: Butterworth, 1995).

Iain Borden, Jane Rendell and Helen Thomas, 'Knowing Different Cities: Reflections on Recent European City and Planning History', Leonie Sandercock (ed.), *Making the Invisible Visible: New Historiographies for Planning* (Berkeley: University of California Press, 1997).

Iain Borden, Joe Kerr, Alicia Pivaro and Jane Rendell (eds), *Strangely Familiar: Narratives of Architecture in the City* (London: Routledge, 1996).

Sara Boutelle, *Julia Morgan: Architect* (New York: Abbeville Press, 1988).

Sophia Bowlby (ed.), *Women and the Designed Environment, Built Environment* (1990), 16(4).

Jos Boys, 'Is there a Feminist Analysis of Architecture?' *Built Environment* (November 1990), 10(1): 25–34.

Rachel G. Bratt, Chester Hartman and Ann Meyerson (eds), *Critical Perspectives on Housing* (Philadelphia, Pa: Temple University Press, 1986).

Denise Scott Brown, 'Urban Concepts', *Architectural Design*, Profile 83 (1990), 60: 1–2.

Cheryl Buckley, 'Made in Patriarchy: Towards a Feminist Analysis of Women and Design', *Design Issues* (1987), 3(2): 3–15.

Marjorie Bulus (ed.), *Women and the Built Environment: An Annotated Bibliography to Promote Curriculum Development in Higher and Further Education* (London: Department of Planning Housing and Development, South Bank Polytechnic, 1987).

Victor Burgin, 'Geometry and Abjection', *AA Files* (Summer 1987), 15: 38–41.

Jude Burkhauser, *Glasgow Girls: Women in Art and Design 1880–1920* (Edinburgh: Canongate, 1993).

Karen Burns, 'A House for Josephine Baker', G.B. Nalbantoglu and C.T. Wong (eds), *Postcolonial Spaces* (New York: Princeton Architectural Press, 1997), pp. 53–72.

Anthea Callen, *Angel in the Studio: Women in the Arts and Crafts Movement 1870–1914* (London: Astragal Books, 1979).

Sue Cavanagh and Vron Ware, *At Women's Convenience* (London: Women's Design Service, 1990).

Zeynep Çelik, *The Remaking of Istanbul: Portrait of an Ottoman City in the Nineteenth century* (Seattle: University of Washington Press, 1986).

——, *Displaying the Orient: Architecture of Islam at Nineteenth-century World's Fairs* (Berkeley: University of California Press, 1992).

——, *Urban Forms and Colonial Confrontations: Algiers under French Rule* (Berkeley: University of California Press, 1997).

Zeynep Çelik, Diane Favro and Richard Ingersoll (eds), *Streets: Critical Perspectives on Public Space* (Berkeley: University of California Press, 1994).

Deborah Chambers, 'A Stake in the Country: Women's Experiences of Suburban Development', Roger Silverstone (ed.), *Visions of Suburbia* (London: Routledge, 1997), pp. 86-107.

'The City', *Differences: A Journal of Feminist Cultural Studies* (Fall 1993), 5(3).

Alison J. Clarke, 'Tupperware: Suburbia, Sociality and Mass Consumption', Roger Silverstone (ed.), *Visions of Suburbia* (London: Routledge, 1997), pp. 132-60.

Doris Cole, *From Tipi to Skyscraper: A History of Women in Architecture* (Boston: i Press, 1973).

Doris Cole and Karen Cord Taylor, *The Lady Architects: Lois Lilley Howe, Eleanor Manning and Mary Almy 1893–1937* (New York, 1990).

Debra Coleman, Elizabeth Danze and Carol Henderson (eds), *Architecture and Feminism* (New York: Princeton Architectural Press, 1996).

Beatriz Colomina (ed.), *Architecture Production* (New York: Princeton Architectural Press, 1988).

—— (ed.), *Sexuality and Space* (Princeton, NJ: Princeton University Press, 1991).

——, *Privacy and Publicity: Modern Architecture as Mass Media* (Cambridge, Mass.: M.I.T. Press, 1994).

Dana Cuff, *Architecture: The Story of Practice* (Cambridge, Mass.: MIT Press, 1991).

Fares el-Dahdah, 'The Josephine Baker House: For Loos's Pleasure', *Assemblage* (1995), 26: 72–87.

Elizabeth Diller and Ricardo Scofidio, *Flesh: Architectural Probes* (New York : Princeton Architectural Press, 1994).

Lamia Doumato, *Architecture and Women: A Bibliography documenting Women Architects, Landscape Architects, Designers, Architectural Critics and Writers and Women in Related Fields Working in the United States* (New York: Garland, 1988).

Louise Durning, *Gender Perspectives in Architectural History: A Working Bibliography* (Oxford Brookes University: Humanities Research Centre, 1995).

Christiane Erlemann, 'What is a Feminist Architecture?' Gisela Ecker (ed.), *Feminist Aesthetics* (London: The Women's Press, 1985), pp. 125–34.

That Exceptional One: Women in American Architecture 1888–1988, Exhibition Catalogue (The American Architectural Foundation, 1988)

Deborah Fausch, Paulette Singley, Rodolphe El-Khoury and Zvi Efrat (eds), *Architecture in Fashion* (New York: Princeton Architectural Press, 1994).

Diane Favro, 'Sincere and Good: The Architectural Practice of Julia Morgan', *Journal of Architecture and Planning Research* (1992), 9(2).

'Feminism and Traditional Aesthetics', *Journal of Aesthetics and Art Criticism* (Fall 1990), 48(4).

Adrian Forty, *Objects of Desire* (London: Thames and Hudson, 1986).

Pauline Fowler, 'The Public and Private in Architecture: A Feminist Critique', *Women's Studies International Forum*, 7(6): 449–454.

Karen Franck, *Nancy Wolf: Hidden Cities, Hidden Longings* (London: Academy Editions, 1996).

Karen Franck and Lynda H. Schneekloth (eds), *Ordering Space: Types in Architecture and Design* (New York: Van Nostrand Reinhold, 1994).

Marco Frascari, 'Maidens "Theory" and "Practice" at the Sides of Lady Architecture', *Assemblage* (October 1988), 7: 16–27.

Alice Friedman, *House and Household in Elizabethan England* (Chicago: University of Chicago Press, 1989).

———, 'A Feminist Practice in Architectural History?', 'Gender and Design', *Design Book Review* (Summer 1992), 25: 16–8.

———, *Women and the Making of the Modern House* (New York, Harry N. Abrams, 1997).

'Gender and Multiculturalism in Architectural Education', *Journal of Architectural Education* (September 1993), 47(1).

Diane Ghirardo, *Architecture after Modernism* (London: Thames and Hudson, 1996).

Charlotte Perkins Gilman, *The Home: Its Work and Influence* (Urbana: University of Illinois Press, 1972).

Rose Gilroy and Roberta Woods (eds), *Housing Women* (London: Routledge, 1994).

Phil Goodall, 'Design and Gender', *Block* (1983), 9: 50–61.

Janie Grote, 'Matrix: A Radical Approach to Architecture', *Journal of Architecture and Planning* (1992), 9(2).

Molly Hankwitz, 'The Right to Rewrite: Feminism and Architectural Theory', *Inland*

Architect (January–February 1991), 52–5.

Dolores Hayden, *Seven American Utopias: The Architecture of Communitarian Socialism 1790–1975* (Cambridge, Mass.: MIT Press, 1976).

———, *The Grand Domestic Revolution* (Cambridge, Mass.: MIT Press, 1981).

———, *Redesigning the American Dream* (New York: W. W. Norton and Company, 1986).

———, *The Power of Place* (Cambridge, Mass.: MIT Press, 1995).

Jonathan Hill (ed.), *Occupying Architecture: Between the Architect and the User* (London: Routlege, 1998).

Francesca Hughes (ed.), *The Architect: Reconstructing her Practice* (Cambridge, Mass.: MIT Press, 1996).

Catherine Ingraham, 'The Faults of Architecture: Troping the Proper', *Assemblage* (October 1988), 7: 7–13.

Jane Jacobs, *The Death and Life of Great American Cities* (New York: Vintage Books, 1961).

Carloyn R. Johnson, *Women in Architecture: An Annotated Bibliography and Guide to Sources of Information* (Council of Planning Librarians, Exchange Bibliography, 1974), 549.

Andrea Kahn (ed.), *Drawing, Building, Text* (New York: Princeton Architectural Press, 1994).

Susanne Keller (ed.), *Building for Women* (Lexington, Mass.: Lexington Books, 1981).

Jeff Kelley, 'The Body Politics of Suzanne Lacy', Nina Felshin (ed.), *But is it Art? The Spirit of Art as Activism* (Seattle, Wash.: Bay Press, 1995).

Magrit Kennedy, 'Seven Hypotheses on Male and Female Principles', 'Making Room: Women and Architecture', *Heresies: A Feminist Publication on Art and Politics* (1981), 3(3), issue 11: 12–3.

Anthony D. King (ed.), *Buildings and Society: Essays on the Social Development of the Built Environment* (London: Routledge and Kegan Paul, 1980).

Pat Kirkham, *Charles and Ray Eames: Designers of the Twentieth Century* (Cambridge Mass.: MIT Press, 1996).

Lawrence Knopp, 'Sexuality and Urban Space; A Framework for Analysis', David Bell and Gill Valentine (eds), *Mapping Desire* (London: Routledge, 1995), pp. 149-61.

David Farrell Krell, *Architecture: Ecstasies of Space, Time and the Human Body* (New York: State University of New York Press, 1997),

Arthur Kroker and Marilouise Kroker (eds), *The Hysterical Male: New Feminist Theory* (London: Macmillan, 1991).

Angel Kwolek-Folland, 'Gender as a Category of Analysis in Vernacular Architecture Studies', Elizabeth Collins Cromley and Carter L. Hudgins (eds), *Gender, Class and Shelter; Perspectives in Vernacular Architecture* (Knoxville: The University of Tennessee Press, 1995).

Suzanne Lacy (ed.), *Mapping the Terrain: New Genre Public Art* (Seattle, Wash., Bay Press, 1995).

Jacqueline Leavitt, 'Feminist Advocacy Planning in the 1980s', B. Checkoway (ed.), *Strategic Perspectives on Planning Practice* (Lexington, Mass.: Lexington Books, 1986).

Lucy R. Lippard, *From the Center: Feminist Essays on Women's Art* (New York: Dutton, 1976).

———, 'Centers and Fragments: Women's Spaces', Susana Torre (ed.), *Women in American Architecture: A Historic and Contemporary Perspective* (New York: Whitney Library of Design, 1977), pp. 186–202.

———, *The Pink Glass Swan: Selected Essays on Feminist Art* (New York: New Press, 1995).

———, *The Lure of the Local: Senses of Place in a Multicentered Society* (New York: New Press, 1997).

J. Little, L. Peake and P. Richardson (eds), *Women in Cities: Gender and the Urban Environment* (London: Macmillan, 1988).

Mimi Lobell, 'The Buried Treasure', Ellen Perry Berkeley (ed.), *Architecture: A Place for Women* (Washington, DC: Smithsonian Institution Press, 1989), pp. 139–57.

Clare Lorenz, *Women in Architecture: A Contemporary Perspective* (London: Trefoil Publications, 1990).

Ellen Lupton, *Mechanical Brides: Women and Machines from Home to Office* (New York: Cooper Hewitt National Museum of Design and Princeton Architectural Press, 1993).

Ellen Lupton and J. Abbott Miller, *The Bathroom, the Kitchen and the Aesthetics of Waste: A Process of Elimination* (Cambridge, Mass.: MIT List Visual Arts Centre), 1992).

Duncan McCorquodale, Katerina Rüedi and Sarah Wigglesworth (eds), *Desiring Practices: Architecture, Gender and the Interdisciplinary* (London: Black Dog, 1996).

Liz McQuiston, *Women in Design: A Contemporary View* (London: Trefoil Publications, 1988)

'Making Room: Women and Architecture', *Heresies: A Feminist Publication on Art and Politics* (New York: Heresies Collective Inc. 1981), 3(3), issue 11.

Thomas A. Markus, *Buildings and Power* (London: Routledge, 1993).

Matrix, *Making Space: Women and the Man-made Environment* (London: Pluto Press, 1984).

'The Meaning of Home', *Journal of Architectural and Planning Research* (Summer 1991), 8(2): 91–180.

Pat Morton, 'A Visit to Womenhouse', Steven Harris and Deborah Berke (eds), *Architecture of the Everyday* (New York: Princeton Architectural Press, 1998), pp. 166–79.

Caroline O. N. Moser and Linda Peake (eds), *Women, Human Settlements and Housing* (London: Tavistock, 1987).

Muf, *Architectural Design* (August 1996), 66(7–8): 80–3.

Kate Nesbitt (ed.), *Theorizing a New Agenda for Architecture: An Anthology of Architectural Theory 1965–1995* (New York: Princeton Architectural Press, 1996).

Barbara Oldershaw, 'Developing a Feminist Critique of Architecture', 'Gender and Design', *Design Book Review* (Summer 1992), 25: 7–15.

L. Ottes, E. Poventud, M. van Schendelen and G. Segond von Banchet (eds), *Gender and the Built Environment: Emancipation in Planning, Housing and Mobility in Europe* (Assen, The Netherlands: Van Gorcum, 1995).

Alberto Perez-Gomez, *Poliphilo of the Dark Forest Revisited: An Erotic Epiphany of*

Architecture (Cambridge, Mass.: MIT Press, 1992).

'A Place for Women in Planning', *Town and Country Planning* (October 1987), 56(9).

Labelle Prussin, *Architecture in Northern Ghana: A Study of Forms and Functions* (Berkeley : University of California Press, 1969).

————, *Hatumere: Islamic Design in West Africa* (Berkeley: University of California Press, 1986).

Amos Rapoport, *House Form and Culture* (Englewood Cliffs, NJ: Prentice-Hall, 1969).

————, *Human Aspects of Urban Form* (Oxford: Pergamon Press, 1977).

Christopher Reed (ed.), *Not at Home: The Suppression of Domesticity in Modern Art and Architecture* (London: Thames and Hudson, 1996).

Jane Rendell, '"Industrious Females' and 'Professional Beauties', or, Fine Articles for Sale in the Burlington Arcade", Iain Borden, Joe Kerr, Alicia Pivaro and Jane Rendell (eds), *Strangely Familiar: Narratives of Architecture in the City* (London: Routledge, 1995), pp. 32–6.

————, 'Subjective Space: A Feminist Architectural History of the Burlington Arcade', in Duncan McCorquodale, Katerina Ruedi and Sarah Wigglesworth (eds), *Desiring Practices: Architecture, Gender and the Interdisciplinary* (London: Black Dog Publishing Ltd, 1996), pp. 216–33.

————, 'Doing it (Un)Doing it (Over)Doing it Yourself: Rhetorics of Architectural Abuse', Jonathan Hill (ed.), *Occupying Architecture* (London: Routledge, 1998a), pp. 227–46.

————, 'Displaying Sexuality: Gendered Identities in the Early Nineteenth-century Street', Nick Fyfe (ed.), *Images of the Street: Representation, Experience, and Control in Public Space* (London: Routledge, 1998b), pp. 74–91.

————, 'Home', 'Pursuit', 'Hell', 'Knowledge', Steve Pile and Nigel Thrift (eds), *City A–Z: Urban Fragments* (London: Routledge, 2000).

Marion Roberts, *Living in Man-made World: Gender Assumptions in Modern Housing Design* (London: Routledge, 1991).

Kristin Ross, *Fast Cars, Clean Bodies: Decolonialization and the Reordering of French Culture* (Cambridge, Mass.: MIT Press, 1995).

Leonie Sandercock (ed.), *Making the Invisible Visible: New Historiographies for Planning* (Berkeley: University of California Press, 1997).

Leonie Sandercock and Ann Forsyth, 'A Gender Agenda: New Directions for Planning Theory', *Journal of the American Planning Association* (1992).

W. Schutte and M. Wilke (eds), *The Wise Woman Buildeth her House: Architecture, History and Women's Studies* (Groningen, The Netherlands: Royal University of Groningen, 1992).

Michael Sorkin (ed.), *Variations on a Theme Park* (New York: Hill and Wang, 1992).

Susan M. Squier (ed.), *Women Writers and the City* (Knoxville: University of Tennessee Press, 1984).

Catherine R. Stimpson, Elsa Dixler, Martha Newlson and Kathryn Yatrakis (eds), *Women and the American City* (Chicago: University of Chicago Press, 1981).

Susana Torre, 'The Pyramid and Labyrinth', Susana Torre (ed.), *Women in American Architecture: A Historic and Contemporary Perspective* (New York: Whitney Library of Design, 1977a), pp. 186–202.

—— (ed.), *Women in American Architecture: a Historic and Contemporary Perspective* (New York: Whitney Library of Design, 1977).

——, 'Space as Matrix', *Making Room: Women and Architecture: Heresies: A Feminist Publication on Art and Politics* (1981), 3(3), issue 11: 51–2.

Georges Teyssot, *The Mutant Body of Architecture* (New York: Princeton Architectural Press, 1994).

Robert Venturi and Denise Scott Brown, *A View from the Campidoglio: Selected Essays 1953–1984* (New York: Harper and Row, 1984).

Robert Venturi, Denise Scott Brown and Steven Izenour, *Learning from Las Vegas: The Forgotten Symbolism of Architectural Form* (rev. ed.) (Cambridge, Mass : MIT Press, 1997).

Anthony Vidler, *The Architectural Uncanny: Essays in the Modern Unhomely* (Cambridge, Mass.: MIT Press, 1992).

——, 'Bodies in Space/Subjects in the City: Psychopathologies of Modern Urbanism', in *The City, Differences, A Journal of Feminist Cultural Studies* (Fall 1993), 5: 31–52.

Lynne Walker, *British Women in Architecture 1671–1951* (London: Sorello Press, 1984).

——, 'Women and Architecture', Judy Attfield and Pat Kirkham (eds), *A View from the Interior: Feminism, Women and Design* (London: The Women's Press, 1989), pp. 90–105.

——, *Cracks in the Pavement: Gender, Fashion, Architecture* (London: Sorello Press, 1993).

——, *Drawing on Diversity: Women, Architecture and Practice* (exhibition catalogue, London: RIBA, Heinz Gallery, 1997).

Sophie Watson, *Accommodating Inequality: Gender and Housing* (Sydney: Allen and Unwin, 1998).

Jeanne Madeline Weimann, *The Fair Women: The Story of the Woman's Building World's Columbian Exposition, Chicago 1893* (Chicago: Chicago Academy, 1981).

Leslie Kanes Weisman, *Discrimination by Design* (Chicago: University of Illinois Press, 1992).

Gerda Werkele, Rebecca Peterson and David Morley (eds), *New Space for Women* (Boulder, Col.: Westview Press, 1980).

Sarah Whiting *et al.* (eds), *Fetish* (New York: Princeton Architectural Press, 1992).

Mark Wigley, *White Walls, Designer Dresses: The Fashioning of Modern Architecture* (Cambridge, Mass.: MIT Press, 1996).

Mabel O. Wilson, 'Black Bodies/White Cities: Le Corbusier in Harlem', *ANY* (1996), 16: 35–9.

'Women and the Designed Environment', *Built Environment* (1990), 16(4).

'Women and the American City', *Signs: The Journal of Women and Culture and Society* (Spring 1980), 5(3).

'Women in Architecture', *Architectural Design* (August 1975), 45(8).

'Women in Design', *Design and Environment* (Spring 1974), 5.

'Women's Voices in Architecture and Planning', *Journal of Architectural and Planning Research* (Summer 1992), 9(2).

Gwendolyn Wright, 'On the Fringe of the Profession: Women in American Architecture',

Spiro Kostof (ed.), *The Architect: Chapters in the History of the Profession* (Oxford: Oxford University Press, 1977), pp. 280–309.

———, *Moralism and the Modern Home* (Chicago: University of Chicago Press, 1980).

———, *Building the Dream: A Social History of Housing in America* (Cambridge, Mass.: MIT Press, 1981).

Index

Numbers in *italics* refer to illustrations
Numbers in **bold** refer to main entries